Footprint
West Coast /

Katrina O'Brien & Andrew Swaffer
2nd edition

G000147614

*The unexpected is what I'm after when I go
trudging along the firm white sand with not a
building or human in sight. True, I'm after solitude
as well, and enough sameness to give me the
peace to think or maybe sing without feeling
self-conscious. But it's the possibility of finding
something strange that keeps me walking*

Tim Winton, *Land's Edge*

West Coast Australia

See colour maps at back of book

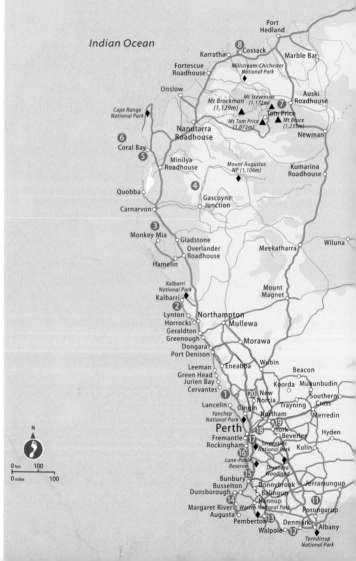

11 Stirling Ranges
Bush-cloaked ranges provide superb hill walking and views

12 Walpole and Denmark
Soaring forests meet granite coasts and snowy beaches

13 Pemberton
Wine, walking and 'tree towers' in the heart of the southern forests

14 Cape-to-Cape region
Coastal walks, wonderful wine, awesome caves and serious surf

15 Bunbury
Ocean beaches, a vibrant town and visiting dolphins

16 Rockingham
Penguin Island and its riot of birdlife (including Fairy penguins) plus the chance to swim with dolphins

17 Fremantle
History meets vibrant culture in WA's most interesting city

18 Rottnest
Perth's 'holiday isle': cute quokkas, great beaches and the best snorkelling around the capital

19 York
Fine colonial architecture and a superb motor museum

20 New Norcia
Australia's unique, historic and fascinating monastic settlement

Contents

Around Perth

Southwest Coast

Timber Towns

South Coast

Midwest

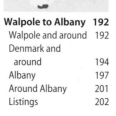

The Gascoyne

The Pilbara

Broome & around

Background

Nature's Window, a rock arch in Kalbarri National Park.

Tight squeeze
Ancient, deep and extremely narrow, the gorges of Karijini National Park are among the most extreme landscapes in Western Australia.

A foot in the door

The people of Australia's west coast cling to land's edge – and for good reason. At their back lies an ocean of desert. Like so many western coastlines across the globe, Australia's can be a wild place. It is hot and dry country with little freshwater and few safe harbours. Much of the state is, in fact, virtually uninhabitable. Its tiny population, vast size and isolation, mean that the west coast is wonderfully unspoiled. There is hardly a high-rise to be found along its entire length and its inhabitants are determined to keep it that way. Solitude is always just around the corner and close encounters of the animal kind are commonplace in a state where the natural world is not outnumbered or overpowered by people.

The obvious thing to be said about Western Australia is that it's big – very big – covering a third of the Australian continent. It's three times larger than Texas and about the same size as Western Europe, yet only two million people, or ten percent of Australians, occupy all this land and three quarters of them live in the state capital Perth. Few visitors ever make it the four thousand kilometres across the Nullarbor to the west coast – most are enticed by the rock, the reef and Sydney harbour – and even most Australians are unaware of the wonders of the west.

Amid the dazzling light of the west coast and the clean air of its constant sea breeze, life seems pared back, easy and uncomplicated, and while you have all the comforts you need, civilization is far, far away. Off the beaten track, the west coast offers an unhyped and unhurried experience – it's a part of the country in which you can still find some secret places and penetrate the heart of the space, sunshine and adventure that Australia has to offer.

Ancient soul

Western Australia is an ancient land, older than most areas on earth, and, if you look closely, it reveals its age. Eroded down into low rounded ranges and vast plains, the west has a timeless quality. The ironstone ranges of the Pilbara are over two billion years old and the Yilgarn plateau of the southwest over three billion years old. These are monumental landscapes of a stark and minimalist beauty; part of the flattest, lowest and driest continent on earth. Age, isolation and harsh conditions have resulted in highly specialized ecologies. Western Australia has more than 6,000 species of plants, which provide stunning wildflower displays in spring, and many unique animals. Of course it may seem like a wilderness out there, without roads, crops, buildings or even ruins, but the truth is that the Australian landscape has been managed, altered and cared for by its indigenous people for an unimaginable length of time. Australian Aboriginals are thought to have lived in the country for around 60,000 years and, despite the turmoil and change wrought by dispossession, their fascinating culture has survived to the present day.

Rock of ages
This otherworldly landscape was created some 20,000 years ago when vegetation and sands were eroded away leaving the Pinnacles, as they are now known, behind.

Frontier spirit

Set against the great age of the land and the tenure of its indigenous people, the man-made environment of the west coast looks young, new and often raw. Many towns on this coast began as a collection of fishing shacks in the 1950s and have only begun to resemble towns much more recently. Most of the Pilbara towns sprang into existence in the 1960s thanks to discoveries of fantastic mineral wealth in the region. Although Perth was established in 1829, earlier than Adelaide or Melbourne, it bears little trace of its history as the same 1960s mining boom provided both the wealth and sense of progress required to demolish the city's oldest buildings. The west coast's modern towns and cities are dominated by functional architecture that reflects its reserved, unsentimental people. West Australians are made insular by ocean and desert. Despite pouring the state's mineral wealth into the nation's coffers, West Australians feel forgotten and ignored by the centres of wealth and power known dismissively in WA as 'the eastern states'. Of course they are proud of their difference too, with a strong sense of living on the frontier and feeling lucky to do so, unmistakably shaped by and bound to their natural environment.

Close encounters
From April to June bands of whale sharks, travelling around the equator, pass through the Ningaloo Reef, offering you a chance to swim alongside these immense and gentle creatures.

1 Wonderful doleful pelicans at Kalbarri. They can often be spotted taking a nap on top of lamp-posts. ▸▸ See page 335.

2 A visit to the southwest of Western Australia will reveal one of the richest plant communities in the world. ▸▸ See page 139.

3 Cable Beach, near Broome, has a long, wide sweep of sand facing west, a perfect place to watch the sun set. ▸▸ See page 288.

4 Fremantle, a port city, is home to the fascinating Western Australian Maritime Museum. ▸▸ See page 97.

5 The sheltered waters of Shark Bay provide a habitat for some amazing marine life, including these adorable baby loggerhead turtles. ▸▸ See page 242.

6 Adventure sports HQ. Thanks to its dependable, strong off-shore winds, Lancelin hosts an Ocean Classic windsurfing race. ▸▸ See page 121.

7 Aboriginal art. Difficult to find but worth seeking out are the Wandjina rock paintings at El Questro Wilderness Park. ▸▸ See page 298.

8 Boat Dock Pier has views across to Busselton Jetty, the longest jetty in the southern hemisphere, at over 1,800 m. ▸▸ See page 146.

9 There's no place like home and rather here than in yours; a termite mound.

10 Take a walk on the wild side on this forest canopy walkway in the Valley of the Giants. ▸▸ See page 193.

11 Quokkas are appealing little wallabies found almost exclusively on Rottnest Island. ▸▸ See page 107.

12 The Lily is a working replica 16th-century Dutch windmill overlooking a wide plain with wonderful views of the Stirling Ranges. ▸▸ See page 210.

Urban ease

Perth is a sprawling, sparkling suburban city, ever expanding up and down the coast, blessed with more hours of sunshine a day than any other Australian city. For the visitor the real appeal lies in experiencing a clean, green well-ordered city that can offer most of the pleasures of big city life, free of smog, traffic and crowds. Fremantle offers the liveliness of a busy port and, just offshore, Rottnest Island is an oasis of pretty beaches and clear warm water. The informal people of Perth seem to live at a slower pace than most urban dwellers, more interested in play than work; eating outdoors, going for a swim, sail or surf or playing a round of golf. What else can you do at the weekend but join in, when the smoke of a thousand lazy backyard barbecues drifts up to dissipate in the brilliant blue skies above?

Corner country

Along its 12,500 kilometre length the west coast is surprisingly uniform north of Perth but the southwest corner, from Perth to Albany, makes a dramatic contrast. This lush, temperate area is the state's playground with its golden surf beaches, acres of vineyards and tall eucalypt forests, populated by an interesting mix of farmers, hippies, surfers, artists and anyone else pursuing 'the good life'. Around the continent's corner at Cape Leeuwin, the cooler southern coast has a grand beauty with its granite-framed bays of pale glacial blue water and snowy sand. The hinterland's dense wet forests harbour relict species like the Tingle, before giving way to vast wheat fields below the blue forested peaks of the Stirling Ranges.

A sparkling modern city, Perth's skyline as night falls.

Shark Bay has a list of attributes as long as both peninsulas to justify its UNESCO heritage area status: dolphins, turtles, rays, stromatolites, turquoise waters, perfect white sand beaches...

Grace underwater

The opportunities to encounter marine wildlife are exceptional. The dolphins of Monkey Mia are well known but perhaps the most tame of what's on offer here. In Coral Bay you can swim off the beach to the reef and find that a green turtle is too busy eating jellyfish to give you more than a quick glance as you snorkel along beside it. On the Ningaloo Reef divers can encounter a flock of giant manta rays moving through the ocean with all the grace of a ballet company or a whale shark swimming by with the inexorable advance of an aircraft carrier. In Exmouth turtles lumber out of the surf by moonlight to lay eggs and are long gone when thousands of baby turtles hatch and flap unsteadily down to the lacy edge of the ocean. Winter brings humpback and southern right whales to migrate along the coast.

Red and raw

The baking hot interior is another world altogether. In Australian terms you don't have to head far inland to leave the sand dunes and coastal scrub behind and encounter intensely red range country. The raw outback reaches its zenith in the Pilbara, in one of Australia's most beautiful yet little known national parks, Karijini. Below the lithe white gum trees and golden spinifex of the plain, stepped gorges narrow to as little as a few metres wide and their deep icy cold pools are only warmed by the sun for a few minutes at midday.

Down anchor

Join the boaters in Geordie Bay, one of the many places to enjoy the sun, sea and sand around Rottnest Island, Perth's very own holiday playground.

Essentials

⁚ Footprint features

Planning your trip

Where to go

Western Australia is the world's single biggest political unit that isn't actually a country. It constitutes a third of an island so big that it isn't even accorded the status of the world's biggest (usually given to Greenland), but rather the smallest continent. Western Australia is not far off the size of India. If you have no more than one or two weeks for a visit, dismiss the idea of trying to see too much of it. Where you choose to visit will primarily be determined by the time of year. Broadly speaking, the far north from October to April is extremely hot, humid and monsoonal. Some enthusiasts extol the delights of the north in the 'Wet', but most visitors will want to enjoy the glorious summer weather in the southern regions at this time and avoid the humidity up north. A visit during May to September opens up the north, but also allows an itinerary to range almost anywhere in the state, though it can be a bit wet and cold down south.

One-week trip

If you've only a few days on your way through, then **Perth** or **Fremantle** make excellent bases and you'll probably have time for an overnight trip down to the **Cape-to-Cape region** to explore the wineries, caves and beaches, or over to **Rottnest Island** to see the quokkas. Interesting day trips from Perth include a quick tour east into the **Perth Hills** to see **Mundaring Weir** and **York**, a circuit north to see **New Norcia** and **Lancelin**, and the short journey south to **Rockingham** to see the penguins and swim with dolphins.

Two-week trip

In addition to the itinerary above, a two-week visit can also allow a longer tour around the south, including a trip along the southern coast to **Albany** before heading back up to Perth. A fortnight is also long enough for a return trip up the coast to **Kalbarri**, or even **Shark Bay**. Alternatively, the more energetic might consider walking parts of the **Cape-to-Cape** or **Bibbulmun Tracks**, or learning to dive, sail or surf off the beautiful beaches around the capital.

Three- to four-week trip

In three weeks you can begin to consider exploring the coast both south and immediately north of Perth, or even the great West Coast trip from Perth to Broome or vice-versa, flying the reverse direction. The latter journey would even allow for a serious side-trip, for instance into the **Millstream-Chichester** or **Karijini National parks**. At least a month is required to see a good spread of most of the highlights detailed in this guide, and to journey the full length of the West Coast between Albany and Broome.

When to go

Climate

As this state is the only one that stretches from the bottom of the country to the top, you can visit WA at any time of year. Generally the state has a superb climate and is sunny much of the time. The northern region is mildly tropical and has a build-up of humidity October-December and occasional monsoonal downpours in January-April,

⦂ Ten great West Coast adventures

- Canoe or abseil in **Kalbarri National Park**.
- Explore the plunging gorges of the **Karijini**, perhaps tackling sections of the fabled '**Miracle Mile**'.
- Gain an understanding of **Aboriginal people** and their culture by staying with them at places like **Lombadina** near Broome.
- Head for the **Ningaloo Reef** to snorkel amongst teeming fish, swim with whale sharks and dive with manta rays.
- Hike a section or two of the **Bibbulmun Track** along the south coast between Pemberton and Albany, or the **Cape-to-Cape Track** between Yallingup and Augusta.
- Sample the caves, wines, and arts of the **Cape-to-Cape region**, and leave some time to sit by the sea, particularly when the whales are around.
- Sleep outside in a comfy **swag** with only the stars and a billy on the fire for company.
- Stay for while on an **outback station**.
- Swim with **dolphins** from one of the towns just south of Perth.
- Take a **sailing trip** from Dunsborough, Fremantle, Monkey Mia or Broome.

Essentials Planning your trip

known as the 'Wet' (a period characterized by high humidity, heat, tremendous monsoonal rainfall and occasional, powerful cyclones). Many roads and tourist facilities close at this time but if you can stand the heat you might enjoy the drama of it. The 'Dry' (May-September) is the best time to visit the Gascoyne and Pilbara as temperatures hover around a delightful 25-30°C (whale sharks swim over the Ningaloo Reef near Exmouth from April-June). As a general rule, the further north you travel, and the further in time from July, the hotter it gets. And hot means very hot: days over 40°C regularly occur in summer in the arid regions, and even Perth averages over 30°C. The central or Mid West region is warm and dry for most of the year with little rain, although spring is the ideal time to visit for the wildflower season. The south, including Perth and the southwest is sunny throughout spring, summer and autumn and these are the ideal seasons to visit. Perth gets an average of 7½ hours of sunshine a day. The southern winter lasts from June-August and this is when this region receives most of its rainfall and gets fairly cold (5-17°C). If you want to see whales though, it will have to be winter or spring when they migrate past the southwest coasts (June-November).

Australia is the driest inhabited continent, and virtually nowhere further than 250 km inland gets more than an average of 600 mm of rain a year. About half the continent, in a band across the south and west, gets less than 300 mm and much of it is desert. The only area in WA that gets significant rainfall spread over more than 160 days a year is the southwest tip.

Holidays and events

School holidays are important to keep an eye on as the state's main holiday areas such as Rottnest, the Margaret River Region, Kalbarri, Monkey Mia and Broome get completely booked out in the appropriate seasons. The main holidays start in mid-December and carry on through to the end of January. Schools also close for the

⬤ *Being a southern hemisphere continent, the seasons are the opposite of those in the*
⬤ *northern hemisphere.*

two weeks after Easter, for two weeks in mid-July, and for another two weeks in early October. Backpackers don't need to be too concerned about visiting at these times as accommodation and tours aimed at that market are less affected.

WA's major festival, the Perth Festival, is held annually in January and February, and the start more or less coincides with state's biggest international sporting event, Tennis' Hopman Cup. ⏵ *See also Festivals and events, page 47.*

⏵ *See also Festivals and events, page 47.*

Tour operators

Australia

All the below are based in Perth.

AAT Kings, www.aatkings.com, and APT, www.aptouring.com.au, are the main 2 national, coach-based, both offer comparable options.

Active Safaris, T08 9450 7776, www.activesafaris.com.au, and **Aussie Outback Safaris**, T08 9593 4464, aussie_outback_safaris@hotmail.com, offers camping trips: 4-days along the west coast up as far as Monkey Mia for around $440.

Avalon Wine Tours, www.avalon-tours.com, offers wine-tasting tours.

All Terrain Safaris, T08 9295 6680, www.allterrain.com.au, has a range of longer west coast tours, some one-way, starting with a five-day trip that goes as far as Coral Bay ($525). Also tours from Broome, Exmouth and Kununurra.

Australian Adventure Travel, T08 9248 2355, www.safaris.net.au, runs 4-day tours up the west coast (Tue and, in winter, Sat, $440) and longer trips further afield, staying in farm stays and sleeping in cabins.

CALM together with the **UWA**, see www.Naturebase.net and contact T08 6488 2433, extension@uwa.edu.au, organize a number of eco expeditions/Landscope research expeditions each year where small numbers of the general public are invited to join them. Trips last 6-10 days, cost $250-500 per day, and conditions are usually pretty basic. Locations are, however, incredible and activities usually revolve around turtle-tagging or the trapping and identification of many other marine and land animal species.

Explorer Tours, T08 9361 0940, www.explorertours.com.au, specializes in following in the footsteps (albeit in a/c 4WDs) of early WA explorers. Tours generally from 8 to 21 days.

Pinnacle Tours, T08 9221 5411, www.pinn

acletours.com.au, is the most luxurious large local coach operator, with several 1-day options to southwest destinations (around $150), 2- to 5-day tours around the southwest ($200 per day, two-day Margaret River daily, other tours depart Sun-Tue), and 3- and 5-day trips (departing Fri and Mon) up the west coast ($150-200 per day).

Planet Perth, T08 9225 6622, www.planettours.com.au, organizes stop-overs in backpacker hostels and tours include the southwest for 4 days (Thu, $495), and the west coast (4 days, Thu, $490).

ROC Tours, T08 9279 6969, www.cycletours.com.au, runs a number of 4 to 11 day mostly outback tours that let you cycle the best bits.

Student Uni Travel, T02-9232 8444, and **Travellers Contact Point**, T02-9221 8744, www.travellers.com.au, specialize in putting together itineraries incorporating bus, plane and train, with a high degree of flexibility.

Venture Winetours Australia, www.venturewinetours.com.au, offers wine tasting tours.

WA Mountain Bike Tours, T/F08 9295 1716, offers a 4-day cycling trip around the southwest for small groups.

Western Travel Bug, T08 9204 4600, www.travelbug.com.au, make use of budget motels on their 2- to 6-day southwest tours (around $130 per day). Departures 3 times a week, including Sat. Also local day tours. Some agents, including:

Wine Tours Australia/NZ, www.winetoursaustralia-nz.com, offers wine tasting tours.

USA

Abercrombie and Kent, 1520 Kensington Rd, Suite 212, Oak Brook, Illinois, 60523-2156, T800-323-7308, www.abercrombiekent.com. Well-established US company offering a diverse range of luxury, locally guided global trips to Australia.

Absolute Australia, 180 Varick St, New York, T212 627 1950, www.absoluteaustralia.com. Has a diverse range of specialist trips to Australia with expert guides.

Earthwatch Research and Exploration PO Box 75, Maynard, MA 01754, USA, T978 461 0081, www.earthwatch.org. Runs excellent eco-tourism trips to Australia in combination with conservation research on Australian wildlife.

UK and Ireland

Australia Travel Centre, 43-45 Middle Abbey St, Dublin, Ireland, T3531-8047188, Australia@abbeytravel.ie. Good source of general advice for those travelling from Ireland.

Contiki, Wells House, 15 Elmfield Rd, Bromley, Kent BR1 1LS, T020 8290 6777, www.contiki.com. One of the world's largest travel companies catering primarily for the 18-35's market with numerous affordable Australian options.

Travelbag, 3-5 High St, Alton GU34 1TL, UK, T0142 088724, www.travelbag.co.uk. Reputable UK based firm offering a good range of general and tailor-made trips to Australia at reasonable prices.

Wildlife Worldwide Chameleon House 162 Selsdon Rd, T020 8667 9158, www.wildlifeworldwide.com. One of the best wildlife oriented global operators offering tailor-made, mainly small group trips to Australia.

Finding out more

The state government tourism body is the **Western Australian Tourist Commission** ① *PO Box X2261, WA 6847, T08 9483 1111, T1300 361351, www.westernaustralia. com*, for brochures/information. There is an office in the UK ① *5th Floor, Australia Centre, The Strand, London, WC2B 4LG, T020-7395 0580*. The state government's own site is *www.wa.gov.au*, and this has some useful links. Backpackers might find **Traveller's Club** (Perth) ① *T08 9226 0660, www.travellersclub.com.au*, and **Travel Lounge** (Fremantle) ① *T08 9335 8776, www.thetravellounge.com.au*, useful sources of information. **Conservation Volunteers** (Perth) ① *T08 9336 6911, www. conservationvolunteers.com.au*, is also useful. **Australian Tourist Commission** ① *T02 9360 1111, www.australia.com, www.aussie.net.au*, can be of great help, and there is also a wealth of all sorts of information to be found on the Federal and government websites, www.fed.gov.au. For details of many Aboriginal cultural centres and tours check out www.aboriginaltouroperators.com.au. Be aware though that the history of the indigenous Aboriginal people, though prodigious in terms of tenure, is sometimes conspicuous by its absence. The preservation and display of the 'European' history of Australia is, as to be expected, much more extensive. Many of the major museums and art galleries are superb, and well worth the time spent wandering their halls and galleries. The best are the group of museums operated under the **Western Australian Museum** umbrella, www.museum.wa.gov.au. Outside of the Perth and the principal cities they can become very parochial, however, and not hugely interesting to non-Australians. As in many countries a **National Trust of Australia (WA)** ① *T08 9321 6088, www. ntwa.com.au*, has been developed to buy and manage buildings of historic and cultural importance that do survive. National parks and reserves generally constitute natural areas of ecological, cultural and/or simply aesthetic importance, and can claim to encompass almost all of Western Australia's most jaw-dropping and sublime natural attractions. **Department of Conservation and Land Management** (CALM) ① *T08 9334 0333, www.naturebase.com.au*, can give further information, including details of visiting and staying in them. Park entry fees are usually $9 a car but for most visitors it is better value to buy a Holiday Pass ($22.50) allowing entry into all WA parks for four weeks. If you plan a longer stay it's worth considering the Annual Pass ($51), valid for 12 months from date of purchase.

Passes can be bought at many parks and VICs or from the **Perth Visitor Centre** in Forrest Place.

Disabled travellers

Disabled travellers to Western Australia will find that although there are a good range of facilities meeting their needs, they can be spread quite thinly, especially outside the major cities. Although all public buildings have to meet certain government standards, the standards actually in place can vary. High profile sights and attractions, and even parks have good access. The key to successful travel, as with any travellers, is planning, and there are several national and state organizations who can help, see below.

As with many major airlines **Qantas** ① T1800 652660 (TTY), has considerable experience with disabled passengers. If you have to be accompanied by a support person on any internal flight, they offer the passenger and the nominated carer a 50 per cent discount off the full-economy or business-class fare. A Carer Concession Photo ID is required. Contact **NICAN** for further details, see below for their details. Guide dogs may be brought into Australia, but are subject to quarantine, with occasional exceptions. Contact the **Australian Quarantine & Inspection Service** ① T02 9832 4025, for further details. The interstate railways generally have facilities for the disabled but public transport in many states is not always well designed for disabled travel unless you have assistance. The major interstate bus operators are pleased to accommodate disabled travellers but prefer notice, though few coaches are equipped with lifts or lowered floors. The major hire car companies have adapted vehicles available. Disabled overseas and interstate parking permits are valid in WA. All **Transperth** carriages are accessible to passengers with disabilities, however, not all the train stations are. Perth **Central Area Transit System** (CATS) ① T08 9322 3326, www.babs.com.au, has a list of particularly well set up B&Bs, buses all have low-floor access, and some have extendable ramps. There is one formal wheelchair space on each bus. When phoning ask for *infoline* for further information.

The guidebook *Easy Access Australia: A Travel Guide to Australia* by Bruce Cameron (updated 2000, ISBN 095775101X), is useful.

Organizations

ACROD, 33 Thesiger Court, Deakin, ACT 2600, T02 6282 4333. The industry association for disability services.
NICAN, PO Box 407, Curtin, ACT 2605, T02 6285 3713. Provide information on recreation, tourism, sport and the arts.
People with Disabilities, T08 9386 6477. A consumer lobby group, also provides information for travellers, including accessible accommodation and transport. Many organizations are equipped for handling TTY calls. For information contact:
Australian Communication Exchange (ACE), T07 3815 7600 or 1800 555677. A free service for TTY users, relaying messages between TTY and hearing phone users.
Telstra Disability Services, GPO Box 4997WW, Melbourne, VIC 3000, T1800 068424, 1800 808981 (TTYs).

Gay and lesbian travellers

Gay & Lesbian Community Services ① T08 9486 9855, www.glcs.org.au, can help with general travel and accommodation advice. Perth's **Pride Parade**, inaugurated in 1990 and held the last two weeks of every October, has in excess of 5,000 participants and over 75,000 spectators. Followed by a popular dance party,

Pride also includes theatre, exhibitions, and a Fair Day. Perth's dedicated gay and lesbian publication is *Shout*, a free newspaper available from city music or book shops. **International Gay & Lesbian Travel Association** (IGLTA), www.iglta.com, is also with a good place to go for travel advice. There are several national magazines keeping lesbians and gays in touch with what's going on, including *Lesbians on the Loose* and *DNA*. Check **www.qbeds.com**, for lesbian and gay friendly accommodation. **Rough Guides** publishes a dedicated guidebook, *Gay & Lesbian Australia*. See also www.gayaustralia guide.com.

Student travellers

If you're a student make sure you have identification as it will be a ticket to much in the way of discounted accommodation, tours and more. There are various official youth/student ID cards available, including the widely recognized **International Student ID Card** (ISIC), www.istc.org, **Federation of International Youth Travel Organisations** (FIYTO) card, www.fiyto.org, **Euro 26 Card**, www.Euro26.org, and **Go-25 Card**. Each also conveys benefits from simply getting discounts, to emergency medical coverage and 24-hour hotlines. The cards are issued by student travel agencies and hostelling organizations. Backpackers will find a **YHA** or **VIP** membership card just as useful.

Travelling with children

Australia is an eminently wonderful and suitable place to take children. Far-fetched stories and rumours about child-eating poisonous snakes and insects, man-eating sharks and crocs, can put parents off – but they shouldn't. If children are aware and sufficiently supervised, Australia will provide a memorable holiday experience for all the right reasons.

If you are concerned about the threat of the rumoured nasty native wildlife a trip to Perth Zoo, or indeed any of the numerous wildlife parks around the state, will soon put your mind at rest that – prevalent as it might be – it's unlikely to feast on your kids. Wildlife in Australia, whether captive or not, offers one of the greatest natural history educational platforms for children on the planet and encounters can become any foreign child's fondest memory.

As far as accommodation is concerned the vast majority of establishments, beyond the usual exclusive retreats for couples seeking a romantic weekend, welcome kids and offer reasonable financial concessions. Tourist-based attractions and activities too, many of which are directed at the children's market, usually offer reduced rates for children and family concessions. When it comes to eating out, like most developed countries some eateries welcome children, while others...don't. In general you are advised to stick to eateries that are obviously child-friendly or ask before making a booking.

In summary there are a multitude of excellent venues to take children or to keep them happily entertained. You will loose count of beaches of course, but we also highly recommend are wildlife parks and the modern museums and theme parks around the state.

Women travellers

In Australia the concept of chauvinism and the archetype Bruce and Sheila (the classic beer drinking male and do-as-you-are-told spouse) is fast becoming an old fashioned myth. Generally speaking women are given all due respect in all but the most backward of outback settlements.

For lone women travellers all the usual common sense recommendations apply. Australia is a big place and given so much space it seems logical you may find yourself alone and 'out there' some of the time. Indeed, the abduction and murder of male and female tourists, especially in the outback has occurred and will no doubt continue to. So try to avoid getting yourself in that situation and always let people know about your intentions. Hitch-hiking alone is not recommended for anybody, but especially women. Other than that, keep your wits and good company about you, especially at night.

Working in Western Australia

To work in Western Australia you will need an appropriate visa (or be a citizen of Australia or New Zealand). These are not easy to come by and you local Australian High Commission can advise on your likely eligibility. Under 30s may, however, be eligible for a temporary working holiday visa. You need a return air ticket or sufficient funds for one, plus sufficient funds for the first part of your holiday. What this actually means in cash terms depends on where you are travelling from – your local Australian embassy can advise. The easiest work to get, though not to do, is generally fruit harvesting or packing. The pay isn't sensational, though hard workers can do alright, but it's sociable and can be fun. The majority of jobs available are fruit picking and tree planting, although there are also some professional, blue collar and service jobs. For information and advice on working in the state see **Workstay WA**, www.workstay.com. au, set up to help travellers on a working holiday visa. The website has a current job vacancies list. Alternatively try www.workingin-australia.com. Other outdoor work can also be found at farms and stations.

> ● *A working holiday visa will be required for casual work, see page 25.*

In the cities work opportunities are usually tipped firmly in favour of women. The hospitality industry (hotels, pubs and bars) is the biggest employer of casual workers. Those with the right qualifications will find medical employment quite easy to come by. Jobs are advertised in local newspapers and on the internet, though the best place to start are the notice boards of backpacker hostels, or contacting them in advance. If working is going to form a major part of your travels, or you are thinking of emigrating to Australia, then consider a publication such as *Live and Work in Australia and New Zealand* by Roberts & McIntosh (updated 2004, ISBN 1854582836).

Organizations

Conservation Volunteers, T1800 032501, www.conservationvolunteers. com.au, organizes volunteer conservation projects. Overnight costs are around $25 per day, including accommodation, food and travel.
Employment National, T02 9200 6800, provides good advice on where in the country to find seasonal work, and have local agencies across Australia helping

find specific employment.
Visitoz, T07 4168 6106, www.visitoz.org, puts you in touch with outback stations looking for workers.
Willing Workers on Organic Farms, T03 5155 0218, www.wwoof.com.au, specializes in matching travellers with their 1,400 affiliated farms and stations. The $50 membership gets you a guidebook on the scheme, friendly advice and insurance against accidental injury.

Before you travel

Visas and immigration

Visas are subject to change, so check first with your local Australian Embassy or High Commission. All travellers to Australia, except New Zealand citizens, must have a valid visa to enter Australia. These must be arranged prior to travel (allow two months) and cannot be organized at Australian airports.

Tourist visas
Tourist visas are free and are available from your local Australian Embassy or High Commission, or in some countries, in electronic format (an Electronic Travel Authority or ETA) from their websites, and from selected travel agents and airlines. Passport holders eligible to apply for an ETA include those from Austria, Belgium, Canada, Denmark, Finland, France, Germany, Greece, Hong Kong, the Irish Republic, Italy, Japan, Netherlands, Norway, Spain, Sweden, Switzerland, the UK and the USA. Tourist visas allow visits of up to three months within the year after the visa is issued. Six-month, multiple-entry tourist visas are also available to visitors from certain countries. Tourist visas do not allow the holder to work in Australia. See also www.immi.gov.au.

Working holiday visa
This visa, which must also be arranged prior to departure, is available to people between 18 and 30 from certain countries that have reciprocal arrangements with Australia, including Canada, Denmark, Germany, Irish Republic, Japan, Netherlands, Norway, Sweden and the UK. Arrangements with Italy and France are pending. The working holiday visa allows multiple entries for one year from first arrival. It is granted on the condition that the holder works for no more than three months for a single employer. Your local Australian Embassy or High Commission issues the visa, for which there is a charge. Application forms can be downloaded from www.immi.gov.au.

Embassies and commissions

A full list can be found at www.dfat.gov.au/ missions. For details of your own embassy or consulate in Australia see the Perth directory, page 92, or visit www.dfat.gov.au/protocol.

Canada 7th Floor, Suite 710, 50 O'Connor St, Ottawa, Ontario, T613 236 0841, www.ahc-ottaw.org.

France (and visa processing for Luxembourg and Belgium) 4 rue Jean Rey, 75724 Paris, Cedex 15, T01 4059 3300/2, www.france.embassy.gov.au.

Germany (and visa processing for Switzerland, Denmark and Norway) Wallstrasse 76-79, 10179 Berlin, T030 8800880, www.australian-embassy.de.

Irish Republic 7th Floor, Fitzwilton Hse, Wilton Terr, Dublin 2, T01 6761517, www.australianembassy.ie.

Italy Via Antonio Bosio 5, 00161 Rome, T06 852721, www.italy.embassy. gov.au.

Japan 2-1-14 Mita, Minato-Ku, Tokyo, T03 5232 4111, www.australia.or.jp.

Netherlands Carnegielaan 4, 2517 KH The Hague, T070 3108200, www.australian-embassy.nl.

New Zealand 72-76 Hobson St, Thorndon, Wellington, T04 473 6411, www.australia.org.nz.

South Africa 292 Orient St, Pretoria, Arcadia 0083, T012 3423781, www.australia.co.za.

Spain Pza Descubridor Diego de Ordás, 3, 28003 Madrid, T091 441 6025, www.spain.embassy.gov.au.

Sweden Sergels Torg 12, 11th Floor, 111 57 Stockholm, T08 613 2900, www.sweden.embassy.gov.au.

United Kingdom Australia House, The Strand, London, WC2B 4LA, T020 7379 4334, www.australia.org.uk.

USA 1601 Massachusetts Ave, NW 20036, Washington DC, T202 797 3000, www.austemb.org.

Customs and duty free

The limits for duty-free goods brought into the country include: 2.25 litres of any alcoholic drink (beer, wine or spirits), and 250 cigarettes, or 250 grams of cigars or tobacco. There are various import restrictions, many there to help protect Australia's already heavily hit ecology. These primarily involve live plants and animals, plant and animal materials (including all items made from wood) and foodstuffs. If in doubt, confine wooden and plant goods to well-worked items and bring processed food only (even this may be confiscated, though Marmite is accepted with a knowing smile). Even muddy walking boots may attract attention. Declare any such items for inspection on arrival if you are unsure. See website www.customs.gov.au for more details.

Vaccinations

None is required to enter Australia, see Health, page 53, for further information.

What to take

If you do forget some essential item you should be able to find it in Western Australia's major cities. Special respect must be paid to the Australian sun. A decent wide-brimmed hat and factor 30+ sun-cream (cheap in Australian supermarkets) are essential. Light, long-sleeved tops and trousers cut down the necessity for quite as much sun-cream, help keep out the mosquitoes and keep you warmer in the early evening when the temperature can drop markedly. Even in the north it can get cold in winter so a few key warm clothes are also a good idea.

❖ *Most larger towns have coin-operated launderettes. The average cost is about $5 for a wash and tumble dry.*

If you're planning on doing some walking or trekking, come as prepared as you would do for wetter climes, including packing some decent boots. The weather can change rapidly, particularly in the south in winter, and trails can get boggy. It is quite easy to get lost on longer treks, so pack a compass and map (see page 40). A sleeping bag is useful in hostels and caravan parks, as linen is not always supplied. In summer a sheet sleeping bag and pillowcase usually suffices. Other useful items include: day bag, waterproof sandals, penknife (with bottle and can opener), padlock and length of light chain for security, head torch, water bottle (such as the *Platypus*), plastic lunchbox and a travel alarm clock. Having said that, other than boots, most walking and camping equipment can usually be hired in the larger cities.

Film can be expensive in Australia so you are advised to stock up before coming to Australia (especially in the USA) or at duty free shops on arrival. See Health, page 53, for medical items.

Insurance

It's a very good idea to take out some form of travel insurance, wherever you're travelling from. This should cover you for theft or loss of possessions and money, the cost of medical and dental treatment, cancellation of flights, delays in travel arrangements, accidents, missed departures, lost baggage, lost passport and personal liability and legal expenses. Also check on inclusion of 'dangerous activities' such as climbing, diving, skiing, horse riding, even trekking, if you plan on doing any.

You should always read the small print carefully. Not all policies cover ambulance, helicopter rescue or emergency flights home. Find out if your policy pays medical expenses direct to the hospital or doctor, or if you have to pay and then claim the money back later. If the latter applies, make sure you keep all records. There are a variety of policies to choose from, so it's best to shop around. Your travel agent can advise on the best deals available.

If you are unfortunate enough to have something stolen, make sure you get a copy of the police report, as you will need this to substantiate your claim.

Insurance companies

Reputable student travel organizations often offer good value policies.
Access America, T1866 8073982, www.accessamerica.com. In USA.
Age Concern, T0800 009966, www.age concern.org.uk. Offers the best policies for older travellers in UK.

Columbus, T0845 3308518, www.colum busdirect.net. In UK.
Direct Travel Insurance, T0190 3812345, www. direct-travel.co.uk. In UK.
Flexicover Group, T0870 9909292, www. Flexicover.net. In UK.
STA, T800 7814040, www.sta-travel.com. US.
Travel Insurance Services, T800 9371387, www.travelinsure.com. In USA.

Money

Currency
The Australian dollar ($) is divided into 100 cents (c). Coins come in denominations of $0.05, $0.10, $0.20, $0.50, $1 and $2. Banknotes come in denominations of $5, $10, $20, $50 and $100. **Exchange rates** (April 2005): 1 Aus $ = US$0.72, £0.40, €0.60.

Banks
The four major banks, the **Challenge/Westpac, Commonwealth, National** and **ANZ**, are usually the best places to change money (and travellers' cheques), though **bureaux de change** tend to have slightly longer opening hours and often open at weekends. Bank opening hours are Monday to Friday, from around 0930 to 1630.

Travellers' cheques
The safest way to carry money is in travellers' cheques, though travellers' dependence on them is fast becoming superseded by the prevalence of ATMs. **American Express, Thomas Cook** and **Visa** are the cheques most commonly accepted. Remember to keep a record of the cheque numbers and the cheques you've cashed separate from the cheques themselves. Travellers' cheques are accepted for exchange in banks, large hotels, post offices and large gift shops. Some insist that at least a portion of the amount is in exchange for goods or services. Commission when cashing travellers' cheques is usually 1 per cent or a flat rate. Hotels rates are often poor.

Debit and credit cards
You can withdraw cash from **ATMs** (cashpoints) with a debit or credit card issued by most international banks. Most hotels, shops, tourist operators and restaurants in Australia accept the major credit cards, though some places may charge for using them. When booking always check if an operator accepts them.

Money transfers
If you need money urgently, the quickest way to have it sent is to have it wired to the nearest bank via **Western Union** ⓘ *T1800 3256000, www.westernunion.com*. Charges apply but on a sliding scale. Complete online services are available with

Travelex, www.travelex.com.au. Money can also be wired by **Amex** or **Thomas Cook**, though this may take a day or two, or transferred direct from bank to bank, but this can take several days. Within Australia money orders can be used to send money. See www.auspost.com.au.

Cost of living/travelling

Accommodation, particularly outside Perth, is good value, though prices can rise uncomfortably in peak seasons. Eating out can be indecently cheap. Around $175 is enough to cover dinner for two at the very best restaurants in Perth and the bill at many still excellent establishments can be half that. Transport varies considerably in price and can be a major factor in your travelling budget. Beer is about $4-6 a throw in pubs and bars, as is a neat spirit or glass of wine. Wine will generally be around 1½ times to double the price in restaurants as it would be from a bottleshop. The general cost of living in Australia is reckoned to be equivalent to the USA and up to 40 per cent cheaper than the UK.

The minimum budget required, if staying in hostels or campsites, cooking for yourself, not drinking much and travelling relatively slowly is about $60 per person per day, but this isn't going to be a lot of fun. Going on the odd tour, travelling faster and eating out occasionally will raise this to a more realistic $80-110. Those staying in modest B&Bs, hotels and motels as couples, eating out most nights and taking a few tours will need to reckon on about $150-250 per person per day. Non-hostelling single travellers should budget on spending around 60-70 per cent of what a couple would spend.

Discounts

Many forms of transport and most tourist sites and tours will give discounts to all or some of the following: students, backpackers, the unemployed, the aged (all grouped as 'concessions' in this guide) and children. Proof will be required, a passport usually sufficient for children or the aged. See also Student travellers, page 23.

Getting there

Air

As Australia is an island nation, and a considerable distance from anywhere except Indonesia and Papua New Guinea, the vast majority of international visitors arrive by air. There are international flights direct to Perth from many cities around the world as well as interstate ones from most other Australian state capitals, see Getting around page 35. However, it is usually possible to book internal Australian flights when booking your international ticket, at lower prices than on arrival. Some do not even require a stated departure and arrival point. If you have any plans to fly within Australia check this out with your travel agent prior to booking.

There are now enormous numbers of high street, phone and internet outlets for buying your plane ticket. This can make life confusing but the competition does mean that dogged work can be rewarded in a very good deal. Fares will depend on the season, with prices much higher during December-January unless booked well in advance. Mid-year tends to see the cheapest fares. **Qantas** is Australia's main international airline and flies from a considerable number of international capitals and major cities. Most other major airlines have flights to Australia from their home countries or Europe.

One-way flight tickets are not necessarily a lot more expensive than half a return fare. If you are contemplating a lengthy trip and are undecided about further plans, or like the idea of being unconstrained, then a single fare could be for you. Australian immigration officials can get very suspicious of visitors arriving on one-way tickets, however, especially on short-term visas. Anyone without long-term residency on a one-way ticket will need to show proof of substantial funds – enough for a stay and onward flight. Discuss your circumstances with your local travel agent or directly with the Australian Embassy or High Commission in your country before committing to a one-way ticket. **Round-the-World (RTW) tickets** can be a real bargain if you stick to the most popular routes, sometimes working out even cheaper than a return fare. RTWs start at around £800 (€1,185 or US$1,750), depending on the season. Perth is easy to include on a RTW itinerary.

When trying to find the best deal, make sure you check the route, journey duration, stopovers, departure and arrival times, restrictions and cancellation penalties. Many cheap flights are sold by small agencies, most honest and reliable, but there may be some risks involved with buying tickets at rock-bottom prices. Avoid paying too much money in advance and check with the airline directly to ensure you have a reservation.

From Europe
The main route, and the cheapest, is via Asia, though fares will also be quoted via North America or Africa. The Asia route usually takes 20-30 hours including stops. There are as yet no non-stop routes (though lookout for the launch of Boeing's 787, which could in theory do London to Perth in one hop), so it's worth checking out what stopovers are on offer: this might be your only chance to see Kuala Lumpur. Stopovers of a few nights do not usually increase the cost of the ticket appreciably. The cheapest return flights, off-season, will be around £600 (€900), with stand-by prices rising to at least £800 (€1,200) around Christmas. Flights to Perth are usually marginally cheaper than to the other state capitals.

Airlines

Air New Zealand, www.airnz.co.uk.
British Airways, www.britishairways.com.
Emirates, www.emirates.com.
Garuda Indonesia,
www.garuda-indonesia.com.
Qantas, www.qantas.co.uk.
Singapore Airlines, www.singaporeair.com.

Agents

Companies dealing in volume can offer better deals than the airlines themselves.

www.cheapflights.com. Online provider.
www.ebookers.com. Online provider.
www.expedia.co.uk. Online provider also offering accommodation and car hire deals.
Flight Centre, T0870 499 5520. Relative newcomer offering good prices.
Flightbookers, T0870 010 7000. Another big player offering good deals.
STA, T0870 160 6070, www.statravel.co.uk, offers special deals for under-26s.
Trailfinders, T0870 814 6614, nationwide.
Travelbag, T01420 80828, www. travelbag. adventures.co.uk. Quotes competitive fares.

From New Zealand
There are direct **Qantas** flights from Auckland, Christchurch and Wellington to Brisbane, Melbourne and Sydney. **Air New Zealand**, www.airnewzealand.co.nz, and **Freedom Air**, www.freedom.co.nz, are the other two main carriers, both offering routes that Qantas do not. Expect to pay a minimum of NZ$1,000 for a return through flight to Perth.

From the Americas
There are direct **Qantas** flights from Los Angeles to Brisbane, Melbourne and Sydney, and from Vancouver and New York to Sydney. The cost of a standard return in the high season from starts from around US$2,200 from Vancouver, US$2,000 from New York, and US$1,700 from Los Angeles. There are also direct flights from Buenos Aires to Sydney.

Airlines

Air New Zealand,
www.airnewzealand.com.
United, www.ual.com.
Air Canada, www.aircanada.com.
Qantas, www.qantas.com.au.
Singapore Airlines,
www.singaporeair.com.

Agents

Hari World Travels, www.hariworld.com,
and **STA,** www.sta-travel.co.uk, have offices
in New York, Toronto and Ontario.
Student fares are also available from
Council Travel, www.counciltravel.com,
with several offices in the USA and
Travel Cuts, www.travelcuts.com, in Canada.

From South Africa

There are direct **Qantas** flights from **Johannesburg** to Perth. **South African Airways**
www.saa.co.za, also flies direct. The flight takes around 11 hours.

Rail

Trainways ① *T132147* or *T8213 4592, www.gsr.com.au*, operates **The Indian Pacific**
service to Perth from Sydney and Adelaide with connections from Darwin, Alice
Springs and Melbourne. An unbroken trip from Sydney takes three days and nights.
The Ghan connects Darwin and Alice Springs to Adelaide (46 hours). **The Overland**
connects Melbourne to Adelaide (10 hours). Unless coming from
Sydney an overnight stopover in Adelaide may be required.
Vehicles can be brought along and sometimes special deals can
make this well worth considering.

‡ *Adult fares get
considerably cheaper
if booked in advance.*

There are three ticket levels on *The Indian Pacific* and *The
Ghan*. The 'Gold Kangaroo' passenger gets a small sleeping cabin, all meals in the
'Gold' dining car, and a lounge. 'Red Kangaroo' passengers have separate lounge and
dining car (meals not included), and either a cabin or day/nighter seat (an ordeal for
some). The seat-only prices are roughly equivalent with interstate buses, with the red
cabins about 2½ times the cost and gold cabins 3½ times. Concessions are good
value, particularly for the long-distance, 'red' seats (Sydney to Perth for as little as
$240!). Great Southern Railway Backpacker Pass ($450) allows unlimited travel in a
'red' day/nighter seat on *The Ghan*, *The Indian Pacific* and *The Overland* for six
months. Pass holders must be members of a recognized backpacker organization (eg
YHA). Upgrades to sleeping berths are allowed, but surcharges apply.

Road

Bus

McCaffertys/Greyhound ① *T131499* or *T07 4690 9950, www.greyhound.com.au*,
have services throughout Australia and it's possible to get a direct, if long ride from
most of the mainland state capitals to Perth, Broome and most of the coastal towns in
between. See Getting around, page 36, for details of travel passes.

Car

Driving to Western Australia involves a trip of at least 1,500 km from anywhere else
in the country and conceivably up to about 5,000 km. Before deciding and setting
out on a self-drive road trip to WA first ensure that the vehicle driver(s) and
passengers are all able, willing, well-prepared and aware of what the journey
involves! Whether coming across the north from NT to the Kimberley and Pilbara, or
from the south across the Nullarbor, and especially via the unsealed Outback
Highway from Yulara, the journey will involve at least one to two days driving across

very hot, arid and sparsely populated regions. See Getting around, page 36, for further information on preparation and driving in Australia. On pages 137 and 211, the routes are given from WA out east.

Touching down

Airport information

Perth Airport, 10 km east of the city centre, has two terminals – domestic and international. With no direct link between the two, transfers are via the perimeter highways. The domestic terminal, Brearley Avenue, has a wide range of services including ATMs, **Travelex** foreign exchange, luggage lockers, cafés and all the major car hire firms. The international terminal, Horrie Miller Drive, is slightly further out. Facilities are just as comprehensive, the **Thomas Cook** foreign exchange counters remaining open before and after all flights. See also Perth Ins and outs, page 62, and the box on page 63.

Taxes

There are currently a number of **departure taxes** levied by individual airports (such as noise tax) and the government. All departure taxes are included in the cost of a ticket, but may not be included in a quote when you first enquire about the cost of a ticket. Almost all goods in Australia are subject to a **Goods and Services Tax** (GST) of 10 per cent. Visitors from outside Australia will find certain shops can deduct the GST if you have a valid departure ticket.

Tourist information

Tourist offices, or **Visitor Information Centres** (**VICs**), can be found in all but the smallest Western Australian towns. Their locations, phone numbers, website or e-mail addresses, and opening hours are listed in the relevant sections of this guide. In most larger towns they have met certain criteria to be officially *accredited*. This usually means that they have some paid staff and will almost certainly mean they are open daily 0900-1700 (except, usually, Christmas day). Smaller offices may close at weekends, but given that many are run entirely by volunteers – something to bear in mind when someone struggles to find an obscure piece of information – the level of commitment to the visitor is impressive. All offices will provide information on accommodation, and local sights, attractions, and tours. Many will also have information on eating out, local history and the environment, and sell local souvenirs, guides and maps. Most will provide a free town map.

Local customs and laws

Anyone travelling from Western Europe or the USA will find Australia's laws and customs very similar to their own, with few unusual prohibitions. In particular laws against recreational drugs are severe and are closely policed. European visitors may

● *Entry to National Trust properties is free to members from UK, USA, Canada, New Zealand,*
● *Japan, Netherlands.*

Touching down

Business hours 0830-1700 Monday-Friday. Many convenience stores and supermarkets are open daily. Late night shopping is generally Thursday or Friday.

Cyclones Cyclone information T1300 659210, www.bom.gov.au/weather/wa. Advice or emergency assistance from **SES**, T1300 130039.

Driving Urban speed limit 50 kph unless otherwise indicated, state maximum 110 kph.

Electricity The current in Australia is 240/250v AC. Plugs have 2 or 3 blade pins and adaptors are widely available.

Emergencies For police, fire brigade or ambulance dial 000.

Fire Seasonal fire bans are managed by local shires. Contact the shire directly or the nearest VIC for advice.

Phone code 08, followed by an eight-digit number.

Road conditions Main Roads Western Australia, T1800 013314, www.mainroads.wa.gov.au. RAC, T1800 999036, also give good advice.

Smoking Illegal in restaurants, cafés and pubs where eating is a primary activity, and on public transport.

Time Western Standard Time: GMT+8 hours. 1½ hours behind SA and the NT, 2 hours behind the eastern states.

Water Generally safe, though not always pleasant! As a precious resource, use sparingly at all times.

Weather Forecasts: T1900 926113, www.bom.gov.au.

Weights and measures All metric.

find traffic penalties being more harshly enforced; there is very little leeway given on speeding and none on alcohol consumption, and parking attendants are ever alert (watch out for 'rear to kerb only' parking spots). Smoking is now illegal where food is publicly available and on public transport. Many towns have banned the consumption of alcohol on selected beaches, in parks and in other public spaces – if this is the case signs will be conspicuous. There are several sensible guidelines for behaviour within national parks, forests and on Aboriginal land (see below) – and many of these are backed by the force of law. In particular are prohibitions against fires during 'fire bans' – again look for signs. Tipping is not the norm in Australia, but a discretionary five-10 per cent tip for particularly good service will be appreciated.

Responsible tourism

All over the world the responsible traveller sticks to the creed of 'take nothing but photographs and leave nothing but footprints'. Of course this should apply to Australia too, where there are also some unique considerations. One of Australia's main attractions is the natural environment and its wildlife, and there are many opportunities for eco-tourism. **CALM** promote a minimal impact bushwalking code aimed at protecting the environment, which is also a useful guide for minimizing your footprint in other natural environments.

Fire is a critical issue in Western Australia's hot dry environments where only a spark is needed to create a fire that can get out of control and destroy an area the size of a small country in a day or two, perhaps threatening lives and property. For this reason, in some areas, there are total fire bans, either for a seasonal period or on days when a high risk of fire is predicted. In extreme circumstances a national park, scenic attraction or walking trail may be closed because the risk of fire is so high. Fire bans or restrictions usually apply in summer (November-March) in the south and during the

⁑ How big is your footprint?

1 Follow the minimal impact bushwalking code for walking and camping. Details can be obtained from any park office. Choose a responsible operator. Ecotourism Association of Australia, T07 3229 5550, www.ecotourism.org.au, promotes ecologically sustainable and responsible products and tourism.

2 Try not to drive at dawn, dusk or at night, both to avoid killing native animals and for your own safety.

3 Water is a precious resource in Australia – don't waste it or pollute it. In dry conditions camp away from waterholes so that animals are not afraid to approach the water.

4 Carrying sufficient water, food and fuel and appropriate clothing or equipment may save your life and avoid danger, expense and inconvenience for those who might otherwise have to rescue you.

5 If you have to pass through gates in national parks or on private property the rule is 'leave them as you find them'.

6 There are many opportunities for recycling glass, plastic, paper etc. Look out for recycling bins in supermarket car parks.

7 Don't feed wild animals – native or feral.

late dry season in the north (July-November). Check fire restrictions before travel with the nearest parks, shire, police or VIC as they may affect your preparations; for example on days of Total Fire Ban you may not even use a camping stove and will have to take food that doesn't need cooking.

Campers should always carry a fuel stove for cooking as many national parks or public reserves forbid campfires or the collection of wood or both. Fallen timber and hollow logs are an important habitat for wildlife.

It is also good practice to keep your walking or camping gear clean between different environments, particularly in the southern forest areas affected by **dieback**, a fungus called *Phytophthora cinnamomi* that attacks the roots of plants. It is spread when soil or roots are moved, possibly via your boots, car or tent. Dieback areas are usually closed to the public but boot-cleaning stations are provided for high-risk walking tracks.

Travellers in Western Australia will also come across 'sacred sites', areas of religious importance to indigenous people, and naturally it is important to respect any restrictions that may apply to these areas. Permission is usually required to enter an Aboriginal community and you may be asked to comply with restrictions, such as a ban on alcohol. If you visit a community, or travel through Aboriginal land, respect the privacy of Aboriginal people and never take photographs without asking first.

For more about environmental issues or get to involved in conservation contact the **Australian Conservation Foundation** ① *T02 9212 6600, www.acfonline.org.au* or **The Wilderness Society** ① *T03 6234 9799, www.wilderness.org.au*. The quarterly wilderness adventure magazine **Wild** ① *www.wild.com.au*, is also a good source of information on current environmental issues and campaigns. Available at newsagents.

Safety → *See also Health, page 53.*

Western Australia certainly has its dangers, but with a little common sense and basic precautions they are relatively easy to minimize. The most basic but important are

Essentials Touching down

against the effects of the **sun**. UV levels can soar in Australia, with safe exposure limits as low as three minutes. A bad burn has ruined many a holiday, and unhealthy exposure can lead to much worse later. As well as sunburn, **heat-stroke** is also a danger, a common result of too much heat and too little fluid.

In Perth and the other major cities, as in almost any city in the world, there is always the possibility of **muggings**, alcohol-induced harassment or worse. The usual simple precautions apply, like keeping a careful eye and hand on belongings, not venturing out alone at night and avoiding dark, lonely areas.

Footprint is a partner in the Foreign and Commonwealth Office's Know before you go campaign www.fco.gov.uk/travel.

In the water

On the beach there is little to trouble the holidaymaker who sticks to the shore and swims between the patrolled flags, but swimmers must be aware of hidden dangers. The principal one is the rip, a strong, off-shore undertow that can sweep even waders off their feet, submerge them and drown them astonishingly quickly. Always look out for signs indicating common rip areas, and ask locals if at all unsure. See the **Surf Life Saving Australia** website, www.slsa.asn.au, for more information. Much publicized, but out of all proportion, is the danger from sharks. There are a handful of shark attacks in Australia each year, and usually one or two are fatal, but this must be balanced against the number of times someone goes for a swim or surf each year – hundreds of millions. Several other sea creatures are far more likely to do you harm, biggest of these are the Estuarine crocodiles ('salties') of the far north. If given the opportunity they will ambush and eat any animal or person careless enough to stray near or into their river or estuary. Always check whether a waterhole or river is likely to be a crocodilian home, and if in doubt assume it is. Australian coastal waters are also home to a host of fish, jellyfish, octopus, urchins, coral and even molluscs that can inflict extremely painful, sometimes lethal stings and bites.

Take precautions. Park rangers and the police are good sources of information. If you have the time learn about the various local poisonous marine creatures, their tell-tale wound-marks and symptoms, and the correct procedure for treatment. See page 53. Tell someone on-shore you are going for a swim. Avoid swimming alone, and keep swimming partners in sight. While snorkelling or diving, do not touch either creatures or coral. Even minor coral scratches can lead to infections, and it doesn't do the coral any good either. Wear a wetsuit or t-shirt and shorts even if the water is warm. This will lessen the effect of any sting and help protect against the sun. Wear waterproof sunscreen, and reapply frequently. If wading around in shallow water, particularly near reefs, wear a pair of old trainers or waterproof sandals. A large number of the little beasties that can do you serious harm do so when you tread on them (they don't enjoy the experience much either). If you are bitten or stung, get out of the water, carefully remove and keep any spine or tissue, seek advice as to appropriate immediate treatment and apply it, and quickly seek medical help. When jumping off rocks into water, always first check that the depth is sufficient.

On land

There are numerous creatures with very poisonous bites on land. Most will only bite, however, if trodden on, cornered or harassed. The most common poisonous spider is the tiny, shy redback, which has a shiny black body with distinct red markings. It regularly sets up shop under rocks or in garden sheds and garages. Outside toilets are also a favourite. There are dozens of venomous snake species. Few are actively aggressive and even those only during certain key times of year, such as mating season, but all are easily provoked and for many an untreated bite can be fatal.

The main dangers while bushwalking are dehydration from a lack of water, heat-stroke, and getting lost. Before setting out seek advice about how to access the start and finish of the track, the terrain you are planning to traverse, how long it will take given your party's minimum fitness level, the likely weather conditions, and prepare accordingly. Park rangers and the police are good sources of information. Learn about the various local poisonous snakes, their seasonal habits, tell-tale wound-marks and symptoms, and the correct procedure for treatment. Plan, if possible, to walk in the early morning or late afternoon when the famous golden glow often takes hold just before sunset. These are also the best times for viewing wildlife. Take a decent map of the area, a compass, and a first-aid kit. Take full precautions for the sun, but also be prepared for wet or cold weather. Take plenty of water, in hot weather at least one litre for every hour you plan to walk (a frozen plastic bottle will ensure cold water for hours). On long-distance walks take something to purify stream and standing water as giardia is present in some areas. Wear stout walking shoes and socks. Tell someone where you are going and when you plan to get back. Avoid striding through long grass and try to keep to tracks. If the path is obscured, make plenty of noise as you walk. If you do see a snake, give it a wide berth. If you need to squat to go to the toilet, or are collecting firewood, bash the undergrowth around your position. If you do get bitten by either a spider or snake stay calm and still, apply pressure to the bite area and wind a compression bandage around it (except for redback bites). Remain as still as possible and keep the limb immobile. Seek urgent medical attention. A description of the creature, and residual venom on the victim's skin, will help with swift identification and so treatment. Anti-venom is available for most spider and snake bites. Avoid walking alone, and keep walking partners in sight. Keep to paths and avoid cliff edges.

Emergency services

Dial ooo for the emergency services. The three main professional emergency services are supported by several others, including the **State Emergency Service** (SES), **Country Fire Service** (CFS), **Surf Life Saving Australia** (SLSA), **Sea-search and Rescue**, and **St John's Ambulance**. The **SES** is prominent in co-ordinating search and rescue operations. The **CFS** provides invaluable support in fighting and controlling bush fires. These services, though professionally trained, are mostly provided by volunteers.

Getting around

Public transport in and around Perth, based on bus and train networks, is generally good and efficient, and often easier than driving. Many of the larger cities also have modest bus services, but some can be curiously regardless of tourist traffic and there is many an important outlying attraction poorly served by public transport, or even missed off the bus routes completely. Some cities are compact enough for this to be a minor irritation, others are so spread out that the visitor must invest in an expensive tourist bus service or taxis to get around. In such places staying at a hostel or B&B with free or low-cost bicycle hire can save a lot of money.

Log on to www.whereis. com.au to view or print out a town or city map in WA.

By far the best way of seeing the west coast is under your own steam, or with a tour operator with an in-depth itinerary. The further from Perth you go, the more patchy and irregular public transport becomes. If short on time and long on funds, flying can save a lot of time and effort. In some cases it is the only real option.

Air

As the biggest state, and one with much profitable mining industry, air travel is common within WA. Though not usually very cheap, a couple of judicious flights can save days of travel if you're short of time. **Skywest** ① *T1300 660088 or T08 9478 9999, www.skywest.com.au*, is the principal state airline with flights from Perth to all the major towns. NT's **Air North** ① *T08 8920 4000, www.air north.com.au*, has connections between Broome, Kununurra and Darwin. **Qantas** ① *T131313, www.qantas.com.au*, provides direct flights between Perth and the main northern towns. If the latter does operate a route they are likely to offer the cheapest fare, usually $100-500 one-way. You could also try **Virgin Blue** ① *T136789 or T07 3295 2296, www.virginblue. com. au*. There are a couple of flight agencies worth checking out: **Flight Centre** ① *T133133, www.flight centre.com.au*; **Harvey World Travel** ① *T02 9567 6099, www.Harveyworld.com.au*; **JetSet** ① *T136383, www.jetset.com.au*; **STA** ① *T1300 733035, www.statravel.com*.

> ☙ *Many provincial airports may not be staffed when you arrive, check with the local VIC regarding transport from the airport to the town.*

Rail

There are limited local lines operated by **TransWA** ① *T1300 6622 05, www.transwa. wa.gov.au*, and integrated into their general schedules. Some journeys alternate between bus and train. Tickets are available at coach and bus stations, and by telephone. See Bus below for contact details.

Road

Bus

If travelling by bus around the west coast, always check the journey duration and time of arrival. Some routes can literally take days, each with 24 hours of travel with just a handful of short meal stops. Many coaches are equipped with videos, but you may want a book to hand. It's also a good idea to take warm clothing, socks, a pillow, toothbrush and ear-plugs. There's a good chance you will arrive in the late evening or the early hours of the morning. If it is the case, book accommodation ahead and, if possible, transfer transportation. At least ensure you know how to get to your accommodation, and try to avoid walking around alone late at night. Also double-check times of connections: many travel arrangements have been disrupted by the discovery that a bus was on a different day than assumed.

TransWA ① *T1300 662205, www.transwa.wa.gov.au*, runs the main train and bus services around the state though their network only extends as far as Kalbarri to the north. If they do operate a route they are likely to be the cheapest option. **Integrity** ① *T08 9226 1339, www.integritycoachlines.com.au*, heads north as far as Port Hedland, while **South West Coachlines** ① *T08 9324 2333*, has the most comprehensive around the southwest. The national coach carrier **McCaffertys/ Greyhound** ① *T131499 or T07 4690 9950, www.greyhound.com.au*, plugs some of the gaps with services right through to Broome and beyond. As well as scheduled routes and fares they offer two jump-on, jump-off passes. The **Explorer Pass** commits you to a set route, valid from 30-365 days, while the slightly pricier **Kilometre Pass** allows travel anywhere on the network over the course of a year. A 2,000-km pass is $328, concessions $295, with each extra 1,000 km costing around $100.

Backpacker and tour buses

There are now several operators who make the assumption that the most important part of your trip is the journey. Over a dozen Western Australian companies offer one-10 day trips around the WA coast and venturing inland – and most can be used as a way of getting from A to B. They are well worth considering, especially if you are travelling alone. In terms of style, price ($75-150 per day) and what is included they

Distances and bus journey times

Accumulated journey times are likely to be longer due to rest stops.		Cervantes to Geraldton	
		205 km	3¼ hours
		Geraldton to Kalbarri	
		155 km	2¼ hours
Perth to Bunbury		Geraldton to Overlander	
180 km	2¼ hours	280 km	3½ hours
Bunbury to Busselton		Kalbarri to Overlander	
53 km	¾ hour	245 km	3¼ hours
Busselton to Margaret River		Overlander to Monkey Mia	
62 km	1¼ hours	155 km	2¼ hours
Margaret River to Pemberton		Overlander to Carnarvon	
140 km	2½ hours	205 km	3 hours
Bunbury to Pemberton		Carnarvon to Coral Bay	
160 km	2¼ hours	245 km	3¼ hours
Pemberton to Walpole		Coral Bay to Exmouth	
120 km	1¾ hours	150 km	2 hours
Walpole to Albany		Carnarvon to Karratha	
117 km	1¾ hours	630 km	9 hours
Perth to Albany		Karratha to Port Hedland	
410 km	6 hours	235 km	3½ hours
Perth to Cervantes		Port Hedland to Broome	
255 km	4 hours	605 km	7½ hours

Essentials Getting around

vary greatly, and it is important to clarify this prior to booking. Some offer transport and commentary only, others include accommodation and some meals, a few specialize in 4WD and bush camping. The latter are not for everyone, but for many will provide an unforgettable experience. Make sure you ask around and chat to some of the operators before committing yourself. Ask about the average age and size of the tour group, the activity level, and details of the itinerary so you can be sure you will see and experience what you want to in a way that suits your ability and comfort level. One of the principal differences between the operators is in the sleeping arrangements they offer. For details of these tour operators, see page 20.

Car, motorbike and bicycle

There is no substitute in Western Australia for having your own transport. As a general rule of thumb consider buying a car for travelling more than three months. If hiring or buying a car, do consider a campervan as an alternative. Long-term bicycle hire is rarely available, and touring cyclists should plan to bring their own bike or buy in Perth.

Traffic congestion is rarely an issue, even Perth has nothing like the traffic of most cities, so driving itineraries can be based on covering a planned distance each day. Up to, say 100 km for each solid hour's driving. The key factor in planning transport is distance. Driving or cycling outside of the main cities is pretty stress-free, but the distances can be huge. Drivers can get very bored – and sleepy. There are a lot of single-vehicle accidents in Australia, and many are a result of driver fatigue.

Also in the country watch out for large animals. Kangaroos and emus can appear seemingly out of nowhere, particularly at dawn and dusk, and sheep and cattle frequently stray onto unfenced roads. Collisions with animals are another major cause of single-vehicle accidents. Such collisions are not simply irritations: hitting a kangaroo, emu or sheep can write-off the vehicle and cause injury. Hitting cattle or a camel is considerably worse. Drive only in full daylight if possible.

On country roads you will also meet road trains. These trucks can be over 50-m long including up to four separate trailers strung along behind the main cab. Overtaking them entails great care – wait for a good long stretch before committing. If you are on a single track bitumen road or an unsealed road pull right over and slow considerably when one comes the other way. Not only can dust cause zero visibility, but you will also minimize the possibility of stones pinging up and damaging your windows.

The general breakdown number is T131111.

The other major factor when planning is the type of roads you may need to use. All the main highways are 'sealed', but many country roads and outback 'tracks' are unsealed, usually meaning a stony or sand surface. When recently graded (levelled and compacted) they can be almost as pleasant to drive on as sealed roads, but even then there are reduced levels of handling. After grading, unsealed roads deteriorate over time. Potholes form, they can become impassable when wet, and corrugations usually develop. These are regular ripples in the road surface, perpendicular to the road direction, and can go on for tens of kilometres. Small ones simply cause an irritating judder, large ones can reduce tolerable driving speeds to 10-20 kph. Generally, the bigger the wheel size and the longer the wheel-base, the more comfortable journeys over corrugations will be. Many unsealed roads can be negotiated with a two wheel-drive (2WD), low-clearance vehicle, but the ride will be a lot more comfortable, and safer in a four wheel-drive (4WD) high-clearance one. Most 2WD hire-cars are uninsured if driven on unsealed roads. Some unsealed roads are designated as 4WD-only or tracks, though individual definitions of some differ according to the map or authority you consult. In dry weather and after recent grading some can be driven in well prepared 2WD cars. At other times they cannot without serious risk of accident, vehicle or tyre damage or getting bogged. If in any doubt whatsoever, stick to the roads you are certain are safe for your vehicle, and you are sufficiently prepared for. Always check with the hire company where you can and cannot take your 4WD vehicle (some will not allow them off graded roads), and also what your liability will be in the case of an accident. Of particular note are the roads in the Pilbara. Although generally passable for 2WD, they are notoriously good at causing punctures on all types of vehicles. Experiencing two or three punctures here on a single trip is not uncommon.

Prepare carefully before driving to remote areas. Even if there are regular roadhouses, try to carry essential spares and tools such as fan belts, hoses, gaffer tape, a tyre repair kit, extra car jack, extra spare wheel and tyre, spade, decent tool kit, oil and coolant, and a fuel can. Membership of the RAC is recommended, as is informing someone of your intended itinerary. Above all carry plenty of spare water, at least 10 litres per person, 20 if possible.

Rules and regulations To drive in WA you must have a current driving licence. Foreign nationals may need an international drivers licence, available from your national motoring organisation. In Australia you **drive on the left**. Speed limits vary between town and country, with maximum urban limits of 50-60 kph and maximum country limits of 100-110 kph. Speeding penalties include a fine, and police allow little leeway. Seatbelts are compulsory for drivers and passengers. Driving under the influence of **alcohol** is illegal over certain (very small) limits and penalties are severe.

Fuel Fuel costs are approximately half that in Britain, twice that in the US, fluctuating between $0.90-1.10 a litre in and around Perth and $1.00-1.35 a litre elsewhere. Anyone driving long distances in WA will soon find that fuel expenses exceed those of food and rival those of accommodation. If budgeting, allow at least $10 for every estimated 100 km.

The RAC ① T131703 or 9421 4444, www.rac.com.au, breakdown service and
motoring organization is affiliated to the **Australian Automobile Association** (AAA),
www.aaa.asn.au, which your home country organization may have a reciprocal link
with. All other Australian states motoring organizations also have reciprocal links.
Note that you will only be covered for about 100 km (depending on scheme) of
towing distance.

Vehicle hire Car rental costs vary according to where you hire from (it's cheaper in
Perth, though small local companies have good deals), what you hire and the
mileage/insurance terms. You may be better off making arrangements in your own
country for a fly/drive deal. Watch out for kilometre caps: some can be as low as 100
km per day. The minimum you'll pay is around $200 a week for a small car. Drivers
need to be over 21. At peak times it can be impossible to hire at short notice, and
some companies may dispose of a booked car within as little as half an hour of you
not showing up for an agreed pick-up time. If you've booked a car but are going to be
late ensure that you let them know. Some companies will offer one-way hire on
certain models and under certain conditions.

Buying a vehicle Buying a vehicle in WA is a relatively simple process provided
you have somewhere you can give as an address. Cars and vans that go the
distance can be picked up from $2,500, or $6,000 for a 4WD. Paying more increases
peace of mind, but obviously increases possible losses when you sell it. If you're
dealing with a second-hand **car dealer** you may be able to agree a 'buy-back' price.
Another factor in favour of dealers is that they usually offer some sort of warranty.
The alternatives are fellow travellers, hostel notice boards, and the classifieds. The
principal advantage to buying privately is cost – vehicles being sold by travellers in
a hurry can be bargains. The **RAC** offers vehicle checks for around $100. An older
vehicle may need a little 'tlc' so the availability of **spares** should be a consideration.
Availability is best for Fords and Holdens, but Toyota parts are also common.

You will need to formally complete the transfer of registration with the transport
department, presenting them with the papers and a receipt (there is a stamp duty
tax of about 5 per cent). Registration must be renewed, in the state the vehicle was
last sold, every six or 12 months. Third-party personal injury **insurance** is included in
the registration, but you are advised to invest at least in third party vehicle and
property insurance, even in comprehensive cover if you cannot afford to lose the
value of your vehicle.

Car hire companies

Australia

Avis, T136333, www.avis.com.
Bayswater, 160 Adelaide Terr, Perth, T08
9325 1000, www.bayswatercarrental.com.au.
Great value.
Budget, T1300 362848, www.budget.com.au.
Delta-Europcar, T1800 811541,
www.deltacars.com.au.
Hertz, T133039, www.hertz.com.
Thrifty, T1300 367227, www.rentacar.com.au.

New Zealand

Avis, T09 5262847.

Budget, T09 3752222.
Hertz, T09 3676350.

North America

Avis, T800 3311084, www.avis.com.
Budget, T800 5270700,
www.budgetrentacar.com.
Hertz, T800-6543001, www.hertz.com.
Thrifty, T800 3672277, www.thrifty.com

UK

Avis, T0990 900500, www.avis.com.
Budget, T0800 181181, www.budget.co.uk.
Hertz, T0990 996699, www.hertz.com.
Thrifty, T0990 168238, www.rentacar.co.uk

Hitching

Hitchhiking, while not strictly illegal, is not advisable. There will always be the odd twisted soul around who will assault or abduct. This is not to say that hitching is more dangerous in WA than elsewhere else, but simply that bad things happen.

Maps

View and print touring and street maps at www.whereis.com.au.
Perth Map Centre, 900 Hay St, Perth, T08 9322 5733, and **Chart and Map Shop**, 14 Collie St, Fremantle, T08 9335 8665, www.chartandmapshop.com.au. Both stock a range of national, state and regional maps and guide books. Also bike maps, Bibbulmun and Cape-to-Cape track maps.
RAC, 228 Adelaide Terr, Perth, T08 9421 4400. Also publish fold-out maps to most areas of the state, only $3 for members.
Streetsmart, series of regional touring maps

are produced by the government and are probably the best maps available for drivers as they are very detailed and note points of interest. These can be bought online at www.landonline.com.au, from bookshops, VICs or from **The Central Map Agency**, T08 9273 7555, 1 Midland Sq, Midland.
UBD Country Towns and Street Directory: Western Australia has good information on towns (excluding Perth) and includes a road atlas for the whole state. The best street directories available for Perth are also published by UBD.

Sleeping

There are a diverse and attractive range of accommodation options, from cheap national park campsites alive with wildlife to exclusive and luxurious retreats. Given the weather and the environment, travelling on a budget does not in any way detract from the enjoyment of a trip. On the contrary, this is a place where nights under canvas in national parks, or preparing your porridge on a campfire under the gaze of a possum is an absolute delight.

If we haven't provided the sleeping option to match your ideal, local VICs can supply full accommodation listings. Booking in advance is highly recommended, especially in peak seasons. Useful websites include: **www.australiatravelsearch. com.au, www.global store.com.au, www.jasons.com, www.travel.com.au** and **www. babs.com.au/wa**. Single rooms are relatively scarce outside of pubs, hostels and roadhouses. Air-conditioning (a/c) is common, but check when booking, and if they don't have it ask how they keep their rooms cool. There are plenty of rooms without a/c in Australia impossible to sleep in during hot weather.

Hotels, motels and resorts

At the top end of the scale are some impressive international-standard hotels and resorts, with luxurious surroundings and facilities, attentive service and often outstanding locations. Rooms will typically start in our **L** range. In the main cities are a few less expensive hotels in the **A-B** range. Most 'hotels' outside the major towns are pubs with upstairs or external accommodation. If upstairs a room is likely have access to shared bathroom facilities, while external rooms are usually standard en suite motel units. The quality of pub-hotel accommodation varies considerably, but is usually a budget option (**C-D**). Linen is almost always supplied.

Motels in Australia are usually anonymous, but dependably clean and safe, and usually offer the cheapest en suite rooms. Most have dining facilities and free, secure parking. Some budget motels will fall into our **D** range, most will be **B-C**. Linen is always supplied.

⚉ Hotel price codes explained

Sleeping codes are based on the cost of a night during the high season. Many places offer discounts during low season or for long stays. Where rooms or units sleep more than two people a nominal extra charge will sometimes be levied for a third and fourth person. Scaled grades indicate a range of rooms of varying standards or styles.	**LL** $300 or over for a double or twin **L** $200-299 for a double or twin **A** $160-199 for a double or twin **B** $120-159 for a double or twin **C** $85-119 for a double or twin **D** $28-42 for a single or dorm, $55-84 for a double or twin **E** $18-27 for a single or dorm, $35-54 for a double or twin **F** $17 or under for a single or dorm

B&Bs and self-catering

Bed and Breakfast (B&B) is in some ways quite different from the British model. Not expensive, but rarely a budget option, most fall into our **B-C** ranges. They offer very comfortable accommodation in upmarket houses. Rooms are usually en suite or have access to a private bathroom. Bathrooms shared by more than two rooms are rare. Hosts are usually friendly and informative. Some B&Bs are actually a semi or fully self-contained cottage or cabin with breakfast provisions supplied. Larger ones may have full kitchens. As well as private houses, self-contained, self-catering options are provided by caravan parks and hostels, and some resorts and motels with apartment style units. Check whether linen is supplied in self-catering accommodation.

National parks, farms and stations

Some **National Parks** and rural cattle and sheep stations have old settlers or workers' homes that have been converted into tourist accommodation, usually self-contained. They are often magical places to stay and include many old lighthouse keepers' cottages and shearers' quarters. **Stations** may also invite guests to see or even get involved in the day's activities. Transport to them can be difficult if you don't have your own. Linen is often not supplied in this sort of accommodation. For options other than those detailed in this guide, see www.farmstaywa.com.

Hostels

Western Australia has a large network of good value hostels (**D-F**). They are popular centres for backpackers and provide a great opportunity for meeting fellow travellers. Most will have at least one double room and possibly singles, sometimes with linen. Almost all hostels have kitchen and common room facilities. A few, particularly in cities, will offer freebies including breakfast and pick-ups. Standards vary considerably, and it's well worth asking other travellers about the hostels at your next ports of call. Most are effectively independent and the best tend to be those that are owner-managed. International visitors can obtain a Hostelling International Card (HIC) from any YHA hostel or travel centre. For this you get a handbook to YHA hostels nationwide and around $3 off every night's YHA accommodation. The hostel associations **NOMADS** ① *To2 9232 7788, www.nomadsworld.com, no membership fee*, and **YHA** ① *To2 9261 1111, www.yha.org.au*, seem to ensure the best consistency of quality. **YMCA** ① *To3 9699 7655, www.ymca.org.au*, and **YWCA** ① *To2 6230 5150, www.ywca.org.au*, hostels, are usually a clean and quiet choice in the major cities.

Caravan and tourist parks

Almost every town will have at least one caravan park with unpowered and powered sites, varying from $10-20 for campers, caravans and campervans, an ablution block

Essentials Sleeping

⁝ Ten great B&Bs and self-contained places to stay

100 Hubble, Fremantle, p100.
Basildene Manor, Margaret River, p168.
The Cove, Denmark, p203.
Donnelly Village, Donnelly, p177.
Lighthouse Keeper's Cottages, Rottnest Island, p109.
The Lily, Stirling Range, p210.

Lonsdales, Bickley Valley, Perth Hills, p119.
McAlpine House, Broome, p290.
Monastery Guesthouse, New Norcia, p122.
Tortoiseshell Farm, near Bridgetown, p184.

and usually a camp kitchen or BBQs. Some will have permanently sited caravans (on-site vans) and cabins. On-site vans are usually the cheapest option (**E-F**) for families or small groups wanting to self-cater. Cabins are more expensive (**C-D**). Some will have televisions, en suite bathrooms, separate bedrooms with linen and well equipped kitchens. Power is rated at the domestic level (240/250v AC) which is very convenient for budget travellers. Joining a park association will get you a discount in all parks that are association members. Associations include: **Big 4**, T03 9811 9300, www.big4.com.au; **Family Parks of Australia**, T1800 682492, www. familyparks. com.au; and **Top Tourist Parks**, T08 8363 1901, www.toptourist.contact.com.au.

Roadhouses
Where roads connect towns more than about 100 km apart there will usually be roadhouses on the way. They vary from simple fuel stops and small stores to mini-resorts with accommodation, small supermarkets, post offices, daytime cafés, evening restaurants and bars. They will often have simple single and double rooms in what look for all the world like converted shipping containers (they often are), known as **dongas**. These usually fall into the **B-C** range.

Camping in national parks
Some national parks allow camping, mostly in designated areas only, with a few allowing limited bush camping. Facilities are usually minimal, with basic toilets, fireplaces and perhaps tank water; a few have BBQs and shower blocks. Enjoyable camping necessitates being well prepared. Payment is often by self-registration (around $3-10 per person), and BBQs often require $0.20, $0.50 or $1 coins, so have small notes and change ready. In many parks you will need a gas stove. If there are fireplaces you must bring your own wood. Collecting wood within parks is prohibited, as logs and twigs are an important habitat for native animals. No fires may be lit, even stoves, during a Total Fire Ban. Even if water is supposedly available it is not guaranteed so take a supply, as well as your own toilet paper. **Bush camping** in national parks is strongly regulated. The key rules are to be particularly careful with fire, camp at least 20 m from any water-hole or course, and to disturb the environment as little as possible. Nothing must be left behind, and nothing removed, even rocks. Toilet waste should be carefully buried, at least 100 m from any water-hole or course.

Bush and roadside camping
There are many spots outside parks where camping is also expressly allowed. On rare occasions there may be basic toilets, water and fireplaces. Out of courtesy and regard for the environment, act as if you were in a national park. Some parking bays allow caravans or campervans to stop overnight. Even if not allowed, stop for a sleep if the choice is between that or driving while very tired. Publications describing free roadside and bush camping spots are widely available.

⦂ Ten great hostels

Baywatch Manor YHA,
Augusta, p169.
Black Cockatoo, Nannup, p184.
Cossack Backpackers,
Cossack, p272.
Cruize Inn, Albany, p204.
Dongara Backpackers,

Dongara, p220.
Dunsborough Beachouse YHA,
Dunsborough, p149.
Kimberley Klub, Broome, p290.
Lancelin Lodge, Lancelin, p122.
Ningaloo Club, Exmouth, p255.
Ocean Beach, Cottesloe, p75.

Campervans

A popular choice for many visitors is to hire or buy a vehicle that can be slept in, combining the costs of accommodation and transport (although you will still need to book into caravan parks for power and ablutions). Ranging from the popular **VW Kombi** to enormous vans with integral bathrooms, they can be hired from as little as $50 per day to as much as $750. A van for two people at around $100 per day compares well with hiring a car and staying in hostels, and allows greater freedom. High-clearance, 4WD campervans are also available, and increase travel possibilities yet further. Kombis can usually be bought from about $2,500. A cheaper though less comfortable alternative is to buy a van or station wagon (estate car) that is big enough to sleep in.

Campervan companies

The following are campervan specialists, though the major car hire companies also have campervans available, see page 39.
Apollo, 141 Adelaide Terr, Perth, T07 3260 5466, www.apollocamper.com.au.
Backpacker, 471 Great Eastern Hwy, Redcliffe, T08 9478 3479, www.backpackercampervans.com.

Britz, 471 Great Eastern Hwy, Redcliffe, T08 9478 3488, www.britz.com.
Getabout, T02 9380 5536, www.getaboutoz.com.
Maui, 471 Great Eastern Hwy, Redcliffe, T08 9277 1000, www.maui-rentals.com.
NQ, 258 Great Eastern Hwy, Redcliffe, T08 9479 3350, www.campervansaust.com.au.
Trailmaster, T08 9478 6666, www.trailmaster.com.au.

Swags

Swags are large lined pieces of canvas that enclose a thin mattress and sleeping bag, for outdoor use, placed directly on the ground. They are very much a part of Australian folklore and are still widely used in the country. There's nothing quite like lying in bed and watching the sun rise in the morning as the cockatoos screech overhead. The main disadvantages to swags are their weight and the space they take up, and also that they are open to the elements and insects.

Eating

Food

The quintessential image of Australian cooking may be of throwing some meat on the barbie but Australia actually has a dynamic and vibrant cuisine all its own. Freed from the bland English 'meat and three veg' strait-jacket in the 1980s by the skills and cuisines of Chinese, Thai, Vietnamese, Italian, Greek, Lebanese and other immigrants,

⦂ Restaurant price codes explained

These prices are based on two-course meal (entrée plus main course) without drinks.

🍴🍴🍴 over $40 a head
🍴🍴 $28-39 a head
🍴 under $27 a head

Australia has developed a fusion cuisine that takes elements from their cultures and mixes them into something new and original. Asian ingredients are easily found in major cities because of the country's high Asian population and might include coriander, lemon grass, chilli, and Thai basil. Australia makes its own dairy products so cheese or cream may come from Tasmania's King Island or Margaret River. Of course there is also plenty of seafood, including some creatures that will be unfamiliar to most travellers like the delicious crustaceans bugs, yabbies, and crayfish (lobster). Mussels, oysters and abalone are all also harvested locally. The fish is a treat too; try the firm white flesh of snapper, dhufish, coral trout and red emperor. WA's isolation and clean environment also ensures that all these ingredients taste as good as possible.

Freshness is the other striking quality of this cuisine, dubbed **Modern Australian**. This is achieved by using produce from the local area, and cooking it in a way that preserves the food's intrinsic flavour. The food shines for itself without being smothered in heavy or dominating sauces. Native animals are sometimes used, such as kangaroo, emu and crocodile, and native plants that Aboriginal people have been eating for thousands of years such as quandong, wattle seed or lemon myrtle leaf.

While you are rubbing your hands with anticipation: a word of warning. This gourmet experience is mostly restricted to Perth and the largest towns. There are pockets of foodie heaven in the southwest, but these are usually associated with wine regions and are the exception rather than the rule.

There are a few special foods that Australians produce and treasure and can be found pretty much throughout WA. The **meat pie** is the favourite Australian fast food, about the size of your palm and filled with mince or steak and gravy. Quality can vary from soggy cardboard to something a French pastry chef would wouldn't be ashamed of. If tempted, your best bet is a fresh one from a bakery rather than a mass-produced one (sealed in a little plastic bag) that sits in a shop's warming oven all day. **Fish and chips** are also popular and these are often good in Australia because the fish is fresh and only light vegetable oils are used for frying.

Vegemite spread is a dark and sticky yeast extract that looks a bit like axle grease. It's the Aussie equivalent of British Marmite, though fans of one usually detest the other. **Tim Tams** are a thick chocolate biscuit, very similar to the Brits' Penguin and reputedly the country's best selling snack. What Brits call crisps, Aussies call chips ('hot chips' are fried chips), with **Twisties** a very Australian favourite.

Damper is bread made of flour, salt and water, best baked out bush in the ashes of a campfire. Nothing beats warm damper slathered with jam and butter. Another Aussie baking favourite is the **lamington**: a block of sponge that has been dipped in chocolate and rolled in coconut. The **pavlova** is a classic Australian dessert, created for the visit of Russian ballerina, Anna Pavlova. The 'pav' is like a cake-sized meringue, served topped with whipped cream and fresh fruit. It is rarely consumed without an argument about whether it was actually invented in Australia or New Zealand. One great icon associated with the outback campfire is **Billy Tea**. It is the fiendishly simple concept of putting a few eucalyptus leaves in with the brew to add that distinctive Aussie flavour. To mix the flavour of the tea leaf with the eucalypt the 'billy can' is held in the hand and swung a couple of times from the shoulders. This is quite a delicate art and can, for the uninitiated, result in considerable drama when the handle breaks, but there we go.

66 99 The quintessential image of Australian cooking may be of throwing some meat on the barbie but Australia actually has a dynamic and vibrant cuisine all its own...

Drink

Australian wine is now imported in huge quantities into Europe and the USA. The industry has a creditable history in such a young country, with several wineries boasting a tradition of a century or more, but it is only in the last 25 years that Australia has become one of the major players on the international scene. The **price** of wine is unexpectedly high given the relatively low cost of food and beer. Even those from Britain will find Australian wines hardly any cheaper at the very cellar door than back home in the supermarket. The joy of Australian wine, however, is in its **variety** and **quality**. There are no restrictions, as there are in parts of Europe, on what grape varieties are grown where, when they are harvested and how they are blended. The 'Mediterranean' climate of much of the south of the country is very favourable for grape-growing, and the soil is sufficient to produce a high-standard grape.

Wineries range in size from vast concerns to one-person operations producing a few hundred bottles a year. **Cellars** range from modern marble and glass temples to venerable, century-old former barns of stone and wood. Some will open for a Saturday afternoon, others every day. In some you'll be lucky to get half a dry cracker to go with a taste, others boast some of the best restaurants in the country. A few are in small town high streets, others are set in hectares of exquisitely designed and maintained gardens. The wonderful thing is that this tremendous mix of styles is found within most of the regions, making a day or two's tasting expedition a scenic and cultural as well as an Epicurean delight. WA has a handful of wine regions, one as far north as Geraldton and several along the south coast. The biggest are the **Swan Valley**, just outside Perth, and **Margaret River**, which is spread over much of the northern half of the Cape-to-Cape region. The latter is one of the most pleasant wine regions in the country. See page 20 for details of operators offering wine tasting tours.

The big two **beer** brands of WA are **Swan** and Emu, both are middle-of-the-road beers available in full and mid-strengths. The state also has a number of small independent brewers, one or two of which are becoming well known even outside the state. These include long-established **Matilda Bay,** producers of the popular **Redback,** and **Little Creatures** who are a little more creative than most of their peers and have a wonderful brewery/bar/restaurant/gallery in Fremantle. Pubs producing their own exceptionally good beers include the **Rose & Crown** in Guildford, and **Matso's** in Broome. Beer is usually served in a 7-oz **middy**, though you can also ask for a 10-oz **pot** or in some pubs a regular British-style **pint**. Beer tends to be around 4-5 per cent alcohol, with the popular and surprisingly pleasant tasting 'mid' varieties about 3½ per cent, and 'light' beers about 2-2½ per cent. Drink driving laws are strict, and the best bet is to not drink alcohol at all if you are driving. As well as being available on draught in pubs, beer is also available from bottleshops (or 'bottle-o's') in cases (or 'slabs') of 24-36 cans ('tinnies' or 'tubes') or bottles ('stubbies') of 375 ml each. This is by *far* the cheapest way of buying beer (often under $1.50 per can or bottle).

The Aussie barbie

"Throw another prawn on the barbie". The image is very familiar to travellers well before they arrive, and for once this is no myth. Aussies love a BBQ, and many households will have a couple a week as a matter of course. Public BBQs are common, often found in town and national parks, and beach foreshores. Unless free, a $0.20, $0.50 or $1 coin will get you 15-30 minutes of heat. You'll need to bring your own utensils. At private BBQs, bringing your own meat and alcohol is the norm, with hosts usually providing salads, bread and a few extra snags (sausages).

Eating out

Restaurants are common even in smaller towns. It is a general, but by no means concrete rule of thumb that the smaller the town the lower the quality, though not usually the price. Chinese and Thai restaurants are very common, with most other cuisines appearing only in the larger towns and cities. In Perth and Fremantle you will find everything from Mexican to Mongolian, Jamaican to Japanese. Corporate hotels and motels almost all have attached restaurants as do traditional pubs who also serve counter meals. Some may have a more imaginative menu or better quality fare than the local restaurants. Most restaurants are licensed for the consumption of alcohol. Some are BYO only, in which case you provide wine or beer and the restaurant provides glasses. Despite the corkage fee this still makes for a better deal than drinking alcohol in fully licensed premises. European style cafés are only rarely found in the country, and as in many western countries the distinction between cafés, bistros and restaurants is becoming extremely blurred.

If you can't do without your burgers or southern-fried chicken or fish and chips then fear not. Australians have taken to fast food as enthusiastically as anywhere else in the world. Alongside these are food courts, found in the shopping malls of cities and larger towns. These have several takeaway options, usually including various Asian cuisines, surrounding a central space equipped with tables and chairs. Also in the budget bracket are the delis and milk bars, also serving hot takeaways, together with sandwiches, cakes and snacks. These make up a fair proportion of the country's cafés, with a few seats inside and often out on the pavement.

If you cook for yourself you'll find just about everything in an Aussie supermarket that you would find in Europe or the USA, and at very reasonable prices. An excellent meal for two can easily be put together for under $20.

Entertainment

As in most 'western' nations, much of the country's entertainment is provided by its pubs and bars. Not only are they a social meeting point but many put on regular live music, DJs, karaoke and quiz nights. The typical Aussie pub is a solid brick and wood affair with wide first floor verandahs extending across the front, and sometimes down the sides as well. These usually have separate public and lounge bars, a bottleshop (off-license) off to the side, and increasingly a separate 'bar' full of pokies (slot machines or one-armed bandits). The public bar often doubles as a TAB betting shop. Pubs and bars vary as much in style as anywhere in the western world. Some pubs are rough as guts and a stranger venturing in is guaranteed a hard stare. Others go out of their way to make a visitor feel welcome. Some haven't

⦂ Ten great pubs

Fitzgeralds, Bunbury, p150.
Gascoyne Junction Hotel, Gascoyne, p255.
Gingin Hotel, Gingin, p122.
Hampton Arms, Greenough, p221.
Matso's, Broome, p291.

Mundaring Weir Hotel, Perth Hills, p119.
Sail & Anchor, Fremantle, p102.
Samson Beach Tavern, Point Samson, p274.
Subiaco Hotel, Perth, p82.
Whim Creek Hotel, Pilbara, p269.

seen a paintbrush since the day they were built, others have been beautifully renovated in styles ranging from modern to authentic outback, saloon to the gimmicky Irish. In some medium-sized towns they also operate a club or discotheque. True nightclubs will only be found in the cities and larger towns, and then usually only open a few nights of the week. They do generally charge an entrance fee, usually around $5-15, though entry will commonly be free on some mid-week nights or before a certain time.

The cinema is popular in Australia and some will have outdoor screens with either deckchair seating or drive-in slots. Expect to pay around $13 for an adult ticket, but look out for early week or pre-1800 specials. Every big city in the country has its major casino. Most are open 24 hours a day and, as well as offering gaming tables and rank upon rank of pokies, also have live music venues and good-value food halls and restaurants. Other indoor pursuits found in most large towns and cities include 10-pin bowling, bingo, karting, snooker and pool halls, and large recreational centres offering everything from swimming to squash, basketball to badminton.

Festivals and events

Most major events and festivals are held in and around Perth, where nearly three quarters of Western Australians live. The year kicks off with the **Hopman Cup**, an international tennis championship that attracts some big tennis names with its unusual format: teams of one male and one female player representing eight nations competing in a 'round robin' format. Held at Perth's Burswood Dome over New Year. For more see www.hopmancup.com.au. The arts year starts with the biggest and the best, **Perth International Arts Festival**, www.perthfestival.com.au. This includes local and international theatre, opera, dance, visual arts, film and music. Held every January-February. Down in Margaret River the main event of the summer is the **Leeuwin Estate Concert**, www.leeuwinestate.com.au, when musical performances are given in the lovely grounds of this premium winery. Held over a weekend in February. Attracting quite a different crowd, the **Margaret River Salomon Masters** international surfing competition is held at Prevelly over a week in mid-April. Waves are also the focus of the **Avon Descent** in early August, a 133-km white water competition on the Avon River from Northam to Perth. Up north, Broome celebrates the Festival of the Pearl, **Shinju Matsuri**, for a week in September. Events include parades, dragon boat racing and the Shinju Ball. In spring, wildflowers are out all over the state but if you are short of time you can see many varieties at the **Kings Park Wildflower Festival**. Held over ten days in late September. In the southwest, the **Bridgetown Blues Festival** is held in late November. See www.australia.com, for exact forthcoming dates.

New Years Day, 2 January 2006, 1 January 2007; **Australia Day,** 26 January 2006, 26 January 2007; **Labour Day,** 6 March 2006, 5 March 2007; **Good Friday,** 14 April 2006, 6 April 2007; **Easter Monday,** 17 April 2006, 9 April 2007; **Anzac Day,** 25 April 2006, 25 April 2007; **Foundation Day,** 5 June 2006, 4 June 2007; **Queen's Birthday,** 26 September 2005, 2 October 2006; **Christmas Day,** 26 December 2005, 25 December 2006; **Boxing Day,** 27 December 2005, 26 December 2006.

Shopping

Tourist shops exploit the cute and cuddly factor of Australian native mammals, so most tourist merchandise seems to consist of soft toy kangaroos and koalas and brightly coloured clothing featuring the same creatures. Other typical items perpetuate the corny Australian stereotypes. Beware of hats strung with corks; not only will you be slapped every five seconds and look foolish but no Australian has ever been spotted wearing one. Corkless hats, however, are a popular and practical souvenir, particularly the distinctively Australian *Akubras*, made from felt in muddy colours. Along the same lines, stockman's clothing made by **RM Williams** is also popular and very good quality. Two of the company's best sellers are elastic-sided boots and moleskins (soft brushed-cotton trousers cut like jeans). The **Driza-bone** long oilskin raincoat is also an Aussie classic. Australian surfwear is sought after world-wide and is a good buy while in the country. Look for labels such as **Ripcurl, Quiksilver, Mambo** and **Billabong**.

Australia is a good place to shop for **jewellery,** and WA is one of the world's greatest producers of gold, pearls and diamonds. There are many talented craftspeople making exquisite metal and bead work. The widest range will be available in the cities but, as in most countries, products are often cheapest at the source and a wonderful memento of place. Look for pearls in Broome or champagne-coloured Argyle diamonds from the Kimberley.

In the tourist shops Aboriginal art designs are as ubiquitous as cuddly toys and printed on everything from T-shirts to tea-towels. Some of these designs can be beautiful but be aware that many articles have no link to Aboriginal people and do not benefit them directly – check the label. **Desert Designs** is a successful label printing the stunning designs of the late, great Sandy Desert artist Jimmy Pike on silk scarves and sarongs. It is possible to buy genuine Aboriginal art and craft but it is more commonly available in country areas close to Aboriginal communities or from Aboriginal owned or operated enterprises. This applies more to craft items such as dijeridus and scorched carvings than paintings and of course there are reputable vendors everywhere but if in doubt ask for more information. Art and crafts bought from reputable sources ensures that the money ends up in the artist's pocket and supports Aboriginal culture, skills and self-reliance.

Many people are keen to buy an Aboriginal **dot painting,** usually acrylic on canvas. Also note that there are different styles of Aboriginal art, often depending on the region the artist comes from. For example the x-ray paintings on bark only come from Arnhem Land. The best Aboriginal paintings sell for many thousands but there are also many thousands of average paintings sold for a few hundred dollars. A good painting will cost at least $800-1500. Simple works on canvas can be as little as $100 and make good souvenirs. Take your time and have a good look around. Visit public and private galleries where you can see work of the highest quality – you may not be able to afford it but you'll learn something of what makes a good piece of Aboriginal art. Some of the qualities to look for are fine application, skilful use of colour and a striking design. The major cities all have commercial galleries selling Aboriginal art.

Sport and activities

In Australia, sport takes on a religious significance for many. Travelling around, you soon start to see just why they are so successful and passionate about it. Even the smallest towns will have a footy pitch or cricket pitch and golf course, and they don't have to be much of a size to have tennis and netball courts, a swimming pool, and a horse-racing track. In most cases there is easy public access at reasonable rates, so if you feel you won't be able to go without a round or a set then bring the minimum of gear and expect to be able to get a game almost anywhere. If you're a real adrenaline junkie then WA can offer quite a range of heart-stopping activities, most of them involving moving quickly over water, slowly but precariously over or under rock, or with gut-wrenching inevitability through nothing but fresh air. Many of the best are offered by specialist tour and hire operators, and if you have some specific goals it is essential to check out your options carefully in advance as the time of year and availability of spaces can make a big difference to what is possible. *Wild Magazine* has a good website, www.wild.com.au, and publishes quite a few walking and adventure guides.

Participation sports

Climbing and abseiling

Although much of Australia is flat as a tack there are a few fabulous **climbing** spots, including a handful on the west coast, notably around **Albany**, the **Cape-to-Cape** region and **Kalbarri**. If scrambling through tight, deep gorges appeals head for the **Karijini**. To find out more get hold of *Climbing Australia: The Essential Guide* by Greg Pritchard or see **www.climbing.com.au**, which also picks out **abseiling** operators.

Cycling and mountain biking

Bicycles are commonly available for hire in cities and major towns, but facilities are scarce otherwise. If you plan to do most of your touring on a bike you will need to either bring your own or buy in Perth, as long-term hire facilities are virtually non-existent. One alternative is to join a cycle-based tour, such as those organized by **Remote Outback Cycles**, www.cycletours.com.au.

Diving and snorkelling

Australia is famous for the **Great Barrier Reef**, and for decades backpackers have made a beeline there to earn their diving spurs. However, increasingly travellers are also heading for the west coast to learn to dive on the lesser known **Ningaloo Reef**, off Coral Bay and Exmouth. This is by no means the only good diving area around this immense coast, however, which boasts a diversity of options from kelp forests and encrusted jetties to wrecks old and new. The seas around Albany, Dunsborough, Busselton, Rottnest Island and the Abrolhos Islands are very popular spots and local operators offer dive trips, tuition and gear hire. If you're content to simply snorkel then the best destinations are Busselton, Rottnest Island, the Abrolhos Islands, Coral Bay and Exmouth.

The websites **www.diveoz.com.au** and **www.scubaaustralia.com.au**, have useful general information as well as fairly comprehensive directories including sites, dive centres and charter boats. **www.divedirectory.net** have details of several multi-day diving trips. Travellers basing their trip on diving around the WA coast should pick up a copy of *Diving Australia* by Coleman and Marsh to decide what sites will best suit them.

Fishing is in some areas the only recreational activity available to locals and is pursued with an almost religious obsession. As you head north surfboards begin to disappear from vehicle roof racks only to be replaced by 'tinnies', short aluminium boats that allow the fishing family to go where they please. Excellent offshore sport fishing is widely available as a day tour, usually for around $150-200. There are several excellent websites on recreational fishing in Australia, with location reports and details of tour operators and retailers, including **www.fishnet.com.au** and **www.sportsfishaustralia.com.au.**

Golf

Almost every town in Australia has at least one golf course, even in the outback, though the feel of the greens may not be too familiar, and most welcome visitors. In WA, the best courses are in and around Perth. **Joondalup**, www.joondalupresort.com.au, and **Kennedy Bay**, www.kennedybay.com, rank in the top five of the country's best public access courses (see **www.ausgolf.com.au.**).

Parachuting and bungy jumping

Many of the several dozen skydiving clubs in WA offer short, usually one-day courses in **parachuting** (also known as 'skydiving'), including a jump or two, and some cut out much of the training by organizing **tandem jumps** where you're strapped, facing forward, to the chest of the instructor. If a quick thrill is all you're after then the latter is the better option as it usually involves 30-60 seconds of freefall, by far the most exhilarating part of the experience, and costs around $250-300. A list of skydiving clubs affiliated to the **Australian Parachute Federation**, T02 6281 6830, can be found at **www.apf.asn.au**.

If you fancy jumping out into thin air without a parachute then **bungy jumping**, leaping off a platform with an elastic rope tied around your ankles, is just about the safest option going. There is an opportunity to make the big leap just south of Perth.

Surfing, windsurfing and kitesurfing

If an Aussie lives near the beach there's a fair bet they'll be a surfer; if they're inland and anywhere near water then waterskiing will probably be the go. This makes for a great many local clubs, tuition and equipment hire. Surfing is generally best in the southern half of the state with famous, and often jealously guarded spots in places as far flung as **Kalbarri** and **Margaret River**. Windsurfing and kitesurfing are also widespread as the west coast is one of the contenders for the best coast in the world for the sports. **Fremantle**, **Lancelin** and **Geraldton** are considered the top spots.

> ❣ Surfies will want to get hold of Mark Warren's Atlas of Australian Surfing.

Websites dedicated to surfing include **www.surfinfo.com.au**, which links to a great many surfie retail and travel businesses, and **www.realsurf.com** which has condition reports from all the major spots around the country. There's also information to be found at **www.windsurfing.org**, with club, holiday and tuition details.

Walking and trekking → See also Safety page 33.

A certain amount of walking is necessary to see many of the west coast's great natural sights, but WA can also boast a great range of short, day and overnight walks, mostly in the many national parks, and even a few excellent multi-day treks. **Bushwalking clubs** are a good source of local advice and often welcome visitors on their regular expeditions. For a comprehensive list of clubs see **www.bushwalking.org.au.**

Starting in Kalamunda, the long-distance **Bibbulmun** walking trail winds its way south through Dwellingup, Balingup, Pemberton and Walpole before finally ending up, 963 km later, in Albany. As well as passing through these picturesque towns the

⁛ Where in the west...

Many of the following creatures, though widespread, are not always easy to see. With patience sightings are likely, if not virtually guaranteed, in their natural environments at the following places (tours and entry fees sometimes apply). Note that koalas, platypus and wombats are not native to Western Australia.

Blue (fairy) wrens Cape-to-Cape region

Corals Busselton, Rottnest Island, Abrolhos Islands, Coral Bay and Exmouth

Crocodiles Broome and the Dampier Peninsula

Dolphins Bunbury, Mandurah, Monkey Mia and Rockingham

Dugongs Monkey Mia and Port Hedland

Eagles and kites Northern WA

Echidnas Common but elusive: try Avon Valley National Park near Perth

Emus Common, 'tame' in Donnelly

Fairy penguins Penguin Island (Rockingham)

Kangaroos Almost anywhere around dawn and dusk.

Manta rays Coral Bay

Parrots Southwest and south coast

Quokkas Rottnest Island

Seals and sea lions Jurien Bay, Leeman and Rockingham

Stingrays Augusta, Hamelin Bay, Coral Bay and Exmouth

Turtles Monkey Mia, Coral Bay, Exmouth and Port Hedland

Whales Albany, Augusta, Dunsborough, Perth, Kalbarri, Coral Bay, Exmouth and Port Hedland

Whale sharks Coral Bay and Exmouth

Essentials Sport & activities

track also winds through several reserves and parks, much of the southern forests and some of the spectacular south coast. There are nearly 50 bush campsites en-route, each with a simple three-sided timber bunk shelter, picnic tables, water tank and pit toilets. Note that there are no cooking facilities, water needs to be boiled or treated, and there is no toilet paper. The whole walk generally takes about six to eight weeks, but few tackle it in a single go and **CALM** have suggestions for various short day sections. The track is by far at its best in autumn and spring. Consider carefully before tackling any of it in high summer or the depths of winter. There is a two-volume guide to the track and a series of eight maps also dedicated to it, all available at the **Perth Map Centre** among other outlets. For more information see www.calm.wa.gov.au/tourism, or contact the **Friends of the Bibbulmun Track**, T08 9481 0551, www.bibbulmuntrack.org.au.

The 140-km **Cape-to-Cape** track follows the coast from Cape Naturaliste to Cape Leeuwin via Yallingup and Prevelly, and takes about a week. Campsites are provided where there are no commercial facilities, but there may be long stretches where no water is available. **CALM** publish annotated maps that cover the entire route ($8), and you can also get advice and information from the **Friends of the Cape-to-Cape**, capetrack@hotmail.com.

Wildlife and birdwatching

The unique Australian wildlife experience is one that goes far beyond meeting friendly kangaroos and coming face-to-face with turtles on the Ningaloo. Almost everywhere you go wildlife surrounds you and can be observed; from parrots in Perth's Kings Park to occasional dolphins off almost any beach on the coast. The concept that almost all of it, beyond the humble roo, is out to clamp its jaws, fangs or stinging tentacles in to you is greatly over exaggerated and certainly not helped with international Reality TV stars like the Crocodile Hunter. True there are many venomous and potentially dangerous creatures out there, but nothing a bit of common sense and respect won't protect you from. On the other hand, you can easily harm the wildlife. Drive sensibly and you will largely avoid hitting small mammals, birds and reptiles; don't disturb the natural environment (including collecting firewood) as this is their home; and don't feed wildlife as animals that get used to being hand fed can become sick, aggressive and dependent. In summary, provided you retain an open mind, patience and open eyes you will return home with an armoury of interesting memories, stories and photographs that will confirm the fact that Australia is one of the best places to encounter wildlife on the planet.

Spectator sport

It's enough to make an Englishman spit. Any sport Australia takes seriously it does very well at. Their cricketers seem to score more runs than anyone else, their rugby players launch themselves for more tries, their swimmers outperform respectably fast fish, their netballers shoot more goals than anyone else, their top tennis players regularly beat even the Americans, and they have recently had world champions in everything from darts to squash. This awful challenge for their opponents converts to a glorious opportunity for visitors to Australia. If you choose to be a spectator at a sport the Aussies really get into, then you're in for a treat: world class competition at relatively low prices. And you'll usually be in the company of thousands of exuberant locals yelling their lungs out.

Australian Rules Football → www.afl.com.au.

This is the classic down-under game, to the casual observer a free-for-all that defies the gods in causing as few broken necks as it does. A derivative of the rough football that was being played in Britain and Ireland in the late 1700s it shares an affinity with Gaelic Football; indeed Ireland and Australia meet to contest an 'international rules' cup.

As with rugby and soccer, it's a winter game, with most leagues playing between March and September. The game is contested on a huge oval pitch, up to 200 m long, between two teams of 18 players each. At each end of the pitch four high posts denote the goal mouth, and it is through these that the teams attempt to get the oval-shaped ball. If the ball goes directly between the central two posts a *goal* is scored and six points awarded. If it goes between one of the central posts and an outer post, or is touched by the defending team on the way, then a *behind* is scored and a single point awarded. Players may kick or *hand pass* the ball in any direction, but not throw it. To hand pass is to punch the ball from the palm of one hand with the clenched fist of the other. If the ball is kicked over 10 m and cleanly caught then the catcher can call a *mark*. He can't be tackled and has time to kick the ball toward goal or a teammate unmolested. The game is split into four quarters, each lasting 25 minutes. Scoring is usually regular, and winning teams with an excess of 100 points are not unusual.

The national league, the **AFL**, is followed most closely, in fact obsessively, though there are enthusiastic state and local amateur leagues throughout the country. Most of the AFL clubs are in and around Melbourne, where the game was invented, but the national league also has two top-flight teams from Perth: the **Fremantle Dockers** and the **West Coast Eagles**.

Cricket

Once the footy seasons ends around September a large number of Australian minds switch, almost like clockwork, to cricket, just another major international team sport at which Australians just happen to be, more or less, better than anyone else. The national side is involved in Test series against England (for the Ashes) and other major cricketing countries and in limited-overs internationals; some of these games are staged at the WACA ground in Perth. There are two interstate competitions, both running from October-February, and involving WA's *Western Warriors* (who play at the WACA). The **ING Cup** is the one-day competition, and the **Pura Cup** decides who has the best four-day team. For round-ups on Australian and international news see www.cricket.org.

Horse racing

Australians are mad about the gee-gees. There are horse racing or *pacing* (horse and trap) tracks all over the country, in all but the tiniest towns, and there are usually a dozen or so meetings every day, and dozens of races to satisfy the most dedicated of punters. Most of the country's betting is via the state **TAB**s, a pooling system similar to the UK's *Tote*. There are some high street TABs, but most can be found in the public bars of the nation's pubs. One of the best independent racing websites is www.racingaustralia.net.

Rugby Union

Rugby Union traditionally had much less of a grass roots following until the national side, the *Wallabies*, won the Rugby World Cup in 1991. In the decade since they can claim to have always rated in the world's top five teams, and frequently vie with arch rivals, the New Zealand *All Blacks*, for status as world's best. Aside from the World Cup (which they won in 1999) and regular international tours, the Wallabies compete in an annual three-way competition (the **'Tri Nations'**) against South Africa and New Zealand. The winners of the Aussie vs Kiwi games gain possession of the much-prized **Bledisloe Cup**, which has been contested by the two countries since 1931. The other major seasonal series is the *Australian Rugby Shield*, the national competition between state capital and country teams held during June-August. See www.rugby.com.au.

Swimming

It doesn't seem fair. Australia doesn't just have one or two international standard swimmers, they have a small poolful. Ian Thorpe (the 'Thorpedo', size 16 feet), Grant Hackett and Michael Klim are all giants on the international scene, often only having each other for serious competition. For this reason the Australian National Championships are the best domestic competition in the world to go and see. They're held in March, see www.ausswim.telstra.com.au, for details.

Tennis

Unlike their swimmers Australia has for a long time had to depend on just one or two brilliant players to keep the male flag flying, and the women's game is surprisingly weak. The boys have got their timing down to a tee: just as Pat Rafter hangs up his racquet, along comes Lleyton Hewitt who looks set to carry the Australian flag for the century's first decade. Australia hosts one of the world's four Grand Slam competitions, the **Australian Open**, www.ausopen.org, in Melbourne in January. Perth hosts the **Hopman Cup**, www.hopmancup.com.au, every January at Burswood Dome, where international teams of one man and woman compete against each other. For round-ups on tennis news see www.tennisaustralia.com.au.

Health

Australia is known as the 'lucky country' and in health terms it is. There are few nasty diseases and the health care facilities are of a very high standard. Australia has a national, government-funded health care scheme called **Medicare**. This, together with the supporting private network, is reckoned to be one of the best health care systems in the world, so you can rest easy with the thought that if you suffer an unexpected accident or illness you should be well looked after. Public hospitals are part of Medicare, a large number of pharmaceutical products are funded or subsidized by the scheme, and most doctors are registered so that their services can also be funded or subsidized by the scheme. Doctors who invoice Medicare directly, so charging the patient nothing on examination, are said to bulk bill. Those that don't bulk bill charge the patient who then has to reclaim the charge from Medicare. Large cities usually have clinics where you can walk in without an appointment. The **Travellers Medical and Vaccination Centre** ('TMVC' or 'The Travel Doctor') operates several clinics around the country.

Australia has reciprocal arrangements with a handful of countries which allow citizens of those countries to receive free 'immediately necessary medical treatment' under the Medicare scheme. The arrangements with New Zealand and the Republic of Ireland provide visitors to Australia with free care as a public patient in public hospitals and subsidized medicines under the Pharmaceutical Benefits Scheme. In addition to these benefits, visitors from Finland, Italy, Malta, the Netherlands, Sweden and the UK also enjoy subsidized out-of-hospital treatment (ie visiting a doctor). Most visitors under the arrangement are covered for their entire stay. Visitors from Malta and Italy, however, are covered for a maximum of six months. If you qualify under the reciprocal

For longer trips involving jungle treks taking a clean needle pack, clean dental pack and water filtration devices are common-sense measures.

arrangement, contact your own national health scheme to check what documents you will require in Australia to claim Medicare. All visitors to Australia are, however, strongly advised to take out medical insurance for the duration of their visit. You do not need to pre-register with Medicare to be entitled to the benefits, but can register on your first visit to a doctor or hospital. Charges can be reclaimed either via the post or in person at a Medicare office, which can be found in all major towns and cities.

There are two main threats to health in Australia. One is global warming, and with that the spread of more tropical diseases such as Dengue Fever. The second are the ever present, poisonous snakes and spiders. Check loo seats, boots and the area around you if you're a visiting the bush.

Before you go

Ideally, you should see your GP or travel clinic at least six weeks before your departure for general advice on travel risks, malaria and vaccinations. Make sure you have travel insurance, get a dental check (especially if you are going to be away for more than a month), know your own blood group and, if you suffer a long-term condition such as diabetes or epilepsy, make sure someone knows or that you have a Medic Alert bracelet/necklace with this information on it.

Items to take with you

Insect repellent Useful to avoid bites. Apply the repellent every four to six hours but more often if you are sweating heavily. If you are a popular target for insect bites or develop lumps quite soon after being bitten, carry an Aspivenin kit. This syringe suction device is available from many chemists and draws out some of the allergic materials and provides quick relief. **Sun Block** The Australians have a great campaign, which has reduced skin cancer. It is called Slip, Slap, Slop. Slip on a shirt, Slap on a hat, Slop on sun screen. **Pain killers** Paracetomol or a suitable painkiller can have multiple uses for symptoms but remember that more than eight paracetomol a day can lead to liver failure. **Ciproxin (Ciprofloaxcin)** A useful antibiotic for some forms of travellers diarrhoea (see below). **Immodium** A standby for those diarrhoeas that occur at awkward times (ie before a long coach/train journey or on a trek). It helps stop the flow of diarrhoea and is of more benefit than harm. **Pepto-Bismol** Used a lot by Americans for diarrhoea. It certainly relieves symptoms but like Immodium it is not

---

An A-Z of health risks

Dengue fever

Symptoms This disease can be contracted throughout Australia. In travellers this can cause a severe 'flu-like illness which includes symptoms of fever, lethargy, enlarged lymph glands and muscle pains. It starts suddenly, lasts for two to three days, seems to get better for two to three days and then kicks in again for another two to three days. It is usually all over in an unpleasant week. The local children are prone to the much nastier haemorrhagic form of the disease, which causes them to bleed from internal organs, mucous membranes and often leading to death. **Cures** The traveller's version of the disease is self limiting and forces rest and recuperation on the sufferer. **Prevention** The mosquitoes that carry the Dengue virus bite during the day unlike the malaria mosquitoes. Which means that repellent application and covered limbs are a 24-hour issue. Check your accommodation for flower pots and shallow pools of water since these are where the mosquitoes breed.

Hepatitis

Symptoms Hepatitis means inflammation of the liver. Viral causes of the disease can be acquired anywhere in Australia. The most obvious symptom is a yellowing of your skin or the whites of your eyes. However, prior to this all that you may notice is itching and tiredness. **Cures** Early on, depending on the type of hepatitis, a vaccine or immunoglobulin may reduce the duration of the illness. **Prevention** Pre-travel hepatitis A vaccine is the best bet. Hepatitis B (for which there is a vaccine) is spread through blood and unprotected sexual intercourse, both of these can be avoided. Unfortunately there is no vaccine for hepatitis C or the increasing alphabetical list of other Hepatitis viruses.

Snakes and other poisonous things

A bite itself does not mean that anything has been injected in to you. However, a commonsense approach is to clean the area of the bite (never have it sutured early on) and get someone to take you to a medical facility. It is better to be taken because the more energy you expand the faster poisons spread. Do not try to catch the snake or spider. You will only get more bites and faster spread of poison for your troubles. For some snake bites a knowledgeable first aider can provide appropriate bandaging and if a poison is on-board specialist anti-venoms will be administered by an experienced doctor.

Sexual health

The range of visible and invisible diseases is awesome. Unprotected sex can spread HIV, Hepatitis B and C, Gonorrhea (green discharge), chlamydia (nothing to see but may cause painful urination and later female infertility), painful recurrent herpes, syphilis and warts, just to name a few. You can cut down the risk by using condoms, a femidom or avoiding sex altogether. Commercial sex workers in Australia have high levels of HIV. If you do have sex, consider getting a sexual health check on your return home.

Sun protection

Symptoms White Britons are notorious for becoming red in hot countries because they like to stay out longer than everyone else and do not use adequate sun protection. This can lead to sunburn, which is painful and followed by flaking of skin. Aloe vera gel is a good pain reliever for sunburn. Long-term sun damage leads to a loss of elasticity of skin and the development of pre-cancerous lesions. Many years later a mild or a very malignant form of cancer may develop. The milder basal cell carcinoma, if detected early, can be treated by cutting it out or freezing it. The much nastier malignant melanoma may have already spread to bone and brain at the time that it is first noticed. **Prevention** Sun screen. SPF stands for Sun Protection Factor. It is measured by determining how long a given person takes to "burn" with and without the sunscreen product on. So, if it takes 10 times longer to burn with the sunscreen product applied, then that product has an SPF of 10. If it only takes twice as long then the SPF is 2. The higher the SPF the greater the protection. However, do not just use higher factors just to stay out in the sun longer. 'Flash frying' (desperate bursts of excessive exposure), as it is called, is known to increase the risks of skin cancer. Follow the Australians' with their Slip, Slap, Slop campaign.

Tuberculosis

Australia has the fourth lowest level in the world for this disease and is well protected by health screens before people can settle there. **Symptoms** Cough, tiredness, fever and lethargy. **Cures** At least six months treatment with a combination of drugs is required. **Prevention** Have a BCG vaccination before you go and see a doctor early if you have a persistent cough, cough blood, fever or unexplained weight loss.

Underwater health

Symptoms If you go diving make sure that you are fit do so. **British Scuba Association** (BSAC) ① *Telford's Quay, South Pier Rd, Ellesmere Port, Cheshire CH65 4FL, UK, T01513-506200, www.bsac.com*, can put you in touch with doctors who do medical examinations. Protect your feet from cuts, beach dog parasites (larva migrans) and sea urchins. The latter are almost impossible to remove but can be dissolved with lime or vinegar. Keep an eye out for secondary infection. **Cures** Antibiotics for secondary infections. Serious diving injuries may need time in a decompression chamber. **Prevention** Check that the dive company know what they are doing, have appropriate certification from BSAC or **Professional Association of Diving Instructors** (PADI) ① *Unit 7, St Philips Central, Albert Rd, St Philips, Bristol BS2 0TD, UK, T0117-3007234, www.padi.com*, and that the equipment is well maintained.

Further information

Websites

British Travel Health Association (UK) www.btha.org. This is the official website of an organization of travel health professionals.

Department of Health Travel Advice (UK) www.doh.gov.uk/traveladvice. This excellent site is also available as a free booklet, the T6, from Post Offices. It lists the vaccine advice requirements for each country.

Fit for Travel (UK) www.fitfortravel.scot. nhs.uk. This site from Scotland provides a quick A-Z of vaccine and travel health advice requirements for each country.

Foreign and Commonwealth Office (FCO) (UK) www.fco.gov.uk. This is a key travel advice site, with useful information on the country, people, climate and lists the UK embassies/consulates. The site also promotes the concept of 'Know Before You Go'. And encourages travel insurance and appropriate travel health advice.

Medic Alert (UK) www.medicalalert.co.uk. This is the website of the foundation that produces bracelets and necklaces for those with existing medical problems. Once you have ordered your bracelet/necklace, write your key medical details inside, so that if you collapse, a medical person can identify you as someone with epilepsy etc.

NetDoctor (UK) www.Netdoctor.co.uk. This general health advice site has a useful section on travel and has an "ask the expert", interactive chat forum.

Public Health Laboratory Service (UK) www.phls.org.uk. This site has up to date malaria advice guidelines. It also has useful information for those who are pregnant, suffering from epilepsy or planning to travel

with children.
Travel Screening Services (UK)
www.travelscreening.co.uk. This is the
author's website. A private clinic dedicated
to integrated travel health. The clinic gives
vaccine, travel health advice, email and SMS
text vaccine reminders and screens returned
travellers for tropical diseases.
World Health Organization www.who.int.
The WHO site has links to the WHO Blue
Book (it was Yellow up to last year) on travel
advice. This lists the diseases in different
regions of the world.

Books
Expedition Medicine (The Royal
Geographic Society) Editors **David Warrell**
and Sarah Anderson ISBN 1 86197 040-4.
**International Travel and Health World
Health Organization Geneva** ISBN 92 4
158026 7.
The Travellers Good Health Guide by Dr
Ted Lankester by ISBN 0-85969-827-0.

Leaflets
The Travellers Guide to Health (T6) can be
obtained by calling the *Health Literature Line*
on T0800 555 777. Advice for travellers on
avoiding the risks of HIV and AIDS (Travel
Safe) available from **Department of Health**,
PO Box 777, London SE1 6XH, UK. The Blood
Care Foundation order form PO Box 7,
Sevenoaks, Kent TN13 2SZ, UK,
T44-(0)1732-742427.

Keeping in touch

Communications

Internet
Internet access, and thus email, is widely available in hostels, hotels and cafés.
Expect to pay about $2 to $5 for 30 minutes.

Post
Most post offices are open Monday to Friday 0900-1700, and Saturday 0900-1230.
Sending a postcard, greeting card or 'small' letter (less than 130 x 240 mm, 5 mm
thick and 250 grams) anywhere in Australia is $0.50 and should arrive within three
days. Postage of larger letters starts at $1. Airmail for postcards and greetings cards
is $1 anywhere in the world, small letters (under 50 g) up to $1.65. Parcels can be
sent either by sea, economy air (a good trade-off option between speed and cost)
or air. Most of the principal or main offices in major towns and cities offer
Post Restante for those peripatetic souls with no fixed address, open
Monday-Friday 0900-1700.

Telephone
Most public payphones are operated by nationally-owned
Telstra www.telstra.com.au. Some take phonecards, available
from newsagents and post offices, and credit cards. A payphone
call within Australia requires $0.40 or $0.50. If you are calling
locally (within approximately 50 km) this lasts indefinitely. **STD**
calls, outside this area, will use up $0.40 in the first 43 seconds
if calling before 1900, and 78 seconds after. Subsequent time
cost $0.40 each time block.

*All WA telephone
numbers are prefixed with
08 if calling from outside
the state. Service
difficulties: T132203,
International service
difficulties: T1221.
Directory inquiries: T1223.
International directory
inquiries: T1225.*

There are no area phone codes. You will, however, need to
use a **state code** for dialling numbers in: ACT/NSW (**02**); VIC/TAS
(**03**); QLD (**07**).

To **call Western Australia** from overseas, dial the international prefix followed by
618, then the eight-digit number. To call WA from ACT/NSW/VIC/TAS/QLD, dial 08

followed by the eight-digit number. You can access the national database of telephone numbers and their accompanying addresses at www.whitepages.com.au. The *Yellow Pages* also has its own site at www.yellowpages.com.au.

To call **overseas from Australia** dial 0011 followed by the country code. Country codes include: **Republic of Ireland** 353; **New Zealand** 64; **South Africa** 27; the **USA** and **Canada** 1; the **UK** 44. By far the cheapest way of calling overseas is to use an international pre-paid phonecard (cannot be used from a mobile phone, or some of the blue and orange public phones).

Worth considering if you are in Australia for any length of time is a **pre-paid mobile phone**. **Telstra** and **Vodaphone** give the best coverage and their phones are widely available from $100. Calls are more expensive of course.

Media

Newspapers and magazines
The *West Australian* is published daily except Sundays, general entertainment listings published daily in *Today* section. *The Australian* is the only national paper. The main current affairs magazine, the weekly *Bulletin*, includes a section of *Newsweek*.

Foreign newspapers and magazines are widely available in the main urban centres. It is also possible to buy special weekly editions of British papers such as the *Daily Mail* and *The Guardian*. There are Asian editions of *Time* and *The Economist*.

TV and radio
There are five main **television** channels in Western Australia; the publicly funded **ABC** and **SBS**, and the independent, commercial stations, **Channel 7** (called **GWN** in country regions), **Channel 9** (WIN in country regions) and **Channel 10**. The ABC aims for Australian high quality content including many **BBC** programmes. The SBS focuses on multinational culture, current affairs, sport and film. The SBS has the best world news, shown daily at 1830.

The ABC broadcasts several national **radio** channels: **Radio National** features news, current affairs, culture and music; **Classic FM** is self-explanatory; and **Triple J** is aimed at a young, 'alternative' audience. There are also many local commercial radio stations that feature a mix of news, talk-back, and music.

Footprint features

Introduction

One of the most isolated cities in the world, Perth is a green, clean and spacious city on the banks of the wide, blue Swan River. The city covers about three times the size of Greater London (with an eighth of the population), contained by coastline to the west and the low Perth Hills of the Darling Range to the east. Although it is about the same age as Adelaide there is little evidence of its past. It's a sparkling modern place, reminiscent of American cities with its freeway, flyovers and dependence on the car.

Perth's best asset is an incredible climate. The sun simply never stops shining and each perfect sunny day is taken for granted. The endless expanse of blue sky and sea is a constant reflection in both the city's skyscrapers and residents' sunglasses. This makes for a city lived in the outdoors where the beaches, ocean, river and parks are the favourite haunts of the friendly, laid-back people of Perth.

History and culture are not major preoccupations of the 'sandgropers', although the city hosts an excellent international arts festival and the port city of Fremantle contains some of the country's finest Victorian buildings. The city centre is often criticized for being soulless by day and empty by night and it is true that it suffers from a lack of inner-city residents. The action in Perth is to be found out in the inner and beach suburbs, where you can watch the sun set into the Indian Ocean, see a film outdoors, go sailing on the river or stroll the café strips.

Don't miss...

1 **WA Art Gallery and Museum** Have a day of culture soaking up the exhibits of these great establishments, page 66.
2 **Kings Park** Admire the view over the city, stroll through the Botanic Gardens and make time for a picnic, page 68.
3 **South Perth** Head for the foreshore and go sailing, waterskiing or parasailing, page 70.
4 **Beach BBQ** Have a late afternoon BBQ at Trigg Beach and watch the sun set into the ocean, page 70.
5 **Hillarys** Check out the aquarium and take a sailing cruise, page 72.
6 **Moonlight cinema** Watch a film at an outdoor cinema, page 83.

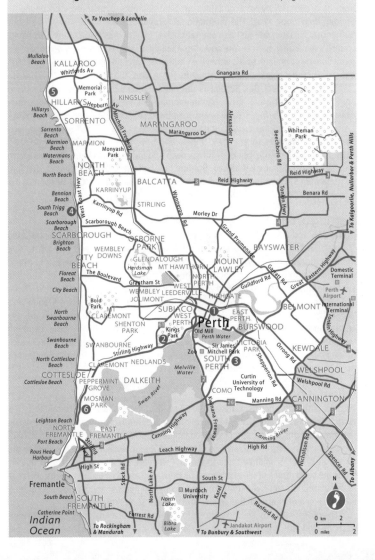

Perth

Ins and outs → *Population: 1.3 million.*

Getting there

Perth Airport, www1.perthairport.net.au, a little over 10 km east of the city centre, has two terminals – domestic and international. With no direct link between the two, transfers are via the perimeter highways (shuttle $9, T9229 8811). The **domestic terminal**, Brearley Avenue, has a wide range of services including ATMs, **Travelex** foreign exchange, luggage lockers, cafés and all the major car hire firms. Transport to Perth is via taxi (around $30), the **Airport Shuttle** minibus, T9277 7958, which meets all flights ($11, you'll need to phone and book to get out to the airport), or the **Transperth** bus (bus stop opposite Qantas terminal, $3, 35 minutes) to the City Busport. Buses leave at least every 30 minutes Monday-Friday, from 0535-2305; every 30-60 minutes on Saturday from 0705-2305; and hourly on Sunday from 0905-2205. The **international terminal**, Horrie Miller Drive, is slightly further out. Facilities are just as comprehensive, the **Thomas Cook** foreign exchange counters remaining open before and after all flights. There is, however, no public bus route from this terminal, so it's either the shuttle ($13, details as above) or a taxi (about $30-35). There are also shuttles to Fremantle, T9335 1614, and Scarborough, T9387 5431.

☃ If you are heading east, beyond Western Australia, leaving from Perth, see page 137 for routes.

Wellington Street Bus Station is the main terminal for interstate coaches and some independent state services. **Greyhound/McCaffertys** ① *on the upper level walkway, (shop 17), T9321 6211, www.greyhound.com.au, Mon-Tue and Thu 0800-1700, Wed and Fri 0800-2000, Sat 0800-1130, Sun 0800-1100 and 1730-2000,* runs the interstate services to Adelaide, Darwin and beyond. **TransWA** ① *T1300 662205, www.transwa.wa.gov.au,* operates most coach and train services within the state from the East Perth Terminal. **Railway Station** on Wellington Street services the four suburban lines, while most metropolitan buses terminate at the **City Busport**. ▶▶ *See Transport, page 89, for further details.*

Getting around

Both Perth and Fremantle have free city centre buses known as CATs (Central Area Transit), T136213, circulating the city on two different routes every seven to five minutes during the day and a less regularly at night. **Transperth**, T136213, www.transperth.wa. gov.au, operates the city's buses, trains and ferries and has several information centres where you can pick up timetables and ask for help. These are located in the Plaza Arcade, at City Busport, the main Railway Station and Wellington Street Bus Station. Urban bus routes tend to radiate out from the city centre, and travelling between peripheral areas, though usually possible, can be a tortuous affair. As it's a fairly flat city Perth is ideal for cycling. Ferries sail from Barrack St Jetty over to South Perth. There are four suburban train lines from Perth station. ▶▶ *See Transport, page 89, for further details.*

Orientation

The core of the city lines the banks of the Swan River from its mouth at Fremantle to the central business district (CBD), 19 km upstream, just north of an open basin known as Perth Water. Perth is contained by the coastline to the west and the low 'Perth hills' of the Darling Ranges to the east, a corridor about 40 km wide. However, sprawl to the north and south is unlimited and in the last 10 years the city has expanded quickly along the sand dunes of the north coast to Joondalup and to the south almost as far as Rockingham. The northern suburbs, serviced by the freeway and the Joondalup train line, are a sea of new brick bungalows and modern shopping malls.

The oldest suburbs are those close to the river, particularly on the northern side such as Dalkeith and Peppermint Grove, and these have always been the most

⁞ Arriving late at night

Suburban buses don't run beyond midnight so you'll need to take a taxi or the airport shuttle to get from the airport to the city (both meet every flight). The Fremantle shuttle should be booked in advance.

Most of the major hotels will check you in at any time, as do some of the hostels , particularly those in Northbridge; try to organize in advance and that they know when you're likely to arrive. If you do get stuck without accommodation in the early hours avoid wandering the streets and head for a 24-hour café such as the **Oriel** in Hay Street, Subiaco.

wealthy and desirable places to live. The beach suburbs close to the city centre such as Cottesloe and City Beach are also affluent. Inner-city suburbs like Subiaco, Leederville and North Perth have become increasingly gentrified and sought after for their location and attractive old architecture.

The city centre is a small grid, just north of the river, of about 2 km by 1 km. The river is bordered by a strip of green lawn throughout the entire city area, and there is a walking trail alongside the river on both north and south banks. However, although the central business district faces the river it is cut off from it by busy roads and freeways – so the foreshore is not quite the asset it could be. South Perth is an attractive area with a wide grassy foreshore heavily used by joggers and picnickers. This is a fashionable suburb with many apartment blocks, making the most of views of the city skyline. Further south lies a large area of well-established middle-class suburbs around the Canning River and inland from Fremantle.

Tourist information

Head for the **Perth Visitor Centre** ⓘ *Forrest Pl, T1300 361351, www.westernaustralia. net, Mon-Thu 0800-1800, Fri 0800-1900, Sat 0830-1230*, the main VIC for the state. You can pick up free maps and brochures for Perth and Fremantle, and booklets on each state region. It acts as a travel agent and sells national park passes. An information kiosk at the junction of Forrest Place and the Murray Street Mall can provide information and help on anything in the city. It is run by volunteers and is not aimed specifically at tourists but it's a good place to ask for directions or advice. There is also a very useful contact point for backpackers, **Traveller's Club** ⓘ *553 Wellington St, T9226 0660, www.travellersclub.com.au, Mon-Sat 0900-2000, Sun 1000-2000*. It offers help and information, has well-used travellers' notice boards, cheap internet use and acts as a tour booking centre. Aside from the VIC, information on national parks can be obtained from the **Department Conservation and Land Management** (CALM) ⓘ *T9334 0333, www.naturebase.net*. CALM produces a small brochure on each park and excellent publications on walking, fauna and flora. It is also possible to visit the **CALM information centres** ⓘ *17 Dick Perry Av, Kensington, Mon-Fri 0800-1700, and 40 Jull St, Armadale, 0900-1400*, to collect brochures but these are out of the way.

Sights

Perth is primarily an outdoor city. A place to soak up the perfect sunny climate by going to the beach, sailing on the Swan River or walking in Kings Park. The city has few grand public institutions and much of its early colonial architecture has been demolished to create a glossy modern city. The most impressive cultural sights are gathered together in the plaza called the Cultural Centre, just north of the railway line, that separates the city from Northbridge. Art Gallery and the Western Australian Museum are both excellent and give a fine insight into the history and culture of the state. Kings Park, just west of the city centre, is the largest green space close to any state capital and is the city's most popular attraction. The park is heavily used by the locals for its views, peaceful walks and picnic spots, café and outdoor cinema. Swan Bells tower also has good city views, and can easily be combined with a visit to Perth Zoo, an unexpected oasis of bush and jungle set back from the river shore of South Perth.

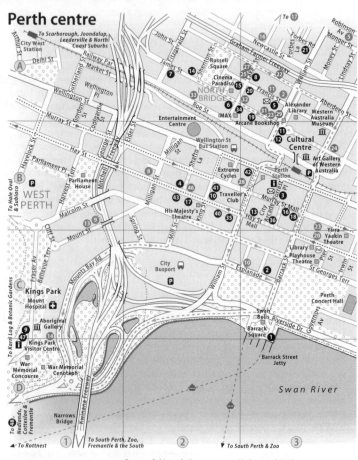

Perth centre

N

0 metres 200
0 yards 200

Central Perth

The city centre is laid out in a grid just north of the river. Four main streets run eastwest within this grid. St Georges Terrace is the commercial district, full of skyscrapers and office workers. Hay and Murray Streets are the shopping and eating streets, while Wellington borders the railway line and is slightly seedier than the rest. Just north of

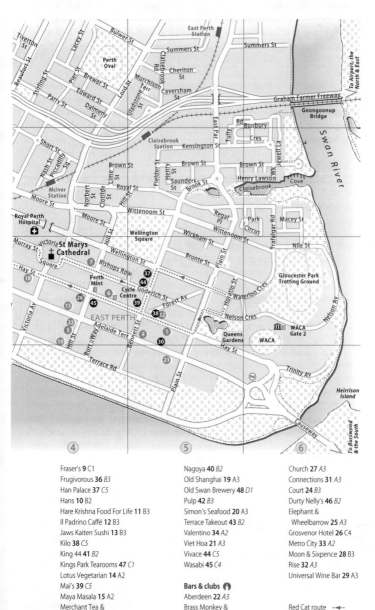

Fraser's **9** C1
Frugivorous **36** *B3*
Han Palace **37** *C5*
Hans **10** B2
Hare Krishna Food For Life **11** B3
Il Padrino Caffé **12** B3
Jaws Kaiten Sushi **13** B3
Kilo **38** *C5*
King 44 **41** *B2*
Kings Park Tearooms **47** *C1*
Lotus Vegetarian **14** A2
Mai's **39** *C5*
Maya Masala **15** A2
Merchant Tea &
    Coffee Company **16** B3

Nagoya **40** *B2*
Old Shanghai **19** *A3*
Old Swan Brewery **48** *D1*
Pulp **42** *B3*
Simon's Seafood **20** *A3*
Terrace Takeout **43** *B2*
Valentino **34** *A2*
Viet Hoa **21** *A3*
Vivace **44** *C5*
Wasabi **45** *C4*

Bars & clubs 🎧
Aberdeen **22** *A3*
Brass Monkey &
    Grapeskin **23** *A3*

Church **27** *A3*
Connections **31** *A3*
Court **24** *B3*
Durty Nelly's **46** *B2*
Elephant &
    Wheelbarrow **25** *A3*
Grosvenor Hotel **26** C4
Metro City **33** *A2*
Moon & Sixpence **28** B3
Rise **32** *A3*
Universal Wine Bar **29** *A3*

Red Cat route ·◄·
Blue Cat route ─◄ ─

The Old Swan Brewery

The Old Swan Brewery occupies a very desirable site on the river between the university and the city. Local Aboriginal people protested for many years against the re-development of the old brewery as the site was an important camping place, initiation site for men and connected with the Waugyl a creator figure, embodied as a snake, who made the southwest rivers and Mount Eliza in Kings Park. Despite many years of wrangling, the Old Swan Brewery is now a luxurious complex of million dollar apartments, offices and two restaurants.

the railway line is Northbridge, a restaurant district. This is reached by a walkway from Forrest Place, over Wellington Street and the Perth Train Station to the Cultural Centre. Northbridge lies just to the west of the plaza, bordered by William Street. The main shopping district is contained within the Hay and Murray Street Malls and the arcades running between the malls.

Art Gallery of Western Australia

ⓘ *Perth Cultural Centre, T9492 6600, www.artgallery.wa.gov.au, 1000-1700, free, guided tours at 1300 Tue-Fri, Sun, Blue CAT route, stop 7, walkway to Perth Train Station, several council car parks on Roe St.*

The gallery forms the southern point of the **Cultural Centre** triangle of public institutions. The main gallery was built in 1979 to house the **State Art Collection** and the clean lines of its featureless exterior walls conceal cool white hexagonal spaces inside. The ground floor is used for temporary exhibitions and this is where the state's most prestigious visiting exhibitions are shown. The central spiral staircase leads to the Aboriginal Art and Contemporary Art collections on the first floor. The gallery's collection of **Aboriginal Art** is one of the most extensive and impressive in Australia, encompassing bark paintings from Arnhem Land, dot paintings by Central Desert artists and works by WA artists such as Jimmy Pike and Sally Morgan. This collection is enhanced by detailed explanations of each painting and biography of the artist. The **Contemporary Art** collection also includes the best of craft and design in ceramics, glass, furniture and metalwork. More traditional work can be seen in the **Centenary Galleries** in the elegant former Police Court building (1905). The emphasis is on Western Australian art from colonial times to the present but also includes painters such as John Glover, Eugene Von Guérard, and Frederick McCubbin's iconic Down on His Luck, 1887. The gallery has an excellent shop stocking fine craft work and a huge range of art books. The spacious, relaxed café opposite does good casual Mediterranean-style food (Monday-Friday 0800-1700, Saturday-Sunday 0900-1700).

Alexander Library

ⓘ *Perth Cultural Centre, T9427 3104, www.liswa.wa.gov.au, Mon-Thu 0900-2000, Fri 0900-1730, Sat-Sun 1000-1730, book to use internet (1 hr), Blue CAT route, stop 7.*

Opposite the Art Gallery is the complementary modern architecture of the state reference library. The **J.S. Battye Library**, on the third level, is a comprehensive collection of WA history titles and archives. Recent national and international newspapers and magazines can be read on the ground floor, where there is also free internet access. The **State Film and Video Archive** is on the first level and visitors can choose a film from the catalogue and use the viewing facilities on request. Other facilities include a café, lockers and a discard bookshop selling ex-library books. The library shop stocks the city's best range of books on WA.

Western Australian Museum

ⓘ *Perth Cultural Centre, T9427 2700, www.museum.wa.gov.au, 0930-1700, free, Blue CAT route, stop 7.*

The natural science collection of the Western Australian Museum came together during the gold boom of the 1890s when the new settlers had the money and leisure to think of fine public facilities. The site held the combined functions of the state library, museum and art gallery until 1955 and sprawls over a large area containing many different architectural styles. The main entrance on James Street joins the Jubilee Building and Hackett Hall. The Jubilee Building was built in 1899 in Victorian Byzantine style, from Rottnest and Cottesloe sandstone. It houses the Mammal Gallery which still displays specimens in their cedar and glass cases from 1903 and bird, butterfly and marine galleries. The beautiful Hackett Hall was built to house the library in 1903 and still retains the original fittings, now a backdrop to the museum's best exhibition, 'WA Land and People'. This is a contemporary look at Western Australia from its ancient geological beginnings to Aboriginal life, European invasion and the ways in which the land has both shaped and been shaped by its residents. Displays on the European history of WA are shown in the Old Gaol, which was built by convicts as a gaol and courthouse and used until 1899 when the prisoners were transferred to Fremantle Gaol. Beyond the gaol is the 1970s Francis St Building, home to meteorites, a blue whale skeleton and fascinating **Aboriginal Gallery**. This is called Katta Djinoong, meaning 'see us and understand us' and goes a long way towards its aim. The exhibition examines the past and present of WA's different indigenous groups, and contemporary issues such as the 'stolen generation'. The Beaufort Street Building, the former Art Gallery, houses temporary and travelling exhibitions. The museum bookshop specializes in Natural and Social Science titles and has an extensive range of books on Aboriginal subjects. There is also a café for light snacks and drinks.

Perth Mint

ⓘ *Hay St, T9421 7223, www.perthmint.com.au, Mon-Fri 0900-1600, Sat-Sun 0900-1300, tours every 30 mins, daily from 0930 to 1½ hrs before close, gold pours on the hour, 1000-1500 Mon-Fri, 1000-1200 Sat-Sun, entry and tours $6.60, children $3.30, concessions $5.50, Red CAT route, stop 10.*

During the 19th century London's Royal Mint established three branches in Australia. The last to be opened, just two years before Federation, was in Perth as a direct result of the gold-rushes that were then gripping the colony and stripping it of ready currency. Built of Rottnest limestone the buildings have endured and the work of the mint has continued to the present day. Although it no longer produces day-to-day currency, it is still the major refiner of WA gold and buys and sells gold at market prices. They also mint a wide range of commemorative medals and coins. Several display rooms are open to the public. Some have windows through to the production area, others contain some of WA's most historic and largest nuggets, and one contains a solid 400 oz gold bar. It's half as big as a house brick but about 10 times as hard to pick up, and you're allowed to have a try. There are regular guided tours and some culminate in a live 'gold pour', quite a spectacular sight.

Swan Bells

ⓘ *Barrack Sq, T9218 8183, 1000-1800, $6, children $3, concessions $3, the bells are rung 1230-1400 Wed-Thu and Sat-Sun, and Tue 1830-2000, Blue CAT route, stop 19.*

It is little known in England that the church bells of St Martin-in-the-Fields, the ones that ring in the new year at Trafalgar Square, are almost brand new and made from Western Australian metals. The original bells, cast in the 1700s from bell metal that was possibly

🔴 *Perth Mint has produced the purest gold ever assayed, so, if you are looking for a gold bar to buy, their shop is the place to buy one.*

first poured a thousand years ago and used to celebrate Captain Cook's home-coming, were found to be stressing the church tower, and it was decided to gift them to WA to commemorate Australia's bicentenary in 1988. Exerting a force of over 40 tonnes the bells needed a substantial bell-tower to house them. Perth not only provided just that, but made the tower the centrepiece of Old Perth Port, a striking, sweeping construction soaring 80 m with twin, copper-clad sails. The bell-chamber is easily accessed and walled with almost sound-proof doubled-glazed windows. These are now the only church bells in the world you can watch without being deafened.

The open-air platform on the sixth floor offers good views of the river and city.

WACA and around

ⓘ *Nelson Cresent, off Murray St, T9265 7222, www.waca.com.au, museum 1000-1500 except match days, $3, children and concessions $1, tours 1000 and 1300, Tue-Thu except match days, $5, children and concessions $2, Red CAT route, stop 6.*
Now used almost exclusively for cricket, the WACA (pronounced simply 'wacker'), parts of which are over a century old, is WA's premier sporting stadium. There are regular tours of the ground and a small but fascinating museum, mostly filled with a hundred years worth of cricketing memorabilia and including a Bradman room. Head for gate 2 for both tours and museum.

Opposite the WACA, the **Queen's Gardens** are a picturesque set of lawns and palm trees set around a series of lily ponds, a surprisingly quiet spot. In the other direction **Gloucester Park** ⓘ *T9221 4110, $11, children free*, is a trotting circuit that holds races every Monday afternoon from 1300 and Friday evenings from 1800.

Kings Park

ⓘ *T9480 3600, www.kpbg.wa.gov.au, 0930-1600, No.33 bus from from St Georges Terr to Fraser Av or Blue CAT bus to stop 21 and walk up Jacob's Ladder, free.*
This huge playground for the city and central suburbs is just about everything you could want a park to be. A large area of natural bush, threaded through with unsigned bush walks, is bordered to the south and east by broad bands of carefully manicured lawns and gardens, these in turn encompassing the excellent **Botanic Gardens**. From many of these are tremendous views across to the city centre and Barrack Street jetty, particularly beautiful at sunset, and very popular with picnickers. The main visitor area is at the end of Fraser Avenue, opposite the **State War Memorial**, one of many memorials in the park as well as one of the best city-viewing spots. In this area are a kiosk ⓘ *0830-1900, to 2100 Sunday*, some superb tearooms and restaurant, the visitor centre and public toilets. Here you can pick up a full map of the park ($1), self-guided walking maps, and details of the various ongoing events and activities.

There are free guided walks from the old Karri log near the centre every day at 1000 and 1400 (bookings not necessary), usually focusing on either the Botanic Gardens or the history of the park, but with variations in winter and spring looking at the local wildflowers and bushland. Walks usually take about 1½ hours, bushland walks about 2½ hours. Also close by the War Memorial is a lookout, and underneath this the **Aboriginal Gallery** ⓘ *Sat-Mon 1200-1600, Tue-Fri 1130-1800, members of the gallery put on a dance performance at the lookout twice a week at 1130 Wed and 1230 Sun*, a workshop and gallery for local artists.

Away from the views is a large area devoted to families with young children. **Hale Oval** has an extensive, imaginative playground, several free electric BBQs with covered seating (though strangely no tables), plus a kiosk-café, **Stickybeaks** ⓘ *T9481 4990, 0800-1700*, with a good range of snack meals and takeaways. There are also events held at the playground, contact the café for details. Other BBQ areas are located at the Pines, off Fraser Avenue, Saw Avenue and Lakeside. The latter two picnic areas are at the west end of the park. Some BBQs, including those in the Pines, are wood- fired with wood provided free, and may be out of bounds in summer.

Central suburbs

The suburbs north of the river and west of the city centre are some of the most attractive in the city. These suburbs all have their own character and most have eating and shopping strips that are more lively than the city centre.

Northbridge is purely a restaurant, entertainment and nightlife precinct, all squeezed into an area of about 1 sq km. There is plenty of variety and cheap eating to be had here but the area has been troubled in the last few years by violence and street gangs. It feels perfectly safe to visit (except late at night) and most of the backpacker hostels are located here so it is full of travellers but it's wise to take precautions.

Subiaco is increasingly taking over from Northbridge as an eating destination, although it is more expensive and too trendy for some. Although Subiaco now has the largest and busiest suburban commercial strip, it had spiritual beginnings far from its current celebration of materialism. It was founded as a monastery, New Subiaco, by two homesick Italian monks who also founded the more famous monastery at New Norcia. There are two small museums here, both worth a look if you have time. **Harvey House**ⓘ *Barker St, T9340 1506, Wed 1000-1600, Sun 1400-1600, $2, children $1*, houses the WA Medical Museum, an exhibition of the history of medicine in WA. **Subiaco Museum**ⓘ *Rokeby Rd, T9237 9227, Tue-Sun 1400-1700, gold coin donation*, has several rooms displaying local artefacts and memorabilia charting the history of Subi from one-time Benedictine monastery to the buzzing suburb that it is today.

West Perth, between Subiaco and the city centre, is mostly a professional suburb where architects, accountants and dentists have their offices. There are also lots of apartments and it makes a very convenient base close to Kings Park, Subiaco restaurants, the city and the freeway. **East Perth**, on the other side of the city centre, is developing into a centre for accommodation and eating but is still fairly quiet and businesslike. It is also a convenient base, although parking can be difficult.

Subiaco

Sleeping		Brew-Ha 3		Zen 10
Amber Rose 1		Buddhabar 4		
		Oriel 6		**Bars & clubs**
Eating		Walk Café 8		Club Red Sea 11
Altos 1		Witches Cauldron 9		Subiaco Hotel 12

Leederville, just north of Subiaco, is an alternative and funky suburb with some great cafés, a lively pub and an arthouse cinema with indoor and outdoor screens.

Heading southwest, the Stirling Highway is an arterial route between the river and coast from the city to Fremantle, and links the leafy, establishment suburbs of Nedlands, Claremont and Cottesloe. **Nedlands** abuts the western border of the University of Western Australia (UWA), the state's oldest university with a beautiful garden campus and an excellent art gallery. **Claremont** has some great shopping and is the haunt of 'ladies who lunch' and their privately educated kids. Further west, **Cottesloe** has one of the city's best and most popular beaches, some great beachside cafés and a seriously laid-back lifestyle.

South Perth, just across Perth Water, has the best city views and a lovely foreshore. This is a great place for sailing or waterskiing and there are hire outlets here during the summer. Several cafés and restaurants are located right on the riverbank and although you might pay a little more for the view, it is a pleasant place to spend a few hours. Alternatively, just head for the eastern end of the foreshore where there are also plenty of good places to picnic, BBQ and walk by the river. In South Perth, the incongruous **Old Mill** ① *T9367 5788, 1000-1600, $2, children $1, by Narrows Bridge, catch a ferry to Mends St jetty, then walk towards the bridge (10 mins) or take bus no's 108, 109 from the Busport*, tucked under the freeway, is an unusual survivor from the early days of the Swan River Settlement in the 1830s. Although the windmill looks quaint, it is technically an industrial site and one of the oldest in the state. It was built in 1835 by William Shenton to grind wheat that fed the young colony. On a windy day the mill averaged 680 kg of flour a day and its location by the river meant that the flour could easily be transported to the city. Incredibly the mill was almost lost when the freeway and Narrows bridge were built in 1955. The government planned to demolish the site to make way for the freeway but there was such public protest that the building was saved and it is now managed by the National Trust. An exhibition in the whitewashed miller's cottage explains the history of the Mill. Also in South Perth, is **Perth Zoo** ① *20 Labouchere Rd, T9367 7988, www.perthzoo.wa.gov. au, 0900-1700, $16, children $8, concessions $12-13, Transperth ferry from Barrack St jetty to Mends St jetty, then 5-min walk*. The zoo covers just 19 ha in a block between the river and the freeway but manages to squeeze in 1,800 animals in attractive natural settings. The three main habitats are the Australian Walkabout, Asian Rainforest and African Savannah. The zoo participates in a native species breeding program, Western Shield, that aims to save the many local WA species close to extinction, releasing zoo-bred animals to the wild. The results of this programme can be seen in the Australian Walkabout, housing creatures such as the tiny Western Swamp Tortoise, one of the world's rarest tortoise species, and the unusual termite-eating Numbat. A highlight of the wetlands area is the horrifyingly large saltwater crocodile. This 50-year-old from Darwin is 380 kg of power and the tank allows you to see him lying underwater. The Asian rainforest is home to elephants, monkeys and orang-utans but the most compelling creatures are the Sumatran tigers, clearly visible through a glass wall. The displays highlight their endangered status. More big cats as well as giraffes, zebra and rhinos can be seen in the African Savannah. The zoo café and shop are located near the entrance. The café menu is limited to junk food but there is also a grassy picnic and BBQ area. On a hot day remember to take a drink or change for the drink machines en route as it can be quite a walk back to the café.

Coastal suburbs

The coastal suburbs are where you'll see Perth locals at their most relaxed. Surf wear is the customary attire and although you may not want to become familiar with a surfer's horny feet you will because bare feet on the street or in shops are entirely unremarkable. These suburbs are mostly residential but most have at least one great café or restaurant on the beach. Swimming is fine at all of the beaches, although there is often a steep shore break. As always in Australia, watch out for rips. If you want the reassurance of lifeguards, swim between the flags at Cottesloe, or Scarborough beaches. City Beach, Floreat and Trigg also often have lifesavers on duty at weekends in summer. Swanbourne is a nudist beach and Trigg is mostly for surfers but the rest are used by all. All west coast beaches are most pleasant in the morning before the sea breeze, known locally as the Fremantle Doctor for the relief it brings, kicks in from the south in the afternoon. The early evening is also a lovely time at the beach, when the sun melts into the Indian ocean and there are often magnificent sunsets.

Cottesloe → *Colour map 1, grid B1. 11 km from city centre, 7 km from Fremantle.*

Perth's most attractive and lively beach suburb, Cottesloe, is the kind of place to make anyone envy the local lifestyle, or persuade them to immigrate here as soon as possible. The blindingly white beaches of Cottesloe and North Cottesloe slope into the clear, warm water of the Indian Ocean and there is usually a bit of a swell for bodysurfing. The beaches attract a hardy band of local swimmers early in the morning who are replaced later in the day by the city's best bodies and bikinis. There are always teenage boys showing off on the pylon and walkers striding along the ocean-side path. The cafés overlooking the ocean are busy from sunrise to sunset, when the sun dips into the sea as if curtsying to Cottesloe alone. It's not glitzy though and owes its contented, laid-back atmosphere to its happy locals who far outnumber visitors. Just inland is the shopping area of Napoleon Street, just off Stirling Highway, full of classy homewares shops catering to the well-heeled residents of the surrounding suburbs.

Cottesloe to Scarborough → *A distance of 12 km.*

One long, sweeping beach extends all the way from Cottesloe to Scarborough, incorporating a nudist section near the military base at **Swanbourne**. This whole stretch of coast is a favourite of surfers and windsurfers alike and swimming can be hazardous. Stick to the patrolled areas.

Mid-way are two small developed enclaves, and these make two of the best spots on the Perth coast if you want to get away from the serious crowds. **City Beach** has an extensive grassy foreshore hard up against a very broad section of beautiful white-sand beach. Facilities include BBQs, picnic tables and toilets and a small complex with a kiosk, café and the best restaurant in Perth that actually hangs over a beach. See Eating page 76 for details of the great eatery, **Oceanus**.

Just a few hundred metres north, **Floreat Beach** is much more modest in scale, but with a superb children's playground, BBQs and some unexpectedly stylish covered picnic tables. There are also two beach volleyball courts; free, collect a ball and net from the kiosk. There is a laid-back, friendly terrace café here, see Eating page 76.

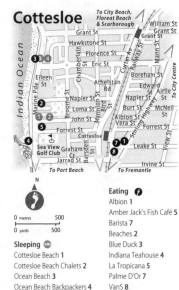

Cottesloe

To City Beach, Floreat Beach & Scarborough

Grant St · William St · Grant St
Hawkstone St
Florence St
Eric St
Chamberlain St
Boreham St
Eileen St
Athelstan Rd · Edward St · Airlie St
Napier Ave · Napier St
Broome St · Loma St · Burt St · McNeil St
John St · Albion St · Vera St
Forrest St · Cottesloe · Forrest St
Marine Pde
Sea View Golf Club · Graham St · Leake St
Jarrad St · Barsden St · Marmion St
Irvine St
Indian Ocean
Railway St · Curtin Ave · Marine Pde · Stirling Highway · Mann St · To City Centre · View St
To Port Beach · To Fremantle

N

0 metres 500
0 yards 500

Sleeping
Cottesloe Beach 1
Cottesloe Beach Chalets 2
Ocean Beach 3
Ocean Beach Backpackers 4

Eating
Albion 1
Amber Jack's Fish Café 5
Barista 3
Beaches 2
Blue Duck 3
Indiana Teahouse 4
La Tropicana 5
Palme D'Or 7
VanS 8

→ *Colour map 1, grid B1. 14 km from city centre, 9 km from Hillarys.*

Where Cottesloe is an almost accidentally popular beach suburb, laid-back and effortless, Scarborough's attractions are more carefully designed. The suburb is dominated by the **Rendezvous Observation Tower**, a multi-storeyed icon built by Alan Bond that somehow slipped through council planning regulations in the 1980s. It is the only skyscraper on the entire city coastline. In front of it a small café strip has developed, separated from the wide beach by a road, narrow grassy foreshore and a thin line of remnant dunes. Facilities are good and family-friendly, including toilets, BBQs, picnic tables, takeaway kiosks and a small cabin hiring out a variety of games, skates and bikes. Around the main junction of the West Coast Highway and Scarborough Beach Road is a cluster of shops and services, including a Coles supermarket. Beyond these are a large number of three- to four-storey holiday apartment complexes. **Scarborough Beach Markets**, held every weekend, pale besides those in the city and Fremantle, but are worth a visit for a well-stocked second-hand book stall.

Scarborough to Sorrento

A kilometre or so north of Scarborough the long sweep of beach that has extended practically all the way from Port Beach finally starts to break into a series of smaller bays and coves. The sand at this breakpoint is called **Trigg Beach**, and it is one of the city's best surfing spots. The beach backs onto large, grassy **Clarko Reserve**, where there are BBQs, covered picnic areas, toilets and changing rooms, and a children's playground. Just to the south, almost on the beach, is the **Trigg Island Café**, see Eating page 76.

A little further north **Mettam's Pool** is one of the few beaches on the Perth coast that favours swimmers and snorkellers over surfers, due to an off-shore reef, close to the surface, that has created a sheltered 'pool'. There are toilets and changing rooms available, and a few picnic tables. Continuing north you will pass the quite average **Waterman's Beach**. Not at all average is the small, funky terrace café across the road, the **BYO Wild Fig**, see Eating page 76.

Hillarys and Sorrento → *Colour map 1, grid A1. 25 km from centre, 27 km from Swan Valley.*

The beach suburbs of Hillarys and Sorrento have put themselves well and truly on the map, particularly for families, by building **Hillarys Boat Harbour**. Primarily containing private moorings the harbour does have a few commercial operations, but has become better known for the shops, restaurants and activities on and around the mall-like **Sorrento Quay**, a pier which almost bisects the harbour and ensures a very well-protected beach. Two major family attractions means the harbour and quay really hum on a weekend and during school holidays, particularly as the harbour also protects a sandy beach.

Aqwaⓘ *Southside Dr, T9447 7500, www.aqwa.com.au, 0900-1700, to 2100 Wed from Nov-Apr, $23.50, children $13, concessions $17.50,* WA's premier aquarium, is an impressive showcase for the sea-life that inhabits the coastal waters around the state. The centrepiece is a large walk-through tank with a good variety of fish, sharks and rays, but the many side tanks are just as fascinating with several devoted to corals and jellyfish. You'll want the Moon jellyfish tank back home in the living room. There are also discovery pools, crocodiles, a theatre showing almost continuous undersea documentaries and a large outdoor seal pool with an adjacent underground viewing room. Regular feeding and educational sessions can easily turn this into a half-day visit. A cheap café serves healthy sandwiches, cheap hot lunches, cakes and drinks. **The Great Escape** ⓘ *slides 0900-1200, 1200-1500, 1500-1800, complex 2100 Fri-Sat during Jan-Feb,* serving as the backdrop to the harbour beach, is a no-nonsense children's attraction with several diversions clustered around the all-important water slides. These are open for three fixed three-hour sessions, so best to arrive just after the start of one of them. Unfortunately everything is priced separately so it can rack up a bit if the kids insist on trying everything. A kiosk supplies drinks and snacks.

🛏 Sleeping

Central Perth *p65, map p64*

Hotels and motels

St Georges and Adelaide Terraces are home to many of the big modern, glitzy hotels in Perth, all with superb balcony rooms overlooking the riverside parks and the river itself. All offer cheaper 'getaway' specials so it might be worth asking what's going.

LL-L Hyatt Regency, 99 Adelaide Terr, T9225 1234, www.perth.hyatt.com. The last of the clutch of international standard hotels strung out along this street. It is arranged around an impressive, massive atrium foyer.

LL-A The Duxton, 1 St Georges Terr, T9261 8000, www.duxton.com. The closest to the city centre and its rooms and services are, by a whisker, the benchmark for the rest. The main restaurant is also seriously good.

A The Melbourne, corner of Hay and Milligan sts, T9320 3333, www.melbourne hotel.com.au. In sharp contrast, is this boutique hotel with 35 rooms in an ornate, restored 1890s pub building. Rooms have TV, en suite, minibar, some with veranda. Also a bar, café and restaurant.

B Criterion, 560 Hay St, T9325 5155, www.criterion-hotel-perth.com.au. A glorious art deco façade does not prepare you for the interior. The hotel has been refurbished to provide 69 comfortable but bland modern rooms, all a/c with minibar. Convenient location in heart of city, also a good brasserie and pub on site.

B New Esplanade, 18 The Esplanade, T9325 2000, www.newesplanade.com.au. Modern hotel with some great views and an almost perfect location. The standard rooms are a little tired, but the deluxe rooms are well equipped and have splendid views. Also underground parking.

B Novotel Langley, 221 Adelaide Terr, T9221 1200. Sandwiched between the much grander **Duxton** and **Sheraton** and does a commendable job at offering a similar experience at a much cheaper price.

B-D Northbridge Hotel, corner of Lake and Brisbane sts, T9328 5254, www.hotelnorth

bridge.com.au. Renovated old corner hotel with veranda. Luxurious hotel rooms (50) with spa and full facilities, bar and mid-range restaurant. 20 budget doubles in the old part of the hotel with shared facilities, TV, fridge.

B Sullivans, 166 Mounts Bay Rd, T9321 8022, www.sullivans.com.au. Just below Kings Park, this comfortable, modern hotel has 68 rooms (some with balcony and river views) and 2 apartments. Also pool, free bikes, parking and café. Convenient location, free city bus (Blue CAT) at door.

C Chateau Commodore, corner of Hay St and Victoria Av, T9325 0461, chateau@ace online.com.au. A slightly tired 1980s purpose-built hotel with very standard en-suite rooms. All rooms are en suite and good value, but particularly the family rooms.

D Jewell House YMCA, 180 Goderich St, T9325 8488, www.ymcajewellhouse.com. An 11-storey tower block with over 200 rooms, catering for the budget market, including simple but clean singles, doubles and family rooms, all including linen. Most floors are single sex. Free off-street parking and a cafeteria supplies seriously cheap breakfasts and dinners, 0700-0900 and 1730-1900.

C Perth City, 200 Hay St, T9220 7000, www.perthcityhotel.com.au. One of Perth's newest, staff are friendly, furnishings bright and cheerful.

Self-contained

B The Alderney, 193 Hay St, T92225 6600, www.alderney.com.au. Has over 60 new, very comfortably furnished, fully self-contained apartments. Each has double and twin bedrooms. Indoor pool and gym and undercover parking are included.

C Riverview, 42 Mount St, T9321 8963, www.riverview.au.com. Stylish, well-equipped studio apartments, all with balconies or patio gardens. Quality with value for couples.

D City Waters Lodge, 118 Terrace Rd, T9325 1566, www.citywaters.com.au. Clean, comfortable studio units (60) overlooking

Langley Park. Each unit has separate kitchen, bathroom, also TV, a/c and phone, serviced daily. Good value.

D **Mountway**, 36 Mount St, T9321 8307, www.mountwayunits.com.au. A considerably less glamorous high-rise block overlooking the freeway and the city. Kitchens are basic, the traffic noise can be considerable and there's no a/c, but these self-contained units are fairly spacious, all have balconies and facilities include internet. Both establishments have off-street parking.

Backpacker hostels

D **Townsend Lodge**, 240 Adelaide Terr, T9325 4143, www.townsend.wa.edu.au. Mostly used for student accommodation, the friendly Townsend has 60 single rooms on separate male and female floors. Lots of facilities include off-street parking and courtyard BBQ. Price drops by a third for stays of 3 nights or more.

D-E **Brittania International YHA**, 253 William St, T9328 6121, britannia@yhawa. com.au. An older crowd and families stay at this large, clean, comfortable hostel with 160 beds. Excellent kitchen and dining facilities. Free breakfast. 24-hr reception. No parking.

D-E **Club Red Backpackers**, 496 Newcastle St, T9227 9969, www.redbackpackers.com.au. This slightly shabby house between Northbridge and Leederville is a real party hostel. All the usual facilities but everything available 24 hrs and an emphasis on a great nightlife. Free pick-ups.

D-E **Coolibah Lodge**, 194 Brisbane St, T9328 9958, www.coolibahlodge.com.au. Quiet, friendly hostel with 6- and 4-bed dorms in restored colonial house. Good doubles with fridge, kettle and sink in newer extension. Small but pleasant courtyard BBQ areas. All rooms a/c. 24-hr reception. Free pick-ups and parking.

D-E **Governor Robinson**, 7 Robinson Av, T9328 3200, www.govrobinsons.com.au. This boutique hostel occupies 2 100-year old cottages and a sympathetic extension in a very quiet street, 10-min walk from the centre. Small but the central room and kitchen have the look and feel of a private home, not a hostel. Fresh, light rooms and

linen, backpack-sized lockers, jarrah floorboards and classy bathrooms. Doubles, some with en suite, are of hotel standard. No pick-ups, street parking. Recommended.

D-E **Hay Street Backpackers**, Hay St, T9221 9880, haystreetbackpackers@hotmail.com. Relatively small, well-maintained hostel with 80 beds in dorms, singles and doubles, some en suite. Clean spacious rooms, swimming pool and a/c, also good on diving advice.

D-E **Northbridge YHA**, 46 Francis St, T9328 7794. One of the best in central Northbridge, this 100-bed hostel is colourful and lively with a lovely spacious outdoor courtyard full of couches and tables. Regular BBQs and football games. Bike hire $15 day. Staff willing to help you find work.

D-E **Underground**, 268 Newcastle St, T9228 3755. Massive central hostel with swimming pool, bar, well equipped kitchen and spacious internet and guest area. Clean and friendly. 24-hr reception. Parking. Recommended.

D-E **Witches Hat**, 148 Palmerston St, T9228 4228, www.witchs-hat.com. Refined and quiet turreted house with 50 beds and shady courtyard. Very clean and modern bathrooms and kitchen, but doubles are small and spartan. 10-min walk from centre of Northbridge. Book ahead if arriving outside office hours, 0830-1230, 1700-2100. Parking.

E **Exclusive Backpackers**, 158 Adelaide Terr, T9221 9991, www.exclusivebackpackers. com. Verges on a boutique hotel for the quality of its 10 rooms, particularly its doubles. Quiet communal areas are characterful and homely, kitchen basic.

E **Murray Street Backpackers**, 118 Murray St, T9325 7627, www.murrayst.com. Not the glamour end of the hostel market, but clean, cheap and very popular with Japanese travellers. Separate floor for women only. Small TV rooms and no outside space. Free internet use and pick ups.

Subiaco *p69, map 69*

C **Amber Rose**, 102 Bagot Rd, T9382 3669, www.amberrose.com.au. B&B with two fresh elegant rooms, both en suite and tea/coffee facilties, in a large 1915 house. Shared guest

● *For an explanation of sleeping and eating price codes used in this guide, see inside the*
● *front cover. Other relevant information is found in Essentials, see pages 40-46.*

sitting room and garden breakfast room.
A 10-min walk to the heart of Subi.
Good value.

Nedlands *p69, map p64*

C **Caesia House**, 32 Thomas St, T9389 8174,
www.caesiahouse.com. Bed and breakfast in
comfortable modern house with 2 en-suite
rooms. Garden pool, excellent breakfast and
very knowledgable hosts, particularly on
nearby Kings Park and its flora.

C **Edward House**, 26 Edward St, T9389 8832.
A similar set-up to **Caesia**, but in an original
Edwardian house, 2 rooms share a bathroom, though rooms are never let to
separate parties.

Cottesloe *p70, map p71*
Hotels and motels

A-B **Ocean Beach**, corner of Marine Pde
and Eric St, T9384 2555, www.obh.com.au.
Recently renovated elegant rooms, some
with ocean views, in a high rise opposite the
beach and next to OBH bars and restaurant.

B-C **Cottesloe Beach Hotel**, 104 Marine
Terr, T9383 1100, www.cottesloebeachhotel.
com.au. Art deco hotel with 13 small rooms.
Comfortable with standard facilities. The best
rooms (6) face the ocean and have a small
balcony. Note that the rooms are above a
very popular and noisy pub.

Self-contained

A-B **Cottesloe Beach Chalets**, 6 John St,
T9383 5000, www.cottesloebeachchalets.
com.au. A complex of 30 modern self-
contained flats close to the beach that sleep
5. Full kitchen, bathroom, and 2 bedrooms
on mezzanine level. The complex also has a
pool and BBQs. Price covers 1-5 people.

Backpacker hostels

D-E **Ocean Beach Backpackers**,
corner of Marine Pde and Eric St, T9384
5111, www.obh.com.au. A stylish modern
hostel owned by the pub next door, this is
a fine place to relax. Light, spacious dorms,
some with sea views and en-suite doubles.
The perfection of North Cott beach lies over
the road but the hostel also offers bike,
scooter, jeep, and surfboard hire. Other
facilities include in-house café, daily van
run to Freo and city, airport pick-ups
on booking.

Hotels and motels

LL-L **Hotel Rendezvous**, T9340 5555,
www.rendezvoushotels.com. The majority
part of the Rendezvous Observation Tower,
is Perth's premier non-city centre hotel. It has
striking views up and down the coast and
facilities include a large number of hotel
restaurants and cafés.

L-B **Sunmoon**, 200 West Coast Highway,
T9245 8000, www.sunmoon.com.au. Striking
new resort-style complex, with a faintly
Asian feel and a wide range of hotel rooms
and self-contained apartments.

Self-contained

A **Sandcastles** and **Seashells**, 170-178 The
Esplanade, T9341 6644, www.seashells.com
.au. Two large resort complexes with 2-3
bedroom self-contained apartments and
some motel-style rooms. Most rooms have
balcony views though there is a lot of car
park between the resorts and the beach.

Backpacker hostels

D-E **Indigo Backpackers**, corner of West
Coast Highway and Brighton St, T9245 3388,
www.indigonet.com.au. A 5-min walk from
the Esplanade, this unpretentious hostel has
60 beds in a variety of singles, doubles,
4-bed and 6-bed dorms. The reception area
doubles as an expensive internet café and
they also offer bike and board hire. Other
facilities include a garden area with BBQ.

Caravan and tourist parks

C-D **Starhaven**, 18 Pearl Pde, T9341 1770.
Closest to the city centre, and is a 10-min
walk from the Esplanade. Cabins and on-site
vans available.

Hillarys and Sorrento *p70*

A **Hillarys Harbour Resort**, 68 Southside
Dr, Hillarys, T9262 7888, www.hillarysresort.
com.au. Well furnished, comfortable and
modern 1 to 3-bedroom fully self-contained
apartments. Most have private balconies or
courtyards overlooking either the harbour or
the courtyard pool.

C **Sorrento House B&B**, 11 Sandpiper St,
Sorrento, T9447 0995, www.sorrentohouse.
com.au. Two bright en-suite rooms sharing a
private lounge and kitchenette. Very friendly
hosts, good facilities and use of the family

pool. A 15-min walk to the harbour. Good value, recommended.

Cherokee Village, 10 Hocking Rd, T9409 9039, www.istnet.net.au/~cherokee. Self-contained cabins, some en suite at this park.

Kingsway Tourist Park, corner of Kingsway and Wanneroo Rd, T9409 9267, www.acclaimparks.com.au. Tourist park with chalets and smaller cabins.

Airport

C-D Perth International, T9453 6677, www.perthinternational.com.au. One of the country's best caravan parks. Self-contained chalets and cabins are well-equipped and comfortable, some with spas, others with the budget-conscious in mind, the grounds immaculate, the facilities excellent, and nothing is too much trouble for the staff. Recommended.

● Eating

Eating in Perth is characterized by location rather than cuisine; it is overwhelmingly an outdoor scene that makes the most of a stable, sunny climate. Many restaurants have very little indoor space and every eating area is crammed with pavement tables or open terraces. Despite Perth's isolation, the food is fresh and varied as it is mostly grown or harvested within the state. Seafood is very good and Asian or Italian food introduced by migrants is very popular. As in the other Australian states most fine restaurants make the best of both produce and flavour with a typically Modern Australian fusion of eastern and western cuisine.

Central Perth *p65, map p64*
There are several food courts in the city which are cheap but can also be dim, messy and crowded. There is a good one upstairs in the City Arcade with an outdoor terrace overlooking Murray St Mall. Also try the basement level of Carillion Arcade and **Old Shanghai** on James St in Northbridge with a good range of Asian stalls (closed Mon).
₸₸₸ Balthazar, 6 The Esplanade, T9421 1206. Indulgent wine bar and restaurant that cleverly combines the traditional crisp lines of folded white table linen with the even crisper lines of the metal and wood architecture. Mediterranean influenced food is matched by the music and supported by an extensive wine list. There's a cheap bar menu for those with shallower pockets and they dig into the cellars to hold wine-tastings every 4-6 weeks. Mon-Fri 1130-2230, Sat 1800-2230. Recommended.
₸₸₸ Fraser's, Fraser Av, T9481 7100. Has for years been one of the city's best in terms of

both food, location and ambience. The view of the city is slightly obscured by trees, but it's still pretty impressive and there are a few terrace tables to make the most of it. Cuisine is mod-Aus, predominantly seafood, with a few grills, and it's supported by an extensive, quality wine list. Buffet breakfasts 0700-1000, 0730 Sun, lunch 1200-1500, dinner 1800-2200.
₸₸₸ Old Swan Brewery, 173 Mounts Bay Rd, T9211 8999. Contemporary space with lots of black furniture and a warehouse feel, with a wide terrace on the river. Modern Australian food with an emphasis on grills, including native meats. Daily 1200-1430, 1800-2200. Also a menu of mid-range café food available Mon-Fri 1000-2300, Sat-Sun 0700-2300.
₸₸ Barre, 825 Hay St, next door to His Majesty's Theatre. A refined and elegant café with dark wood fittings and white linen tablecloths. The menu is less formal, with glammed-up burgers, pizzas, salads and pasta. Lunch only Mon-Fri, dinner when performances are running next door.
₸₸ Brass Monkey Brasserie, corner of William and James sts, T9227 9596. This brasserie on the balcony is one of the most pleasant places to dine in Northbridge. The creative Modern Australian menu changes regularly to reflect the use of fresh seasonal produce but is not precious. Mon-Thu 1200-1500, 1800-2200. Fri 1100-2200. Sat 1700-2200. Sun 1200-1600. Recommended.
₸₸ Café Bocca, Shafto Lane, 872 Hay Street, T9226 4030. Stylish, contemporary Italian in a lovely shady courtyard by a tranquil fountain. Most tables outdoors. Mon-Thu 0730-1530, Fri 0730-2200.

¶¶ **Dusit Thai**, 249 James St, T9328 7647. Elegant and ornate Thai serving consistently fresh and creative food. Lic and BYO. Thu-Fri 1200-1400, Tue-Sun 1800-2100.

¶¶ **Emperors Court**, 66 Lake St, T9328 8860. The city's best Cantonese restaurant in soothingly dim and calming rooms. Seafood and Cantonese claypots are specialities. Mon-Fri 1100-1500, Sat-Sun 1000-1500. Daily 1730-2300.

¶¶ **Kilo**, 202 Hay St, T9221 7777. Specializes in just that: kilos of freshly steamed mussels in a choice of sauces. Also a few grills, salads and lighter lunchtime specials. Open to 2100 daily, from 1100 Mon-Fri, 1800 Sat, 1200 Sun.

¶¶ **King Street 44**, T9231 4476. Inventive Modern Australian cooking, each dish on the menu accompanied by a wine suggestion. A large, noisy brasserie-style space that is always popular with socialites and foodies. Great for breakfast, or just coffee. Daily 0700-2100.

¶¶ **Palace**, 73 Bennett St, T9325 8883. Is a traditional Chinese with a very regal dining room. The food is very good and you can eat cheaply. Open Mon-Fri 1200-1500, Mon-Sat 1800-2300, Sun 1800-2130.

¶¶ **Simon's Seafood**, 73 Francis St, T9227 9055. Long established and comfortable restaurant serving the freshest of fish and seafood. Good value set menus. Licensed and BYO. Mon-Fri 1200-1430, Mon-Sat 1800-2100.

¶¶ **Tansawa Tei**, 1 Shenton St, T9228 0258. Elegant and contemporary Japanese overlooking the park. Set menus are good value for the whole culinary experience but lunch or a light meal can be had for under $15. Mon-Sat 1200-1430, 1800-2230.

¶¶ **Valentino**, corner of James and Lake sts, T9328 2177. Enormous fashionable Italian with plenty of pavement tables. All the standards but the menu includes some Asian dishes too. Also sandwiches and breakfasts. Daily 0800-2300.

¶ **Annalakshmi**, Jetty 4, Barrack St, T9221 3003. Friendly Indian vegetarian buffet where all profits go to various food and arts charities and there is no set price – you simply pay what you feel you can afford. They also put on monthly displays of Indian dancing, usually on the Sat closest to the full moon. Open Mon-Fri 1200-1430, Mon-Sat 1830-2130. No alcohol allowed.

¶ **Arirang**, 91 Barrack St, T9225 4855. Unusual Korean BBQ restaurant with a stylish, contemporary interior. Charcoals are brought to the table for you to cook your own meat in a central well to combine with rice and sauces. Good fun with a focus on the best fresh food and Korean culture. Dinner mid-range. 1130-1630, 1730-2130.

¶ **Chef Han's Cafe**, 245 William St, T6328 8122. Very busy large noodle bar with most dishes under $10. Flavour makes up for very bland surroundings. Daily 1100-2200.

¶ **Connie's**, 156 Adelaide Terr. Serves up a good value breakfast and hot buffet lunch, including roasts and veggie options, but is also a good place to grab a coffee and relax. Some terrace tables. Open Mon-Fri 0730-1530, Sat 0800-1230.

¶ **Frugivorous**, City Arcade, Murray St Level. For the new breed of juice junkies: fresh juices, smoothies, booster drinks and soups.

¶ **Hans**, 500 and 822 Hay St and others. Chain of slightly scruffy casual restaurants, always packed for their good value Thai, Japanese and Chinese dishes.

¶ **Hare Krishna Food for Life**, 200 William St, T9227 1684. A bargain, the Hare Krishnas offer an all-you-can-eat veggie buffet of curry, pasta, chutneys, desserts and drinks. Daily 1200-1430. Takeaway from 1700-1800.

¶ **Il Padrino Caffé**, 198 William St, T9227 9065. Welcoming and casual Italian, lined with owner Nunzio's claims to fame. He was voted the world's best pizza maker in 2001 in an international contest. Also makes pretty mean pasta and traditional meat-based dishes. Good value specials every Tue. Tue-Fri 1100-1500, 1700-2100, Sat 1700-2100.

¶ **Jaws Kaiten Sushi**, Hay St Mall. A true sushi bar with seats in a horseshoe facing the very cheap dishes whizzing past on the conveyor belt. Always a busy lunch spot for office workers. Daily 1130-1800.

¶ **Lotus Vegetarian**, 220 James St, T9228 2882. A buffet with veggie versions of Chinese, Indian and Malaysian favourites. Also a good range of salads, tasty western desserts and non-alcholic drinks. The surroundings are fairly simple but its good value food with friendly service. Thu-Sun 1130-1430 Tue-Sun 1800-2100.

¶ **Mai's**, 51 Bennett St, T9325 6206. A decidedly unsexy, traditional Vietnamese with a much more attractive cheap menu. BYO, open Mon-Fri 1130-1430, daily 1730-2100.

Matsuri, 250 St Georges Terr, T9322 7737. Sushi takeaway bar on the QV1 Plaza. Mon-Fri 1200-1430, daily 1800-2200.

Maya Masala, corner of Lake St and Francis St, T9328 5655. Wonderful Indian food in quite groovy, contemporary style. Specialities are dosa, thali, curries and tandoori but also particularly perfect Indian sweets. Prices are almost too good to be true. Licensed and BYO. Tue-Sun 1130-1430, 1730-2100. Recommended.

Nagoya Sushi, 777 Hay St. Efficient and cheap sushi bar, decked out in stainless steel, lots of pavement tables. Mon-Sat 0900-2100, Sun 1100-1700.

Tak Chee, 182 William St, T9328 9445. Authentic cooking from Penang in a no-frills environment. Noodle, rice and meat dishes all under $10. Mon-Tue, Thu-Sun 1130-1430, 1730-2100.

Terrace Takeout, Cloisters Arcade (off Hay St), T9322 1241. Small eat-in area and high quality takeaway including inventive sandwiches, soups, smoothies.

Viet Hoa, 349 William St, T9328 2127. Vietnamese and Chinese in this large, businesslike restaurant. Always very busy and great value. Most dishes under $10. Daily 1000-2200.

Vivace, 71 Bennett St, T9325 1788. Terrace pizzeria and café with a bright, fresh dining area. Also takeaway. Licensed and BYO.

Wasabi, corner of Hay St and Hill St. Principally a Japanese takeaway but has eat-in tables. Open 1030-1430, 1700-1900 Mon-Fri.

Cafés

Many cafés stay open later on Fri night.
Bocelli's Espresso, a large bustling outdoor café in the heart of Forrest Pl, a good place for a casual bite while watching the crowds. Gourmet sandwiches, cakes, drinks, also breakfasts. Daily until 1800 (2100 Fri).

Coffee Beans Express, 45 Francis St, next to post office. A rare lunch bar where you can grab a basic toasted sandwich or a drink from the fridge, with sunny yellow chairs for patrons on the plaza. Mon-Fri 0600-1700.

Dôme, James St. A good place for breakfast, coffee or sandwiches, this café is on a busy corner and has daily newspapers and lots of outdoor tables. Mon-Fri 0700-2200, Sat-Sun 0800-0200.

E Cucina, 777 Hay St, next to City Park. Smart Italian food and, around the corner, a straight-up espresso bar for city workers on the run.

Kings Park Tea Rooms, Frasers Av, is slap bang next to Frasers and nearly its equal in terms of setting. Cheap light lunches include pizza, and cream teas are available in the afternoon, plus it's licensed. 1000-1700.

Merchant Tea and Coffee Company, 183 Murray St Mall (and others). An elegant respite from the mall, lined with dark wood and with cool high ceilings. Sandwiches, cakes and coffee ordered at the counter. Also pavement tables. 0700-1900 (0900 Sun).

Mount Street Café, 42 Mount St, T9485 1411. Has a bit of a monopoly in this part of Perth, but is by no means complacent. The tiny front terrace is a pleasant place to hang out with a coffee and the excellent mid-range food is fresh and healthy. 0730-1700 daily, to 2200 Fri.

Subiaco *p69, map p69*

Subiaco is fast becoming central Perth's social hub. Rokeby Rd, between Bagot and Roberts sts, is the main strip, with several good options along Hay St.

Altos, 424 Hay St, T9382 3292. Dark, atmospheric dining room suited to the serious business of eating top-quality cuisine. The menu is tight on choice, but supported by a considerable wine list. Open Mon-Fri 1200-2200, Sat 1700-2230.

Witches Cauldron, 89 Rokeby Rd, T9381 2508. Formal restaurant with a traditional feel only slightly off-set by pictures of pointy-hatted ladies. Cuisine is modern Australian and dependably good. Mostly seafood, chicken and steak grills with a few veggie options. Open 1200-1500 Mon-Fri, 1800-2200 daily.

Buddhabar, 88 Rokeby Rd, T9382 2941. Hip Indian that puts as much creativity into its music and surrounds as its curries. Relaxed and friendly, their late night 'supper clubs' give a whole new cultured meaning to a late-night curry. Open Thu-Sat 1200-1430, Tue-Sun 1800-2200, Fri-Sat 2300-1300.

Oriel, 483 Hay St, T9382 1886. A real rarity – a quality, licensed, 24-hr eatery – and a Subi institution. Breakfast is 0100-1130, and 'lunch' from 1200-2445. A wide-ranging menu includes everything from a sandwich to scotch fillet, there are lots of Asian and Mediterranean dishes. Cakes are also superb.

¶ **Zen**, Seddon St car park, T9381 4931. Traditional, licensed Japanese with seriously cheap takeaway lunch specials. Open Tue-Sat 1200-1400, Tue-Sun 1800-2200.

Cafés

There are several good cafés in Subiaco and they can all be relied upon for a decent coffee. The below are located on pedestrian walk-throughs, and so have appeal of larger outdoor areas away from road traffic.

Brew-Ha, 162 Rokeby Rd. Fresh coffee and tea, by the packet or the cup. Comfy chairs and laid-back style make this a good spot to enjoy the morning paper. 0630-1800.

Walk Café, Forrest Walk. Cool, contemporary and relaxed with plenty of outside tables. Light lunches have a Greek slant and come in big serves. 0730-1800.

Leederville p69

This inner-city suburb has developed an alternative vibe and small café scene around the junction of Oxford and Newcastle St. At its heart is the arthouse **Luna Cinema**. The **Leederville** pub is also a big draw for the area. The shops are all independent establishments selling books, clothing, homewares and music.

¶¶ **Giardini**, 135 Oxford St, T9242 2602. Sophisticated Italian with good service and a modern twist to the cooking. Large, relaxing space has cane chairs and lots of greenery. Daily 0730-2100.

¶ **Kailis Bros Fish Café**, 101 Oxford St, T9443 6300. An unusual but elegant seafood restaurant that shares an open space with a fresh fish market. You can even select seafood to be cooked for you. Every kind of fish and seafood, Greek mezze plates, dips and wonderful seafood platters. Daily 0830-2130. Also takeaways.

¶ **Banzai**, 741 Newcastle St, T9227 7990. A slick modern sushi and noodle bar. Also has internet access.

¶ **Cino to Go**, 136 Oxford St and others, T9242 4688. A small lively chain of cafés with excellent coffee, cakes and pannini, daily 0700-2300.

¶ **Eminem**, 224 Carr Pl, T9227 7407. Small refined Turkish restaurant with deep blue, burgundy and green contemporary furnishings. Traditional dishes or a set menu for $30.

¶ **Hawkers Hut**, 150 Oxford, T9444 6662. For Asian food under $10 try, open daily for lunch and dinner.

Claremont p69

Eating in Claremont can usually be found in a small area around Bay View Terr and Stirling Highway.

¶¶¶ **Kuppa**, 37 Bay View Terr, T9284 5400. The outdoor terrace is the place to be seen in this very sophisticated, fashionable restaurant. Excellent fusion food leans toward the casual with wood-fired pizzas, stir fries and divine salads. Mon-Tue 0700-1700, Wed-Fri 0700-2030, Sat 0800-2100, Sun 0900-1430.

¶¶ **Pronto**, 16 Bay View Terr, T9284 6090. Always buzzing for its clever combination of effusive, charming service, colourful smart room and good-value pizzas and pasta. Mon-Sat 0730-2200.

Cafés

Dôme, 31 Carrington St, T9386 3099. Busy French-bistro style café with fine coffee, cakes, gourmet sandwiches and light meals. Mon-Wed 0700-2200, Thu-Sat 0700-2300, Sun 0700-2100.

Yo! Juice, in Claremont Arcade. A juice bar.

Nedlands p69

Nedlands is more spread out but there are some good places only a short distance from public transport.

¶¶¶ **Jojo's**, Broadway Jetty, T9386 8757. One of Perth's finest water-view restaurants, the main dining room is very formal in a plush comfortable way, with a few tables on the jetty boardwalk. The menu is dominated by seafood, complemented by a quality, WA-orientated wine list. Open 1200-1500 Wed-Fri, Sun and daily 1800-2200. The adjacent café is slightly cheaper and far less formal, with more boardwalk tables, though still an expensive option. Open daily for breakfast and lunch, 0800-1100 and 1130-1500.

¶¶ **Kafeneon**, 31A Hampden Rd, T9386 6181. Charming and long-established Greek restaurant with quiet, garden tables, warm

Perth Eating

service and delicious spanokopita. Tue-Fri 1200-1430, Tue-Sat 1800-2100.

† **Hot Box**, 38 Broadway, T9386 6600. For takeaways, fresh noodles, rice, curries, pasta under $10.

Cafés

Barrett's Bread, 19A Broadway. Bakery café with an awesome selection of French and Italian breads and pastries. Great place for a quick coffee and cake or picnic supplies. Mon-Fri 0630-1730, Sat-Sun 0630-1530.

South Perth *p69*

With a million-dollar view over Perth Water to the city, you'd expect a host of restaurants and cafés to enjoy it from, but there are only a handful. **Boatshed's** view is the best, and **Gandhi** and **Bookcaffé** don't have one.

††† **Boatshed Cafe**, Coode St Jetty, T9474 1314. On the river foreshore facing the city skyline, this airy, open restaurant is smart but unfussy. Daily 0700-2100. Modern Australian food that steals flavours from every major world cuisine. High prices are alleviated by BYO only policy, no corkage charge.

††† **Coco's**, corner of South Perth Esplanade and Mends St, T9474 3030. One of Perth's swankiest establishments, specializing in seafood and grills and frequently changing menus. Specials depend on what's looking best at the markets. Open daily 0900-2130.

†† **Bellhouse**, Mends St Jetty, T9367 1699. Warm upmarket food café with lots of golden wood fittings, perched at the end of the jetty. The menu is mostly seafood, with a few snack options, also breakfast at the weekends. Meals 1200-1600, 1800-200 daily and 0830-1100 Sat-Sun.

†† **Gandhi**, 33 Mends St, T9367 7733. Small funky Indian by night, café by day. Also a wide range of reasonably priced breakfasts and cheap lunches including salads and pastas as well as curries. 0630-2130.

Cafés

Boatshed Café has a cheap kiosk on one side with outdoor tables so the impecunious can also enjoy the view, selling drinks, fish and chips, scones and muffins. 0700-2000.

Mill Point Caffé Bookshop, 254 Mill Point Rd. Sells a good range of new books that you can purchase then read to your hearts content over a coffee. Open daily 0900-1730.

Cottesloe *p70, map p71*

Most mid-range restaurants are cheap for lunch.

†† **Indiana Tea House**, 99 Marine Pde, T9385 5005. This mansion above the surf club and Cottesloe Beach is a colonial-style restaurant with echoes of the Raj in its cane armchairs and fine linen. The food, mostly seafood, is very good and the ocean views magnificent but this is one of the most expensive restaurants in the city. Very pleasant for afternoon tea. Daily 1000-2100 (Sun 2000).

†† **Palme D'Or**, 16 Napoleon St, T9385 1412. French patisserie and café that becomes a fine restaurant Fri-Sat 1830-2200. Simple, authentic cooking with suberb flavour. Café Mon-Sat 0800-1700.

†† **Blue Duck**, 151 Marine Pde, T9385 2499. A long-standing Cottesloe favourite, the café hangs above the beach with mesmerizing views. Particularly good for breakfast, light lunches include wood-fired pizzas and inventive salads (cheap), more emphasis on fish and seafood for dinner. Daily 0630-2000. Recommended.

†† **La Tropicana**, 88 Marine Pde, T9286 1111. Holding out against the slickness of other establishments, this unpretentious neighbourhood café has a colourful, alternative feel. Breakfasts until 1200 specialize in eggs, the rest of the food is a modern Australian mix with some lighter options (cheap) like salads and tarts.

†† **Ogdens Bar and Grill**, Albion pub, is a smart, 'cook your own' grill with a good selection of salads and other accom-paniments. Daily 1200-1400, 1800-2100.

†† **VanS**, 1 Napoleon St, T9384 0696. A classy but casual café with sophisticated sand-wiches, salads and platters to share. Simple pasta and seafood dishes that let the quality of the ingredients shine. Mon-Sat 0900-2200.

† **Amberjacks Fish Café**, corner of Marine and John St. Tue-Sun 1100-2000. Head here for fish and chips on the beach.

† **Barista**, 38 Napoleon St, T9383 3545. Funky café with a great mix of light Asian and Mediterranean dishes and some thoughtful options for kids. Daily 0630-2200.

† **Beaches**, 122 Marine Pde, T9384 4412. Always busy, most of this café's seating is arranged under a Norfolk pine outside. Extensive breakfast menu (served all day) and sandwich menu. Daily 0630-1700.

Cottesloe to Scarborough *p70*

♥♥♥ ♣ **Oceanus**, City Beach, T9385 7555, has a large wood-beamed dining room with floor-to-ceiling windows overlooking the ocean. Most seating is indoor with a few tables on a small balcony to the side. The expensive fusion cuisine is excellent and the service friendly and attentive. Breakfast choices, from 0800-1030, include an optional continental buffet. Lunch 1200-1430, dinner 1800-2130. Mezze, snacks and coffee available all day. The upper floor houses a showcase gallery for WA artists.

♥ **Costa Azzurra**, Floreat Beach, T9285 0048, serves a good range of cheap, light Mediterranean meals from 0700-2200 in summer, 0900-2100 in winter. Again the café is beachside with tables overlooking the ocean. In summer their Latino dance evenings on Wednesdays give you the chance to strut your stuff.

Scarborough *p72*

♥♥♥ **Brighton Beach**, corner of Esplanade and Brighton St, T9341 8699. A traditional Italian specializing in seafood and steaks with a small range of cheaper alternatives. Much of the restaurant sits on an enclosed, vine-covered terrace. 1800-2230 Mon-Sat.

♥♥ **Jimmy Dean's**, 2nd Floor, Esplanade, corner of Manning St, T9205 1271. Friendly American diner with a range of quality grills and cheap burgers, some good value mid-week lunch specials. Some balcony tables have good ocean views. 1100-2330.

♥♥ **Villa Bianchi**, corner of Esplanade and Scarborough Beach Rd, T9245 2001. Large earthy Italian café with a long, thin, ever-busy veranda. The light bites are consistently good and the café has become a mainstay of the suburb. 0700-2230. Recommended.

♥ **Peters by the Sea**, Esplanade. A takeaway and the automatic choice for locals. They serve up excellent fish and chips, kebabs and souvlaki, and even provide covered terrace tables. 0900 to past midnight.

Scarborough to Sorrento *p72*

♥♥ **Trigg Island Café**, Trigg Beach, T9447 0077, a large, sunny and very popular place with a beachside terrace. Dependably good, light mid-range meals include pastas, salads, seafood and grills. Open all day, main meals 0930-1430 and 1800-2030. Their takeaway kiosk is open daily, school holidays only.

♥ **BYO Wild Fig**, corner of West Coast Dr and Elsie St, Waterman's Beach, T9246 9222, Latino music Fri-Sat nights and Sun afternoons, food 0700-1630 Sun-Wed, to 2130 Thu-Sat, is relaxed, people- and eco-friendly and the staff denote all tips and corkage to charity. It serves lots of tasty snacks and salads, juices and smoothies, and has live latino music. Recommended.

Hillarys and Sorrento *p72*

♥♥♥ **Portofinos**, Southside Dr, T9246 4700. Stylish Italian restaurant with a Romanèsque interior and large covered terrace. Extensive menu includes pasta, oysters, salads and wood-fired pizzas, plus breakfast at week-ends. Mon-Fri 1100-2100, Sat-Sun 0900-2130.

♥♥ **Jetty's**, Sorrento Quay, T9448 9060. Large smorgasbord affair with endless good food at reasonable prices. Seafood is always on a menu that changes its theme each month. Inside and boardwalk tables. Open 0700-1030, 1200-1530, 1730-2200. Café area open all day.

♥♥ **Volcanoes**, Sorrento Quay, T9246 4210. Serve up a range of southern American dishes, influenced by the hot flavours of Mexico. Good range of seafood.

♥ **Spinnakers**, Northside Dr, T9203 5266. Ploughs its lone furrow on the 'opposite' side of the harbour to all the rest. Its great position is enhanced by friendly service, fresh simple meals and a bright, cheerful décor. The few covered tables on the outside decking are the ones to go for. Open 0700 for breakfast, with lunch 1100-1500. Coffee and terrific cakes to 1730. Recommended.

Perth Bars & clubs

🟠 Bars and clubs

Central Perth *p65, map p64*
See the clubbing website www.teknoscape. com.au, for details of club nights and events.

Aberdeen, 84 Aberdeen St, T9227 9361. Serious posing joint crammed with sexy young things on Fri-Sat nights. Lots of open space to pack them in, music loud enough to aid assessment by looks alone and a dedicated band room. Closed Thu and Sun.

Brass Monkey, corner of William and James sts, T9227 9596. Northbridge's classiest pub and a distinctive landmark, built in 1897. Mellow old front bar, quiet courtyard seats and the Tap Room for serious beer drinkers and sports watchers. Excellent brasserie upstairs, sophisticated wine bar next door.

Court, 50 Beaufort St, T9328 5292. Gay venue with DJs 6 nights a week, live shows and karaoke. Also pool tables, bar snacks and a beer garden.

Durty Nelly's Irish Pub, Shafto Lane, T9226 0233. A standard 'Irish' pub with a dark, cosy interior enriched by a typically Perth addition; a large outdoor terrace on the lane. Irish dishes and Australian pub food 1130-1430, 1700-2100. Covers band Fri-Sat.

Elephant and Wheelbarrow, 53 Lake St, T9228 4433. British-style pub popular with backpackers. 15 British and Irish beers on tap, live covers and retro music Wed-Sun, cheap pub grub and pleasant shady terrace.

Grapeskin Wine Bar, 209 William St, 9227 9596. Stylish, contemporary bar and cellar attracts an sophisticated crowd of beautiful people. Also has good menu of grazing and sharing food available 1100-2200. Bar Mon-Thu 1100-2400, Fri-Sat 1100-0200.

Grosvenor Hotel, corner of Hay and Hill sts, T9325 3799. Also has a large outdoor terrace, well shaded and with lots of tables. A contemporary, stylish feel has been grafted into this old pub, but the menu is cheap, combining a traditional counter meals with a few spicy snacks. Available 1130-2000. Original live music Thu-Sat evenings and acoustic Sun afternoons.

Moon and Sixpence, 300 Murray St. Very British, popular with backpackers wanting a drink in the sun. Over 15 beers are on tap.

Rosie O'Grady's, corner of James and Milligan, T9328 1488. Typical 'Irish' pub, dark and green cosiness and a good range of British and Irish beers. Live music Thu-Sun.

Universal Wine Bar, 221 William St, T9227 6711. Hip without being slick, the Universal's long room opens to the street but becomes dim and jazzy towards the back. Good cheap snack menu of burgers, salads and sandwiches. Live blues and jazz every night. Mon-Fri 1130-2400, Sat 1600-0200.

Clubs

Connections, 81 James St, Northbridge, T9328 1870. A Perth institution, this welcoming gay club has been running for 25 years and promises disco glory. Tue-Sat 2200-late, Sun from 2100. Free entry for first hour.

Hip-E Club, corner of Newcastle and Oxford (rear of Leederville Village), T9227 8899, www.hipeclub.com.au. 70s and 90s psychedelica and backpacker specials (Tue). Tue-Wed, Fri-Sat from 2100.

Metro City, 146 Roe St, Northbridge, T9228 0500, is a huge commercial dance club with 10 bars and a 18-25 crowd.

Rise, 139 James St, Northbridge, T9328 7447, www.rise.net.au, or **The Church**, 69 Lake St, T9328 1065, for trance, techno and house.

Subiaco *p69, map p69*

Bars

Subiaco Hotel, corner of Rokeby Rd and Hay St, T9381 3069. Large historic hotel refurbished in smart, contemporary style, and now the social hub of Subi. Three main areas: edgy public bar serving up cheap counter meals, 1200-2300 with RnB cover bands Thu, Sat, DJs Fri; lounge bar with comfy sofas and easy chairs; and **Subiaco Café**, the hotel's upmarket, mid-range terrace restaurant, jazz band on Wed and Sat nights. Café meals 0700-2345.

Clubs

Club Red Sea, 83 Rokeby Rd, T9382 2022. Laid-back music bar playing familiar dance tracks from the mid-90s to present. A safe and relaxed haunt of the 25-30 crowd, it gets very busy and often only members get in. Call ahead during the day to secure entry. Open Fri-Sat from 2100.

Leederville *p69*

Leederville, 742 Newcastle St, T9444 8388. Is known for a heaving Sun session in the beer garden, live music, podium dancing and 5 bars.

Claremont *p69*

RedRock, 1 Bay View Terr, T9384 0977. Trendy corner pub with large posing terrace and lots of standing space, attracts style-conscious yuppies. Live music Thu-Sun, usually funk, swing, jazz or DJ. Free pool Sun.

Nedlands p69

Captain Stirling, 80 Stirling Highway, T9386 2200. Stylish old pub renovated in colonial style, popular with an older crowd. Excellent food daily 1200-2200.

Steve's Nedlands Park, 171 Broadway, T9386 3336. Relaxed pub close to the university and the river that is an institution for students and former students. Large, mellow beer garden and stylish food 1200-1500, 1800-2100. Live music on Sun, karaoke Wed.

Cottesloe p71, map p71

Cottesloe is renowned for its Sunday session. Sun afternoons in the extensive beer gardens of the 'Cott' or the 'OBH' attract thousands of svelte, tanned beach boys and girls. Shades, attitude and surf attire essential.

Cottesloe Beach Hotel, 104 Marine Terr. The mustard-coloured art deco Cott has an ocean-facing balcony (although the view is not quite as good as the OBH) and a contemporary stylish bar. The session is most popular here and the pub has live music Wed-Sat. The pub also has an ATM and a pleasant colourful café, daily 0700-2200.

Ocean Beach Hotel, corner of Marine and Eric, used to be distinguished by a chocolate brick tower, now painted a tasteful white to the relief of locals. The long back bar has pool tables but the front bar is the one to head for at sunset. Picture windows overlook the ocean in a large wood-lined room.

Entertainment

The main agency is **Ticketmaster7**, infoline T1900 933666, bookings T136100, www.ticketmaster7.com. Ask for the nearest retail outlet. Theatre tickets are usually handled by **BOCS Ticketing**, T9484 1133, www.bocs ticketing.com.au. BOCS ticket outlets: Perth Concert Hall, His Majesty's Theatre, Play-house Theatre and Subiaco Theatre Centre.

Cinema

Indoor

Screening details are published daily in the West Australian newspaper.

Ace Cinema, 500 Hay St, Subiaco, T9388 6500.

Cinema Paradiso, 164 James St, Northbridge. T9227 1771. Arthouse features.

Hoyts Cinecentre, corner of Murray and Barrack sts, T9325 2844. Mainstream releases.

Imax, 14 Lake St, Northbridge, T9328 0600. Large format IMAX films.

Luna, 155 Oxford St, Leederville, T9444 4056, www.lunapalace.com.au. Mainstream and alternative features.

Windsor Twin, 98 Stirling Highway, Nedlands, T9386 3554. Old fashioned, small arthouse cinema.

Outdoor

One of the best things to do in Perth is to see a film at an outdoor cinema. You can usually take a picnic and nothing beats having a drink while you recline in a deck chair and gaze at the stars during the slow bits. Season limited to summer only.

Camelot, T9385 4793, 16 Lochee St, Mosman Park. Recent releases in a fairly classy setting. Venue licenced and wood-fired pizzas available.

Luna Outdoor Nextdoor, Leederville, T9444 4056, www.lunapalace.com.au, aims to screen films that can't be seen elsewhere such as Japanese horror or cult skate flicks. Picnics OK but venue is licenced so no BYO.

Somerville Auditorium at UWA, T9380 1732, and **Joondalup Picture Garden**, T8400 5888, at Edith Cowan University in Joondalup both screen arthouse and foreign films from the Perth International Arts Festival (Jan-Mar). Tickets or at the door or from **BOCS** and www.perthfestival.com.au, but beware hefty service charge. Arrive by 1800 for a good seat at the picturesque Somerville.

Sunset Cinema, www.sunsetcinema.com.au, Kings Park, screens popular favourites and cult classics (Jan-Mar). Tickets from **Ticketmaster7**, T136100, www.ticketmaster7.com.au, or gate.

Sport

AFL (Australian Rules)

West Coast Eagles and the **Fremantle Dockers** both play at the Subiaco Oval. Each have home games, once a fortnight on either a Sat or Sun, from the end of Mar to

Aug. See www.afl.com.au for fixtures. Tickets from **Ticketmaster**, T1300 136100. Tickets go on sale 2 weeks before a match and often sell out, so it pays to book.

Cricket
Western Warriors, T9265 7222, www.waca.com.au. The state side play at the WACA during summer, and the ground also occasionally hosts international matches.

Theatre

Contact **BOCS** for theatre tickets and current performances.

Belvoir Amphitheatre and **Quarry Amphitheatre**, both lovely stone amphitheatres in classical Greek style. Look out for events.

Entertainment Centre, on Wellington St. A venue for large shows, music concerts and sporting events. Tickets from the box office or **Ticketmaster7**.

His Majesty's, 825 Hay St, T9265 0912. A beautiful Edwardian theatre and the state's main venue. Also home of the WA Ballet and WA Opera companies.

Perth Concert Hall, 5 St Georges Terr, T9231 9900. The main venue for classical performances, particularly from the West Australian Symphony Orchestra.

Playhouse, 3 Pier St, T9325 3355. Modern proscenium arch theatre and home of the Perth Theatre Company, producing contemporary and classic works with local and national performers.

Regal, corner of Hay St and Rokeby Rd, Subiaco. Puts on a wide range of local and touring shows and performers. Bookings BOCS.

Subiaco Theatre Centre, 180 Hammersley Rd, Subiaco, T9382 3385. A major venue set in lovely gardens near the top of Rokeby Rd. A 300-seat auditorium and smaller studio performance space.

Yirra Yaakin, 65 Murray St, T9202 1966. A Noongar company that produces Aboriginal theatre using Aboriginal writers, directors, designers and production staff.

❀ Festivals and events

Perth has just one major festival and lacks major sporting events due to its isolation and small population. Most events are held during spring and summer.

Jan Hopman Cup, www.hopmancup.com.au. A tennis championship held at Burswood Dome running for a week. International teams of 1 man and woman from each country, compete against each other. Attracts some big tennis names but there are fears Perth may lose the event to another state in the next few years.

Jan-Feb Perth International Arts Festival, the main event of the year, including hundreds of events all over the city. This includes the best local and international theatre, opera, dance, visual arts and music. The cultural centre acts as a focus point, alive with activity from 1730-0300. A film festival is also part of the programme, held outdoors from Dec-Mar at the Somerville at UWA and Joondalup Pines at Edith Cowan University. Programs are widely available from Dec, all festival tickets from BOCS. For more info T9380 2000, www.perthfestival.com.au.

Jan-Feb Fringe Festival, held at the same time as the main arts festival, Fringe is a celebration of all art forms and all artists, anyone can perform so its an exciting mix of the riveting and the soporific. Pick up a programme in Jan.

26 Jan Skyworks, held every Australia Day, is a fireworks show set to music broadcast on a local radio station. It is Perth's most popular event, attracting 400,000 people who picnic in Kings Park and along the Swan River foreshore to watch the fireworks. You need to get a position many hours before the show starts.

Late Feb Rottnest Channel Swim, about 1,200 people race from Cottesloe Beach to Rottnest (20 km). It's all over pretty quickly but fun to watch the start and finish.

Early Aug Avon Descent, a 133-km white water competition on the Avon River from Northam to Perth. It's always an exciting event, involving some portage, but gets hairy when water levels are low and kayaks or rafts get stuck on rocks.

Late Sep Kings Park Wildflower Festival is a huge indoor and outdoor display of native plants and flowers. This is a good way to see the state's incredible variety of wildflowers if you're not able to get to the wildflower country (mid-west region) during the Sep-Oct wildflower season. Held for 10 days. **Oct** Pride Festival is a celebration of gay and lesbian arts, culture and entertainment.

Ends with a fantastic parade through the streets of Northbridge and a dance party. For more info T9227 1767, www.pridewa.asn.au. **Dec** Artrage Festival, www.artrage.com.au. Bi-annual alternative arts festival including theatre, dance, music, street performers, comedy and visual arts. Perth and Fremantle.

○ Shopping

Perth's compact shopping area consists of the parallel Hay St and Murray St Malls and the arcades connecting them. The shopping also contines west along Hay St as far as King St, which is a trendy pocket of fashion and homewares shopping, galleries and cafes. The city has 2 major department stores, **Myers** in Forrest Pl, and **David Jones** occupying a block between the Malls. These both sell almost everything and David Jones has an excellent food hall.

Shopping hours are Mon-Sat 0900-1730 with the exception of late-night shopping until 2100 in the city on Fri, and in the suburbs and Fremantle on Thu. On Sun, city hours are 1200-1800, Fremantle 1000-1600.

Arts and crafts

Australian Woodcraft Galleries, 207 Murray St, T9324 1333. Fine work in native timbers; furniture and homewares.
Craftwest Gallery, 357 Murray St, T9226 2161. A gallery and shop featuring the very best of contemporary Australian design, including ceramics, glass work, jewellery, textiles, sculpture and wood work. Mon-Thu 0900-1730, Fri 0900- 2100, Sat 0900-1700.
Creative Native, 32 King St, T9322 3398. Large commercial Aboriginal art gallery and shop. Also good books on Aboriginal art.

Books and maps

The main chains are **Dymocks** and **Angus and Robertson**, both have branches in the Hay St Mall and can be found in suburban shopping centres.
All Foreign Language Bookshop, 101 William St, T9485 1246. Mon-Sat 0900-1700. A good range of guide books as well as books in over 100 languages.
Arcane Bookshop, 212 William St,

Northbridge, T9328 5073. Small jewel with literary fiction, film, drama, feminist and gay titles.
Bookcaffe, 137 Claremont Crs, Swanbourne, T9385 0553, and **Mill Point Caffé Bookshop** 254 Mill Point Rd, South Perth, T9367 4567. Independents with knowledgeable staff and pleasant cafés.
Book Sale Ltd, 158 Murray St Mall, has very cheap street directories.
Elizabeth's Second hand Bookshop, 820 Hay St, T9481 8848. Perth's best second-hand range. Also suburban branches including 375 Roberts Rd, Subiaco, T9381 5886.
The Lane Bookshop, Theatre Lane, Claremont, T9384 4423. Fine range of literary, arts and travel titles and knowledgable, helpful staff.
Map World, 900 Hay St, T9322 5733. Maps and guide books for every state and country. Full range of topographic maps, also bike maps, Bibbulman and Cape-to-Cape track maps.
Mosaic, 11 Rokeby Rd, Subiaco. Lots of quality fiction and non-fiction, mostly displayed face-out.
Supernova Books, 135 William St, T9322 5910. Sci-fi and fantasy. Also see Art Gallery of WA, WA Museum and Alexander Library.
Wisdom Books, 432 Hay St, Subiaco, T9382 2817. An excellent independent specializing in new age, history, literature and home.

Clothes

The best clothes shopping is found in Subiaco and Claremont. The Subiaco Colonnades on Hay St is one of the most exclusive shopping areas, full of the best Australian and international designers. Bay View and St Quentins Terraces in Claremont are full of fashion boutiques and Rokeby Rd in Subiaco is also a good spot. Claremont is shoe heaven with at least 5 shoe shops. The shops listed below are all in the city centre.

Elements, 375 Hay St. Has a great surf and swimwear range with brightly coloured separates and downstairs a factory outlet with some serious bargains, particularly boardshorts and 1-piece swimsuits.

Emporio, 672 Hay St Mall. Shoes, 3 floors of trendy designs.

Outback Red, Plaza Arcade. Bushwear such as boots, hats and moleskins.

R M Williams, upstairs in the Carillion Arcade. Sell rugged country wear such as boots, hats and moleskins.

Star Surf, 328 Murray St. Good surfwear.

Underground Surf Sports, corner Plaza Arcade and Hay St Mall. Good for surf and swimwear.

Vidlers, 14 Station St, Cottesloe. Despite the daggy appearance this has the best range.

Zomp, Trinity Arcade. For classy shoes.

Food and drink

Central Perth *p65*

There are many Asian supermarkets in Northbridge, on William St between Newcastle and Brisbane.

Kakulas Brothers, 183 William St, Northbridge. T9328 5744. A cornucopia of groceries and delicatessen food such as cheese, meats, nuts and dried fruit.

Lamont's, corner of St Georges Terr and King St, T9321 9928. Gourmet food and wine products, also the best quality takeaways – Mediterranean-influenced pasta, salad, risotto, sandwiches and cakes. Picnic hampers can be ordered (by 1500) and delivered. Mon-Fri 0700-1900.

Vintage Cellars, 726 Hay St Mall. Handy bottle shop in town centre.

Subiaco *p69*

Chokeby Rd, 175 Rokeby Rd. Chocolate specialists, bursting with both hand-crafted and European goodies.

Earth Market, 375 Hay St. Organic food store and café. Open Mon-Fri 1000-1800, Sat 0900-1600.

Farmers Direct, corner of Rowland St and Hay St. A handy 24-hr food store.

Food, 151 Rokeby Rd, T6380 2000. Upmarket deli and café serving cakes, light lunches, and preparing gourmet picnic hampers and takeaway hot meals. Open Mon-Fri 0800-1800, Sat-Sun 0900-1700.

Tea for Me, corner of Rokeby Rd and Church St. Nearly 100 different, flavoured Ceylon teas, available in leaf or as tea-bags. Customers are welcomed with a cuppa. Also exquisite ceramic tea-sets. Open Mon-Sat.

Leederville *p69*

Kailis Fish Market, 101 Oxford St. Every kind of fresh fish and seafood available relatively close to the city centre.

Claremont *p69*

Claremont Fresh, 333 Stirling Highway. A fruit and veg market, also selling seafood, bread and some groceries. Daily 0700-1900.

Fresh Provisions, in the Bay View Centre, corner of Stirling Highway and Leura Av. A small supermarket open 24 hrs.

Peter's Choice Butchery, 3 St Quentin Av. Sells takeaway pastas and curries by weight.

Jewellery

The city centre is awash with jewellery shops. For cheaper imported jewellery try the Subiaco or Fremantle markets.

Antika, City Arcade. There is none better for silver jewellery in the city.

Esola, 5 Napoleon St, Cottesloe. This is the top of the pops.

Linney's, 37 Rokeby Rd, Subiaco. Specialize in WA pearls, diamonds and gold. Open Mon-Fri and Sat morning.

Rosendorf's, 673 Hay St Mall. One of the best, for Argyle diamonds, Broome pearls and Australian opal in a classy environment.

Markets

The king of Perth markets is actually to be found in Fremantle but the runners up would be the popular weekend markets in Subiaco. These markets are all fairly permanent well-established affairs.

Canning Vale Markets, 280 Bannister Rd, Canning Vale, just east of Jandakot airport.

● *Cancer Foundation shops are useful for cheap Sun Smart clothing, sunglasses and* ● *sunscreen half the price of the commercial brands.*

Huge flea market with hundreds of stalls. Sun 0700-1400. During the week this is Perth's wholesale market for meat, fish, flowers and fruit and veg.

Galleria Art and Craft Market, Cultural Centre. Only a few stalls but often worth a look for pottery and high quality souvenirs. Sat-Sun 0900-1700.

Pavilion Market, 2 Rokeby Rd, Subiaco. Indoor market with about 50 stalls selling jewellery, clothing, pottery. Also a good food hall. Thu-Fri 1000-2100, Sat-Sun 1000-1700.

Station St Markets, Subiaco. A slightly less permanent feel and cheaper goods than the Pavilion markets over the railway line with more stalls, inclding fruit and veg, and there is often live entertainment. Sat-Sun 0900-1700.

Wanneroo Market, 33 Prindiville Dr, Wanneroo, 22 km north of city centre. A huge a/c indoor market selling everything and anything. Also has two food halls. Sat-Sun 0900-1730.

Music

78 Records, 918 Hay St, T9322 6384. A huge selection, also a ticket outlet for some gigs and sells music mags.

CD Library, on Wellington St (just east of William St). To sell or trade CDs.

Complex Records, 42 William St, T9322 4850. Dance, experimental, electronic, jazz, techno and house.

Jays Juke Box, 8 Forrest Walk, Subiaco. A friendly CD store strong on local, Aboriginal and world music, also jazz and blues. Open Tue-Sat.

Rokeby Records, 18 Rokeby, Subiaco. Has a big, mainstream range.

Wesley Classics, opposite Wesley Arcade. Classical CDs.

Wesley Megastore, Wesley Arcade, off William or Hay sts.

Zenith Music, Bay View Centre, Claremont, T9383 1422. One of Perth's most comprehensive selections of CDs, also instruments and sheet music.

Outdoor

Kathmandu, 884 Hay St.

Mainpeak, 415 Hay St, Subiaco, T9388 9072, www.mainpeak.com.au. Well stocked store, strong on local knowledge. Trekking slide shows year-round, also hire of almost all gear except boots. Maps for Bibbulmun and Cape-to-Cape tracks. They have another store at 31 Jarrad St, Cottesloe, T9385 2552, which also hires out sea-kayaks.

Midland Army Navy Disposal, 360 Murray St. Good for cheaper gear.

Paddy Pallins, 895 Hay St, opposite Map World.

Shimensons Budget Backpacker Supplies, 148 William St, T9321 8784. For cheaper gear.

▲▲ Activities and tours

4WD tours

Design a Tour, T9841 7778, takes 10 days to 4WD to Broome and include Karijini ($1,500, departs most Thu, Mar-Oct).

Travelabout, T1800 621200, www.travel about.au.com. For direct 4WD trips to Alice Springs. It also heads down to the southwest and up around the coast as far as Darwin.

West Coast Explorer, T9418 8835, makes it all the way to Darwin in 18 days ($2,150, also departs Thu).

Backpacker buses

Easyrider, T9446 1800, www.easyridertours. com.au, offers jump-on, jump-off up to Exmouth, Broome and around the southwest.

Nullarbor Traveller, T1800 816858, info@the-traveller.com.au, runs excellent 9-day adventure trips to Adelaide ($770-824, concessions $735-789), departing most Sun.

Boat cruises

For maximum time at Rottnest, take an early trip from Fremantle. Several companies operate cruises on the Swan River from the Barrack St Jetty.

Aqwa, see page 72, has its own boat that alternates in summer between trips to the seals and dolphins in local Marmion Marine Park (2 hrs, 0800 and 1030, Thu-Fri, Sun, $85), and day-long snorkelling expeditions to Rottnest (0800 Mon, Wed, Sat, $155). Entry to Aqwa included.

Boat Torque, T9421 5888, www.boattorque.com.au.

Boat Torque Cruises, Sorrento Quay, T9246 1039. Operates a ferry over to Rottnest, 2-4 times a day ($50 day-return, children $14.50, concessions $40). It also offers several package tours to the island, sunset cruises ($17, children $6, concessions $11) and whale-watching excursions during the Sep-Nov season (2 hrs, $30, children $12, concessions $20).

Captain Cook, T9325 3341, www.captain cookcruises.com.au. Cruises range from short runs to Fremantle, lunch and dinner cruises (around $20-85), to gourmet winetasting trips upriver to Swan Valley ($100).

Decoy, T9581 2383. Paddle-boat that steams out every Sun in summer, 1400- 1700, for a jazz cruise.

Mills Charters, T9246 5334, www.millschart ers.com.au. Also head out from Sorrento Quay deep-sea fishing most days depending on demand at 0630 ($120), and also offers 3-hr whale- watching trips ($45, children $25). Its glass-bottom boat goes out for several short cruises a day to the marine park. (Nov-Apr, 30 mins $14, children $8, concessions $10).

Oceanic Cruises, T9325 1191, www.oceanic cruises.com.au, leaves from Barrack St, and calls at Claremont on some trips (1 hr, $16). To Rottnest Island, return fares around $65, children $30, with several departures a day from 0845. Also Fremantle.

Cycling tours

Remote Outback Cycle Tours, T9279 6969, www.cycletours.com.au, offers superb 4WD and cycle combination tours to Uluru in NT ($880). The 6-day trip leaves about once a month between May-Oct.

WA Mountain Bike Tours, T/F9295 1716. Head into the forests of the Perth Hills for day or half-day guided trips.

Diving

Aqwa, Hillarys Boat Harbour (see page 72). You can arrange to scuba or snorkel with either the sharks or seals ($90).

Australian Diving Academy, T9364 7878, www.ausdiving.com.au. Run PADI courses and dive trips to Rottnest.

Sorrento Quay Dive Shop, Northside Dr, T9448 6343, www.sorrentoquaydive.com.au.

Has gear for hire (full kit $55 per day) and also organizes dives to both the Marmion Marine Park limestone reef (Thu-Fri, Sun, 2 hrs, $85 inc gear) and Rottnest (Sat, full day, $120). 1-week PADI courses $450, snorkel hire $15 per day.

Golf

Perth has many excellent courses that welcome visitors and have relatively low fees.

Burswood Park, Burswood Casino Complex, Great Eastern Highway, T9362 7576. Great city views and central location. Equipment hire available.

Vines Resort, Verdelho Drive, Swan Valley, T9297 0777. A 36-hole championship course along banks of Ellen Brook, good facilities nearby at the resort. Hosts the Heineken Classic in late Jan/early Feb, Australia's richest tournament.

Wembley, the Boulevard, Floreat, T9484 2500. Two 18-hole layouts, also driving range, pro shop and bar.

Kayaking and rafting

Rivergods, T9259 0749, www.rivergods. com.au. Heads out daily from Sep-Jun to Penguin Island off Rockingham to see the penguins and seals ($95). Trips further afield and personalized canoeing and rafting trips also available.

Wildside Adventures, T1300-886688. Raft the local Murray (Jul-Oct) and Collie rivers (dam-fed, Feb-Mar). Day trips around $150.

Kitesurfing

This fast-growing sport of surfing harnessed to a parachute offers awesome power and speed, and is generally practiced off the beaches between Cottesloe and Fremantle.

Choice Kitesurfing, T0438 382638, choicekitesurfing@yahoo.com. Lessons, beginners $100 for 2 hrs, int/adv $80 per hr.

Local sightseeing tours

Black Swan Tours, T9296 2568, www. black swantours.com.au. Offers a number of different Swan Valley options, geared toward small groups.

Out & About, T9377 3376, oaat@multiline. com.au. Takes small groups visiting wineries plus the chocolate and cheese factories.

Planet Perth, T9225 6622, www.planettours. com.au. Has a couple of local options, including an afternoon in Swan Valley ($50) and an evening BBQ tour to Caversham Wildlife Park ($55).

Super Roo, T9367 5465, super_roo@iprimus. com.au. Heads out Mon, Wed and Fri on a backpacker orientated whizz around Kings Park, coastal suburbs and Swan Valley ($95). **Swan Gold**, T9451 5333, www1.swangold. com.au. Runs a range of trips including Swan Valley (Fri and Sun pm, $55), a 'Dolphins & Forests' day (Mon-Sat, $88), the **Avon Valley** (Fri, $88) and a summer run to **Penguin Island** (Mon, Wed, Fri and Sun pm, $55).

Parasailing
South Perth Parasailing, Mill Point Rd, T9313 3897. Daily in summer.

Sailing
Funcats, Coode St Jetty, South Perth, T0408 926003, www.funcats.com.au. Surfcat hire for $23 per hr, free tuition. Daily 0930-1830, Oct-Apr.
Wind Dancer, Hillarys Boat Harbour, T/F9448 2496. Available for charter for a wide range of sailing excursions ($650 per day, max 12 passengers) and also heads out for half-day cruises about once a week depending on demand ($35 per person).

Scenic flights
Sunset Coast, T9298 829. Offers a range of flights from Jandakot Airport. A 1-hr flight over Perth, Beaches and Rottnest is $110, min 2 people.

Shopping tours
Aussie Shopping Tours, T9343 9900. Whisks you around a selection of wholesalers and factory outlets not usually open to the public. Clothes are the chief target.

Skating
The Scarborough foreshore hire-van hires in-line skates for $7 per hr or $18 per day, and it's the same price for bike hire.

Skydiving
WA Skydiving Academy, T1800 245066, www.waskydiving.com.au. Tandem freefall from $220, assisted freefall with full training $525.

Surfing and bodyboarding
There is an artificial reef called Cables, just south of Cottesloe Beach, ensuring consistent breaks all year round. Whalebone Classic is a Malibu competition attracting about 5,000 people over a weekend in mid-Jul. For more info on surfing or surfboard and snorkel hire, go to **Fun's Back Surf**, 120 Marine Parade, T9284 7873.
Bluewater, 21 Scarborough Beach Rd. Hires out bodyboards for $10 per day.
Cordingley, Esplanade, Scarborough, T9341 5688. Good range of surfwear and hire out surfboards ($30 for 5 hrs) and bodyboards ($10 for 4 hrs). Open daily.
Indigo Backpackers has a few fairly ropy surfboards available for $5 a day.

Waterskiing
Wake Up WA, Narrows Bridge, South Perth, T0402 476 487. Waterskiing, wakeboarding and knee boarding is $20 for 15 mins, tuberiding $10 for 10 mins. Tue-Sun 0800 to sunset, Nov-Apr.

⊜ Transport

Air

Skywest operates flights daily to **Albany**, **Broome** (Mon-Sat), **Carnarvon**, **Esperance**, **Exmouth**, **Geraldton**, **Kalgoorlie** (Sun-Fri), **Karratha** (Sun-Fri), and **Port Hedland**. **Qantas** provides daily direct flights to **Kalgoorlie**, **Karratha**, **Port Hedland** and **Broome**. It also has daily flights to most state capitals (except Hobart), **Alice Springs** and **Yulara** ('Ayers Rock'/Uluru). **Virgin Blue** fly daily to **Adelaide**, **Melbourne** and **Sydney**.
Airlines Air New Zealand, 44 St Georges Terr, T9326 0910. British Airways, 77 St Georges Terr, T9425 7711. Garuda Indonesia, 40 The Esplanade, T1300 365331. Malaysia Airlines, 56 William St, T9263 7007. Qantas, 55 William St, T9225 8282. Royal Brunei, 216 St Georges Terr, T9321 8757 or 131223. Singapore Airlines, 178 St Georges Terr, T9265 0500. Skywest, Perth Domestic Airport, T131300. South African Airways,

Ticket to ride

Transperth routes extend beyond Hillarys to the north, out to the Swan Valley and Perth Hills, and south as far as Mandurah. Fares are worked out according to how many zones you cross. The central suburbs are encompassed by zone 1, and zone 2 extends to include Fremantle, Cottesloe, Scarborough and Midland. Tickets are valid for two hours, and cost $2 for travel within one zone, $3 for two zones. A multi-zone DayRider ticket is available for $7.50 after 0900 and is valid all day. Buying tickets in packs of 10 saves about 15 per cent. FamilyRider ticket is a real bargain: two adults, plus up to five children, travel anywhere and back for $7.10. It's available all day weekends, after 0900 school holiday weekdays, after 1800 Monday-Thursday, and 1500 Friday. Standard tickets, DayRiders and FamilyRiders can be purchased on board buses and ferries, and at train stations. Bulk tickets have to be bought at Transperth info centres, or the many newsagents and retail outlets that stock them.

68 St Georges Terr, T9322 7388. **Virgin Blue**, T136789.

Bicycle

As a fairly flat city Perth is ideal for cycling. Pick up detailed maps of cycle routes, Bikewest Perth Bike Map Series ($6) is good. **Extreme Cycles**, corner of Wellington and Queen sts, T9481 5448, is a cycle shop that offers repairs and a useful service for cyclists. For $2 per day you can store your bike safely, shower and secure your gear in a locker. **Cycle Centre**, 282 Hay St, near Perth Mint, T9325 1176, sells new and second-hand bikes from about $100 and offers visitors a buy-back scheme.

Bike hire costs around $25 a day. **About Bike Hire**, T9221 2665, www.about bikehire.com.au, Causeway car park, Riverside Drive, East Perth. Mon-Sat 1000-1700, Sun 0900-1700. **Bike Force**, 365 Rokeby Rd, Subiaco, T9209 2900, www.bikeforce.com.au, other branches in South Perth, Midland and Fremantle.

Bus

Local
The free city centre buses, CATs, T136213 take 2 circuits. **Blue Cat** travels around Northbridge, through the city centre, and around Riverside Drive and Mounts Bay Road. Buses every 8 mins from 0650-1820 Mon-Fri, and every 15 mins from 1820-0105 Fri, 0830-0100 Sat, and 1000-1700 Sun. **Red Cat** heads to East Perth just short of the WACA, and to West Perth as far as Outram St. The service runs much of the length of Hay St in a westerly direction, and Murray St the other way. Buses every 5 mins from 0650-1820 Mon-Fri, and every 45 mins from 1000-1815 Sat-Sun. Both Red and Blue services run within 200 m or so of the Wellington St stations, the Blue Cat stops at both the City Busport and Barrack Square (for the Barrack St Jetty). No CAT services on public holidays.

Selected bus services from City Busport: **Airport** (domestic terminal), 37, 39; **Fremantle** (Queen St) via East Perth, 106, 111; **Fremantle** (Railway Station) via **East Perth**, 105; **Kalamunda**, 285, 287, 303; **Kings Park Rd**, **Nedlands**, **Claremont**, 103, 104; **Mandurah**, 107; **Rockingham**, 866.

Long distance
The majority of services are run by the state-owned company **TransWA**, Perth Business Centre and main stations, T1300 662205, www.transwa.wa.gov.au, whose routes extend right around the southwest, east as far as Norseman, and north as far as Kalbarri and Meekatharra. There are a handful of other operators that may prove more convenient. **South West Coachlines**, 3 Mounts Bay Rd, T9324 2333, has a couple of southern routes, including one terminating at **Dunsborough**, and another to

Manjimup. Integrity, 554 Wellington St, T1800 226339, www.integritycoach lines.com.au, runs a route up the **Brand Highway** via **Geraldton** and **Coral Bay** to **Exmouth** (1930, Thu and Sun), and another that continues onto **Broome** (0800, Mon and Fri). This Broome service also offers connections via shuttles to **Kalbarri** and **Monkey Mia** but 24 hrs' notice is required. Given the sparsity of land transport in some parts of the state, **McCaffertys/Greyhound**, 554 Wellington St, T131499, usually considered an interstate operator only, provides a few further, very useful options. Their main northbound service leaves Perth (Wellington St Bus Station) at 0845, travels up the Brand Highway through **Geraldton**, stops at **Carnarvon** and **Port Hedland**, and continues on via **Broome** and **Kununurra** to **Katherine**. This goes onto **Darwin** (60 hrs). A separate service heads up to **Exmouth** at 2000 Wed, Fri and Sun, calling at all the major coastal towns from Cervantes northward. Its eastbound service to **Adelaide** (40 hrs) via **Kalgoorlie** leaves at 1530 Fri.

Selected services

TransWA routes from Perth Railway Station or East Perth Terminal:
Albany via **Mt Barker**, daily, GS1, GS2; **Albany** via **Timber towns**, daily, GS3; **Bunbury**, **Cape-to-Cape** towns, Sun-Fri, SW1; **Geraldton** via **Dongara**, Sun-Fri, N1; **Kalbarri** via **Geraldton**, Mon, Wed, Fri, N1; **Northam**, **York**, Sun-Wed, Fri, GS2; **Pemberton** via **Cape-to-Cape towns**, Sun-Thu, SW1; **Pemberton** via **Bridgetown**, Mon, Wed, Sun, SW2.

Car

Perth is a fairly easy place to get around by car and there are no special restrictions or toll fees. The freeways are the arterial routes and entry and exit points are marked by large green signs. Kwinana Freeway services the southern suburbs, the Mitchell Freeway services the northern suburbs. The Graham Farmer Freeway is a short stretch just north of the city centre that connects the Mitchell Freeway to the Great Eastern Highway (and airports). The speed limit in built-up areas is 50 kph, unless signposted otherwise.

Car hire Bayswater, T9325 1000, www.bayswatercarrental.com.au, is one of the best value of many operators in the city, though they do not have a depot at either airport terminal.

Car parking Council car parks in Roe St, behind train station. Restricted meters in the city centre, several car parks off Riverside Drive and better value ones by the WACA.

Car servicing Ultra Tune, 25 Newcastle St, Northbridge, T9227 5356, www.ultratune.com.au (many other branches around the city).

Ferry

See also Boat cruises above.

Transperth operates ferries from Barrack Street Jetty over to South Perth. Those to Mends St are the best for the zoo and main restaurants. Take the Coode St ferry for the Boatshed and for surfcat hire. The former leave every 20-30 mins daily from 0750-1915, and also to 2115 Sat-Sun during Sep-Apr. Last return ferry is at 1930 (2130 Fri-Sat during Sep-Apr). Coode St ferries depart a few times a day from 0705-1805 Mon-Fri, and at 1230, 1530 Sat-Sun. No returns on weekends, last return 1820 Mon-Fri.

Taxi

There are dozens of taxi ranks around the city. A few are: outside Perth Sation of Wellington St, southwest corner of of junction of Adelaide Terr and Hill St, opposite the Melbourne on south side of Hay St. Also **Black & White**, T131008. **Swan**, T131330.

Train

Local

There are four suburban lines radiating like spokes from Perth station. All run regular services from early morning to past midnight. To the north the Joondalup line stops at **Leederville** and **Stirling** (change for Scarborough Beach) on the way, while the Fremantle line calls at **Subiaco**, **Claremont** and **Cottesloe** (with a 15-min walk to the beach). The Midland line has stops at **East Perth** (for TransWA services) and **Guildford** (the Swan Valley), and trains to **Armadale** call at **Burswood**. Fares are as per the bus services.

Long distance

TransWA, Perth Business Centre and main stations, T1300 662205, www.transwa.wa. gov.au, most useful rail services are the Prospector line to **Toodyay**, **Northam** and **Kalgoorlie**, and the Australind line to **Bunbury**. *The Indian Pacific*, T1300 132147, www.gsr.com.au, heads out to **Adelaide** (43 hrs) and **Sydney** (70 hrs) at 1155 every Wed and Sun.

❶ Directory

Banks The major banks have ATMs on Hay St Mall and Murray St Mall. They are also liberally located in all the central suburbs. Foreign exchange: **American Express**, Hay St Mall, T9221 0693. Mon-Fri 0900-1700, Sat 0900-1200. **Thomas Cook**, Hay St Mall, corner of Piccadilly Arcade. Mon-Fri 0845-1645, Sat 1000-1400. **Chemists** 24 hr chemists: Beaufort Street Chemist, 647 Beaufort St, Mt Lawley, T9328 7775.
Dentists Lifecare Dental, 419 Wellington St, T9221 2777. Daily 0800-0800. Medicare, T132011. For claims or to register visit city office in Wesley Arcade (upstairs) off William or Hay St. **Embassies and consulates Canada**, 267 St Georges Terr, T08 9322 7930. **Germany**, 8th Floor, St, George's Court, 16 St Georges Terr, T08 9325 8851. **Irish Republic**, 10 Lilika Road, City Beach, Perth, T08 9385 8247. **Italy**, 1292 Hay St, West Perth, T08 9322 4500. **Japan**, Level 21, The Forrest Centre, 221 St Georges Terr, Perth, T08 9480 1800. **Netherlands**, 1/88 Thomas St, West Perth, T08 9486 1579. **Spain**, 23 Barrack St, Perth, T08 9225 5222. **Sweden**, Courier Australia, 23 Walters Dr, Herdsman, Perth, T08 9204 0900. **UK**, Level 26, Allendale Sq, 77 St Georges Terr, Perth, T08 9224 4700. **USA**, 13th Floor, St. George's Court, 16 St Georges Terr, Perth, T08 9202 1224.
Hospitals Royal Perth, Wellington St, City, T9224 2244. Sir Charles Gairdner, Hospital Av, Nedlands, T9346 3333. **Internet** Free at Alexander Library, 1 hr only, bookings required, T9427 3104. Traveller's Club, 499 Wellington St, T9226 0660. **Medical centre** Perth Medical Centre, 713 Hay St, T9481 4342, bulk bills. Open Mon-Thu 0800-1800, Fri 0800-1700, Sat 0900-1500. **Police** 1 Hay St, East Perth, T9222 1048. **Post** Forrest Pl, Mon-Fri 0800-1730, Sat 0900-1230, Sun 1200-1600. Poste Restante: (take photo ID to collect mail) Mon-Fri 0800-1700.

⁞ Footprint features

Introduction

The region around Perth presents a microcosm of the southern half of the state with some exceptional beaches, wildlife encounters, extensive bushland, a wine region and some of WA's oldest European heritage. Much can be seen on day trips from Perth, or included on longer itineraries to the southern or northern parts of the state.

Fremantle is Perth's port and effectively a suburb of the city. It is by no means eclipsed, however, and a visit to Perth is incomplete without time spent in this small historic outpost. It's also the principal jumping-off point for Rottnest Island, the penal settlement turned playground that has the beaches in the region. The Swan Valley is Perth's very own wine region, less than an hour's drive from the city centre, and a pleasant place for lunch in a vine-covered courtyard on a sunny day.

Running parallel to the coast, about 30 km inland, the Perth Hills provide an extensive network of walking, mountain-biking, and horse-riding tracks. It is from here that the Bibbulmun Track starts its winding, 963-km route to Albany in the south. To the east, beyond the Perth Hills, lies the fertile Avon Valley where the Avon River flows through low, bare hills and pockets of woodland. Some of the state's oldest colonial settlements are found here, such as the charming town of York.

Heading north into a more arid region, the sand dunes of Lancelin are well worth seeing at sunset and can be combined with a visit to the incongruous monastical settlement of New Norcia. To the south of Perth stretches an almost unbroken line of coastal development, including the towns of Rockingham and Mandurah. While they can't compete with the really spectacular attractions further south, both towns are worth a look for their relaxed pace, water activities and dolphins.

Don't miss

1 **Fremantle** Eat fish and chips on the wharf, explore its maritime character and take the night tour of Fremantle Prison, page 96.
2 **Rottnest Island** Cycle and snorkel your way around Rottnest Island, page 106.
3 **Swan Valley** Tour a winery and stop for lunch, page 111.
4 **Yanchep National Park** With its tranquil lakes and bountiful birdlife, a day spent here is very relaxing, page 120.
5 **Lancelin dunes** Sit atop the dunes at sunset, page 121.
6 **New Norcia** Contemplate the lives of the monks here, page 121.
7 **York** Walk the streets and visit the Motor Museum, page 124.
8 **Rockingham** Swim with the dolphins, page 128.
9 **Lane Poole Reserve** Canoe the Murray River through this reserve, near Dwellingup, page 132.

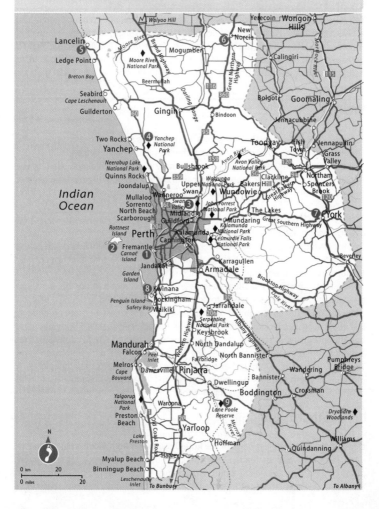

Fremantle → *Colour map 1, grid C1. Population: 45,000.*

Ports are not usually known for their charm but Fremantle is a fine exception. Founded at the same time as Perth, Fremantle has kept the 19th-century buildings that Perth has lost and retained its character and spirit. A strong community of immigrants and artists contribute to the port city's alternative soul. 'Freo', as the locals call it, is full of street performers, markets, galleries, pubs and restaurants as well as fishing boats and container ships. Many Southern Europeans have settled here and their simple Italian cafés have merged into the busy 'cappuccino strip' of the olive-tree-lined South Terrace. Fishing Boat Harbour has become an alternative hub of eating and entertainment activity, and manages to mix some seriously good restaurants in with some of the country's biggest fish and chip shops. Fremantle's lively atmosphere draws people from all over Perth, particularly at weekends, and it makes an interesting base for travellers. ▶▶ *For Sleeping, Eating and other listings, see pages 100-106.*

Ins and outs → *20 km from Perth centre, 7 km from Cottesloe.*
Travel Lounge① *16 Market St, T9335 8776, www.thetravellounge.com.au, 0700-2300*, acts as a general booking agent and net café but are also happy to provide information and advice to all travellers. The **VIC**① *Kings Sq, T9431 7878, ftb@iinet.net.au, Mon-Fri 0900-1700, Sat 0900-1500*, is located in the town hall. Also try www.freofocus.com.au and www.fremantlewesternaustralia. com.▶▶ *For transport details, see page 105.*

Sights

There are some interesting historic sights in Freo but it is also well worth having a walk around the well-preserved port precinct of the 'west end'. Phillimore and Cliff Streets and the surrounding streets contain some lovely Victorian buildings, such as the Customs House, painted in muted colours with hardly a hint of the passage of time. Freo's sights are best reached on foot with plenty of refuelling café-stops.

The Roundhouse
① *Between High St and Bathers Bay, T9336 6897, 1030-1530, gold coin donation.*
As convicts did not reach the Swan River colony until 1850, Western Australia's oldest building need not necessarily be a gaol, but the fact remains that it is. Not actually round, the 12-sided 1831 building was built on the commanding promontory of Arthur Head, and the precinct still affords good views over the boat harbour and across to off-shore islands. Built as a prison for immigrant and native wrong-doers, it was too small to house the large number of British convicts and slowly became redundant, last being used as a lock-up in 1900. For a while it was used as police living quarters, but fell into disuse when the headland became a favoured site for defensive gun batteries. The precinct has also been the site of lighthouses and, from 1900-37, a Time Ball, looked to by mariners and locals alike to accurately fix their timepieces. A mock-up of the apparatus has been erected and is activated, complete with the accompanying cannon-fire, every day at 1300.

Port Authority Building
① *1 Cliff St, T9430 3555, www.fremantleports.com.au, guided tour daily 1330, free.*
Fremantle's docks are just north of the Roundhouse and from Victoria Quay you can often see massive ships loaded with sheep for live export negotiating the narrow passage. Presiding over all shipping movements is the modern Port Authority; its tower is far higher than any other structure in Freo and naturally has superb views.

Western Australian Maritime Museum

ⓘ *Victoria Quay Rd, T9335 8921, www.mm.wa.gov.au, main museum 0930-1700, $10, children $3, concessions $5; submarine tours daily every 30 mins, 1000-1600 (1¼ hrs), $8, children $3, concessions $5 (buy ticket at museum first); Shipwreck Galleries, Slip St, 0930-1700, free tours 1000, 1100, 1400, 1500, gold coin donation.*

The striking new Western Australian Maritime Museum sits on the quay looking out towards the western horizon. The six themed galleries look at WA's past and future as a community on the edge of the Indian Ocean. With significant historic objects and boats that highlight the state's sporting and adventure heritage (such as *Australia II*, the yacht that wrestled the America's cup from the US in 1983), the exhibitions tell many fascinating stories of human endeavour. Part of the new museum, the *Oberon* class submarine **HMAS Ovens**, was commissioned in 1969 and saw active service for over 25 years. It is 90 m long and had a crew of over 60. Today it is in dry-dock and part of the WA Maritime Museum. The submarine is in very much the state it was when decommissioned in 1995, giving a rare glimpse into the strange lives of the submariners who crewed it. The fascinating and entertaining tours are conducted by volunteers, many of whom are former or serving submariners.

Housed in a complex of old dock buildings the original Maritime Museum is now called the **Shipwreck Galleries** and is primarily dedicated to the preservation and display of artefacts from the principal WA shipwrecks, mostly of the Dutch East India Company. Intermingled with the recoveries are numerous charts, logs and journals from the period and the combination presents an interesting historical overview of European exploration of Australia's west coast. There is everything from cannon to candelabra recovered from wrecks such as *The Zuytdorp* and *The Zeewijk*, but the most fascinating gallery has to be the one dedicated to *The Batavia*. A large part of the ship's hull is on display, plus a replica cabin, and most chillingly of all the hacked skeleton of one of those murdered on the Abrolhos, see *The Batavia*, page 218.

Fremantle Prison

ⓘ *The Terrace, T9336 9200, www.fremantleprison.com.au, entry by tour only (every 30 mins from 1000-1700 (1¼ hrs), $14.90, children $7.50, concessions $11.50, candlelight tours Wed and Fri eve, bookings required, $18.90, children $9.90, concessions $14.50).*

With the first consignment of convicts in 1850 it became clear to the governors of the Swan River colony that a much bigger prison than the Roundhouse would be required. The building of Fremantle Prison was one of the first tasks to be undertaken by the first convict groups and took about five years to construct. In this time they built themselves a prodigious set of buildings in a huge walled enclosure, the main cell block dominating and brooding over an expansive parade ground. Such was the solidity of construction that the prison was still in use in 1991.

‡ *If you have time, book onto one of the spooky night tours (around 1900).*

Fremantle History Museum

ⓘ *1 Finnerty St, T9430 7966, www.museum.wa.gov.au, Sun-Fri 1030-1630, Sat 1300-1700, gold coin donation.*

Set on a low hill overlooking the main town is an impressive but imposing gothic limestone building dating back to the 1860s. It was built by the convicts to house those of their colleagues who had gone 'mad' and were deemed a danger to fellow inmates and their jailers, but although still a part of the convict system it seems to have been built with considerably more flair than the stolid penitentiary just down the road. It remained an asylum, for both convicts and immigrants, until 1909 when the last of the patients were transferred to new premises in Claremont. It was planned to be allowed to run down, but at the last moment was deemed suitable as a shelter for elderly women. The US Navy took it over as their HQ during the Second World War, after which the building's very existence hung in the balance, sometimes in the shadow of imminent demolition, always gradually deteriorating. The building was finally converted to a museum and arts centre between 1965 and 1972. The magnificent wooden staircases and floors and spacious high-ceilinged rooms are ideal for its current purpose. The museum is dedicated to the history of Fremantle and the building itself and houses some excellent displays. There are free tours once or twice a day.

Fremantle Arts Centre
ⓘ *T9432 9555, www.fac.org.au, 1000-1700, free.*
Also in the former asylum, the centre is run by a dynamic arts organization and is well worth a visit. Fremantle Arts Centre holds regular exhibitions of contemporary visual arts and crafts, runs arts courses and literary events, acts as a small but respected publisher and hosts free music in the courtyard every Sunday 1400- 1600

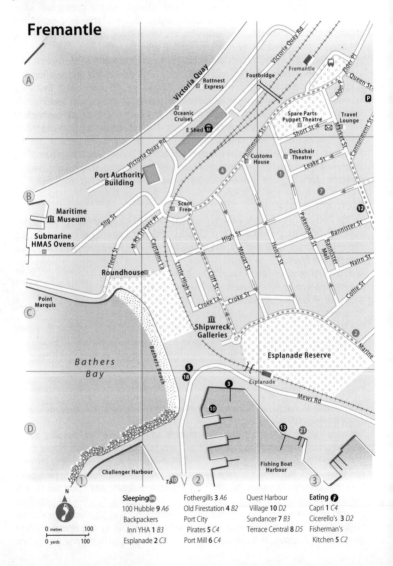

Fremantle

N

0 metres 100
0 yards 100

(January-April). The music ranges from jazz and folk to funk and classical and is usually a very mellow affair on the lawn. Pick up a program for Arts Centre events at the VIC or at the Centre. There is also an excellent craft shop selling the best of local work at great prices and a small bookshop. The leafy courtyard café is also excellent, serving cakes, coffee and light, healthy lunches, daily 1100-1400.

Beaches

There's a beach just to the north of the harbour, but it's not the area's best. Head north of the river to **Port** and **Leighton** beaches or more south. Port Beach is a safe swimming beach, although like all west coast beaches, best in the morning before the afternoon sea breeze gets going. That same breeze is heaven for windsurfers and Leighton is a good spot for it. It's worth coming here on a windy day to watch the rainbow-coloured sails skimming across the sea; **Surf Club** café is a good spot to do so from.

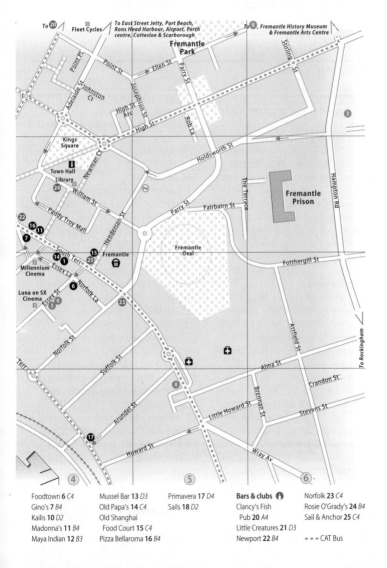

			Bars & clubs	Norfolk 23 *C4*
Foodtown 6 *C4*	Mussel Bar 13 *D3*	Primavera 17 *D4*	Clancy's Fish	Rosie O'Grady's 24 *B4*
Gino's 7 *B4*	Old Papa's 14 *C4*	Sails 18 *D2*	Pub 20 *A4*	Sail & Anchor 25 *C4*
Kailis 10 *D2*	Old Shanghai		Little Creatures 21 *D3*	
Madonna's 11 *B4*	Food Court 15 *C4*		Newport 22 *B4*	= = = CAT Bus
Maya Indian 12 *B3*	Pizza Bellaroma 16 *B4*			

⦂ Oh islands in the sun

Garden Island is connected by bridge to Rockingham but the public have no access by road. It is about 3 km long and ½ km wide and has been both a holiday resort and a naval base over the last century. It was once the home of the secret Z-Force involved in clandestine missions against the Japanese in the Second World War. Since 1978 it has been the permanent home of a naval support facility with public access restricted to certain small areas in daylight hours, via private boat only. **Carnac Island**, just to the north, is a fraction of its size. The whole island is a nature reserve, home to populations of Australian sea lions, fairy penguins and shearwaters. Snorkelling in the clear surrounding waters over the fish and coral is a popular activity. Carnac Island can be visited by private boat or on a commercial cruise but no overnight camping is allowed. See Activities and tours, page 104, for details.

⊜ Sleeping

Fremantle *p96, map p99*
See also Bars and clubs, for options in Pubs.
Hotels
LL-L Esplanade, corner of Marine Terr and Essex St, T1800 998201, www.esplanade hotelfremantle.com.au. Freo's flagship, an elegant Federation hotel that has been the automatic choice for many visitors for over a century. Facilities include 2 courtyard pools, smorgasbord, à la carte restaurants, fitness centre and bike hire. Many of the 259 rooms have access to the never-ending balconies.

Bed and breakfast
If you're looking for a hosted, heritage B&B in Fremantle you're going to be spoilt for choice and the following are just a selection. All have friendly, knowledgeable hosts who serve up excellent breakfasts. Most, however, do not have parking facilities.
A-B Fothergills, 20 Ord St, T9335 6784, www.babs.com.au/fothergills. Large, stately colonial house with 2 spacious en-suite rooms, subdued but luxurious, and a very pleasant upstairs balcony. Breakfast in a sunny conservatory. Some parking.
A-B Port Mill, 17 Essex St, T9433 3832, www. babs.com.au/portmill. The white-washed rough stone walls and tight cottagey stair-case make it hard to believe this new building isn't just as old as the 1863 flour mill opposite. 3 bright en-suite rooms with balconies; the front 2 have great views.

A-B Terrace Central, 83 South Terr, T/F9335 6600, www.users.bigpond.com/port fremantle. Bright and breezily decorated 1890s cottage, 8 spacious en-suite rooms. Continental breakfast.

Self-contained
L-A Quest Harbour Village, Mews Rd, Challenger Harbour, T9430 3888, www. questwa.com.au. Modern, luxury apartments perched in a great spot between Challenger and Fishing Boat harbours.
A 100 Hubble, 100 Hubble St, East Fremantle, T9339 8080, www.100hubble. com. A private oasis sheltered by high whitewashed walls, this charming place is utterly original and quite magical. Sleeps 6, 4 in a cosy converted railway carriage. The kitchen fits into a wooden wheelhouse, shower in a red telephone box, bathroom in the garden. Also a lawn, BBQ, sun lounges, sun deck and lots of tranquil corners for a snooze. Recommended.
A-B Westerley, T9430 4458, www.fremantle. com/westerley. Manage a number of com-fortable and centrally located properties including studios, converted warehouse and town houses.

Backpacker hostels
D-E Backpackers Inn YHA, 11 Packenham St, T9431 7061. Has 41 rooms and good facilities. Doubles are pricey but en suite.

D-E Port City Pirates, 11 Essex St, T9335 6635. One of the smallest and quietest hostels with only 50 beds, including singles and doubles. It still has a good range of facilities, however, including a courtyard BBQ, internet, and very friendly management.

D-E Sundancer, 80 High St, T1800061144, www.sundancerbackpackers.com. The best of the big hostels and very well positioned. Rooms and communal facilities are bright and clean, and the sunny rear courtyard has a spa. On the ground floor is a purpose built room for the disabled. This is not the place to go for an en-suite double, however, unless toilet privacy is simply not your thing.

E Old Firestation, 18 Phillimore St, T9430 5454, www.old-firestation.net. Has a laid-back atmosphere and lots of freebies, including off-street parking. It is also good at tracking down employment and has cheap curries for residents downstairs at Bengal.

Caravan parks

Coogee Beach, Cockburn Rd, T9418 1810. Another 4 km further south, with direct beach access.

Fremantle Village, Cockburn Rd, T9430 4866, www.fremantlevillage.com.au. 3 km south of the city centre on the coast road.

❼ Eating

Fremantle *p96, map p99*
The choice in Fremantle is staggering and it's a favourite eating destination for those who live in Perth. With its sunny climate, almost every restaurant and café has outdoor or pavement tables and many have been built to open onto the street so that they barely seem to have walls at all. The city's large Italian population have helped to build a very continental culture of coffee drinking, posing and long, leisurely hours of eating. Italian food and seafood predominate, there are few Asian flavours here. The main eating areas are South Terr and around the Boat Harbour. It is said that it's hard to find a bad meal in Freo, and the following does not even begin to exhaust the possibilities.

₮₮₮ Mussel Bar, 42 Mews Rd, T9433 1800.

Large, contemporary dining room with sloping glass windows looking out over the harbour, giving it the feel of a ship's wheelhouse. Excellent mussels, but also a range of seafood and grills. Open Tue-Sun 1100-2200, plus Mon in summer.

₮₮₮ Red Herring, 26 Riverside Rd, East Fremantle, T9339 1611. Considered one of the best seafood restaurants in Perth and running out of wall space for its awards, this contemporary restaurant sits on pylons over the river. Central sushi and oyster bar makes for a terrific appetizer. Save room for the fine dessert and cheese menu. Excellent wine list and wine-matching suggestions.

₮₮ Madonna's, 16 South Terr, T9336 5811. Massive, slick warehouse-style café, restaurant and bar with lots of shiny wood and glass surfaces. Mediterranean food manages substance as well as style but you come here to be seen above all. Lounge bar upstairs Fri-Sat only. Mon-Fri 1000-2100, Sat-Sun 0800-2200.

₮₮ Primavera, on the corner of Marine Terr and Arundel St, T9335 1744. One of the town's favourite Italian venues, specializing in risotto, pasta, seafood freshly caught by the owner's brother, and homemade gelati. Licensed, with an extensive list of WA wines, but also BYO. Open all day, Tue-Sun, lunch 1200-1430, dinner 1830-2130.

₮₮ Sails, above MacDonalds, 47 Mews Rd, T9430 5050. Occupies an unlikely spot above the burger-master, but once upstairs the hustle and bustle fades, the cane furniture beckons and so does the impressive ocean view to the off-shore islands and beyond. The menu, which borders on the expensive, takes inspiration from a multitude of sources but seafood is a strong theme and is consistently good. 1200-1500, 1800-2100.

₮ Capri, 21 South Terr, T9335 1399. This is the real thing: classic old fashioned Italian cooking in a simple wood panelled room. No fuss, no frills but wonderful flavours. Many seafood dishes. 1200-1400, 1700-2200.

₮ Cicerello's, on the harbour itself. A dominating boatshed-style building that serves up portions to hundreds of tourists every day from about 0930-2030.

₮ Fisherman's Kitchen, a little further away

● For an explanation of sleeping and eating price codes used in this guide, see inside the
● front cover. Other relevant information is found in Essentials, see pages 40-46.

from the harbour, behind MacDonalds. Away from the crowds and uses cholesterol-free oil. Open 1100-1900 daily.

♥ **Foodtown**, on Essex St. Another food hall. Fish and chips jostle with sushi, noodles, Thai, Italian and Chinese, plus there's a bar. Open 1100-2100 Tue-Sun, to 2200 Fri-Sat.

♥ **Juice Works**, in South Terr Piazza. A tasty juice bar.

♥ **Kailis** massive boatshed-style building, similar to Cicerello's.

♥ **Left Bank**, 15 Riverside Rd, East Fremantle, T9319 1315. A large, open pub on the river that concentrates on its food. Café-style menu downstairs with burgers and salads and very popular breakfasts, go early at the weekend. Classy mid-range restaurant upstairs with some romantic balcony tables. Café daily from 0700, restaurant Mon-Sat from 1200. One of the more popular spots for the traditional Perth Sun session.

♥ **Maya Indian**, 77 Market St, T9335 2796. The authentic Indian food has won many awards and it's always busy. A short, tradi-tional menu, BYO only. Tue-Sun 1800-2200.

♥ **Old Shanghai Food Court**, Henderson Mall. Good food from Japanese to juices and lots of pavement tables in the mall. Dead cheap. Wed-Thu 1100-2100, Fri-Sat 1100-2130.

♥ **Pizza Bella Roma**, 14 South Terr, T9335 1554. The best pizza and chilli mussels in an unpretentious setting. BYO. Lunch and dinner Tue-Sun.

♥ **Surf Club**, Port Beach Rd, T9430 6866. Casual café on the beach with an open air pavilion for those with sandy feet and a smarter glassed-in area. Breakfasts, light meals and a focus on fish and seafood. Lunch 1100-1700 daily, dinner 1800-2030 (summer only).

Cafés

There are dozens of cafés in and around Fremantle, and most can be relied upon for great coffee and service.

Fremantle Arts Centre, see Sights, has a peaceful café, great for coffee or lunch.

Gino's, 1 South Terr, T9336 1464. One of the original Italian cafés, Gino's has stuck to its simple formula of fast, honest Italian food and great coffee. Lots of space inside and out, order at the counter. Mon-Fri 0600-2200, Sat-Sun 0600-2300.

Old Papa's, 17 South Terr, T9335 4655. Along with Gino's, one of Freo's old survivors but perhaps trading on its reputation. Extensive breakfast menu, cheap pasta and pizza, good gelati. A bargain can be had between 1700-1830 when you pay an amount that matches the time you order. Daily 0545-2130.

🔾 Bars and clubs

Fremantle *p96, map p99*
Bars

Clancy's Fish Pub, 51 Cantonment St, T9335 1351. A bit out of the way but one of the most relaxed pubs in Freo, Clancy's has a funky, alternative feel and great food available all day (1200-2100). The menu concentrates on fish and seafood but pasta, noodles and cakes are also on offer. The veranda is a fine place for a quiet drink. Always packed for the Sun session. Recommended.

Little Creatures, 40 Mews Rd, T9430 5555. A former boat shed and crocodile farm, now a cool, cavernous brewery and bar. Excellent, inventive cheap food, including wood-fired pizzas, mussels and tapas, available all day. Open from 1000 Mon-Fri, 0900 Sat-Sun, to at least 2300.

Newport, on the corner of Market St and South Terr, T9335 2428. A lively, relaxed pub smartened up with polished floors and aluminium chairs. Pool tables, atrium courtyard, dedicated room for top-40 style bands on Fri-Sun, DJs Thu.

Norfolk, corner of Norfolk St and South Terr, T9335 5405. A really social pub with a great enclosed stone courtyard, huge on Sunday afternoons. Live jazz on Sat afternoons and evenings. Cheap bar food available daily 1100-2100. The 9 rooms are some of the town's best pub options **C**).

Rosie O'Grady's, 23 William St, T9335 1645. Pleasant, airy and spacious Irish theme pub (a chain). The walls and slate floors are green of course but the heritage building has been cleverly converted to Australian- style drinking rather than dark and cosy Irish-style. Cheap and hearty Irish-themed food (daily 1100-2100) and 17 bland but comfortable hotel rooms (**β-C**). Live music every night.

Sail & Anchor, 64 South Terr, T9335 8433. The pub that started the boutique beer and good food revolution in Freo around the time of the Americas Cup. The 100-year old pub has recently had a stylish revamp in muted greys and is more popular than ever. The pub has a micro-brewery producing many of the beers sold on site. The courtyard area does cheap wood-fired pizzas and casual light meals, while the elegant brasserie offers fine mid-range Modern Australian cuisine on the balcony. Also a good bottle shop and brewery tours Mon 1700, Sat 1100, Sun 1000.

Clubs
Although Fremantle is not the automatic choice for Perth clubbers there are a couple of options.
Kulcha, on South Terr.
Metropolis, on South Terr.

Ⓔ Entertainment

Fremantle *p96, map p99*
Cinema
Luna on SX, 13 Essex St, T9430 5999. Fremantle's grooviest cinema, with a good value double-feature on Sun afternoons.

Theatre
Deckchair Theatre, 33 Packenham St, T9430 4771, www.deckchairtheatre.com.au. Puts on contemporary, home-grown productions, often with a Fremantle or multicultural theme.
Spare Parts Puppet Theatre, 1 Short St, T9335 5044, www.sppt.asn.au. Produces inventive children's entertainment.

Ⓕ Festivals and events

Fremantle *p96, map p99*
The city held its 1st **Fremantle International Jazz Festivals** in **Jan** 2002 as part of the Perth International Arts Festival, and plan to hold the event annually over the **Australia Day weekend** in the future. Contact BOCS for ticketing details (T9484 1133, wwwbocs ticketing.com.au.); weekend passes around $150, day passes $75-80. For details see www.fremantlefestivals.com. The **Fremantle Festival** is held annually in mid-**Nov** at various venues around the city. Over 120,000 people flock to the city to see and participate in dozens of events featuring local and world

music, dance, acrobatics and art. For information contact the VIC or T9432 9728.

Ⓞ Shopping

Fremantle *p96, map p99*
There is some excellent shopping in the port city. Although the major chains are here, in or around High St Mall, there are also many quirky and interesting shops that help to give Fremantle its character. Fremantle shopping hours are generally 0900-1730 with the exception of late night shopping on Thu until 2100. Most shops are also open at the weekend. The Fremantle Markets are the best in WA, still held in the original Victorian market hall. The markets have a fresh fruit and vegetable section and sell clothes, jewellery, art and all manner of other things. The Henderson Mall entrance leads to shops selling wonderful fresh food such as bread, cheese and fish so it's a good place to stock up for a picnic. Open Fri 0900-2100, Sat 0900-1700, Sun 1000-1700. The E Shed Markets do not match up to this high standard, but still have a few jewellery, clothes and craft shops worth a look if you're waiting for a ferry. Open Fri-Sun 0900-1800, foodcourt and cafés open to 2000.

Arts and crafts
Creative Native, 65 High St. One of several indigenous art shops on this strip. This is aimed more at the casual tourist than the serious art buyer, though it does have a good range of didgeridoos.
Fremantle Arts Centre, 1 Finnerty St, T9432 9569. Excellent quality craft work (ceramics, wood, textiles, jewellery) by WA artists and very reasonable prices.
Indigenart, 82 High St. Stock authentic high-quality Aboriginal art, sculpture and craftwork.
Japingka, 47 High St. Stock authentic high-quality Aboriginal art, sculpture and craftwork.

Bookshops
Chart and Map Shop, 14 Collie St, T9335 8665, www.chartandmapshop. com.au. For maps and guides check out their excellent range.
Elizabeth's Second hand Bookshop,

3 William St, T9430 6700.

New Edition, 50 South Terr, T9335 2383. Daily 0930-2230. One of Freo's most loved shops in the heart of the cappucino strip. great range of literature, art, travel and design books and an atmosphere conducive to hours of browsing.

Clothing and jewellery

There are a few cutting-edge fashion boutiques in Market St.

Artisans of the Sea, corner of Marine Terr and Collie, T9336 3633. Classy shop selling jewellery made with Broome pearls.

Edna Beverage Co, 56 South Terr, T9430 4577. Amusing beer-related clothing and souvenirs.

Eros, 79 Market St, T9335 2141. One of the best clothing boutiques on this street.

Jalfreezi, South Terr Piazza, T9433 3340. A good range of attractive and cheap Indian clothing. Also visit the Fremantle Markets for this kind of clothing.

Krazy Tees, corner of Market St and South Terr. Has unusually inventive 'slogan' T-shirts.

Zingara, Fremantle Markets (opposite the Market Bar). High-quality silver jewellery.

Food

The first stop has to be the markets.

Interfoods, 4 South Terr. For delicatessen foods and Italian groceries.

Kakulas Sister, 29 Market St. Sells delicatessen foods and Italian groceries

The Mill Bakehouse, 52 South Terr. Sells fresh bread.

Music

Record Cellar, 63 South Terr. Open daily and has a small but select range of 1950-90s vinyl and a few CDs.

Record Finder, 87 High St. A much larger affair with a huge stock of vinyl. Open daily.

Outdoor

Army & Navy, on the corner of Packenham and High sts.

Getaway Camping, 66 Adelaide St. Tents, swags, sleeping bags and other camping equipment.

Wilderness Society Shop, 12 William St, T9335 9512. Posters, cards, calendars and Green gifts.

▲ Activities and tours

Fremantle *p96, map p99*

Boat cruises

See also Sailing below.

Captain Cook Cruises, T9325 3341, www.captaincookcruises.com.au. Runs several cruises from East St Jetty. These include daily cruises to Perth (90 mins), and lunch cruises (3 hrs).

Extreme Tours WA, T9337 3928, www. extremetourswa.com.au. Takes a large powerboat out from the Fishing Boat Harbour for 3 different open-air trips: 2 head out to sea for 30 high-speed mins, the other makes the journey up to Perth and back (2½ hrs). Trips go according to demand.

Oceanic Cruises, T9325 1191, www.oceanic cruises.com.au. Also leaves from East St for Perth, up to 4 times a day, and calls at Claremont. Fares are a little cheaper and the journey is a bit quicker (1 hr). It also offers a couple of excellent buffet lunch cruises. One heads out to Carnac Island and includes a trip in a glass-bottomed boat, guided beach walk and use of snorkel gear.

Rottnest Express, T9335 6406, www.rott nestexpress.com.au. Takes its boat *Sea Eagle* out to cruise past Garden Island every Sun from Victoria Quay 4 hrs, basic BBQ included. Whale-watching tours in season (Sep-Nov).

Diving

Australian Diving Academy, T9364 7878, www.ausdiving.com.au. Runs PADI courses and dive trips to Rottnest.

Dolphin, 1 Cantonment St, T9336 6286, freodive@dolphindiveshop.com. Organizes several boat dives, including wreck and night dives, and have hire facilities. It also runs a 'snorkel with seals' on Wed.

Golf

Fremantle Public Golf Course, Montreal St, T9336 3933. Daily 0530-1900 (18 holes).

Local sightseeing tours

Fremantle Tramswest Tours, T9339 8719, www.tramswest.com.au. Trundle around Fremantle on their buses-dressed-as-trams on 4 different routes every day. Tours range from 45-90 mins and $8-12, some including short harbour cruises. The best quick introduction to Fremantle is its Historical Trail (45 mins,) which leaves at 1000, 1200, 1400 and 1600. It also has a 5-hr combined tram/ boat tour of Fremantle and Perth (1000, 1400), and a weekly evening tour that takes in the prison and the harbour, fish and chips included.

Parasailing
Fremantle Parasailing, Fishing Boat Harbour, T0417 188502. Offers a quick parasail for around $70 and also ski-tubing.

Sailing
Leeuwin, T9430 4105, www.leeuwin.com, is Fremantle's resident tall ship, a magnificent 3-masted vessel that dominates Victoria Quay when it is moored there. It sails out on a variety of trips depending on season. In summer it is based in the port and there are lots of opportunities to get aboard for a day sail, mostly at weekends. Most last from 3-5 hrs and cost $55-100. **Oceanic Cruises**, T9325 1191. Heads out on summer Sun for 4-5 hrs on their 30-m sailing schooner, the *MV Oceanic*. It sails down past Carnac and Garden islands, stopping briefly for a BBQ and a swim, and is great value.

◉ Transport

Fremantle *p96, map p99*
See also Activities and tours for getting around Fremantle. For more information, www.transperth.wa.gov.au or T136213.

Air
The private Airport Shuttle runs between Perth airport and Fremantle approximately hourly from 0830-1715 and 2000-2330. Bookings essential, T9383 4115. Fares $20 single, groups $25 for two, $10 each for 3 or more, family tickets $35. A cheaper ($3.60, concessions $1.60) but much longer option from the domestic terminal is to take either the No 37 or 39 buses to the City Busport (see page 62) and change. A taxi will be around $40-50. The main service between the City Busport and Fremantle is the 105 which runs every 30-60 mins, daily from at least 0900-2330 (45 mins). Single tickets $3.

Bicycle/scooter
Bike hire from **Fleet Cycles**, 66 Adelaide St, T9430 5414. Mon-Fri 0900-1730, Sat 0900-1700, Sun 1100-1700.

Scooter hire from **Scoot Freo**, 2 Phillimore St, T9336 5933, hires out scooters and 3-wheel, 2-person scootcars. Minimum age 21. Open Mon-Fri 1000-1600, Sat-Sun 0900-1700. Closed if wet.

Bus
Local As well as the many scheduled services (see below), the free Fremantle CAT circles around the town in a figure of 8 that stretches from the railway station to the History Museum, and from Victoria Quay to south of the hospital. Buses leave every 10 mins or so, 0730-1830 Mon-Fri and 1000-1830 Sat-Sun. The main bus terminal is in front of the railway station.
Long distance Selected bus services from Fremantle: **Booragoon**, **City Busport**, **East Perth**, 105; **City Busport**, **East Perth** (from Queen St), 106, 111; **Cottesloe**, **Stirling Highway**, **Kings Park**, **St Georges Terr**, 103, 104; **Cottesloe**, **Claremont**, 70; **Port Beach**, **Cottesloe Beach**, **Scarborough**, 381 (weekdays); **Port Beach**, **Cottesloe Beach**, **Scarborough**, **Hillarys**, 582 (weekends only during Oct-Apr); **Rockingham Bus Station**, 126 (weekdays only), 920.

Car
Hire from **Ace**, T92211333, www.acerent. com.au; **Perth**, T9430 4322, www.perth renta car.com.au. Car parking is cheapest at Victoria Quay, maximum 3 hrs). All day for $5 just north of the railway station and south of the harbour. Car servicing from **M&L Wilding**, 218 South St, T9430 9805.

Ferry
Fremantle presents the cheapest options to **Rottnest**, saving around $15 on the return fare ($45-50) from Perth. **Oceanic Cruises**, T9335 2666, www.oceaniccruises.com.au, and **Rottnest Express**, T9335 6406, www.rott nestexpress.com.au, both offer services daily from **Victoria Quay**. The latter also have several ferry/hotel packages worth looking at. **Boat Torque Cruises**, T9430 5844, leaves from **Rous Head Harbour**. With any ferry parking will be an additional $5-8 a day. See also boat cruises above.

Swan, T9444 4444, Black & White, T9333 3333. From Perth it's about $40-45.

Train
The Fremantle Line runs between Perth and Fremantle via **Subiaco**, **Claremont** and **Cottesloe**. Services every 10-15 mins from 0530-1630 and every 30-60 mins from 1900-0200. Sunday services at similar times from 0700-2400. The journey takes about 30 mins.

ⓘ Directory

Fremantle *p96, map p99*

Banks ATMs for the major banks on Adelaide St between Point and Queen sts. Interforex, next to VIC. Daily 0800-1930. **Hospital** Fremantle Hospital, corner of Alma St and South Terr, T9431 3333. **Internet** Travel Lounge, 16 Market St, 0700-2300. **Library** 8 William St, T9432 9766. Mon-Thu 0930-2000, Fri-Sat 0930-1700. **Police** Henderson St, T9430 1222. **Post** 13 Market St.

Rottnest Island → *Colour map 2, grid B4.*

Rotto, as the locals call it, once a penal settlement, is now Perth's holiday playground. Just 20 km west of the city, it feels a long way from the metropolitan commotion. Generations of Perth families have come to frolic here every summer and it's a traditional place to celebrate the end of school, university or parental control. The entire coast is one long cordon of quite magical sandy bays and clear aquamarine water, and so understandably, come summer, many beaches get very busy. However, even at this time, you'll find almost deserted stretches towards the western and southern parts of the island. The off-shore reefs are full of brightly coloured fish, exotic corals and limestone caves, and littered with wrecks. The island itself is 11 km long and 4 km wide and covered in low bushy scrub with some patches of eucalypt woodland. Much of this provides cover for the island's famous small wallaby, the quokka, after which the island was dubiously named. There are few permanent human residents as the island is carefully managed to preserve the environment and scarce water resources. The number of overnight visitors is kept to a sustainable level and cars are not allowed▶ For Sleeping, Eating and other listings, see pages 108-110.

Ins and outs

Getting there There are two ways of getting to Rotto, by air and ferry. The cheapest way is to get public transport from Perth to Freo and then catch the ferry to Rottnest. **Getting around** As only essential service vehicles and buses are allowed on the island, there are just two principal choices if you want to see more of the island than

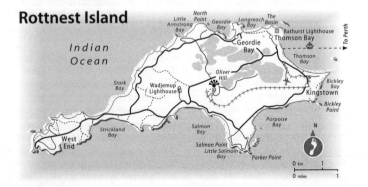

Quokka spotting

When the Dutch explorer Willem Vlamingh encountered Rottnest Island he encumbered it with a name that suggests the opposite of its natural beauty. In Dutch Rottnest means 'rat nest'. Europeans simply had no language to describe the unique Australian fauna. The 'rats' Vlamingh saw were the small wallabies (Setonix bracyurus), that still populate the island. Now commonly known as the *Quokka*, from the *Noongar* word, these appealing wallabies are about 30-cm high. Although most closely identified with the island, the habitat of Quokkas actually spreads along the southwestern coastal region. However, they are endangered there due to predation by foxes and habitat loss. There are a few left in Dwellingup, the Stirling Ranges and on Bald Island, but Rottnest is the last bastion of a sizeable population; there are about 8,000-10,000 on the island. Even so, they suffer in summer because freshwater supplies are much lower than they were before settlement. Constant interaction with people, to their detriment, has also made some of them quite tame so you have a very good chance of seeing some. Visitors are now asked not to touch or feed them. If you're not venturing beyond the settlements you should always be able to find them hanging around the shop at Geordie Bay, alongside the Garden Lake boardwalk behind the Lodge, and at the short boardwalk opposite the turn-off to Kingstown Barracks.

Thomson Bay Settlement: bikes and buses. There is also a train service going to and fro from between the south end of the Settlement and Oliver Hill lookout. ▸▸ *See under relevant departure point for ferry details and see Transport, page 110, for other details.*

Tourist information VIC① *T9372 9752, Thomson Bay Settlement, 0815-1700*. Also in Thomson Bay is a small shopping mall with a post office, ATM, takeaway, general store, bakery and clothes/gift shop. The general store stocks books, pharmaceuticals and a bottle shop. There is a similarly stocked store at Geordie Bay. Both open daily. The island has a nursing post T9292 5030, police station T9292 5029, and rangers office T9372 9788. See also www.rottnest.wa.gov.au.

Background

Until 7,000 years ago Rottnest was a peninsula, attached to the mainland. Since the connecting bridge drowned, a result of the ending of the last ice age, the island was abandoned by any Aboriginals who may have been living there and the new island christened *Wadjemup* by the mainland local peoples. In 1696 the island was first visited by Europeans in a Dutch vessel commanded by Willem de Vlamingh. Seeing the island swarming with the small wallabies, the Dutch considered the island a 'rats nest' and named it accordingly. As well as the quokkas, as they are known to the Noongar, the island is home to a variety of animals and flora marooned when the island was cut off. The fact that it was an island close to a European colony doomed it to become a penal settlement, but this time with a difference. A few convicts were shipped over, but for the most part it was used to imprison Aboriginal 'criminals' who incurred the authorities' displeasure on the mainland. Many of the buildings constructed for this purpose still remain in and around the island's only village, known simply as the Settlement. For the last 80 or so years the island has served a dual purpose as holiday destination and military encampment, with the latter moving out in the 1980s.

Around Perth Rottnest Island

While **Thomson Bay Settlement** has the ferry terminal, is the main settlement and has most of the island's services, it is also something of an open air museum, and the general layout is claimed to be Australia's oldest intact streetscape. Most interesting is the part of the Lodge known as the **Quod,** and the heritage precinct in front of it. Once one of the most feared places on the island, it was built in 1838 to house dozens of Aboriginal 'criminals' in horrendous conditions. There were still prisoners on the island when it was converted into a tourist hostel in 1911. Most of the current double rooms were once two cells holding about 10 men. The **museum and library** ⓘ *museum 1100-1600, token entry fee; library 1400-1545, free,* just behind the general store in the mall, are the main repositories of the island's history. Museum displays include the early days as a prison for Aboriginal men, island shipwrecks, military use and its development as Perth's holiday isle.

Also in Thomson Bay the original **Salt Store** has a small gallery and exhibition that focuses on the island's early colonial history. Further afield there is an interesting walk south through the dunes at Kingstown Barracks to the **Bickley Battery.** The 45-minute stroll takes you past several ruined buildings that were once gun emplacements, built in the 1930s to defend Perth against any interlopers. Almost in the centre of the island is **Oliver Hill** ⓘ *tours on the hour from 1000, token entry fee or included in cost of the train from Thomson Bay, 1 hr to walk, 30 mins to cycle, the lighthouses are closed to the public,* used during the Second World War as another gun emplacement. Underground is a small maze of underground tunnels.

Beaches are what Rottnest is all about for most visitors. There are over a dozen picture-postcard bays with white-sand beaches and usually clear, intensely blue water. Reefs lie just offshore from some beaches and many are enclosed by dramatic limestone headlands. The most sheltered are along the north shore and these also get the busiest, especially the **Basin,** the most picturesque bay on the island. The Basin has covered picnic tables and toilets, adding to its popularity. Other small bays a bit further from Thomson Bay include **Little Armstrong** on the north shore and **Little Salmon** on the south. The water can get choppy in the afternoons at the latter. **Longreach** and **Geordie** are long sweeping bays overlooked by accommodation and often crowded with boats. **Salmon Bay** in the south is of a similar scale, clear of boats and can be good for boogie boarding, though there are no facilities. Diving and snorkelling is excellent off Rottnest, with a large variety of wrecks, fish, corals and limestone caves. Particularly good snorkelling spots can be found off Parker Point, where there is a marked out trail, Little Salmon Bay, parts of Salmon Bay and the Basin.

● Sleeping

Rottnest Island *p106*

Most of the accommodation on the island is in self-contained cottages, villas or cabins, and all need to be booked through the **Accommodation Office,** T1800 111111 or 9432 9111 (which also hires out televisions and video recorders - videos from Family Fun Park). Thomson Bay has the most accommodation and accordingly has a resort feel about it. There are also options at the former military Kingstown Barracks, and also at Geordie Bay on the north coast. During the Dec-Jan summer period it is virtually impossible to find a room, cabin or patch of ground on the island unless you've booked it

months in advance. The best chance you will have is at the YHA. Even outside of this period weekends commonly see the island booked almost full, so either plan well ahead or plan for a mid-week visit. There is a maximum stay for visitors of 2 weeks in summer, 3 weeks in winter.

Hotels and hostels

Some of the ferry companies offer ferry/accommodation/bike packages that may shave a few dollars off the cost.

L-A Rottnest Lodge, Thomson Bay, T9292 5161, www.rottnestlodge.com.au. The island's premier establishment which incorporates many of the early colonial prison buildings, including the Quod. Rooms are furnished in contemporary style and most face onto various courtyards, the pool or the Quod. A few face a lake, but this can smell a little in high summer.

A **Quokka Arms**, Thomson Bay, T9292 5011, quokkaarms@rottnestisland.com. Converted from a former residence for the Western Australian Governor, has a dozen motel-style rooms, mostly around an adjacent courtyard, but some overlooking the bay. They are a little cheaper than those at the Lodge, especially in winter, but the accommodation lacks the ambience of the other establishment.

D-E **Rottnest Youth Hostel** (YHA), T9372 9780. Occupies part of the red-brick military Kingstown Barracks built in 1936, 1 km south of Thomson Bay. Facilities are good, and the staff are friendly and helpful. The office is open daily 0730-1730.

Self-contained

There is a wide choice of accommodation on the island, almost all around the eastern bays, ranging from beautifully renovated colonial cottages to small huts. Each is reasonably well equipped, and you just need to bring sheets and pillowcases. In size most range from 4 to 8 beds, though there are a few larger ones around Kingstown Barracks (up to 18 beds). Of the hundreds available the following represent a few of the best options. Prices drop considerably if you're staying more than 1 night. At certain times of year, however – principally school holidays – the demand for accommodation is such that it is allocated by ballot about 6 months beforehand. Ballot application forms can be found on the Rottnest website. Kingstown is, strictly speaking, an alcohol-free area. Bookings for all these are through the Accommodation Office, up to a year in advance.

L **Commander's House**, more isolated than most in an inland position, but with fine views down across the ocean.

L **Lighthouse Keeper's Cottages** (villas 547 and 548) are in a wonderful shore-side spot next to Bathurst Lighthouse, with front verandas looking across to Perth. Slightly cheaper than **Commander's House**. Recommended.

A **Geordie Bay**, modern, villas all have good views across the bay and immediate access to the beach.

C **Caroline Thomson**, the best budget option, cabins in Thomson Bay.

Camping

There is a small area set aside for camping in Thomson Bay – it is not allowed over the rest of the island. Adults $8 per night, children $4. Booking sites in peak times is as necessary as booking cabins and villas, and can be done through the Accommodation office. The camping area is an alcohol-free zone.

⊘ Eating

Rottnest Island p106

♥♥♥ ♥ **Rottnest Lodge**, see Sleeping, is surprisingly reasonably priced given its decidedly upmarket feel. Breakfast is a full buffet from 0700-1000, with choice of buffet (1200-1400) or à la carte (1200-1530) for lunch. The evening menu (1800-2100) is pricey, but the food is the best on the island.

♥♥ **Dôme**, part of the gallic-style chain, central to Thomson's Bay with terrace views over the harbour. Open 0700-2100. Serves up simple meals from Thai chicken curries to steak and Guinness pies. The place gets very busy but there are no bookings.

♥♥ **Quokka Arms**, has 2 dining options and as the only pub on the island is the life and soul of the ongoing party. Meals available 1200-1400 and 1800-2100.

♥♥ ♥ **Tearooms**, just along from the Dôme, the long boardwalk also looks out over the harbour. Open 0700-2100, they are slightly cheaper and less highbrow than their neighbours, but nevertheless offer a good range of breakfasts and hot meals. All the establishments above are licensed.

♥ **WA Caterers**, Kingston Barracks. A seriously cheap, no-frills catering outfit that produces buffet and set meals 3 times a day every day. Meals are filling, usually very tasty and nutritious, though the whole experience brings 'school dinners' to mind, and you may

● For an explanation of sleeping and eating price codes used in this guide, see inside the
● front cover. Other relevant information is found in Essentials, see pages 40-46.

actually find yourself in the company of large numbers of school kids. Excellent value though. Meals at 0700-0845 (0800-1000 Sun), 1200-1400, and 1800-2000. Meal tickets bought at the hostel reception, about 100 m away, shave a dollar off the price.

▲ Activities and tours

Rottnest Island p106
Astronomy
Astro Tours, T0417 949958. Take small parties and several large telescopes out beyond Geordie Bay for 2 hrs of commentated star-gazing. This is one of the best tours of its kind. Nightly, 2000 Nov-Mar.

Boat and kayak tours
Capricorn Kayak Tours, T9438 1911, www.capricornkayak.com.au. Takes small groups out sea-kayaking around some of the island's best off-shore spots. From 2 hrs to a full day, Oct-May.
Small, covered, glass- bottomed boats can be hired at Geordie Bay ($20 for ½ hr) from 0930-1730, T0407 009283.
Underwater Explorer, T0400 202340. A large glass-bottomed boat that heads out several times a day on a variety of short cruises that include a 45-min 'wreck & reef' tour, and longer snorkelling trips (1½ hrs).

Diving
As a rule of thumb the wind comes from the east in the morning and the southwest in the afternoon. Precisely where it is best to jump into the water around the island depends on the weather and prevalent wind direction. In general it is best to be in the lee of the wind, but before deciding where to head for have a chat with the people at **Malibu Diving**. Malibu Diving and the VIC sells an excellent, very detailed but inexpensive guide to Rottnest snorkelling.
Australian Diving Academy, T9364 7878, www.ausdiving.com.au. Offers trips from Perth and Fremantle.
Malibu Diving, T9292 5111, www.rottnest diving.com.au. This outfit is happy to advise on the best spots. It hires out kit and organizes a variety of boat dives daily from $60 per dive depending on kit supplied.

Golf and bowls
Golf and Country Club has a 9-hole course and a bowling green. Club hire available. 0830-110, 1400-1900 Tue-Sat in summer, 0900-1630 daily in the main winter season.

Local sightseeing tours
A 2-hr bus tour sets off around the island a few times each day, with full commentary on the human and natural history of the island. The tour includes visits to Wadjemup Lighthouse and the West End. Adults $22, children $11, concessions $16.50.
Rottnest Voluntary Guides, conduct guided walks daily around Thomson Bay, mostly focusing on the island's penitential and military history. In summer the programme is extended to include evening walks that include star-gazing and ghost stories. Gold coin donation appreciated, see VIC for current programme.

Surfing
There are a few good breaks around the island, notably at Stark Bay, Strickland Bay, North Point and Salmon Point. These are all reef breaks, however, and not suitable for beginners. Surf and bodyboards can be hired from **Malibu Diving**, for $20 a day.

Tennis
See VIC or Geordie Bay store for bookings of Thomson Bay and Geordie Bay courts. Racket hire available. There are also courts at Kingstown Barracks and these are free for hostel residents.

⊘ Transport

Air
Rottnest Air Taxi, T9292 5027, offers return trips from Jandakot airport, east of Fremantle. Fares from $66 per person, depending on numbers. Once on the island they also offer quick scenic flights from $25.

Bicycle
Bikes can be brought over on the ferries, and the ferry companies also offer bike hire. Hire on the island is from **Rottnest Bike Hire**, T9292 5105, which has a wide range to suit all ages including some tandems and electric wheelchairs (from $15 per day). Open 0830-1700. Beware however. The coast road

around the island undulates over the dunes like a roller-coaster. The slopes may be short, but they are often quite steep and cycling is a tiring business, so avoid single speed bikes. Also note that there is no fresh water west of either Geordie Bay or Kingstown Barracks – and you should take plenty if there in summer.

Bus
A free Courtesy Shuttle bus operates every 30 mins between Geordie Bay, Longreach Bay, Thomson Bay Settlement, the airport and Kingstown Barracks. Services between 0800-2100. Bayseeker bus travels clockwise right around the coast road, but doesn't get out to the West End. It operates a jump-on, jump-off system with 16 stops on the circuit

and goes about every 20-40 minutes. A day fare is $7, children $3.50, concessions $5. Services from 0830-1700.

Ferry
Ferries run from Barrack Street Jetty in Perth, Fremantle and Hillarys. See the Transport sections at the departure point for details.

Train
Not exactly a comprehensive service, but a pleasant ride anyway. Travels between the south end of the Settlement and Oliver Hill lookout. Fare includes a tour at Oliver Hill, except for the last ride of the day. Two-hour round trips hourly from 1030-1430. Tickets $15.40, children $7.70, concessions $11, available from the VIC.

Swan Valley → Colour map 1, grid B3.

The Swan Valley is Perth's very own wine region, just a 45-minute drive from the city. In truth it's half a valley, bordered to the east by the Darling Range, but running flat to the west all the way to the northern Perth suburbs. It was settled early in Perth's history, providing better agricultural land than further down the Swan River, and vines were being grown by 1836 at what is now Houghton's, the valley's best known winery. All sorts of other fruit and vegetables are also grown here, much by small-scale farmers, and it seems that almost every other house has a sign outside advertising table grapes and rock melons. At the southern end of the valley is Guildford, an inland port established in 1829, but falling out of favour early in its history, which helped preserve many early Victorian buildings. ▸▸ *For Sleeping, Eating and other listings, see pages 113-116.*

Ins and outs
Getting there and around Frequent trains leave from East Perth station to Guildford and Midland, but this is not the ideal way to tour the valley. Ideally you need your own transport, or take a tour. A taxi to or from the airport will be about $30, nearly double that from Perth.▸▸ *See Activities and tours, page 115, and Transport, page 116, for further details.*
Tourist information The main VIC① *on the corner of Meadow and Swan sts, T9379 9400, www.swanvalley.com.au, 0900-1700,* for the region is in Guildford.

Sights

Wineries
There are some 30 wineries in the region, ranging from one of the largest producers in the state to several one-person operations. Most offer wines in the $15-30 range. Cellar door hours vary widely, and Monday to Tuesday is probably the worst time to visit as some of the smaller wineries keep these as their days off. Most wineries charge $2 for a tasting, usually refundable from a purchase, and many have cafés or restaurants, most of which have outdoor vine-covered courtyards. See Eating, page 114, for a range of eating options in wineries and cellar door only wineries.

The Swan Valley is not just a haven for wine buffs. If you're interested in early Perth history this is also a good place to trace some of the earliest developments in the colony. WA's oldest church, **All Saints**, was built on the furthest spot Captain Stirling reached in his exploration of 1827. The simple red-brick building, over 160 years old, is still in use today and is usually open to visitors.

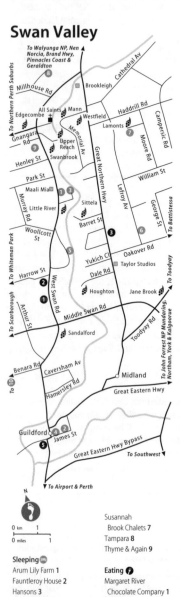

Swan Valley

Susannah
Brook Chalets 7
Tampara 8
Thyme & Again 9

Sleeping 🛏
Arum Lily Farm 1
Fauntleroy House 2
Hansons 3
Perth Big 4 10
Rose & Crown 4
Settlers Rest 5
Strelley Brook 6

Eating 🍴
Margaret River
  Chocolate Company 1
Old Cottage Café 2
Swan Valley Cheese
  Company 3
Whiteman's Abroad 5

The arts scene has been building for some time and there are now a number of seriously exciting artists in the valley. Antonio Battistessa, the 'Wizard of Fire', has been creating ornate iron sculptures and furniture for years and his work can be found all over Perth. His studio, **Battistessa** ⓘ *T9296 4121, 0900-1600, corner of Campersic and Neuman rds*, is continuously growing. **Maalinup** ⓘ *West Swan Rd, T9296 0704, 1000 -1700*, is an Aboriginal owned and operated cultural centre with work-shops and two galleries. The premier room exhibits a few fine original artworks, wood carvings and didgeridoos, the other houses the more run-of-the-mill works found in many gift shops. Jude Taylor, the proprietor of **Taylor Studios** ⓘ *510 Great Northern Highway, T9274 3435, opening hours vary so call ahead*, can seemingly turn her hand to almost anything and the studio houses a brilliant collection of art, sculpture and furniture. **Lamonts winery** has a gallery featuring many local and WA artists.

Guildford → *Colour map 1, grid B3.*

Guildford, 20 km from Perth, 16 km from Mundaring, retains many old buildings from its early founding as the agricultural base to supply the Swan River Colony, but as yet makes very little of them other than as accommodation. The **courthouse** and **gaol** complex ⓘ *corner of Swan and Meadow sts, 0900-1600, token entry fee*, dates back to 1841 and as a museum now has a collection of colonial memorabilia. Entry to these also includes a peek inside one of the original settlers cottages, constructed around 1880. Next door is **Guildford Potters** ⓘ *T9279 9859, Mon-Fri 0930-1500, Sat-Sun 0930-1600*, a commercial operation that displays work from over 20 local potters. On show is a wide range, mostly a mix of practical, rustic ceramics with some fairly esoteric decorative pieces.

Some 15 km north of central Swan Valley, this 18 sq km block sits on the western escarpment of the Darling Range at the point at which the Avon River winds its way through to the plains to the west. It's a river that draws many visitors, particularly during the **Avon Descent** ① *T9571 1371, $9 per car*, in the first weekend in August when competitors brave the length of Syds Rapids in their race downstream. Permanent water and a good supply of native tucker also made this a fine spot for the area's first inhabitants and one of the park's shorter trails describes some of the local Aboriginal stories. There are two parking areas, both with toilets and wood-fired BBQs. The further of the two, adjacent to Boongarup Pool, tends to be the quieter and is closer to the rapids. Three longer circular bush walks head off from the car parks, the shortest, the Kangaroo Trail taking about 1½ hours, and the longest, the Echidna, taking about four hours. The latter reaches the highest point in the park (260 m) and you'll get views across the Avon valley.

Whiteman Park → *Colour map 1, grid A3.*

① *T9209 6000, www.whiteman park.com.au, 0830-1800, 0900-1700 Mon-Fri, entry via Lord St, where the no 335 Midland-Ellenbrook bus drops off 3 times a day Mon-Fri, pick-ups from main gate usually possible.*

Covering over 3,000 ha of natural and regenerated bush, Whiteman Park, 20 km from Perth, is the most family-orientated of Perth's peripheral parks, focusing on children's activities, picnic facilities and visitor attractions rather than extensive bush-walking. The park hosts equestrian and shooting centres but the main visitor area is at the **Village**, with extensive picnic facilities (and associated car parks) around nearby **Mussel Pool**, a small lake and area of wetland. The picnic facilities are impressive: dozens of gas fired ($1 for 10 minutes) and wood-fired BBQs with firewood provided free. There are vast lawned areas and quite a few covered tables, some of which can be booked ahead.

In the village are the visitor centre, café, a few craft shops, children's playground and pool, and the **Motor Museum of WA** ① *T9249 9457, 1000-1600, $6, children and concessions $3*, which has the largest collection of vintage vehicles in the state. Adjacent is a separate **Tractor Museum** ① *Wed, Sat-Sun, 1100-1600, gold coin donation*. During 2005 these are being joined by the **Transport Heritage Centre** ① *trams/trains operate 1200-1500, $4, children and concessions $2*, where tourist trains and vintage trams will snake through the bush and connect the village with Mussel Pool. Another new attraction in the park is **Caversham Wildlife Park** ① *T9248 1984, www.cavershamwildlife.com.au, 0830-1730, $13.50, children $6, concessions $10*, relocated from Arthur Street, West Swan. This park holds the largest collection of animals in the state. They have over 200 species of birds, mammals and reptiles from all over the country, and a few from overseas. Highlights include the wombats, some of which can be met and 'cuddled'.

As well as the static attractions Whiteman Park plays host to a series of regular child and adult-orientated events throughout the year, including concerts and funfairs.

● Sleeping

Swan Valley *p111, map p112*

L-A Hansons, 60 Forest Rd, T9296 3366, www.hansons.com.au. The place to stay if your pockets are deep enough. A modern boutique hotel with 10 contemporary, crisp white rooms, all en suite with own balcony or courtyard, the expensive mod-Aus cuisine is also hard to beat and is accompanied by

the valley's best wine list. Breakfast included. Great views, pool. Meals 0800-1030, 1900-2100. Recommended.

A-B Arum Lily Farm, West Swan Rd, T9296 0402. Has hosted B&B rooms in the elegant homestead and a self-contained cottage that sleeps 6. Both properties are ancient by WA standards, and are furnished in keeping.

B **Settlers Rest**, George St, T/F9250 4540, www.settlersrest.com.au. Historic, beautifully furnished 3-bedroom weatherboard cottage in a quiet, central spot. Open fires, a/c and traditional verandas.

Similar restored settlers' cottages include:
Moulton's Cottage, 27 Meadow St, Guildford, T9279 9543.

Strelley Brook, Lefroy Av, T9296 1876.

Thyme and Again, Merrich Estate, West Swan Rd, T9296 0750.

Cheaper self-contained and B&Bs include:
C **Susannah Brook Chalets**, Bisdee Rd, T9296 4733, www.susannahbrookcottages.com.au. 2 adjacent en suite, a/c cabins in a quiet bush setting near **Lamonts**. Bed-sit style with limited kitchenette. One of the valley's cheapest options.

C **Tampara** Anglesea Cres, T9297 3221, www.tampara.com.au. A large modern home purpose-built in colonial style as a traditional B&B. 3 rooms include 1 en suite double. Large grounds, pleasant gardens. Very welcoming hosts serve up a seriously good breakfast. Good value.

There are a handful of caravan parks in the valley, including:
Perth Big 4 at 91 Benara Rd, T1800 679992, perthholiday@bigpond.com.au.

Guildford p112

L-C **Rose & Crown**, 105 Swan St, T9279 8444, rcrown@iinet.net.au. This grand old coaching inn is officially the oldest pub in WA, and does indeed ooze its early colonial character. The 4 rooms upstairs are sumptuous, unashamedly old-worldy, but scale dramatically in price. Also modern motel rooms available. All rooms en suite. Meals available include substantial breakfasts 0700-0900, simple cheap light lunches 1200-1500 and mid-range dinners 1800-2100 Mon-Sat.

A-B **Fauntleroy House**, 4 James St, T9379 0270, www.fauntleroyhouse.com.au. A large old Federation home, now a traditional B&B with a welcome swimming pool.

⊘ Eating

Swan Valley p111, map p112
Restaurants (in wineries)
Wines by the glass and bottle available at all these wineries

▼▼▼ **Sandalford**, 3210 West Swan Rd, T9374 9366, www.sandalford.com. One of the 2 heavyweights in the valley, Sandalford offers more than most to the visitor. The extensive range of wines is split between the cheaper Element Range and the Premium Collection at $18-30, and it offers a full appreciation and tasting session as part of a guided tour. The cuisine is modern Australian with a strong Italian influence, and uses a lot of fresh, simple flavours. Restaurant hours are generous, 1000-1500 daily and 1800-2100 Sat-Sun. It also serves up a buffet breakfast ($20) Sun 0800-1100. A 3-course lunch and the full appreciation tour are included in its gourmet boat trip on the luxurious Miss Sandalford, which makes the trip from Barrack St Jetty, Perth. Cellar door open daily 1000-1700. Wine appreciation tour daily 1100, 1400 and 1500. 75 mins, $18. Swan river cruise daily 1000, return 1430 by bus. $129, bookings required.

▼▼ **Little River**, 6 Forest Rd, T9296 4462. 1000-1700 daily, café closed Thu. Wines $15-30. A little bit of rustic France in the Swan, both food and wine being strongly gallic influenced. Casual and a lá carte menus, and cream teas. Homemade desserts and ice-creams. Wines include the rare viognier.

▼▼ **Sittella**, Barrett St, T9296 2600. Claims one of the valley's best views from its large covered wooden deck. Inside tables are in a large, contemporary but earthy dining room. Open for lunch and tastings Wed-Sun 1100-1600. Recommended.

▼▼-▼ **Lamonts**, Bisdee Rd, T9296 4485. A large family-run winery with a shady alfresco area serving light lunches and a more formal dining room serving a lá carte. Well respected wines include a good Shiraz and Merlot. Wed-Sun 1000-1700, evening meals Sat 1700-2200.

▼ **Jane Brook**, Toodyay Rd, T9274 1432. A small family-run winery with a large covered decking area devoted to serving up substantial gourmet platters. Plain Jane range is good value at $15, while more traditional vintages go for $20-30. Mon-Fri 1000-1700, Sat-Sun 1200-1700.

▼ **Swanbrook**, Swan St, T9296 3100. Wines $13-25, also cheaper 2-litre casks. This smallish winery doesn't attract the buses making it a great spot for a quiet lunch.

Inside and outside dining areas. Inventive tapas and light lunches, with a spit-roast option on Sun. 1030-1600 daily.

Cafés (in wineries)

Edgecombe, Gnangara Rd, T9296 4307. Family-run, one of the most laid-back and welcoming wineries in the valley. Wines $13-20, 0900-1800 daily. Its unpretentious shop also sells an excellent range of home-produced jams, sauces and produce. It serves up a simple light lunch or cream tea.

Houghton, Dale Rd, T9274 9540. The valley's expansive elder statesman and now produces some of the most popular wines in Australia. Wines $12-40. 1000-1700. Its cheaper ranges are consistently good and always good value. It has a small museum, gallery and simple café but the big draw is its long lawn dotted with tall jacaranda trees. Picnickers welcome, though platters, ploughmans and pizzas are available.

Cellar door only

Mann, Memorial Av, T9296 4348. A 1-man operation continuing 3 generations of expertise in producing a smooth, dry Méthode Champenoise. A bargain at $18, the cellar door remains open, Sat-Sun and most weekdays 1000-1700, from Aug to when the 500 annual cases have gone, usually in Jan. Jack Mann has also produced an entirely new variety of grape, the *Cygneblanc*, though the wine is a little pricier at $30.

Upper Reach, Memorial Av, T9296 0078. Produces some of the valley's finest wines, particularly their Semignon and Chardonnay. It is also in a very picturesque location and welcome picnickers. Sat-Sun 1100-1700.

Westfield, Memorial Av, T9296 4356. The real McCoy with tastings in the cool 1927 cellar, surrounded by dozens of aromatic barrels. Its Chardonnay is just one of several highly regarded wines, but new vintages are still only $15-25. Mon-Sat 0900-1700, Sun 1100-1600.

Restaurants

††† **Whiteman's Abroad**, 34 Johnson St, Guildford, T9379 2990. Excellent dining

either inside in a beautiful colonial house or alfresco in the gardens. Lunch, cream teas and dinners available Wed-Sun 1030-2100, and gourmet breakfasts from 0900 Sun. Recommended.

Cafés

Margaret River Chocolate Company, 5123 West Swan Rd, T9250 1588. Housed in a smart, high-ceilinged new building, has a long counter in front of a huge wall of chocolate, within which is a window onto the chocolate-making activities beyond. The wide range of delicious chocs can be bought singly or by the bag, and the café has a range of coffees, cakes and panninis. Open daily 0900-1700, café 1000-1600.

Old Cottage Café, West Swan Rd, T9250 3638. Quaint 1915 weatherboard cottage with polished jarra floors and traditional verandas, now serving light lunches, cream teas and mid-range dinners. Mostly Italian-influenced home cooking with a few good veggie options. 0830, to 1700 Mon, Wed, 2100 Thu-Sat and 1930 Sun.

⦿ Shopping

Swan Valley Cheese Company, on the Great Northern Highway, T9296 0600. Open 0900-1700 daily. If you're into Italian cheeses then call in.

▲ Activities and tours

Swan Valley *p111, map p112*

Boat Torque Cruises, T9421 5888. Heads up from Barrack St Jetty in Perth daily.

Brookleigh, Great Northern Highway, T9296 2603, www.brookleigh.com.au. Organizes scenic and winery rides of 1-5 hrs, leaving most days ($45-100). Pick-ups can often be arranged.

Epicurean Tours, T0427 766717, www.epicurean.com.au. Take out small groups for knowledgeable and indulgent trips around the valley.

Sandalford, see page 114, for a more luxurious sailing option.

Swan Valley Tours, T9299 6249, www.svtours.com.au. Offers various wine

---

🎈 *For an explanation of sleeping and eating price codes used in this guide, see inside the*
⚫ *front cover. Other relevant information is found in Essentials, see pages 40-46.*

and gourmet tours with pick-ups from central Perth or Guildford.

Wagon Winery Trails, T0412 917496, www.swanvalleywa.com. Take the decidedly slow option in horse-drawn 'pioneer' wagons. Lots of different packages, but none of them go very far from their starting-point in Upper Swan.

⊖ **Transport**

Swan Valley *p111, map p112*
There are frequent train services between **Midland**, **Guildford** and **Perth**. Last trains leave Midland at 2400 Mon-Fri, 0130 Sun (ie Sat night) and 2330 Sun.

The Perth Hills

The sharp, 400-m high western escarpment of the Darling Ranges runs parallel to the coast about 30 km inland, forming a natural eastern border to the rapidly expanding Perth suburbs, and a western border to WA's huge and ancient inland plateau. Large areas of the scarp have been set aside as reserves and parks, preserving the characteristic gum woodlands and providing city-dwellers and visitors with an extensive network of bush-walking, mountain-biking and horse-riding tracks. Some of the valleys that snake inland have been cultivated by European settlers to produce fruit, vegetables and grapes. Although not as well known as the more extensive producers on the coastal plain in Swan Valley, several wineries have been established, and some can claim the prettiest settings near Perth. ▸▸ *For Sleeping, Eating and other listings, see pages 119-120.*

Ins and outs

There are some buses from Perth and Midland. An excellent way of getting a flavour of the hills forests is by bike, and there are a number of circular trails. ▸▸ *See Activities and tours and Transport, page 120, for details.* The main VICs are in Kalamunda ① *11 Headingly Rd, T9293 0299, Fri-Sun 1000-1500*; and Mundaring ① *7225 Great Eastern Highway, T9295 0202, 1000-1600*. CALM office ① *1 km east of Mundaring Weir on the Mundaring Weir Road, T9295 1955, Mon-Fri 1000-1630*, holds a good stock of brochures and maps including those for the Bibbulmun Track ($6 each), and will advise on current trail accessibility.

Kalamunda → *Colour map 2, grid B2. 25 km from Perth, 25 km from Mundaring.*

Kalamunda has grown to be a good-sized modern town, seemingly built around a central shopping centre and shoving its history to the fringes. Its main claim to fame is as the northern terminus of the prodigious **Bibbulmun Track**, but the **Kalamunda History Village** ① *Railway Rd, T9293 1371, 1000-1500 Mon-Thu, Sat, and 1330-1630 Sun, $4, children $1, concessions $3*, is well worth a stroll around. Although a small example of an 'assembled' village, all the dozen or so buildings and their copious contents are authentic and well laid out around the town's original railway station. A good insight into life in WA around the early 20th century.

Gooseberry Hill and the Zig Zag → *15-km loop driving circuit.*

From Kalamunda it is worth driving out on Williams Sreeet to Gooseberry Hill, where the road winds one-way down to close to the base of the scarp. At almost every point along the series of switchbacks there are sweeping views of the coastal plains and Perth city centre. No entry fees apply. The road comes out on Ridge Hill Road. Turn right, left into Helena Valley Road, right again into Scott Street for the Great Eastern Highway. Turn left, then left again for Kalamunda Road and the Roe Highway.

⁝ The Bibbulmun Track

Started in the 1970s the long-distance Bibbulmun walking trail was last upgraded in 1998 and is now well marked along its entire route. Starting in Kalamunda it winds its way south through North Bannister, Dwellingup, Balingup, Pemberton and Walpole before finally ending up, 963 km later, in Albany. As well as passing through these picturesque towns the track also winds through several reserves and parks, much of the southern forests and some of the spectacular south coast. There are nearly 50 bush campsites en-route, each with a simple three-sided timber bunk shelter, picnic tables, water tank and pit toilets. Note that there are no cooking facilities, water needs to be boiled or treated, and there is no toilet paper. None of shelters are accessible by private vehicle, a great idea on the part of designers. There are also a few B&Bs that offer pick-ups and drop-offs to sections of the track. The whole walk generally takes about 6-8 weeks, but few tackle it in a single go. CALM have suggestions for various short day sections. The track is by far at its best in winter and spring, think twice, and then again before tackling any of it in high summer. There is a two-volume guide to the track and a series of eight maps also dedicated to it, all available at Perth's **Map World** amongst other outlets. For more information see www.bibbul muntrack.org.au or www.calm.wa.gov.au/tourism/ bibbulmun_splash.com, or contact the **Friends of the Bibbulmun Track** on T9481 0551.

Around Perth The Perth Hills

Bickley Valley → *Colour map 2, grid B2.*

Reached by taking Mundaring Weir Road from Kalamunda and then turning right into Aldersyde Road, Bickley Valley is one of the most picturesque of several small valleys that have been partially cultivated for fruit and wine. Fairly steep-sided, it is a patchwork of native forest, pasture and groves of fruit trees, always with a green, lush feel even in the heat of summer. There are a handful of small wineries dotted along and just off Aldersyde Road and Walnut Road, but they are only open for tastings at weekends. At the far end of the valley is the **Perth Observatory** ① *Walnut Rd, T9293 8255, www.wa.gov.au/perthobs, day tours 1st Sun in the month 1400 (1½ hrs), other days as per demand, $6.50, children and concessions $4.50, viewing nights $17, children and concessions $12 – 2 sessions each evening, the last of which sometimes stretches beyond the usual 1½ hrs*, which regularly holds viewing nights throughout the year. Each month they generally have a week of 'night sky' evenings, when the moon is fuller and visible, and a week of 'deep sky' nights, when the moon's absence allows even more to be seen, including other galaxies. Parties of 12 usually get to see six objects through three separate telescopes. These evenings are some of the best value of their kind, and bookings are essential. Also day tours, more appropriate for children, which include a slide show and sometimes sunspot viewing.

Mundaring → *Colour map 2, grid B2. 40 km from Perth, 55 km from Northam.*

Straddling the Great Eastern Highway with its thunderous, constant traffic, Mundaring is a modern town of pale-coloured brick with glimpses of an earlier history peeping through the cracks. Its chief attractions lie outside the town itself, west along the highway at **John Forrest National Park**, and south at **Mundaring Weir**.

John Forrest National Park → *Colour map 2, grid B2. 30 km from Perth,*
10 km from Mundaring.

ⓘ *$9 per vehicle, T9298 8344. Access is via looping Park Road, off the highway, a side*
road taking you into the visitor area where a fee applies. At the visitor area are a few
facilities including bush BBQs and picnic tables and a ranger station.

The first formal reserve in WA, declared in 1900, John Forrest is still one of the biggest
parks dedicated to preserving the original wildlife and gum woodlands of the scarp,
extending about 4 km along the side of the Great Eastern Highway and 5 km north.

The main draw of the park is its walking trails, best undertaken in winter or spring
when the brooks are flowing. It is absolutely riddled with them, but many are unmarked
so take care to stick to the signposted trails. If you are after a short introductory stroll the
Glenn Brook Trail takes about 45 minutes from the visitor area and winds its way easily
around the Glen Brook Dam that you will have seen on your right while driving in. The
trail is relatively flat, has views across the dam and passes a large number of
wildflowers in spring. Considerably more challenging is the **Eagle's View Walk Trail**, a
six- to seven-hour loop that takes in much of the park's area and scenery. Taking the
clockwise option the walk begins with an uphill section to a lookout, with views over the
coast plain to Perth, then along a pretty valley that is also thick with wildflowers in
spring. The return section undulates up and over a couple of rocky ridges, once again
affording views of Perth, but this time also over much of the park in the foreground.

Mundaring Weir → *Colour map 2, grid B2. 8 km from Mundaring, 16 km from Kalamunda.*

In 1895, with the Kalgoorlie goldrushes in full swing, WA's Engineer-in-Chief, CY
O'Connor, was given the task of supplying water to the new goldfields. Over 500 km
inland, in one of Australia's driest areas, the task seemed to many impossible but it
simply had to be done to sustain the new cash cow and O'Connor was the man on the
spot. His solution was simple, but challenged the technology of the day. He proposed
building a massive reservoir in the Perth Hills near Mundaring and from there a
pipeline all the way to Kalgoorlie. The scheme was widely derided as unworkable, but
O'Connor got his green light. The dam, enlarged to 40 m high in the 1950s and still
performing its intended purpose, is a testament to his vision and capability, but sadly
he didn't live to see it in operation. He killed himself weeks before the initial trials in
1902, a result of the intense pressure and harassment the scheme brought him.

Today a small huddle of houses sits in the forest to the north of the main dam
wall, amidst them the excellent pub built to cater for the original workers and
engineers, and a YHA hostel. A little beyond the village the **C Y O'Connor Museum**
ⓘ *T9295 2455, 1030-1500 Mon, Wed-Fri, and 1200-1700 Sun, $3, National Trust*
operated, utilizes the original pump-house and carefully details the development of
the gold-rushes and the building of both dam and pipeline. In the other direction the
Hills Forest Discovery Centre ⓘ *for a programme, T9295 2244, or click the 'tourism*
and recreation' icon at www.naturebase.com, is an activity-based educational centre
with a programme of regular day tours and part-day activities. Many are designed for
kids, but there are a number of notable exceptions, including moonlit canoeing, 4WD
training drives, Aboriginal bush tours, fishing workshops and fauna discovery
walks.Opposite the centre, the **Kookaburra Cinema** ⓘ *T9295 6190, nightly Nov-Apr,*
current releases, has an outdoor screen and seating.

There are a few walking trails in and around the weir. The **Weir Walk**, following
yellow-collared posts, takes a little less than an hour and winds around the area
between the pub and the weir, over the weir (gates close at 1800), around the picnic
areas to the south and through the pumping station complex. It formally starts
outside the museum but can be started outside the pub. The **O'Connor Trail**,
following the green-collared posts, starts opposite the pub at the village hall (now a
craft centre), and follows a loop through the forest, past the discovery centre and
cinema on the way. Allow about two hours.

🌐 Sleeping

Kalamunda p116

C**Lady Muck**, 22 Mundaring Weir Rd, T9257 2475, www.ladymuck.netfirms.com. A small, modern home-style B&B with 3 rooms, 1 en suite, and an engaging, friendly host. Breakfast is a substantial continental.

D**Kalamunda Hotel**, 43 Railway Terr, T9257 1084, kh@iinet.net.au. Built in 1902, has 3 simple upstairs doubles, but all en suite with a/c. Downstairs, the traditional bars have been smartly refurbished, the dining room serves a wide range of good meals for most budgets and there are some covered tables out front. Meals daily 1200-1500, 1800-2100.

Bickley Valley p117

B**Brookside Vineyard**, 5 Loaring Rd, T9291 8705. Has a charming new garden cottage, built and furnished in the style of the adjacent Federation homestead. Open-plan with combined living and bedroom, wood-fired heater, en-suite bathroom, and veranda. Substantial breakfast, family pool and optional evening meals for $35.

B**Lonsdales**, 181 Walnut Rd, T9293 8106, www.wantree.com.au/~ lonsdale. Secluded modern B&B built of jarrah, straw and recycled bricks, and sitting in a secluded spot amongst gum woodland. The large open-plan guest wing, with mezzanine sleeping area, is full of interesting nik-naks from many years of travel, and a perfect spot for simply chilling out. Garden pool, lots of wildlife and full breakfast. Recommended.

Mundaring p117

L**Loose Box**, 6825 Great Eastern Highway, 2 km west of Mundaring, T9295 1787, www.loosebox.com. Everything about this place exudes quality and indulgence. The restaurant, a winner of a constant stream of state and national awards since it opened in 1980, is a century-old weatherboard house, now opened up into several formal dining areas. The seriously expensive cuisine is classical French, with Australian influences, using local produce (much of it grown in the kitchen gardens. Meals Wed-Sat 1900-2200, Sun 1200-1400. Bookings recommended. In

the garden are 6 luxury chalets, available as part of a lunch or dinner package Wed-Thu and Sun, and room only Mon-Tue, Fri-Sat. Recommended.

Mundaring Weir p117

C**Mundaring Weir Hotel**, T9295 1106, www.mundaringweirhotel.com.au. A grand old pub hotel perched on the hill above the weir pump stations, and a favourite Sun destination for locals and city-dwellers when a lamb spit-roast is prepared for lunch. The main bars capture a feel for the pub's century of history, but you'll be likely to head for the garden tables, some covered. Fresh, inventive meals are mostly cheap, available 1200-1430 daily, 1800-2000 Fri-Sat. Accommodation in 8 external motel-style units, each with an open fireplace, grouped alongside the pubs pool. Room/dinner packages only, Fri-Sat.

E**Djaril-Mari**, YHA hostel, T9295 1809. A small relaxed hostel with 24 beds in 4-bunk dorms and another 2 6-bunk rooms in a separate cottage with its own facilities. General facilities aren't extensive, but clean and comfortable and include a wood-burning stove in the pleasant lounge area, and well-equipped kitchen.

🍴 Eating

For further options, see Sleeping above.

Kalamunda p116

🍴🍴**Thai on the Hill**, on the corner of Haynes Rd and Railway Rd, Kalamunda, T9293 4312. Has a pleasant rich-red formal dining room and serves up Thai food with an extensive range of cheaper veggie options. Licensed, open 1800-2200 Tue-Sun.

🍴**Fish & Chip Shop**, behind the café, open 1630-2000.

🍴**Le Paris-Brest**, Haynes St, Kalamunda, T9293 2752. Something of a cultural oasis in Kalamunda, a small, cheerful Gallic corner providing a patisserie and café, on-going art exhibitions, and monthly live jazz on their wraparound terrace. Everything is

🍷 *For an explanation of sleeping and eating price codes used in this guide, see inside the front cover. Other relevant information is found in Essentials, see pages 40-46.*

home-made, including all the cakes and icecream. 0700-1730 Tue-Sun and public holidays, jazz on the 1st Sat of each month.

Bickley Valley *p117*

♔ **Packing Shed**, T9291 8425, almost next door to **Brookside**. The restaurant of the **Lawnbrook Estate**, now much better known for its food than its wine. Essentially a barn with a large brick terrace, the excellent food is appropriately country Mediterranean style, spiced with the odd curry. Open for lunches and teas, 1000-1800 Sat-Sun.

▲ Activities and tours

The principal 40-km loop trail heads out from Midland, up the scarp and through John Forrest National Park, steers well clear of the highway and drops around to Mundaring. Much of the return to Midland is along the route of the Old Eastern Railway. From Mundaring a connecting 15-km loop heads south through the state forest to Mundaring Weir. Free trail notes and maps are available from CALM offices.

⊜ Transport

Metropolitan buses for **Mundaring** leave from the train station at **Midland**. Buses to **Kalamunda** leave Perth City Busport several times a day. There are direct TransWA coaches from **East Perth** that call at **Mundaring**, leaving at 0715 Mon, 0800 Tue, Thu and Sun, 0930 Thu, and 0900 Fri.

North of Perth

The coastal road north of Perth runs as far as Lancelin at present but within a few years the sandy 4WD track between Lancelin and Cervantes will finally be sealed. This will create a coastal route all the way from Perth to Geraldton and will bring much change to the string of sleepy fishing and holiday towns between the two cities. Yanchep National Park makes a fine day trip from Perth, with its tranquil lakes and birdlife, but it is worth continuing north for a night in Lancelin. It is windsurfing heaven but if you are weedy of arm then come for the dunes. Lancelin has a long expanse of silky dunes that are magical at sunset and only a short walk from the town centre. Inland, the appealing town of Gingin lies on the Brand Highway and can make an interesting stop on the way to or from Geraldton. Further east, the curious settlement of New Norcia straddles the Great Northern Highway. New Norcia is a small community of Benedictine monks living a contemplative life in their grand edifices, as road trains thunder past. ➤ *For Sleeping, Eating and other listings, see pages 122-123.*

Yanchep National Park → *Colour map 2, grid B2. 50 km from Perth, 80 km from Lancelin.*
Perched just inland, 15 km away from Perth's northernmost suburbs, lies one of the region's best parks. Encompassing two lakes, **Loch McNess** and the larger **North Lake**, the area was earmarked as a nature reserve in 1905, but the park has developed slowly since then and has also seen military use. Yanchep has a wide range of attractions for the visitor. Its bush-covered dunes, teeming with Western Grey kangaroos, overlay a large network of limestone caves, two of which are readily accessible by the public. There are many walking trails, threading their way through and around heathland, gum woods and wetland, and there are opportunities for overnight hikes, with camping at the far end of North Lake. As well as the wild roos there are two animal enclosures, one for kangaroos and emus, and a large koala enclosure where they actually get to live their lives up trees. The park is also home to dozens of bird species. Simply sitting by the lakes in summer you are likely to see flocks of galahs and black cockatoos, not to mention the inquisitive ducks. There are several picnic areas with BBQs and some covered tables.

The park puts on a constant programme of activities, especially in summer, some free some not (contact the visitor centre for a current programme). Most take place in the area between the visitor centre, Loch McNess and the **Yanchep Inn**. Aboriginal

performances of dancing, didgeridoo playing and weapons throwing take place
regularly throughout the day. There are also cultural talks and demonstrations about
the area's traditional Aboriginal lifestyle. Rowing boats on Loch McNess can be hired
at the visitor centre. There is public access to two caves. There are regular tours of the
Crystal Cave, a still active and therefore quite damp cave, and the public can also
book to explore **Yonderup Cave**, now dry. Occasional adventure caving trips are also
organized for Yonderup. The park has its own nine-hole golf course. Several short
walks of around 2 km (one hour) head around Loch McNess and the caves area, all
described on the free map you will receive on entering the park. For details of the
longer and overnight walks contact the visitor centre. The koalas spend most of their
time high up in the trees, but a few are brought down occasionally during the day to a
smaller area where you can have your photograph taken with them.

The **VIC** ① *T9561 1004, yanchep@calm.wa.gov.au, $9 per car, per activity, $6.50,
children $3.50, concessions $5*, is close to the park entrance, next to a kiosk
and tearooms.

Lancelin → *Colour map 2, grid A1. Population: 1,500. 130 km from Perth, 75 km from Gingin.*
At the current end of the coastal highway, Lancelin is a small, spread out fishing town
that has become a firm favourite of windsurfers and kitesurfers during the main
October-May season. The strong dependable off-shore winds are also responsible for
the naked dunes that run for a couple of kilometres just inland of the town. They make
an excellent venue for sandboarding, and are also used by local trailbikers,
four-wheel drivers and tour operators, but they are at their most striking when devoid
of traffic and lit up by a strong sunset when they fleetingly turn blush pink. The dunes
start about 1 km north of town, and you should arrive about 25 minutes before sunset
to get the full effect. The town beaches are not the coast's best but a few decent surf
breaks, snorkelling and diving spots help make this a popular destination. The town
has all the basic services, including ATMs in the **Gull** service station and **Crayside
Tavern**. There is no public transport to or from Lancelin.

Gingin → *Colour map 2, grid A2. Population: 600. 80 km from Perth, 225 km from Dongara.*
A tiny, picturesque rural town, Gingin sits inside a loop of Gingin Brook and is the
centre of a thriving agricultural community. Beef cattle are traditionally farmed here
but increasingly olive tree plantations are dominating the area. The town has a fine
grassy park by the brook and a few lovely old stone buildings, such as **St Lukes
Church** (1860) and **Dewars House** (1880), an unusual two-storey private residence.
There are a few basic services on Brockman Street and an excellent pub on Jones
Street between the brook and railway line. Just outside town, **Colamber Bird Park**
① *Mooliabeenee Rd, T9575 1575, Wed-Mon 0900-1600, $5, children and concessions
$3*, is well worth a visit. Australian parrots are displayed in large cages and a walk-in
aviary around a central lawn and picnic area. Great for kids with a playground that will
keep them out of nipping distance, cream teas available. To the west of Gingin, Gingin
Brook Road (32 km) runs between the Brand Highway and the main coast road to
Guilderton and Lancelin.

New Norcia → *Colour map 2, grid A2. Population: 50 130 km from Perth, 80 km from Gingin.*
New Norcia is one of the most unusual settlements in Australia. A small community of
Benedictine monks live a traditional Benedictine life of work and prayer within an
astonishingly grand setting on the hot and dry Victoria Plains. The first Bishop of
Perth, Dr John Brady, was concerned for the welfare of Western Australia's indigenous
people and thought 'the blessing of civilization and religion' would save them. He
persuaded two Spanish monks to come to Australia to establish a mission and they
set off from Perth on foot for the Victoria Plains in 1846 to do so. Dom Rosendo
Salvado, the first Abbot, aimed to encourage local Aboriginal people to become

Around Perth North of Perth

farmers and to educate Aboriginal children within a self-sufficient religious community. It is hard to say how successful he was but the second Abbot, Torres, pursued markedly different aims. New Norcia became less of a bush mission and more of a monastic community and centre for education. Torres was also an architect and during his short stint from 1901 to 1914 most of the enormous, elaborate buildings were constructed or simple existing buildings, such as the Abbey Church, were given a face-lift. These days there are only 16 monks but they employ a workforce of about 60 to keep the place running. Much of the place is off-limits but there is an interesting **museum** and **art gallery** ① *T9654 8056, www.newnorcia.wa.edu.au, 0930-1700 Aug-Oct, 1000-1630 Nov-Jul, $6.50, children under 12 free, concessions $5.50, tours daily 1100, 1330. $13.50, children u12 free (2 hrs)*, that focuses on the history of the mission and displays some of New Norcia's rare and valuable artwork and treasures. A shop sells high quality pottery, souvenirs and things the monks make, including olive oil and the renowned preservative-free New Norcia bread, baked daily in a wood-fired oven and served in many Perth restaurants.

❣ To see more of New Norcia, take a guided tour, which visits the monastery, colleges and Abbey Church. Visitors can also join the monks for prayers or early morning mass.

● Sleeping

Yanchep National Park p120

C Yanchep Holiday Village, 56 St Andrews Dr, 10 km from the park near the small coastal settlement of Yanchep, T9561 2244, www.yanchepholidays.com. Small number of self-contained apartments around a central pool area, surrounded by bush.
C Yanchep Inn, 200 m north of visitor centre, T9561 1001. Four motel rooms. Pub serves counter and restaurant meals Mon-Fri 1130-1500, 1730-2000, Sat-Sun 1130-2000.

Lancelin p121

B-C Windsurfer Beach Chalets, T/F9655 1454, Hopkins St. Has a few inexpensive self-contained units. Can also organize a variety of houses for short-stays in the town.
C Lancelin Inn, north end of town, T9655 1005. Has motel style en-suite rooms and a mid-range dining room overlooking the shore. Meals daily 1200-1400 and 1800-2000.
D-E Lancelin Lodge, south end of town on Hopkins St, T9655 2020, www.lancelinlodge. com.au. Has just about everything you look for in a hostel. Great rooms and communal facilities, friendly, pool, lots of freebies including bikes, and excellent local knowledge. They will even pick up from Perth (cost involved). Recommended. There are 2 caravan parks, both with on-site vans and both close to the shore. The one at the north end, T9655 1115, is also close to the dunes.

Gingin p121

C Gingin Hotel, 5 Jones St, T9575 2214. The owners of this old 2-storey pub have brought city style to the country. Imaginative rustic decor, good coffee and a lovely outdoor terrace. Hearty mid-range meals of grills and pies using the plentiful local produce, daily 1200-1400, 1800-2030. Also clean and tidy motel and hotel rooms. Recommended. Backpackers can also be accommodated (E) and this can often be linked to agricultural work in the district, contact **Gingin Labour Hire**, T9575 1001.
C Neergabby Organic Farm, Gingin Brook Rd, 15 km west of Brand Highway, T9575 7667, www.wabba.asn.au/members/neer gabby. Peaceful B&B in a rammed earth and timber building by the brook. 3 elegant, en-suite, classic rooms. Also outdoor spa, dinner by arrangement.
Shell Roadhouse, corner of Brand Highway and Dewar Rd, T9575 2258. Roadhouses are not usually known for their tucker but this is an exception. Good country meals daily 0700-2100. It also runs the caravan park next door, sites and cabins.

New Norcia p121

There are only 2 options for sleeping.
C Guesthouse, T9654 8002. 8 comfortable twin en-suite rooms around a courtyard within the monastery. The price (a recommended donation) includes 3 meals of the same fare as the monks, although the

dining room is separate. Male guests may be asked to eat with the monks. Book in advance, especially at weekends.

C **New Norcia Hotel**, T9654 8034, built for parents visiting their children in the colleges next door. The exterior is fit for a king, indeed Abbot Torres hoped the King of Spain would visit, but inside it is a pretty simple country pub with 17 tired twin and single rooms. Shared facilities and no meals included.

● Eating

Lancelin *p121*

♣♣ **El Tropo**, main shopping strip, T9655 1448. Best in town, even though it's done out like a beach shack. Evenings only.

♣♣ **Endeavour Tavern**, T9655 1052. Characterful, modern but rustic, with lots of rough timbers and bare antique brick. The pub garden overlooks the shore and ocean. DJs and live music every weekend.

♣♣ **Offshore Café & Store**, near the boat ramp at the south end, T9655 2828. Licensed or BYO, cheerful and unpretentious and serves lots of cheap rice dishes, seafood and pizzas. Open daily 0900-2100.

New Norcia *p121*

♣♣-♣ **New Norcia Hotel** has lunches daily 1200-1400 and dinners of grills, seafood and pizzas, Mon-Sat 1800-2000. There is also a roadhouse where you can get fast food and takeaways, open daily 0800-2000. The general store next door sells groceries.

▲▲ Activities and tours

Lancelin *p121*

Aqua Jack, T9655 1693, alex@wind speed.net.au. For boat fishing tours. Surf-cam and weather updates at www.ocean classic.org.

Desert Storm Adventures, T9655 2550, info@desertstorm.com.au. Runs a jacked-up yellow bus with simply enormous tyres, claiming to be the world's biggest 4WD. Tours (1¼ hrs, $40) several times a day into the dunes for a bit of a roller-coaster drive and a spot of sandboarding.

Lancelin Surfsports, T0655 1441. Sandboard hire.

Sandcruza, T0403-430079. Will take parties of 1-5 into the dunes for photography or sandboarding for $75 per party (45 min).

Werner's, T9655 1553, windslanc@hotmail. com. Hire (from $15 per hr) and lessons.

● Transport

Some TransWA buses (N1) pass through **Gingin** on their way north, departing **East Perth** at 0830 Mon-Sat, 1730 Fri and 0930 Sun. Other services (N2) head to **Geraldton** via **New Norcia**, leaving at 0930 Tue, Thu, 1700 Fri, 1145 Sun. **Integrity**, Wellington St Bus Station, Perth, T9226 1339, www.inte gritycoachlines.com.au, also operates a service up the west coast, stopping at **Gingin**. Run Sun-Fri.

Avon Valley

The area just to the east of the Darling Range is threaded through by the Avon River (as in 'have', not 'grave'), and is a picturesque country of rolling hills, pasture and woodland. Early European settlers soon found it to be one of the most fertile regions around Perth, and substantial urban and agricultural progress was already being made when the gold-rushes began in the 1890s. That saw the area's importance increase yet more as a goods marshalling point and the last place to collect water. Some of the oldest towns in WA can be found here, full of historic buildings, including York, one of the most attractive towns in the state. ▸▸ *For Sleeping, Eating and other listings, see pages 126-127.*

Avon Valley National Park → *Colour map 2, grid B2. 65 km from Perth, 35 km from Toodyay.*
ⓘ *$9 car, camping $5 person, both payable at self-registration stations.*

Avon Valley is a pretty and peaceful small park around a section of the Avon River. The steep-sided valley is covered in woodland and granite outcrops. The park has an interesting mix of flora and fauna as it includes the northern limit of jarrah and the wandoo woodland found in drier country to the east. Marri and grass trees are also common in the park. Euros, western-grey kangaroos and more than 90 species of birds live in the park. In the 1860s this area was one of the most inaccessible in the Darling Ranges and was used as a hide-out by bushranger Moondyne Joe. More law-abiding types still use it as a hide-out from the city; there are a handful of tranquil camping spots, each with wood BBQs, picnic tables and pit toilets. Valley Campsite is the most popular, often used for launching canoes although the river retreats to a series of pools in summer and autumn. The campsites are about 10 km along steep unsealed roads. There are great views over the valley from Bald Hill and you can clamber around the rocks here.

Toodyay → *Colour map 2, grid B3. Population: 400. 85 km from Perth, 27 km from Northam.*

Like York, its more famous southern neighbour, Toodyay (pronounced 'Two-jay'), has retained a fine collection of Victorian buildings, and also sits alongside the Avon. At this point the river is frequently dry, though its setting is one of prettiest in the area, with several low hills surrounding the small town centre. Toodyay is now closely associated with **Moondyne Joe**, the complex bushranger who for some time in his chequered career camped in the hills around the town. At the beginning of November the town hosts the annual **WA Jazz Festival** (tradjazzwa@bigpond.com).

A visit to the well-preserved and informative **Old Gaol** ① *Mon-Fri 1000-1500, Sat-Sun 1000-1600, $2, children and concessions $1, follow main Stirling Terr west under the railway bridge, turn left and follow to Clinton St, approx 1 km*, illustrates Moondyne Joe's story, and gives another grisly reminder about the shocking treatment the early colonial authorities meted out to the local Aboriginals.In the main street is **Connor's Mill** ① *Stirling Terr, 0900-1700, $2.50, children and concessions $2, entry via the VIC*, a building that had careers both as a flour mill and a mini power station. It has been restored, with authentic machinery, to a semblance of how it probably looked in its flour-grinding days. The **Cola Café** on Stirling Terrace, is well worth a visit to see the extensive collection of Coca-Cola memorabilia. The VIC ① *T9574 2435, www.gidgenet. com.au/toodyay, Mon-Sat 0900-1700, Sun 1000-1700*, is adjacent to the mill.

Northam → *Colour map 2, grid B3. Population: 6,000. 95 km from Perth, 500 km from Kalgoorlie-Boulder.*

Chosen early in the 20th century as the main rail junction for the region, Northam is still the Avon Valley's principal service town. Although there is little hard grist for the tourist mill, a stroll around town will reveal many Victorian buildings, several good pubs and the surprisingly wide **Avon River**, bridged for pedestrians by the longest suspension span of its kind in Australia. This pleasant stretch of water also has another claim to fame, the country's only breeding population of introduced white swans, a novel sight to Perth weekenders, more familiar to many international visitors. During the first weekend in August, the town is packed for the **Avon Descent** race. The river can get very white in places on its 133-km way downstream, but the start here is noted more for the screams of spectators than participants.

The town has the usual services, mostly along Fitzgerald Street or in the adjacent shopping centre, including a cinema. The VIC ① *Grey St, T9622 2100, northam@ avon.net.au, 0900-1700*, which houses an exhibition on post-war immigration to the area, is by the river and suspension bridge.

York → *Colour map 2, grid B3. Population: 3,000. 95 km from Perth, 35 km from Northam.*

In 1830 European settlers from the Swan River Colony explored the country east of the Darling Range and were delighted to find the Avon Valley. It seemed so fertile that Governor Stirling felt that success of his new colony was assured and one of his companions suggested the area be called Yorkshire as the rolling green hills reminded him of home. Land was grabbed eagerly and the district has been a

Moondyne Joe

Englishman Joseph Johns, convicted of stealing food in 1848, was transported to the Swan Valley colony in 1853. A non-violent and slightly eccentric man, his career as a criminal was chequered with many visits to Toodyay and Fremantle prisons (the latter building him his own 'escape-proof' cell) and as many escapes. As a felon-at-large and bushranger he frequently took to the area near Toodyay, known to the local Aborigines as *Moondyne* and now the Avon Valley National Park, so gaining his nick-name by a sympathetic public. Then, and now, seen as a somewhat comic figure, his final years were extremely sad, his mind succumbing to dementia. He was incarcerated in an asylum, but could never be convinced it wasn't prison and still repeatedly escaped until his quiet death in 1900.

successful agricultural region ever since. Situated by the Avon River, York experienced a short boom in the 1890s when gold was discovered in the east of the state. At the time York was the easternmost rail terminus and the last source of fresh water but was soon passed by when both water and rail reached Kalgoorlie. Northam was chosen as the major rail junction to the goldfields and became the regional centre, leaving York with a magnificent collection of 19th-century buildings to be left in peace for another century. The town is now an appealing, friendly place with museums, cafés, antique and bookshops along the main street that draw lots of visitors from Perth at weekends. York is also known for its festivals; vintage cars in July and jazz at the end of September.

The chief attraction of York is its remarkable 19th-century streetscape, mostly built between 1880 and 1910. It is well worth a stroll up and down the main street, Avon Terrace, and some of the back streets (local guide and architecture expert Adelphe King can be booked for personalized tours, T9641 1799). The most impressive building is the **Town Hall**, a magnificently opulent Edwardian hall of red brick and yellow columns. Visitors are welcome to explore the building. Also prominent in Avon Terrace are the post office and courthouse, both designed by architect George Temple-Poole in the 1890s and built of brick and Toodyay stone.

A map featuring the main buildings is available from the VIC.

Old Gaol and Courthouse ① *Avon Terr, T9641 2072, 1000-1600, small admission fee,* are managed by the National Trust. An influx of land-grabbing Europeans naturally dismayed the Aboriginal people of the area who began to attack the new settlers in the mid-1830s. Soldiers were sent to York to protect the settlers so the town had a strong military and later police presence from its earliest days. The complex began as mud-brick in the 1840s and grew into the grand formal buildings of the courthouse in the 1890s. Visitors can stroll through the courthouses, cell block, stables and a troopers cottage dressed in the furnishings of 1867.

Next door is the **York Motor Museum** ① *116 Avon Terr, T9641 1288, 0930-1500, $7.50, children $5.50, concessions $6.50,* a $20 million private collection of classic cars and sports cars whose highlight is its grand prix racers. The cars range from an 1886 Benz to a 1979 Williams FW07 Cosworth. About 50 of them are kept in working order and are driven around the town in age order during the **Festival of the Cars** in July.

In the oldest part of York, the eastern side, is the **Residency Museum** ① *Brook St, T9641 1751, Tue-Thu 1300-1500, Sat-Sun 1200-1600, $3, children $1.* The building housing the museum was constructed in the 1840-50s for the Government Resident and Magistrate. It now houses a collection of photographs, clothes and household items. In spring and autumn the town blooms with white roses, the York Rose, and the **Historical Rose Garden** ① *2 Osnaburg Rd, T9641 1469, Oct-Nov, Apr-May,* opens. It has more than 500 roses in a formal setting among rosemary and lavender, a nursery and tearoom.

York is also known for its antique shops and galleries. Most are on the main street but two good ones are just behind it. **Jah-Roc** ① *7 Broome St, T9641 2522, daily 0900-1700,* is a large gallery and studio complex. The gallery mostly shows woodcraft, and there is also a shop and café. The **Convent Gallery** ① *21 South St, Sat-Sun 1000-1700,* shows furniture, ceramics and art.

For more information contact the friendly and helpful VIC ① *81 Avon Terrace, T9641 1301, www.yorktouristbureau.com.au, 0900-1700.*

● Sleeping

Toodyay *p124*

C **River Valley Lodge**, just behind the Cola Café, T/F9574 5764, madacsi@avon.net.au. Centrally situated, 2 double, 2 family rooms plus a lounge in an unhosted block. Continental breakfast included.

D-E **Victoria**, Stirling Terr, T9574 2206. Pub accommodation, good value hotel and motel rooms, 'backpacker' rooms, cheap counter meals and à la carte on the adjacent terrace. Meals daily 1200-1500, 1800-2100. **Avonbank**, Railway Rd, T9574 2612, is the closest caravan park, has on-site vans.

Northam *p124*

Many of the other hotels have standard share rooms (**D**).

A-B **Shamrock Hotel**, 112 Fitzgerald St, T9622 1092. Has been splendidly renovated in keeping with its Victorian heritage. Rooms are luxurious without being fussy, the main bar is uncluttered and comfortable and the food is consistently good. The restaurant is mostly mid-range, open Mon-Sat 1830-2000. The café serves seriously cheap buffets Tue-Fri 1130-1430, Wed 1800-2000. Also open for cheap lunches Sat-Sun 1030-1500.

C **Liddelow on Avon**, 38 Broome Terr, T/F9622 5647. Just over the river, though close to the suspension bridge, so an easy walk to town. One of the few B&Bs in town, is a century-old.

E **Northam Guest House**, 51 Wellington St, T9622 2301. The most budget-conscious will head here, 30 basic rooms, mostly doubles, twins and singles and use of a kitchen. It ain't pretty but it is clean and very secure.

York *p124*

Unsurprisingly there are a good number of heritage and heritage-style B&Bs in the area, mostly in the **A-B** price range, though bargains can be had off-season (Dec-Mar) when Perth weekenders find it too hot.

B **Langsford House**, T9641 1440, langs ford@westnet.com.au. One of the most authentic heritage experiences, is this traditional B&B, a small brick manor full of period antiques. At peak times a bit pricey, the 4 en suite rooms can be up to half-price midweek.

B **York Cottages**, Morris Edwards Dr, T/F9641 2125, yorkcottages@wn.com.au. Modern and fully self-contained – more luxurious than their ancient counterparts. Both have open fires and can sleep up to 6.

C **Avon Motel**, 10 William St, T9641 2066. Has the cheapest en suites in town.

C **Kookaburra Dream**, T9641 2936, www.yorkbackpackerswa.com.au. A very pleasant, friendly hostel in a suitably old building with dorms and twins. Good facilities and extras make this the best budget option.

C-D **Castle**, 97 Avon Terr, T9641 1007, castlehotel@westnet.com.au. The best of the 3 pubs in town. Its renovations have been in a simpler style and much truer to its Victorian origins. The more expensive motel rooms are en suite, more comfortable, and larger than the hotel rooms, but lack the latter's simple character.

Mt Bakewell Caravan Park, 2 km north of town on Eighth Rd, T9641 1421. Well-managed with well-equipped on-site vans.

● *For an explanation of sleeping and eating price codes used in this guide, see inside the*
● *front cover. Other relevant information is found in Essentials, see pages 40-46.*

Eating

Toodyay p124

†-†**Cola Café**, Stirling Terr, T9574 4407, is the town's best café, a shrine to that great god of commerce. Styled as an American diner, specialities are burgers and omelettes, shakes, juices and of course the great drink itself. Open daily 0900-1700, Fri 1830-2100.

Northam p124

†-†**Fitzgeralds Hotel**, 174 Fitzgerald St, T9622 5511. A good eating alternative to the Shamrock, considerably hipper, does cheap lunches daily 1200-1400 and mid-range evening meals 1800-2100. A long terrace in the adjacent pedestrianized street is a good spot for lunch or a drink and it has live bands every Fri.

†**Café Fiumé**, in the VIC building. The veranda here is a pleasant place for a light lunch or coffee. It hangs over the riverbank. Open daily 0900-1700.

York p124

†**Greenhills Inn**, 8 Greenhill Rd, 22 km from York along the road to Quairading, T9641 4095. If time and transport allow try to get out to this pub, has loads of character, full of antiques and an interesting mix of locals. The restaurant does excellent modern Australian meals, about $40 for a 3-couse set menu. Bed and breakfast is also available (**B**).

†-†**Café Bugatti**, 104 Avon Terr, T9641 1583. The town favourite with great coffee and a good range of traditional Italian dishes such as osso buco and veal parmigiana, and cheap pasta. Warm timber dining room lined with motoring memorabilia. Open Wed-Mon 0900-1500, Fri-Sat 1800-2000.

†-†**Castle** pub, 97 Avon Terr. Serves a range of unpretentious but very palatable meals from 1200-1430 Wed-Sun and 1800-2030 daily, with seriously cheap counter meals also available. On a sunny day the rear courtyard is a great spot for scran or a drink.

†**Jah-Roc Café**, 13 Broome St, T9641 2447. Funky café within the mill complex making casual café food such as burgers and salads. Daily 1000-1700, Fri-Sat 1800-2000.

†**Jules Shoppe**, 119 Avon Terr, T9641 1832. A good spot for a bite of lunch with a few tables on the pavement. Wholesome food including falafel, kebabs, veggie sandwiches, homemade pastries, biscuits and muffins. Open Thu-Tue 0800-1700.

†**Yorky's Coffee Carriage**, South St, T9641 1554. Novel café in a railway carriage parked by the riverbank. Basic outdoor seating and a simple cheap menu of morning and afternoon tea, burgers, fish and chips, quiche and lasagne. Open Thu-Sun 1000-2000.

Transport

TransWA Prospector train service leaves **East Perth** for **Toodyay** and **Northam** (1½ hrs) 1-2 times a day, continuing on to **Kalgoorlie**. Their GS2 bus service to **Albany** calls at both **Northam** and **York** (2 hrs), departing at 0900 Mon, Fri, 1700 Tue, 0945 Wed, 1800 Fri, and 1300 Sun.

South of Perth

The coast immediately south of Fremantle is not the state's prettiest and the region sometimes gets dismissed as a serious destination. From Rockingham the scenery improves, however, and both Rockingham and Mandurah do have their charms, not least the dolphins that live in the waters off both cities. There are tours to see or even swim with dolphins, and the experience here or in Bunbury is usually considerably richer than up at Monkey Mia. Inland the Darling Range continues south and harbours several forested parks and reserves, which reward the time and effort required to visit them. ▸▸ *For Sleeping, Eating and other listings, see pages 132-136.*

The coast to Rockingham

There may be a lot of coast between Fremantle and Rockingham, but it's not the sort of coast that need detain you. The area does seem to attract recreational and theme parks, however, and these may be worth a look if time allows.

Araluen Botanic Park ① *Croyden Rd off Brookton Highway, T9496 1171, www.araluenbotanicpark.com.au, 0900-1800. $7, children $4*, is thought by many to be the best of its kind around Perth. Set amongst the waterfalls, rock pools and tall woodland of the hills, the park features exotic species such as magnolias, rhododendrons and camellias and is known for wonderful flower displays. Facilities include BBQs, picnic areas, a restaurant and takeaway kiosk. Best in spring, especially when the tulips are out.

Aviation Heritage Museum ① *on the corner of Kwinana and Leach Highways, T9311 4470, www.raafawa.org.au, 1000-1600, $12, children $5, concessions $8, bus No 866 from Perth or Rockingham*, is one of the country's best military aircraft museums, with over 30 planes. There's a selection from the Second World War, including a Lancaster bomber, and several Australian aircraft. A separate wing documents the development of flight and space travel.

Cables Waterski Park ① *3 Troode St off Rockingham Rd, Spearwood, T9418 6111, 0945-2000 Nov-Apr, Mon-Fri 1145-1900 and Sat-Sun 0945-1900, May-Oct; pools $4, skiing $18 per hr, waterslides $6, slingshot $25*, has a range of activities in and out of the water, including cable waterskiing, waterslides and pools, mini-golf, children's playgrounds the 'slingshot' upside-down bungy.

Adventure World ① *179 Progress Dr, Bibra Lake, T9417 9666, www.adventure world.net.au, 1000-1700 Oct-Apr (closed Tue-Wed school days), $36, children $29, concessions $32*, is a theme park incorporating a wildlife park and over 30 fairground rides and attractions. On the same road is **Bungee West** ① *T9417 2500, call for opening times*, offering bungy jumps and abseils down their purpose-built tower.

Rockingham → *Colour map 2, grid B2. Population: 72,000. 30 km from Fremantle and Mandurah.*

The coast south of Fremantle extends along three long bays, each overlooked by suburbs, naval establishments and industry. **Mangles Bay**, the furthest south, is sheltered to the west by Garden Island and forms the northern shore of a roughly square peninsula now occupied for the most part by the city of Rockingham and its suburbs. A thin line of dunes or grassy foreshore just separates these developments from the many excellent beaches that slope gently into relatively calm seas. The combination of usually flat water plus afternoon breezes can make southern **Safety Bay** a popular spot for windsurfers. Its foreshore is virtually undeveloped, with just a few beach facilities, including BBQs, toilets and picnic tables around the junction of Safety Bay and Malibu Roads. **Rockingham Beach**, on the north shore, does have a few cafés and a couple of hotels. The roads leading away from this beach also mark the original commercial centre of the city, though there are larger and more modern shops and services along Read Street in the centre of the peninsula. The waters around the peninsula teem with wildlife and have been declared a marine park, see Penguin Island below. The **VIC** ① *43 Kent St, T9592 3464, www.rockinghamwa.com, Mon-Fri 0900-1700, Sat-Sun 0900-1600*, close to Rockingham Beach, acts as an agent for much of the city's holiday homes.

Penguin Island

① *T9528 2004, www.annabella.net/seatours.html, penguin feeds $5, children $3.30, concessions $4.40, half price for ferry passengers, island ferry $12.50 return, children $9.50, concessions $11.50, island cruises $28.50, snorkel cruises $35-59.*

Just off the southwest corner of the Rockingham Peninsula, opposite the third main beach area off Arcadia Drive, is tiny Penguin Island, known locally as 'Pengos'. Just 1 km long it has the feel of a miniature Rottnest, a similar landscape of scrub overlying undulating dunes on a limestone base. There are no quokkas here, but there are birds by the thousand, including seagulls, shearwaters, terns and a substantial colony of fairy penguins. Because of this riot of birdlife, and also a few visiting sea lions, the island is a sanctuary, and is mostly off-limits. You can access many of its

⁙ Fairy penguins

Also known as Little penguins, these tiny birds, the smallest penguins, have colonies right around Australia's southern coasts. The Penguin Island colony is the largest in WA with about 600 breeding pairs. They like to nest in small natural caverns, under thick vegetation or in sand burrows. They spend most of the day out at sea feeding, normally only coming in at dusk or even remaining out at sea for several days. Activity on land increases around March when they start to get frisky. Egg laying happens from May to October with incubation taking about 35 days.

beaches, plus the Island Discovery Centre, an information kiosk with a small, enclosed amphitheatre behind. At the centre of several rows of seating is a large glass tank, freely accessible to wild penguins, many of which know they'll get a modest feed there at 1030, 1230 and 1430 daily (weather permitting). This is well worth a look even though you are likely to see penguins while walking around the island. Another key attraction of the island is the wealth of snorkelling to be done just off its beaches, particularly the eastern ones where there is a small wreck. While on the island you may see sea lions on the beach, and they or dolphins may come and check you out while

⁙ *Wading out to the island along the narrow sandspit is not recommended. Dozens of people get stranded, and several have drowned.*

snorkelling. Snorkel hire is available at the kiosk by the jetty opposite the island ($15 per day), and sea kayak hire ($13 per hour). There are surf breaks on the western side of the island. There are also a variety of cruises around the island to see and swim with the local sea lions.

Serpentine National Park → *Colour map 2, grid B2. 55 km from Perth, 30 km from Rockingham.*

This park is named for the river that flows through it and is dammed at two locations. The **Serpentine Falls** are the main attraction and accessible by an easy 15-minute walk from a picnic site. The falls are not high; the river flows over smooth and gently sloping granite into a pool and is only really impressive after good rains. There is a popular campground on the northeastern side, accessible from the small town of **Jarrahdale**, a timber town for workers cutting jarrah in the area. The park was originally set aside as a flora and fauna reserve in the 1890s when local naturalists realised all their timber would soon be gone. Unfortunately, the reserve only lasted for a couple of decades until the government permitted it to be cleared for orchards but the falls area was retained. It is a pleasant place for a picnic or walk and just off the main South Western Highway. There are good views of the plain from Baldwins Bluff, a walking trail through woodland to the granite bluff above (6 km, two hours).

Mandurah → *Colour map 2, grid C2. Population: 50,000. 110 km from Bunbury, 20 km from Pinjarra.*

Mandurah straddles the Mandurah Estuary, a narrow channel that flows into **Peel Inlet**, an enormous body of water just to the south of the town. Naturally water activities dominate, and the place is in the process of transforming itself from a sleepy seaside town into an expensive and desirable place to live. During the late 1980s and the 1990s new suburbs were created on the south side of the estuary by digging canals, now full of flashy homes with boats tied at the door. The northern side is presently under development as a residential ocean marina. Things will change further when the freeway and train line from Perth reach Mandurah in a few years time. The town has traditionally had a large retiree population and is also popular with WA families during school holidays for boating, fishing, and swimming.

Mandurah is closely identified with crabs, which can be picked up in the estuary and are celebrated in an annual crab festival in March. Dolphins are also often seen in the estuary and are the focus for regular boat cruises. Two of the best beaches are Blue Bay and Silver Sands, both calm swimming beaches.

Mandurah was settled by Thomas Peel in 1830. The name is a corruption of the Noongar word *mandja* meaning meeting place. Peel and others were settlers from the Swan River colony who chose land grants in this area to develop for agriculture. Many surviving buildings such as **Christ's Church** and those of **Café Pronto** date from the 1870-1890s when the town developed, thanks to sawmilling nearby and the arrival of the railway. There are few recognizably old buildings left but the oldest part of town is the land around the junction of Mandurah Terrace, Pinjarra Road and the old bridge. There is a small museum here, **Mandurah Community Museum** ① *Tue, Sun 1300-1600, donation*, in school buildings dating from 1900. The old bridge spans the estuary at the southern end of Mandjar Bay, and the struts underneath are a very popular fishing spot. Cross the bridge to see one of Mandurah's oldest buildings, **Halls Cottage** ① *Sun 1000-1600*. Built in 1832 by farmer Henry Edward Hall, it has been restored and heritage listed. To see more pick up a brochure for the heritage artwalk trail from the VIC. Back on the eastern bank is another old house that once belonged to a local named Tuckey, who had a fish cannery next door. Tuckey's house is now used for the best commercial gallery in the area, **Fishbone** ① *1 Mandurah Terr, T9535 2111, Tue-Sat 1000-1700, Sun 1200-1700, free*, and there are plans to combine the gallery site with a pub. The gallery sells local work: paintings, ceramics, sculpture and furniture. Another gallery worth a look is the one in the **Mandurah Performing Arts Centre** ① *T9550 3900, free, Mon-Fri 0900-1700, Sat 1000-1600, Sun 1300-1700*, the glass-fronted building that dominates the boardwalk precinct.

The **VIC** ① *75 Mandurah Terrace, T9550 3999, www.peeltour.net.au, Mon-Fri 0900-1630, Sat-Sun 0930-1600*, sits just behind the attractive boardwalk area at the northern end of Mandjar Bay.

Down the coast to Bunbury

The 100-odd km south to Bunbury can be covered by heading inland to Pinjarra, with perhaps a diversion to Dwellingup then south on the South Western Highway, see below. Slightly slower is the Old Coast Road. After staying close to the coast for about 10 km, this road cuts slightly inland, the long **Yalgorup National Park** separating it from the sea. The park preserves a large area of coastal vegetation, particularly Tuart and Peppermint woodlands, and also encompasses several lakes. The largest of these, **Clifton Lake**, is the very rare home of a colony of **thrombolites** – small, dome-like structures built up by the photosynthetic process of billions of microbes. The process involves drawing in water rich in calcium carbonate and this slowly accumulates in layers as the microbes die. (This is a different process to that which forms the stromatolites in Cervantes and Shark Bay which are basically layers of sediment trapped in slime.) The thrombolites line the wide white shore of Lake Clifton as far as the eye can see and make an arresting site on a fine day. A boardwalk has been built a short way out over the water, ensuring a close-up view of a scene that would have been a lot more common 600 million years ago. To get to the boardwalk follow the sign for the **Cape Bouvard Winery** about 27 km south of Mandurah. The winery, open daily and about 3 km off the highway, is 100 m from the boardwalk and they have a large lawn and picnic tables available for customers and tasters. A second access point to the park is off Preston Beach Road, about 10 km south of the thrombolites.

Shortly before Bunbury, about 6 km after the turn-off to Binninup Beach, take the right-hand Cathedral Road. The adjacent unsealed Buffalo Road heads into **Leschenault Peninsula Conservation Park**, another area of preserved coastal vegetation, also with a campground. Cathedral Road is the scenic route into Bunbury, hugging the shore of picturesque Leschenault Inlet and passing early on by a couple

⦂ The 'Battle' of Pinjarra

Pinjarra, named for the local Bindjareb tribe, was settled early in the colony's history. As such, it swiftly became a flashpoint of antagonism between the indigenous people and the settlers, both sides wanting control of the relatively fertile land. A series of incidents finally led the Bindjareb to seek blood retribution on the invaders and a young man called Hugh Nesbit was speared to death in an ambush. This prompted Captain Stirling to take action. In an act of punitive revenge, he and about 25 other well-armed men ambushed the Bindjareb at a site just south of the town on 28 October 1934. Accounts vary as to the immediate effects on the people, Stirling estimated about 15 killed, all men. Bindjareb oral histories put the figure well above this, possibly over 100, and most of these women and children. The long-term effect on the Bindjareb was dire. The survivors did not dare take on the settlers again and had to simply retreat in the face of their expansion. One of their own customs forbade the eating of certain totemic animals after an older custodian had died. This, coupled with the loss of available resources, almost certainly led to hardship and starvation.

of spots where you would be unlucky not to see a fair mob of kangaroos. At the end turn right back onto the Old Coast Road then right again after the bridge into Estuary Drive. This brings you out onto Koombana Drive, turn right to head into the centre of Bunbury, see page 142.

Pinjarra → *Colour map 2, grid C2. Population: 2,000. 85 km from Perth, 24 km from Dwellingup.*

A medium-sized service town, Pinjarra straddles both the Murray River and South Western Highway about 20 km inland from Mandurah. There is a long, lawned riverside park on the western bank, overhung with gum trees, with a few picnic tables and a BBQ next to the pedestrian suspension bridge. Opposite this, and also near the road bridge, is the **Edenvale Complex**. This small group of buildings dates back to the 1880s and includes the impressive house built by a prominent local parliamentarian, Edward McLarty. One of his sons, Duncan Ross, became Premier of WA in 1947 and the house has a long association with state politics. Part of the house is now the town's **VIC** ⓘ *T9531 1438, Mon-Fri 0900-1700, Sat-Sun 1000-1600*. The rear part is a tearoom. Much of the rest of the complex is now used for art and craft shops and studios. See page 136 for details of the Etmilyn Forest Tramway.

  Ravenswood Sanctuary is a large residential and golf development 3 km west of Pinjarra. It is home to **Bellawood Parrots** ⓘ *T9531 1457, Wed-Mon 1000-1600*, one of WA's best parrot centres, with two large walk-through aviaries, 50 of Australia's 55 parrot species, walking trails and a 'treetop' boardwalk.

Dwellingup → *Colour map 2, grid C2. Population: 400. 24 km from Pinjarra.*

Still a timber milling town, Dwellingup is a sleepy settlement in the hills surrounded by extensive jarrah forests. Although it has a long history in the timber felling and milling industry there is little of this heritage left to speak of as most of the town was razed to the ground by a fierce bushfire that swept through in 1961. The focus of the town is now switching more and more to providing activities that best show off the extensive natural attractions around the town, primarily the forest and the Murray River. Facilities are modest, including a pub, store, post office and an expensive petrol station. See page 136 for details of the Etmilyn Forest Tramway.

Around Perth South of Perth

North of town the **Forest Heritage Centre** ① *Acacia St, T9538 1395, www.forest heritagecentre.com.au, 1000-1700, $5.50, children $2.20, concessions $4.40, signposted 1 km from the VIC*, is a leaf-shaped set of buildings showcasing the process of carpentry from 'forest to furniture'. Outside are several bushwalks, from 5 to 20 minutes long, each focusing on a different aspect of the forest, from Aboriginal use to tree types, canopy viewing to wildflowers. Inside are a forest interpretative centre, carpentry workshops and finally a gallery and shop selling exquisite handmade wooden furniture and turned items. West of town the **Marrinup Reserve** is the site of an old Second World War internment camp, now a pleasant picnic and bushwalking spot.

The **VIC** ① *Marrinup St, opposite the pub, T9538 1108, www.murray.wa.gov.au, 1000-1500*, and has a good range of local maps and guides. The local **CALM** office ① *Banksiadale Rd, T9538 1078, dwell.dis@calm.wa.gov.au*, is close by.

Lane Poole Reserve → *Colour map 2 grid C2.*

① *T9538 1078, camping $10 per night for 2 adults, firewood available in Dwellingup, but gas stoves only are allowed from Dec-Mar, detailed map and guide available at the VIC, the best time to visit the forests around Dwellingup are spring and autumn.*

South of Dwellingup, 7 km down Nanga Road, is the northern boundary of Lane Poole Reserve, an extensive area of pretty jarrah aand marri forest through which the Murray River runs for several dozen kilometres. There are a number of bush and riverside campsites, most with fireplaces, picnic tables and toilets. The Bibbulmun Track passes through the reserve and the river, though long and flat in parts, has some stretches of white water, particularly during winter and spring. There are also other walking and mountain-biking trails, and lots of swimming spots. The roads within the reserve are unsealed.

Dryandra Woodlands → *Colour map 3, grid A4. 160 km from Perth, 140 km from Dwellingup.*

Dryandra is within the wheatbelt region and is a vital remnant of the kind of vegetation that used to cover the area before it was cleared for farming. The reserve is formed from 17 blocks of bush and is a major focus of conservation in the state. Species of mammals that were nearly extinct have been saved by Western Shield, a CALM programme of wildlife conservation, involving fox control and breeding enclosures. The park is best known for the numbat, an ant and termite-eating marsupial that feeds in daylight hours but is difficult to see because of its keen senses of hearing and smell. This striped creature looks a bit like a large squirrel and can stand on its hind legs. You'll need to stay upwind or it will scamper off as soon as it gets a whiff of you. Other rare animals of the Dryandra are the woylie and tammar wallaby. The reserve is also a haven for birds and bird-spotters have counted about 130 species here. The woodland is open, consisting mostly of wandoo, powderbark and brown mallet, with many walk trails looping through the bush. It is a special and peaceful place where you may see some of WA's rarest animals if you are patient. A nocturnal viewing area should be completed shortly and this will allow viewing of some of the older mammals of the breeding program. The nearest town to pick up supplies is Narrogin, a large farming community 27 km east, and you can get CALM brochures on Dryandra from the Narrogin VIC ① *Earl St, T9881 2064, Mon-Fri 0930-1630, Sat-Sun 1000-1600.*

● Sleeping

Rockingham *p128*

Self-contained apartments, units and holiday homes are the big thing in Rockingham. Many apartments and homes can only be rented by the week, contact the VIC for options. There are a number of B&Bs in town, all priced around $80-90.

L-B Beachside Apartments, 58 Kent St, T9529 3777, www.annabella.net/beachside. html. At the top end of the market with several smart modern 1 to 3-bedroom apartments overlooking the Rockingham foreshore and beach.

C **Pelican's Landing**, 352 Safety Bay Rd, T9592 3058, www.pelicans.com.au. Has the best ocean views over Safety Bay from its breakfast and lounge room. Some en suite.

C **Waikiki Hotel** pub, 434 Safety Bay Rd, T9592 1388, right opposite the main southern beach facilities. Has 16 comfortable motel units, refurbished.

D **CWA Apartments**, 108 Parkin St, T9527 9560, 200 m back from northern Palm Beach. At the budget end of the market.

Mandurah *p129*

Most accommodation in town is holiday units and houses. Contact the VIC for more options as it acts as a booking service. Thanks to Mandurah's proximity to Perth occupancy and prices rise at weekends and on public and school holidays. Book ahead at these times.

L-A **Dolphin Houseboats**, T9535 9898, www.dolphinhouseboats.com. Ocean Marina. Attractive and comfortable 6- or 8-berth houseboats. Most with bunks, kitchen, bathroom and eating area. Price applies to boat so good value for 4-8. Prices rise steeply for weekends and public holidays.

L-A **Quest Apartments**, 20 Apollo Pl. T9535 9599, www.questapartments.com.au. Elegant serviced apartment complex on the southern shore, the town's only accommodation facing the canals. Apartments have 1-3 bedrooms and full kitchen, complex also has BBQs, pool, spa and boat pens.

B-C **Atrium**, 65 Ormsby Terr, T9535 6633, www.the-atrium.com.au. Multi-storey hotel with 118 smart a/c rooms around a central atrium furnished with plants and indoor pool. Also restaurant, outdoor pool, BBQs, tennis courts, saunas.

C **Foreshore Motel**, 2 Gibson St. T9535 5577, mandurahforeshore@bigpond.com. Good location a few steps from the foreshore café strip, a/c rooms with TV, phone, fridge, tea/coffee.

C-D **Mandurah Caravan Park**, 603 Pinjarra

Rd, T9535 1171. Large park with chalets and cabins, pool, kiosk and playground.

D-E **Belvedere**, 153 Mandurah Terr, T9535 1213. Small quiet caravan park close to town centre with on-site vans and cabins.

Pinjarra *p131*

D **Exchange Hotel**, 10 George St, T9531 1209. Backs onto the riverbank and has a handful of patio tables at the rear. Rooms include a few singles. Cheap meals daily 1200-1400, Mon-Sat 1800-2000.

D-E **Fairbridge Village**, 10 km up the highway, T9531 1177, www.fairbridge.asn. au. A large activity and education centre. Now catering mainly for large groups, they have a few self-contained cottages that are good for families and small groups. Facilities include a snack shop, free sports (including swimming, tennis, adventure playground), bushwalks and BBQs. Own linen required.

Dwellingup *p131*

There are a handful of B&Bs in the forest surrounding the town.

C **Berryvale Lodge**, 1082 Williams Rd, T9538 1239, www.berryvalelodge.com.au. A large rammed-earth home with a comfortable 1st floor dedicated to guests. The owners run a berry and stone-fruit farm, so expect plenty of stewed fruit for breakfast. 1 en-suite double, double and a twin share a bathroom.

C-D **Dwellingup Community Hotel/Motel** Marrinup St, T9538 1056. A large, friendly open-plan pub with cheap counter meals, bands during the afternoon 'Sunday sesh', cheap hotel rooms, including singles, and a few external motel rooms. Meals daily 1200-1400 daily, Mon-Sat 1800-2000.

E **Forest Heritage Centre** has a few dorms suitable for backpackers.

Lane Poole Reserve *p132*

Nanga Bush Camp, T9538 1300, www. nangabush.com. Just by the entrance to the reserve (follow the main road around to the right across 'one-lane bridge'), and right by the river. Primarily catering for large school groups, they have a few self-contained bush cabins, expensive for 1-2 people, good value for 6-10.

For an explanation of sleeping and eating price codes used in this guide, see inside the front cover. Other relevant information is found in Essentials, see pages 40-46.

There are good campsites at Congelin Dam.
E Dryandra Village, T9884 5231. Comfortable self-contained accommodation within
the reserve in the settlement. Simple but
charming timber workers' cottages are
equipped with a full kitchen and BBQ but
own linen required.

● Eating

Rockingham p128

With so much ocean it's a shame not to eat
within sight of it.
❦❦ **Pengos**, at the ferry 'terminal' opposite
Penguin Island, T9528 2004. A simple café
with a surprisingly inventive lunch and
dinner menu, concentrating on seafood
and grills. Open 0800-1800 Mon-Tue,
0800-2100 Wed-Sun. Adjacent is a
takeaway kiosk with a few covered
outdoor tables, open daily 0800-dusk.
❦❦-❦ **Winstons**, T9527 1163, on the main
Rockingham Rd cappuccino strip. Open for
breakfast and meals daily 0730-2000. Snacks
and coffee outside of main mealtimes.
Pavement tables.

Mandurah p129

Picnic tables and free BBQs on the foreshore.
❦❦ **Amalfi**, Boardwalk, T9582 7144. A stylish
wood-furnished space by the water. This is a
pleasant place for coffee, mediterranean
lunches or seafood mains. Wed-Sun
1100-2100.
❦❦ **Café Pronto**, on the corner of Mandurah
Terr and Pinjarra Rd, T9535 1004. 0700-2100.
One of the best places to eat in town, this
relaxed brasserie takes up 2 historic old
houses on a busy corner. Food is a good mix
of seafood, steak and Asian dishes like
curries, stir frys and warm salads. Also more
snacky light meals (cheap), wood-fired
pizzas and extensive all-day breakfast menu.
❦❦ **Stage Door**, Mandurah Performing Arts
Centre, T9550 3900. Bar and brasserie with
stunning water views and boardwalk tables.
The menu has a great range that reflects the
variety of their punters. Seafood and grills
and plenty of lighter meals. Jazz on Sun from
1500. Daily 0900-2100.
❦ **Cicerellos**, Boardwalk, T9535 9777. A
branch of the famous Fremantle restaurant,
this place does upmarket fish and chips and

is licensed but has no table service. Pleasant
balcony tables upstairs, overlooking the bay.
Also takeaway.
❦ **Foreshore Takeway**, 25 Mandurah Terr.
Fish and chips to eat on the grass opposite.
❦ **Penang House**, 45 Mandurah Terr, T9535
8891. One of the town's most popular
restaurants. Good Chinese and Malaysian
dishes under $15. BYO. Daily 1130-1430,
1630-2100.
❦ **Ruffinos**, Scotts Plaza, 52 Mandurah Terr,
T9534 9906. Italian family restaurant with 18
types of pizza and 30 varieties of pasta.
Traditional Italian mains are mid-range.
Leave room for the gelato. BYO. Tue-Fri
1700-2100, Sat-Sun 1100-2100.
❦ **Taku Japanese Kitchen**, Scotts Plaza, 52
Mandurah Terr, T9582 7308. Small dining
room and cheap sushi, sashimi, noodles and
teriyaki meats. Also takeway. Tue-Sun
1130-1430, 1800-2130.

Cafés

Dôme, Boardwalk, T9581 1666. A franchise
café but one of Mandurah's most popular,
opening onto the boardwalk. Wonderful
coffee and cakes, light meals (cheap), daily
papers and magazines. Daily 0700-2100.
Reading Room Book Café, 15 Mandurah
Terr, T9535 1633. Welcoming and
idiosyncratic café that stands out from the
clones, with couches, books to read, games
to play and pavement tables. Wholesome,
homemade food includes light meals and
cakes. Daily 1000-1700.
Simmo's Icecream, Boardwalk. Ice-cream
choices under the slogan 'delicious
dilemmas', plus waffles, coffee and drinks in
an attractive room overlooking the Mandjar
Bay. Daily 1000-2200.

Pinjarra p131

❦❦ **Redcliffe Barn**, the most stylish eatery
around, open daily out at the **Sanctuary**.
❦ **Tea Rooms**, in the Edenbridge complex.
Open daily around 1000-1600 for lunch
and afternoon teas.

Dwellingup p131

❦❦ **Millhouse**, McLarty St, T9538 1122. The
town's little touch of class, a chic restaurant,
café and chocolate-maker that's
unfortunately only open Fri-Sun, daily some
school holidays. Hours vary so phone ahead.

▲ Activities and tours

Rockingham p128

Boat hire

Sound Boat Hire, T0402 841862. Hires out a variety of boats and water craft.

Cycling

The entire peninsula foreshore makes for a pleasant ride. Bikes can be hired during Dec-Apr from a van at Safety Bay Beach, T0411 299945, $16 for ½ day.

Diving

Subanautics Diving, T9524 4447, malibu@vianet.net.au. Organizes boat dives out to the marine park and runs courses.

Dolphin cruises

The bays around Rockingham are home to about 130 dolphins, many of whom have been become familiar with, and friendly to people.

Rockingham Dolphins, www.dolphins.com.au. Runs 2 excellent tours to see them, both operating daily between mid-Sep and May. Dolphin Watch cruise (T0409 090011, $50, children $25) leaves the Yacht Club jetty, the Esplanade, Rockingham, at 0830, returning about 1100. Swim with Dolphins cruise (T9591 1333, $165 including snorkelling gear, wetsuits and lunch) leaves the jetty at 0730, returning around 1200-1300. There are Perth bus pick-ups for both tours from the Wellington St Bus Station (costs a bit more).

Fishing

Shikari Charters, T9528 1602. Organizes deep-sea fishing trips from around $100 per person.

Mandurah p129

Boat hire/cruises

A free Mandurah Boating Guide is available at the VIC, with a map of local waters and details of boating regulations.

Mandurah Boat Hire, T9535 5877. Has runabouts and punts for hire, bait, crab nets and tackle. Daily 0700-1900. Pontoons $35-45 hr, dinghys $30 hr.

Mandurah Ferry Cruises, Boardwalk jetty, T9535 3324, www.mandurahferrycruises.com. Good-value lunch cruise up the Murray River, past canals, dolphins and the Peel

Inlet, 3-course lunch at a restaurant en route included. Tue-Sun 1000-1500, $48. Tickets on board or at VIC.

Cycling

Mandurah is very flat and ideal for cycling. For maps and routes pick up a free cycle guide from the VIC.

Cycles Mandurah, 152 Mandurah Terr, T9535 3490. Bike hire $15 day, repairs and parts. Mon-Sat 0815-1730.

Diving

Noted for wreck dives. Ask at the VIC or dive shops for locations and advice.

David Budd Diving Academy, corner of Mandurah Terr and Tuckey St, T9535 1520. Offers hire and lessons.

Mandurah Diving Academy, 17 Sholl St, T9581 2566. Offers hire and lessons.

Dolphin cruises

Swimming with wild dolphins in WA is prohibited by CALM but some operators are granted licences to permit supervized encounters.

Dolphin Encounters, T0407 090284. Mandurah's only operator, departures from VIC. The 2½-hr cruise operates Nov-Jun only in the Mandurah Estuary and it is possible to swim ($140) or watch ($90), all snorkelling equipment provided. Bookings essential. Note that tours were suspended at time of writing but it was hoped they would be operating at some point during 2005. There are also enjoyable dolphin-spotting cruises in the estuary several times a day, which also run into the canals for a gawk at the real estate.

Mandjar, T9535 3324. Leaves from boardwalk jetty at 1030, 1230, 1430 ($12, 1 hr). Tickets on board or at VIC. People swimming or boating in the estuary, near the southern shore, are also likely to see dolphins.

Fishing/crabbing

Blue Manna crabs can be caught in the Peel Inlet and Mandurah Estuary in summer and autumn. The Fisheries Dept of WA sets rules on methods, size and quantity, check with the VIC. Equipment can be hired from the boat hire businesses and **Tuckey's Tackle and Dive**, 2 Mandurah Terr.

Aqualib Marine Charters, T9535 6553. Deep sea and game fishing, skipper has been fishing Mandurah waters for 15 years.

There are 2 major golfing resorts north of Mandurah.

Meadow Springs, T9581 6360.
Secret Harbour, T9524 7133, www.secret harbourgolflinks.com.au. Links course.

Tours

Kwillana Dreaming runs excellent tours that introduce travellers to the Noongar culture and history in the Mandurah region. Eco-tour of flora and fauna, Canoe tour on Goegrup Lake and Serpentine River (both $95, 5 hrs), and half-day tours around the city ($45, 3 hrs). Bookings and pick-ups from VIC, also pick-ups from Perth.

TramsWest, T9550 3999. Buses disguised as trams run short orientation trips around town. City sights and canals, daily 1000, 1100, 1400 (45 mins). Dawesville Cut and Peel Inlet Tour, daily 1300 (1 hr). Depart from VIC, buy tickets on board.

Pinjarra p131

Etmilyn Forest Tramway, T9221 4444, www.hothamvalleyrailway.com.au, for a current timetable. From the railway station over the river this heads up to Dwellingup and beyond to the Etmilyn forest. Restored trains, some pulled by steam engines, make the journey several times a week. Steam trains are used whenever possible at weekends during May-Oct.

Dwellingup p131

Dwellingup Adventures, T9538 1127, dwgupadv@westnet.com.au. Organizes a variety of self-guided rafting and canoeing tours along the Murray. They range from half-day excursions (from $60 for a 2-person canoe), to overnight hike/canoe adventures, camping out in Lane Poole reserve (from $60 to $115 for a 2-person canoe, depending on starting point from Dwellingup). Hires out camping gear (tent plus stove $22 per day).
School of Wood, based in the Forest Heritage Centre, runs short 1-5 day courses alongside their 2-year diplomas. Participants come away with their own self-made box, chair or even mandolin, constructed from the finest WA or Tasmanian timbers, and for around half the cost you'd see it in the shop. Contact the centre for a programme, courses around $120 per day.

⊙ Transport

Penguin Island p128

A ferry leaves for the island from the third main beach area off Arcadia Drive every hour, daily, from 0900-1500, last return 1600.

Serpentine National Park p129

TransWA's *Australind* train line stops at **Serpentine** and **Pinjarra** on its way to **Bunbury**. Services leave Perth daily.

Rockingham p128

Rockingham lies under the umbrella of Perth's metropolitan bus network. There are frequent services daily: north to **Perth**, south to **Mandurah**, and also various routes around the peninsula. The main bus station is in the centre of the peninsula on the corner of Council Av and Clifton St. Aside from the metropolitan services, Rockingham lies on both **TransWA's** and **South West Coachline's** (T9324 2333) main southbound routes. Some TransWA services, which leave from the central Read St shopping centre, head for **Bunbury**, **Busselton**, and the Cape-to-Cape towns. Other buses call at Bunbury before heading through the Timber Towns to **Pemberton**. South West Coachline's have similar though shorter services, daily to **Dunsborough**, Mon-Fri to **Manjimup**.

Penguin Island p128

The ferry does not operate Jun to mid-Sep, when the island is closed to visitors.

Pinjarra p131

TransWA's *Australind* train line stops at **Serpentine** and **Pinjarra** on its way to **Bunbury**. Services leave Perth daily.

Mandurah p129

TransWA bus services leave from the corner of Sutton St and Davey St for **Bunbury**, **Busselton**, and the Cape-to-Cape towns, while others call at Bunbury before heading through the Timber Towns to **Pemberton**. South West Coachline's have similar, shorter services, **Dunsborough** and **Manjimup**. Metropolitan bus There are services from Dower St to **Rockingham** (No 168, connections to **Fremantle** Mon-Fri only on No 126), and **Perth** (No 107).

Routes east

The most direct route east is to take the highway out through Midland and Northam (see page 124) and continue on through the Goldfields towns of Coolgardie, and possibly Kalgoorlie-Boulder, to the Eyre Highway. This crosses the infamous Nullarbor Plain to Ceduna, the first major town in South Australia. The adventurous might wish to consider the unsealed Great Central Road (the 'Outback Highway'), that runs from Laverton, north of Kalgoorlie, through the isolated settlement of Warburton and then on to Yulara, the tourist resort for visitors to Uluru ('Ayers Rock').

Northam to Kalgoorlie-Boulder → *Kalgoorlie 500 km from Northam, 185 km from Norseman, 360 km from Laverton.*

The Great Eastern Highway passes through a handful of wheatbelt towns before striking out across the scrub to the original WA goldfield town of **Coolgardie**. It is possible to stay here, and then continue directly to Norseman, but **Kalgoorlie-Boulder**, www.kalgoorlieandwagoldfields.com.au, makes a much more interesting stopover and involves a detour of about 60 km. The pubs, the **Super Pit**, Langtrees brothel, and the **Mining Hall of Fame** are the principal attractions. **Norseman**, also has a still-operating goldmine, but is a much smaller town. There's little to see but this is the last opportunity to grab groceries and reasonably priced fuel before Ceduna, and the accommodation options are all very welcoming.

Great Central Road ('The Outback Highway') → *Laverton to Yulara is 1,000 km. Only diesel is available on this road.*

Laverton has the last decent supermarket and cheapest fuel before hitting the dirt road to the 'red centre'. It also has a post office, car hire, the **Desert Inn pub and motel** (T9031 1188), and **Desert Pea Caravan Park** (T9031 1072). Though it is sometimes successfully tackled in a 2WD, the Outback Highway is

> **!** *If you have the time it is definitely worth starting your eastern journey by first heading south.*

generally considered a 4WD-only route, and even then it is recommended to travel in a well-prepared and self-sufficient convoy. From Laverton, it's 315 km to the **Tjukayirla Roadhouse** (T9037 1108, diesel and meals daily 0800-1800, plus accommodation). From here it's a further 255 km to the small town of **Warburton**. Here, there is a **roadhouse** (T8956 7656, 0800-1700 during the week, 0900-1500 at the weekend). If you do get out this way, don't miss a visit to the **Tjulyuru Cultural Centre** ⓘ *T8956 7966, www.tjulyuru.com, Mon-Fri 0830-1600, donation*, part of a grand scheme to bridge the gap between the local Ngaanyatjarra and non-Aboriginal people. Further fuel and food are available at **Giles**, 230 km from Warburton, and the Docker River roadhouse, another 100 km further in NT. The **Warakurna Roadhouse** ⓘ *Giles, T8956 7344, 0830-1800 Mon-Fri, 0900-1500 Sat-Sun (NB Central Standard Time)*. For current road conditions contact T1800 013314 (WA section) and T1800 246199 (NT section). Separate permits are required for traversing Aboriginal lands in both WA and NT. Contact the **Ngaanyatjarra Council** ⓘ *8 Victoria Av, Perth, T9325 4630*, for WA, and the **Central Land Council** ⓘ *31 Stuart Highway, Alice Springs, T8951 6320*, for NT. For more information on the highway contact the **Outback Highway Development Council** ⓘ *T9323 4300, www.outback-hwy.gov.au*, or see the appropriate Westprint map.

The Eyre Highway → *Eucla 725 km from Norseman, 505 km from Ceduna.*

In a country with a lot of long, straight and quiet roads the **Nullarbor** is a legendary drive which takes on almost mythic qualities to both those who have and haven't driven it. What is really striking is how flat the entire landscape is. It is pretty likely your backside will take on the same contours after two to three days of driving but fortunately there are a few interesting stops to break the journey, such as caves and blowholes around **Cocklebiddy**, the sand dunes and beach around the telegraph station at **Eucla**, and whalewatching and spectacular cliffs at the **Head of Bight**.

The first roadhouse, 195 km from Norseman, is **Balladonia** (T9039 3453, C-E). It has an interesting heritage museum. Range of accommodation, from deluxe to backpacker and camp sites. Petrol and food available 0600-2100 summer, 0800-2030 winter.

The unmarked turn-off to **Cocklebiddy Cave** is at the rear of a small parking bay, 245 km from Balladonia, 54 km from Caiguna, and 10 km short of the Cocklebiddy Roadhouse. One of many huge caves under the plain, this is the most accessible and a rewarding excursion. The track, rough but fine for 2WD when dry, passes a sign for Nuytsland Nature Reserve after 100 m then interweaves its way for 10 km to the cave. Wear sturdy shoes for the steep and rocky climb down and take a good torch each. If you've any plans to stay in the area, take the time to stay at the **Eyre Bird Observatory** (T9039 3450, B), occupying an old telegraph station 40 km off the highway from the roadhouse and right on the coast. Staff will collect you if you are in a 2WD vehicle. All-inclusive except for linen, advance bookings essential. Recommended. The highway drops down through the Madura Pass 95 km after Cocklebiddy, to the **Madura Pass Oasis** (T9039 3464, 0630-2000, D-E), a large resort-style roadhouse at the base of the escarpment. Halfway along the next 185 km to Eucla, the **Mundrabilla Roadhouse** (T9039 3465, 0530-2300, D) has the cheapest petrol for several hundred kilometres in either direction.

Eucla makes a good stop just before the South Australian border. It was home to one of Australia's busiest telegraph stations in the 1880s, sending more than 11,000 messages a year, but the ruins of the station and the old settlement are disappearing fast under sand dunes. **Eucla** (T9039 3468, 0600-2200, C-E) has motel, budget rooms and camping. A large fibreglass whale and a disconcerting snake collection distinguish the **Nullarbor Roadhouse** (T8625 6271, 0700-2200, C-E), 190 km from Eucla. Motel units and backpacker type accommodation. **Whale watching flights** (in spring) can be taken from here. Contact **Whale Air** ① *T8625 6271*, who also flies a 3½-hour Nullarbor Air Safari. The turn for the Head of Bight, a cliff-top whale watching platform, is another 15 km, and the large town of **Ceduna** a further 285 km.

⁑ Footprint features

Introduction

Some of the most beautiful and varied country in Western Australia is packed into the southwest, particularly the neat rectangular notch of the Capes region. Within 100 km or so lie flawless beaches, a classy wine region, sophisticated restaurants and galleries and acres of tall forests. From Cape Naturaliste to Cape Leeuwin you can go caving in limestone caves, reef and wreck diving, surf some of Australia's best waves, walk some of its best coastal trails, watch whales in winter, and swim with dolphins further north in the region's main town of Bunbury. What are few and far between are high-rise blocks, traffic jams and crowded beaches. It's the kind of place that people come for a day and stay for a week, with plenty to keep you occupied for double that time.

Naturally this abundance of natural beauty is no secret. It is Western Australia's favourite corner for a holiday and this means it is still relatively the busiest and most developed area outside Perth. For all that, this region simply can't be missed. If you want to escape there are still plenty of wild and quiet places to be found in the southwest, from cool remanants of woodland like that around Wellington Dam to beaches, such as Cosy Corner and Indijup, that stay miraculously free of the main crowd.

Don't miss...

1 **Koombana Bay** Meet the inquisitive dolphins, page 145.
2 **Busselton** Dive or snorkel off the jetty to see vivid soft corals and sponges, page 147.
3 **Cape-to-Cape Track** Walk some of the track, page 152.
4 **Wine tasting** Spend a day or two wine tasting in the Margaret River region, page 160.
5 **Margaret River** See the flying display at the Eagles Heritage Centre, page 162, and take a canoe trip of discovery up the river, page 160.
6 **Cosy Corner** Have a swim or a walk on this beach, page 165.
7 **Jewel Cave** Visit this spectacular cave, near Augusta, page 165.
8 **Augusta** Witness a humpback whale breaching off Augusta, page 165.

Ins and outs

Getting there and around
The ideal way to explore this region is to drive yourself as there is so much to see and no great distances to endure. There are two main routes south from Perth to Bunbury: the coastal route via the Kwinana Freeway and Old Coast Road; or the inland route, the South Western Highway. From Bunbury, the inland route veers southeast, reaching the coast at Walpole. To reach the southwest coast, take the Bussell Highway southwest to Busselton. Once in the Capes region there are two main routes to Augusta. The Bussell Highway is the faster and most direct inland route, passing through Cowaramup and Margaret River. Caves Road runs parallel to the highway but is closer to the coast. This is a narrow and windy route but definitely the more scenic, providing access to the caves and beaches of the region.

For those relying on public transport **TransWA** coaches leave the East Perth Terminal to Bunbury (three hours), Busselton (four hours), Dunsborough (4½ hours), Yallingup, Margaret River (5½ hours), and Augusta (six hours) at 0830 and 1220 Sunday-Thursday, 0830 and 1700 Friday. **South West Coachlines**, T9324 2333, buses leave from the City Bus Port, Mounts Bay Road, daily at 0845, 1315 and 1745 for Bunbury and Busselton, with connections for Dunsborough. There are no train services in this area except for the TransWA *Australind* line between Perth Railway Station and Bunbury. Two services daily (2¼ hourrs). ⇥ *See individual transport sections for more details.*

Best time to visit
The region has a mild climate but is at its best in summer, although spring and autumn are also very pleasant. Winter (June-August) is often cold (15-18°C) and wet, although excellent for whale watching around Augusta. The southwest coast is an extremely popular holiday destination for the people of Perth so all weekends, public holidays and school holidays are busy but the whole region gets booked out well in advance over summer (Christmas to end January) and prices rise accordingly.

Geographe Bay

The long sweep of Geographe Bay from Bunbury to Cape Naturaliste provides some of this region's calmest and warmest beaches, particularly the further west you travel, culminating in crescents of serene perfection close to the tip of the Cape. Of the three towns on this bay, Bunbury is the second largest city in the state but still has wild dolphins swimming into a city beach most days. Busselton and fast expanding Dunsborough are sleepier holiday towns offering superb water activities such as reef and wreck diving, whale watching and looking at the marine life under Busselton jetty as it hangs in the current like party streamers. ⇥ *For Sleeping, Eating and other listings, see pages 148-152.*

Bunbury → *Colour map 3, grid A2. Population: 28,000. 180 km from Perth, 100 km from Margaret River, 160 km from Pemberton.*

Sitting on Koombana Bay, at the northern end of the beautiful sweep of Geographe Bay, is Bunbury, the major port for the southwest. It is far from a natural harbour though, as the original shape of the coastline has been dramatically altered by cutting a channel through the **Leschenault Peninsula** to the sea and the construction of boating and shipping harbours. Major exports include mineral sands, alumina and woodchips and, until recently, industry has come first in Bunbury and has been

Diving in the bay

The bay north of Busselton and Dunsborough is a huge sea-grass plain, known as a good place to spot the beautiful common sea dragon. As well as the amazing 'reef' under Busselton Jetty, there are two other artificial reefs in the bay, plus the limestone contour called 4-Mile Reef that runs east-west across it. This is covered in many types of corals and sponges, attracts whales and is about 18-m deep. The first Artificial Reef is a collection of constructions made from old car tyres, covering about 1 ha under about 21 m of water, and now harbouring a large array of marine life. Most recetnly, and spectacularly, the HMAS Swan is rapidly building its own collection of sealife, and is an unforgettable dive, definitely the star attraction in the bay. The warship was sunk in 1997 in 30 m of water off Eagle Bay near Dunsborough.

allowed to dominate the coastline. However in the last few years grain silos have been demolished and train yards moved to create a far more attractive foreshore. There are also plans to develop a boardwalk on the bay lined with cafés and apartments. The city's greatest natural attraction, however, is its resident population of dolphins who live in Koombana Bay and swim in to the beach regularly. Bunbury also has a sophisticated 'cappuccino strip' along Victoria Street, good shopping and beautiful ocean beaches on Geographe Bay. It's an appealing and relaxed place with the services of a large city and the slow, sunny pace of a small seaside town.

Ins and outs

Getting there There are regular bus services down the coast from Perth taking about three hours. ►► *See Transport, page 151, for further details.*

Getting around Despite its sprawling, and rapidly increasing size, the town centre is very compact and almost everything of interest can easily be reached on foot.

Tourist information The VIC ⓘ *Carmody Place, T9721 7922, www.justsouth.com. au, 0900-1700*, is housed in the former railway station in the centre of town.

Sights

A good way to take in the sights of the town is by foot. This walk starts at the VIC in the century-old railway station. Walk beside the inlet towards the roundabout. This area is known as **Bicentennial Square** and was formerly an ugly area of railyards. Head straight across to the tall, white **grain silos**. Several were demolished but these remaining ones have been heritage listed and there are plans to turn the silos into a hotel complex and the foreshore into a boardwalk precinct of cafés. The **old timber jetty** ahead, dating from 1864, was used for all shipping until the 1970s. Just to the left of the jetty are Jetty Baths Beach where you once would have seen neck-to-knee bathing costumes. Head west along Wollaston Street to reach Marlston Drive and the **Marlston Hill Lookout**. The hill was used for whale watching when that was a less innocent pastime. Follow the road around to reach Ocean Drive and walk past the black and white checked **lighthouse** to Ocean Beach. This is a good spot for a swim. The rocks here are basalt, very rare in Australia, formed from lava flow 150 million years ago. Head back towards the town centre along Clifton Street and turn right into Victoria Street. The **Bunbury Tower** dominates the street and is a useful landmark. It was built to resemble the prow of a ship and is full of private and government offices. Stroll past the shops and cafés and the **Rose Hotel**, built in 1898, then turn right up Prinsep Street to Wittenoom. The pale pink building on the corner dates from 1883 and is a former convent and chapel. The convent is now used as the **Regional Art**

Gallery and holds regular exhibitions of work by artists and craftspeople of the southwest. With your back to the tower continue along Wittenoom Street to the next corner to see one of Bunbury's oldest buildings, the old post office and courthouse (1855). Continue around the corner into Stirling Street. On the right by Anzac Park is Stirling House, built as a home for the town clerk in the 1880s. Pass the park and turn right into Parkfield Street. About 100 m down this street are the city's cathedrals. **St Patricks** ① *Hayward St, T9721 8380, 1000-1700, $5, children $3, concessions $4*, on the right, was built in 1921. Its steeple was lost in a shipwreck so it went without until 1967. The pews are made of local jarrah. The more modern **St Boniface**, on the left side, has lovely stained-glass windows and native blackbutt floors and ceiling.

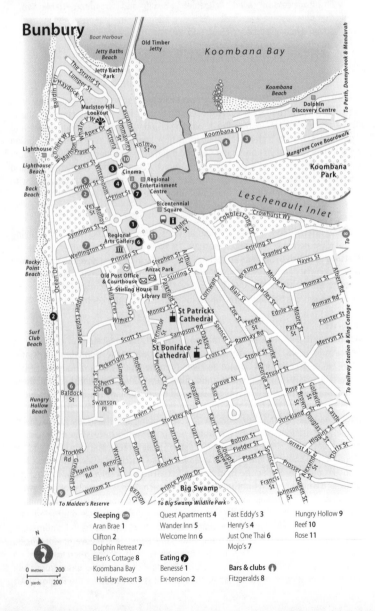

Bunbury

Sleeping 😴
Aran Brae **1**
Clifton **2**
Dolphin Retreat **7**
Ellen's Cottage **8**
Koombana Bay
   Holiday Resort **3**

Quest Apartments **4**
Wander Inn **5**
Welcome Inn **6**

Eating 🍴
Benessé **1**
Ex-tension **2**

Fast Eddy's **3**
Henry's **4**
Just One Thai **6**
Mojo's **7**

Bars & clubs 🍸
Fitzgeralds **8**

Hungry Hollow **9**
Reef **10**
Rose **11**

N

0 metres   200
0 yards   200

Retrace your steps to Stirling Street, cross the road and continue along Victoria Street, then turn right down Wellington Street to return to the VIC.

Bottlenose dolphins have been visting the beach in front of the **Dolphin Discovery Centre** for many years and it is estimated that about 100 live in Koombana Bay. To encounter these curious locals you can simply wade in off the beach, take a short cruise into the bay, kayak through their territory or go on an outstanding swim tour. See page 151 for details of the tours. The **Dolphin Discovery Centre** ① *Koombana Dr, T9791 3088, www.dolphindisco very.com.au, 0800-1700 Nov-Apr, 0900-01400 May-Oct, $4, children/concessions $2, 1.5 km from town centre,* manages dolphin beach encounters and conducts research into the Koombana Bay pods. It is a non-profit community organization run mostly by volunteers on donations and sponsorship. The centre has a small museum that explains the biology and behaviour of dolphins and other local marine creatures and shows excellent short videos about the Koombana Bay dolphins. The main attraction though is the interactive zone, an area of shallow water that has been roped off to allow encounters between dolphins and people. Volunteer guides are on hand to ensure that visitors behave correctly but you are allowed to stand waist deep in the water or even float with a mask and snorkel as the dolphins approach you. The crowds are usually small, especially if you arrive early (0800-0900) which is also when you have the best chance of seeing the dolphins. The focus is on keeping the dolphins wild so they are not fed except for a few individuals who have become used to feeding in the past. These dolphins are fed about 500 g of local fish (one to two per cent of their daily intake) but this happens irregularly and not usually in front of tourists. The dolphins generally visit the interactive zone more frequently in summer. Cruises and swim tours leave from the beach and should be booked at the centre. Facilities include a café, shop, and showers but bring own snorkel gear. The centre welcomes travellers into its volunteer programme if they are can be involved for at least three days a week for three months.

Bunbury has two **mangrove colonies** which are remarkable for their southerly position. The nearest mangroves in the state are found on the Abrolohos Islands, off Geraldton, some 600 km further north, and become more common in the far northern regions. Bunbury's mangroves are believed to date from 10,000 years ago and were once much closer to the coastline. In the years since European settlement the coastline has moved 200 m further west. There are short boardwalks through the colonies and these are a great place to see water birds. **Mangrove Cove** walk is opposite the Dolphin Discovery Centre on Koombana Drive and focuses on shipwrecks that have occurred in the bay with an artistic series of shelters and lookouts. The **Big Swamp** walk is a wetland just to the south of the city, close to the coast, and attracts water birds such as herons and swans. Long necked turtles can also be seen there. The 100-m boardwalk connects to a 2-km circuit of the swamp and a bird hide.

Adjacent to the Big Swamp is the **Big Swamp Wildlife Park**. Its main ticket office also houses a swamp interpretative centre, well worth a look if you're about to walk around the swamp and boardwalks, and entry to this is free. The wildlife park has a few free-roaming kangaroos, some emus, a wombat and a large aviary, but there's nothing here to really get excited about. On the other side of Bunbury Plaza shopping centre, is **King Cottage** ① *Forrest Av, T9721 7546, 1400-1600, $3, children $0.50, concessions $2,* the home of the pioneering King family from 1880 to 1920 and is furnished as it would have been around 1900.

Around Bunbury

Leschenault Peninsula Conservation Park

This is a long, thin peninsula of sand dunes and peppermint woodland that divides the ocean from the Leschenault inlet, just north of Australind. The park can be

⦂ Jetty tales

The Busselton Jetty is the longest in the southern hemisphere at 1,841 m. Originally constructed out of jarrah in 1865, the jetty was built to allow swifter and easier loading of timber from the shore to awaiting ships. By the early 1900s sand build-up, partly caused by the jetty itself, had extended the shoreline out some 70 m, and had decreased the depth further out. The far part of the jetty was extended in 1911 and a spur added that could carry a railway, so increasing the efficiency of loading. Shipping use continued until 1972 and in 1978 much of the original part of the jetty was destroyed by Cyclone Alby, though the railway spur and extension survived, leaving the boomerang shaped structure you see today. In 1999 a fire created a huge hole in the structure and effectively cut off the last 200 m. In this case it meant fishermen could no longer reach the end of the pier and this has been very beneficial. It has allowed the already vigorous growth of soft corals and sponges to continue unhampered, and for marine life to proliferate. Species brought down by the offshore Leeuwin Current, normally only found much further north, have found a home alongside more local inhabitants and the community under the jetty, adhering to the massive piles is spectacularly colourful.

accessed at the northern end from the Old Coast Road. Unsealed roads lead to Buffalo and Belvidere Beach, both popular for fishing and with no facilities. From the highway it is 7 km around the shore of the inlet to a lovely camping area among shady peppermint and Tuart trees. In Australind, a Discovery Centre on the foreshore provides information on the park.

Collie River Valley → *Colour map 3, grid A2. 50 km from Bunbury.*

Set amidst extensive peppermint and jarrah forests, Wellington Dam is one of Perth's principal reservoirs. There is a viewing area over the dam, and a small café (0830-1630). The Collie River flows downstream from the dam to Leschenault Inlet and there are a few bush camps on the way, including a campground at picturesque **Honeymoon Pool**, a popular swimming spot. Facilities here include fireplace BBQs (firewood supplied April-November), picnic tables, toilets and tank water. Camping fees $10 per couple. Access to the dam, and a lakeside campground, is via the sealed Wellington Weir Road that heads south from the main Coalfields Road between Bunbury and Collie. Honeymoon Pool is accessed via an unsealed road off this. For more details, T9734 2051, www.collieriver valley.org.au.

The roads south of the dam and pool are unsealed, meet up and continue south to the sealed road that threads back through the **Ferguson Valley**, a fledgling wine area, to Bunbury. Alternatively another unsealed road heads in the opposite direction through the forests to the old milling area of **Wellington Mill**. A sealed road from here heads to the tiny community of **Lowden** and the main road back to Bunbury via **Donnybrook**. The whole area is interlaced with unsealed and 4WD tracks and there are a number of isolated sleeping options.

Donnybrook → *Colour map 3, grid A2. 35 km from Bunbury, 30 km from Balingup.*

A small, well kept town, Donnybrook serves as the focus for a thriving apple orchard area. Roadside apples, and much other fruit, are commonly available but the best product of the area has to be the **Old Goldfields** ① *T9731 0311, www.oldgoldfields. com.au, Wed-Sun 0930-1630, daily in school holidays, $2, includes wine-tasting;*

wines $15, ciders $3 per small bottle, signposted off the Capel Rd. This enterprising
orchard, centred around the towering poppet-head of a now-defunct goldmine, has a
café, picnic garden, small goldfields interpretative shed and also produces wine. The
ciders are strong but smooth and include an unusual, zesty ginger brew. Backpackers
seeking casual work will find plenty of picking during November to June by contacting
the harvest office ① *T9731 2400, www.workstay.com.au*. The town has a fantastic
hostel set up specifically to cater for working backpackers, though you certainly don't
have to be picking to stay there.

Busselton → *Colour map 3, grid B2. Population: 10,500. 55 km from Bunbury, 45 km from*
Margaret River.

Busselton is a laid-back town, originally one of the main export ports for WA's timber,
now simply a relaxed family holiday town with a large number of tourist parks and
motels strung out along the Bussell Highway.

The town has a wonderful piece of heritage from its days as a port, **Busselton Jetty**
① *$2.50, children and concessions $1.50, trains daily unless windy, on the hour,*
1000-1600, tickets $7.50, children and concessions $5.50, divers with scuba equipment
$13, a very pleasant walk that conceals beneath its timbers a riot of marine life
including some amazingly colourful soft corals. There is public access to the jetty 24
hours a day, with a small charge for walkers which goes toward the jetty's restoration. It
takes about 25 minutes to walk the 1,600 m to the 'cut', but if your legs don't fancy it a
small tourist train heads out there too. The Interpretative Centre at the base of the jetty
has many superb photographs of life under the jetty's tip. By donning a mask and
snorkel and getting into the water by the weather station just before the cut you will be
able to see much of the coral and fish life living on the piles. You're still 8 m from the
bottom, however, and to really appreciate
this wonderful artificial reef up close a
scuba dive is necessary, at night if
possible. If you don't want to get wet the
new **Under Water Observatory** ① *T9754*
0900, 1000-1600, $20, children $11.50
(pier entry and train ride also);
interpretative centre free, offers the next
best thing – an opportunity to catch a lift
down into an underwater glass-walled
room located near the end of the pier.

Stretching away on either side of the
jetty the beach is a beauty, with lots of
white sand sloping gently into the clear
water. The grassy foreshore around the
jetty has plenty of shade and there are
toilets by the café. The **Old Courthouse**
Complex, at the end of Queen Street, now
houses art and craft stalls instead of
criminals. There is a tearoom in the
adjacent old post office. The **VIC** ① *38*
Peel Terr, T9752 1288, www.downsouth.
com.au, Mon-Fri 0830- 1700, Sat-Sun
1000-1400 (1600 in summer), is also the
TransWA bus terminal. South West
Coachlines stop around the corner on
Albert Street.

Busselton

Sleeping ●
Busselton
  Backpackers **1**
Caravan Parks **7**
Esplanade **2**
Geographe **3**
Jacaranda **4**
Kookaburra **5**
Paradise **6**

Eating ●
Cod Rocks **1**
Equinox **2**
Geographe Pizza **3**
Goose **4**

N

0 metres   200
0 yards   200

Southwest Coast Geographe Bay

Dunsborough → *Colour map 3, grid B1. Population: 1,500. 24 km from Busselton, 45 km from Margaret River.*

Sharing the same long north-facing beach as Busselton, Dunsborough is as much a holiday town as its neighbour, in fact more so for its proximity to Cape Naturaliste and the region's main wine area. The beach remains shallow way out to sea and there are extensive grassed and bush foreshore areas which separate it from the town. Other than heading for the beach there is not a great deal to do in the town itself, and most visitors use it as a base to explore the northern part of the Capes region, dive the **HMAS Swan** (see page 143) and head out on the various tours. The helpful **VIC** ① *T9755 3299, www.downsouth.com.au, Mon-Fri 0900-1700, to 1600 Sat, and 1000-1600 Sun*, is in the dominating Dunsborough Park Shopping Centre, and can supply details of the many private holiday homes and units available for let in the town.

● Sleeping

Bunbury *p142, map p144*

L-C Clifton, corner of Clifton and Molloy sts, T9721 4300, www.theclifton.com.au. Well placed for both the centre and back beach, this luxurious hotel has expensive suites within an impeccably refurbished Victorian manor house, Grittleton Lodge, around which the modern part of the hotel is built. The restaurant is also the best in Bunbury.

A-B Quest Apartments, corner of Koombana and Lyons Drive, T9722 0777, www.questapartments.com.au. Smart, contemporary apartments (52) in a complex a few mins walk from the town centre. 1- and 2-bed apartments have full kitchen and laundry, studio apartments have a kitchenette. Tennis court, pool and BBQs.

B Ellen's Cottage, 41 King Rd, T9721 4082. Historic self-contained farmers cottage built by a convict in 1878. Handmade beams and glass, open fires, cottage garden, and claw foot bath. Modern kitchen and laundry appliances but no TV or phone. Breakfast basket supplied.

C Aran Brae, 5 Sherry St, T9721 2177. B&B with an en-suite garden apartment, private courtyard and BBQ, and a very warm, Irish welcome.

C-D Welcome Inn, Ocean Dr, T9721 3100. Well positioned, friendly motel, overlooking the back beach and a 10-min stroll from Victoria St.

B-D Koombana Bay Holiday Resort, Koombana Dr, T9791 3900, www.kbhr.com.

au. Well maintained caravan park opposite the Dolphin Discovery Centre with 3-bedroom chalets, en-suite cabins and en-suite sites. The complex has a pool, campers kitchen, shop, café and tennis courts, and is the closest to town.

D-E Dolphin Retreat YHA, 14 Wellington St, T9792 4690, dolphinretreatbunburyyha@iinet.net.au. A smaller, family-run option.

D-E Wander Inn, 16 Clifton St, T9721 3242, wanderinnbp@yahoo.com. Excellent friendly and clean backpackers in a great location by the cafés and the beach. Singles, twins and doubles make up many of the 54 beds. Lovely, shady back garden and BBQ area, and all the usual facilities. Also bike hire. Recommended.

Donnybrook *p146*

E Brook Lodge, Bridge St, T9731 1520, www.brooklodgecom.au. Has over 80 beds, mostly in 3-bed dorms. 4 doubles have their own share kitchen and bathroom. On the edge of town, the hostel is set in large grounds and the excellent facilities include lots of outdoor areas, and 5-a-side soccer pitch. There's even a café and bar! Recommended.

Busselton *p147, map p147*

A-D Esplanade Hotel (the 'Nard'), Marine Terr, T9752 1078, www.thenard.com. Pleasant dining rooms serving cheap counter meals, front terrace tables and a

● *For an explanation of sleeping and eating price codes used in this guide, see inside the front cover. Other relevant information is found in Essentials, see pages 40-46.*

range of rooms from the simple to luxurious. Live music every Fri, meals Mon-Sat 1200-1400, daily 1800-2000, to 2030 Thu-Sat.

C Geographe, West St, T9752 1451, geoguest@iinet.net.au. B&B.

C Jacaranda, West St, T8752 1246, www.westnet.com.au/jacaranda. B&B with home-cooked food, gardens and hot spa.

C Prospect Villa, T9752 2273, prospect_villa@optusnet.com.au. This B&B is the oldest house in the town.

C-D Paradise, Pries Av, T9752 1200. The closest motel to town and one of the cheapest. Standard motel doubles plus a 'lodge' with a few good value singles, a television room and kitchenette.

E Busselton Backpackers, 14 Peel Terr, T9754 2763, backpackers@bsnbpk.com. A quiet converted home that sleeps 17 in small dorms and doubles. Nothing fancy here but it's clean and spacious, has a large covered BBQ courtyard and, like the town, is a good place to unwind.

Kookaburra, Marine Terr, T9752 1516, of a number of caravan parks along the highway, this one is the closest to the centre.

Dunsborough *p148*

Most of the really luxurious accommodation is out of town toward the cape or the wine district. There are a few budget choices, the last hostels before Margaret River.

A Ocean View, Geographe Bay Rd, T9756 8934, www.oceanview-villas.com. A complex of 4 modern, brightly coloured and cheerfully furnished houses, all facing the beach with 1st floor balconies overlooking the ocean. Each has 3 double bedrooms, small terrace and well-equipped kitchen. Recommended.

C Grevillea Cove, 5 Grevillea Cove. 1 of a handful of modern B&Bs in the town, and has a couple of en-suite doubles.

B-D Dunsborough Lakes, Caves Rd, T9756 8300. The town's only caravan park, a little out of town but spacious with a good range of facilities and entertainment.

C-E Dunsborough Inn, 50 Dunn Bay Rd, T9756 7277, www.dunsboroughinn.com. A modern brick complex, with half a dozen pretty open-plan self-contained units and a separate budget section with doubles, twins, triples and quads. Clean and comprehensive hostel-style communal facilities include a

games room and garden BBQ area. The friendly owners often take guests out on snorkelling trips when they have time.

D Dunsborough Beachouse YHA, 201 Geographe Bay Rd, T9755 3107, dunsborough@yhawa.com.au. The most homely and liveliest with 70 beds in small dorms and a few pretty doubles and twins. Fantastic beachside position with a huge rear garden overlooking the ocean, excellent facilities including bike hire. The big drawback is the 40-min walk to town, but the manager drives in a couple of times a day and gives lifts. Pick-ups usually possible if pre-arranged.

🍴 Eating

Bunbury *p142, map p144*

See also Bars and clubs below for pub fare.

¶¶¶ Louisa's, The Clifton, Clifton St, T9721 4300. As the **Grittleton** is the benchmark for Bunbury's accommodation, so Louisa's is for its restaurants. Fine heritage dining rooms complement the excellent fusion cuisine. Tue-Fri 1200-1400, Mon-Sat 1800-2100.

¶¶ Mojo's, Victoria St, T9792 5900. Sleek and stylish place offering all day breakfast and cheap café menu that varies from classy versions of nachos, burgers and fish and chips to pastas, salads and nibbles plate. Evening meals change to mid-range modern Australian, daily 0830-2200.

¶ Fast Eddy's, corner of Victoria and Clifton sts, T9791 3000. The 24-hr American diner.

¶ Just One Thai, 109A Victoria St, T9721 1205. BYO. Authentic Thai cooking with a good range of seafood dishes. The food is good enough to make this one of the city's most popular restaurants. Tue-Fri 1200-1400, daily 0600-2100. Also takeaway.

Cafés

Benessé, 83 Victoria St, T9791 4030. The best coffee on the strip can be found in this laidback understated café. Food is casual and light and it's a good place for an informal dinner as the menu stays that way in the evening. Daily 0700-2100.

Ex-tension, Ocean Dr, T9791 2141. Hanging over the beach the café is a good spot to catch a sunset, though the décor is a little ordinary. Mid-range grills and seafood, other cheap options and also a kiosk. Open Mon-Tue 0700-1500, Wed-Sun 0700-2100.

Henry's, corner of Victoria and Clifton sts, T9792 4060. Genteel style with raffia chairs, pavement tables and unhurried coffee. Mostly cheap meals, from wraps to pasta, burgers to salads.

Busselton p147, map p147

¶-¶ **Blend**, 6 Prince St, T9751 2300. Offers the best cuisine in town, including excellent breakfasts and light lunches. Most of the seating is in a shady patio courtyard. Also open all day for coffee and snacks. Open Tue-Sat 0900-2100.

¶-¶ **Equinox**, T9752 4641. A large, friendly café on the foreshore near the jetty. All tables are inside, but there are large panoramic windows overlooking the beach and jetty. Light lunches and evening meals include snacks and platters. Separate take-away kiosk has a few tables underneath the huge adjacent Moreton Bay fig trees. Daily 0800-2100, kiosk to 1800, later peak summer.

¶ **Codrocks**, Kent St. One of the takeaways includes this fish and chip shop, open daily to 2000, which also sells fresh and frozen seafood.

Dunsborough p148

¶¶¶ **Bay Cottage**, Dunn Bay Rd, T9755 3554. An unassuming looking restaurant on the outskirts of town whose modern Australian food is excellent, with service to match. Open Tue-Sat 1800-2030. Recommended.

Cafés/delicatessen

Artézen, 234 Naturaliste Terr, T9755 3325. Best value in town, this chic but earthy café serves an interesting range of light meals including crêpes, salads and pitta pizzas, and is a good spot to chill out. Recommended.

Newberry, 6 Newberry Rd, off Naturaliste Terr, T9755 3631. Combines a bookshop, gallery and café. Tue-Sun 1000-1600.

Bay Gourmet, 233 Naturaliste Terr, T9756 8368. One of a few delicatessens selling fine foods. Prepare picnic hampers and platters.

Dunsborough Bakery, 14 Naturaliste Terr. Renowned for quality bread and pastries.

🅐 Bars and clubs

Bunbury p142, map p144

Fitzgeralds, 22 Victoria St, T9791 2295. In a former warehouse, this pub stands out from the crowd. The old brick walls are hung with rare Guinness prints, there is a mellow room full of richly upholstered couches and a spacious outdoor courtyard. Friendly staff and great, cheap bar meals 1800-2200. Open Thu-Sat 1800-0300, Sun 2000-2400. Recommended.

Hungry Hollow, 316 Ocean Dr, T9791 5577. The only pub with views over the ocean, this cheerily decorated brasserie does breakfast at weekends and meals daily.

Reef, Victoria St, T9791 6677. Bunbury's principal party pub. Lots goes on here, mostly Wed-Sat, and it all goes on until the early hours. Check out their collection of odd-shaped pool tables.

Rose, Victoria St, T9721 4533. This 100-year-old pub with iron lace verandas is an elegant place for a drink, and is often where the evening starts for Bunbury locals. Large range of imported beers and 40 wines by the glass. Cheap bar meals and snacks 1200- 1400, 1800-2000. Also 25 motel rooms and 10 hotel rooms with shared facilities (**C-D**).

Dunsborough p148

Dunsborough Tavern, T9755 3657, is the only pub. It has a large open-plan bar serving cheap counter meals daily 1200-1400, with cover bands on Fri and DJs on Sat.

🅔 Entertainment

Busselton p147

Cinema, 27 Albert St, T0418 933556, single screen showing a thoughtful range of current releases. Also advise what's on at the drive-in screen further down the highway.

Grand Cinemas, corner of Victoria and Clifton sts, T9791 4455.

Nautical Lady is a centre with a range of activities for children including mini-golf, water slides, in-line skate area and flying fox, each costing from $2.50-5 for a go or session. Their lookout tower is a good place to get a photo of the jetty, $2.50. Open daily 0930-2130 summer, 1000-1700 winter.

Regional Entertainment Centre, Blair St, T9791 1133. Regular performances of music, dance, theatre and film.

○ Shopping

Bunbury *p142, map p144*
Bunbury Book Exchange, 20 Prinsep St.
Sells second-hand books.
Busselton Books, 26 Queen St. Also sells
second-hand books.
Dymocks, Prince St. New books for sale.
Rose and Leo's Book Exchange, 42
Wellington St. Second-hand books.
Youngs, Stephen St, T9721 5004.
Sells new books.

▲ Activities and tours

Bunbury *p142, map p144*
Taking a boat cruise into the bay allows
you to see the dolphins in their own
environment and engaging in natural
behaviour such as catching fish or raising
calves. There are several pods living in the
bay and the tour operators **Naturaliste
Charters** usually know where the dolphins
can be found. They love riding the bow wave
and the guides swear they line up to take
turns at it. During the summer, the swim
tours take a similar route by boat but stop at
places the dolphins are known to engage in
play. Swimmers don wetsuits and snorkelling
gear and jump in for about 15 mins at a time.
To see the dolphins underwater, hear them
clicking and whistling and have them swim
around you is an unforgettable experience.
Do keep in mind that while sightings are
likely, they are not guaranteed.
Dolphin cruise daily 0930, 1100, 1400. $33,
children $22, concessions $27-30.
Swim tour daily 0800, 1100, Dec-Apr. $115.
Bookings at the discovery centre, T9791
3088, www.dolphindiscovery.com.au.
South West Yacht Charters, T9721 7664,
www.swyachtcharters.com.au. This outfit has
a variety of yachts for hire, and sailing courses.

Busselton *p147, map p147*
Each of the 2 dive operators offer regular
boat dives to the jetty and the *Swan* and
equipment hire. Contact both to see what
they're running and who's got places. Expect
to pay from $150 for a 2-dive trip including
gear, and $70-100 for a single jetty dive.
Dive Shed, 21 Queen St, T9754 1615,
www.diveshed.com.au. Marginally cheaper
and also offers an introductory dive at the

jetty for $65. It won't count towards a
qualification, but this is a terrific place to get
a taster. Open daily.
Southern Skydivers, T0439 979897. Do a
tandem parachute jump for $320.

Dunsborough *p148*
The main dive season is Nov-Apr; not much
happens Jul-Aug. You'll pay about $160 for a
2-dive trip to the *Swan*, including gear hire,
and about $95 for a single dive.
Cape Dive, Naturaliste Terr, T9756 8778,
www.capedive.com. Has dozens of dive
combinations, mostly focusing on the *Swan*.
It also runs PADI dive courses.
Dunsborough Horse World, Genoli Rd,
T9756 7706. Offers a variety of horse rides.
Dunsborough Outdoor Sportz,
Dunsborough Park Shopping Centre, T9756
7222. Hires out a wide range of stuff
including a boat, waterskis, boogie boards,
bikes, skates, fishing rods, tennis racquets,
and camping gear. Open daily.
Naturaliste Charters, T9755 2276, www.
whales-australia.com. Runs deep-sea fishing
day trips from Dec-May ($130, 0700-1500)
and whale watching trips daily.
SeaEco, T/F9755 2039, www.seaeco.com,
a trim 34' yacht, heads out daily on various
2-to 4-hr sailing cruises. Good value ($35-60).
Also runs whale watching trips daily
(Sep-Dec, 1030, 4 hrs, $60).
Taste the South, T9756 7958, tastethesouth
@netserv.net.au. Runs informative, flexible
and fun minibus tours around Margaret River
region. $48 for ½ day, $68-90 for a full day.

○ Transport

Bunbury *p142, map p144*
Bus
Local A metropolitan bus service, T9791
1955, www.bct.com.au, serves some of the
more outlying suburbs, and the Railway
Station. Buses depart from the bus station
next to the VIC, with most fares $2 (children
and concessions $0.80). No Sunday services,
frequency of buses on other days varies
considerably. Buses from the Railway Station
to town leave every 20-40 mins, Mon-Fri
0730-1800, Sat 0740-1415.
Long distance TransWA services to the
Cape-to-Cape region depart from the
railway station at 1205 Sun-Fri, 1545 Sun-Thu

and 2035 Fri. The 1545 and 2035 services call at the VIC 20-30 mins earlier. Services to **Donnybrook** and the **timber towns** (**Pemberton** 2½ hrs) leave the VIC daily at 1130, the railway station at 1200. All services continue on to **Albany** (6½ hrs) (Wed and Fri services do not stop at Pemberton or Northcliffe). South West Coachlines services leave from Bicentennial Sq 3 times daily. The **Busselton** services go at least twice a day.

Car

Hire from **Avis**, 55 Forrest Av, T9721 7873. **Bunbury Cheaper**, 4 Mervyn St, T9721 4822. Cheap older model cars but no bombs.

Taxi

Taxi T9721 2300.

Train

The *Australind* goes to **Pinjarra**, **Serpentine** and **Perth** daily at 0600 and 1445.

Busselton *p147, map p147*
TransWA bus services leave from the VIC for **Perth** every day. Services to the **Capes** also daily. **South West Coachlines** also operate daily north and south services.

Car servicing at **Gull**, corner of Albert and West sts, T9752 1274.

❻ Directory

Bunbury *p142, map p144*
Banks Major banks have branches and ATMs on southern end of Victoria St, except **Commonwealth** on Stephen St. **Hospital** Bunbury Regional, Bussell Highway, corner of Robertson Drive, T9722 1000. **Internet** Internet Planet, Victoria St. Mon-Thu 0900-1900, Fri 0900-1800, Sat 1000-1800. **Police** 29 Symmons St, T9791 2422. **Post** Corner of Victoria and Stirling sts.

Busselton *p147, map p147*
Banks Major banks have branches and ATMs on Queen St. **Chemist** Amcal, Boulevard Shopping Centre, Prince St, T9752 4200. Mon-Fri 0830-1800, to 2000 Thu, Sat 0830-1600. **Hospital** Mill Rd, T9752 1122. **Police** Queen St, T9754 1222. **Post** Prince St.

Cape to Cape

It is no exaggeration to say that this tiny section of the west coast from Cape Naturaliste to Cape Leeuwin is one of the most gorgeous regions in Australia. West Australians will tell you that it's busy and over developed but it's a quiet backwater compared to many of the beauty spots of the east coast and local residents are trying hard to preserve its low-key and non-elitist nature. Fortunately, much of the coast is protected by the Leeuwin-Naturaliste National Park, accessible by road at a few points but best seen on a section of the wonderful Cape-to-Cape Walking Track. Just inland is a network of limestone caves and patches of thick karri forest to explore. Margaret River is at the centre of the region and is the focus for a top-end wine and gourmet food industry as well as the arts and crafts produced by the region's strong artistic community. Tiny Augusta, at the southern end of the region, is a great spot for whale watching in winter and a reminder of what the west coast towns used to be like; simple, slow and unsophisticated. ▶▶ *For Sleeping, Eating and other listings, see pages 167-172.*

Cape Naturaliste → *Colour map 3, grid A1.*

The cape is a wild triangle of hardly developed land where you can find a perfect beach and peaceful isolation less than half an hour's drive from Dunsborough and Busselton. Dunsborough sits at its eastern corner on Geographe Bay and a string of spectacular quiet bay beaches stretch to the tip where there is a lighthouse. These beaches all have dazzling fine white sand, turquoise water and shallow safe swimming. Tall trees and vegetation can grow right down to the shore on this side. The western coast takes the full force of the prevailing southwesterly breeze and is a wilder surf coast that is mostly inaccessible until you reach Yallingup at the western base of the cape.

Cape Naturaliste Road

> *Check the wind direction before setting off for the beach. If it's blowing from the west, head for an east-facing beach, and vice versa.*

Cape Naturaliste Road leads out to the cape and there are small settlements on the calm eastern side of this road. Take a detour along the Eagle Bay Meelup loop to see something of the coastline. **Castle Rock Beach** is a small sandy cove that was once the site of a whaling station. There are shady picnic tables, BBQs and toilets. Further along is **Meelup Beach,** the most popular on the cape. The beach was named by the Noongars of the Wardandi people who lived in the coastal region from Bussleton to Augusta. The name means 'place of the moon' because the moon rises from the sea at certain times of the year. Meelup is a long sandy beach with scrub almost to the shore so you can sit on the grass under a tree to escape the sun for a while. There are also picnic tables and toilets here. The next beach is Eagle Bay, although there are small beaches all the way along the coast from Meelup and plenty of places to stop. Head for one of these if you want the beach to yourself. **Eagle Bay** has a settlement of holiday homes and a café-kiosk. The coastal road terminates here and you need to take Eagle Bay Road uphill to re-join the main road to the cape, passing Wise winery on the way.

Sugarloaf Rock

A further 4 km northwest on the main road is the turn-off to Sugarloaf Rock. This is the only point to access the western coast of the cape and the 3-km sealed road leads to the striking formation named for a cone of sugar (sugar was once sold wrapped in a twist of paper). The pale slabbed rocks lean at 45 degrees and create small sheltered pools. The rock is home to a small colony of rare red-tailed tropic birds in summer. It's an idyllic swimming spot in calm weather, dramatic in wild weather and a fine place to take a bottle of wine and watch the sun set into the ocean.

Bunker Bay and Cape Naturaliste Lighthouse

Back on the main road, turn right after 1 km to reach **Bunker Bay**. This is the most beautiful sandy beach on the eastern side but there are no facilities here so it is less frequented that the others. At the western end of the beach is a pretty cove with granite boulders and sheltered pools and the appropriately named Shelley Beach. From here you can walk to the lighthouse. **Cape Naturalise Lighthouse** ⓘ *T9755 3955, 0930-1600, $7, children $3,* is just 2 km further along the main road, set back from the coast by a few kilometres. The 23-m lighthouse was built in 1903 from limestone quarried at Bunker Bay and is still in use today. The light is operated automatically now and on electricity rather than the oil and kerosene used in the past. Guided tours allow access to the lens and balcony and a small museum in a lighthouse keeper's cottage.

There is a walking track along the coast from **Dunsborough to Eagle Bay** (6 km) that starts from Forrest Street on the far western edge of Dunsborough. Ask at the Dunsborough VIC for a map or directions. The long-distance **Cape-to-Cape** walk starts from the Cape Naturaliste Lighthouse car park and traverses the western coastline of the cape, see below. There are also several short walking tracks from the lighthouse to the coast and this is an excellent spot for **whale watching**, September to November. Access to the walks from lighthouse grounds is free and the lighthouse shop has a detailed walking trail map ($2.20). The Whale Lookout track is the shortest to the coast and leads to watching platforms (40 minutes return). The **Cape Naturaliste Track** leads to the far western end of the cape and an area called the Pinnacles for some rock formations, while the Bunker Bay track leads around the coast to the bay.

Cape to Cape

Sleeping
Cape Lodge 1
Empire Retreat 3
Erravilla 4
Wildwood 5

Cape-to-Cape Track (1)

The first section of the track follows a fairly flat path along 50 m cliff tops most of the way to Yallingup (14 km). There are no facilities along the way. You could also consider walking as far as Yallingup, stay overnight in the caravan park and walk back. The first walk from the Cape to Sugarloaf Rock (3½ km) makes a pleasant introduction to the track and a good short walk. You could have a swim at Sugarloaf and return to the cape car park (7 km return). The southern part traverses some really interesting scenery and some of the track's best short sections. From the southern end of Smiths Beach it is only 2 km to Canal Rocks, passing through coastal heath and tea-tree on its way across the granite headland. A further 2 km from Canal Rocks to Wyardup provides magnificent views of the rock formations and south to Cape Clairault. From Cape Clairault you can walk a loop by heading south across the cape and then dropping down to the beach and following the rocks and beaches north, back around to Indijup Beach (7 km). It is 20 km from Cape Naturaliste to Wyardup.

Yallingup and around

Yallingup → Colour map 3, grid B1.

Population: 100. 10 km from Dunsborough, 20 km from Wilyabrup wineries.

This tiny beach settlement spreads down a hill to a long beach and reef-protected lagoon. To the north and south are isolated and pristine surfing beaches. The main attractions are swimming, surfing, and the NgILGI Cave, although Yallingup also makes a mellow base close to the wineries and galleries just inland. At the top of the hill is the venerable Caves House, a caravan park, and shop. Follow the road downhill to reach the beach and the main area of holiday homes. By the beach there is a grassy foreshore with playground and BBQs. Also a café, gallery and **Yallingup Surf Shop** ① *T9755 2036, 0900-1700,* hiring out surfboards and beach umbrellas (deposit and ID required).

: Wonder walk

The spectacular **Cape-to-Cape Track**, or part of it at least, is a must if you are staying in the area for any length of time. This track follows the coastline from Cape Naturaliste to Cape Leeuwin (140 km) and is a superb way to see coastal and forest scenery in the region, much of it inaccessible by car. The walk, rated as one of the best coastal walks in the country, is mostly within the **Leewin-Naturaliste National Park**, a narrow strip less than 10 km wide in places, along a limestone ridge. Unusually for a long Australian track it is accessible year-round, rarely either too hot or cold, though it's not at its best on wet wintry days or scorching summer ones. There are regular road access points so it is easy to walk short sections or day trips and these are suggested at appropriate points in the text. Unfortunately the nature of the track allows for hardly any loop trails, and so most short or day walks will involve returning along the same path unless you can arrange a pick up. Basic campsites reserved for walkers can be used along the way. Tents, water and fuel stoves must all be carried and waste carried out. The track is administered by **CALM** who produce an excellent pack ($8) containing walk maps and notes in five sections covering the whole route. There are no charges or permits. For more information contact CALM in Busselton, T9752 1677, CALM in Margaret River T9757 2322, or see www.naturebase.net. A few companies organize guided walks along the track. **Environmental Encounters**, T9375 7885, www.environmentalencounters.com.au, periodically run seven-day fully supported trips that cover the entire track, for around $1,000.

Surfing lessons are available from **Yallingup Surf School** ① *T9755 2755, for $70 (less for if more than one).* There are several walking trails around Yallingup, such as the **Wardanup Hill loop** (5 km, 2½ hours), from the beach car park. This heads uphill past NgILGI Cave and a lookout and circles back to the coast. You can access the Cape-to-Cape track from the foreshore.

NgILGI Cave

① *Caves Rd, T9755 2152, www.downsouth.com.au, 0930-1630 (last entry 1530), $15, children $6 (cash only); tours every 30 mins on the half hour, adventure tours $70, 3 hrs, daily at 0930 but bookings essential, about 1 km east of Yallingup.*

This cave was the first to be opened to the public in 1901 and launched tourism in the area. It is a beautifully deep and decorated limestone cave, with magnificent shawls, stalagmites, stalactites and helictites. NgILGI cave (pronounced nil-gee) is thought to be about 500,000 years old and is named for an Aboriginal creation myth. NgILGI was a good warrior spirit who

> : *The cave has 95 per cent humidity and there are many steps so asthmatics may find the exertion uncomfortable.*

lived by the sea. Wolgine, an evil spirit lived in the cave and had been drying out local waterholes and tempting children into the cave. NgILGI whipped up a storm, cutting the cave off from the sea and driving Wolgine deep into the cave and out through the present entrance. It then became his own *nurilem* (cave). Entry to the cave is only by semi-guided tour. A guide takes you down into the cave and another remains in the main chamber but once inside you are free to wander about at your own pace. Most

● *Yallingup is a* Noongar *word meaning 'place of love'; so you never know what might* ● *happen here...*

people take about an hour to look around. There are also adventure tours which involve wriggling though some tight spaces, climbing and crawling around areas not normally seen by the public. Wear enclosed boots and clothes to get grubby in.

Beaches around Yallingup

Much of the Cape-to-Cape coast is actually inaccessible to anyone but walkers, but Yallingup is at the end of one of three sealed roads in quick succession that lead to a series of rocky headlands and almost impossibly perfect beaches.

Some 5 km south of Yallingup, Canal Rocks Road leads both to Canal Rocks and Smiths Beach. **Smiths Beach**, one of the most popular in the area thanks to the adjacent caravan parks, stretches all the way from Yallingup, a long, broad stretch of white sand sloping gently into the sea. The sea itself is often not so gentle, but when it's calm and the sun is shining the iridescent blues and greens of the water make an arresting sight. **Canal Rocks** is a bare rocky headland with a maze of fissures worn so deep and wide as to create a series of islands, separated by canal-like channels and pools. Snorkelling and swimming can be a lot of fun here, but beware the very strong currents and swells created by the narrow channels that can make such pursuits very hazardous. A narrow bridge connects the mainland to the first island. The small adjacent bay is a popular boat-launching site and there are public toilets in the car park.

About 10 km south via Wyardup Road, but just a magnificent 2-km cliff-top walk via the Cape-to-Cape track, are **Wyardup Rocks** and **Indijup Beach** stretching to **Cape Clairault**. The rocks, similar to though not quite as broken up as Canal Rocks, are immediately adjacent to the beach, which is easily a match for Smiths. The main difference between the two spots is that the latter rocks and beach have no facilities, except some toilets at the south end of the beach, and consequently far less people, often none at all.

Wardan Aboriginal Cultural Centre

ⓘ *Injidup Springs Rd, T9756 6566, www.wardan.com.au, 1000-1600 Wed-Mon.*

On the way out to the beach look out for the new Wardan Aboriginal Cultural Centre. Inside the rammed-earth walls, the centre aims to give visitors insight into the Bibelmen Mia culture through an art gallery, interpretive centre and 1-km bushwalking trail demonstrating traditional plant uses.

Yallingup Shearing Shed

ⓘ *T9755 2309, Sat-Thu 1000-1600, shearing demonstrations at 1100 and sometimes 1500. $5.50, children $3.50.*

This is an unusual diversion in the area, 6 km from Yallingup on the Wildwood Road. Principally a sheep farm, part of the woolshed is now a fairly uninspiring knitwear shop. Most of it, however, is still very much a shearing shed and the owners ensure that there are sheep to be shorn all year round. Lively demonstrations happen every day except Friday (when shearers go to the chiropractor), and spectators get to take part in much of the process save the actual clipping.

Northern Margaret River wine area

The area between Dunsborough and Yallingup, the northern of three principal areas that together have become famous as the Margaret River Wine Region, is covered in a maze of picturesque, mostly sealed lanes, with a gallery or winery seemingly around every corner.

Wilyabrup Valley wine area, to the south, is the core of the Margaret River Wine Region. It is a few kilometres north of Gracetown and Cowaramup with most of the wineries packed along Caves Road and slightly inland between Metricup and

Harmons South roads. Mildly hilly, many of the wineries have large, scenic dams with
cafés and restaurants taking full advantage of them. As a rule most wineries,
particularly the smaller, cellar-door-only ones, do not charge for tastings and are open
daily. As well as wine there are also opportunities to taste cheese, chocolate, coffee
and beer. ➼ *See map,s page 154 and 158, for the location of wineries and galleries.*

Around Dunsborough and Yallingup

Goanna Gallery ① *Hayes Rd, T9756 8096, 1000-1700*, houses local art and craft work
in a small scale bush setting. The gallery has a café serving cheap food, homemade
cakes, jams and preserves and a outdoor terrace. **Gunyulgup Galleries** ① *Gunyulgup
Valley Dr, T9755 2177, 1000-1700*, is the finest in the southwest, set in a grand formal
space overhanging a lake and surrounded by bush. High quality paintings, sculpture,
jewellery, glass and ceramics. **Happs** ① *Commonage Rd, T9755 3479, 1000-1700*, is a
welcoming, rustic winery and pottery. There is an extensive and unusual range of
wines, such as Marsanne and Viognier, but the most popular is Fuchsia, a light pink
made from 19 red varieties. Also a few preservative-free wines. No food sold but
picnickers are welcome. The pottery is attractive domestic ware. **Wicked Ale Brewery**
① *3 Hemsley Rd, T9755 2848, Wed-Mon 1000-1600*, is a small brewery making
speciality beers such as chilli, chocolate, ginger and passionfruit. Bar and beer
garden. Pool tables and darts. It's part of a small complex of rural arts and crafts
businesses. **Yallingup Galleries** ① *Walker Rd, T9755 2372, 1000-1700*, is surrounded
by bush with a focus on paintings and furniture and a good range of prices. During
busy holiday periods special exhibitions are held at the Garden Art Studio.

    The main small cluster of wineries in this northern end of the region is on, or just off
Wildwood Road. **Rivendell** ① *T9755 2090, www.rivendellwines.com.au, 1030-1700,
from 0900 Sun*, complement their wines with a rambling gardens, tearoom and
restaurant serving a wide range of options from an inexpensive Sunday brunch to
mid-range country-style lunches and cream teas. Wines $12-22. Also accommodation
(A). **Abbey Vale** ① *T9217 6700, 1030-1630*, is a small cellar door built adjacent to their
large lake. It has a veranda and rear gardens. Picnickers welcome if they buy a bottle.
Cheese platters available. Best known for their Dry Verdelho. Wines $14-25.

    South of the main area, on Caves Road are the following. **Clairault** ① *off Pusey
Rd, T9755 6225, 1000-1700, restaurant 1200-1530 daily, 1800-2100 Sat and Nov-
Easter on Fri*, is around the block from Driftwood. Either head south then left, left and
left again, or north and keep going clockwise. This is the largest family owned and run
winery in the region, and has one of the most stylish tasting and dining rooms, a
smooth assemblage of polished timber, contemporary furniture and rich tones.
Attention to culinary detail is just as close, the excellent expensive international
cuisine available. Swagman's Kiss, is their drink-now range, premium Clairault range
priced $20-40. **Driftwood** ① *T9755 6338*, is unusual for having a restaurant open daily
for lunch and dinner. They have the same expensive menu for both sittings and the
modern Australian cuisine is consistently good.

Wilyabrup Valley wine area → *Colour map 3, grid B1. 30 km from Busselton, 20 km from Margaret River.*

The short stretch of Caves Road that passes through this area is the epicentre of the
entire Margaret River wine region with over a dozen wineries along 5 km of bitumen.

    Cullen ① *T9755 5277, 1000-1600*, a large solid-looking building, much of it leased
to a large restaurant, serves substantial platters and cheeseboards all day, as well as
mid-range meals that use local produce with an Asian influence. The homemade cakes
are excellent and can be eaten with a coffee out on the deck. Wines $17-35.

    Evans and Tate ① *T9755 6244, 1030-1630*, a little further south from **Moss
Brothers**, right on the corner of the Metricup Rd turn-off, is a perennial favourite of WA
restaurants with a very well respected and reasonably priced range of wines $14-18.

Moss Brothers ⓘ *T9755 6270, 1000-1700*, is the most northerly winery. Its $18-30 premium range includes an excellent Shiraz, but the Drummond Hill label still has a some very drinkable wines at around $15. It usually has a good stock of museum wines.

Pierro ⓘ *T9755 6220, 1000-1700*, has a rustic, unpretentious and friendly rammed-earth and jarrah cellar door that hints little at the superb quality of their $20-60 wines. The smooth top-of-the-range Chardonnay is considered one of the very best wines in the region and both their Pierro and Fire Gully ranges are highly sought after. All their wines are available for tasting if they haven't sold out.

Vasse Felix ⓘ *T9756 5000, www.vassefelix.com.au, 1000-1700, restaurant 1200-1500*, at the end of it's own tree-lined driveway, is still making some of the region's best wines and is particularly well-known for its flagship Heytesbury Chardonnay. Now owned by the influential Holmes à Court family, the winery has a separate café and excellent 1st floor restaurant. A large exhibition and performance space is becoming a key WA arts venue.

After **Evans and Tate** there are a few more wineries along Metricup Road that are well worth the visit. **Grove** ⓘ *T9755 7458, www.thegrovevineyard.com.au, 0900- 1600*, is a stylish fusion of companies and ideas sharing the same buildings and the objective of offering the visitor something a bit different. Premium wines are complemented by a boardwalk café that hangs over the large, lily covered dam. Its mid-range international menu has a few unusual twists and there are plenty of grazing options. In a larger adjacent building is a purpose-built glass cool room, featuring a range of international and Australian cheese and chocolate for tasting. Also in here is the **Yahava KoffeeWorks** who import, blend and roast about a dozen coffees, daily tastings at 1130 and 1500. **Woody Nook** ⓘ *T9755 6547, 1000-1630*, is about as laid-back and rustic as it gets around here. It's not relaxed about the wine-making, however, and the Cabernet Sauvignon and Sauvignon Blanc are consistently good. Its ports are very fine too. The unpretentious café serves appropriately hearty meals such as mid-range pies, curries and grills and always offers a cheap three-course set menu, 1200-1500. Also morning and afternoon teas.

Off Metricup Road, Harmons Mill Road heads down to the Bussell Highway. Along it are a couple more small wineries quietly producing superb wines, and the Margaret River Chocolate Factory. **Hay Shed Hill** ⓘ *T9755 6305, 1030-1700*, is almost next door to **Willespie** with wines $15-50. One of the friendliest wineries in the region, with a rare sense of humour. It's one of the prettiest too, occupying a series of large white weatherboard buildings in keeping with the traditional old hay shed. Their flagship wines are a treat, a rich velvety Pinot Noir and an equally good Cabernet Sauvignon. Picnickers are welcome on the front lawn and if they're not busy staff will be happy to help you plan a tasting day.

Willespie ⓘ *T9755 6248, 1030-1700*, was the first of the wineries and has recently experimented with a full-bodied Shiraz with success. The small first floor cellar door has a small veranda on where unfussy and inexpensive cheese platters, sandwiches and cream teas are served.

Southwest Coast Cape to Cape

Wilyabrup Valley wineries

Sleeping 🛏
Taunton Farm
Caravan Park 1

Wineries 🍷
Clairault 13
Cullen 1
Evans & Tate 2
Fermoy 3

Grove 4
Hay Shed Hill 5
Moss Brothers 6
Palandri 7
Pierro 8
Treeton 9
Vasse Felix 10
Willespie 11
Woody Nook 12

A handful of wineries are now pioneering the area to the east, along the Bussell Highway. **Palandri** ① *T9755 5711, www.palandri.com.au, 1000-1700*, is a new powerhouse in the region, serious about providing the whole experience in an innovative hangar-like space. Several ranges and crisp, drinkable wines aimed at a worldwide market. Wines $15-45. There is also a café offering unusual breakfasts and light, café-style salads and platters ($15-20) matched to wine varieties. Lots of wine merchandise and playstations to distract the kids.

Treeton Estate ① *Treeton Rd, T9755 5481, 1000-1800*, just outside Cowaramup, has small, rustic, wines for $18. Its later opening hours are just one of the reasons to make this the last stop of the day. The whites are extremely drinkable, light summer wines, and packaged patés, water biscuits and Margaret River cheeses at supermarket prices are also sold. A plate, knife and a few cool, covered outdoor tables help you unwind.

Cowaramup → *Colour map 3, grid B1. 35 km from Busselton, 10 km from Margaret River.*

Though your nose won't miss the pungent and ripe smells of cheese-making and dairying in this area, Cowaramup itself is a 'blink and you'll miss it' settlement on the Bussell Highway. It is worth a stop though for a couple of interesting businesses. The **Margaret River Regional Wine Centre** ① *T9755 5501, www.mrwines.com, Mon-Sat 1000-1900, Sun 1200-1800*, stocks almost every wine made in the region and can ship mixed cases anywhere in the world. It also acts as an information centre, can help plan a wine-tasting itinerary based on your tastes and time, and has wine tastings, often from wineries without a cellar door.

Cape-to-Cape Walk Track (2)

The second stretch of track from **Wyardup** to **Gracetown** (27 km) is more broken than that to the north and south, a series of rugged cliffs and headlands and a few small sandy coves. The walk mostly follows cliff tops with only a few descents to beaches. To the east there is nothing but vineyards so it is a peaceful stretch with no sealed road access. From Cape Clairault the next 4 km along the cliff top is a good place to see whales and dolphins in season. In the southern half of this section you'll see the 40-m granite-gneiss **Willyabrup Cliffs**, a strong draw for climbers and abseilers. This section could be walked from Gracetown although a fairly long day (22 km return). With a 4WD it is possible to drive to the end of Juniper Road and walk along the track for about 5 km to the cliffs and return.

Gracetown → *Colour map 3, grid B1. 32 km from Yallingup, 11 km from Cowaramup.*

Gracetown is a tiny coastal settlement due west of Cowaramup. The houses cluster on a hillside, above the white sand and rock outcrops of Cowaramup Bay. The bay is good for fishing from the rocks on a calm day when the water shimmers with patches of turquoise but can also put on massive surf when a swell is running. The **Cape-to-Cape Track** follows the coast closely at this point along cliff tops so the views are particularly good and it's only 11 km north to the climbers' playground of Wilyabrup Cliffs. Facilities at Gracetown are limited to a general store ① *0700-1900*, with petrol and phone and a café, the **Sea Star**.

Cape-to-Cape Walk Track (3)

The third section of the track, 31 km from Gracetown to Redgate Beach, passes through several settlements. There is quite a bit of bush walking in fairly low country and some fine swimming and surfing beaches. After following the beach at Gracetown, the track passes along a cliff top to **Ellensbrook**, where you can look around the Bussells' old homestead, see page 161, and **Meekadarabee Cave**. There is a nice campsite nearby, beside the stream. The track then continues inland until veering to the coast again near **Cape Mentelle**, a high limestone headland. From here it's not far to the beautiful beach at the mouth of Margaret River. This is a good short walk to do from the rivermouth (3 km return) to see the Cape Mentelle cliffs and Kilcarnup on the northern side. The trail then heads up behind **Prevelly** and **Gnarabup** (you'll probably want to detour here to sit in a café or stay overnight). The coast is not reached again until 3 km north of **Redgate**, a picturesque beach with no facilities.

> ❧ There is a walk and cycle trail from Prevelly to Margaret River but no public transport.

Margaret River and around → *Colour map 3, grid B1. Population: 3,000.*

100 km from Bunbury via Highway, 55 km from Augusta via Caves Road.

The Margaret River and around is famous for two things: wineries and surf. The region produces some of Australia's best premium wines and the surf is also exceptional. Contrary to many travellers' expectations, neither are in Margaret River itself, but it does make a convenient base for these attractions. Most of the wineries are to the north, almost as close to Dunsborough as Margaret River, and the beach is to be found at the river mouth near the small settlement of Prevelly.

Margaret River

Margaret River town sits on the southern side of the river, 10 km inland from the beach, and a busy street of shops and restaurants has developed along its main street. The town acts as a focus for the talent in the region and has some wonderful restaurants, galleries, and accommodation that are the equal of any in the country.

On the northern riverbank is a small Rotary Park with BBQs, picnic tables and toilets. A footbridge leads to the **Old Settlement Museum** ① *T9757 9335, Mon-Sat 1000-1700, Sun 1230-1700*, a reconstruction of a 'pioneer settlement' of the group settlers of the twenties. The complex includes buildings such as a blacksmith shed and you can feed kangaroos. There is a tearoom serving cream teas. The Rotary Park is the trailhead for a walk/cycle trail to **Ten Mile Brook Dam**. This is a pleasant riverbank trail (15 km return) through karri, blackbutt, and jarrah forest to a picnic site by the dam.

There are some talented artists and craftspeople in the southwest region and visiting galleries is another enjoyable aspect of the area. Many studios are in the countryside but there are a few galleries in Margaret River that showcase regional work. **Jahroc Gallery** ① *83 Bussell Highway, T9757 2729*, shows a fine range of painting, sculpture,

Margaret River

0 metres 200
0 yards 200

Sleeping 🛏
Basildene Manor **6**
Bridgefield **1**
Inne Town Backpackers **2**
Margaret River Guesthouse **3**
Margaret River Lodge **7**
Margaret River Tourist Park **8**
Margarets Forest **4**
Peppermint Brook Cottages **5**
River Chalets **9**
Riverview **10**

Eating 🍴
Arc of Iris **1**
Goodfellas **2**
Margaret River Fish & Chips **3**
Margaret River Hotel **4**
Urban Bean **5**
VAT 107 **6**

Bars & clubs 🍸
Settlers Tavern **7**
Wino's **8**

Southwest Coast Cape to Cape

Surf's up

As well as linking its name indelibly to the wines between the capes, Margaret River has also become the moniker for the region as a surf destination and it is common to hear or read about 'Margaret River surf breaks', even though only a couple are anywhere near the river mouth itself and none are near the town as it's 10 km inland. Whatever the name, the succession of west-facing beaches between the capes, particularly the northern half, many of which are only accessible by a long walk, are famous for their surf breaks and regarded as the best in Western Australia. The best of the best are around Gracetown, particularly the 'womb', described by one local surfy as the place to go 'if you want a lot of water up your nose'. Others to check out are 'three bears', 'grunters' and 'lefties'.

woodwork and jewellery. Almost next door is **Margaret River Pottery** ① *91 Bussell Highway, T9757 2848*, with a large range of Ian Dowling's distinctive 'chun blue' glazed stoneware. Ask the VIC for a list if you wish to go on a gallery crawl.

Margaret River hosts a lively **Wine Festival** ① *T9758 1903, www.mrwinefest.org.au*, over 10 days in November. Events include wine master classes, comparative tastings, art exhibitions, cooking classes and outdoor concerts. On some days during the festival special bus routes operate to events at wineries and galleries ($25 day).

The **VIC** ① *Bussell Highway, T9757 2911, www.margaretriverwa.com, 0900-1700*, has a room showcasing the wineries of the region and can help with bookings.

Ellensbrook → *13 km from Gracetown, 13 km from Margaret River.*
① *House: Sat-Wed 1000-1600), $4, children $2, concession $3; Grounds: daily, donations appreciated.*
One of the earliest houses in the district, Ellensbrook was built by Alfred and Ellen Bussell in 1857. The homestead was part of a farming property and was carefully sited by a stream fed by a natural spring. It has been restored by the National Trust and is a fine example of a European pioneer house, built with local materials such as driftwood for beams and paperbark sheets for the roof. In the early days the Bussells established no more than subsistence farming but later had success with beef and dairy cattle. Ellensbrook is a wonderful place to spend a few hours; the immaculate lawn surrounded by trees is a fine picnic spot, there is a beach just down the road and a lovely short walk. The **Meekadarribee Trail** (1,600-m loop) is a shady walk through forest, leading along the banks of Ellen Brook to a cave grotto and waterfall. Endangered black cockatoos are often seen by the water.

Prevelly and Gnarabup → *Colour map 3, grid B1. 9 km from Margaret River.*
Another coastal settlement spilling downhill among dense coastal tea tree, **Prevelly** is Margaret River's closest beach and where the legendary international surf competition, **Margaret River Masters**, is held in April (www.salomonmasters.com). Surfers Point, at the northern edge of Prevelly, is a powerful reef break and the surfers' car park there is a great place to watch the action on a big day. Around the corner is a perfect crescent of beach where the eucalypt green of Margaret River meets the aquamarine of the Indian ocean and the only sign of civilization is a small car-park. In front of Prevelly itself the beaches are hidden by high sand dunes. At the southern end is **Gnarabup Beach** where a humble but picturesque café perches above the water. This is also the site of obtrusive high-density modern housing, a controversial development that goes to the heart of the future of the Capes region. Facilities at Prevelly and Gnarabup are limited to a café and general store.

The small but select number of wineries around Margaret River itself mostly lie along or just off Boodijup Road, the turn-off to which is just south of town.

Leeuwin Estate ① *T9757 6253, www.leeuwinestate.com.au, 1000-1630*, may not quite be the oldest winery in the region, but is the best known. Apart from a stylish expensive restaurant, excellent wines and fascinating art gallery, the key feature of the winery is its gently sloping lawned amphitheatre. Here they host the Leeuwin Concert Series every summer (February), a few days of mostly classical performances that are the Southwest's premier event. Book well ahead for tickets ($100-plus) and accommodation.

Minot's ① *off Exmoor Drive, opposite the Eagles Heritage Centre, T9757 3579*, 'Cellar door' is simply a modest table outside the owners' bungalow home. They produces a light, refreshing Semillon Sauvignon Blanc ($13), and a fabulously rich, velvety Cabernet ($23) that is well worth going out of the way for. They try to be open 1000-1700, but phone ahead if possible. **Redgate** ① *Boodijup Rd, T9757 6488, 1000-1700*, is nothing fancy but its range of reds and whites is well respected, and it welcomes picnickers to the few covered tables on the front terrace. Wines $15-35.

Swallows Welcome ① *Wickham Rd, T9757 6348*, is a few kilometres east of this core group, on the other side of the Bussell Highway. It is another very small operation, and one where a visit can be memorable. Call ahead to make sure the owner is around. **Voyager** ① *T9757 6354, 1000-1700*, is arguably the most scenic winery in the region. Landscaped rose gardens and white-washed walls surround a gleaming white Cape Dutch-style cellar door and restaurant. Both wines and the expensive cuisine are multi-award winning, lunches 1200-1430. Both it and **Leeuwin** are well signposted a little way past Exmoor Drive. Wines $20-40.

Xanadu ① *T9757 3066, 1000-1700, tapas from 1000, meals 1200-1600 and on Sat 1700-2100*, is first on the right, after about 4 km. Everything about this place is smart and savvy, but casual. The three ranges of wines hit both palate and wallet in the right place and the mid-range meals, served inside the huge, heavy beamed and earthy building, or in the large grassy courtyard, are the equal of those you'll get at much pricier establishments. Options include BBQ-yourself and kids menus, and children also have an outdoor playground and indoor games. Wines $14-40. Recommended.

Eagles Heritage Centre

① *Boodijup Rd, T9757 2960, www.eaglesheritage.com.au, 1000-1700, displays 1100 and 1330 (1 hr), $10, children $5, concessions $8.*

Dedicated to rescuing and rehabilitating birds of prey, this is currently the only wildlife park of its kind in Australia. Those fully rehabilitated are released back into the wild, those permanently damaged, either physically or psychologically, are cared for at the centre for the rest of their lives. Incredibly, many of the beautiful birds brought in have been deliberately harmed, shot or poisoned. In every state except NT it is actually possible to obtain a license to shoot Wedgetailed eagles. These are Australia's largest bird of prey and down to less than 10,000 breeding pairs after decades of deliberate, government-sponsored persecution, the result of an erroneous belief that they prey on sheep. A century ago there were around a million pairs and the birds were a major factor in keeping down populations of feral mammals, they are now listed as endangered. Although you can stroll around the aviaries, try to time a visit for one of the wonderful flying displays.

Cape-to-Cape Walk Track (4)

The fourth section of track from Redgate to Hamelin Bay (29 km) is one of the best because it offers a lot of variety and traverses a wide section of the Leeuwin-Naturaliste Park so feels much more remote than the last section. If you're

Harmony at Ellensbrook

The Bussell family were one of the first European families in the region and have left their names behind in Busselton and Gracetown. The Bussell brothers arrived at the Swan River Colony in 1830 from England and travelled to Augusta to try and found a settlement there. It wasn't very successful so the settlers explored further north in search of fertile farming land. John Bussell came across Margaret River and is thought to have named it after his cousin. His younger brother, Alfred Bussell, bought land further north, now Busselton. He transported provisions for soldiers from Augusta to Vasse and came to know the region and the local Noongar people very well. Ironically the soldiers were stationed in Vasse to protect new settlers from attacks by the dispossessed Noongars. Much of Alfred's knowledge came from the Noongar people and when he decided to move south with his young family in 1857 he took a Noongar guide who showed him to the freshwater oasis at Ellensbrook, a traditional summer camping place.

Alfred and his family seem to have had a good relationship with local Noongar people and even to have relied heavily each other. Noongars lived with the Bussells at Ellensbrook and worked on the property, clearing and farming. When two small daughters were lost in the bush for days it was a Noongar boy who found them and saved their lives. Noongar Sam Issacs saved many lives in 1865 when the *Georgette* foundered off Redgate Beach and he galloped for help, finding Alfred and Ellen's daughter Grace. Both were awarded medals from the Royal Humane Society. NgILGI was abandoned at the property as a baby and was brought up and educated with the Bussell children. The family lived at Ellensbrook until 1865, when Alfred built a grander property, Wallcliffe near the Margaret River mouth. Ellensbrook was run by several daughters but Edith looked after it the longest and turned it into a home for destitute Aboriginal children from the northwest, from 1899-1917. Descendants of the Bussells owned Ellensbrook until 1956.

walking south it also has the advantage of finishing at Hamelin Bay where there are the comforts of a caravan park, shop and stunning swimming beach. Following the coast closely from Redgate, the section from the cliff and caves of Bob's Hollow to Conto's is magnificent. You are close to the edge of high cliffs with excellent views back to Redgate and south to Cape Freycinet. When you reach Conto's there is a campground and you can also walk up to Caveworks, where you can explore Lake Cave and visit the café. After leaving Conto's the track passes through the beautiful karri trees of Boranup Forest for 8 km, before rejoining the beach for 5 km along sand to Hamelin Bay. Redgate to Conto's makes a spectacular short walk (8 km) but ideally with a pick-up at one end.

Caves Road to Augusta → *Cave Works 17 km from Margaret River.*

Boodijup Road comes out on Caves Road, 2 km north of the turning to **Redgate Beach**. This white-sand beach has many off-shore reefs creating rock pools suitable for swimming and snorkelling. Thanks to its isolation and lack of facilities it's also one of the quietest of those accessible by sealed road. It was the scene of a dramatic rescue in 1865 when Grace Bussell and Sam Issacs rode a line out to the *Georgette*, a ship in

66 99 The near part of the bay is a long, wide beach of the finest white sand, sloping off into a maze of seaweed covered reefs and deep sandy troughs...

severe distress in heavy surf, and rescued every one of those still aboard. Three km south of the turn-off Caves Road passes **Calgardup Cave** ① *T9757 7422, 0900-1615, self-guided, allow 1 hr, $10, children $5*, the first of a series of caves for which the road was named. There are 300 known caves in the region, riddling the limestone base like holes in a cheese, but less than a dozen are open to the public. Calgardup, managed by CALM, is a relatively shallow cave and so easily accessed with all routes inside via boardwalks. It has an array of coloured decorations, a lake and a stream. Just around the corner is **Mammoth Cave** ① *T9757 7514, 0900-1600, allow 45 mins, $15.50, children $6.50*, one of several managed by the Augusta Margaret River Tourism Association (AMRTA). With a huge opening chamber the cave was a long-standing shelter for Aboriginal tribes and many species of animals. Over 10,000 fossil fragments have been found here, including bones from several extinct animals such as the cow-sized Zygomaturus, a relative of the wombats. Not the most spectacular of caves, entry is self-guided via boardwalks, includes a personal audio, and some of the cave is accessible to wheelchairs.

Some 3 km south of Mammoth is a right turn into Conto Road. This is sealed the short distance to **Cave Works** ① *T9757 7411, 0900-1700, free with any AMRTA cave ticket, otherwise $3, children $2, adjacent is a welcome café, 0830-1700*, the local cave interpretation centre. The displays describe the geology of the region and how the caves formed, the fossils found in the caves and the scant life that still occupies them, and has a mock-up of a small cave, complete with cave decorations. Cave Works is also the entry point for **Lake Cave** ① *entry by tour, on the ½ hr from 0930-1530, allow 1 hr, $15.50, children $6.50*, a relatively small but beautiful and peaceful chamber whose entire floor is covered by a shallow lake. Due to its depth most of the decorations are almost pure white. One unusual feature is the 'suspended table', a section of horizontal flowstone that has had its foundation washed away and hangs just above the lake, held up by two 2-m columns. Access is via 300-odd steps into a sink-hole.

Conto Road becomes unsealed after Cave Works and heads 3 km down to **Conto Beach** and the bush campground of **Conto Field**, the closest such campsite to a beach in the region. It is a stunning piece of coast and you are unlikely to have to share it with anyone if you explore a bit. Back on Caves Road, 2 km south of Conto Road, is **Giants Cave** ① *T9757 7422, 0930-1530 during school and public holidays, self-guided, allow 1 hr, $10, children $5*, another self-guided cave (you can explore for as long as you like) with a series of massive chambers. This is one of the more adventurous with several ladders and some scrambling required – wear stout shoes.

Just south of Giants Cave is the start of an unsealed scenic drive that runs parallel to Caves Road for 14 km. It winds through the heart of the **Boranup Forest** ① *T9757 2322, bush-camping fees: $6 adult, $2 children, facilities include toilets, picnic tables, fireplaces and wood*, a large area of karri forest that was clear-felled in the 1800s and has been allowed to grow back naturally. Though no really massive trees remain the regrowth is impressive and the drive is worth the 15 minutes' extra driving time. Towards the far end is a lookout over the forest to the plains beyond, and a bush campground. If, instead of hitting the dirt, you stick to the bitumen you will pass **Boranup Gallery** ① *0930-1630 or later*, almost immediately on the left, the best for the beauty of West Australian hardwoods and the skill of local craftspeople. The adjacent café is a good spot for a cheap light lunch or simply a cuppa.

The quickest route to Augusta from this area is to head for **Karridale** and head south. There are handful of services at Karridale, including the last fuel before Nannup some 75 km away, plus **Fox Studio Glass**, about 200 m down the road east to Nannup. It is a small gallery of the work of Alan Fox, a master glass artist who has been refining his skills for almost 30 years (he reckons on 20 years' practice just to become competent in glass blowing). The longer route, continuing on Caves Road, heads past the turning for Hamelin Bay, and then passes **Jewel Cave**.

Hamelin Bay, 40 km from Margaret River, 20 km from Augusta, is a long beach can be driven on by 4WD vehicles, has a boat ramp and extensive caravan park, and is accessible via sealed road. This generally makes it the busiest of beaches south of Margaret River. However, it's also the best place to see the **stingrays** that will often come in for a feed off certain beaches in the south of the Capes region. A small colony of them practically live around the boat jetty and can easily be enticed in with a small amount of fish bait. The bush **caravan park** (T9758 5540, D-E) has a few on-site vans and cabins, and a small, scantily-stocked shop.

South of the bay, 9 km by partially unsealed road and 5 km via the Cape-to-Cape Track, are a couple of the most beautiful beaches in this part of the world. **Cosy Corner** is a 2-km wide bay sheltered by a series of off-shore rocks and reefs. The near part of the bay is a long, wide beach of the finest white sand, sloping off into a maze of seaweed covered reefs and deep sandy troughs. Further around a long rocky shelf sits at the base of the high dunes that surround the bay. This shelf is punctuated by holes that become a series of spectacular blowholes during heavy seas. Thanks to its lack of facilities and unsealed access, Cosy Corner and its smaller adjacent bays can be virtually deserted even when Hamelin Bay is heaving.

Jewel Cave ① *T9758 4541, entry by tour, on the hour 0930-1330 and 1530, allow 1 hr, $15.50, children $6.50*, is 9 km from Augusta. If you can only see one cave then try to see this one. It is the largest and one of the deepest caves open to the public. The decorations are fantastic, especially the helictites and straws. There is also a good short walk through karri trees at the site.

Cape-to-Cape Walk Track (5)

The last section from Hamelin Bay to Cape Leeuwin (29 km) is one of the wildest and most remote. There is a caravan park at the start but no other settlements along the route. Starting at Hamelin Bay the trail follows the beach before climbing up to the headland and Foul Bay Lighthouse, then dropping to the idyllic Cosy Corner beach. This section from Hamelin Bay to Cosy Corner makes a wonderful **day walk** (6½ km one way). Following the coast past the blowholes and Cape Hamelin, the track then traverses a long and utterly lonely beach before heading uphill closer to the cape and reaching good lookouts. From Skippy Rock it is a short walk over rocks, beach and bush to the waterwheel at Cape Leeuwin. This section (3 km) passes some interesting 'gour' pools, layers of scalloped stone, and is a pleasant **short walk** to do from Augusta. If you've walked the whole Cape-to-Cape track hobble immediately to the Augusta pub (8 km) or persuade someone to give you a lift. Unfortunately there is no public phone at the Cape. Alternatively use the phone at Hamelin Bay to book accommodation in Augusta and ask to be picked up.

Augusta → *Colour map 3, grid B1. Population: 1,100. 90 km from Nannup, 125 km from Pemberton.*

Augusta hugs the west bank of the **Blackwood River** mouth, the region's largest river, and continues a little way down the eastern side of Cape Leeuwin. The town claims to

⦂ The curious cape cruises

Humpback and **Southern Right** whales cruise past the capes during their yearly migration north from Antarctica. They hang about Cape Leeuwin from around June to August, then head up the coast, coming close to shore at Gracetown and Sugarloaf, before spending another three months or so around Cape Naturaliste. There are whale-watching boat tours from Augusta (June to September) and Dunsborough (September to December) which often get very close to the whales due to their great curiosity. If you can pick your time then head south, as during this period the Humpbacks are particularly active, often breaching, spy-hopping and waving to tourists.

be one of Western Australia's first settlements, but in fact almost all the original 1830 settlers, including the industrious Bussells, had cleared out by 1840 leaving the place to the sealers and whalers. It got going again only in the 1860s. The town's interesting history is illustrated by the many exhibits and photographs in the **Augusta Historical Museum** ① *Blackwood Av, T9758 1948, 1000-1200, 1400-1600, $2, children $0.50*, including a fascinating section on the mass strandings of whales that happened here. In May 1986, 114 False Killer whales beached themselves just outside the river mouth and hundreds of volunteers succeeded in rescuing 96 of them. This is thought to be the most successful largescale rescue of its kind to have happened anywhere.

Although it has most services, including an ATM, Augusta has a friendly, small town feel. The main street is on a rise above the riverbank, looking down on the town jetty, though a better spot to sit and gaze about the river is actually a few hundred metres further south at Turner Street Jetty where **stingrays** will sometimes come in to feed if a little bait is dropped in the water, and pelicans and seagulls will already be waiting. The grassy foreshore has picnic tables, and an excellent café and takeaway are just across the road. The best spots for a swim at any time of year are 2 km south of town at **Flinders Bay Settlement**. By the jetty is popular, though nearby **Granny's Pool**, a shallow area enclosed by rocks, is safer still. The helpful **VIC** ① *T9758 0166, aupro@netserv.net.au, Mon-Fri 0900-1700, Sat-Sun 0900-1300*, is at the far end of the main shopping drag

---

Cape Leeuwin → *Colour map 3, grid B1.*

Most of Cape Leeuwin, the southern end of the capes' low coastal hill range, is part of the national park and so free of development. The cape marks the geographical point at which the Southern and Indian Oceans meet, though there is seldom any physical sign of meeting currents. As the most southwesterly point of the Australian mainland, it was often the only part of Australia ships saw (and still see) before reaching their final port, making the many offshore reefs and rocks a huge danger to shipping.

The kilometre-long promontory at the end of the cape was long seen as an ideal place for a **Lighthouse** ① *T9758 1920, promontory precinct open daily 0845-1700, free, lighthouse tours every ¾ hr from 0900-1115 and 1300-1600, $6, children $3, 8 km from Augusta, may not run if very windy, phone first to check*, though interstate financial arguments delayed building until the 1880s. The still-functioning lighthouse is the fourth tallest in the country yet, as a guided tour reveals, once built the reefs still

● *In 2001 Cape Leeuwin Lighthouse received the furthest ever delivered pizza – all the way* ● *from New York in 24 hours.*

proved dangerous. Just two years before the sinking of *Titanic* the White Star Line lost another liner, the *Pericles*, here in almost dead calm seas, possibly because the skipper was trying to cut the corner. Luckily good weather and sufficient lifeboats enabled all 463 souls aboard to get safely to shore. There is not a great deal to see on the tour except the excellent views from the top, but the guides' plentiful tales make it well worth the trip. Still on the promontory shore, though outside the lighthouse precinct, is the hundred-year old **waterwheel** that used to supply the keepers' cottages with fresh water. Now partly calcified and covered in moss it is a favourite spot for local photographers. For an excellent view over the entire promontory take the unsealed scenic drive just before the waterwheel car park. The main lookout is about 1 km along this road on the left.

● Sleeping

Cape Naturaliste *p152*
A-D Wise, Eagle Bay Rd, Eagle Bay, T9756 8098, www.wisewine.com.au. This winery has 5 lovely self-contained chalets that are very good value, especially the romantic (**D**) 'Dolls House' for 2. All have outdoor dining tables and pot belly stoves or fireplaces for winter, linen provided.

Yallingup and around *p154*
Coastal prices soar in the peak Dec-Jan period when even an unpowered tent site will set you back over $30. In terms of luxury accommodation, there are a couple of real treats in store. If you want to stay in Yallingup for a week or more try the local real estate agent for a huge range of holiday home rentals. Try **Caves Realty**, Caves Rd, Yallingup, T9755 2002, www.cavesrealty. com.au.
LL-L Cape Lodge, Caves Rd, T9755 6311, www.capelodge.com.au. Cape-style boutique hotel with beautiful grounds, within which are discretely placed half a dozen garden and lake suites. Rooms are contemporary and comfortable, the friendly service cannot be faulted, and the small conservatory restaurant simply enhances the experience.
LL-L Empire Retreat, Caves Rd, Yallingup, T9755 2065, www.empireretreat.com. Private and luxurious resort in bushland owned by a homewares company. 10 suites are decorated in sumptuous contemporary style with Indonesian and Japanese influences (and if you like it you can buy it!). Most with spa and balcony. Also guest lounge, kitchen, BBQ, spa and lots of bushwalks.
L Erravilla, Blythe Rd, T9755 1008, www.erra villa.com. Peaceful mansion in 54 ha of bush

with 6 spa suites. Each room is spacious and decorated in earth tones with fine textiles and furniture. Warm hospitality, excellent, personal service and a good location close to major wineries and beaches. Substantial healthy breakfast included.
A Chandler's Villas, Smiths Beach, T/F9755 2062, www.chandlerssmithsbeach.com.au. 3 widely separated tiers of rammed earth and wood self-contained cottages, all with panoramic views over Smiths Beach, a 5-min walk away. Each sleeps up to 6.
A Rivendell, T9755 2090, www.rivendell wines.com.au. Accommodation in a large self-contained log chalet sleeping up to 20. Min 2 nights and 6 people.
A Wildwood Valley B&B, Wildwood Rd, T9755 2120, www.wildwoodvalley.com.au. 5 comfortable rooms, all with en-suite or private bathroom. Extensive guest areas include a snooker room.
B-D Canal Rocks Beach Resort, Smiths Beach, T9755 2116, www.canalrocks.com.au. Has a wide range of slightly pricier options from luxurious spa apartments with beach views to on-site vans and camp sites. It's a short walk to the beach and facilities include a shop, open 0730-2200, takeaway and the Rocks café.
B-D Yallingup Beach, T9755 2164, www. yallingupbeach.com.au. This holiday park has superb views, cabins, on-site vans, kiosk and grassy sites.

Northern Margaret River wine area *p157*
There is less accommodation in the Wilya-brup Valley area than around the town centres, but the area has the richest concentration of wineries and makes a very

good base for exploring the whole region.

L **Karriview Lodge**, Caves Rd, Cowaramup. T9755 5553, www.karrieview.com.au. Set in 19 ha of bush, the place has been designed to have the cosy feel of a ski lodge. 12 rooms decorated in individual country style. There is also a restaurant, tennis court, golf driving range, sauna and outdoor spa.

B **Sunset Ridge**, Peake St, Cowaramup, T9755 5239. Self-contained apartment in a modern brick house, down a quiet lane. Port and choccies on arrival, peaceful and comfortable.

B-D There is also a caravan park with cabins and on-site vans at Gracetown, T9755 5301, close to Caves Rd, 3 km from the beach.

C **Noble Grape**, Bussell Highway, Cowaramup, T9755 5538, www.babs.com.au/noble grape. 6 comfortable motel rooms arranged around a pretty garden courtyard and decorated with florals and reproduction antiques. More character then usual. Continental breakfast included.

C **Taunton Farm**, Bussell Highway, Cowaramup, T9755 5334, www.tauntonfarm.com.au. A friendly place with a few spacious, well-priced cottages alongside the shady, lawned sites. Still a working dairy and sheep farm, the campground is far enough from the highway that the only sound you'll hear is mooing. Recommended.

Margaret River and around
p160, map p160

L **Basildene Manor**, Wallcliffe Rd, T9757 3140 www.basildene.com.au. The finest accommodation in the area. Built in 1912, this historic stone house sits in lovely grounds. Joined to a sympathetic modern extension, the manor has 17 splendid rooms, several guest lounges, outdoor pool and a welcoming, homely feel. Recommended.

L-B **Margarets Beach Resort**, Walcliffe Rd, Gnarabup Beach, T9757 1227, www.assured hospitality.com.au. Self-contained apartments and houses in the new Gnarabup development. Styles vary, some with spa or balcony but all very smart and fully equipped. Rates jump in high season (Jan and long weekends). Beach house rates are based on 4 sharing so good value.

A **VAT 107**, 107 Bussell Highway, T9758 8877, www.vat107.com.au. Four elegant contemporary spa suites above the acclaimed restaurant.

B **Margarets Forest**, 96 Bussell Highway, T9758 7188, www.assuredhospitality.com.au. A complex of stylish and contemporary self-contained studios and apartments in the centre of town, most with full kitchen, spa, BBQ and deck overlooking bush by the river.

B **Riverglen Chalets**, Carters Rd, T9757 2101, www.riverglenchalets.com.au. Spacious timber chalets in a beautifully landscaped bush setting a short walk from town. Some chalets sleep 8, some with spa and woodfire. All have kitchen, balcony, BBQ. Linen included.

B-C **Prevelly Park**, T9757 2374. Caravan park opposite the beach with cabins, vans, cottages and shady camping sites.

C **Bridgefield**, 73 Bussell Highway, T9757 3007, bridgefield@westnet.com. Lovely National Trust listed guesthouse close to the river with 4 jarrah-lined traditional rooms, brass beds and antiques. Warm hospitality and excellent continental breakfast. The only flaw is traffic noise, mostly during the day. Excellent value.

C **Margaret River Guest House**, Valley Rd, T9757 2349. A former convent in a quiet side street with beautiful English garden, this B&B has 8 comfortable rooms, some opening onto the veranda. Breakfast (cooked and continental) is something of an event and you may not need to eat again for days.

C **Peppermint Brook Cottages**, Mann St, T9757 2485, www.bushlandcottages.com.au /peppermint. Brick self-contained cottages close to town, simple but affordable. 2 bedrooms, linen included.

C-D **Riverview**, 8 Willmott Av, T9757 2270. A range of cabins but only the most expensive ones have cooking facilities.

C-E **Surf Point Lodge**, Riedle Drv, Gnarabup Beach, T9757 1777, www.surfpoint.com.au. Has a luxurious 'hostel' section which has backpacker accommodation with dining and cooking facilities and chic TV room. Bike and boogie board hire. Watch out for extras like videos and internet.

D **Margaret River Tourist Park**, 44 Station Rd, T9757 2180. Timber cottages with

---

● *For an explanation of sleeping and eating price codes used in this guide, see inside the*
● *front cover. Other relevant information is found in Essentials, see pages 40-46.*

kitchen and en suite, pool and good shady, grassy tent sites.

D-E Inne Town Backpackers, 93 Bussell Highway, T9757 3698. Small hostel that has the major advantage of being in the centre of town. Dorms and doubles. Hard-working managers ensure a good atmosphere.

D-E Margaret River Lodge, 220 Railway Terr, T9757 9532, www.mrlodge.com.au. Backpackers in quiet bush location about 2 km from town centre. This place also has a good vibe and lots of ideas and activities. Rammed-earth buildings, pool, BBQs and bike hire. Pick-ups from coach stop.

Augusta p165

A Augusta Sheoak Chalets, on the road to the main golf course, T9758 1958, www.she oakchalets.com.au. Well-appointed wooden chalets in a quiet inland spot. Sleeping 2, 8 or 16, the chalets have wonderful views across pasture and forest to the Blackwood River. Price is actually **C** most of the year.

B-D Augusta Hotel/Motel Blackwood Av, T9758 1944, www.augusta-resorts.com.au. Resort-style pub hotel with a large rear lounge bar, terrace and tiered beer garden with sweeping views across a couple of paddocks to the river and beyond. Over 50 motel rooms, a couple of self-contained 2-bedroom cottages, and a backpackers lodge. Counter meals 1200-1400, 1800-2030, plus a mid-range restaurant in summer.

C Juniper's East Bank Studio, T9758 1693, www.mronline.com.au/accom/juniper. Artistic and utterly peaceful self-contained cottage for 2 in the tiny cluster of houses on the far side of the river. Utilities include a couple of bikes, and a boat can be hired. There is no bridge so the owners will ferry you over, though you can make the 40-km drive if you choose. Recommended.

C-E Baywatch Manor YHA, 88 Blackwood Av, T9758 1290, enquiries@baywatchmanor. com.au. A clean, friendly, purpose-built hostel built on the lines of a large house. Most of the 36 beds are in comfortable singles, twins and doubles, some en suite, with 2 small single-sex dorms. Linen included. Communal facilities excellent, including a garden, and upstairs balcony with extensive views. Recommended. It also has a number of good value self-contained cottages and units dotted about town (**B-C**).

E Doonbanks, T9758 1517. The closest carvan park to town, with a few cabins.

E Westbay Retreat, T9758 1572, has a few very on-site vans plus the most stylish toilet block you're ever likely to see.

⑦ Eating

Cape Naturaliste p152

ᵗᵗᵗ **Wise**, Eagle Bay Rd, Eagle Bay, T9756 8098, is the only winery in the southwest with ocean views, though a distant backdrop to vines and forest. A beautiful restaurant with outdoor terrace has been built to fully appreciate it. Modern Australian cuisine, daily 1200-1500, Fri-Sat 1800-2000. Book at weekends or for a balcony table. The cellar door offers a range of crisp, fruity whites and spicy reds, priced from $14-28. Cellar door daily 1000-1700. Also accommodation (**A-D**).

ᵗ **Eagle Bay Café**, Eagle Bay Meelup Rd. This is more of a general store but there are few outdoor tables where you can have a drink or some takeaway-style food. It also does wood-fired pizzas from 1730-1830 but these must be ordered by 1600. Daily 0730-1830.

Yallingup and around p154

See also the wineries in the travelling text above.

ᵗᵗᵗ **Lamont's**, next to Gunyulgup Gallery, T9755 2434. A relatively new venue, the food here is some of the best in the region. An open modern space and tables on a deck overlooking a lake. Fusion food using fresh, local ingredients such as Pemberton marron. Platters are also available to be collected or eat on the deck. Daily 1000-1800, Sat 1000-2030. Recommended.

ᵗᵗᵗ-ᵗ **Rocks Café**, Smiths Beach, T9755 2116. Serves meals in the simple dining room or on the outside deck. Breakfasts all day from 0730, cheap light lunches 1130-1730 and mostly expensive dinners 1800-2030.

ᵗ **Simmo's**, 105 Commonage Rd, T9755 3745. About 40 flavours of ice-cream made to an 'old Irish recipe'. The venue has a BBQ area, mini golf and playground – pretty touristy but the ice-cream is good. Daily 1030-1700.

Northern Margaret River wine area p

See also the wineries in the travelling text above and Shopping below for other foodies treats.

Sea Star, 4 Bayview Dr, Gracetown, T9755 5000. A casual sea-themed café with bay views and a shady outdoor terrace. Uncomplicated food such as salads, pasta, fish and steak, mid-range evening menu. Wed-Mon 1000-2000.

Margaret River and around
p160, map p160

See also Bars and clubs below.

Vat 107, 107 Bussell Highway, T9758 8877, has won awards placing it as one of the best in the country. Eating here is worth every cent. The food is an innovative mix of local produce and Asian elements, although inspiration has also been taken from Mediterranean and Middle Eastern cooking. Warm, unstuffy service and original contemporary decor. Breakfast 0900-1130, lunch 1130-1800, dinner 1800-2030. Recommended.

Arc of Iris, 151 Bussell Highway, T9757 3112. Funky little café full of art and handmade furniture. A long-standing locals' favourite for tasty, interesting and good value food. BYO. Thu-Sun 1200-1400, daily 1800-2030. Recommended.

D'Vine, Margaret River Hotel, see Bars and clubs, is a sophisticated bistro with a large outdoor courtyard serving wood-fired pizzas, a mix of grills, seafood, 'Mediterrasian' dishes. 1700-2100. Takeaway pizzas too.

Goodfellas, 97 Bussell Highway, T9757 3184. Lively pizza and pasta café with an upstairs balcony. BYO. Daily 1800-2030.

Margaret River Fish & Chips, 137 Bussell Highway, T9757 3808. Set back from the street in Town Sq, this is a top quality fish and chip joint. Wed-Sun 1600-2000.

Urban Bean, 157 Bussell Highway, T9757 3480. Deservedly popular, the outdoor terrace is always filled with people watching the street action. Casual and unpretentious, the café serves great coffee, cakes, sandwiches and salads from the counter. Also sells a range of local produce. Daily 0700-1700.

Augusta *p165*

August Moon, corner of Ellis St and Allnutt Terr, T9758 1322. Cheap but popular Chinese that does seriously cheap 'twilight specials' daily to 1800. Open Mon-Tue 1730-2000, Wed-Sun 1200-1400, 1700-2000.

Colourpatch, Albany Terr, T9758 1295. One of a number of cafés, this is a simple, cheerful place with cheap meals to match and a terrace overlooking the river. Open daily 0830-1930. Also has a Fish and chip shop section. Recommended.

🜚 Bars and clubs

Wilyabrup Valley *p157*

Bootleg Brewery, Pusey Rd, at the northern tip of the area, just off Johnson Rd, T9755 6300, www.bootlegbrewery.com.au. Open daily 1000-1630, wholesome lunches 1200-1500. The European-style beers include a brown ale, wheat beer, pilsner and a more Australian light. They are available for tasting at the large bar, and for purchase by the glass or large stubby. A large beer-garden is pleasant spot to quaff a beer, particularly on a Sun when a band gets going and the place stays open to 1900.

Margaret River and around
p160, map p160

Margaret River Hotel, Bussell Highway, T9757 2655. A classy and civilized pub with lots of outdoor terrace tables. Karaoke Thu, bands and DJs Fri-Sat. Also some pleasant hotel rooms upstairs (all en suites) but these can be noisy (**B-Q**).

Settlers Tavern, 114 Bussell Highway, T9757 2398. A traditional Aussie pub with no frills. A grassy beer garden on the streetfront, pool tables, TVs and TAB. A refuge for those who dislike the town's increasing yuppiness, it's also a busy live venue Wed-Sat, see blackboards for current programme.

Wino's, 85 Bussell Highway, T9758 7155. Hip wine bar full of understated art. It's not snooty though – the emphasis is on having fun with wine and food and the staff are very friendly and knowledgeable. Huge range of local wines by the glass and an excellent 'grits' menu, lots of small $5 nibble dishes, so you can eat (and spend) as much as you wish. Also mid-range mains in a casual fusion style. Daily 1100-late.

⛰ Activities and tours

Margaret River and around
p160, map p160

Adventure sports

Adventure IN, T9757 2104, abseil@yahoo. com.au. Organizes all sorts of activities for individuals and small groups, including caving, abseiling, bushwalking, canoeing and rock climbing.

Outdoor Discoveries, T0407 084945, outdoor@iinet.net.au. Again different sorts of adventure sports for individuals and groups.

Canoeing

Bushtucker Tours, T9757 1084, www.bushtuckertours.com. Runs one of the most interesting and fun tours in the southwest. The 4-hr trip ($45, children $25), which leaves the river mouth daily at 1000, takes in a bit of a paddle, a short bushwalk, a cave tour and a bushtucker picnic. The guides are bursting with information and the finale will leave you gasping. A similar tour without the caving leaves at 0930.

Surfing

24-hr surf report T1900 922 995.

Beach Life Surf Shop, 117 Bussell Highway, T9757 2888. Board hire from $20 ½ day. Also book lessons here for **Margaret River Surf School**. Group lessons at 1000 daily, $45 per person including equipment.

Walking and cycling

A brochure on walking and cycling trails can be bought from the VIC ($2).

Wine tasting

Margaret River Lady, T9757 1212, www.thewinetourco.com.au. There are number of options including this personal tour in a Bentley, perfect if you're loaded or out to impress.

Margaret River Tours, T04-1991 7166, www.margaretrivertours.com. A little less hard on the purse, vehicles range from minibuses to 4WDs.

Augusta *p165*
Bicycle hire

Leeuwin Souvenirs, Blackwood Av, next to post office, T9758 1695. Second-hand books and exchange. Cheaper at the YHA for guests.

Boat cruises/hire

Augusta Marine, T9758 0808, hires out a variety of motor boats.

Miss Flinders, operated by the hotel, is a covered motor-cruiser that heads up the Blackwood River, the largest and one of the most unspoiled rivers in the southwest. Wildlife encounters, including with dolphins, are common, commentary is informed and enthusiastic, and some cruises include afternoon tea or evening BBQ. Enquire at hotel or VIC for current schedule.

Sea Dragon, T9758 4003, takes to the water daily at 1100.

Turner Caravan Park, T9758 1593, has surfcats available in summer.

Golf

9-hole par-3 course on Allnutt Terr ($4, honesty box).

Augusta Hardware, club hire, $15 a day.

Whale watching

Naturaliste Charters, T9755 2276, www.whales-australia.com. Heads out 1000 daily, Jun-Aug, and see whales almost every day (3 hrs, $48, children $27, concessions $42). Do not miss this tour if there are whales around.

○ Shopping

Northern Margaret River
wine area *p156*

Candy Cow, Cowaramup, T9755 9155. Makes fine fudges, nougat and boiled lollies (sweets). Daily 1000-1700.

Fonti Farm, Bussell Highway, Cowaramup, T9755 5400, at the end of Harmons Mill Rd. Here the best known dairy in WA, the **Margaret River Cheese Company**, produces a range of rich cheeses, yoghurts, and ice-cream. This is just a sales outlet but there is a window that allows you to see the action in the dairy. Daily 0930-1700.

Margaret River Chocolate Factory, Harmons Mill Rd, T9755 6555. Open 1000-1700. It always has about 20 different varieties of choccies available, based on the old milk, white and plain favourites. These bases are available for tasting as small buttons. It also sells a range of homemade jams, sauces, pickles etc. A small café serves cake, coffee and panninis all day.

Margaret River and around
p160, map p160

Down South Camping, 144 Bussell Highway, T9757 2155. Camping equipment but no hire.

Margaret River Book Exchange, Town Sq,
Bussell Highway. Second-hand books.
River Tales, Bussell Highway between
Willmott and Forrest, T9757 2746.
New books.

Transport

Margaret River and around
p160, map p160
TransWA northbound bus services leave
from Charles West Rd at least once daily.
Services south depart Sun-Fri. Some buses
continue on to **Nannup** and **Pemberton**.
Taxi, T9757 3444.

Augusta *p165*
TransWA northbound bus services leave
opposite the newsagents at least once a day.

Services to **Nannup** and **Pemberton** depart
Tue, Thu and Sun.

❶ Directory

Margaret River *p160*
Banks Major banks branches and ATMs on
Bussell Highway. **Chemist** Margaret River
Pharmacy, 146 Bussell Highway, T9757 2224.
Daily 0830-1800. **Internet** Cybercorner, 72
Willmott Av, T9757 9388. Mon-Sat 0800-
2000, Sun 1300-1700. **Post** Corner of Will-
mont Av and Town View Terr. **Police** 20
Willmott Av, T9757 2222. **Usful addresses**
Margaret River Environment Centre, 50
Townview Terr, T9758 8078. Community
centre where you can learn about local
environmental issues.

❧ Footprint features

Introduction

In stark contrast to the red, barren earth of the north, this area is all about growth and forests of very tall trees. The timber towns of Nannup, Balingup, Bridgetown, Manjimup and Pemberton all sit within the region's vast expanse of forest and grew up when a timber industry developed in the southwest in the late 19th and early 20th centuries. Many areas were cleared and opened up for dairy farming and agriculture by the group settlers of the 1920s; British immigrants persuaded to settle here after the First World War by promises of free land to farm. Most of them had no idea they would have to clear it first.

Timber mills provided work and prosperity for much of the 20th century but the few mills left now operate on reduced hours. These towns have suffered in the last few decades and are now hoping, some reluctantly, that tourism will keep them alive. Those who visit these days will be able to enjoy magnificent walking, driving through tall karri forests and climbing to dizzying heights on a few of the giant fire-spotting trees.

Nannup and Pemberton are the most attractive towns, full of characteristic timber workers cottages. Both are still small and fairly undeveloped, but with good facilities in beautiful surroundings. Bridgetown and Manjimup are both larger, less interesting places that have survived on agriculture and by supplying regional services.

⁞ Don't miss...

1 **Bibbulmun Track** Walk through towering forest, along sandplains and beside rugged coastline, page 177.

2 **Greenbushes** Stare into this pit, over 300-m deep and a little over that across, page 178.

3 **Tree climbing** Climb one of the fire-spotting trees, near Pemberton, page 180.

4 **Warren National Park** Come here and camp by the river, the Ritz has nothing on this place, page 182.

5 **Yeagerup Dunes** Explore the coast around these dunes where beach meets forest and there's not a highrise nor ice-cream kiosk in sight, page 182.

6 **Salmon Beach** Stroll along this perfect beach, near Windy Harbour, page 182.

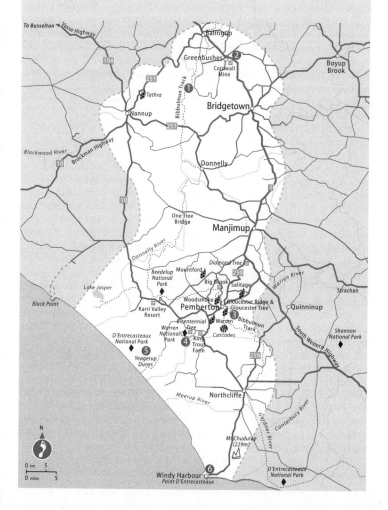

Ins and outs

TransWA has daily bus services from Perth railway station (train to Bunbury then coach) to Balingup, Greenbushes, Bridgetown, and Manjimup that leave at 0930. On Wednesday and Friday it also calls at Pemberton (5½ hours) and Northcliffe. Nannup is served by a service between Pemberton and Augusta in the Capes region. During the week, **South West Coachlines** buses leave from the City Bus Port, Perth, and call at Balingup, Greenbushes, Bridgetown and Manjimup.

Nannup and around

Nannup → *Colour map 3, grid B2. Population: 800. 60 km from Busselton, 90 km from Augusta.*

A pretty, historic town by the banks of the Blackwood River, Nannup sits in an idyllic green valley surrounded by forest. The main street, Warren Street, is full of trees and timber cottages with bull-nosed tin verandas. Europeans settled here by the river, where they found a ford useful for travellers to rest and water their horses or bullocks. It is a sleepy and peaceful place to unwind but is likely to develop rapidly in the next few years when the Mowen road is sealed, providing a short cut to Margaret River. Canoeing on the Blackwood or walking in the forest are the main things to do and there are a few excellent restaurants and places to stay. The busiest time of year is during the **Nannup Music Festival**, held on the Labour Day weekend in early March. Nannup is also noted for its flowers, particularly in spring (August-September) when masses of tulips blossom and wildflowers carpet the forest. ▶ *For Sleeping, Eating and other listings, see pages 184-188.*

One sight you won't see is the **Nannup Tiger**. Some locals believe that *Thylacines*, better known as the extinct Tasmanian Tiger, live in the jarrah forest around Nannup. Needless to say there has been no proof of this but several businesses in town use the tiger as a logo. The town does have one old survivor though, one of the few timber mills still operating in the region, the **Nannup Timber Processing Mill** ① *Vasse Highway, Mon, Wed, Fri 0930, free, meet at the mill office, enclosed shoes must be worn, enquiries to the VIC.* Tours take visitors into the mill to watch the saw operators cut a round jarrah trunk into square planks used for floorboards and other building material. Most of the waste, such as bark, is reused as garden mulch and the rest burnt in the dalek-shaped iron furnace. There is a **Gemstone Museum** ① *125 Warren Rd, T9756 1182, Thu-Tue 0900-1200, 1300-1730, entry by donation,* just north of the Mill, which holds a small amateur collection of rocks, gems, bottles and badges. It's really only for the dedicated rock hound. Gardeners will enjoy **Blythe Gardens** ① *11 Brockman St, opposite VIC, daily dawn to dusk, $1, children free,* established by longtime locals from a cow paddock behind the pub. It is full of natives and exotics, such as a tree dahlia, ginko and Paulownia. In the main shopping area on Warren Street there are a few antique shops and timber furniture shops.

Just outside the town centre are a few lovely spots for walking or camping in the forest. Cross the river, heading north, and take the first left into Mowen Road. In wildflower season turn left again into Barrabup Road to access the **Wildflower Drive**, a pretty short loop through forest, banksia, orchids and other wildflowers. Continue along Mowen Road and follow signs for **Barrabup** and **Workers Pools** (9 km from Nannup), tranquil emerald green swimming holes surrounded by forest. Each has camping sites, picnic tables and BBQs. Timberline walk trail links the two pools. Visit the CALM office ① *Warren St, Mon-Fri, 0900-1600,* for more walking suggestions.

The VIC ① *4 Brockman St, T9756 1211, nannuptb@compwest.net.au, 0900-1700,* is in the former police station at the northern end of town by the riverbank and bridge.

Nannup sits on the confluence of several major roads and highways. The Vasse Highway runs directly from Busselton, and the Brockman Highway from Augusta, both in the **Southwest**, see page 139. In addition to these the unsealed Mowen Road comes almost directly from Margaret River. The Vasse continues south through the Karri Valley to **Pemberton** (75 km), though there is a slightly longer option via the much forested Brockman Highway, turning right at Sears Road through **Donnelly** and then **Manjimup** (85 km). The Brockman itself passes through a small stand of karri trees just after the turn, and then carries on to **Bridgetown** (45 km). The most scenic road north of the town is via the Blackwood Valley to **Balingup** (40 km). This valley, a patchwork of forest, plantations and pasture, is often quite steep-sided and the road hugs the river the entire way.

Donnelly → *Colour map 3, grid B2. 32 km from Nannup, 27 km from Manjimup.*

In the middle of extensive jarrah and karri forests, Donnelly is a timber milling town that closed down in the early 1970s. The 36 former workers cottages, each with their own small garden and front veranda, are spaced evenly around a loop road in the forest and are now all available for holiday rental. Facilities are scant, the small shop doubling as reception and tearooms, but there are a few sporting activities available, including tennis and a flying fox. The real attraction is the forest itself, and the wildlife. For good or ill, emus and kangaroos have been hand fed over the years and are now more or less tame. Pellets can be bought from the shop, but even without them you are likely to have several guests in the garden. Birdlife is also prolific, particularly kookaburras, 28s (the green parrots with a yellow collar) and black cockatoos. **Donnelly River Holiday Village** ① *T9772 1244, www.donnelly-river-holiday-village. com.au, 0830-1700*, is where to go for bookings. Linen and towels not supplied. The **Bibbulmun Track** passes close to the village.

The Bibbulmun Track

This is one of the most tranquil, appealing and easy sections of the 'Bibb'. Soon after leaving the quaint wooden houses of Donnelly, the track begins to follow the Donnelly River past its attractive falls, pools and log bridges. Further south, after leaving the Donnelly River Valley, the track passes through Beedelup National Park by Beedelup Falls, then the Big Brook Dam and Arboretum just before reaching Pemberton. This southern section can make a good two to three day walk: it is 11 km from Pemberton to **Pemberton Forest Stay** near the Big Brook Dam, and a further 13 km from here to the campsite in Beedelup National Park.

> ⁑ *The section of track from Balingup to Pemberton is a classic forest section, passing through magnificent jarrah, karri and yarri (blackbutt) country.*

Balingup to Bridgetown

Balingup → *Colour map 3, grid B2. Population: 500. 65 km from Bunbury, 26 km from Bridgetown.*

Not yet in the heart of the timber region, tiny Balingup is surrounded by hilly pastoral country. For those walking the **Bibbulmun Track**, which passes through the town, Balingup is very welcome. There is not a great deal to do here, other than have a look around the **Old Cheese Factory** ① *Nannup Rd, 0900-1700*, which claims to have the biggest collection of craft in Australia. The extensive premises are indeed full of a wide range of items, such as carved wombats – cute little momentos in various timbers costing $30-300. There is also a cheap café. The **VIC** ① *T9764 1818, www.balingup.asn.au, 1000-1600*, is just off the main street. Check here for details of walks around the town. There are good views over the pretty vale Balingup sits in from the top of the track leading to **Balingup Heights**. ▶ *For Sleeping, Eating and other listings, see pages 184-188.*

For Sleeping, Eating and other listings, see pages 184-188.

Greenbushes → *Colour map 3, grid B3. 10 km from Balingup, 16 km from Bridgetown.*

With the distinct feel of a ghost town, there would be little reason to visit Greenbushes if it wasn't for the **Cornwall Mine**. This open-cast pit, dug to extract various metals including lithium, tin and tantalum, is over 300-m deep and a little over that across. There are good views of it from the lookout, open daily 0800-1700. The town also has an **Eco-cultural Discovery Centre** ① *T9764 3883, Sat-Sun 1000-1400, $2, children $0.50*, giving an overview of the environment in the southwest. It also has information on local bushwalks.

Bridgetown → *Colour map 3, grid B3. Population: 2,100. 46 km from Nannup, 37 km from Manjimup.*

A service town for the local agricultural area, Bridgetown nestles alongside the Blackwood River, and is not without its charms. The surrounding, sharply undulating hills, partly forested, are very scenic, but the town itself struggles to offer much to the visitor except during the second week of November when major garden and blues festivals run nearly back-to-back.

    Bridgedale House ① *T9761 1508, Sat-Sun 1000-1430 (other days and times subject to availability of volunteers), $3.30, children $1.65*, encapsulates the spirit of much of Bridgetown's history, and that of the timber region. It was the first house in the district, built in 1862 by John Blechynden who was shown the valley by local Aborigines, and enlarged over time. After almost being lost to the bulldozers in the 1960s it has been restored by the National Trust. Entry includes an informative tour of the house. Just over the bridge from the house is a riverside park, and adjacent to this the caravan park which hires out canoes (0800-1600, $11 per hour). **Centenary Outdoor Pool** ① *corner of Steere and Gifford sts, daily Nov-Easter, Mon-Fri 0900-1900, Sat 1000-1700, Sun 1200-1700. $2.20, children $1.10*, is a welcome spot on a hot day. The **VIC** ① *Hampton St, T9761 1740, tourist1@iinet.net.au, 0900-1700*, houses a small artefact museum and a collection of framed jigsaws.

Manjimup and around → *Colour map 3, grid B3. Population: 4,400. 120 km from Walpole, 160 km from Mt Barker.*

Manjimup is the major service town for the central timber region. The area has a fruit and vegetable industry, and grows tree seedlings and plantation trees such as Tasmanian blue gum for paper pulp. There is not much to interest travellers but if you have the time and inclination a visit to the **Manjimup Regional Timber Park** ① *corner of Rose and Edwards sts, T9771 1831, 0900-1700, entry by donation*, by the VIC can be interesting. There is an Age of Steam museum, timber museum, historic hamlet, lookout tower and pleasant grounds.

    About 20 km west of Manjimup are the **Four Aces**, four karri giants from 67-79 m high and a short forest walk. **One Tree Bridge** is another picnic and walking site around a pioneer bridge but both of these areas are pretty out of the way unless you are walking the Bibbulmun Track. **Perup Ecology Centre** ① *T9771 7988*, is open to tours and groups only. Some 50 km east of Manjimup, it is worth the trip for anyone who loves wildlife. About 30 mammal species native to the southern forests can be found here, observed from hides and walk trails, and there are also daily tours and spotlighting night tours. Call for details of tour operators taking trips to the centre. If staying overnight accommo- dation is in rammed-earth houses with a shared kitchen.

    About 9 km south of Manjimup, just off the main highway, the **Diamond Tree** is one of the original fire-spotting trees. Standing 51-m high, several metres above the surrounding canopy, there are all-round views from the platform at the top. Two great things about the Diamond Tree are that you don't need to pay to get into a national park to get to it, and it's less well known than either the Gloucester or Bicentennial Trees, so draws fewer people.

The South Western Highway continues on to Walpole, and if you are heading for Pemberton there are three roughly equidistant routes. By taking Channybearup Road, 1 km before the Diamond Tree, and then left into the unsealed Tramway Trail, you can drive right through some of the most beautiful parts of the local karri forests, and past either **Big Brook Arboretum** or **Big Brook Dam**. Immediately before the Diamond Tree, Eastbourne Road winds mostly through pastoral country before coming out just north of Pemberton. Alternatively the Vasse Highway, 6 km beyond the tree, passes a couple of wineries, including **Salitage**, on the way to the town.

Pemberton

Pemberton sits in a valley surrounded by tall karri, jarrah and marri trees and national parks. Like most of the timber towns it grew up around a timber mill and the town is full of identical wooden workers' cottages that lend Pemberton a quaint toy-town feel. The mill still operates, although on reduced hours and many workers have lost their jobs. It is likely to close in the next few years and the town is slowly shifting its focus to tourism and other ventures. Pemberton is central to an emerging wine region, a couple of superb woodcraft galleries and wonderfully scenic bushwalking and driving country amid the soaring forests. ▶ *For Sleeping, Eating and other listings, see pages 184-188.*

> ❢ *Look out for wildflowers during September to November, this is when the forest looks its best.*

Sights → *Colour map 3, grid B3. Population: 1,000. 31 km from Manjimup, 31 km from Northcliffe.*

Most sights revolve around forest and fishing. One of the most popular ways to see the forest is to take a **Pemberton Tram** ① *Railway Cres, T9776 1322, 1045, 1400 to Warren River ($18, 2 hrs), varying times according to tram availability (Sep-Apr) to Northcliffe ($34, 5½ hrs); steam trains $28, 3 hrs, check timetable.* The trams run along disused lines to Warren River Bridge and Northcliffe. There are a couple of stops where you can get out and wander in the forest. There are also steam train trips 21 km north to Lyall on weekends (April-October). Trainspotters can enquire about driving courses. To see what can be done with all this timber don't miss the **Fine Woodcraft Gallery** ① *Dickinson St, T9776 1399, 0900-1700,* one of the best in the region with its superb collection of timber furniture and homewares. **Peter Kovacsy Studio** ① *Jamieson St, T9776 1265, Mon-Sat 0900-1700,* also has some fine work, by one craftsman who specializes in inlay work. There are free one-hour tours of the local karri **timber mill** ① *Brockman St, T9776 1825, Mon-Thu 0900, 1100, 1330, tours leave from Forest Information Centre, enclosed shoes must be worn,* which show how the logs are cut up and processed and the Forest Information Centre keeps some brochures and articles on the contentious subject of logging although the tour itself is apolitical. The efficient **VIC** ① *0900-1700, T9776 1133, www.pembertontourist.com. au,* is on the main street which becomes Brockman Street where the Vasse Highway passes through the town centre. It sells a good brochure on 30 walks in the area ($3.30). The VIC has a **Karri Forest**

Pemberton

To Golf Course
Pemberton Trams
Railway Cres
Swimming Pool Rd
Hospital Av
Hoppie Cres
Ellis St
To Peter Kovacsy Studio
Guppy St
Karri Forest Discovery Centre
To Mountford Winery & Big Brook Dam
To Nannup, Northcliffe & Augusta
Club Rd
Swimming Pool Rd
Brockman St
Pine St
Kelly St
Dean St
Karri St
To 3, 4, 5, Salitage Winery, Manjimup & Albany
Vasse Highway
Forest Information Centre
To Brockman Hwy
Dickinson St
Cemetery Rd
Timber Mills
Fine Woodcraft Gallery

N
0 metres 200
0 yards 200

Sleeping 🛏
Pemberton 1

Pemberton
Backpackers 2
Glenhaven 3
Lavender Berry
Farm Cottages 4
Treenbrook
Cottages 5
YHA 6

Wisteria House 7

Eating 🍴
Café Mazz 1
Jan's Diner 2
Pembee Fish Café 3

⦂ Living towers

From the 1950s to the mid-1970s, when aerial observation became the preferred method of fire-spotting in the region, there were eight fire-spotting towers around Manjimup and Pemberton used by the local communities to pinpoint fires when smoke was seen. These were not, however, constructed from the ground up, but used living karri trees as enormous central pillars. The trunks were stripped of branches and metal rungs pinned in, curling around and up the trunk to form a sloping ladder. The tree was then topped at a point at which the trunk was still strong and a platform constructed atop it. As well as still being a back-up to the planes, two of the original trees are now open to the public, the 64-m **Gloucester Tree**, in Gloucester Discovery Centre which aims to reveal the secrets of the karri forest. It is pretty tired but has an interesting short film about life in the forest.

National Park, and the 51-m **Diamond Tree**. In 1988 another was 'constructed', with less damage to the tree, in Warren National Park: the **Bicentennial Tree**. At 75 m this is the most challenging, but also the most rewarding. All three will give most people the willies, particularly on the way down when you have to look down at your feet (and thus the ground) the whole way. Only four people are allowed at the top of each tree at one time, so try to avoid the crowds by arriving in the early morning or late afternoon. Climbing can be dangerous in the wet or when windy so watch your step. There is enough clearance around all three to get a good photo of each but you will need a fairly wide-angle lens, about 28 mm.

Around Pemberton

This is a large area, but there are many worthy attractions around. The Pemberton wine region lies in a cooler, wetter area than the Margaret River wine region so cool climate varieties such as Sauvignon Blanc, Semillon, Pinot and Merlot dominate. There are about 10 cellar doors, a few with good restaurants, and they are often picturesque with rows of vines rolling downhill to meet karri forest. The Bibbulmun Track passes through the Pemberton, on its way down to the coast. The knee-wobbling climbing trees are also good fun and beyond the forest, lies the coastal D'Entrecasteaux National Park, an untouched wilderness of monster sand dunes and wild shores. ▸▸ *For Sleeping, Eating and other listings, see pages 184-188.*

Wineries

Gloucester Ridge's ① *Burma Rd, T9776 1035, 1100-1700, lunches 1130-1430,* Sauvignon Blanc and Cabernet Sauvignon are particularly good of the dozen or more wines available for tasting. Wines $17-40. The restaurant opens onto a deck over the vineyard and offers local produce like marron and trout (mid-range). Also a good value cheese platter ($10) served with a glass of wine.

Mountford ① *Bamess Rd, T9776 1345, www.mountfordwines.com.au, 1000-1600,* is one of the region's oldest vineyards so wines have more intensity and complexity than some. All wine is grown, made and bottled on the estate so these are pure Pemberton wines using the region's classic white and red varieties. Lovely timber and rammed-earth cellar door, art gallery and unusually they also make traditional English cider, including a scrumpy from the barrel. Wines $15-25.

Salitage ⓘ *Vasse Highway, T9776 1771, 1000-1600*, 10 km east, is Pemberton's grandest winery with some of the best of the region's wines. Wines $17-40. The restaurant overlooks the vineyard in summer or the wine-making operations in winter and offers mid-range modern Australian (Fri-Mon 1200-1430). Also tours at 1100 daily.

Warren ⓘ *Conte Rd (unsealed), 3 km from Pemberton, T9776 1115, 1100-1700*, is a small family-owned winery producing superb wines specializing in reds that are made for cellaring. Such is their belief in ageing the wine properly that they don't make it available for tasting or sales until it's at least five years old. Wines $15-30.

WoodSmoke Estate ⓘ *Kemp Rd, T9776 0225, 1030-1600*, is a new winery producing Sauvingnon Blanc, Cabernet Sauvignon and Cabernet Franc, and Semillon. Hand pruned vines and hand-picked grapes, this is a small, friendly winery with a rustic cellar door. Wines $18-25.

Gloucester National Park → *Colour map 3, grid B3. Vehicle entry $9.*

This relatively small park marks Pemberton's southern boundary and also extends to the east. From Pemberton's main street, a 3-km route, which doubles as the Bibbulmun Track, is clearly signposted to the park's first access point, the site of the **Gloucester Tree**. One of the eight original fire-trees used in the mid-20th century, it reaches 64 m and was named for the visiting Duke of Gloucester who helped drill some of the holes. There are toilets and several picnic tables here. The park's second public access point is 6 km out on the Northcliffe Road, an unsealed 2 km road to the **Cascades**, a series of rocky rapids in the East Brook – impressive after heavy rain in winter, disappointing if it's dry. There are a few short easy walks from the tree.

Big Brook

Just north of town the Big Brook dam supplies water for the town and the trout hatchery. It is a beautiful stretch of water surrounded by tall karri forest and a lovely spot for a picnic or drive. There are usually lots of parrots and fairy wrens flitting about and the route gives the feeling of being deep in the forest. The road is unsealed and mostly one way, forming a loop of about 12 km off Stirling Road. There is a walking circuit of the dam (4 km) and picnic tables by a small stretch of sand. The Rainbow Trail is part of the loop and passes through an arboretum planted in the 1920-1930s of Californian redwoods, cyprus and Victorian mountain ash. The **Bibbulmun Track** passes along the dam to Pemberton and it is a very pleasant walk from town along the track (about 6 km one way).

Founders Forest

The Founders Forest is another pretty picnic and walking spot surrounded by karri trees. The forest is significant because it was visited by government minister Lane-Poole in 1913. He knew the land had been cleared in 1875 yet there was a 'fine crop of karri' standing almost 40 years later. This proved to a sceptical government that karri could be successfully regrown and should be kept as forest and not all cut down for agriculture. The area became the first under management of the Forestry Department. It is reached by following Pemberton Road North for 9 km, then continuing along the unsealed Smiths Rd for a couple of kilometres.

The Bibbulmun Track

To walk from Pemberton to **Walpole** would take you about 10 days (192 km) but this is a fascinating transitional section, changing gradually from tall karri forest to the low vegetation of sandplains and the rugged southern coastline. Just outside Pemberton the track passes the **Gloucester Tree** (3 km) and the **Cascades** (8 km), both of which make pleasant day excursions from town. Following old rail trails, the track descends into the **Warren River Valley** and reaches Warren campsite on the valley rim with lovely views of the forest canopy (22 km from Pemberton). Around **Northcliffe** the track becomes less wild, skirting farmland and logging areas before finding the quiet Gardner River and entering D'Entrecasteaux National Park, reaching Gardner campsite 15 km from Northcliffe. The vegetation changes to jarrah woodland and low swampy areas deeper into the park where there is a delightful campsite by **Lake Maringup** (15½ km from Gardner campsite). Swinging east, the track enters the **Shannon National Park** before traversing the **Pingerup Plains** with its granite outcrops and views to Broke Inlet and the coastal dunes beyond. From the blocky granite **Woolbale Hills** campsite it is 11 km down to the coast at **Mandalay Beach**. With your own transport, this would make a fine day or overnight walk (road access at the beach). From Broke Inlet Road, off the highway, you can access the Pingerup Plains and climb **Mount Pingerup** (7 km return).

Warren National Park → *Colour map 3, grid B2.*
The unsealed Old Vasse Road, which runs from 12 km west of Pemberton to 8 km south, passes right through the heart of another reserve of old growth karri forest, now encompassed by Warren National Park ① *vehicle entry $9, camping $10.* Nearer the Northcliffe Road end is the **Bicentennial Tree**, the 75 m living lookout constructed in 1988. There are wonderful views over the surrounding canopy at the top and a surety of wobbly legs for those who make it up there. Also off the through road is a 9 km one-way loop route called the **Heartbreak Trail** which runs down to the banks of the Warren River and then follows its course amongst the stately karri trees for about 5 km. There are several beautiful riverside camping and picnic spots along the way, and a high lookout near the end which looks out over the river valley.

Beedelup and Karri Valley → *Colour map 3, grid B2.*
Beedelup National Park, 20 km west on the Nannup road, is a small park based around a low waterfall. Like the Cascades the **Beedelup Falls** are a bit of a (not-so) damp squib in the dry. Even in winter the falls are not especially spectacular but there is a pleasant boardwalk loop constructed around the falls (600 m). Car entry to the park is $9. Just beyond the park is an area known as Karri Valley, a stand of old growth forest, and the **Karri Valley Resort**, see Sleeping.

D'Entrecasteaux National Park → *Colour map 3, grid C2.*
This is a large area of wilderness along the coast south of Pemberton. Stretching 130 km from Black Point south of Nannup to the border of the Walpole-Nornalup National Park in the east, the park was reserved on the request of local foresters to stop coastal development. Most of it is inaccessible and all except one route in require extensive 4WD experience. However there are good tours into the park, from operators in Pemberton and Walpole. If you can get there it is a stunning area of almost untouched beaches, cliffs, heathland and forest. Immediately south of Pemberton are the **Yeagerup Dunes**, a spectacular place where the forest abruptly meets high creamy dunes. In fact the dunes are mobile and fast swallowing the forest. **Lake Jasper** is the largest freshwater lake in the southwest and currently the subject of controversy. Environmentalists are aghast at plans to mine the area for ilminite, a mineral sand. The area is ecologically fragile and contains a significant archaeological site (4,000-year-old stone artefacts) but mining may still go ahead. The only sealed road access is south of Northcliffe, leading to **Windy Harbour** (25 km). There is a fishing shack settlement there and a campground ($5) but the real attraction is **Salmon Beach**, 3 km west by unsealed road. This is a perfect long stretch of sand below high, rugged cliffs. Picnic tables and toilets by the car park are the only facilities. From the beach take the loop drive back to Windy Harbour via Point D'Entrecasteaux for wonderful coastal views. **Mandalay Beach** is another beautiful beach at the eastern end of the park, just 12 km from Walpole. There is a

⁞ Fruits of the forest

Western Australia's most beautiful hardwood, **jarrah**, grows in the inland region from the Darling Range to Manjimup. It is a deep red wood that is not susceptible to termites, unlike karri, and so has been used extensively as a building material. It is such a fine wood that it is also often used for handmade furniture and woodcraft. The tree grows to about 40 m and has a stringy grey-brown bark. It typically has a leafy crown, creating a large, shady canopy. Before logging and clearfelling the canopy inhibited the growth of seedlings and kept fuel for bushfires to a minimum. Jarrah trees live for about 300 years.

Marri are often found near jarrah. These are also known as redgum for the sticky gum oozing from its rough, grey bark. Its height varies from 10 to 60 m, depending on the quality of soil. Marri has beautiful white blossoms in summer and is an important food source for bees and birds. Winemakers like to have marri near their vines, so parrots will leave their grapes alone.

The forest of the southern region between Manjimup and Walpole is dominated by **Karri**. Growing to 90 m and as slender and smooth as a telegraph pole, karri is the most easily recognizable of the forest trees. It has pale grey bark that peels in strips, revealing a peachy pink trunk. Karri only grows on red clay loams that receive more than 750 mm of rain a year. It is the third tallest hardwood in the world and lives for 250-300 years. The timber looks very similar to jarrah, a dark red colour, but is not used for construction as termites, or white ants, love it. This hasn't stopped it being cut down though as it can still be used for woodchips.

Timber Towns Around Pemberton

CALM campground just after the highway turnoff to this beach, called Crystal Springs. Vehicle entry into the park is $9, camping $10.

Northcliffe → *Colour map 3, grid C3. 31 km from Pemberton, 100 km from Walpole.*
The timber mill no longer operates at Northcliffe but there is still a small population supporting a few services, and a large forest park in the centre has a several pretty picnic areas. As well as some accommodation, the settlement also has a supermarket, café, petrol station and small VIC ① *T9776 7203, Mon-Fri 0930- 1600, Sat-Sun 1000-1400.*

Shannon National Park → *Colour map 3, grid C3.*
Sitting astride the main highway south to Walpole, and named for the river that runs north-south through it, Shannon was a karri logging settlement in the 1940s with a mill employing 160 men. The mill closed in 1968 and logging stopped in 1983 but amazingly there is hardly a trace of this activity now. The park is best known for the **Great Forest Trees Drive**, a 48-km one-way unsealed loop road through varied forest country, linked to radio stops telling tales of the timber-cutting days. It crosses the highway at two points so you can just do half of it. The southern half, the first turn you see if driving south, is the best as it takes you to **Big Tree Grove** within 5 km, a small but impressive cluster of karri trees around 85-m high and over 300 years old. At the far end of this part of the drive, near the highway, is a peaceful campsite and basic eight-bed lodge. Call CALM ① *T9776 1207,* for bookings. There are also some walking trails in the park, see the information board at the campsite. Car entry is $9 and camping $10.

Nannup and around *p176*

B Holberry House, Grange Rd. T9756 1276, www.holberryhouse.com. A large, stone guesthouse on a hillside above Nannup in beautiful grounds. Traditional country style, 6 rooms, spacious guest lounge and conservatory. Friendly, knowledgeable hosts and plenty of books and newspapers. Outdoor pool.

B Redgum Retreat, Nannup to Balingup road, T9756 2056, www.babs.com.au/red gum. One of the few licensed guesthouses.

C Blackwood River Cottages, River Rd, 2 km southwest of Nannup on road to Augusta, T9756 1252. Self-contained accommodation, secluded timber cabins surrounded by bush.

C Nannup Bush Cabins, Barrabup Rd, 5 km from town, T9756 1170. Good self-contained accommodation, secluded timber cabins surrounded by bush.

C-D Nannup Hotel, 12 Warren Rd, T9756 1080. The town's workmanlike pub has motel units and rather bare hotel rooms improved by old timber furniture and floors.

D-E Black Cockatoo, 27 Grange Rd, T9756 1035, www.blackcockatoo.nannup.net. This backpackers in an old timber cottage and huge garden is something special. The owners have combined their interests in the environment, arts and spirituality to create a unique and welcoming place to stay. Herb and vegetable gardens, dorms with patchwork quilts, 2 gorgeous rooms for couples, and a teepee in the garden in summer. Campers can use the lawn and facilities for $11. It is popular so book ahead. Recommended.

There are 2 caravan parks by the river, run by the VIC. Sites and 1 cabin. Campers should also consider the sites at Barrabup Pool and, close to Balingup on the Nannup to Balingup road, Wrights Bridge, a campground ($5 per site) and picnic site in a forested loop of the river. Facilities include fireplace BBQs and toilets, and swimming is allowed.

Balingup *p177*

C PJ's, 109 Jayes Rd, T9764 1205. A friendly B&B 1½ km from the town centre. 3 en-suite double rooms, in a 1927 cottage with jarrah floors and pressed-tin ceilings.

D Balingup Backpackers, T9764 1049, www.wn.com.au/hotbunks. Simply a self-contained extension to the post office with a dozen beds in 5 rooms. Large lounge and adequate kitchen.

Balingup Heights, 1 km off the Nannup Rd, up a very steep unsealed road, T9764 1283, www.bluewren.com.au. 4 self-contained wooden cottages of varying size, each isolated from the others and cleverly contrived to be both in a forest setting and have expansive views over neighbouring valleys.

Greenbushes *p178*

D-E Exchange Hotel, T9764 3509. A friendly pub built in 1907, renovated in keeping with its history. Both the cheap counter and mid-range brasserie meals are a cut above average pub fare and the hotel rooms are good value. Meals 0500-0900, 1200-1330 and 1800-2030.

Bridgetown *p178*

B Ford House, Eedle Terr, T9761 1816, www.fordhouse.com. A former winner of WA's B&B of the year. This 1896 former magistrate's cottage has seen hardly any changes since it was built, but has been very well maintained. 2 doubles and 2 singles, comfortably furnished in keeping, share a bathroom. The owners have built another house, **Aislinn**, in a similar weatherboard style to Ford, but with 2 large, significantly more luxurious en -suite rooms. The rear gardens of both back onto the river.

C Tortoiseshell Farm, 12 km east of Bridgetown, partly via unsealed roads, T/F9761 1089. A modern B&B farmhouse with serious character, wonderful hosts and sweeping veranda views. Rough red stone walls enclose an open-plan jarrah-floored living area, complete with pool table, old tin ads and one-armed bandits. Dinners by pre-arrangement, $25. Call ahead for directions. Recommended.

C-D Freemasons Arms, Hampton St, T9761 1725. A large traditional pub with a friendly public bar, cheap counter meals Thu-Fri 1200-1330 and 1830-2030 daily.

Live cover bands or DJs on a Fri give the place a swing and there is a choice of simple hotel double rooms or en-suite motel units. The only, lacklustre, caravan park, T9761 1053, is on the far bank of the river, 1 km from the town centre. On-site vans and cabins.

Manjimup and around *p178*
C Lavender Cottage, Manjimup, T9777 1760. Pretty self-contained white weatherboard cottage in the English-style garden of a larger house. Breakfast included.
D Manjimup Hotel, Giblett St, Manjimup, T9771 1322. Has a smart lounge bar and serves cheap but adventurous counter meals, and there's a generous and inviting salad and veggie bar. Both single and double hotel and motel rooms available. Meals daily 1200-1400, 1800-2030.
There is also a site-only caravan park close to town.

Pemberton *p179, map p179*
The busiest period is in Jan and it is often very quiet in winter when you may get a good discount if you ask. Accommodation in the area is dominated by self-contained cottages, usually timber or rammed earth and surrounded by bush.
A-B Pemberton Hotel, Brockman St, T9776 1017, www.pembertonhotel.bestwestern. com. 30 luxurious rooms in shades of navy and taupe furnished with modern art and timber furniture, some with spa, balcony and kitchenette.
B Treenbrook Cottages, Vasse Highway, 5 km northwest of town. T9776 1638, www.treenbrook.com.au. 4 charming, rustic cottages made of mud brick and local timbers. 2 bedrooms, full kitchen, woodfire, BBQ, and lots of bushwalk trails in the adjoining forest.
B-C Lavender Berry Farm Cottages, Browns Rd, 4 km from town, T9776 1661, www.wn.com.au/lavenderberryfarm. 4 comfortable self-contained rammed-earth cottages overlooking a lake and the berry farm. Wood fires, leather couches, BBQs.

D Pemberton YHA, Stirling Rd (8 km from town). Budget cabins along with free BBQs and friendly roos. Details from the VIC.
D-E Caravan park, Pump Hill Rd, T9776 1300, also has some timber cabins.
D-E Pemberton Backpackers Forest Stay, 7 Brockman St. T9776 1105, pembertonyha@westnest.com.au. Old timber building in the main street with a large central lounge and woodfire, grassy lawn and BBQ, utilitarian kitchen and standard bunk rooms. Also bike hire and some seasonal work.

Big Brook *p181*
D-E Pemberton Forest Stay, Stirling Rd. T9776 1153, www.pembertonforeststay.com. Peaceful hostel-style accommodation in bush near the dam. Beds are in 6 former timber workers' cottages, each with 2 bedrooms, own kitchen, lounge, fireplace. Outdoor BBQ shed, bike hire, volleyball court and rescued kangaroos to feed. If you want to splash out, take the Zamin cottage ($72 double) exclusively.

Warren National Park *p182*
Camping is possible here. See section.
A-B Marima Cottages, Old Vasse Rd, T/F9776 1211, www.marima.com.au. Each set at the boundary between the encircling forest and a modest paddock, very smart, a favourite evening haunt of kangaroos, in a relict block within the park.

D'Entrecasteaux National Park *p185*
Camping is possible here. See section.

Beedelup and Karri Valley *p182*
L-A Karri Valley Resort, T1800 245757 or 9776 2020, www.karrivalleyresort.com.au, on the shores of Lake Beedelup to the west of Pemberton. Has a series of wooden self-contained chalets, motel-style rooms and a restaurant. Though the experience isn't cheap it is possible to fish for trout straight off some verandas here. The office is open daily 0900-1800 and a wide range of generally inexpensive activities, all open to non-residents, includes horse trail-riding, guided bushwalking, canoeing, trout fishing, animal night-spotting and bike hire.

Timber Towns Around Pemberton Listings

🎈 *For an explanation of sleeping and eating price codes used in this guide, see inside the*
● *front cover. Other relevant information is found in Essentials, see pages 40-46.*

D-E **Caravan park**, T9776 7276, B&B rooms, on-site vans and backpacker beds ($10).
D-E **The pub**, T9776 7089, has some standard rooms and cheaper rooms with shared facilities for backpackers and walkers.

Shannon National Park *p183*
Camping is possible here. See section.

❼ Eating

Nannup and around *p176*
There are 2 excellent restaurants in town.
♯♯ **Hamish's Cafe**, 1 Warren Rd, T9756 1287. Lively place in a corrugated-iron building full of art, sculpture and recycled materials. Generous, casual meals such as pasta and grills. Wed-Fri, Sun 1000-1430, Fri 1830-2030.
♯♯ **Mulberry Tree**, 62 Warren Rd, T9756 3038. Formal fine dining in a cottage with lots of character. The food features local produce and Latin American, Caribbean and Asian flavours. BYO. Tue-Sun 1100-1500, 1800-2100.

Cafés

Blackwood Café, Warren Rd. Takeaways, fast food, Mon-Fri 0800-2000, Sat-Sun 0900-2000.
Blackwood Wines, Kearney St, a 30-min walk from the VIC along the river bank. A good place for lunch, do a good sharing platter and homemade quiches, salads and soups. Thu-Tue 1200-1400.
Good Food Shop, a few doors down from Blackwood Café. Wholesome snacks and lunches, daily 0900-1630. The bakery also makes pizzas Mon-Sat from 1830.
Tathra, T/F9756 2040, Nannup to Balingup Rd. A fruit winery with a café and a humble 19th-century woodman's slab cottage, furnished much as it was when first built.

Bridgetown *p178*
♯ **Cidery**, Gifford St, T9761 2204, www.thecidery.com.au. Sells their own strong brewed ciders and beers from a large barn. The dry cider is particularly good, 6 per cent alcohol and a good bite. Cheap lunches at weekends, otherwise bring a picnic (if you buy a drink or 2). Open Wed-Sun 1100-1600.
♯ **Tongue & Groove**, Eedle Terr. Scrumptious and interesting light lunches Fri-Sun 1000-1700 in the small blonde-wood café.

Manjimup and around *p178*
Cafés
Graphiti, T9772 1283, out towards One Tree Bridge. A nice café, Wed-Sun 1000-1700.
Slice of Heaven, Rose St. The most pleasant café in town, serves up foccaccias, wraps and light lunches, Mon-Fri 0900-1700 and Sat 0900-1300.

Pemberton *p179, map p179*
♯♯-♯ **Pemberton Hotel**, T9776 1017. A traditional old place with a huge modern café and accommodation wing. Hotel meals are cheap and standard favourites are served in a pretty old dining room daily 1200-1400, 1800-2000.

Cafés
Café Mazz, part of the stylish, modern wing in rammed earth and local timber. The food here is a more modern mix of flavours and fresh local produce, cheap salad, foccaccia and burger lunches and mid-range evening mains. Daily 0700-2030.
Coffee Connection, Dickinson Rd, at the Fine Woodcraft Gallery, T9776 1159. The best café in town by a long stretch, this place has fabulous coffee, cakes and a very small menu of light lunches. Small terrace surrounded by quiet bushland. Daily 1000-1600.
Jan's Diner, in the centre, for a simple burger or toastie.
Lavender Berry Farm, Browns Rd, T9776 1661. Has a fragrant garden and a café with wholesome food such as pies, pancakes and Devonshire teas. Daily 0900-1730. You can also pick your own berries.
Pembee Fish Café, Brockman St. A bright, casual café for fish and chips or pizza to eat in the small colourful dining room or takeway. BYO.

Wineries *p180*
The wineries around the town provide some of the best food in and around Pemberton and some may be open for evening meals at weekends, see that section for details.

Warren National Park *p182*
Old Vasse, about half-way along the Old Vasse Rd in Warren National Park. Completely surrounded by the park, a relict freehold block on which is a simple but stylish rammed-earth café, daily 1000-1600.

⁞ Gone fishing

There are several places around Pemberton that farm trout in large dams and offer the opportunity to catch a fish or two for supper. Such is the density of fish stocks that you usually don't need to be an expert angler to get a bite. There is usually a hire charge for the rod, possibly a fishing charge, and fish caught are usually charged at around $15 per kg. A reasonably sized fish, enough to feed one person, is around 300-400 g. Although more patience and/or skill will be required at Beedelup Lake, fish caught here are free. There is a limit of two fish per person per day and rod hire for the resort Activity Office is $10. You can also fish for trout, perch and marron in any of Pemberton's rivers and streams if you have your own gear but you need a licence (obtain at the post office). The VIC can give more information on licensing, sizing and locations. Marron is a small freshwater crayfish that carries a lot of meat for its size and is absolutely delicious. Marron season is January-February, trout September-April.

Beedelup and Karri Valley *p182*
⁞⁞⁞⁞ **Karri Valley Resort**, T9776 2020. The restaurant is open 1100-2030, serves cheap light lunches, cream teas and very good evening meals (expensive). The views across the lake are great but there is no deck or outside tables. Opposite the adjacent Activity Office, however, is a small lakeside grassed area, teeming with ducks and swans, which has a free BBQ and picnic tables.
King Trout Farm, 8 km south, T9776 1352. Both trout farm and log-cabin café so they'll happily cook the fish you catch. If 2 people share a rod the all-up cost of a self-caught, restaurant-cooked fish lunch will be about $15 each, otherwise there are several cheap seafood options including a good value 'marron taster'. They also deliver to Pemberton accommodation excellent platters, plenty for 2, for $50. Open Fri-Wed 1030-1600.

▲ Activities and tours

Nannup and around *p176*
Blackwood River Canoeing, T9756 1209. ½-day paddles ($25) or extended trips with equipment and transport to canoe a section of the river for 2-5 days (from $35 day).

Pemberton *p179, map p179*
Pemberton Discovery Tours, T9776 0484, www.wn.com.au/pdt. Excellent 4WD trips into D'Entrecasteaux National Park and the Yeagarup Dunes and Warren National Park. Beaches, river, and forest with a lively and flexible guide. Also winery tours. From $40 ½ day, $80 full day.
Pemberton Hiking Company, T9776 1559, pemhike@wn.com.au. Guided walks with a knowledgeable local and environmentalist. Also canoeing on the Warren, Yeagarup Dunes on foot, night walks and 2-5 day wilderness walks. Can plan any tour to suit.

Beedelup and Karri Valley *p182*
Karri Valley Resort runs a wide range of activities, all available to non-residents, including horse riding.

⊖ Transport

Bridgetown *p178*
TransWA buses leave from the Boat Park for stops to **Bunbury** at 0940 Mon-Tue and Thu, and 1247 Sat-Tue and Thu (change to *Australind* train for **Perth** if necessary). **Pemberton** buses depart 1702 Mon, Wed and 2007 Sun. Additional daily 1317 services continue on to **Albany**, though the Wed and Fri buses don't call at Pemberton. **South West Coachlines** heads to **Perth** at 0700 Mon-Fri, and to **Manjimup** at 1800 Mon-Fri.

Pemberton *p179, map p179*
TransWA buses leave from the VIC for stops to **Perth** at 0845 Mon, Tue, Thu,

and for **Bunbury** at 1120 Sat-Tue and
Thu (change to **Australind** train for **Perth**).
Buses to **Northcliffe**, **Walpole** (2 hrs),
Denmark and **Albany** (3½ hrs) leave at 1421
Sat-Tue and Thu. Its **Nannup** and **Capes**
region buses depart 0630 Mon, Wed and Fri.

Car servicing at **BP**, Brockman St,
T9776 1288.

❶ Directory

Pemberton *p179, map p179*
Banks Bankwest ATM on Brockman St.
Chemist Pemberton Pharmacy, Brockman
St, T9776 1054, Mon-Fri 0830-1730, Sat
0830-1200. **Hospital** Hospital Av, T9776
1209. **Internet** Telecentre, next to VIC,
T9776 1745. 1000-1630, Sat 1400-1800.
Laundry Pemberton Wash House,
Brockman St. **Police** Ellis St, T9776 1202.
Post Corner of Brockman St and Ellis St.

South Coast

Footprint features

Introduction

From Walpole to Albany and beyond, the long southern coastline is all about granite. Weathered into smooth rounded boulders, headlands and islands, granite forms striking bays and archipelagos on this coast. It also breaks down into impossibly fine, clean sand, leaving the water as clear as liquid glass. Some of the most beautiful beaches in the country are found here, especially around Denmark and Albany. The catch is that the water is bracing at best – this is the southern ocean and there's nothing between you and Antarctica. This makes summers mild and winters surprisingly cold, although the latter is the best time to see southern right whales who sojourn near the historic town of Albany. The south coast also receives relatively high rainfall which nourishes the rare tingle trees of the Valley of the Giants and tall karri forest down to the shoreline around Walpole and Denmark.

Further inland, the low granite range of the Porongorup National Park provides gentle walks and good views of the more dramatic Stirling Ranges, rising above the state's vast wheat plains. This magnificent region of forest, hills, beaches and wilderness offers superb walking, as well as canoeing, boat cruises and coastal drives.

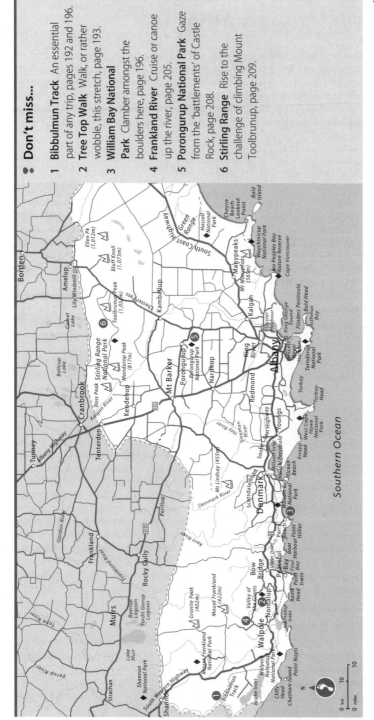

South Coast

• Don't miss...

1 **Bibbulmun Track** An essential part of any trip, pages 192 and 196.

2 **Tree Top Walk** Walk, or rather wobble, this stretch, page 193.

3 **William Bay National Park** Clamber amongst the boulders here, page 196.

4 **Frankland River** Cruise or canoe up the river, page 205.

5 **Porongurup National Park** Gaze from the 'battlements' of Castle Rock, page 208.

6 **Stirling Range** Rise to the challenge of climbing Mount Toolbrunup, page 209.

0 km   10

0 miles   10

N

Southern Ocean

Walpole to Albany

The most striking thing about this stretch of coast is its abundance of natural attractions and how few people there are visiting them. Most of your exploring – whether in forests, up granite knolls, down quiet rivers or along white-sand beaches – will be uninterrupted by people. The only exception is the Valley of the Giants, a preserved area of soaring old growth forest with both tree-top and forest floor walks, but even here you'll not exactly be crowded out. ▸▸ *For Sleeping, Eating and other listings, see pages 202-207.*

Walpole and around

Walpole → *Colour map 3, grid C4. Population: 500. 120 km from Pemberton, 65 km from Denmark.*

Walpole is a tiny town, with the minimum of services, that sits on the northern shore of Walpole Inlet, itself a watery outpost from Nornalup Inlet. The main street shops hug one side of the highway, the foreshore area being undeveloped. The scantiness of the town often causes travellers to suppose that the only reason to visit the area is the Tree Top Walk. In actual fact the natural forest and coastal attractions are such that many who come for a night end up staying several.

The inlets and the town are almost entirely enclosed by the **Walpole-Nornalup National Park**, which extends for several kilometres in each direction and encompasses one of the best preserved coastal forest and heath areas in the state, commonly called the Nuyts Wilderness Area. The Bibbulmun Track runs right through the area and town, and several sections of it, some of the best on its entire course, can easily be done as day walks using the town as a base. A shorter, 2-km loop walk through karri forest runs directly from behind the VIC. The extremely helpful VIC ① *T9840 1111, walpole.southernforests.com.au, 0900-1700*, is opposite the main shopping strip.

The Bibbulmun Track

The walks around Walpole are some of the best on the track, combining magnificent tall karri and tingle forest with coastal scenery, riverside and beach walking. It is also a convenient place to attempt short sections. **Mount Clare to Walpole** is 10 km and descends gradually to the town with good views over the Walpole-Nornalup Inlet. The next section from **Walpole to Frankland** (17½ km) follows the shore of the inlet before rising to Hilltop Lookout and passing by the Giant Tingle Tree. Walking through stunning forest follows until you reach the campsite at Frankland River, an isolated and pristine spot. From **Frankland to Giants** (13½ km) is another fine forest section that passes the Valley of the Giants treetop walk before ending at a campsite nearby. The next section **Giants to Rame Head** (15½ km) moves through forest, through the renowned patch of red flowering gum to the coast at Conspicuous Cliff and a campsite on the headland. Also consider a long distance walk from **Walpole to Denmark** (115 km, six to seven days), a fantastic week of walking and easily accessible by public transport.

Giant Tingle Tree and Circular Pool

Opposite the turn to Coalmine Beach is another, unsealed road to the fair but unremarkable **Hilltop Lookout**, and then, 5 km from the highway, to the **Giant Tingle Tree**, a 400-m walk from the carpark. This is said to have the widest girth of any living tree in Australia, but is burnt out, hollow and seems to cling precariously to life. It is a magnificent old survivor but perhaps less impressive than a circumference of 25 m suggests. Just beyond the tree the road hits a T-junction. The one-way right turn

Shiver me tingles

There are three types of tingle tree, the Red, Yellow and Rates Tingle. The one most commonly referred to simply as tingle is the Red Tingle. It has grey stringy bark similar to jarrah but can be distinguished by its height and wide buttressed trunks. Red Tingle reaches 70 m high and 20 m wide at the base, although the bases are often burnt out and hollow. These trees are only found in a tiny patch of the country around Walpole, close to the Deep, Bow and Frankland Rivers. The tingle are believed to be relict species from the Gondwanan period 65 million years ago when the climate was wetter and have only survived in the wettest areas of the southwest. These rare stars of the Tree Top Walk are not harvested for the timber industry. The Yellow and Rates Tingle can only be distinguished by looking at their leaves and gumnuts closely, but both are generally smaller trees.

deposits you back on the highway near Nornalup, the one-way left heads the long way back to Walpole with an optional 8-km loop up to **Circular Pool**, a picturesque part of the Frankland River, overhung by giant karri and a good place for a swim.

Valley of the Giants
① T9840 8263, the walkway 0900-1700, last entry 1615, $6, children $2.50.
On the other side of Nornalup, 12 km from Walpole, is the **Valley of the Giants**, an area of forest with a high density of good-sized karri, tingle and other trees. In 1996 CALM opened the 600-m **Tree Top Walk** here, a sloping steel walkway suspended up to 40 m above the forest floor and passing several forest giants at canopy level. Although the walkway does sway, the sense of awe most people feel is enough to make them forget their vertigo, and the clever design means no steps are involved, making the entire walk wheelchair accessible. A separate forest floor walk, the **Ancient Empire**, identifies several species of giant forest tree and introduces you to a few striking individuals, notably Grandmother Tingle who looks like she could have had a starring role in *Lord of the Rings*.

Peaceful Bay, Mandalay Beach and Conspicuous Cliffs
There are two ocean beaches accessible by unsealed road within 25 km of Walpole, and another at **Peaceful Bay**, that can be reached via sealed road. **Mandalay Beach** is reached via Crystal Springs bush campground and national park entry fees apply ($9 per car). The beach at **Conspicuous Cliffs** is the most beautiful in the area that can be reached by a 2WD vehicle, a long sweep of broad sand with the subtle but impressive cliffs a towering eastern backdrop. The unsealed Ficifolia Road connecting the cliffs with Peaceful Bay is named for the many red flowering gums that line it. These eucalypts flower in a range of vibrant oranges, reds and pinks during the summer. The tree has been introduced all over the world, but its origin is in this area of bush.

The lookout at Conspicuous Cliffs is a popular spot for whale watching July-August and October-November when whales can often be seen on their migrations.

Other wonderful beaches and bays in the area include **Shell Beach** and **Blue Holes**, the site of the annual Salmon Camp, all only accessible by 4WD or boat. Some are visited as part of local boat cruise and 4WD tours.

Bird and Reptile Discovery Centre
① T9840 8335, www.valleyofthegiantsbirdandreptilediscoverycentre.com, 0900-1700 Oct-Apr, otherwise 1000-1600, $9, children $4.

On the road to Denmark, 300 m off the highway, this modest-sized bird park has an excellent collection of some of the world's most brightly coloured parrots and macaws. The birds are well cared for and held in large cages in a pleasant, grassy garden and in a walk-in aviary. Some of their rescued and hand-reared birds roam free about the park and visitors are invited to be perched upon, a memorable and unusual opportunity.

Mount Frankland → *Colour map 3, grid C3. 30 km from Walpole (10 km unsealed).*

Inland from Walpole, Mount Frankland is a bald lump of granite sticking out of the forest that almost seems to have been forgotten by the tourism authorities. It is left off brochures and not signposted until the last turn-off. This hill's charms should not, however, be underestimated. The 15-minute ascent to the summit, via concrete steps and a metal ladder, seems over before you've started, leaving all the more time to admire the 360° views. To the south the inlets can be distantly glimpsed, to the north the forest seems to stretch away forever, broken only by a few other peaks. By taking the **Loop Walk** on the way back down you extend the total walk to a little over an hour, hiking right around the base of the exposed granite cap, threading your way between towering karri trees. There are fireplace BBQs and a toilet back at the car park and camping is permitted; this is an amazing spot to see either sunrise or sunset.

Denmark and around

The small, appealing town of Denmark lies on the western bank of the Denmark River as it flows into Wilson Inlet. The hills above the inlet are cloaked in karri trees and outside its narrow entrance lie some of the most stunning beaches and headlands on the southern coast. William Bay National Park, 18 km to the west of Denmark, includes the magical Greens Pool, Elephant Rocks and Madfish Bay, scattered with leviathan granite boulders. The picturesque temperate location has attracted artists and winemakers and their galleries and cellar doors are found along the Scotsdale and Mount Shadforth roads in the hills above town. ▶▶ *For Sleeping, Eating and other listings, see pages 202-207.*

Denmark → *Colour map 3, grid C5. Population: 5,000. 55 km from Mt Barker, 55 km from Albany.*

Denmark's population of alternative lifestylers help to give the town more of an edge than the tourist towns of the Cape region. During the 1990s the town boomed but distance from Perth and the lack of employment slowed down subsequent development. The commercial centre is limited to the junction of the highway and Strickland Street and the grassy banks of the wide river have been left to picnickers and walkers. The attractions of Denmark are mostly natural ones, or outside the town centre. Within town, the small **Historical Society Museum** ① *Mitchell St, T9848 1781, Thu 1000-1600 or by appointment, entry by donation*, is dedicated to the lives of early settlers in Denmark. The days of timber workers and group settlers are illuminated by old photographs, machinery and tools. Denmark Environment Centre ① *25 Strickland St, T9848 1644, Mon-Fri 1000-1600, Sat 1000-1300*, is a focus for conservationists and greenies in the area and is a good place to go to pick up publications on flora and fauna or information on any green events. There is a great glass and tile mural by a local artist on the back wall but strangely it is almost obscured by the car park. The VIC ① *T9848 2055, www.denmarkvisitorcentre.com.au, 0900-1700*, is halfway along Strickland Street.

Wilson Inlet and Ocean Beach → *11 km from Denmark.*

Ocean Beach Road heads straight down to Wilson Head, though a slightly more scenic option is to detour via Hollings Road to the **Rivermouth**, and then via **Poison**

Point. There is a lookout here and a 300-m walk down to the tiny deserted promontory – a good place to see the many water birds living on the inlet, including black swans and the ubiquitous pelicans. A spit of sand usually blocks the ocean entrance to Wilson Inlet and this extends round the external Ratcliffe Bay in a long sweep. The near-side section, **Ocean Beach**, is popular with locals and holidaymakers alike. The sealed road ends at the lookout just above Ocean Beach; continue along the unsealed road for a succession of ever better views. Where the road ends you can look directly south at **Wilson Head** where a shelf of rock, extending some 100 m east, creates fantastic waves. The view gets better if you scramble the 200 m down the path to the boulders below.

Mount Shadforth and Scotsdale scenic drives → *Full loop about 45 km.*

From Denmark two roads heading northwest have been designated as tourist drives – you can drive both as a continuous loop, though this will involve an unsealed section. **Mount Shadforth Road** winds west along the range of hills culminating in Mount Shadforth (300 m) after 10 km. There are a succession of excellent views both inland and south over the inlets, and it's hardly worth the trouble going out to the official lookout, especially if you stop for a coffee at the **Observatory** ⓘ *Dec-Mar, Wed-Sun 1000-1700*. There are a couple of galleries and wineries along the way. **David Rich** ⓘ *T9848 3849, www.davidrich.com.au, Thu-Sun 1100-1700*, skilfully captures the rich colours and movement of the coastal ocean in pastels, and his pictures are very affordable.

Beyond Mount Shadforth an unsealed section leads to McLeod Road. A left turn here runs down to the highway, almost opposite the turn-off for **William Bay National Park**, see page 196, and close to **Bartholomews Meadery** ⓘ *T9840 9349, 0930-1630*. This honey farm produces a selection of meads (honey wines), honey,

South Coast Denmark & around

Around Denmark

To Mt Barker
To Mt Barker
The Edge
Scotsdale Rd
Harewood Forest
Somerset Hill
Barker Rd
Pentland Alpaca & Tourist Farm
McLeod Rd
Howard Park
To Albany
Shadforth Rd
David Rich
Denmark
Mt Shadforth (300m)
South Coast Highway
To Walpole
Bartholomews Meadery
Ocean Beach Rd
Poison Point
Wilson Inlet
Mt Hallowell (280m)
Monkey Rock
Nullaki Peninsula
William Bay National Park
Greens Pool
Waterfall Beach
Lights Beach
Madfish Bay
Ocean Beach
Ratcliff Bay
Wilson Head

N

0 km   2
0 miles   2

Sleeping
Cove 1
Karma Chalets 2
Koorabup Motel 3

Mt Lindsay View 4
Ocean Beach 5
Rivermouth 6
Waterfront 7

Eating
Observatory 2
Waterfront 3

····· Bibbulmun track

honey ice-cream and beeswax products, and has a buzzing see-through hive right by the counter.

Backtracking, the right turn off the unsealed section of Mount Shadforth Road onto McLeod Road heads up to the western end of the 'tourist' section of **Scotsdale Road** after passing **Somerset Hill Winery** ① *T9840 9388, 1100-1600, wines $16-35, include the top-end Methode Champenoise*. A true cellar built recently on Mediterranean lines, with the bubbly ageing on a series of racks. Almost on the Scotsdale Road junction is the **Pentland Alpaca and Tourist Farm** ① *T9840 9262, www.pentlandalpacafarm.com.au, 1000-1600, $10, children $5, concessions $9*, a rustic attraction with paddocks and pens containing farm and native animals, including koalas. Visitors may enter many of the areas.

The 20 km drive back to Denmark heads through a mix of pastoral and forest country, and past a few more wineries and galleries. The **Edge** gallery ① *3 km up unsealed Harewood Rd, T9840 9237, Wed-Sun 1000-1700*, has an interesting collection of artworks, glass creations, ceramics and sculpture. Close to the town centre is the **Howard Park Winery** ① *T9848 2345, 1000-1600, wines $14-75*. These people regularly make some of the best wines in the region, including their 'drink-now' range, *Madfish*, which has received international recognition.

William Bay National Park → *Colour map 3, grid C4. Greens Pool 18 km from Denmark.*

The granite that makes up much of the south coast takes on some of its most spectacular sculpted forms in the gentle headland at the east end of William Bay. Mesmeric **Greens Pool** is a clear sandy bay, sheltered not by an island or reef but by a collection of domed boulders scattered for several hundred metres about 100 m offshore. At the end of the sealed road and a safe swimming beach, the pool is a very popular family destination. Parking in the Elephant Rocks car park, just 50 m along the unsealed section, gives just as quick walking access to the pool, but also to **Elephant Rocks**, a cluster of gigantic boulders nuzzling the nearside of a tiny sandy inlet, more like beached whales than elephants. The whole ensemble never fails to awe, in fair weather or foul. The unsealed road leads, after 3 km, to **Madfish Bay**, a broad sandspit connecting the mainland to a long rock island. In strong seas waves come around both ends of the island to meet at the middle of the spit. Not always recommended as a swimming spot, this is nevertheless well worth a visit.

The Bibbulmun Track

The section west of Denmark makes an excellent short day walk or overnight walk. From Wilson Inlet Holiday Park, 6 km south of town, the track rises through huge granite outcrops to **Mount Hollowell**, where there are great views of the inlet (6 km one way). After descending to the coast you reach a campsite close to the beautiful beaches of **William Bay** (15 km from Denmark). Another good section is the track through **West Cape Howe National Park**, where there are not only spectacular coastal views but views inland to the Porongorups and Stirling Ranges. If a pick-up can be arranged (try **Denmark Tours**) the ideal section would be from Tennessee Road South car park to **Cosy Corner** car park (21 km to Torbay campsite, 2½ km to Cosy Corner the following day). Walkers heading straight through need to get over the inlet to (or from) the Nullakai Peninsula. Check with Denmark VIC for current ferry arrangements.

Denmark to Albany

There are two routes between these settlements and taking the more scenic Lower Denmark Road rather than the South Coast Highway provides views of the coastline and access to **Cape Howe National Park** ① *South Coast Highway, T9845 2028, Fri-Tue 1000-1600*. The area is known as **Torbay**, after Torbay Head in the national park. Just before the road splits there is a fine gallery, **Woodworks**, showing the impressive work of Dean Malcolm.

After turning down the Lower Denmark Road there is a right turn almost immediately onto Eden Road. This leads down to the shores of Wilson Inlet and meets the Bibbulmun Track. There is also a blueberry farm, **Eden Gate** ① *T9845 2003, Dec-Apr, Thu-Mon 1030-1600*, where you can pick your own or try their ice cream, jam and wines. Back on the main road, there is a general store 2 km further on at **Youngs Siding**, a reminder of the days when Denmark and Albany were connected by a railway line that followed the route of this road. The line was used to transport timber felled in the Torbay region in the late 1890s. The next turn-off leads to Lowlands Beach at the western edge of Cape Howe National Park. Tennessee South Road is sealed for 4 km but unsealed for the last few kilometres to the beach. There is also a good place to eat nearby, **Emily's Country Kitchen** ① *Tennessee South Rd, T9845 1133, morning and afternoon teas and lunches*.

Cape Howe National Park is a small park with cliff and coastal scenery, most of it is only accessible to walkers and 4WD vehicles. The main entrance is further east, along the sealed Cosy Corner Road, from Lower Denmark Road. At Cosy Corner beach there is a general store. Continue along the unsealed road to **Shelley Beach**. There are great views from the hang-gliding ramp above the long sandy beach. The Bibbulmun Track passes both beaches and these can be a good start or finish point if you can arrange transport. There are few self-contained places to stay in this area, see Sleeping. From the Cosy Corner turn-off it is a further 26 km east to Albany.

Albany → Colour map 3, grid C5. Population: 20,500. 385 km from Margaret River, 410 km from Perth, 480 km from Esperance.

Albany has a small city centre making it a relaxed and friendly place and many enjoy the mild climate (Albany is often 10 degrees cooler than Perth in summer). There are great national parks in every direction but Torndirrup National Park is the closest and has some impressive granite rock formations, cliffs and magical ocean beaches. The main activity in winter is whale watching, although strangely one of Albany's busiest attractions is the whaling station where the giants were chopped up as recently as 1978. ▸▸ *For Sleeping, Eating and other listings, see pages 202-207.*

Ins and outs
The VIC ① *Princess Royal Drive, T9841 1088, www.albanytourist.com.au, Mon-Fri 0830-1730, Sat-Sun 0900-1700*, is housed in the former railway station on the waterfront, a timber building constructed in the 1880s. ▸▸ *See Transport page 206, for details.*

History
Albany is the site of the first European settlement of Western Australia, thanks to the state's finest natural harbour, Princess Royal Harbour within King George Sound. The sound was officially discovered by George Vancouver, captain of the *Discovery*, in 1791, who landed on a beach with a freshwater stream 'the colour of brandy but exceedingly well tasted'. He laid claim to the land in the name of King George III and named the inner harbour after the Princess Royal as it was her birthday. He sailed away shortly afterwards to explore the far west coast of North America but his charts led Matthew Flinders to enter the harbour in search of shelter in 1801. Flinders wrote detailed notes on the Aboriginal people he met, describing their kangaroo-skin capes and fascination with his red-coated soldiers.

The French arrived two years later on Baudin's voyage of exploration and indirectly caused the British settlement of Albany. In NSW and in England the activities of the French were watched anxiously for fear they would claim and settle parts of Australia. In the same way that Tasmania and Victoria were settled immediately after Baudin's expedition, in 1825 the British authorities decided to order settlement of King George Sound to forestall the French who were reported to be continually present in the southern coastal waters that year. In 1826 Major Edmund Lockyer set out from Sydney in the *Amity* with a small party of soldiers and convicts and established a town site in Princess Royal Harbour that he named Frederickstown. When James Stirling founded a new colony at Swan River (Perth) in 1829 control of the southern settlement passed from Sydney to Perth and the name was changed to Albany. The town's position on the main shipping route to the eastern states ensured its survival and it became a busy port. However its importance quickly declined after Fremantle's harbour was built in the 1890s.Whaling and the harvesting of karri, jarrah and sandalwood timber were important industries, although all were eventually exhausted and replaced by agriculture.

Sights

Despite the advanced age of Albany in Western Australian terms, the first impression is not of its heritage but its beautiful natural harbour. The city sits on the northern shore of Princess Royal Harbour and King George Sound and overlooks both the curving arm of the peninsula and the granite islands of the sound. The main street,

❣ The VIC has brochures on a historic walk in the centre.

York Street, runs downhill to the waterfront and it is here that Albany's history becomes more visible, in the simple Residency and Gaol by a 19th-century sailing ship and the Victorian buildings of Stirling Terrace.

The earliest settlement in Albany was established on the waterfront, just to the west of the modern port facilities. Major Lockyer's party stepped ashore at the spot where the Residency still stands and the first encampment was made on flat high ground just above, now called Foundation Park. A replica of Lockyer's ship, the **Brig Amity** ① *0900-1700, $2.50, children $0.55, access from museum*, has been built and stands roughly in the place that the original ship moored in 1826. At the time the brig was owned by the colonial government in Sydney and used as a government supply vessel. She carried a party of about 45 people, as well as supplies and livestock for the new settlement, although today the boat looks hardly big enough for one family and a telly. The *Amity* was reconstructed by local boat builders in time for the 150th anniversary of its arrival in 1976. Visitors can clamber all over the boat and below deck to see the cramped conditions sailors of the 19th century had to put up with.

The **Residency**, just next door, was built in 1850 and originally used as a storehouse for the convict hiring depot nearby. In 1873 it became the home of Government Residents, responsible for administration of the settlement and exploration of the area. Later magistrates lived in the building until 1953 when the last moved out complaining of damp and cold. The Residency now houses the **West Australian Museum – Albany** ① *Residency Rd, T9841 4844, www.museum.wa.gov. au, 1000-1700, free*, and displays on the region's geological and social history. The site includes the Eclipse Building, housing the Eclipse Island lighthouse optic and displays related to the ocean. There is also an Artisans' Gallery, selling leather products, and a museum shop selling a range of interesting books on local history and wildlife.

Behind the museum lie the high, spiky walls of the **Old Gaol** ① *Stirling Terr, T9841 5403, 1000-1615, $4, children $2.50 (price includes entry to Patrick Taylor Cottage)*, set with broken glass to dissuade nimble escapees. The gaol was actually built in 1852 as a convict depot where convicts were housed while they laboured on the town's roads. It was converted to a gaol in 1873 and used for police quarters. The Albany Historical Society now runs the Old Gaol as a museum of early European local history. Some cells have displays on the ghoulish crimes of their inhabitants, such as Frederick Bailey Deeming, who put several wives under concrete.

Patrick Taylor Cottage ① *Duke St, T9841 6174, 1300-1615, $4, children $2.50 (price includes entry to Old Gaol)*, is just up the hill, on the street behind Stirling

Terrace. This is considered to be the oldest wattle and daub building in the state. Built in 1832 it was purchased by a British gentleman, Patrick Taylor, in 1834. He married Mary Yates Bussell, whom he had met on the voyage from England. Mary was a member of the Bussell family who settled in the Southwest Capes region. The humble and cosy cottage has been furnished with clothing and furniture of the period. There are also many historic buildings along Stirling Terrace, east of York Street. The most striking is the red brick **Old Post Office** with its turrets and clock tower. The 1870 building housed the courthouse, mail room, customs office and bond store. It has recently been occupied by the University of Western Australia to be used as the Albany campus.

The city sits between two hills, **Mount Melville** and **Mount Clarence**, both of which have impressive viewpoints that can be driven to (within 100 m or so). Mount Clarence was the site of Australia's first dawn ANZAC Day service in April 1930. Further to the east, forming the northern headland of the Ataturk Entrance, is the city's third major hill, **Mount Adelaide**. It is atop Mount Adelaide that the city's defences were

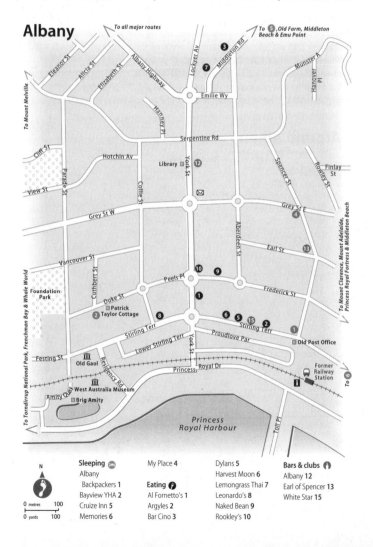

Albany

Sleeping	My Place **4**	Dylans **5**	**Bars & clubs**
Albany		Harvest Moon **6**	Albany **12**
Backpackers **1**	**Eating**	Lemongrass Thai **7**	Earl of Spencer **13**
Bayview YHA **2**	Al Fornetto's **1**	Leonardo's **8**	White Star **15**
Cruize Inn **5**	Argyles **2**	Naked Bean **9**	
Memories **6**	Bar Cino **3**	Rookley's **10**	

N

0 metres 100
0 yards 100

chiefly constructed at the end of the 19th century. **The Forts** ⓘ *0900-1700, $3, children $1, concessions $2, café closed Mon,* is the common name for the **Princess Royal Fortress**, actually less a fortress and more a barracks and gunnery station. Gun emplacements were first put into place at the end of the 19th century to guard against the imagined threat from both France and Russia, and were beefed up for the duration of the Second World War, though a shot was never fired in anger.

📍 *If you like military history the Forts makes an excellent excursion and can occupy up to half a day.*

Many of the dozen or so existing buildings, from barracks to ammunition storage pits, have been restored and either convey their original use or have been converted to museums, notably of the Australian Light Horse. The extensive grounds also contain a couple of good lookouts and two large gun turrets from Second World War naval vessels, including one from HMAS *Sydney*, which are open for inspection. The tearoom serves light lunches and cream teas.

The Old Farm at Strawberry Hill ⓘ *Middleton Rd, 1000-1600, $3.30, children and concessions $2.20, National Trust,* between the city centre and Middleton Beach, see below, was the very first farm in WA and the small complex sports a number of buildings from the 1830s. One original cottage is now a tearoom, very much in the English style. The main two-storey building, dating from 1836, was the family home of Captain Sir Richard Spencer, Albany's Government Resident of the time, and is now furnished as it might have been a century or so ago.

The nearest decent beach to the city, **Middleton Beach**, is at the northern base of the hill, 4 km from the city centre via road or 5 km via the pleasant walking track that comes around the headland from the end of Princess Royal Drive. This beach has a

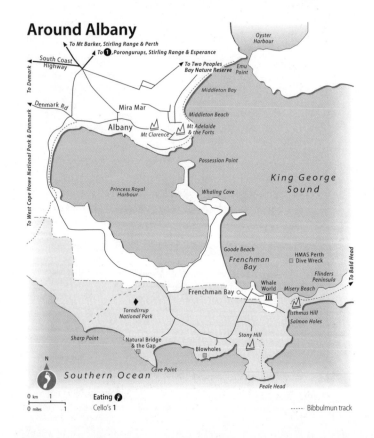

Around Albany

To Mt Barker, Stirling Range & Perth
To ❶, Porongurups, Stirling Range & Esperance
South Coast Highway
To Denmark
Denmark Rd
To West Cape Howe National Park & Denmark
To Two Peoples Bay Nature Reserve
Emu Point
Oyster Harbour
Middleton Bay
Mira Mar
Middleton Beach
Albany
Mt Adelaide & the Forts
Mt Clarence
Possession Point
Princess Royal Harbour
Whaling Cove
King George Sound
Goode Beach
Frenchman Bay
HMAS Perth Dive Wreck
Flinders Peninsula
Whale World
Misery Beach
Frenchman Bay
To Bald Head
Torndirrup National Park
Isthmus Hill
Salmon Holes
Sharp Point
Natural Bridge & the Gap
Stony Hill
Blowholes
Cave Point
Peale Head
N
Southern Ocean
0 km 1
0 miles 1

Eating ❶
Cello's 1

----- Bibbulmun track

grassy foreshore with a BBQ and picnic tables, toilets, showers and changing rooms. The small adjacent suburb boasts a couple of cafés, a large hotel and several other accommodation options. Another 4 km north along the shore of Middleton Harbour is **Emu Point**, the western headland at the entrance to **Oyster Harbour**. On the harbour side of the point is a small, more sheltered beach with a safe swimming enclosure and boat hire. The beach also has a grassy foreshore with BBQs, picnic tables and toilets, plus an adjacent café and restaurant.

Around Albany

HMAS Perth

This ex-Navy warship was sunk in King George Sound in November 2001 to create a new marine environment and dive site. Thanks to the sound's clean and well oxygenated waters the wreck soon began building its own eco-system – locals were finding as much growth in the first three months as many new wrecks get in their first year. This, one of the latest of Australia's artificial reefs, is close to one of its first, the whale hunter **Cheynes III**, sunk in 1982. Commercial dives to both wrecks are available from Albany.

Torndirrup National Park → *Colour map 3, grid C5. Return drive around 60 km.*

Occupying the ocean-side part of the peninsula that forms the southern arm of both Princess Royal Harbour and King George Sound, Torndirrup protects one of WA's most striking stretches of granite coast. The final 6 km of Frenchman Bay Road winds through the inland part of the park, with a series of side roads, mostly sealed, leading to the coast's most spectacular landmarks. The first of these, **Sharp Point**, is accessed by an unsealed road just past an 80 km sign and shortly before the Rangers Residence. A short loop walk at the point gives excellent views up and down the coast. The first sealed turn-off, after the information bay, leads to the **Gap** and **Natural Bridge**. The first is a 25-m deep chasm perpendicular to the cliff edge, a real wave trap that sees the sea thumping into the rocks, shooting spray sometimes up as far as the lookout (take care to stay behind the rails when the seas are heavy). A similar chasm 50 m away is bridged at the end by a massive natural arch. The third access road is for the **Blowholes**, a series of cracks in the granite foreshore that in heavy seas can erupt into geysers of spray and foam. At quieter times the 30-minute return walk is worth it for the views up and down the coast, including the impressively bulbous promontory of **Peak Head**. There is a 2½ hour return walk to the head from **Stony Hill**, a couple of kilometres from Blowholes. Views from the hill range over much of the park. Salmon Hole Road leads to **Salmon Holes**, a beautiful sandy beach below a ring of protective low hills. An offshore reef creates a beach-side pool, said to shelter migrating salmon in rough seas. Also off this road, an unsealed turn heads down to **Misery Beach**, a beautiful white-sand cove on the sheltered side of the peninsula, and **Isthmus Hill**. A path leads up over the shoulder of the hill (20 minutes return), with views over Salmon Holes and King George Sound, and then on another 5 km to the end of the peninsula at Bald Head. Allow six hours return for this excellent hike. Frenchman Bay Road ends at the small community of **Frenchman Bay**, with its lovely little beach, complete with BBQs and picnic tables. There are places to stay here, see Sleeping.

Whale World

ⓘ *Frenchman Bay Rd, 20 km from Albany, T9844 4021, www.whaleworld.org, 0900-1700, tours on the hour 1000-1600 (40 mins), $18, children $9, concessions $14.*
This former whaling station turned museum treats its history and subject matter in a laudably even-handed way, offering a rare glimpse into the inner life of this emotive

industry. Most of the extensive complex comprises the old whale-processing buildings, preserved more or less as they were the day the station closed in 1978. These include the open-air cutting and flensing decks, cooking rooms, oil processing and storage facilities, and even one of the last hunting ships, now dry-docked. All allow virtually full access. One shed houses various skeletons and pickled remains. Displays, films and diaramas leave little (except, thankfully, the notorious smells) to the imagination, so this may not be for you if you're squeamish, but a fascinating couple of hours can be spent here. The main building also houses a wonderful collection of prints by wildlife artist Richard Ellis, depicting over 60 marine mammals, plus a gift shop and cheap café with indoor and terrace tables overlooking the harbour.

Two Peoples Bay Nature Reserve

ⓘ *T9846 4276, visitor centre 1000-1600, daily in summer, otherwise Wed, Sat-Sun.*

Just to the east of Albany, about 35 km by road, is another magical bit of coastline, Two Peoples Bay, where granite domes slope into the sea and sand. The bay was named for a meeting between Frenchman Captain Ransonnet of Baudin's exploratory expedition and James Pendleton, captain of an American brig that had just arrived for sealing and whaling. The pair are thought to have had a good whinge about the British and then named the bay Baie des Deux Nations in memory of the meeting. The reserve has some very rare fauna, in fact two species previously thought to be extinct have been found here, the Noisy scrub bird and Gilbert's potoroo. The potoroo is a distant relation of wallabies and is a small nocturnal creature that digs for truffles. You are unlikely to see either of these creatures but there is a good visitors centre where you can learn more about them. Little Beach – a smooth white one, scattered with boulders – tends to be more peaceful than the fine beaches of Frenchman Bay. At the picnic ground by the visitors centre there is a 2-km walking circuit with several lookouts providing views over the bay and towards Mount Manypeaks. The road is not sealed but fine for 2WD. Camping is not allowed.

> ❢ *The reserve has one of the best beaches in the area, Little Beach.*

⊕ Sleeping

Walpole and around *p192*

B Riverside Retreat, South Coast Highway, near Nornalup, T9840 1255, www.riverside retreat.com.au. The best located of the many self-contained cottage establishments in the area, with splendid views over the eastern end of Nornalup Inlet. The 6 chalets are clean, well-equipped and comfortable rather than luxurious, and sleep up to 8.

C Inlet View, 58 Walpole St, T9840 1226. Not an outstanding B&B, but the welcome is very warm and it has good views over Walpole Inlet.

C Stargazers, Jacksonii Av, off Allen Rd 5 km from Walpole, T9840 1553, stargazers@wn. com.au. Another unremarkable modern B&B, but with very welcoming, friendly hosts and

a great position overlooking a wide dam and hilltop forest. All meals can be prearranged, telescope available for stargazing.

C Tingledale Cottage, off Hazelvale Rd, T9840 8181, www.tingledalecottage.bizland. com. Charming, isolated wooden cottage in a forest setting with outdoor spa. Semi self-contained, all meals can be arranged, breakfast included.

C Walpole Hotel, corner of Boronia Av and South Coast Highway, T9840 1023. Standard motel rooms.

D Tingle All Over YHA, Nockolds St, T9840 1041, tingleallover2000@yahoo.com.au. Clean and well-presented budget rooms, share bathroom and kitchen.

There are 4 caravan parks in the area:

> ● *For an explanation of sleeping and eating price codes used in this guide, see inside the*
> ● *front cover. Other relevant information is found in Essentials, see pages 40-46.*

Rest Point Caravan Park, Rest Point Rd, T9840 1032. Has the best location, overlooking Walpole Inlet, and is about a 2-km walk from Walpole.

Coalmine Beach, T9840 1026, is a similar distance away and is very close to Nornalup Inlet. The latter has the better facilities, both have cabins, neither have on-site vans.

Valley of the Giants Eco Park, South Coast Highway, Nornalup, T9840 1313, and **Peaceful Bay**, T9840 8060, both have on-site vans. It is also possible to hire houseboats to cruise around the inlets, though there is a minimum 2 nights.

L Houseboat Holidays, T/F9840 1310. Has 10-, 6- and 4-berth boats available, expensive for 2 people, but around $40-60 per person per night if you fill them up.

Denmark p194

There is a lot of accommodation around Denmark, particularly self- contained chalets and cottages. Contact the VIC if none of these fit the bill.

A-B Karma Chalets, South Coast Highway, T9848 1568, www.karmachalets.com.au. 8 luxury houses on stilts, some with spas, backing onto karri forest. Superb views over the inlets.

B The Cove, Payne Rd, T9848 1770, www.thecovechalets.com. Sits on about 20 ha of mixed karri, jarrah and tingle forest, threaded through with bushwalks which wind directly down to the inlet. The 5 hand-built wooden cottages sleeping from 2-20: 'Sanctum' and 'Tingle' are particularly charming. The hosts are bushwalkers and happy to do Bibbulmun drop-offs and pick-ups.

B-C Waterfront, 63 Inlet Dr, T9848 1147, www.denmarkwaterfront.com.au. A good range of accommodation in this complex among karri trees on the inlet shore 2½ km from town. 2 level studios with balcony and motel rooms are all bright and cheery and built in a rustic timber and earth style.

C Koorabup Motel, South Coast Highway, T9848 1044. Has a few rammed-earth units, plus motel rooms with bush-view balconies.

C Mt Lindesay View, corner of Mt Shadforth and McNabb rds, T9848 1933, members.westnet.com.au/mtlindesayview. Modern, purpose-built bungalow B&B with 3 comfortable en suite rooms and views over the valleys to the north. The welcome

extends to an breakfast and optional evening meals (3 courses, $25).

E Blue Wren Travellers Rest YHA, 17 Price St, T9848 3300, www.bluewren.batcave.net. 20 beds in backpacker hostel, in an old timber worker's cottage extended for modern dorms and bathrooms. Clean with central location.

Ocean Beach, T9848 1105. Caravan park in a beautiful location near the mouth of the inlet.

Rivermouth, T/F9848 1262. Of several caravan parks, this is the closest, on-site vans.

Denmark to Albany p196

Contact the Denmark VIC for more information about accommodation in Cape Howe National Park.

A Chalet Arunga, in Cape Howe National Park, T9845 1025, www.denmarkwa.com/arunga, is a luxurious option.

B Cape Howe Cottages, Tennessee South Rd, western edge of Cape Howe National Park, T9845 1295, www.capehowe.com.au. 2 private self-contained houses. Bibbulmun Track drop-offs and pick-ups by arrangement.

C Torbay View Haven, Cosy Corner Rd, T9845 1065, a motel.

Albany p197, map p199

L-A Esplanade Hotel, Flinders Pde, opposite Middleton beach, T9842 1711. Albany's top-rung establishment with both ocean-view rooms and self-contained apartments.

A Albany Houseboat Holidays, Elizabeth Rd, Bayonet Head, T/F9844 8726, www.albanyhouseboats.com. A range of house- boats, sleeping 2-6, for use in Oyster Harbour. Minimum 2 nights, these can be an excellent deal for groups or families, especially in the winter off-season when the owners are open to negotiation.

B-D Middleton Beach, end of Middleton Rd, T9841 3593. Excellent caravan park with cabins and facilities.

B-E Rose Gardens, 45 Mermaid Av, Emu Point, T9844 1041. Caravan park with on-site vans, and a store and fuel.

C Memories, 118 Brunswick Rd, T9842 9787, memoriesbandb@bigpond.com. 3 en-suite rooms in an 1880s house overlooking the harbour. This B&B has warm hosts, cooked breakfasts and complimentary biscuits, chocs and port in your room.

C My Place guesthouse, 47 Grey St East, T9842 3242, myplace@iinet.net.au. 8 spacious and clean units with full kitchen, laundry, BBQ.

C-D Discovery Inn, 9 Middleton Rd, 200 m from beach, T9842 5535, www.discovery inn.com.au. Guesthouse with 12 rooms, some en suite and a couple of small 'backpacker' dorms. Full cooked breakfast can be taken in the pleasant central courtyard.

D Cruize Inn, 122 Middleton Rd, 1 km from beach, 2½ km from city centre, T9842 9599, www.cruizeinn.com. That rarest of things, a bright and breezy guesthouse run on the laid-back lines of a backpacker hostel. 2 twins, 2 doubles, lots of facilities including open-plan kitchen and lounge room, and bike hire. Pick-ups available. Recommended.

D-E Albany Backpackers, corner of Stirling Terr and Spencer St, T9842 5255, www. albanybackpackers.com.au. Lively hostel with some vivid wall paintings. Activities arranged, such as pasta, pool and video nights. Coffee and cake chinwag every night at 1830.

D-E Bayview YHA, 49 Duke St, T9842 3388, www.yha.com.au. Friendly, clean and quiet backpackers with lots of space, sea views and good facilities. Bike, board and snorkel hire.

Torndirrup National Park *p201*

C Island View, 10 Austin Rd, T9844 4767. Modern B&B with superb views over Goode Beach and beyond.

C-D Frenchman Bay, T9844 4015. Friendly caravan park with a good spot close to the beach and a small store and café.

⊘ Eating

Walpole and around *p192*

⫲-⫲ Tea House, Nornalup, T9840 1422. The smartest café in the area, with a jarrah-floored, cane-chaired dining room, outdoor deck and mellow tunes. Open at 1000, they serve light lunches, salads and paninis daily 1200-1500, and inventive dinners Wed-Sat 1800-2000.

⫲-⫲ Top Deck, Walpole, T9840 1344. Usually the preferred choice, a café that takes care to

serve consistently good food. Open all day from 0830 for breakfast, lunch 1100-1430 and mid-range dinner 1800-2000.

⫲-⫲ Walpole Hotel, T9840 1023. Serves cheap counter and brasserie meals every day, 1200-1400 and 1800-2000. Its biggest social nights are Wed (darts competition), Thu (pool competition) and Fri.

Denmark *p194*

⫲ Bandaleros, Hollings Rd, T9848 2188. Popular restaurant opposite the river with cosy timber décor. A very international menu can include bangers and mash, Vietnamese chicken salad and fettucini Napolitana! Licensed or BYO. Open 1800-2030 Mon-Sat.

⫲ Denmark Hotel, Hollings Rd, T9848 2206. The pub has a large, modern dining room overlooking the river and does cheap(ish) pub meals a cut above the usual, including some Asian food as well as the standard steak and schnitzels.

Cafés

Lushus Café, 18 Hollings Rd, T9848 1299. Colourful place full of original art and laidback locals. The blackboard menu offers lots of choice and may include dishes such as curry, noodles or turkish bread. Daily 0830-1700 and evenings over summer and major holidays.

Mary Rose, North St. A more traditional tearoom-style place that is also a pleasant place for a coffee or a simple lunch. Daily 1000-1630.

McSweeneys Gourmet Café, 5b Strickland St, T9848 2362. Small rustic establishment with outside tables and serving the best café food in Denmark. Open 0900-1700 Mon-Fri, 0900-1500 Sat. Recommended.

Mount Shadforth and Scotsdale scenic drives *p195, map p195*

⫲⫲-⫲ The Observatory, Karri Mia, Mt Shadforth Rd, T9848 2600. Stylish dining room and an outside deck, both with superb views over the inlets. Not particularly inventive menu but the food is excellent. Cheap light lunches, more formal in the evening. Open all day, breakfast 0800-1030 Sat-Sun, lunch and dinner 1130-1500, 1800-2100 daily. Recommended.

Albany *p197, map p199*

See also Bars and clubs below.

▼▼▼ **Leonardo's**, 166 Stirling Terr, T9841 1732. Local, fresh produce with an Italian influence, served in a series of intimate, formal dining rooms. Mon-Sat 1830-2030. BYO.

▼▼ **Al Fornetto's**, 132 York St, T9842 1060. A reliable favourite for excellent Italian food, including pasta, pizza and traditional mains. Always busy so book. Daily 1800-2030.

▼▼ **Argyles**, 42 Stirling Terr, T9842 9696. A cosy bistro with warm brick walls and expansive cane armchairs. The tasty and satisfying modern Australian food is good value and there is a prix fixe menu ($20) available from 1730 daily.

▼ **Dylans**, 82 Stirling Terr, T9841 8720. Casual place that does breakfasts, burgers, pancakes and ice-cream sundaes. BYO. Daily 0700-2030.

▼ **Lemongrass Thai**, Middleton Loop, T9841 7650. Try this place for takeaways, open Tue-Sun 1700-2100.

Cafés

Bar Cino, 338 Middleton Loop, T9841 5550. Sleek joint in subdued shades of purple at the top end of town, with a good range of tapas, salads and stylish casual food. Open Tue-Sat 0700-2030.

Harvest Moon, 86 Stirling Terr, T9841 8833. One of Albany's best, this homely and wholesome café makes great vegetarian bakes, quiches, soups and fresh salads. Couches, newspapers, mellow music. Also books. Recommended.

Naked Bean, 14 Peels Pl, T9841 1815. Seriously good coffee, gourmet lunches and the best cakes in town in an attractive, contemporary space. Open Mon-Fri 0800-1700, Sat 0800-1600.

Rookley's, 36 Peels Pl, T9842 2236. The best position and outdoor terrace tables to watch the action on York St. Excellent gourmet sweet and savoury pies, fresh bread and pastries. Open Mon-Fri 0900-1730, Sat 0830-1600.

Range Retreat is a simple place for fast food and drinks, open daily 0800-2100.

Around Albany *p201*

▼▼▼ **Cello's of Church Lane**, corner of Hassell Highway and Church Lane Rd, 25 km from Albany, T9844 3370. Considered the best in the region, imaginative food served in an historic homestead overlooking the Kalgan River. Fri-Sat 1100-1700 and 1830-2030, Sun 0930-1700. BYO. Recommended.

⬤ Bars and clubs

Albany *p197, map p199*

Albany, 244 York St, T9842 3337. A smart and busy pub, its street terrace is one of the town's most popular spots on a sunny day. Restaurant meals daily 1200-1430, 1800-2100.

Earl of Spencer, corner of Earl and Spencer sts, T9841 1322. Built in the 1870s this fine pub has seen stints as a boarding house, ale house and grocery store. It's cosiness, traditional decor, English and Irish beers, and excellent food make it about as close to a real English pub as you'll find in WA. Meals (cheap) Mon-Sat 1200-1400, daily 1800-2100. Smoking is not allowed. Lovely courtyard and live folk, jazz or blues every weekend.

White Star, 72 Stirling Terr, T9841 1733. Welcoming relaxed pub that has been smartened up with trendy corrugated iron and distressed walls, but its not overdone. Popular with visitors and locals, Thu is a big backpacker night. Counter meals Mon-Sat 1200-1400, daily 0600-2100.

⬤ Shopping

Albany *p197, map p199*

Albany Campers, T9841 8601. Camper trailer, tent and equipment hire.

Angus & Robertson, 240 York St. Has a large range of new books.

Gemini, 70 York St. Secondhand books and exchange.

Harvest Moon, 86 Stirling Terr. Offers the opportunity to break a browse the book shelves with a coffee.

Stirling Terrace Bookcafé, 168 Stirling Terr. Gives you the opportunity to drink coffee while you browse.

⬤ Activities and tours

Walpole *p192*

Tree Top Canoe Hire, contact VIC for details.

Wild Over Walpole, T9840 1036, www.wow wilderness.com.au. Enthusiastic, informative and entertaining boat cruises around the inlets (2½ hrs, $30) or, on most Sun, memorable trips up the Frankland River (3½ hrs, $40). Departures 1000 daily from the jetties near the pub.

Denmark *p194*
Little River Discovery, T9848 2604. 4WD day tours by local naturalists to West Cape Howe National Park ($70), Valley of the Giants ($75) and short local tours (from $22) to see wildflowers, birds, beaches or wineries.
Boat and canoe hire on the river by Berridge Park, Sep-Apr 0900-1600.

Wilson Inlet and Ocean Beach *p200*
South Coast Surfing, T9848 2057, Ocean Beach. Private lessons $50 for 2 hrs. One day group lessons $35 per person including wetsuit and board hire.

Albany *p197*
Albany Escape, T9844 1945, escape@albany is.com.au. Offers a number of tours including to the Stirling Range (full day, $88), William Bay and Tree Top Walk (full day, $88 not including entry fees), and Torndirrup and Whale World (½ day, $44 not including entry fees). The latter tour goes regularly at 1245 Mon, Wed, Fri and 0830 Sun.
Albany Scenic Day Tours, T1800 625900. Runs a range of winery and coastal tours, including one to Two Peoples Bay. Half day $40-55, full day $90.
Bay View YHA and **Cruize Inn** each have bikes plus a range of surf gear.
Kalgan Queen, T9844 1949. Half-day cruises from Emu Point up the Kalgan River in a glass-bottom boat to explore Albany's history and wildlife. And wine-tasting cruises.
Silver Star II, T04-2893 6711, www.whales. com.au. Heads out daily, Jun-Oct, at 0930 and 1300 for 2½ hr whale-watching trips ($45, children $25, concession $38).
Spinners, T9841 7151, www.spinners charters.com.au. Offers full-day ocean fishing trips for around $160.
At Emu Point you can hire pedalos, surfcats at weekends and daily during school hols.

HMAS Perth *p201*
South Coast Diving Supplies, T/F98 417176, www.divealbany.com.au, and

Albany Dive, T04-2966 4874, www.albany dive.com. Expect to pay around $160 for a twin-dive boat trip.

Transport

Walpole *p192*
TransWA buses leave from the post office for the **timber towns** and **Bunbury** at 0943 Sat-Tue and Thu, and 1018 Mon and Thu (the latter Mon and Thu services do not stop at **Northcliffe** or **Pemberton**). All have immediate onward connections to **Perth**. Eastbound buses to **Denmark** and **Albany** depart 1627 Sat-Tue and Thu, and 1552 Wed and Fri.
Car servicing from **Walpole Motors**, Nock-olds St, T9840 1315. Bike hire from **Norm's Tyre & Hire**, T9840 1297. $15-22 per day.

Denmark *p194*
TransWA buses leave from the VIC for **Walpole**, the **timber towns** and **Bunbury** at 0847 Sat-Tue and Thu, and 0922 Mon and Thu (the latter Mon and Thu services do not stop at **Northcliffe** or **Pemberton**). All have immediate onward connections to **Perth**. Eastbound buses to **Albany** depart 1723 Sat-Tue and Thu, and 1648 Wed and Fri.
Car servicing at **Talisman Motors**, South Coast Highway, corner of Welsh St, T9848 1372.

Albany *p197, map p199*
Skywest flies daily to **Perth**. Love's Bus Service, T9841 1211, operates a handful of services around the northern city suburbs, all starting and terminating at Peels Place. The 301 heads out along **Middleton Road** to **Middleton Beach** and **Emu Point** at 0845, 1100, 1305 and 1450 Mon-Fri, and 1030, 1210 Sat. TransWA buses leave from the VIC for **Denmark**, **Walpole**, the **timber towns** and **Bunbury** at 0800 Sat-Tue and Thu, and 0835 Mon and Thu (the latter Mon and Thu services do not stop at **Northcliffe** or **Pemberton**).
Car hire from **Albany Car Rentals**, 386 Albany Highway, T9841 7077. **Budget Rent-a-car**, 255 Albany Highway, T9841 7799. Car servicing at **De Jonge Mechanical Repairs**, 52 Cockburn Rd, T9842 2293. Taxi, T9841 7000.

Around Albany *p201*
There are no public services to **Torndirrup National Park.**

🛈 Directory

Walpole *p192*
Banks No ATMs in the town. **Chemist** Silver Chain supermarket has basic supplies and can get prescriptions overnight. **Internet** Telecentre, T9840 1395. Open Tue-Fri 0900-1700, 1000-1400 in winter. **Post** Main St. **Useful contacts** CALM, Main St, T9840 1027. Mon-Fri 0800-1700.

Denmark *p194*
Banks Several banks and ATMs on Strickland St. **Chemists** Denmark Pharmacy, South Coast Highway, T9848

1711. Mon-Fri 0900-1700, Sat 0900-1200. **Hospital** Denmark District, Strickland St, T9848 1201. **Internet** Telecentre, Strickland St, T9848 2842. Mon-Fri 1000-1600. $8 hr. **Police** South Coast Highway, T9848 1311. **Post** Stickland St.

Albany *p197, map p199*
Banks Several banks and ATMs on York St. **Chemist** Amcal, 262 York St, T9842 2036. Daily 0900-2100. **Hospital** Albany Regional, Warden Av, T9892 2222. **Internet** Several, including Eco Tourist Centre, corner of York and Stirling Terr. **Medical centre** Southern Regional Medical Group, 32 Albany Highway (near York St roundabout), T9841 2733. **Police** 210 Stirling Terr, T9841 0555. **Post** Corner of York and Grey sts.

Mount Barker and around

Mount Barker is a service town for the surrounding agricultural region but unlike most towns of that description it has a bit of character. The area was explored by Europeans in the 1830s, mostly settlers from Albany looking for good agricultural land. In the past the region was known for apples, sheep and cattle but now, like much of the southwest, the earth is fast being covered by vines. Wildflowers are also grown commercially and there are many young plantations of Tasmanian blue gums that will be used for paper and woodchips. The main appeal for visitors is Mount Barker's location just west of the Porongurup National Park and south of the Stirling Range National Park. Both are beautiful forested hill ranges with great peak walks and the Stirling Ranges, in particular, has an incredible diversity of flora. The wildflowers in spring are wonderful and draw many visitors. ►► *For Sleeping, Eating and other listings, see pages 202-207.*

Ins and outs
The VIC ① *T9851 1163, www.mountbarkerwa.com, Mon-Fri 0900-1700, Sat 0900-1500, Sun 1000-1500*, is in the old railway station on the Albany Highway. It's very efficient and can provide maps for a driving route around the region, taking in wineries, wildflowers and St Werburghs Chapel. ►► *See Transport page 211 for details.*

Mount Barker → *Colour map 3, grid C5. Population: 1,700. 50 km from Albany.*
Just north of the town centre is a cluster of some of Mount Barker's oldest buildings, now restored and smelling of roses. The **Old Police Station** was built by convicts in 1867 from local ironstone cemented with mud. For 20 years, until a lockup was added to the stables building, prisoners were tied to a log out front during the day and if required to spend a night in custody, the prisoner would be firmly secured to the leg of the police constable's kitchen table. The buildings are now used as a **museum** ① *T9851 1631, Albany Highway, ½ km north of VIC, Sat-Sun 1000-1600 or by appointment, $4, concessions $2,* by the local historical society.

During the wildflower season it is well worth visiting the local **Banksia Farm** ① *Pearce Rd, off Muir Highway, T9851 1770, 0900-1700 (Aug-Nov), 1000-1600*

(Mar-Jun) or by appointment Dec-Feb, guided tours $11, self-guided tours $5.50, which displays an impressive collection of these unique Australian flowers. To the southwest of town, the lovely old **St Werburghs Chapel** ⓘ *St Werbergh's Rd, off Muir or Albany Highways, visitors welcome,* was built for the local settlers in 1872 from local timber and clay. The design is simple, and services are still held there by candlelight.

Wineries

The first vines were planted in 1867 but most vineyards in the region were established much more recently. Riesling has been the most successful variety, although

> ‡ *The VIC has a comprehensive list of cellar door locations and opening hours.*

chardonnay and shiraz are also doing well. There are around 20 cellar doors around Mount Barker and most are fairly small and friendly places with picnic areas but no food on offer (with the exception of Plantaganet)

Goundrey ⓘ *Muir Highway, T9851 1777, Mon-Sat 1000-1630, Sun 1100-1630,* the region's flagship, is an impressive, modern cellar door, 10 km south of town. The winery has won many awards for reasonably priced and drinkable wine. A good range of whites, reds, and a few sweet wines. Tours at 1130 and 1500 (the morning tours usually get to see the bottling line). Wines $13-26.

Plantaganet ⓘ *Albany Highway, T9851 2150, Mon-Fri 0900-1700, Sat-Sun 1000-1600,* is right in town so ideal for those without transport. A small, rustic cellar door offers tastings of dry whites, dry reds and a few fortifieds. A small café has cheese platters (1200-1500), cakes and coffee. Wines $15-35.

Porongurup National Park → *Colour map 3, grid C5. 22 km from Mt Barker, 50 km from Albany.*

Despite the proximity of the Porongurup Hills to the Stirling Range, these massive **granite** domes have a very different geological background to their taller neighbours and are thought to be about twice their age. The national park is a small area of forest encompassing the Porongurup Range, only about 12 km long and a

> ‡ *There are no campsites in the park and there are no entry fees.*

few kilometres wide. The range rises out of tall **karri forest**, a relic from a wetter climate that has managed to survive in the conditions provided by the ranges. Karri usually grows further south, between Manjimup and Walpole. The typical karri forest understorey flora and fauna has also survived here and

wildflowers stage a brilliant display in spring. Walking in the Porongurup range is very enjoyable as most walks include both gentle forest trails and fantastic views of the Stirling Range and King George Sound from the top of sheets and boulders of granite. You also have a good chance of seeing western grey kangaroos, brush wallabies and lots of birds if you walk quietly, particularly in the late afternoon. There are two main entry points, both from the northern side. Bolganup Road leads from the main settlement area to a shady clearing where there are picnic tables and BBQs. This is the start of several walk trails. The next entry point is Castle Rock Road, unsealed but only 1 km long, about 6 km further east, and gives access to the **Castle Rock** and Balancing Rock trail only.

One of the park's attractions is **Tree in the Rock**, a karri that appears to be growing from the centre of a large boulder. The tree is only about 100 m from the Bolganup picnic area and you will pass it if you walk the **Nancy Peak circuit**. This is a steady uphill walk through forest up to three peaks: Hayward, Nancy and Morgans. The highest is Nancy at a little over 600 m. Once you reach the first peak you walk along the ridge and there is little further uphill walking. The southern coast and the Stirling Range are clearly visible from the top. There is a short, steep descent from Morgans and then you follow a wide easy forest path back to the picnic area (5½ km, two hours). This is a good walk but if you only have time for one, then head for **Castle Rock**. An easy uphill walk through forest leads to Balancing Rock, a huge 180-tonne boulder that appears to be sitting on its narrowest point, like an upstanding egg. From here you can access the top of adjacent Castle Rock, though it is a bit of a scramble. You need to squeeze through two sets of massive rocks to reach a ladder. Climb the ladder to a platform and you are in the 'castle', a tall group of boulders that enclose you and feel strangely like battlements. There are magnificent views of the Stirling Range, laid out on the horizon like a Hollywood set, and you will want to stay up here for ages. Return by the same route (4 km, 1½ hours return).

Stirling Range National Park → *Colour map 3, grid B6. Loop drive (some unsealed) approximately 180 km from Mt Barker, 260 km from Albany.*

ⓘ *Vehicle entry $9 payable at Bluff Knoll turn-off, park ranger, T9827 9230.*

The Stirling Range is an island of pointy bush-clothed peaks, rising sharply from an endless expanse of flat, cleared farmland. The ranges are formed from uplifted quartzite, sandstone and shales and were once ancient seabeds. Rippled stone found all over the ranges is a reminder that they lay under a shallow sea about 500 million years ago. The park is particularly noted for its incredible diversity of flora: there are over 1,500 plant species within the park, an area about 65 km by 20 km. The wildflowers are wonderful here in spring and the park has some unusual species of orchids and mountains bells (Darwinias). The park has many peak walks giving views over the surrounding plains and a scenic drive running east-west through the ranges. This unsealed drive (50 km) is best done westward in the morning and eastward in the afternoon. It is also worth a drive up the sealed road to the Bluff Knoll car park for good views of the ranges, even if you don't walk. There are a few picnic areas and lookouts but essentially the park is undeveloped. Dieback is a problem here, requiring some areas to be closed to visitors, as are bushfires caused by lightning strikes. There is still much evidence of the bad fires of 1996.

> ♟ *If planning extended walks in the park, we recommend Mountain Walks in the Stirling Range by Tony Morphett.*

Walking in this national park is really for those who enjoy climbing peaks. Most of the highest peaks can be climbed but two stand out. **Bluff Knoll** (1,073 m), the distinctive prow-like peak at the eastern end of the park, is the highest point in the south-west (second highest in WA) and for many visitors this is the one to tick off, if only because it is the only one accessed via a sealed road. The walk starts at the car park and ascends 656 m to the summit. It is a steady uphill walk, along a good formed path, through scrub to a saddle, before swinging around to the summit plateau. The wildflowers are ever present, but fantastic in spring, and there are good views of the coast from the saddle (5 km, 2-3 hours return). The best views in the park are, however, from **Toolbrunup Peak** (1,054 m). This narrow conical hill, with two prominent shoulders, can be seen from Bluff Knoll though is more impressive from the scenic drive. It is a more challenging and interesting walk (ascending 630 m) but only for those who are fit, agile and enjoy scrambling over large boulders. Despite the daunting look of the peak from the western side, the route approaches from the east and is tiring. The first half ascends through forest along scree and gravel paths before reaching a boulder field. After an extended, steep scramble the route reaches a saddle and from there it is a short clamber up to the summit, where there are 360° views of the whole Stirling Range, Porongurups and the surrounding plains.

There is a two- to three-day wilderness walk, **Stirling Ridge Walk**, from Ellen Peak to Bluff Knoll but you should talk to the CALM ranger (T9827 9230) if considering this. **Stirling Range Retreat** can arrange pick-ups and drops-offs for day walks or extended walks. They also run good-value short guided walks and slide nights during wildflowers season (September-October). Carry plenty of water and check the forecast. Weather can change rapidly on the high peaks and low cloud can cause wind chill and obscure the route.

Mount Barker p207

Mt Barker is not a tourist town so prices remain reasonable all year. The busiest time is wildflower season from mid-Aug-Oct.

B-C Abbeyholme, Mitchell St, T9851 1101, www.abbeyholme.com. B&B in a fine stone house built in 1869. 2 elegant en-suite rooms with whitewashed walls and antique furniture, large guest lounge, cooked brekkie. Also a small self-contained timber cottage.

D Plantagenet, 9 Lowood Rd, T9851 1008. Standard hotel rooms above the pub with shared facilities and slightly more expensive self-contained motel rooms.

D-E Chill Out Backpackers, 79 Hassell St, T9851 2798. Modern, comfortable hostel in a large A-frame about 1 km south of the VIC. Singles, doubles and dorms, spacious living area and a great music collection.

D-E Caravan park, Albany Highway just north of town, T9851 1691, with cabins, on-site vans and basic dongas.

Porongorup National Park p208

Porongorup settlement is little more than a shop and service station, which triples as a tearooms and a small, simple hostel.

A-C Karribank, T9853 1022, www.karribank. com.au. Opposite the YHA, this is the area's upmarket option, an old farm turned guesthouse is a genteel retreat with some beautifully furnished century-old cottage rooms and cheaper chalets.

C Bolganup Homestead, T9853 1049. Next to the shop, a classic farm homestead has been split into 3 large self-contained apartments. Good value for 2, bargain for 4-6.

C-E Porongurup Range Tourist Park, T9853 1057. Has on-site vans and cabins, plus an excellent camp kitchen and common room.

E YHA, T9853 1110, A handful of rooms and basic but serviceable facilities.

Stirling Ranges National Park p209

B-C The Lily, Chester Pass Rd, 12 km north of Bluff Knoll turn-off, T9827 9205, www.thelily. com.au. No visit to the Stirlings is complete without a trip here. This arresting and inspiring mini 'complex' of rescued and hand built buildings (solely by the owner) includes a fully working replica 16th-century Dutch windmill, various 'outbuildings' with elegant and homely rooms and an excellent café/ bistro in a transferred and restored 1924 railway station. The buildings sit on a slight rise on a wide plain with fantastic views to the ranges. Tue-Sun 1000-1700, candlelit dinners by arrangement. Recommended.

B-E Stirling Range Retreat, Chester Pass Rd, opposite Bluff Knoll turn-off, T9827 9229, www.stirlingrange.com.au. Self-contained chalets, cabins, vans, campsites and pool (Nov-Mar). Friendly, helpful staff can advise on walking and arrange pick-ups and drop-offs. Managed as bush retreat for native animals so can be a good spot to see wildlife. There is a **park campsite** ($10) at Moingup Springs, just off the Chester Pass Rd, with toilets and BBQs. Obtain permit on arrival.

● Eating

Mount Barker p207

🍴 **Plantagenet** pub has a good reputation for its food, particularly steak, served in a very ordinary dining room Mon-Fri 1200-1400, Mon-Sat 1800-2000.

Fifteen Streets Berry Farm, Orient Rd, 4 km south of town. At the weekend you can get lunches and cream teas.

Lockwoods Bread Shoppe, is a pleasant old fashioned bakery café, Mon-Fri 0900-1730, Sat 0900-1200.

Porongorup National Park p208

🍴 **Karribank's**, T9853 1022. Country-style restaurant, open all day, meals 0830-0930, 1200-1430 and evenings from 1830, bookings appreciated.

🍴 **Maleeya's Thai Café**, 1376 Porongurup Rd, 6 km west of Porongurup, T9853 1123. Wonderful authentic Thai food comes out of the kitchen at this bamboo nursery and souvenir shop. There are only 6 tables so book ahead. BYO only. Thu-Sun 1800-2000.

Stirling Ranges p209

See also **The Lily**, in Sleeping above.

Bluff Knoll Café, almost opposite Stirling Range Retreat.

⊖ Transport

Mount Barker *p207*
From Albany northbound buses to **Perth** go
via **Mount Barker** depart at least once a day
from 0900 Mon-Sat, and 1315 Sun.

The route east

Albany to Esperance → *Distance: 480 km.*

The road to Esperance is a long and mostly featureless one, but there are a few places along the way where you can break the journey and a magnificent wilderness within the **Fitzgerald River National Park**. There are petrol stations roughly every 100 km.

At **Ravensthorpe**, 290 km from Albany, the South Coast Highway meets the meandering route back to Perth, which heads through the wheatbelt and can take in **Wave Rock** at Hyden. Ravensthorpe has a VIC, pub and caravan park.

Hopetoun, 50 km off the highway due south of Ravensthorpe, is a little coastal town that provides the best access to Fitzgerald River. Tourist information is available from **Barnacles Café**, where you can get homemade fare. There are some places to sleep: **Hopetoun Motel and Chalet Village** (T9838 3219) and the pub on the foreshore, **Port Hotel** (T9838 3053). Hopetoun also has a supermarket, fuel and caravan park.

The wilderness of **Fitzgerald River National Park** ① *$9 car, camping at Point Ann and Hamersley Inlet, for more information contact CALM ranger, T9835 5043*, stretches between Bremer Bay and Hopetoun, and inland almost as far as the highway. It is one of the state's most important national parks and has been registered as a UNESCO international biosphere reserve. It contains about 1,900 plant species in an area of almost 330,000 ha. Most of the park is covered in low scrub leading to a string of granite ranges and peaks close to the coast. Hammersley Drive passes south of **East Mount Barren**, 12 km west of Hopetoun, and you can climb to the top (3 km, 2½ hours) along a ridge for views along much of the park's coastline.

The last town on the south coast is **Esperance**, a port town dominated by an industrial wharf. The town overlooks the **Archipelago of the Recherche**, a beautiful wide bay full of more than a hundred granite islands. It is one of the most isolated towns in the state and a practical place, with few frills or buildings of character. What draws visitors are the stunning beaches and coastal scenery both to the west on Great Ocean Drive and, further out, to the east of the town in the **Cape Le Grand** and **Cape Arid National Parks**, where blinding sandy coves and coastal heath frame granite headlands. The contrast of snow-like sand and aquamarine water deepening to sapphire blue has captivated visitors since Captain Jean Michel Huon de Kermadec discovered this coast in 1792 in L'Esperance. For more information on Esperance contact the **VIC** ① *Dempster St, T9071 2330, www.visitesperance.com, 0900-1700*.

Across the Nullabor and beyond

From Esperance it's 200 km north to the small gold-mining town of Norseman and from there 720 km east to the WA border. If you are heading to the eastern states take a deep breath because it's a further 1265 km from the WA/SA border to Adelaide. For brief details of **Norseman**, and the trip across the **Nullarbor**, see page 137.

South Coast The route east

‡ Footprint features

Introduction

A dry, semi-arid region, the Midwest divides the green hills of Perth and the Southwest from the near desert regions further north. The Batavia Coast is a long, straight stretch of coastline battered by wind. The narrow beaches and high white dunes gradually rise to the limestone cliffs of Kalbarri. At Cervantes, limestone columns, the Pinnacles, protrude from the sand, eerily reminiscent of the stone circles of northern Europe.

There are few bays and natural harbours along this coastline, and it is only interrupted by slow-flowing rivers. In such dry country freshwater is the key to survival so almost every town is clustered around a rivermouth. Some of these, such as Dongara, are old settlements, used as ports by early pastoralists. Others, such as Cervantes and Kalbarri, are relatively young towns that sprang up as a collection of fishing shacks in the last 50 years. Life in these coastal towns is dominated by the crayfish, a small tasty lobster that commands high prices overseas and has made the fortune of many a local fisherman. The major port of Geraldton, one of the states largest cities, has superb windsurfing conditions and excellent diving and snorkelling on the coral reefs of the Houtman Abrolhos islands 60 km offshore.

Inland, much of the country has been cleared and there is a narrow wheat-growing area as far north as Northampton. This region is well known for its spectacular wildflowers in spring when the midwest is carpeted in flowers after good winter rains. The wildflowers are best seen just inland but are also found along the Brand Highway and in the Kalbarri National Park. There is no doubt, however, that Kalbarri is the queen of the midwest. This small seaside town can boast a beautiful location, fine beaches, and a national park with stunning river and coastal gorges.

❗ Don't miss...

1 **Pinnacles** Watch the sun rise or set on forest of rocks, page 216.
2 **Beagle Island** Swim with the sea lions off this island, page 217.
3 **Greenough Hamlet** Peer into the past at this 1860's settlers village, page 219.
4 **Dongara** Become a crayfisherman for a day, page 221.
5 **Abrolhos** Take a flight to this island and snorkel in the crystal clear water, page 225.
6 **Kalbarri** Gallop on a trusty steed along the beach here, or learn to sail on a surfcat in its sheltered rivermouth, page 231.
7 **Kalbarri National Park** Canoe the gorges or explore further on an overnight camping trip, page 235.

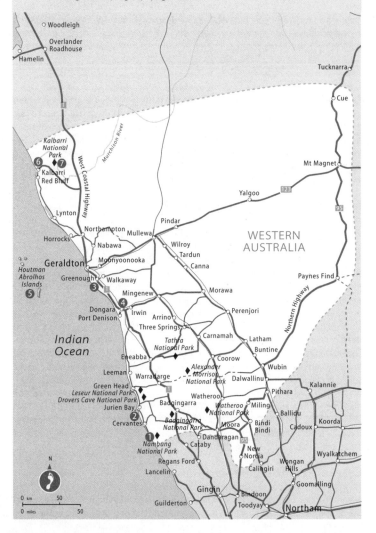

Midwest

Batavia Coast

This coastline is named for the Batavia, *a Dutch trading ship that was wrecked on the Houtman-Abrolhos Islands in 1629, close to Geraldton. The* Batavia *is famous for the gruesome behaviour of its survivors but it is only one of many shipwrecks on this coast. Strong westerly winds and an absence of safe, sheltered harbours meant ships were regularly smashed onto the reefs and rocks of this unforgiving coastline. The settlements of Cervantes, Jurien Bay, Leeman and Green Head are all crayfishing towns of utterly functional architecture. They hold little of interest except for the Pinnacles in the Nambung National Park, near Cervantes and the possibility of swimming with sealions at Jurien Bay and Green Head. Further north, the old twin towns of Dongara-Port Denison are good places for a relaxed overnight stop and the historic settlement on the Greenough flats is worth exploring. Geraldton is a large city where you can stock up on supplies and explore its excellent maritime museum focusing on the story of the* Batavia. *It is also good for watersports; the windsurfing is known worldwide and there is excellent diving and snorkelling both on a brand new artificial reef and on the coral reefs of the Houtman-Abrolhos islands 60 km offshore.*
▸▸ *For Sleeping, Eating and other listings, see pages 220-222.*

Cervantes → *Colour map 4, grid B1. Population: 500. 225 km from Perth, 25 km from Jurien.*
Cervantes is a small crayfishing community built in the last 30 years on flat sandy land by Ronsard Bay, sheltered by an offshore reef. The town has the good fortune of being the closest to Nambung National Park and its famous Pinnacles, although most people visit the park on a daytrip so the town remains essentially undeveloped. The most exotic thing about Cervantes is its Spanish street names. The town was named after an American whaling ship wrecked just offshore in 1844 but the street names were chosen from *Don Quixote* (by Miguel de Cervantes).

Nambung National Park and the Pinnacles → *Colour map 4, grid B1.*
19 km from Cervantes, 6 km unsealed.
This national park protects an otherworldly forest of spiky rocks rising out of a yellow sandy desert. The Pinnacles are one of the most recognizable images of Western Australia and they are certainly a striking sight, one well worth making a detour for. Dutch sailors passing by in the 17th century marked them on their charts and likened them to the crumbling remains of an ancient city. The rock formations are surprisingly extensive, covering an area of several square kilometres, and there are thousands of them, taking varied forms from narrow towers 5-m high to modest stubs. There is some debate about the geological origin of the Pinnacles but the consensus is that deep cracks and hollows created by plant roots filled with a hard quartz limestone. These shapes and columns were left exposed when much of the vegetation cover and top sands eroded away some 20,000 years ago. The best time to see the park is in the soft light of early morning or at sunset, although sunset is quite busy with tour groups. A 3 km loop road (sandy but hard packed and perfectly suitable for 2WD) traverses the main area of formations and you can stop along the way and walk among them. There are two picnic spots by the beach on the way out, at **Kangaroo Point** and **Hangover Bay**; the latter is the best for swimming and has gas BBQs. Park entry fee $9 car or $3.40 per person.

Cervantes to Dongara → *Distance: 160 km.*
This coastal route passes through sand dunes with the occasional glimpse of the ocean or a few fishing shacks, and the small fishing communities of Jurien, Green Head, and Leeman. The coastline is long and flat here and the largest of the three

townships, Jurien Bay, has created an artificial boat harbour for safe anchorage. Swimming, windsurfing, snorkelling and surfing are all popular activities along this stretch of coast, although youll need your own gear. All of the towns are very similar; a collection of functional shacks and bungalows, boat ramps and jetties, and a few basic services.

Jurien Bay has a shopping centre on the corner of the main street, Bashford Street, and Roberts Street. Tourist information is available from the BP service station ① *T9652 1444*. There is a supermarket ① *0730-1800*, with an ATM and two pleasant cafés. The main appeal of this area for visitors is the chance to swim with sealions, who live in large colonies on Fisherman Islands, north of Jurien, and **Beagle Island**, north of Leeman.

Between Jurien and Green Head there are three national parks, all strictly 4WD only, with rough sandy and rocky tracks. **Drovers Cave National Park** and **Stockyard Gully National Park** have limestone caves (without decoration) and the latter a 270-m riverbed tunnel that you can walk through. **Lesueur National Park** has over 900 species of plants, one of the most diverse collections of flora in the state. There is a short walking track up Mount Lesueur (3 km return), a low flat-topped laterite mesa. For more information, contact the Cervantes CALM ranger ① *T9652 7053*. For tours contact **Turquoise Coast Enviro Tours**.

Green Head has little more than a general store and caravan park ① *T9953 1131*, but it does have a lovely swimming and picnic spot at **Dynamite Bay**. The bay is a tiny cove with rocky limestone headlands and there are covered picnic areas, showers, toilets and BBQ. **Leeman** is slightly larger, housing workers from a mineral sands mining venture at Eneabba. The foreshore area has a few picnic tables and BBQs. Basic shops on Nairn Street, parallel to the main coast road and Spencer Street, between Nairn Street and the foreshore. Leeman also has a Telecentre on Spencer Street, for internet access.

Badgingarra to Dongara → *Distance: 155 km.*

Badgingarra, 200 km out of Perth and a few kilometres past the Cervantes turn-off, is many peoples first stop north on the Brand Highway if theyre not going via the coast. **Badgingarra Roadhouse** ① *T9652 9051, 0600-2000*, is all that most people see of the tiny town, and frankly all they need to. The roadhouse has a tearoom. The town sits amidst the much bigger **Badgingarra National Park**, a wildflower wonderland in season. There are few trails in the park, but a short walk that is worth the time, especially in spring, heads a short way east from the highway opposite the roadhouse turn-off.

From Badgingarra the highway continues 75 km north to **Eneabba**, another tiny settlement, with a pleasant surprise. As well as the **roadhouse** ① *0630-1930*, and pub, its outdoor community swimming pool ① *1200-1700, 1800-1930 Mon, Wed-Fri, 1200-1800 Sat-Sun*, can provide a welcome break on a hot day. Dongara is a further 80 km up the road, with a short diversion via **Port Denison** sign-posted a few kilometres before.

Dongara and Port Denison → *Colour map 4, grid A1. Population: 1,900. 65 km from Geraldton.*

Dongara and its sister town Port Denison are sited 3 km apart at the point at which the Irwin River meets the Indian Ocean. Dongara is a historic town, retaining many buildings over a century old and with a picturesque main street lined with huge mature Moreton Bay Fig trees. It was first settled in the 1850s as the centre of a new agricultural area. From its earliest days the river mouth was used as stop-gap port and a jetty was built in the 1860s to ease transport of goods. The present day port exhibits much less of its history and is dominated by an extensive

⁞ Strolls up the banks of the Irwin River or along the extensive expanse of South Beach are recommended.

The Batavia

The Batavia was some ship, twice as big as the later *Endeavour*. It embarked on its maiden voyage to the Dutch East Indies in 1628 with a rich cargo of currency, jewels, provisions and, as it turned out, mutineers. Following usual practice, the ship rounded Cape Horn and headed east, setting out over the Indian Ocean and planning to turn north after sighting the 'Southland'. That was Commander Pelsaert's plan at any rate. Skipper, Jacobsz, and the senior merchant, Cornelisz, had other ideas. Previous animosity with the Commander and rampant greed persuaded them to a new plan: to murder all but a handful of like-minded crew and take to a life of piracy.

Before the mutiny was sprung, however, fate intervened. On the 4 June 1629 the ship ran permanently aground on the reefs of the Abrolhos islands, though no life was lost. At first the situation was dire, much of the water was spoiled and little food was recovered. The ship carried two boats, capable of carrying 50 or so people onward to the Indies. In a shameful move the Commander and Jacobsz slipped away in these under cover of darkness, with 40-odd able crew and the lion's share of the water and provisions. Pelsaert intended to return as quickly as possible with a larger ship, but in his heart must have assumed none would survive to be rescued.

Some few did indeed die of thirst, but within days a great storm dumped rain by the bucket load onto the huddle of small islands. Their new inhabitants were able to channel much of it into barrels, while at the same time discovered that the islands offered plentiful food in the way of fish, shellfish and seals. Survival seemed possible, even probable.

They hadn't, however, reckoned on one of their own number. Cornelisz harboured plans of taking over the expected rescue ship, recovering the Batavia's treasure and still living a piratical life. But that meant eliminating the majority of the survivors before the rescue ship arrived. He re-recruited his fellow mutineers and began a campaign of terror that makes Lord of the Flies seem like a tea-party. About 125 people were gradually isolated and foully murdered, one young boy was decapitated simply to settle a bet on the sharpness of a sword. When Pelsaert did eventually return it was to discover Cornelisz and his well-armed band besieging a larger and unarmed, though admirably resourceful group led by a common soldier, Weibbe Hayes.

Cornelisz and the other most dangerous ring-leaders were hung by Pelsaert on the spot, though some mutineers were brought back to Batavia for more visible punishment. Two were given a last-minute reprieve by the commander and marooned on the mainland, their fate still unknown. Pelsaert was dead within a year, some say of shame, but his career would certainly have ended shortly after. Jacobsz was arrested and is last heard of rotting in a Javan prison, unwilling to confess his planned role in the mutiny despite the testimonies of several co-conspirators. Weibbe Hayes received a handsome promotion and has become something of a Dutch legend. Relics from the wreck of the Batavia are housed in the Western Australian Museum in Geraldton and the ship's hull is preserved in the Maritime Museum in Fremantle.

modern harbour. There are beaches north and south of the towns, **Harbour Beach**
being very sheltered and **South Beach** a kilometre-long expanse of hard-packed sand
on which vehicles are allowed. Town services are comprehensive, including banks
and a hospital.

The **Irwin District Museum** ① *Waldeck St, T9927 1323, adjacent to the VIC,
Mon-Fri 1000-1600 when volunteers are available*, has photographic displays and
memorabilia that explore local history, shipwrecks and, somewhat oddly, the
phenomenon of rabbits in Australia. It also manages **Russ Historic Cottage** ① *corner
of Point Leander Dr and St Dominics Rd, Sun 1000-1200, $2.50, children $0.50*, a
pioneer dwelling built in the 1870s and now restored and furnished in keeping with
the period. The **Old Mill** (1894), visible from the highway, is being restored by the
National Trust but is not yet open. The VIC ① *9 Waldeck St, T9927 1404, ddtic@wn.
com.au, 0900-1700 Mon-Fri, 0900-1400 Sat-Sun*, occupies part of the old Post
Office, which also houses the library.

Greenough → *Colour map 4, grid A1. 41 km from Dongara, 24 km from Geraldton.*

Greenough Flats is a long flat area of relatively fertile ground, sandwiched between
the coastal dunes and a low inland limestone ridge, and extending about 30 km
south of Geraldton. From the south the area of principal interest starts at the **S Bend
roadhouse and caravan park** ① *T9926 1072*. Here the main highway turns sharply to
the right while the old road carries straight on for about 6 km before a right turn into
McCartney Road heads over a convict-built bridge and back on to the highway. Dont
be fooled by the unsealed turn-off, it reverts to tarmac within 200 m. Taking this
diversion misses nothing, and takes you past the **Hampton Arms**, a characterful 1863
pub which incorporates the **Rare & Antique Bookshop**. Opposite McCartney Road a
2-km unsealed track leads to **Lucys Beach**, a wild and windswept stretch of coast,
much favoured by fishers and surfers, with some impressively spiky weathered rocks
exposed at low tide. The last 600 m of the track are 4WD-only or a walk.

Greenough Hamlet
① *T9926 1084, 0900-1600, $4.50, children and concessions $2.50.*
On the other side of the highway from McCartney Road is Greenough Hamlet. This
settlers village, dating back to the 1860s, is now uninhabited and maintained as an
open-air museum by the National Trust. The dozen buildings include two churches
and several cottages, half of them accessible and furnished to lesser and greater
degrees as they might have been over a hundred years ago. Most interesting is the
court and gaol building, the cells of which powerfully demonstrate the contempt in
which Aboriginals were held. There are several displays in the entry building and also
a tearoom serving a variety of snacks and excellent afternoon teas.

The road behind the Hamlet leads, after 15 km of bitumen and 5 km of unsealed
road, to **Ellendale Pool**, a picturesque and shaded swimming waterhole and free
camping spot, with basic toilets. Further up the highway, past the wind-tortured
leaning trees is the **Pioneer Museum** ① *T9926 1058, Tue-Sun 1000-1600, $3,
children $1, concessions $2*, another of the Flats pioneer homes and now a folk
museum stuffed full of everyday artefacts from the late 1800s. Several rooms are
open and give a good idea of how a well-to-do family of the period lived. There are
sheltered picnic tables out the front.

Greenough Rivermouth
Greenough River winds down from the Moresby Ranges to meet the ocean 12 km south
of Geraldton at Greenough Rivermouth. A sandbar turns the lower reaches of the river
into one long lake most of the time and there are walking trails up along both banks for
several kilometres. At the beach are toilets and some shelter. Alternatively, **Greenough
River Cruises** leave the mouth most days for genteel and informative cruises upriver.

● Sleeping

Cervantes *p216*
C Cervantes Pinnacles Motel, Aragon St, T9652 7145. Large modern motel with 40 standard rooms, pool, bar and restaurant.
D-E Cervantes Lodge and Pinnacle Beach Backpackers, 91 Seville St, T9652 7377, www.cervanteslodge.com.au. Clean, comfortable, attractive and welcoming hostel and B&B, with a range of rooms from dorms to ensuite doubles. Excellent facilities include a licensed café, the *Don Quixote*, and pool. Recommended.
The caravan park on Aragon St, T9652 7060, has cheap, clean cabins and vans.

Cervantes to Dongara *p216*
C Jurien Bay Hotel Motel, Padbury St, Jurien Bay, T9652 1022.
C Tamarisk Court, corner of Tamarisk and Nairn sts, Leeman, T9953 1190. Range of self- contained units.
C-D Jurien Beachfront Holiday Units, corner of Cook and Grigson sts, Jurien Bay, T9652 1172.
Caravan park, Jurien Bay, T9652 1595.
Caravan park, Leeman, T9953 1080, with units, chalets and vans at the southern end of town on Thomas St.

Badgingarra to Dongara *p217*
Western Flora, T9955 2030, 22 km north of Eneabba, is a caravan park on the Brand Highway. Great place if you are a wildflower enthusiast as just west of the wildflower district. Chalets, vans, cabins, backpacker beds and guided wildflower walks.

Dongara and Port Denison *p217*
Dongara is blessed with a range of extremely good value accommodation.
C Dongara Hotel, 12 Moreton Terr, T9927 1023, dongarahotel@wn.com.au. Motel rooms, large bar and separate restaurant.
D Lazy Lobster, 49 Hampton St, Port Denison, T/F9927 2177, lazylobster@bigpond.com. Self-contained chalets.
D Priory Lodge, 11 St Dominics Rd, T/F9927 1090, is an old inn-turned-convent-turned-inn, has a public bar, beer garden opposite the river. 17 spacious, doubles and singles

with high-ceilings and plain decor. No en suites but there is a guest kitchen and lounge.
E Dongara Backpackers (YHA), 32 Waldeck St, T9927 1581, dongarabackpack@west net.com.au. A charming and friendly hostel in a converted cottage and 1906 railway carriage (the Snorient Express). Some doubles, lots of freebies, pick-ups, garden with BBQ and excellent local knowledge. Recommended.
Dongara Denison Tourist Park, 8 George St near South Beach, Port Denison, T/F9927 1210. One of 4 caravan parks here with cabins, on-site vans and sites in a shaded bush setting. Some sites overlook the ocean.

Greenough *p219*
B-C Greenough River Resort, T9921 5888, members.westnet.com.au/grenor. On the short road to Greenough Rivermouth is this modern, rambling motel, a 2-min walk from the river. It has a mid-range restaurant and 15 semi self-contained rooms, mostly grouped around an attractive pool area.
C Rock of Ages B&B, T/F9926 1154, rockofages@westnet.com.au. An 1857 thick, stone-walled cottage, opposite the Pioneer Museum, originally built by WAs Convict No 2, John Patience. Its been beautifully restored, furnished mostly in period as a B&B, and has a small garden with gazebo spa and BBQ. 3 double rooms share a single bathroom. Recommended.
D Bentwood Olive Grove, T/F9926 1196, is set back off the Brand Highway. Has a single, self-contained cottage. Private garden with BBQ, access to the family pool, and optional breakfast. One double, one 4-bunk room. Comfortably and cheerfully furnished, and excellent value.
D Hampton Arms, Company Rd, T9926 1057. One of WAs great historic pubs, the bookshop simply adding to the feel of antiquity. There's a small bar, a ballroom turned mid-range restaurant, and a small number of suitably characterful rooms.
Caravan park, T9964 9845, just back from the mouth of the river. On-site vans and cabins, a good-sized shop and takeaway, open daily to 2000, and also hires out canoes.

❼ Eating

Cervantes *p216*
🍴 Ronsard Bay Tavern, Cadiz St, T9652 7041. Has a large dining room (meals daily 1130-1400, 1830-2030) and a public bar. There is a small shopping centre with a general store and takeaway shop near here.

Cervantes to Dongara *p216*
🍴 Café Rusca, at the shopping centre, Jurien Bay, a large Mediterranean-style place open for lunch and dinner, Tue-Sat.
🍴 Beaches of Leeman, Spencer St, Leeman. Has fast food, takeaways and drinks, daily.
🍴 Indian Ocean, Jurien Bay, at the shopping centre, does all-day breakfasts.

Badgingarra to Dongara *p217*
🍴 Eneabba Sands Tavern, Eneabba, T9955 1077. Has pool and table tennis tables and serves bar snacks and grills daily 1200-2130.

Dongara and Port Denison *p217*
🍴 Southerlys, Point Leander Dr, Port Denison, T9927 2207. A smart, casual modern bar and restaurant with a large front terrace over the road from the foreshore. Cheap bar meals daily 1200-1400, 1800-2000, while the mid-range restaurant is open 1800-2100.
🍴 Tokos, corner of Moreton Terr and Point Leander Dr, T9927 1497. Slightly more traditional in both decor and cuisine. Open Wed-Fri 1200-1400 and 1830-2030 daily.
🍴 Coffee Tree, 8 Moreton Terr, T9927 1400. Has a small terrace under one of the larger fig trees and is a pleasant spot to sit and watch the world go by. All-day breakfast, sandwiches and salads, BYO, coffee and cake. Daily 0800-1600.
🍴 Dongara Hotel, 12 Moreton Terr, T9927 1023, dongarahotel@wn.com.au. Has a large bar and a separate restaurant. Meals in both include a go at a salad and veggie bar. Bar meals 1200-1400, evening meals in the restaurant from 1830-2000. On Fri evenings they have bands in the bar and a buffet in the restaurant ($16.50).
🍴 Priory Lodge, 11 St Dominics Rd, T/F9927 1090. Has a public bar and a beer garden opposite the river. Simple, cheap and wholesome meals daily 1200-1400,

1800-2000, spit roasts most Sun, live regular weekend live music, and free sausage sizzles every Tue night.

Greenough *p219*
🍴 Hampton Arms, Company Rd, T9926 1057. Has a small bar, a ballroom turned mid-range restaurant serving simple grills, seafood and gourmet pies, 6 double rooms and a covered rear courtyard. Wed-Sun 1000-2200 , meals 1130-1430, 1800-2030.

▲ Activities and tours

Cervantes *p216*
As well as many tours available from Perth, there are also 2 Cervantes operators.
Happy Day Tours head out most days at 0800 for a 3-hr tour ($25). Good value, though youll miss the deep colours of sunrise or sunset. Book via **Greyhound**, T132030.
Turquoise Coast Enviro Tours, T9652 7047, www.holiday-wa.net/tcet. Run by ex-ranger Mike Newton, who offers personalized 4WD tours of many of the national parks in the area (most are only accessible by 4WD). His all day tour starts with the Pinnacles and also takes in Lesueur and Stockyard Gully parks. Prices vary according to group size and duration.

Cervantes to Dongara *p216*
Jurien Fishing & Dive Charters, Jurien Bay, T9652 1109. Organizes regular swimming with sea lion tours. Prices vary according to size of party. Mornings are usually the best time for a tour and there is a minimum numbers requirement, so book ahead. It can also organize whale watching (Oct-Dec), sea-fishing and diving excursions.

Dongara and Port Denison *p217*
Lobster fishing is possible with a couple of the local cray-boat captains. They will take out temporary crew for around $20 a day during the Nov-Jun season. You will need to take your own provisions. Book via the VIC.
Arkell Air Charter, T9927 1267. Runs a variety of flights from $55. The operator also organizes excellent day trips to the Abrolhos Islands that can be as cheap as $100 per person.

Backtrack Tours, operated by the hostel, offers 3-hr mini bus tours ($29) in and around town, including a trip to a local sheep station and a visit to the Lobster Logistics Centre in Port Denison.

Icon Charters, Port Denison, T9927 1256. Trips aboard boats include sea lion interaction (6 hrs, $150), whale watching (2 hrs, $40), sunset tours (1 hrs, $25) and sea fishing (7 hrs, $120). All are numbers dependent and are available Jul-Oct.

Greenough Rivermouth *p219*
Greenough River Cruises, T9926 1717, cruise@wn.com.au, leaves the mouth most days for cruises up river. Tue-Sun 1030, other times as per demand. Morning or afternoon tea, or sunset BBQ included.

☻ Transport

The Batavia Coast *p216*
TransWA passes through the region on 3 routes. The main (N1) services to Geraldton (6 hrs) leave East Perth terminal at 0830 Mon-Sat, 1730 Fri and 0930 Sun, stops include **Gingin**, **Dongara** and **Greenough**. The morning Mon, Wed and Fri services continue on to **Kalbarri**. McCaffertys/ Greyhounds has a service to Exmouth from Perth leaving at 2000 Wed, Fri and Sun, calling at major coastal towns from **Cervantes** northward.

Geraldton and around

Many West Australians dismiss Geraldton as a large and uninteresting port city. It is true that the citys emphasis is firmly on industry and it hasn't developed with aesthetics in mind; an enormous silo and industrial wharves dominate the southern end of Geraldton and a series of functional rock groynes obscure the coastline. It does, however, have a fantastic sunny climate and strong, reliable westerlies make it a mecca for windsurfers. It is also the base for dive and snorkel tours out to the Houtman Abrolhos Islands, a remote group of coral islands teeming with fish and only inhabited for a few months a year by local crayfishermen. Geraldton itself has many interesting sights (some of which are free) and all the services of a large town if you are heading north this will be the last place to find such services for many, many hundreds of kilometres. ▸▸ *For Sleeping, Eating and other listings, see pages 226-229.*

Ins and outs
The VIC ① *T9921 3999, www.geraldtontourist.com.au, www.kalbarri.com/geraldton, Mon-Fri 0830-1700, Sat 0900-1630, Sun 0930-1630*, is located in the Bill Sewell Complex, along with a simple café and a backpacker hostel. The fine two-storey sandstone buildings were part of a district hospital built in 1884. ▸▸ *See Transport, page 228, for details.*

Geraldton → *Colour map 4, grid A1. Population: 20,000. 425 km from Perth, 480 km from Carnarvon.*

Geraldton can make the unusual but welcome claim that many of its main tourist attractions are free, or involve a token donation. Some of these, particularly the gallery and museum, are of a very high standard. The waterfront area around the museum is being developed into a townhouse and marina complex and this is likely to become an attractive, lively part of the city.

Sights
Lighthouse Keepers Cottage ① *Chapman Rd, Bluff Point, 3 km north of town centre, Thu 1000-1600, $1,* houses the main research office of the Geraldton Historical

Society, and is stuffed full of their records and pictures. Public access is restricted to a couple of rooms in this unusual 1876 blend of lighthouse and keepers cottage. There used to be another lighthouse on the beach and the two were used as a line-of-sight by shipping to guide them through the difficult mouth of the harbour.

Old Geraldton Gaol Craft Centre ① *Chapman Rd, T9921 1614, 1000-1600, free*, located just south of the Bill Sewell tourist complex, is a whitewashed old gaol built in 1858 and last used in 1986. There are 16 cells along a central corridor and several exercise yards. Information sheets along the corridor explain some of the history of the gaol including amusing correspondence between the gaoler and his boss. The gaol is rather run down but has been taken over by an army of craftspeople who look after it and sell their work from the cells. Exhibitions are sometimes held in the adjacent former police quarters. Teddies, pottery, and baby clothes are some examples of the craftwork produced.

Western Australian Museum Geraldton ① *1 Museum Pl, T9921 5080, www. museum.wa.gov.au, 1000-1600, donation*, on the other side of the railway line from the gaol, is an impressive new museum focusing on the maritime and so appropriately has been built next to the sea. A wall of glass overlooks the ocean and the floor of warm, polished timbers is evocative of a ships deck. Opened in May 2002, the hangar-like museum has an open central space used as a gallery for temporary or touring exhibitions. The northern end leads into the Shipwreck Hall, the heart of the museums collection. The dimly lit space contains relics from the wrecks of the *Batavia* and *Zuytdorp* and tells the stories of those ships and others of the Dutch East India company wrecked on the midwest coast or the Abrolhos Islands in the 18th century. The deliciously chilling tale of the *Batavia* wreck is borne out by a skull bearing axe

Midwest Geraldton & around

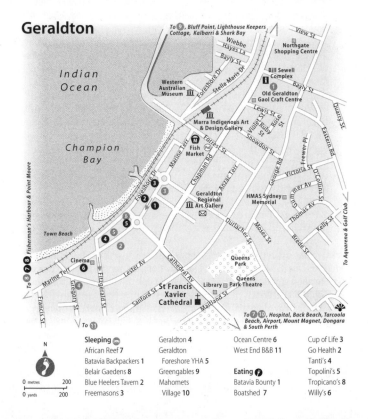

Geraldton

N

0 metres 200
0 yards 200

▪ Heavenly toil

Monsignor John Hawes is an interesting Midwest figure who left his imprint on the region with a series of distinctive and original church buildings. Hawes was born in Richmond, Surrey in 1876, the son of a London solicitor, and was inspired as a boy by the architecture of Canterbury Cathedral. He trained as an architect during the time that the Arts and Craft movement was advocating a return to simple organic decoration and natural materials. In 1901 he converted to High Anglicanism and was ordained two years later. His lifelong task of helping others began in the London slums, before he sought missionary work in the Bahamas. After a few years Hawes converted to Catholicism and it was when he was in Rome studying for the priesthood that he met Geraldton's Bishop Kelly, who was there on a recruting drive. Hawes agreed to move to Western Australia and was allocated the Murchison Goldfields region.

Arriving in 1915, he brought the plans for a new cathedral for Geraldton with him and construction began the following year. Because of delays and the scale of the work, the Cathedral of St Francis Xavier was not completed until 1938. In the meantime Hawes led a hardworking life as parish priest in Mullewa and designed many church buildings in the region. It is possible to see his work in the midwest towns of Mullewa, Morawa, Yalgoo, Northampton, Perenjori and Tardun. All of his buildings were made of local stone and are quite different from each other but he aimed to catch 'the rhythm of a poem in stone' with his solid Mediterranean style buildings with their domes, tiles, round arches and simple whitewashed interiors. Hawes constructed some of the smaller buildings with his own hands, "tormented with flies and scorching summer sun" as he put it and worrying that his cracked hands would catch on his silk vestments on Sunday. He always lived among very humble surrounds but as he aged he began to long for a simpler monastic life of Franciscan poverty. He also wanted to leave Australia, writing "I shall be only too glad to leave this prosaic and mundane land full of hotels, beer, wool and sheep".

At 64, feeling worn out, he told his bishop he was going on holiday to Europe and never came back. He settled on the Bahamas where he became a hermit known as Father Jerome, but even there the local bishop pestered him to design churches and colleges. He was buried on Cat Island in the Bahamas in 1956. Brochures on the Monsignor Hawes Heritage Trail can be purchased at the Geraldton VIC.

marks. Other exhibits include the Aboriginal Gallery which aims to help visitors understand the significance of the region to Aboriginal people past and present. The museum shop stocks an exceptional range of books on the sea, wildlife, aboriginal issues and local history.

HMAS Sydney Memorial ① *Mt Scott, accessible from carpark on Gummer Av*, on a small rise overlooking the city, is a new and beautiful landmark built in 2001 to remember the victims of the HMAS *Sydney* tragedy. This Australian naval ship was lost in 1941 when it engaged a German raider, the *Kormoran*, disguised as a Dutch merchant ship. None of the 645 crew survived and the ship has never been found although it is thought to have sunk off Carnarvon. The loss was more keenly felt because the *Sydney* was already famous, having sunk an Italian ship off Crete in the first year of the Second World War. The crew paraded as heroes through the streets of Sydney, feted by thousands, less than a year before the tragedy. Each aspect of the memorial carries significance. The silvery dome is a filigree of 645 seagulls, traditional symbols of the souls of lost sailors. The design was inspired by a flock of silver gulls that swooped over the crowd during the mournful notes of the Last Post when the site was dedicated in 1998. The stele represents the prow of the *Sydney* and echoes the form of a standing stone, used in ancient British times as grave markers. Naturally, there are also excellent views of Geraldton from the site.

Geraldton Regional Art Gallery ① *24 Chapman Rd, T9921 6811, Tue-Sat 1000-1700, Sun-Mon 1330-1630, free*, is housed in the former Town Hall, built in 1907. A public campaign in the 1980s saved this elegant civic building from being demolished and shortly afterwards it was converted into the gallery. A large contemporary space on the ground floor is used for regular touring exhibitions, while the small permanent City of Geraldton collection is usually hung upstairs. This contains contemporary art of the 1990s focusing on Geraldton and the midwest region or local artists. Earlier artworks include paintings by Elizabeth Durack, a Hans Heysen and Robert Junipers *Pilgrimage* (1962). The gallerys wonderful shop stocks high quality art, craft, ceramics and jewellery made by local artists and from countries such as Morocco and India.

St Francis Xavier Cathedral ① *open daily, guided tours at 1000 Mon and 1400 Fri*, the towns Catholic cathedral, is a splendid edifice in golden stone built between 1916 and 1938, and designed by the indefatigable Monsignor John Hawes, see box page 224. To some, the inside of the building, with its grey and orange stripes, will seem fairly psychedelic.

At the **Fishermans Harbour** during the crayfishing season it is possible to tour the **Live Lobster factory** ① *T9921 7084, Mon-Fri 0930, Nov-Jun, free, closed-in shoes must be worn, 3 km from the town centre on West Ends northern shore*, to find out more about this valuable industry. The one-hour tour includes an explanatory video and youll get to see the unloading and sorting of the crays, plus the live holding tanks. **Point Moore Lighthouse**, at the far end of West End, is a rare all-steel building and was imported from England in sections in 1878. It was commissioned after the *Africa* ran aground on a reef (now called African Reef) off Point Moore in 1863, though failed to prevent at least two other vessels coming to grief in later years. Closed to the public, it is nonetheless an impressive structure.

There are plenty of beaches around the town. **Pages Beach**, on the north shore of West End, is the most family-orientated with safe swimming, toilets, BBQs, playground and a large grassed area for picnics. Those at **Point Moore**, at the end of West End, get the brunt of the wind and are generally the preserve of windsurfers. To the south of the point, **Greys Beach** is pretty scruffy but things improve past Separation Point where **Back Beach** and **Tarcoola Beach** have decent stretches of white sand and offer good surfing, though swimming can be dangerous. **Town Beach**, accessed via Foreshore Drive, is as the name suggests the nearest beach to the centre of town. Sheltered, it's perfect for a cooling afternoon dip. A long series of beaches also stretch north from town, offering surfing breaks at **Bluff Beach** and beyond.

Around Geraldton

Houtman Abrolhos Islands

The Houtman Abrolhos Islands (commonly just called the Abrolhos) are a maze of low coral islands lying 60 km west of Geraldton. Essentially built-up reefs, they are uninhabited, except for a few crayfishermen in the short island season (Mar-Jun). Their low-lying nature and treacherous outlying reefs mean they are very difficult to spot and they are the final resting place of at least 19 vessels, including the ill-fated

Batavia. Indeed the name Abrolhos is thought to be a corruption of the Portugese words for 'keep your eyes open'. The principal attraction for visitors however, are the crystal clear waters and huge diversity of sealife. As the recipient of the final gasp of the warm tropical currents that spill down Australia's west coast, the islands encompass the world's most southerly coral reefs but also have a rich variety of more temperate species, a mix quite fascinating to marine biologists. They are also home to sea lions, turtles and dozens of species of sea birds. Snorkelling and diving here is outstanding for coral gardens and many types of reef and pelagic fish. The islands can reached either via air or sea, but air is the better option for a short trip as the views are wonderful and the sea crossing can be a bit rough.

Geraldton to Northampton → *52 km via coast road.*
There is little of particular interest on the main coast road, except the **Oakabella Homestead** ① *T9925 1033, 0900-1600, tours $4, 20 mins, usually conducted on demand*, 3 km down an unsealed side-turn 32 km out of Geraldton. The century-old homestead, largely furnished in keeping and reputedly haunted, is open for tours which also take in the grounds and a small folk museum housed in an unusual and historic barn. The pleasant tearoom, in a modern but sympathetic building, serves cheap light lunches as well as cream teas.

An alternative route, about 20 km longer than the coastal route, heads up along Chapman Valley Road via Nabawa. Along the way are three **wineries**, one right on the road, the other two both 3 km off on unsealed side-roads. The first, and most accessible is **Ego Creek** ① *T/F9938 1052*, 8 km from the city. Unfortunately only open on Sundays (though it's worth checking to see if this has changed), it offers half a dozen red and whites, all very palatable, but best of all has scrumptious cheap platters and puds available on its huge, covered veranda. With views over Geraldton and the ocean, this is a top spot to while away an afternoon. Open 1130-1800, wines around $15. Recommended. The right-hand turn to **Red Hill** ① *Murphy Norris Rd, T9920 5034, redhill.modnet.com.au/winery*, is another 15 km on. Wine tasting weekends 1000-1700, wines $10-15. It has a 1904 thick stone-walled cottage as backpackers accommodation, and will pick you up from town if you stay a couple of nights. Its very scruffy and basic and cheap, with 12 beds in 3 rooms, but out of the way and not uncomfortable. Temporary work is often available. **Chapman Valley Wines** ① *Howatharra Rd, T9920 5148, www.chapmanvalleywines.com.au*, is sign-posted off to the left. Tastings by appointment.

● Sleeping

Geraldton *p222, map p223*
The VIC can advise on and book other motels. See also Red Hill winery, page 226.
A-C Ocean Centre Hotel, corner of Fore-shore St and Cathedral Av, T9921 7777, www.oceancentrehotel.com.au. Right on the foreshore in the middle of town, with lots of balcony rooms overlooking the harbour, an upmarket, motel-style set-up with expensive in-house restaurant. All rooms en suite.
B-C African Reef, corner of Willcock Dr and Broadhead Av, T9964 5566, www.africanreef.com.au. Another motel resort, this time overlooking Tarcoola beach, 3 km south. All rooms en suite with a/c and kitchenettes. The terrace café, open all day, has one of the

best locations in town, with sweeping views around Port Grey Bay to West End.
B-C Greengables, Hackett Rd, T9938 2332, www.wn.com.au/greengables. A large, modern family home with 4 B&B guest rooms, 2 en suite, 6 km from town. Hosts are very welcoming and create a homely atmosphere. Set 2-course dinner available. Pick-ups by arrangement, pool, internet.
C Mahomets Village, Willcock Dr, T9921 6652, mahometsvillage@wn.com.au. 14 self-contained, well-equipped units a short walk from Back Beach.
D-E Blue Heelers Tavern, 185 Marine Terr, T9921 1133. One of several pubs offering cheap accommodation.

E **Batavia Backpackers**, on the corner of Chapman and Bayly sts behind the VIC, T9964 3001. A clean and friendly, if somewhat spartan, 100-bed hostel in a heritage building with large verandas. Good private storage space and close to bus stop.

E **Geraldton Foreshore YHA**, 172 Marine Terr, T9921 3275. A great place to relax for a few days, this homely 50-bed hostel in a spacious old house faces a small swimming beach. There are sunny, enclosed verandas, hammocks, and 3-4 bed dorms with lovely old wooden furniture. Recommended.

Belair Gardens, Willcock Dr, T9921 1997, is the best positioned carvan park with on-site vans and a good range of facilities and cabins.

🍴 Eating

Geraldton *p222, map p223*
In contrast to Geraldton's relatively cheap accommodation and many free sights, the restaurants in town are generally pretty pricey. See also nearby wineries, page 226.

🍴🍴 **Boatshed**, 357 Marine Terr, T9921 5500, Is the town's seafood specialist, with a nautically themed dining room and a more atmospheric stone-walled, covered courtyard. Open Tue-Sun 1800-2030.

🍴 **Tantis**, 174 Marine Terr, T9964 2311. Of a number of Thai and Chinese restaurants try this one, open Mon-Sat 1730-2200, Thu-Fri 1100-1400. Offers takeaway too.

🍴 **Topolinis**, 158 Marine Terr, T9964 5866. An airy restaurant serving pizza and pasta; café food and offer takeway. Mon-Sat 0900-2100, Sun 0800-2000.

🍴 **Tropicanos**, Point Moore. A cheap and cheerful café with views across to the ocean and resident windsurfers. Substantial, break-fasts (excellent buffet on Sun), lunches and evening meals. Loads of choice, Mediterr-anean and Asian cooking. Licensed, but free BYO. Sun-Fri 0800-2000, to at least 2400 Sat. Recommended.

Cafés

Batavia Bounty, 127 Marine Terr. The best of the bakery-cafés and has a few pavement tables in the middle of the shopping area. Open Mon-Fri 0700-1630.

Cup of Life, 84 Marine Terr. A bookshop/café, open daily.

Go Health, 122 Marine Terr. A juice and sandwich bar with internet ($2 for 15 mins). Open daily 0830-1600.

Willys, 239 Marine Terr, next to the cinema. Serves up heroic portions of fish and chips (1 is enough for 2 people), though the batter is a bit greasy. Open Thu-Sun 1130-1400, Wed-Mon 1630-2000 year-round, but every lunch and dinner in summer.

🍷 Bars and club

Geraldton *p222, map p223*
Much of the scene revolves around 2 pubs, both at the northern end of the main shopping area.

Freemasons Hotel (the Freo), 79 Marine Terr, T9964 3457, has 2 main bars, one café style, the other with an Irish theme. It has live bands or DJs every Fri-Sat, a local jam session on Thu and mellower tunes on a Sun afternoon. The bar meals are excellent, daily 1200-1430, 1800-2030, and there's a cook-your-own area out the back. The accommodation upstairs has 50 new bunkbeds, mostly in twins or quads, veranda access and a small lounge/kitchenette.

Breakers Tavern, 41 Chapman Rd. Stages a variety of live bands, in its single large bar, every Fri-Sun, and often Wed-Thu.

🎭 Entertainment

Geraldton *p222, map p223*
Queens Park, Cathedral Av, T9956 6662. An impressive, modern theatre designed on traditional lines. It hosts visiting and local productions from dance to comedy, bands to pantomime. A grassed outdoor amphitheatre is the venue for open-air evening films from Jan-Apr.

🛍 Shopping

Geraldton *p222, map p223*
Marine Terr, between Fitzgerald and Forrest sts, is the main shopping precinct in town, though a large mall with a **Coles** and **Target** budget department store, is just north of the

Midwest Geraldton & around Listings

🎈 *For an explanation of sleeping and eating price codes used in this guide, see inside the*
🎈 *front cover. Other relevant information is found in Essentials, see pages 40-46.*

VIC at Northgate. Also check the Museum shop for a good selection of new books. There are several shops selling street surfwear, and some even selling boards, along Marine Terr.

Geraldton Fish Market, 365 Marine Terr. Fresh seafood, including crays, can be purchased at the supermarkets or here, open Mon-Fri 0830-1730, Sat 0830-1200.

Marra Indigenous Art and Design Gallery, Chapman Rd, T/F9965 3440, in the old Railway Station. This is a good place to meet some of the local Marra people and see a range of paintings (a few quite exquisite), textiles, woodwork and ceramics. Open Mon-Fri 0830-1500. The Art Gallery shop also has excellent local work.

Read A Lot Books is the towns independent and well-stocked general bookshop, tucked away in Geraldton Shopping Centre (shop 13) on Chapman Rd.

▲ Activities and tours

Geraldton *p222, map p223*
Aerial tours
Geraldton Air Charter, T9923 3434, members.westnet.com.au/geroair, and **Shine Aviation Services**, T9923 3600, www.abrolhos.com.au. Both fly regular tours to the **Abrolhos**. On some of these they land on 1 or more of the main islands, allowing a closer look and perhaps some snorkelling. Minimum of 2 passengers, flights start at around $130 for 1 hr. Both companies also offer excursions up coast to **Kalbarri** and **Shark Bay**. You can also take a flight up in a Tiger Moth with *Shine*. See also *Arkell Air Charter* in Dongara, page 221, for another, excellent value, flight option.

Diving
The clean waters off Geraldton can be excellent for diving, but winds and silt from the Chapman River also often ruin visibility. The best time is mid-Feb to mid-May. The waters are also now the home of Australias newest artificial reef, the South Tomi, an illegal fishing boat that was seized by Australian Fisheries. Phone **Batavia Coast Dive Academy**, 153 Marine Terr, T9921 4229, www.bataviacoastdive.com, ahead for current conditions. They hire out scuba gear for shore dives and run one morning boat dive a day, according to demand and conditions (about 2 hrs). Open Mon-Sat 0830-1700, Sun 1000-1400.

Golf
Geraldton Golf Club, Pass St, T9964 1911. The closest course to the town centre and welcomes visitors.

Surfing and windsurfing
Geraldton calls itself, not unreasonably, Australias windsurfing capital, and there are good wind and water conditions for most of the year.

Batavia Coast Surf Academy, T0418 903379. Offers day courses in surfboarding for $99, including all equipment.

Sail West, Point Moore, T9964 1722, www.sailwest.com.au. Hires out windsurfers and surfboards from their shop next to the lighthouse. Open Mon-Fri 0900-1700, Sat-Sun 1000-1700, when the wind is above 20 knots.

Swimming
Aquarena, Pass St, T9921 8844. A large new complex with indoor and outdoor pools, slide, spa and steam room. Open Mon-Fri 0530-2100, Sat-Sun 0700-1900.

● Transport

Geraldton *p222, map p223*
Air
Skywest has daily flights from **Perth**.

Bicycle
Bike hire is available from **Bike Force**.

Bus
Local   There are several local bus services to and from Anzac Terrace, T9923 1100. The circular 800 service is free, as are the 201 and 501 services between the terrace and Northgate Shopping Centre (adjacent to the VIC). Services run Mon-Sat, 2-5 times a day, the 800 service more frequently in the mornings.

Long distance   There is at least 1 daily TransWA service to **Perth** from the railway station, many leaving at 0830. The **Northampton** and **Kalbarri** service leaves 1440 Mon, Wed and Fri. **McCaffertys/ Greyhound** northbound services leave the

VIC at 1625 daily (**Port Hedland**) and 0205 Mon, Thu and Sat (coastal towns to **Exmouth**). **Perth** buses depart 1250 daily, and 0100 Tue, Fri and Sun (coastal route).

Car
Parking is metered and restricted in the town centre. Free and unrestricted at the railway station. Car servicing at **Axis**, 284 Marine Terr. T9921 2411. Fill up with cheap fuel at the 440 Roadhouse, 10 km north of town. Cheapest at **Gull**, opposite VIC; 24-hr services at **BP Tarcoola**, Brand Highway, and **Gull 440 Roadhouse**, North West Coastal Highway.

Geraldton *p222, map p223*
Banks All the main banks, with ATMs, have branches along Marine Terr or Chapman Rd.
Chemist Fountains, 113 Marine Terr, T9921 1755. Mon-Sat 0830-2000, Sun 1000-1300, 1700-2000. **Hospital** Geraldton Regional, Shenton St, T9956 2222.
Internet Free at the library. Open Tue-Sat 0930-1300, Sun-Fri 1300 to at least 1630. Otherwise try Go Health. **Police** Marine Terr, T9923 4555. **Post** 50 Durlacher St.
Taxi T9921 7000.

Kalbarri and around

Although Kalbarri is a very young town the surrounding district is notable for its part in early West Australian settler history. Northampton is an old mining town, partly built by the labour of convicts based at nearby Lynton. Port Gregory, and Horrocks further south, are now both just sleepy beach settlements popular with locals for cheap family holidays. Lynton guards much of what little early European history survives in the area, while the rock art near Horrocks harks back to an even earlier era. Unless staying at tranquil Willow Gully, see page 233, the journey to Kalbarri need not detain you for long. Once there, this lovely town has plenty to keep you occupied for days but it is also a beautiful spot for doing nothing at all. ▶ *For Sleeping, Eating and other listings, see pages 233-236.*

Northampton → *Colour map 4, grid A1. Population: 800. 105 km from Kalbarri, 225 km from the Overlander roadhouse.*

This historic town on the Nokanena Brook was the first of Western Australias mining towns. Galena, lead ore, was found in the bed of the Murchison River in 1848 and the following year the Geraldine Mining Company was formed to exploit deposits of lead and copper in the area. Welsh and Cornish miners were brought out from Britain for their expertise and many of their descendants still live in the area. Port Gregory was used to export the lead to Britain and a convict-hiring depot was established at Lynton for convict labour on roads, buildings and in the mines. Port Gregory wasn't the safest anchorage though so a new lead port was opened at Geraldton in 1861 and a 54-km railway linking Northampton and Geraldton, built in 1879, was the first government railway in WA. The town still has many fine old stone buildings, but little is made of them. Northampton exists to service the surrounding wheat district and lies on the main highway north. However, its passing trade has dropped off significantly since the coast road to Kalbarri was sealed in 2000 and there are few facilities for visitors. The liveliest time to be in Northampton is the **Airing of the Quilts,** when handmade quilts festoon the verandas of the town. This is held on a Saturday in October check the date with the VIC ① *T9934 1488, Old Police Station, Hampton Rd, Mon-Fri 0900-1500, Sat 0900-1300.* It also has brochures for a heritage walk.

At the southern end of Northampton, the long stone building is the former home of Captain Samuel Mitchell and now the site of the **Chiverton House Museum** ① *Hampton Rd, T9934 1215, Thu-Mon 1000-1200, 1400-1600, $2.20, children $0.50.*

Mitchell was the mining engineer for the Geraldine Mine and a respected member of the community with 14 children. He had the house built by convicts around 1868. The museum has a sprawling, ordinary and dusty collection of domestic equipment, photographs, clothes, and farm machinery. Further up the main street is a fine Catholic church, **St Mary in Ara Coeli**, built in 1936 to a design by talented architect-priest Monsignor John Hawes. Its rough-hewn stone and restrained decoration is typical of Hawess work, although he had originally planned a more Byzantine style. The Priest of Northampton, Father Irwin, insisted on a Gothic design and Hawes agreed but the whitewashed interior with its round arches and shutters retains a Mediterranean feel. The jarrah roof is particularly fine. The impressive two-storey building next door is the former **Sacred Heart Convent** and was also designed by Hawes.

Horrocks → Colour map 4, grid A1. 24 km from Northampton 55 km from Lynton.

Horrocks is a tiny fishing and family orientated tourist town at the end of an 18-km off-shoot from the Northampton-Kalbarri road. Nestled amidst high sand dunes the settlement crowds around a grid of former squatters huts, now made more respectable by formal legislation and the permanency that comes with it. They face a long beach, remarkably sheltered for this coast because of a reef about 200 m from the shore, which makes this a good spot for safe swimming and snorkelling, though the natural habour is also used by a small fishing fleet. Aside from many happy children in summer this is a quiet spot. A grassy foreshore has BBQs and covered picnic tables. The general store has a limited supply of groceries, fuel (much more expensive than Geraldton) and also operates as a takeaway. Other facilities include tennis courts and a nine-hole golf course.

Around Horrocks

About 2 km back towards Northampton is an unsealed right hand turn to **Bowes Beach**. After a rough 3 km drive it leads to a beach very popular with both surfers and fishermen, and bush camping is allowed. It's well worth stopping just 50 m down the track, even if a beach visit isnt in your plans, for a very short path up the slope leads to the **Willigulli Rock Art Site**. Of undetermined age, there are several images, mostly of stencilled objects created by the blowing of white, yellow and red pigments. Hands are ubiquitous, but the images also include the local native yams and boomerangs. They were made by the **Nanda** and their ancestors, a peaceful people who, on the arrival of Europeans, were already living a settled existence with stone huts, deep wells and the beginnings of an agriculture based on yams. It has been suggested, controversially, that they learnt some of their ways from Wouter Looes and Jan Pelgrom, the two men from the *Batavia* marooned on this coast back in 1629.

Lynton → Colour map 4, grid A1. 40 km from Northampton, 65 km from Kalbarri.

Squeezed between the low Menai Hills and the coastal sandhills, a rosy future was anticipated for the township of Lynton. Captain Henry Ayshford Sandford was the first arrival, setting up a considerable farm property in 1852. His house, now being gradually restored, sits prominently on the side of the hill, the upstairs veranda begging a tearoom. The house, plus the original flour mill and impressive stables, can be visited for a gold-coin donation. Afternoon teas are currently available in the stables and well placed BBQs are also available for overnight visitors. It's a 10-minute scramble from the main property up to the top of the Menai Hills. From here there's a view over the dunes to the ocean and north up to the **Pink Lake**, an aquaculture farm harvesting the intensely red algae *Dunaliella salina*. By the main entrance are the remains of the **Lynton Convict Settlement**, established in 1853 to hire out convicts to the surrounding mines but abandoned just three years later.

The most picturesque coastal town in the state, Kalbarri sits at the mouth of the Murchison River where it winds through shoals of sand to the ocean. At the entrance a triangular rock rises above the surf and marks the difficult zig-zag passage through the reef to the ocean. The reef protects the calm waters of the inlet, forming a safe harbour for the crayfishing fleet moored here and a tranquil place for swimming, sailing and fishing. A long grassy foreshore lines the riverbank and the town is laid out along the foreshore, facing the sparkling blue water of river and ocean.

Kalbarri Wildflower Centre ① *T/F9937 1229, 1 km north of town, behind the tourist info bay, Jun-Nov, 0900-1700, $3.50, children free, tours daily at 1000*, has a large number of the local wildflowers in a small area bordering the national park. A 2-km trail takes in hundreds of species, bursting into flower during July-October.

Kalbarri Oceanarium ① *north end of Grey St by the jetty, T9937 2027, www.kalbarriexplorer.com.au/oceanarium, 1000-1600, $6, children $4,* is a modest-sized but well-stocked outfit with a dozen tanks featuring most of the species of fish and crustaceans that can be found in the sea off Kalbarri. Includes a tank of seahorses and a childrens touch pool.

On a similar theme, and close by, there's a newly opened **Seahorse Sanctuary** ① *Grey St, www.seahorsesanctuary.com.au,* opposite the marina. The owners, both biologists, have set the venture up to conserve seahorses and other marine life by bredding them and selling them to aquariums and collectors (at present most such creatures are taken from the wild).

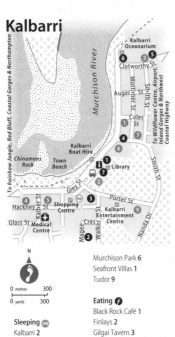

Kalbarri

N

0 metres 300
0 yards 300

Sleeping 🛏
Kalbarri **2**
Kalbarri Backpackers **7**
Kalbarri Beach Resort **3**
Kalbarri Riverfront **4**
Kalbarri Riverfront
  Budget Units **5**
Murchison Park **6**
Seafront Villas **1**
Tudor **9**

Eating 🍽
Black Rock Café **1**
Finlays **2**
Gilgai Tavern **3**
Grass Tree **4**
Jakes **5**
Jetty Seafood Shack **6**
Jonah's **7**
Syrups **7**

Rainbow Jungle ① *3 km south on Red Bluff Rd, T9937 1248, 0900-1700, Sun 1000-1700, $9.50, children $3.50,* claims to be the foremost Australian parrot breeding centre and is certainly one of the more impressive aviaries in the country. Privately developed, most of the many parrots fly around in very large enclosures, well watered and with lots of ferns and other plants. Visitors get to stroll amongst them, and can stay for a picnic and make use of the BBQs. Worth a visit even on a hot day.

Opposite Rainbow Jungle is a parking bay for an ocean **beach**. Once on the sand it is about 4 km north to **Chinamans Rock** and beach at the mouth of the Murchison River, and 800 m south to **Jakes**, Kalbarris well-known surf break. This is not recommended for beginners, though the bay just before it is great for boogie-boarding, as is **Red Bluff** beach 1 km further south.

Murchison House Station ① *T9937 1110, access to the station is via tour only (4 hrs), they leave most days and include morning tea,* is one of WAs most historic properties. It was established in 1848 by Charles Von Bibra to grow supplies for his convict lead-miners and also breed horses for the Indian Army. The station has had a colourful history, witnessing the fatal crash of one of the three planes involved in WAs first commercial flight, and later as the home and playground of Prince Mukramm Jah, the 8th Nizam of Hydrabad. Most of the stations income now comes from feral goats and Brahmin cattle. The original homestead and old woolshed are still standing and the area around the current homestead is littered with the Princes playthings, including several decrepit military vehicles and gigantic earth-movers. A visit it recommended.

The VIC ① *Grey St, T9937 1104, www.kalbarri.com, 0900-1700*, opposite the foreshore, is helpful.

Kalbarri National Park → *Colour map 4, grid A1.*
① *For information call CALM ranger, T9937 1192, $9 per vehicle (inland gorges only).*
The Murchison meanders through deep gorges of spectacular red and white banded rock with the most striking formations and tight loops of riverbed enclosed within the park. In winter and spring, the park is also renowned for its beautiful display of wildflowers. On the route running east to the highway, you can see many blooms including Banksias, grevilleas, Kangaroo paws, the appropriately fluffy lambswool and brightly coloured featherflowers. The park also extends along the coast and contains high coastal cliffs, gorges and magical sheltered coves. Along the coast road, the heath is dominated by the waving stems of white plume grevillea, also called smelly socks for its less than pleasant locker-room fragrance. The dramatic gorges and cliffs, cut by the sea into rugged notches and rock platforms, are quite different from the inland gorges. This wealth of natural beauty in the park is complemented by a great range of tours, activities and services. There are many excellent lookouts over the gorges and a few walking tracks aimed at reasonably agile walkers.

‡ *The inland gorges can be extremely hot in summer so the park is busier in winter. If you are around in summer make sure you take plenty of water and only walk early morning and late afternoon.*

Coastal gorges South of the river mouth, the ocean beaches gradually rise to a long stretch of golden sandstone cliffs. This southern coastline is also part of the national park and there are a series of excellent lookouts and tracks down the rock platforms and beaches. **Red Bluff** is the imposing knoll that can be seen from the town beaches and is the first of the park lookouts, 5 km from town. There is an 800-m return walk to the top of the bluff from where you can see the whole coastline and this is also a great spot in calm weather for whale watching in winter. A loop walk from **Mushroom Rock** to **Rainbow Valley** takes about 1-1½ hours and allows you to explore the rock platforms and the arid hillside. **Pot Alley Gorge** is a delightful narrow gorge with interesting rocks and a pretty beach the ideal place for secluded swimming or sunbathing. **Eagle Gorge** also has a good sandy beach reached from a track by the lookout but less protected, and extensive rock platforms to explore (8 km from town). **Shellhouse Grandstand** is named for a rock that looks like the Shell service station sign if you see it from a boat and a natural amphitheatre formed by rock platforms. Towards the southern end the cliffs become higher and less accessible but more impressive. The last two lookouts, **Island Rock** and **Natural Bridge**, are both remnants left behind by the cliffs as they retreat before the waves, and are particularly beautiful at sunset.

Inland gorges There are three main points to access the inland gorges, all situated at scenic bends and loops in the rivers course, and all via unsealed roads. Shortly after leaving town there is also a great lookout over Kalbarri called **Meanarra Hill**, reached by a short walk from the car park. After a further 11 km the first park turn-off is on the left. This leads to Natures Window (26 km) and Z Bend (25 km). **Natures Window** is a rock arch that overlooks a tight bend in the river called **The Loop**. The walk around the Loop is excellent, following the ridge at first and then dropping down to the riverbed (8 km, three hours). At **Z-bend** (a few km drive away) there is a lookout over a right angle in the gorge and with some careful rock hopping you can get down to the river and explore. Take the unmarked but well-used track to the right of the lookout. This is also a lovely place for a swim as the river does not flow all year round and is often a series of calm shallow pools. You need to return to the main road and travel another 24 km to get to **Hawks Head** and **Ross Graham**. These are both good lookouts and there are easier tracks down to the river. It is possible for experienced walkers to tackle the 38 km (four days) from Ross Graham Lookout to The Loop or shorter two-day walks but you must notify the ranger and plan carefully. There are picnic tables and toilets at all car parks. Natures Window and Z Bend also have gas BBQs.

● Sleeping

Northampton *p229*

D Jidamya Ostriches B&B, Barron St, just outside town, T9934 1024, www.country cousins.com.au/jidamya. Includes a full breakfast as well as interaction with their large feathered stock. Single occupation and evening dinners (by pre-arrangement) are almost embarrassingly good value.

D Miners Arms, main street, T9934 1281. This top pub is marginally the most characterful of 3 very ordinary establishments. Serves meals Mon-Sat 1200-1330, 1800-2000. En-suite motel rooms at the back too.

E Old Convent, main street, T/F9934 1488. Looks extremely impressive from the road but inside is a bit stark and functional. It sleeps 40 in a variety of rooms from one double and a 10-bed dorm, and has a clean communal kitchen and lounge area. Some rooms are accessed from the wide 1st-floor veranda.

E Railway Tavern, T9934 1120. More expensive though better quality than those at the bottom pub.

Horrocks *p230*

C Willow Gully, T/F9934 3093, members. westnet.com.au/nhp, back on the main road. This farm was convict-built sometime before 1861. No longer an agriculturally run property the owners have restored a fine one-bedroom workers cottage for holiday rental. Its thick, rough stone walls are whitewashed to keep out the summer heat. The very warm welcome, simple but fine furnishings, flagstone courtyard and neat kitchen garden make this a great retreat.

D Killara Cottages, T9934 3031. Has 12 large, basic but well-equipped cabins. Good value, but in peak holiday season you can only take them for a week (a snip at $220 for two), and youll need to book.

Horrocks Beach Caravan Park, T/F9934 3039. Has on-site vans as well as sites, also a small café, tennis and golf hire.

Lynton *p230*

D-E Lynton-on-Sea Farmstay, T9935 1040. The property owners are now Lyntons entire population. A small number of simple but clean twin dongers and a self-contained modern cottage with 2 twin bedrooms. Own linen required.

Kalbarri *p231*

The bulk of accommodation available is in complexes of self-contained units, all very much designed to a common plan and mostly located on the foreshore. The competition means high standards, generally well-equipped kitchens, good laundry facilities and many have on-site pools. Almost all are designed for families, with 2 or 3 bedrooms. Prices can drop considerably in low season.

B Seafront Villas, T9937 1025, www. kalbarri seafrontvillas.com.au. One of the better examples.

B Kalbarri Beach Resort, T9937 1061, www.kalbarribeachresort.com.au, has over 100 units.

C Kalbarri Hotel, T9937 1000, is the only motel in town, has a few doubles and twins.

● For an explanation of sleeping and eating price codes used in this guide, see inside the
● front cover. Other relevant information is found in Essentials, see pages 40-46.

C **Kalbarri Riverfront**, T9937 1032, www.westnet.com.au/fg, has 2 units, but they are 2 of the best positioned and furnished in town. Recommended.

C **Kalbarri Riverfront Budget Units**, the owners of **Kalbarri Riverfront** also manage this, the only budget units on the foreshore, which are considerably more pleasant inside than they look from the outside. Contact Ray White, T9937 1700, www.kalbarriaccommo dation.com.au, for details of many houses to let around the town.

C-D **Murchison Park**, corner of Grey St and Wood St, T9937 1005. Of those in town this is the best situated and has some waterfront sites, cabins, on-site vans and a good range of facilities.

C-D **Red Bluff Caravan Park**, Red Bluff Beach Rd, 4 km south of town, T9937 1080. Has sites and cabins, some en suite and a/c, a camp kitchen, takeaways and fuel. Adjacent to Red Bluff car park it's about 150 m from the beach.

D **Tudor**, Porter St, T9937 1077. Has the best value cabins.

E **Kalbarri Backpackers & Bunks**, T9937 1430, members.westnet.com.au/kalbbacpak. A hostel, has decent facilities (including a pool) and this is just about the only place likely to have a walk-in bed during peak season!

❼ Eating

Northampton *p229*
❦ **Northampton Cafe**, at the northern end of town. Does simple sandwiches, burgers and drinks and is open daily until 1700.

Kalbarri *p231*
The 2 pubs provide the other options for a substantial lunch. Both do cheap to mid-range meals daily, 1200-1400 and 1800-2030.

❦❦ **Black Rock Café**, 80 Grey St, T9937 1062. The best spot in town, open daily 0700-2000. Dinners can verge on the expensive and breakfast and lunch are also pricey but the foreshore location, consistently good food and unhurried, friendly service always make it a good spot. BYO only. Recommended.

❦❦ **The Grass Tree**, just up the road from **Black Rock Café**, T9937 2288. Gives **Black Rock** a good run for its money however.

❦ **Echoes**, shopping centre, Porter St, T9937 1033. Has a pleasant 1st-floor balcony overlooking the river. Evenings only, Wed-Mon 1730-2030, licensed.

❦ **Finlays**, Magee Cres, off Walker St, T9937 1260. Provides a BBQ feed with plenty of outdoor seating. Deliberately a bit rough and ready, the seafood and salads may not sensationalize your tastebuds but they will satisfy your stomach. Gets very busy with tourists in summer and you cant book so get there early at busy times. BYO only.

❦ **Gilgai Tavern** is the best place for quality.

❦ **Jakes**, in the grounds of the **Kalbarri Beach Resort**, T9937 2222. Serves a substantial, good value feed, daily from 1730-2030. Buffet roast on Sun.

❦ **Jetty Seafood Shack**,oOffers the best value portion of fish 'n' chips.

❦ **Jonahs**, next to the VIC, generally serves up the best (and most expensive) fish, open daily in the evenings.

❦ **Syrups**, healthfood outlet, pizza and pasta, and Chinese.

❶ Bars and clubs

Kalbarri *p231*
Gilgai Tavern, over the road from the hotel, is the town's quieter option, occasional live music.

Kalbarri Hotel is the larger place with a dancefloor, large bar and restaurant area, betting shop, bottle shop, plenty of covered outdoor tables and is the social hub of the town, has occasional live music.

❷ Entertainment

Kalbarri *p231*
Kalbarri Entertainment Centre, Porter St, T9937 1105. Has a crazy golf course and childrens trampolines. It also hires out bicycles and golf clubs for use on the separate 9-hole course. Half-set hire is $11, and it's another $11 for green fees. It is happy about collection the night before an early morning game.

❍ Shopping

Kalbarri *p231*
There are a few local jewellery makers making some outstanding stuff, including

some of the coolest silver you'll see in Australia. Local gift shops stock some of it, but for his full range of silver pendants see the designer, Paul, some evenings at the backpacker hostel or call him direct, T9937 2121, www.paulsgallery.com.au.

There are 2 supermarkets in town, both open daily, and also meat and seafood specialists.

▲ Activities and tours

There are dozens of river, sea and bus tours available, plus a good many adventure activities. All can be booked via the VIC. Some can be very demanding in hot weather, check what is supplied and be well prepared with drinks and for the sun.

Kalbarri p231
4WD
Kalbarri Backpackers & Bunks, corner of Woods and Mortimer sts, T9937 1430, has a 4WD car available, local use only. Insured for unsealed roads, it's handy for getting out to the inland gorges.
Kalbarri Safari Tours, T9937 1011, kalsaf@ wn.com.au. Runs a variety of very enjoyable trips, from sandboarding the massive coastal dunes near Port Gregory ($65), to 2-day driving and trekking expeditions into Kalbarri National Park ($138, all-inclusive).

Abseiling
Kalbarri Abseil, T9937 1618, heads out most mornings to the Z Bend gorge and conduct abseils on the red cliffs above the river ($65, children $55).

Aerial tours
Kalbarri Air Charter, T/F9937 1130, kalbarriair@wn.com.au. Offer a range of flights from a 20-min zip along the coast cliffs ($40, children $30) to an excellent morning excursion up to **Monkey Mia** ($195, children $120). Aircraft can also be chartered by groups for trips further afield.

Boat cruises/hire
Two licensed boats offer virtually identical cruises up river. Morning trips (3-4 hrs) are $35 and include a sausage sizzle, sunset cruises (2-3 hrs) are $27. Both fishing boats offer sunset coastal cruises ($24-44, children

$15-25), and whale and dolphin watching trips according to demand.
Kalbarri Boat Hire, T9937 1245, on the beach opposite the VIC. Open daily and has a wide variety of boats available, from canoes to small motor boats, windsurfers to catamarans. Prices vary from $12-30 an hr. If youve ever wanted to learn to sail, this is an excellent spot to have a go.
Murchison Boat Hire, T/F9937 2043, iasue @wn.com.au. Has larger seagoing motor boats for DIY fishermen and divers, from $125 per day. Fishing gear hire available.

Bus tours
Kalbarri Coach Tours, T9937 1161, www. wn.com.au/coachtours. Offers a variety of short trips from a jaunt round town to tours of the national park (from $39 a half day), and day trips up to **Shark Bay** ($125).

Camel safaris
Kalbarri Camel Safaris, 3 km south on Red Bluff Rd, T9937 1211. 45-min bush rides $20, children $15.

Canoe trips
Kalbarri Adventure Tours, T9937 1677, www.kalbarritours.com.au. Runs more adventurous day trips into the inland gorges ($65). This is a great way to see what the national park has to offer if you have just a day to do so. Recommended.
Kalbarri Boat Hire, takes groups a short way up the Murchison for a gentle paddle around the lower reaches of the river. Bush breakfast included (4 hrs, $55, children from $25).

Dive and fishing
Kalbarri Explorer, T9937 2027, www.kalbarriexplorer.com.au. Runs day sea-fishing trips for $150.
Kalbarri Sports & Dive, Kalbarri Arcade. Fishing tackle ($15 per day), snorkel ($15), scuba gear ($60) available, Mon-Sat 0830-1730, also Sun in summer. Tank refills $6.
Reefwalker, T9937 1356, www.reefwalker. com.au. Runs day sea-fishing trips for $150.

Horse riding
Big River Ranch, 2 km north of town, T9937 1214, www.wn.com.au/bigriverranch. Has a range of bush and beach rides from 1-4 hrs.

⊖ Transport

Kalbarri p231

Bicycle/scooters

From end to end Kalbarri is about 2 km, and the closest coastal gorges are 5 km south, so you can do a lot of getting around without your own transport. Bicycles and tandems can be hired at the Kalbarri Entertainment Centre, Porter St, T9937 1105.

Scooter hire from Jonahs fish and chip shop on Grey St. Also one and one-seaters.

Bus

The main (N1) services to Geraldton (6 hrs) leave East Perth terminal at 0830 Mon-Sat, 1730 Fri and 0930 Sun; on Mon, Wed and Fri go to Kalbarri. TransWA services leave the VIC for **Northampton**, **Geraldton** and **Perth** at 0710 Tue, Thu and Sat. McCaffertys/ Greyhound northbound services leave at 0430 Mon, Thu and Sat (coastal towns to **Exmouth**). Its **Perth** buses depart 2255 Mon, Thu and Sat (coastal route). A local shuttle service, on a Mon, Thu and Sat, connects with the main daily north- and southbound services (at the Ajana turn-off). The **Integrity** service north to **Broome**, runs Mon and Fri from Ajana turn-off (reached vis shuttle from Kalbarri).

Car

Car servicing from **Kalbarri Auto Centre**, Atkinson Dr, T9937 1290.

Taxi

Call, T9937 1888.

⊖ Directory

Kalbarri p231

Banks ATM in Kalbarri Arcade.
Internet At several cafés and shops. All around $5-6 per hr, though the hostel is cheaper. **Chemist** Kalbarri Arcade, T9937 1026. Open Mon-Fri 0900-1730, Sat 0900-1230. **Medical centre** Glass St, T9937 0100. **Police** Grey St, T9937 1006. **Post** Kalbarri Arcade. **Useful contacts** CALM office 1 km north of town, T9937 1140.

Routes north

Northampton to the Overlander roadhouse → *Distance: 225 km.*

From Northampton the North West Coastal Highway leaves the northern end of the wheat belt and plunges into native scrub, now largely utilized for keeping stock animals such as sheep and cattle. The vast paddocks are not fenced off from the road so this is not a stretch of road to undertake at dawn or twilight. For several hundred kilometres the drive is remarkable only for its uniformity and only wildflowers in season save it from serious monotony. The last hint of interest is the picnic spot at Galena bridge over the Murchison River, about 60 km from Northampton, and just past the Kalbarri turn-off. From there it is another 120 km to **Billabong**, the site of a roadhouse and hotel.

The Wildflower Way → *See page 338 for an overview of WAs wildflowers.*

During the months from July to September, it is well worth considering the route from Perth to Moora (preferably via New Norcia), and from there to Mullewa via Carnamah, Perenjori, and Morawa to Mullewa. The quality and richness of the wildflowers along the way varies from year to year, depending chiefly on the amount of rainfall the region receives the preceding winter, but can be quite fantastic. The VICs at Mullewa and Morawa are happy to advise on the years blooms and the best places to seek them out on your way through. In this region you can see orchids, everlastings, grevilleas, smoke bush and many other species but it is particularly known for the unusual wreath flower, Lechenaultia macrantha. This region is also interesting for the unusual church architecture of Monsignor John Hawes.

Morawa is a wheat-growing area where 70 per cent of native vegetation has been cleared, but great diversity in flora remains in reserves and on roadside verges. The Church of the Holy Cross in Davis Street is one of John Hawes designs, of local stone with Cordoban roof tiles and green tropical shutters. For more information contact the VIC ① *main street, T9971 1421, or shire office on Prater St*, T9971 1004, from June to September only.

Mullewa, 550 km from Perth, 100 km from Geraldton, has one of Hawes finest works, The Church of Our Lady of Mount Carmel, a romantic Mediterranean style with solid stone walls to keep out the sun. The Priest House nearby is maintained as a museum of Hawes life. For more information contact the VIC ① *Jose St, T9961 1505, or the shire office on Padbury St, T9961 1007, 1000- 1200*, July to October only.

From Mullewa you can choose to head out to the North West Coastal Highway at Geraldton or inland to Mount Magnet (245 km) and the Great Northern Highway. If heading inland **Yalgoo**, 120 km east of Mullewa, is a charming old gold mining town with a lovely John Hawes chapel, the Dominican Chapel of St Hyacinth. Ask at the shire office for the key and a heritage trail booklet to explore Yalgoo.

Great Northern Highway → *Mt Magnet 345 km from Geraldton, 200 km Meekatharra.*
If you're heading north towards the central Pilbara or the Kimberley the Great Northern Highway can save a few hundred kilometres when compared to the coastal highways. The route splits from the Brand Highway just north of the Swan Valley and continues via **New Norcia** through wildflower country to the vast inland plains beyond the small town of **Wubin**, 270 km from Perth. From here the towns and fuel stops become considerably more scarce, the 290 km to Mount Magnet interrupted by just one fuel-stop midway at Paynes Find.

Mount Magnet is one of the most active of the Midwest goldfield towns, though there is still activity at both **Cue** and **Meekatharra** further north. The Pilbara town of **Newman**, 430 km north of Meekatharra, marks the start of the rich iron-ore mines of the northwest.

⬤ Sleeping

Northampton to the Overlander roadhouse *p236*
C **Billabong Hotel**, Billabong, T9942 5980. Modern, has a bar and café, motel rooms, caravan sites but no kitchen. Rooms are en suite and have a/c, and guests can use the swimming pool. Internet $5 for 15 mins.
C **Shell roadhouse**, Billabong, T9942 5919, adjacent to the Billabong Hotel. The smiles are a pleasant contrast to Billabong, though its rooms aren't en suite. Standard cheap meals available at both from 0600 to after 2000. Bar and fuel to about 2200.
D-E **Overlander**, Billabong, T9942 5916. Another friendly roadhouse and marks the turn-off to Denham and Monkey Mia, 24-hr. Fuel is usually no more expensive than at Billabong, and fractionally cheaper than Shark Bay. It has an ATM, a good range of cheap meals is available 0600-2400, internet access, and the standard accommodation is basic but clean and includes linen and air

conditioning. Backpacker beds are the same without linen. Also caravan sites, camp kitchen and television room.

The Wildflower Way *p236*
Morawa has a small motel, T9971 1060, and a caravan park. Mullewa has a caravan park with sites only (enquire at **Yarrumba** service station on Jose St).
C **Railway Hotel**, Mullewa, T9961 1050. Motel and hotel rooms here.
B&B accommodation in the old pub at Pindar, 26 km east of Mullewa on Mt Magnet Rd, T9962 3024.
Tallering Station, T9962 3045, 14 km from Pindar, has good wildflower sites, a craft shop, meals and accommodation in the homestead, shearers quarters, dorms or powered sites, available Jul-Oct only. Yalgoo has a pub, site-only caravan park, general store and petrol.

The Gascoyne

• Footprint features

Introduction

The hot and arid Gascoyne region sits betweentwo distinct
hooks on the shoulder of the coastline – from Shark Bay in the
south to the North West Cape in the north, and inland for a
few hundred kilometres. In the waters off this region marine
life is abundant; in the rest of the country, only the Great
Barrier Reef can rival them.

The sheltered waters of Shark Bay harbour dugongs and
turtles as well as dolphins, who come in to shore to be fed by
hand at Monkey Mia. Further north, a coral fringing reef lines
the coast for over 250 km, the Ningaloo Reef. When the coral
spawns in March each year it attracts the world's largest fish,
the whale shark, to feed on this caviar-like soup for several
months. Snorkelling alongside them as they feed is one of the
most thrilling experiences this great island nation can offer.
On a wonderfully accessible level, at some points, the reef
comes so close to shore that you are able to snorkel among
coral, fish, turtles and rays straight off the beach. Come
summer you can watch the turtles laying and hatching.

Heading east is a landscape of red dirt and open spaces,
and here you'll encounter the hospitality of outback country.
The Kennedy Range is a rare break in the Gascoyne's relatively
flat interior and orientated such that early morning overnight
campers are treated to a rich morning glow lighting up its
steep east-facing cliffs.

✷ Don't miss...

1 **Monkey Mia** Keep your eyes peeled for turtles on a turtle-tagging tip, page 245.
2 **The Blowholes** See the waters erupt, page 249.
3 **Kennedy Range** See day break on the eastern cliffs, page 250.
4 **Exmouth** Swim with the hungry whale sharks, page 252.
5 **Cape Range National Park** Camp out on the beach by night and come the morning wake up with a swim and a snorkel, page 253.
6 **The outback** Stay for a night or two at an outback station, such as Bidgemia or Giralia, page 255.
7 **Coral Bay** Quad-bike through the dunes, page 258.

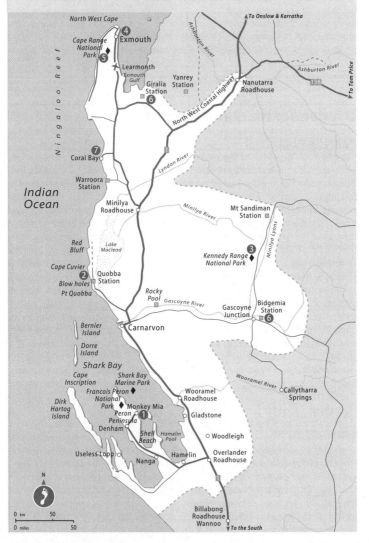

The Gascoyne

Shark Bay

Shark Bay is formed by two long peninsulas lying parallel to the coast, like the prongs of a fork. The middle prong is the Peron Peninsula, and the western prong is formed by the Zuytdorp Cliffs and Dirk Hartog Island. These are the most westerly bits of land in Australia, forming an extraordinary sheltered marine environment in its countless small bays. The waters of Shark Bay are always a startling turquoise and as clear as a swimming pool thanks to its shallowness; the average depth of the bay is 10 m and much of it is no deeper than 1 m. It is most famous for its colony of dolphins, some of whom come into shore at Monkey Mia, but there are also dugongs, turtles, rays and sharks living in these waters and all are easily seen on a boat trip or from the shore. The land is also a refuge for wildlife. Although its low arid scrub and red sand looks too harsh and barren for anything to survive, the Francois Peron National Park is the focus for a program to save endangered native species. The small town of Denham and the tourist facilities at Monkey Mia provide comfortable lodging for visitors but most of the Shark Bay region is a wilderness. Shark Bay was declared a World Heritage Area in 1991 for its rare stromatolites, extensive seagrass beds, endangered animals and natural beauty. ▸▸ *For Sleeping, Eating and other listings, see pages 245-247.*

Overlander roadhouse to Denham

Hamelin Pool → *Colour map 5, grid C1. 35 km from the Overlander, 105 km from Denham.*
Hamelin Pool is a wide shallow estuary on the eastern side of Shark Bay. It elicits great scientific interest today because of the resident colonies of **stromatolites**. These boulder-like formations are the direct result of sediments becoming trapped by thin organic mats of cyanobacteria over thousands of years. These dark, stumpy colonies, squatting in the inter-tidal area, are about 3,000 years old. In pre-Cambrian times, over 600 million years ago, these communities were one of the dominant features of life on earth, but now thrive only in those places where just about every other kind of life finds it very tough going. A boardwalk extends out over the stromatolites into the bay, and though the action is subdued to say the least, it is striking to consider that this is a window into an almost inconceivably distant past.

In the 1880s this spot was chosen as the site of one of WA's **telegraph repeater stations** ⓘ *T9942 5905, 0830-1730, $5.50, children and concessions $3*, because of its relative ease of provisioning by sea. The original station is now a modest museum, partly devoted to an explanation of the stromatolites (including a video and a very rare aquarium colony), partly to preserve the heritage of the telegraph system. The shady compound with its green lawn is something of an oasis in the baking hot conditions favoured by stromatolites, and the tearoom is a welcome place to grab a cold drink.

Hamelin Pool to Denham

There are a couple of sights worth stopping for on this stretch, first **Shell Beach**, 50 km from Hamelin. At Hamelin you'll have noticed that the white sand underfoot is actually crushed shells. Shell Beach is one of the most accessible examples of a beach entirely made up of tiny white shells, and it slopes gently into the bay for hundreds of metres. The shells are the bivalve cardiid cockle, a type of saline-tolerant cockle only found in Shark Bay. Deep under the beach the shells cement together when rainwater dissolves their calcium carbonate and the resulting coquina limestone has been readily utilized around Shark Bay as a building material. Some 20 km short of Denham a 4-km unsealed side-road leads to **Eagle Bluff**, a 40-m high headland that gives great views

⁝ Predators ousted from paradise

Project Eden aims to make Peron Peninsula the largest conservation area in Australia and has had great success since its inception in 1995. It is protected by a 2-m high electrified fence and a cattle grid has been placed where the fence meets the road. In case any nimble-footed predators are tempted to tiptoe over the grid, there are also recordings of barking dogs, activated by movement, and high-pitched sonar recordings to deter them. About 50,000 baits a year are laid on the peninsula (and nearby stations) to kill foxes and it is thought that there are few, if any, left on the peninsula. Feral cats are more difficult to eradicate as they won't take baits if live marsupials are on the menu. Traps have caught about 3,000 cats since 1995 and seem to be keeping numbers down. Native fauna such as emus, echidnas, monitors and bird species have flourished since predators have been reduced and CALM has begun to reintroduce other native species such as malleefowl, bilbies and woylies. All of these species have begun breeding and seem established on the peninsula. Scientists hope to soon release viable populations of banded hare wallabies and western barred bandicoots. In the future CALM intends to provide ways for visitors to be able to observe these native animals in the wild.

straight into a broad expanse of pale clear water below. Extensive boardwalks make it easy to find vantage points from which you may spot some of the region's wonderful marine life, including rays, turtles, sharks and dolphins.

Denham → *Colour map 5, grid C1. Population: 1,200. 375 km from Kalbarri, 330 km from Carnarvon.*

Denham is a small friendly town that services much of the ever increasing tourist trade on its way to Monkey Mia, 30 km away on the eastern side of the Peron Peninsula. Denham sits on the western side of the peninsula, well protected from the open ocean by long and narrow Dirk Hartog Island. The main industry is fishing, replacing the industry that brought Europeans, Malaysians and Chinese people here in the 1850s: pearling. Recently the pearl industry has been revived and pearl farms have been established in the bay, producing fine black pearls. The town is laid out along a pleasant grassy foreshore, with BBQs and sheltered picnic tables, and provides basic services such as fuel and a supermarket. The helpful **VIC** ① *close to the corner of Knight Terrace and Durlacher St, T9948 1253, www.sharkbay.asn.au, 0900-1700*, is in a small souvenir shop on the main street,

Francois Peron National Park → *Colour map 5, grid C1.*

① *For more information contact CALM, Knight Terr, Denham, T9948 1208, $9 car, camping $10 for 2, visitor centre daily 0800-1630.*
Named for a French naturalist who explored Shark Bay as part of Baudin's expedition on the *Geographe* and *Naturaliste* in 1801 and 1803, the Francis Peron covers the northern tip of the Peron Peninsula, from the Monkey Mia Road north to Cape Peron, an area of 40,000 ha. A dramatic series of cliffs and bays, where red rocks merge into white sand and turquoise sea, encloses a dry and arid region with many salt-pans (birridas) dotting the low sandy plains. Despite the unpromising look of the land early

European visitors called 'useless', the peninsula was used as a sheep station from the 1880s until 1990, when the government bought the station and created the park. The vegetation here is significant because the flowering plants of the southwest – grevilleas and hakeas – reach their northern limit in the park and meet the acacias typical of northern regions. The park is also notable for **Project Eden**, part of the *Western Shield* nature conservation programme to reverse the decline of native mammals caused by fox and feral cat predation. The park is home to malleefowl, bilbies, woylies, bandicoots, the Shark Bay mouse and many other species. This mostly nocturnal wildlife is not often seen but thorny devils are common and dolphins, dugongs and turtles may be spotted from the cliffs at Cape Peron. There is a **visitor centre** at the old station homestead that aims to educate visitors about Project Eden, and an outdoor hot tub fed by an artesian bore that visitors are welcome to use. The homestead is usually accessible by 2WD (10 km, unsealed) but the rest of this peaceful, remote place is only accessible by high clearance 4WD.

❉ The sturdy electric fence just before Shell Beach is feral-proof, designed to keep out foxes and cats.

Monkey Mia → *Colour map 5, grid C1. 30 km from Denham.*

ⓘ *For more information contact CALM, T9948 1366, calmmonkeymia@wn.com.au. Day pass $6, children $2 (valid for one day and following morning). Holiday pass $9, children $4 (valid for 4 weeks).*

Dolphins have lived in Shark Bay for millennia but the current encounters with humans only began in the 1960s when fishermen began to hand feed dolphins. The dolphins were happy to accept a free feed and visited settlements regularly. By the 1980s word began to spread of a place called Monkey Mia where people fed and swam with dolphins. Even though the place is incredibly remote, over 800 km from Perth and 330 km from Canarvon, the pull of wild dolphins is irresistible and has made the area internationally famous. Each year Monkey Mia seems to get busier and things are very different from the informal encounters of the past. Interaction with the dolphins is carefully managed to keep them wild and minimize the impact of hundreds of visitors a day. One of the best things to do in Monkey Mia is to leave the beach and take a boat cruise and see the dolphins in their own environment, as well as many other incredible animals such as dugongs and turtles. Despite the number of visitors Monkey Mia itself is just a small low-key resort. The visitor centre overlooking the beach where the dolphins swim into shore has displays on the biology and behaviour of dolphins and shows videos on marine life.

Dolphin encounters

Free spirits wanting to commune with nature may be a little disappointed with the Monkey Mia experience. This is how it works: the dolphins swim into a section of beach by the jetty that is closed to boats and swimmers. When the dolphins arrive people line up along the beach, perhaps for 100 m or more. You are not allowed to enter the water beyond your knees, and a CALM officer will stand in the water making sure that the dolphins are not touched or disturbed. The dolphins are often only a few feet away and nuzzle the officers' calves like dogs wanting their dinner while the officers chat about the dolphins. When the CALM officers decide to feed the dolphins everyone is asked to step out of the water and a few lucky souls are picked to come forward and give a dolphin a fish. Only mature female dolphins are fed and their three daughters and they get no more than a third of their daily requirements so they will not become dependent on handouts. Once the feeding is finished the dolphins usually swim away, but if they don't you can step

❉ Don't put sunscreen on your legs as it irritates dolphins' eyes.

⁝ Temptresses and turtles

The clear waters of Shark Bay are home to a far more mysterious and rare creature than the friendly dolphin. This is the Sirenia, named for the mythical sirens of the sea luring sailors to their doom. When you see the portly, brown body and broad snout of a dugong it is hard to believe that sailors once mistook them for mermaids, but apparently from a distance their ample figures and mermaid-shaped tail set sailors' hearts pounding.

The dugong is a type of sea cow and is similar to the only other surviving Sirenia, the manatee of the Caribbean. An average dugong is about 3 m long, 300 kg and can live more than 70 years. About 10,000 dugongs live in Shark Bay, the second largest population in the world. These animals graze on seagrass and they are able to live so successfully in Shark Bay because it has the largest and most diverse seagrass meadows in the world. Over thousands of years the seagrass has had a powerful influence on the environment of the bay. For starters

the meadows inhibit tidal flow, a factor in the hypersaline conditions that have resulted in the growth of stromatolites and tiny bivalve cockles. Seagrass also provides food and shelter for hundreds of animals in the food chain, creating Shark Bay's rich marine environment.

The turtle is another magnificent animal that feeds on the seagrass and there are estimated to be about 6,000 turtles in the world heritage area; mostly green turtles and the endangered loggerhead turtles. The loggerheads breed and nest on Dirk Hartog Island from August-January and hatchlings emerge around February-March. CALM conducts research trips during this period and volunteers can sometimes join in to count and tag nesting turtles (contact **Landscope** ⓘ *T9380 2433, extension@ uwa.edu.au, for details*). Green turtles and dugongs are often seen from boats, although dugongs are notoriously shy. Also look out for green turtles around the jetty at Monkey Mia and while swimming as they are often seen close to shore.

back in the water to your knees again. Even in such crowded and controlled conditions it is wonderful to be so close to these wild dolphins. When they roll on their sides and look up at you you can't help feeling that these creatures really are as curious about you as you are about them (or maybe they're just wondering where you're hiding the fish).

To get the best out of the experience plan to spend the whole day at Monkey Mia or make it an overnight trip. The dolphins usually arrive about 0800 and after they have been fed the main crowds disappear on their tour buses. Dolphin feeding is allowed three times between 0800 and 1300 and there is a good chance that the dolphins will reappear and you'll have a more intimate encounter. Take an afternoon and sunset cruise and you can't fail to have an awesome day.

⊜ Sleeping

Hamelin Pool *p242*
D **Hamelin Pool Telegraph Station**, T9942 5905. Campers can use the lawns, and they and the day customers can use the sheltered BBQ facilities. There are also caravan sites and a single a/c cabin, sleeping up to 4.

Denham *p243*
There is a fair range of reasonably priced accommodation here, mostly in self-contained units and caravan parks. The busiest season is the winter-spring season (Jul-Oct) but all school and public holidays

and the Dec-Jan Christmas period are also usually booked out well in advance.

B Heritage Resort Hotel, corner of Knight Terr and Durlacher St, T9948 1133, www. heritageresort.net.au. Large hotel with the best rooms in town, some with ocean views and small balconies.

B-E Bay Lodge (YHA), Knight Terr, T9948 1278, www.baylodge.info. Has motel rooms, some facing the ocean, self-contained chalets, and several units grouped around the pool set aside as 2-6 bed backpacker dorms with small kitchens, a TV area and bathroom. Free shuttle to Monkey Mia, 0745.

C Denham Lodge, Durlacher St, T9948 1264, www.denhamvillas.com. Has some of the best presented and equipped self-contained units, many with ocean views.

C-D Shark Bay Holiday Cottages, 3 Knight Terr, T9948 1206, www.sharkbaycottages. com.au. Simple self-contained cottages opposite the beach. All a/c with TV, clean and comfortable. Also pool and laundry.

Denham Seaside, at the northern end of Knight Terr, T9948 1242. Best positioned of the 3 caravan parks, good facilities too.

Monkey Mia *p244*
A-C-E Dolphin Resort, T9948 1320, www.monkeymia.com.au. Has a few very comfortable beachfront villas, self-contained cabins, safari canvas 'condos' (all a/c), on-site vans, backpacker dongers and camping sites. Residents' facilities include a pool, campers' kitchen and BBQs. The complex also has a small expensive store with fuel pumps, open 0700-1800, a bar and food outlets.

❼ Eating

Hamelin Pool *p242*
Hamelin Pool Telegraph Station, T9942 5905. Serves snack lunches and excellent cream teas, daily 0830-1730.

Denham *p243*
🍴 **Old Pearler**, corner of Durlacher St and Knight Terr, T9948 1373, is the most visible example of a building made of shells

(coquina limestone blocks). While it certainly has the most character, the food does not always live up to the cosy rustic interior and is priced well above other places in town.

🍴-🍴 **Heritage Resort Hotel**, corner of Knight Terr and Durlacher St, T9948 1133. The food lives up to the generally high standards of this place. The evening buffets on Tue and Fri-Sun are particularly popular, though all evening meals include a dive into the salad bar. Meals 1200-1500, 1800-2100. Live retro cover band Sun, sometimes Fri-Sat.

🍴 **Bay Café**, next to the VIC, has good cheap meals at this very simple and casual place. Lunches lean toward burgers and smoothies but the evening menu offers more interesting meals of fish, seafood as well as chicken and steak dishes. Daily 1000-1530, 1700-2100.

Monkey Mia *p244*
🍴 **Boughshed** serves as the resort restaurant. While the food is OK and it's a great place to sit and watch the beach, you pay for the privilege. Instead, you could grab something from the takeaway and eat on the grass in front of the café and enjoy the same view. Meals 0700-1400, 1830-2030.

🍴 **Dolphin Resort**, T9948 1320. Has a takeaway café serving pizzas, burgers etc. from 1000-2000 and an overpriced café bar.

▲▲ Activities and tours

Denham *p243*
Majestic Tours, T9948 1627, www.ozpal. com/majestic. 4WD tours to Shell Beach and Eagle Bluff (½ day, $65), Stromatolites and telegraph station (full day $125) and Francois Peron National Park (full day $125). There is also an adventure tour to Steep Point, on the rugged western peninsula (15 hrs).

Outback Coast, T9948 1445, outbackcoast 4wd@wn.com.au. This company offers very similar tours at slightly lower prices but the charter is exclusive so you need to be able to get 4 people together.

Shark Bay Air Charter, T9948 1773, www. ozpal.com/sharkbayair. Flights are a good way to see these peninsulas and sharks, dugongs and dolphins are visible from the

● For an explanation of sleeping and eating price codes used in this guide, see inside the
● front cover. Other relevant information is found in Essentials, see pages 40-46.

air. Flights over Monkey Mia and Peron Homestead, Denham, Monkey Mia and Francois Peron National Park, Steep Point, Useless Loop and salt lakes, Zuytdorp Cliffs (prices range: $50-115).
Sportfishing Safaris, T9948 1846, www.sportfish.com.au. Day trips from $145.

Monkey Mia *p244*
Beach volleyball
Use of the court is free, ask to borrow a ball at the resort reception.

Boat cruises
Two operators offer cruises into the bay.
Aristocat 2, T9948 1446, www.monkey-mia. net. Has a large enclosed cabin, making it slower to move around, but perhaps more reassuring for those sensitive to the sun. They offer similar cruises at the same prices (except the afternoon cruise which is not specifically a dugong cruise). Daily cruises 0900, 1100, 1330, sunset.
Blue Lagoon Pearl, T9948 1325. A small glass-bottom boat that takes visitors out to the pearl farm where you can learn about the industry and buy pearl jewellery. Daily at 1100 from the jetty (1hr, $10). Buy tickets for all cruises from the booths on the boardwalk.
Shotover, T9948 1481, www.monkey miawildsights.com.au. An 18-m open catamaran. No central cabin means excellent all-round views, and there are large nets slung between the hulls that you can sit in, as well as plentiful deck seating. Shade is provided by the sail and an awning. Polaroid sunglasses are handed out that make it much easier to see animals underwater. Daily cruises: short morning cruise 0900 (1 hr, $34), wildlife spotting 1030 (2 hrs, $49), dugong-spotting cruise 1300 (2½ hrs, $54), sunset cruise (1½ hrs, $44).

Boat and snorkel hire
Westcoast Watersports offers kayak hire ($12 hr), electric glass-bottom boat hire ($30 hr) and snorkel hire ($3 hr) from the marquee at the end of the beach. Snorkel hire from VIC, $10 day.

Cinema
Contemporary movies are shown at the small outdoor amphitheatre most Mon-Sun nights. The 2 film shows are $8.

Walking
A short loop walk around Monkey Mia (2 km) takes you past an ancient Aboriginal site and provides good views from a low ridge. Pick up a walksheet from the visitor centre.

⊖ Transport

Denham *p243*
Bicycle
From **Shell** garage.

Bus
A shuttle, T9948 1627, meets some **Greyhound/McCafferty's** services at the *Overlander*. These 0545 and 1800 Mon, Thu and Sat shuttles meet both north- and south-bound coaches. Bookings required. **Bay Lodge** run a gratis shuttle to Monkey Mia, departing 0745 and returning 1630. Non-residents welcome if seats are available and they pay an $8 donation to the Silver Chain nursing organization.

Car
Hire from **Shark Bay Car Hire**, T9948 3032. 4WD hire from $110 day, which allows exploration of the national park.

Taxi
It's a $40 one-way trip to Monkey Mia, T9948 1331.

Monkey Mia *p244*
Bike hire is available at reception for $13 a day but they are not really up to the ride to Denham (about 4-5 hrs return). See above.

❶ Directory

Denham *p243*
Banks Bankwest ATM at **Heritage Resort**.
Hospital Emergency care (24 hrs) at **Silver Chain Nursing Post**, 35 Hughes St, T9948 1213. No chemist, but some basic supplies available at **Foodland**. **Internet** At VIC.
Post Back of newsagent on Knight Terr.

The northwest

The area vies with the Nullarbor for the title of Australia's driest stretch of coastline, and so it's something of a surprise to find lush banana plantations surrounding the port town of Carnarvon. This is an anomaly though with the rest of the region struggles for water. By far the biggest draw is just off-shore from the impressive beaches, the Ningaloo Reef. This runs parallel to the coast from south of Coral Bay to north of the North West Cape and although the reef's corals may not be quite as colourful as other major reefs, the fish and other sealife it harbours are second to none. Coral Bay is still only a small holiday resort, struggling to stretch its resources to cope with the thousands of visitors who come to wade off the beach, to snorkel over the reef and swim with giant manta rays. Exmouth, one of the youngest towns in WA, is the other side of the Cape to the reef, but acts as the base to explore the pristine Cape Range National Park and the long part of the Ningaloo that lies just metres off the shore. Exmouth is also the base for those wanting to experience one of life's true wonders: swimming with whale sharks. ▸▸ *For Sleeping, Eating and other listings, see pages 254-261.*

Overlander roadhouse to Carnarvon → *Distance: 200 km.*

The vegetation gets a little more sparse and scrubby but there is little else to enliven this featureless drive. One bright spot is the welcoming **Wooramel roadhouse** (E), 75 km from the **Overlander**, which pumps the cheapest fuel since Geraldton, also breakfasts, snacks and burgers, ATM, single and double a/c dongas. Meals and fuel 0600-2100. Just short of Carnarvon, the highway north is interrupted by a T-junction (the T-junction in local parlance), the focus of a cluster of 24-hour roadhouses, fruit plantations and caravan parks. Turn left for the town centre, 5 km away, right for the Blowholes, Quobba, the Kennedy Range, and destinations further north.

Carnarvon → *Colour map 5, grid C1. Population: 6,900. 480 km from Geraldton, 370 km from Exmouth, 360 km from Nanutarra roadhouse.*

Of many ports set up by settlers in the mid-1800s along the west coast, Carnarvon is one of the few survivors and has consolidated its early prosperity by making the most of the water that flows in great volume down the Gascoyne River. Most of the time the mighty riverbed is exposed as a wide ribbon of sand but the Gascoyne flows deep underground all year round and it is tapped by local fruit growers for irrigation. Consequently, Carnarvon appears as something of an oasis among the dry, scrubby plains to the north and south. Vast plantations of banana and mango trees are mingled with colourful bougainvillea, poinciana trees and tall palms. Other than a couple of plantations with tours and tropical cafés, Carnarvon has few tourist pretensions, but does make a useful base for exploring the rugged coastline to the north, including the Blowholes, and the impressive Kennedy Range, 200 km inland. A lot of Australians and backpackers come to Carnarvon for work, as attested by the many caravan parks, see below.

Sights
The town centre sits by the shore of an artificial ocean inlet, the Fascine. Over the inlet are Babbage and Whitlock Islands, cut off from the mainland by the Fascine and a swampy section bridged by a causeway. **Babbage Island** has an unremarkable ocean beach and the remains of the original port facilities, the long town jetty.

One Mile Jetty ① *train runs every 45 mins May-Sep, otherwise most weekends, T9941 4309, $4.50, children and concessions $2.50; cottage 1000-1300, gold coin donation*, is the main feature of the town's Heritage Precinct on Babbage Island, curiously named after Charles Babbage, the English mathematician and inventor of the first mechanical computer. The jetty was built at the close of the 18th century and began to fall into disrepair in the 1970s but was rescued by the community in the late 1990s. Visitors can walk out along the jetty for a $2 coin donation or catch a train from the adjacent kiosk. Also part of the precinct are a rail shed, surrounded by the rusting hulks of various engines, carriages, tractors, boats and engineering paraphernalia, some of historical interest, and the genteel **Lighthouse Keeper's Cottage**. The cottage is now furnished as it might have been in the 1920s.

Piyarli Yardi, an Aboriginal Cultural Centre, is being built just outside the centre of town, and promises to be a major attraction. Contact the VIC for advice on an opening date, expected during 2005. Close to the main T-junction is an O.T.C. dish, part of a **satellite tracking station** set up in 1963 to assist NASA with communications during the orbital Gemini and Moon-landing Apollo programmes. Up to 180 people once worked at the station, which was a crucial part of the communications set-up that guided the space vehicles. As much so, in fact, as the centre at Parkes in NSW, the 'star' of the Australian movie, *The Dish*. The station ceased operations in 1986 but the dish is now one of Australia's most unusual lookouts, with steps up to a first-floor 'landing' giving great views across the surrounding plains, plantations and ocean.

The VIC ① *corner of (the main) Robinson St and Camel Lane, T9941 1146, cvontourist@wn.com.au, 0900-1700*, is very helpful and friendly.

Carnarvon

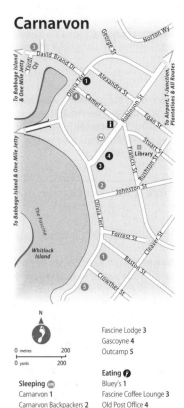

N

0 metres 200
0 yards 200

Sleeping 🛌
Carnarvon **1**
Carnarvon Backpackers **2**
Fascine Lodge **3**
Gascoyne **4**
Outcamp **5**

Eating 🍴
Bluey's **1**
Fascine Coffee Lounge **3**
Old Post Office **4**

Excursions

The **plantations** of Carnarvon are the most attractive and unusual aspect of the town. It is well worth driving along South River Road to see the plantations and buy fruit from roadside stalls. Two of the plantations, **Munro's** and **Westo- by** (see Eating below for further details), are open to the public where you can learn something of the industry on a tour and try the local produce in their cafés. The water that nourishes the fruit trees is also used to encourage a delightful profusion of trees, palms and flowering plants and café tables are placed under the deep shade they provide. On a hot day it feels at least 10 degrees cooler in these gardens and it's well worth stopping for respite from the dull highway.

The Blowholes are a bit of a drive from Carnarvon, some 75 km, but they are good fun and the road is sealed all the way. This is a very rocky, sharp coastline with waves crashing on jagged shelves and reefs even on a calm day. At the blowholes site water surges under a rock platform and is forced up a narrow channel to eject a roaring jet of water 10-m high in calm weather, double that in rough weather. You can't miss the sign at the junction of the Quobba Road: 'king waves kill'. This is a way of telling you that it is easy to be swept off the rocks by a huge wave so stand well back when looking at the blowholes and watch the ocean carefully.

Just one unsealed kilometre south of the blowholes is **Point Quobba**, where there are a few fishing shacks and a campsite. The rocky sites are $5, there are toilets but no showers or fresh water. There is also a small sandy beach and an excellent **snorkelling** site, between the beach and an island. You'll need to take your own gear but you'll see lots of colourful fish, coral and even turtles if you're lucky.

Heading north from the junction the road becomes unsealed, reaching the **Quobba Station Homestead** ① *T/F9941 2036, quobba@wn.com.au*, after 10 km. This is a working sheep station that also provides accommodation and a small shop for the hordes of locals who love to fish along this coastline. There are eight basic fishing shacks (**D-E**), two comfortable cabins (**C**), none air-conditioned, and camping sites ($5 per person per day). The shop is open 1000-1600 most days. Drop in for a map and advice if heading further north. The road continues north for about another 100 km along pale rocky cliffs and scrub-covered dunes. This remote rugged country is a fishermen's and surfers' paradise.

After 21 km, past the second bitumen mining road, is a 3-km station track (2WD) to the cliff edge. There are good views south to **Cape Cuvier** and its salt and gypsum loading facility. You might see sharks in the clear water below the cliffs and the last remnants of the *Korean Star*, a bulk carrier ship wrecked during a cyclone in 1988. Another 25 km north is **Red Bluff**. The long wide beach below the bluff offers sheltered swimming and is a fantastic surfing spot. Camping is permitted here and there is another small shop, open irregularly. Note that camping outside the three spots mentioned is not permitted by the station owners. After Red Bluff you pass into **Gnaraloo Station**, which also allows limited camping. The surf is so good that major surfing competitions have been held here but it's a long drive on a very rough track.

Working in Carnarvon

The fruit picking and packing season extends for most of the year from April-January, while the fishing season is April-September. Getting a job as a deckhand is generally the better paid and more interesting, but is certainly harder work. Expect to earn upward of $10 an hour. The backpacker hostel can help find work, otherwise you'll need to do the rounds of the plantations and boats yourself.

Kennedy Range National Park → *Colour map 5, grid B2. Eastern bluffs 245 km from Carnarvon.*

① *For more information CALM office, Denham, T9948 1208; road conditions, T9941 077; no entry fee or camping fees.*

The Kennedy Range forms a dramatic flame-coloured mesa, 75 km long, running north to south. Sheer sandstone walls rise above a skirt of scree slopes, spreading down to the plains below. The range is all that remains of a plateau that elsewhere has been worn away, down to the current level of the Lyons River Valley plain. The range is a long drive from anywhere (see Transport for route details) on an unsealed road but this park offers the chance to experience the outback, and perhaps a local station stay. Much of the range is inaccessible but on the eastern side there are three narrow gorges that can be explored and a campsite right at the base of the 100-m cliffs. Each gorge is less than a kilometre apart and there are short walks along the creek beds. The Kennedy Range contains such interesting rocks that you'll wish you had a geologist with you. In fact, the sheer variety of the rock shapes and colours is so captivating that it is hard to remember to lift your head and look at the stunning cliffs

Jaw dropping

Imagine swimming with a shark the size of a bus, in water a kilometre deep. You stand on the back of boat all suited up in snorkel, fins and wetsuit and the divemaster shouts 'go, go, go' like Murray Walker at a grand prix. Adrenalin surges and suddenly you're looking through your mask at a mouth as big as a cave coming straight for you. Shock paralyses for a second as your mind screams get out of the way!

Swimming with whale sharks may be one of the most memorable and exciting things you do in your lifetime. The whale shark is a plankton feeder that isn't the slightest bit interested in gobbling you into its wide gaping mouth but is alarmingly huge when you are only a few metres away. These rare gentle beasts can reach 18 m but are more often seen at 4-12 m. Little is known about them except that they travel in a band around the equator and arrive to feed at the Ningaloo Reef after the coral spawning in March and April. The sharks swim just under the surface as sunlight sparkles on their blue-grey bodies and delicate pattern of white spots. When spotted by a boat, snorkellers jump in and

accompany a shark for a while, just like the fleet of remora fish that hang around its mouth and belly. Some sharks seem mildly curious about their new fluro-coloured gasping, flapping friends but others seem about as bothered as an elephant by a gnat. However the interaction has only occurred for about ten years and it is not known what impact swimmers have on the whale sharks.

Fishermen had seen a few on the Ningaloo Reef over the years but it wasn't until the late 1980s that marine biologists began to realise just how unusual but regular these sightings were. During the 1990s tours were developed to take visitors out to swim with the whale sharks and it has become big business in Exmouth. CALM have developed strict guidelines for swimming and boating around them, and it is hoped that this will keep the whale sharks undisturbed. Of course these are wild creatures and sightings are not guaranteed (although you will generally get a second trip for free if you don't see any). Experiences can vary from hectic five minute swims to magical forty minute floats but are always extraordinary.

above. The cliffs themselves are at their best at dawn when they can take on some seriously impressive yellow, orange and red hues. The campsite has a toilet but no other facilities. Take plenty of water. Roads are fine for 2WD except after heavy rain, when the roads will be closed.

The **southern gorge** has the longest and hardest walk (3 km return), including an optional scramble up the sides of the gorge to the plateau edge above. The unmarked track passes several rock pools and waterfalls before reaching a final high waterfall, heavily frequented by feral goats by the look (and smell) of the place. Of course 'waterfall' in this region means about the same as 'river': most of the time there is no water in either. The **middle gorge**, **Temple Gorge**, is an easier, more open walk (1½ km return). Look for marine fossils in ledge caves above the car park of both walks. The northern gorge has a stunning series of cliff faces and rock weathered to honeycomb (½ km). Again, you can climb to the top where there is an unexpected landscape of red sand dunes covered in spinifex and scrub, but there is no path. Take great care if you do this as the sandstone is very crumbly and loose.

Carnarvon to Coral Bay

Minilya → *Colour map 5, grid B1. 140 km from Carnarvon, 225 km from Exmouth.*

On the south side of the course of the eucalypt-flanked Minilya River is a shady picnic area with BBQs and toilets. Customers of the spotless **D Minilya Roadhouse**① *T9942 5922, just over the bridge, 0600-2200, meals to 2100*, get to use their air-conditioned bathrooms, a rare treat along this long stretch of road! Dedicated to quality, the roadhouse serves above-average cheap meals and takeaways, has comfortable donger rooms, an en suite four-bed cabin, all air conditioned, and lawned caravan sites. It also sells the last relatively inexpensive fuel if you're heading north. Soon after Minilya the highway forks. Take the left turn for Coral Bay and Exmouth, continue right for Karratha and Broome.

Waroora → *Colour map 5, grid B1. 55 km from Minilya, 60 km from Coral Bay.*

An unsealed detour off the main road leads to the coastal sheep station of **D Warroora** ('Worra') ① *T9942 5920, warroora@bigpond.com*. One of four neighbouring stations that have allied to help protect this beautiful piece of coastline and the offshore **Ningaloo Reef**, Warroora has about 50 km of beaches, all accessible by 4WD only. In some places the reef is just metres offshore and there are consequently some wonderful snorkelling and diving spots. Camping is allowed all along the coast ($5 per person per day), and there are basic but comfortable twin donger rooms near the homestead with an ablution block and BBQs. Own linen required. Water is very restricted, and there are no supplies available, so bring your own. Call in to the homestead office to pay your fees and get a map.

Coral Bay → *Colour map 5, grid B1. 240 km from Carnarvon, 150 km from Exmouth.*

This pretty shallow bay is just a notch in a long coastline of white sand, dunes and desert but this is the most accessible spot on the north west coast where the **Ningaloo coral reef** gets within 50 m of the shore. The reef is full of colourful fish, clams, sea cucumbers, rays and even the odd turtle, though the coral itself is more notable for its intricate shapes and forms than any vibrancy of colour. All you need to do is grab a snorkel, mask and fins and wade in. There are also a variety of boat trips that take you further out onto the reef to snorkel or dive with manta rays, turtles and whale sharks, or spot humpback whales, dugongs and dolphins; near Utopia for anyone who loves marine wildlife. The settlement itself is a small, relaxed beach resort where you can walk barefoot from your door to the beach in two minutes. Coral Bay is changing fast though and each year there are more operators, activities and visitors. There is no independent VIC, and half a dozen local tour operators have set up booking offices that sell their, and usually most of their competitors', tours. For superb free information on the Coral Bay environment and wildlife, call into the **Coastal Adventure Tours** office and internet café in the Coral Bay Shopping Centre. Facilities are modest, but there is a supermarket, newsagent, a few gift shops and fuel is also available.

Exmouth → *Colour map 5, grid A1. Population: 3,100. 615 km from Tom Price (Karijini), 555 km from Karratha.*

Exmouth sits on the eastern side of the North West Cape, facing the calm waters of the Exmouth Gulf and seperated by the low hills of Cape Range from the pristine beaches of the Ningaloo Marine Park. Despite the marine riches of the cape, the town doesn't have a coastal feel. It's a practical place that was built to service the local military bases and to withstand the seasonal cyclones of this region. A self-sufficient community of American naval staff lived on the Harold E. Holt Naval Communications station from 1967 until 1992 when the Australian Navy took over management of the base. Thirteen VLF towers dominate the northern tip of the cape and are taller than the Eiffel Tower. Until recently some buildings at the station were used for tourism ventures but after the 11 September terrorist attacks security has been tightened and the base is effectively closed for the present.

Exmouth's proximity to the **Ningaloo Reef** and its extraordinary wildlife make it a special place for eco-tourism. It is possible to swim with whale sharks, watch turtles laying and hatching, spot migrating humpback whales, snorkel over coral from the beach, and dive on almost untouched sites. There are also red rocky gorges and campsites by perfect beaches in the Cape Range National Park. The only drawback is the intense heat and aridity of the cape – most people visit in winter when temperatures drop to 25-30°C. Exmouth is well set-up for travellers, with a good range of accommodation, tours and activities to make the most of what it has to offer. The helpful **VIC** ① *Murat St, T9949 1176, www.exmouth-australia.com, 0900- 1700*, is on the main through road.

Cape Range National Park → *Colour map 5, grid A1. 50 km from Exmouth.*

① *Milyering 0930-1600; park T9949 2808, 24 hrs, $9 per vehicle or $3.30 per person, camping $10 for 2 people, ranger collects camping fees.*

Cape Range National Park is an unforgiving, rocky strip of land on the western side of North West Cape, adjoining the Ningaloo Marine Park. The low red hills of Cape Range form a spine running down the middle of the cape, gashed by gorges that are all dry as a bone except the tranquil Yardie Creek Gorge, at the southern end. The glittering turquoise sea fringing the park just seems to emphasize its aridity and kangaroos have to seek shade under bushes only knee high. However, this is the place to access the wonderful Ningaloo Reef and at places such as Turquoise Bay the reef is only metres from shore so you can snorkel off the beach among a dazzling parade of fish. The park's **Milyering Visitor Centre** is 13 km inside the northern park boundary. It houses an interpretative centre and a small shop with a limited range of drinks and snacks. **Turquoise Bay**, a beautiful white swimming beach, is a further 10 km south. There are a few shade sails and a toilet here but no other facilities. About 15 km from Milyering is **Mandu Mandu Gorge**, where there is a 3 km (return) walk into the dry gorge. Right at the end of the sealed road is **Yardie** Creek, a short gorge with sheer red walls above the creek and a colony of black-footed rock wallabies. Yardie Creek has a picnic area, a boat cruise along the creek at 1230 and a

Exmouth To ④, Ningaloo Lighthouse, Cape Range National Park & Ningaloo Reef

Sleeping	Ningaloo Club 6	Eating
Excape	Ningaloo	Grace's Tavern 2
Backpackers 3	Lighthouse	Sea Urchin 3
Exmouth Cape	Caravan Park 4	Whaler's 4
Tourist Village	Ningaloo Lodge 2	
(Pete's	Potshot 3	
Backpackers) 1		

The Gascoyne The northwest

short, rocky track (1½ km return) along the northern side of the gorge. There are also two gorges that can be accessed from the eastern side of the cape, **Shothole Canyon** and **Charles Knife**. There are great views of the gulf from these rugged gorges but the roads are unsealed and very rough.

Exmouth to Nanutarra Roadhouse → *Colour map 5, grid B2.*

Nanutarra roadhouse 280 km from Exmouth, 265 km from Karratha, 335 km from Tom Price.

If heading north there is a sealed short-cut connecting the Exmouth Road with the North West Coastal Highway. Halfway along this road is **L-A,D Giralia** ① *T9942 5937, raeblake@bigpond.com, 130 km from Exmouth*, and one of the best station stays in the region. They have four en-suite doubles and twins in the main homestead and guests in these rooms are fully catered for. Also close to the main house, completely rebuilt following the devastation of Cyclone Vance in 1999, are a self-contained cottage, a pretty quadrangle of simple air-conditioned donger rooms and a bush camp. There are basic kitchen facilities but the friendly hosts cook up a cheap meal every evening. There are several 4WD tracks on the station, some leading to the tidal flats of Exmouth Gulf 30 km north, well known locally for excellent fly fishing.

A little further on from Giralia is the turn for **Yanrey Station** ① *T9943 0686, yanreystation@bigpond.com*, notable for offering residential courses for would-be Jackaroos and Jilleroos.

North West Cape

Sleeping ⌂
Ningaloo Club **1**
Ningaloo Lighthouse
Caravan Park **2**
Ningaloo Reef Retreat **3**

Camping ▲
Kurrajong **4**
Lakeside **5**
Mesa Camp **6**
Neds Camp **7**
Osprey Bay **8**
Pilgramunna **9**
T-Bone Bay **10**
Tulki Beach **11**
Yardie Creek **12**

After the following junction with the main highway the slow greening of the landscape continues and the monotous flat becomes punctuated with low hill ranges, the first signs of the main Pilbara ranges. The change is a sight for sore eyes after the west coast scenery, as is the first appearance of rivers with (some) water in them. Yannarie is the first of these, 45 km from the junction, where bush camping is allowed. If you fancy a splash. However, it's worth hanging on for the **D Nanutarra Roadhouse** ① *T9943 0521*, by the Ashburton River which always has some decent-sized waterholes. The roadhouse has a few air-conditioned donger rooms, camp sites and a licensed café. Meals 0630-2200, fuel to 2400. It marks one of the north's major junctions, and from here it's 120 km to **Onslow**, 270 km to **Karratha**, and 350 km to **Tom Price**.

◉ Sleeping

Carnarvon *p248, map p249*
B Outcamp, 139 Olivia Terr, T9941 2421, is the only B&B in town. Although associated by family connections to the historic stations to the east, this is a new family home, comfortable but lacking character. Luckily this is more than made up for by

the welcoming, knowledgable hosts and excellent breakfasts. It has 5 twins and doubles, none en suite.

C **Fascine Lodge**, David Brand Dr, T9941 2411. A comfortable upmarket motel with bar, restaurant, pool and airport pick-ups. Of the 4 pubs, 2 are worth a mention.

C **Gascoyne**, 88 Olivia Terr, T9941 1412. Has been the town's gastronomic mainstay for some years with an inoffensive dining room and shaded rear courtyard.

D-E **Carnarvon**, 28 Olivia Terr, T9941 1181. Has been opened up to the waterfront with glass walls and an alfresco beer garden, serving as both bistro and café. Both pubs have basic motel accommodation and serve meals 1200-1400 and 1800-2030, though the latter will be serving coffee and cake in the afternoons.

D-E **Carnarvon Backpackers**, 97 Olivia Terr, T9941 1095, carnarvon.backpacker @big pond.com. Very much a workers' hostel. They can help find jobs and run a daily shuttle bus in season to the major employers. The facilities are pretty scruffy, and this hostel won't be everyone's cup of tea, but they are the only place that will open for the early morning buses.

Carnarvon Tourist Centre, Robinson St, T9941 1438, is the closest of the many caravan parks here. Has a good range of cabins, on-site vans and sites.

Norwesta, on the main T-junction, T9941 1277, is a caravan park with reasonably priced a/c vans.

Kennedy Ranges *p250*

Camping is free at a designated spot in the visitors area. There are also 3 options, to suit most budgets, within 70 km, 2 of these outback station stays.

L **Mt Sandiman Station**, T/F9943 0550. 100 years-old, this is the closest to the visitor area (45 km north), and offers both homestead dinner/B&B and camping. They also run 4WD tours up to the top of the ranges.

L-A **Bidgemia Station**, 11 km east of Gascoyne Junction on the banks of the river, T9943 0501, bidge mia@wn.com.au. Has 2 sets of rooms: 5 twins in a spacious Mediterranean-style a/c house within the

pleasant homestead gardens, and another 5 simple but comfy twins designated as shearers' quarters. Similar to **Mt Sandiman**, the tariff is pricey but includes all meals and drinks with the station owners, and use of the welcome pool. Impromptu tours (both 4WD and flights in their small twin-seater) may be thrown in when convenient. Recommended.

D **Gascoyne Junction Hotel**, T9943 0504. A classic outback tin pub with a friendly bar full of decaying memorabilia, a games room and shady beer garden. All the single and double donga rooms are a/c, and there are also camping sites. Drinks, basic supplies and fuel available 0800-2000.

Coral Bay *p252*

Coral Bay is always booked out weeks in advance for school and public holidays. All establishments are on the main street, Robinson St.

L-B-E **Ningaloo Reef Resort**, T9942 5934, www.coralbay.org/resort, is the bay's only resort-style hotel, with many rooms having ocean views and direct access to the central pool. Don't be tempted by the backpacker rooms unless it's your only option.

A-D **Bayview Coral Bay**, T9385 6655, www.coralbaywa.com. A great range of accommodation from self-contained villas with sea views, motel-style rooms, chalets, cabins, on-site vans and grassy caravan and camping park. All are bright, clean and a/c. The villas and motel rooms have TV and linen is supplied.

C **People's Caravan Park**, T9942 5933. Mostly caravan and grassy camping sites, some with views of the bay. Currently 2 en-suite, a/c cabins.

D-E **Ningaloo Club**, T9385 7411, www.ning alooclub.com. A large new hostel arranged around a pool-filled central courtyard with a pleasant communal deck area to one side. The kitchen is small but well-equipped. Linen is included, rooms are simple, comfortable and some doubles have a/c. Cheap internet and continental brekky for guests. Recommended.

The Gascoyne The northwest Listings

A-C-E Potshot, Murat Rd, T9949 1200. The town's largest resort complex, covering a huge area with different accommodation types in brick poolside units. Standard motel rooms, self-contained apartments, as well as modern, well-equipped villas across the road. Also runs **Excape Backpackers** which has modern but characterless a/c dorms, large industrial kitchen and use of resort facilities.

B-C Ningaloo Lighthouse Caravan Park, 17 km north of town on Yardie Creek Rd, T9949 1478, www.ningaloolighthouse.com. Well run park with lots of trees and grassy sites, and smart self-contained chalets, all with private veranda and BBQ. The 'Lookout' chalets perch high above the park and have wonderful sea views. Also shop, pool, tennis court, snorkel hire, cheap fuel and daytime café (Apr-Oct).

B-C-E Exmouth Cape Tourist Village (Pete's Backpackers), Murat Rd, T9949 1101, www.exmouthvillage.com. A range of a/c, en-suite cottages and cabins are available exclusively, or as mini backpacker dorms. Also grassed and shady caravan and camp sites. It also runs the airport/ 'Greyhound' shuttle and the on-site **Village Dive** centre. Recommended.

C Ningaloo Lodge, Lefroy St, T9949 4949, www.ningaloolodge.com.au. Comfortable motel with twins and doubles courtyard pool and communal kitchen, dining, television and games rooms.

C-E Ningaloo Club (formerly Marina Beach), Market St, 3 km south of town, T9949 1500. A full, surprisingly luxurious hostel complex almost completely under canvas. Large, en-suite safari tents make up 6-bed dorms and premium doubles, other doubles in 2-person tents. Excellent communal facilities include open-air pool, chill-out deck, café-bar and camp kitchen. Direct beach access, free pick-ups and free bikes. Recommended.

Coral Coast, on-site dive operators, has a number of internet terminals.

Cape Range National Park *p253*
A-B Ningaloo Reef Retreat, T9949 4073, www.ningalooreefretreat.com. The only commercial accommodation within the park itself. It has 4 comfortable 4-bed, en-suite safari tents overlooking the beach and ocean, plus a small kitchen, chill-out area and ablution block. The price includes all meals, drinks (BYO alcohol) and activities including guided kayaking and snorkelling. The budget option is in a swag. Recommended.

Camping
There are lots of camp grounds within the park, mostly close to the beach and some with bush toilets. There is no fresh water available so bring your own, though drinks are available at Milyering. The VIC and CALM have a comprehensive list that details the qualities of each site. Only Lakeside, near Milyering, is close to a good snorkelling site. No bookings are taken so call ahead for availablility of spaces during the Apr-Oct peak season.

---

❷ Eating

Carnarvon *p248, map p249*
Plantations
Fascine Coffee Lounge, Robinson St, near the foreshore. The best of a small handful of unimaginative cafés in the town centre. Open Mon-Fri 0800-1500, Sat 0800-1300.

Munro's, South River Rd, T9941 8104. Opposite the river bed, this plantation café is known for excellent food, such as sweet and savoury scones, banana and mango smoothies. Tours at 1100. Open Sun-Fri 1000-1600 (Jun-Oct), Sun-Thu (Nov-May). When heading north turn left off the highway just before the Gascoyne bridge.

Old Post Office, Robinson St, T9941 1800. Aside from the plantations, the only pukka non-hotel restaurant, serving mostly mid-range pizza and pasta on the large alfresco deck. Open Tue-Sat 1700-2200, though reports indicate it is often unaccountably closed, so book ahead.

Westoby, 500 Robinson St, T9941 8003. Fairly close to the town centre, this plantation has entertaining informative tours at 1100 and 1400. The café, under a massive poinciana tree, serves snacks such as fish and chips as well as banana sundaes and mango ice blocks. Open Wed-Mon 1000-1600, Fri 1800-2100 (bookings essential on Fri night).

Kennedy Ranges *p250*
Gascoyne Junction Hotel, T9943 0504. Serves cheap meals available daily, 1200-1400 and 1800-2000 from Apr-Oct, otherwise the publican will usually be happy to see what he can throw together.

Coral Bay *p252*
All establishments are on the main street, Robinson St.
¶¶ **Fins**, Robinson St, T9942 5900. A Greek taverna-style terrace restaurant, shading into expensive, but BYO and easily the best food in town, arguably the region. Breakfasts, coffee and snacks all day from 0730, evening dining 1700-2100. Bookings essential during busy periods. Recommended.
¶¶-¶ **Ningaloo Reef Resort**, T9942 5934. Meals and snacks to 2000, happy hour in the main bar from 1730-1830 Tue and Fri. Don't be tempted by the backpacker rooms unless it's your only option.
¶ **Ningaloo Reef Café** is part of **Bayview Coral Bay**. This is a colourful, licensed, open space with a simple cheap menu of fish, steak, pasta and pizzas. Also takeaways, open daily 1730-2130.

Exmouth *p252, map p253*
¶¶¶-¶¶ **Potshot**, has 2 dining options. The shady pool-side bar serves steak and seafood meals 0700-1830 and (in peak season) 1830-2100, and a pricier bistro at the other end of the complex, open 1130-1400 and 1830-2100.
¶¶ **Whaler's**, Kennedy St, T9949 2416. The town's main restaurant, with plenty of tables on a covered terrace. Open 0830-1500 for a good range of breakfasts and light lunches, and 1830-2100 for mostly Italian-influenced meals. Licensed.
¶¶-¶ **Grace's Tavern**, Murat Rd, T9949 1000, tucked behind **Ampol** on Maidstone Cres. Serves counter meals from 1130-1400 and 1830-2100.
¶ **Exmouth Cape Tourist Village**, on Wed and Sun evenings they have a BYO pool-side fish BBQ ($9.50).
¶ **Golden Orchid**, main shopping area, T9949 1740. Chinese restaurant, does cheap lunch specials and is open Mon-Fri 1130-1400 and 1700-2200 daily.

Cafés
Continental Café, in the shopping area, good for breakfast, smoothies, sarnies, coffee and cakes from 0800 daily to 1700 Mon-Sat, 1300 Sun.
Sea Urchin Café, T9949 1249. A cheap and cheerful BYO terrace café offering the best value seafood in town, as well as a good range of mains and snacks. A portion of fish and chips is usually enough for 2. Open evenings only 1700-2130. Recommended.

O Shopping

Exmouth *p252, map p253*
Second-hand from the **Bookshop**, corner of Pelias St and Murat Rd. Open Tue-Fri and morning Sat-Sun from Apr-Oct, otherwise 1000-1300 Tue-Sat. New books from **Sharpe Newsagency** in the main shopping area.

▲ Activities and tours

Carnarvon *p248, map p249*
Stockman Safaris, T9941 2421, stockmansafaris@wn.com.au. Offers a range of excellent 4WD outback tours that include combinations of the rarely visited western escarpment of the Kennedy Range, authentic station homesteads and the rugged coast north of Quobba. Day trips from $150, 3-day camp/station excursions around $600. Call ahead for the current programme.
Tropicair, T9941 2002, www.tropicair.com. au. Planes available for charter.

Coral Bay *p252*
Boat hire
Glass-bottomed canoes available from the hire caravan at the far end of the main beach. **Coral Bay Boat Hire**, T9942 5810, has motor boats from $70 per half day.

Diving
Ningaloo Reef Dive Centre, Coral Bay Shopping Centre, T9942 5824. Dive trips (full day, 2-dive safaris $165) and PADI tuition (open water courses start every Sat, $360), plus a discover scuba day, including dives at 2 bay sites ($185). Full gear hire $70 per fay, open 0730-1730. Dive medicals can be arranged in Coral Bay.

Fish feeding

Occurs at the main beach every day at 1530. You only need to get in up to your knees.

Fishing

Mahi Mahi, T/F9942 5874, mahimahi1@bigpond.com. Offers half, full day ($140) and overnight game-fishing trips, also whale watching and snorkelling. This isn't the only option if full or not operating.

Glass-bottomed boats

There are 3 boats offering 1- to 2-hr cruises over the coral, each of which stop for snorkelling sessions at some of the best off-shore spots. Snorkel hire is included and the gear can usually be retained for the rest of the day for snorkelling off the beach.

Coral Bay Charter, T9942 5932. Very experienced and their 2-hr ($35) trips at 1015 and 1230 usually visit 2 snorkelling spots.

Manta rays

A couple of boats offer snorkelling trips out to swim with these massive but gentle rays. **Coral Bay Adventures**, T9942 5955, www.coralbayadventures.com.au. Marginally the more expensive (half day, $115), but a spotter plane increases the chances of finding rays. **Ningaloo Reef Dive Centre** offers half-day trips to dive with mantas for $150.

Quad bikes

Quad-Treks, T9948 5190, quadtreks@bigpond.com. The more experienced of 2 companies operating these 4-wheel motor-bikes out along the dunes and beaches. These are fantastic fun and you find yourself spending much of each trip working out how you can afford one when you get home. Options include 3-hr snorkelling trips to some favoured turtle spots ($65), and sunset trips which include more challenging terrain and the thrill of a return run in the dark.

Sailing cruises

Coral Breeze, T9948 5190, admin@coastaladventuretours.com. A fairly small catamaran that heads out for 4-hr wildlife spotting and snorkelling trips and 2-hr BYO sunset cruises. This is one of the most peaceful and rewarding ways of seeing the bay, and the cruises are excellent value.

Snorkelling

Snorkel hire at the caravan at the far end of the main beach ($5.50 per half day). Unless you specifically want to see turtles, sharks or rays, then it is hard to beat simply snorkelling straight off the main beach (head out beyond the 5 knot sign just south of the main beach then drift back toward the moorings). If you want to be fairly sure of seeing turtles then head out on the appropriate boat or quad-bike trip. Most boat operators offer a half-day snorkel, including the **Ningaloo Reef Dive Centre** ($50) and **Ningaloo Experience**, T9942 5877 ($55). Sep-Jan is the breeding season for the local reef sharks, and baby ones can be seen by their dozens during this time in Skeleton Bay, just to the north of the main beach.

Tours

Tracks up and down the coast from Coral Bay are 4WD only. There is a profusion of booking offices, and most will sell most of the tours available, making shopping around a confusing business.

Mermaids Cave, T9942 5955, Coral Bay Shopping Centre. Has a small information booth inside and are a good 1st port of call. **Coral Bay Adventures** can organize a variety of flights from a 30-min wildlife tour to a 2-hr 'Ninglaoo Odyssey' that includes a fly over the Cape Range.

Whale sharks

Although Exmouth is hailed as the world's whale shark 'capital', a couple of Coral Bay boats do offer snorkelling trips to try and find them in season (Apr-Jun). They include **Coral Bay Adventures** (full day $310).

Whale watching

Most of the larger boat operators and **Ningaloo Reef Dive Centre** offer tours to see humpbacks in season (Jun-Nov).

Exmouth *p252, map p253*

4WD

Ningaloo Safari Tours, T9949 1550, www.ningaloosafari.com. Neil McLeod runs knowledgeable and enthusiastic 4WD tours into Cape Range National Park, including Shothole Canyon, Charles Knife Rd, 4WD over the top of the range to Yardie Creek and a snorkel at Turquoise Bay. Lunch and tea

breaks included (full day, $155).
Recommended.

so can usually find good dive spots any time of the year.

Boat tours
Exmouth Diving Centre, Potshot Hotel, hires out snorkel sets, while you can pick up a set at the **Lighthouse Caravan Park** for $15 for 24 hrs.
Ningaloo Chase T9949 1500, www.ninga loochase.com.au, runs day trips to look for turtles, for $65, which also include a hike into Yardie Creek.
Ningaloo Ecology, T9949 2255, runs 2-hr (0900, $35) trips from the Tantabiddi boat ramp. The glass-bottom boat heads out a few hundred metres to the reef and is a good way to see some fish, coral and turtles if you don't snorkel. The 2-hr trip includes about an hr of snorkelling off the boat and includes town transfers.
Ningaloo Reef Retreat, T9949 4073, www.ningalooreefretreat.com, takes people out from their secluded beach. Encounters with turtles are likely. Half-day, $60.

Camping adventures
Ningaloo Chase has a canvas beach-side camp just south of Yardie Creek. Overnight visits are $185, 2 nights $345, and include transfers, meals, drinks (BYO alcohol) and activities.
Ningaloo Reef Retreat, beachside, and close to a spectacular snorkelling area, offer a similar, though slightly less structured experience, actually within the national park. Overnight swag stays are $155, including the brilliant kayak trip described above.

Diving
Diving on the Ningaloo can be exceptional, with hundreds of species of fish and coral. There are a number of operators in town, each with their own specialities. Some are run by or associated with town accommodation.
Coral Coast, T9949 1044, dives off the nearby disused navy pier, home to around 200 fish species.
Exmouth Dive Centre, Potshot Hotel, T9949 1201, www.exmouth diving.com.au, has one of the widest ranges of single day options.
Village Dive, T9949 1101, www.exmouth diving.com, specializes in the Muiron Islands,

Fishing
Several boats run game-fishing trips, though the choice is reduced during whale shark season.
Exmouth Game Fishing Charters, T9949 2920. Serious game fishing (also fly fishing) on *Indizari*, top quality tackle.
Ocean Quest Charters, T9949 111, offers full and half-day trips. Flexible and friendly.

Kayaking
Capricorn Kayak Tours, T9949 4431, www.capricornkayak.com.au. Offers various options from a sunset paddle and BBQ at Bundegi ($55) to multi-day camping safaris (5-days for $795, minimum 4 people). Apr-Oct only.
Ningaloo Reef Retreat takes small groups out from their friendly beach-side camp to the **Blue Lagoon**, one of the finest snorkelling sites on the whole reef. You kayak about 1 km offshore to the lagoon where you have a very good chance of seeing turtles and huge cow-tailed stingrays, as well as fish and pristine corals. Cost $90, including lunch and town pick-up. Combine with a beach snorkel and swag overnight for an extra $5. Recommended.

Mini-bus tours
Exmouth Cape Tourist Village runs day trips to the see the main national park spots, including a Turquoise Bay snorkel, for $95, Wed, Fri and Sun.

Quad-bikes
Coastal Quad Bike Tours, T9949 1607. Full day, half day ($100) and 1-3 hr (2 hrs, $50) tours on Exmouth Gulf, some combined with fishing and snorkelling.

Snorkelling
As always in WA, remember that conditions on the beach are best in the morning before the wind arrives, particularly for snorkelling when you want a calm, flat sea.

If you have your own transport you can snorkel from many beaches in the Cape Range National Park where you can expect to see a great variety of fish and coral, although the coral is not very brightly coloured, and perhaps turtles, rays and reef sharks (harmless!). The best site is Turquoise Bay but take care as there is a very strong current and a break in the reef. From the beach walk south around the corner and another 100 m down the beach before entering the water. The current will drift you north and you should get out at the sandspit on the corner to avoid the channel leading to the gap in the reef. Check conditions at the park entry booth or Milyering before snorkelling here – high tide is the worst time. A daily bus service stops at Turquoise Bay.

Swimming
Paltridge Memorial Swimming Pool
Payne St. Aside from the beaches, this outdoor pool is a good spot to cool off on a hot day. Open 0600-0730 and 1000-1800 Mon-Fri, 1200-1800 Sun. $2.40, children and concessions $1.30. The very average town beach is 2 km south of the town centre.

Turtle watching
Turtles come ashore in the Cape Range National Park to breed and lay eggs and it is possible to have the extraordinary and rare experience of watching them do so. Nesting turtles lumber onto the northern end of the cape (Hunters, Mauritius, Jacobsz and Jansz beaches) during Nov-Feb, at night just before high tide and for 2 hrs afterwards. Hatchlings emerge from Jan-Apr between 1700-2000 and scamper to the water's edge. Turtles must not be disturbed by noise, light or touching – it is very important to follow the CALM code of conduct for turtle watching (pick a copy up at their office in town) or the turtles may stop nesting here.
Ningaloo Safari Tours, T9949 1550. Run an evening turtle watching tour ($40) in season (Nov-Mar).

Whale sharks
For many people the sole reason to venture up to Exmouth, a successful swim with a whale shark is simply one of the most awesome experiences Australia has to offer. They come in to feed off the reef from Apr-July, though at the fringes of the season they are generally fewer and smaller. Come during May-Jun for the best chance of

seeing a real biggie (12-m sharks are not uncommon). Half a dozen boats offer day trips to snorkel with them for around $300, and most offer a free follow-up trip if they fail to find one first time around.
Exmouth Dive Centre is one of the best operators. It also includes diving and snorkelling time. You will need to be comfortable with a snorkel, and be a reasonably strong swimmer if you catch a shark going faster than it's 'amble' pace.

Whale watching
Humpback whales migrate along the Ningaloo between Jul-Oct, and most of the dive and boat operators run whale-watching trips during that period.

Cape Range National Park *p253*
Ningaloo Reef Retreat, T9949 1776, operates a bus service between Exmouth and Turquoise Bay, with stops including the Sea Breeze Resort, Lighthouse Caravan Park, Tantabiddi and Milyering. The outward service leaves the main shopping area at 0850, arriving Turquoise Bay at 1025 ($22 return). The return service leaves the bay at 1445. Services daily from Apr-Oct, otherwise Mon-Tue and Fri-Sat. Day passengers to Turquoise Bay can borrow a snorkel set for free.

⊖ Transport

Carnarvon *p248, map p249*
Air
There are regular **Skywest** services to **Perth**. The airport is a 10-min walk from town or a cheap taxi ride, and there are 2 hire car agencies out there: **Avis**, T9941 1357, and **Budget**, T9941 2155.

Bus
Local A bus, T9941 8336, operates from Alexandra St on Mon, Wed and Fri. Services include an 0930 run to Babbage Island and the jetty, returning 1145, and a 1030 bus to Westboy Plantation, returning 1415. During the winter season a steam train occasionally trundles from the island side of the pedestrian bridge opposite the Gascoyne pub, over Babbage Island to the jetty. Call T9941 4309 for operating days. If the train isn't operating, the same route can be traversed on foot (about 6 km return).

Long distance Greyhound/McCafferty's northbound services leave the civic centre at 2255 daily (**Coral Bay** and **Broome**). **Perth** buses depart 0615 daily.

Car
Servicing from **Carnarvon Motor Wreckers**, Campbell Way, T9941 1621.

Taxi
Call T131008.

Kennedy Ranges *p250*
Just north of the main Carnarvon T-Junction is an unsealed right turn onto Gascoyne Junction Road. This becomes sealed for a fair way, before becoming unsealed again round about the turn-off for Rocky Pool, 38 km from the highway. This permanent waterhole in the Gascoyne River is a popular camping spot in winter and there is a toilet close by. Gascoyne Junction is a tiny, dusty community another 130 km on with a hotel and expensive, but very handy fuel. Turn left at the crossroads for the Kennedy Range, straight on for Bidgemia Station.

Coral Bay *p252*
Air
A shuttle bus to Coral Bay, T9942 5955, meets every **Skywest** flight into Exmouth's Learmonth Airport ($65) if booked in advance, though its about $20 cheaper to catch the coach to Exmouth then the scheduled buses back down.

Bus
Greyhound/McCafferty's northbound services leave the Ningaloo Club for Exmouth at 1400 Mon, Thu and Sat. **Carnarvon** and **Perth** buses depart 1400 Mon, Thu and Sat (mid-west coastal route), daily at 0305.

Exmouth *p252, map p253*
Air
35 km south of Exmouth, a shuttle, T9949 1101, meets each of the daily **Skywest** flights on request. **Allen's**, **Budget** and **Avis** hire

cars. **Skywest** has daily flights to **Perth**.

Bus
Greyhound/McCafferty's buses depart southbound 1445 Mon, Thu and Sat (mid-west coastal route). If heading to **Broome** and **Katherine** you will need to catch the shuttle service, T9949 1101, that leaves daily at 2255. This connects with th eastbound GX620 service at the Giralia turn-off (1-hr wait), and also with the daily southbound GX850 service.

Car
Car hire from both **Allen's**, T9949 2403, and also from **Exmouth Cape Tourist Village**. Car servicing can be had from **Exmouth Automotive & Boating**, Griffiths Way, T9949 2795.

Taxi
Call T0409 994933.

🛈 Directory

Carnarvon *p248, map p249*
Banks Major banks and ATMs on Robinson St. **Chemist** Amcal, Boulevard Centre, T9941 1547. 0830 Mon-Sat, 0900 Sun, closing 1800 Mon-Fri, 1300 Sat-Sun. **Hospital** Carnarvon Regional, Cleaver St, T9941 1555. **Internet** At the Library, Stuart St, 0900-1730 Mon-Wed, Fri, 1300-2000 Thu and 0900-1200 Sat. **Police** Robinson St, T9941 1444. **Post** Camel Lane.

Exmouth *p252, map p253*
Banks One bank branch, plus ATMs in the 2 supermarkets (open daily). **Chemist** Exmouth Pharmacy, main shopping area, T9949 1140. Open from 0900 Mon-Sat, closing 1730 Mon-Fri, 1230 Sat. **Hospital** Lyon St, T9949 1011. **Internet** Cheapest at **Ningaloo Blue**, corner of Kennedy and Thew sts. Open daily 1000-1900. **Police** Riggs St, T9949 2444. **Post** On Maidstone Cres. **Useful contacts** CALM, 22 Nimitz St, T9949 1676. Open Mon-Fri 0800-1700. Brochures and park advice.

The Pilbara

Footprint features

Introduction

The Pilbara has iron in its ancient dark-red stone and its very soul. In fact it contains so much iron that some rocks give a dull ring when you tap them, and it is this mineral that the region is primarily known for. Almost half of Australia's mineral wealth is mined and exported from the region and almost every town has been created by mining companies in the last few decades.

Most of the Pilbara's population lives on the coast in the industrial ports of Dampier and Port Hedland or residential suburbs such as Karratha, Wickham and South Hedland, but the most striking and distinctive landscapes of the Pilbara are found inland. It is a region of stark beauty and grandeur where just two colours dominate – red and gold. Stony, rounded ranges extend in every direction, sitting like pincushions across the landscape, covered as they are in spinifex grass and bleached to a mellow gold. This scenery is seen at its best in one of Australia's finest national parks, Karijini. Here, deep, narrow gorges have been carved into the Hamersley Range to create an oasis of rock pools and waterfalls, some reached only by fantastic nerve-jangling adventure routes. Millstream-Chichester National Park is another area of rugged landscape relieved by water and has idyllic, palm-lined campsites by spring-fed pools. It's not all roses though; the locals also have to take the Pilbara's isolation, cyclones, and unrelenting heat in their stride. Try to visit in winter to avoid the last two.

The Pilbara

✥ Don't miss...

1 **Karratha** Discover some of Pilbara's unique original rock engravings, page 267.

2 **Cossack** Stay overnight at this virtually deserted but charming coastal town, page 268.

3 **Cemetery Beach** Witness one of the wonders of the wild; turtles laying eggs or eggs hatching, page 270.

4 **Port Hedland** Experience industry where everything is done on a big scale: take a cruise around the harbour and see gigantic ore ships up close and tour around one of the huge coastal industrial sites, page 275.

5 **Millstream-Chichester National Park** Take the plunge and cool off in the freshwater pools and then climb to the top of Mount Herbert to watch the sunset, page 276.

6 **Karijini National Park** Climb Mount Bruce and explore the gorges, page 278.

Pilbara coast

The tidal flats and mangrove swamps of this section of the West Australian coast wouldn't win any beauty contests, but the coastal towns of the Pilbara are impressive in their own way. Forty percent of Australia's mineral wealth is exported from these towns and the scale of operations required is staggering. Much can be seen from viewing platforms or on mine-site tours. The services provided for workers are excellent, and useful for travellers so these towns are comfortable places to rest and replenish supplies. The offshore island groups, the Mackerel and Montebello Islands, and the Dampier Archipelago, offer excellent fishing, diving and snorkelling in clear turquoise water. They're not easy to get to, but a trip out can be quite an experience for those who make the effort. ➤➤ *For Sleeping, Eating and other listings, see pages 272-276.*

Onslow and around

One of Western Australia's most isolated coastal towns, tiny Onslow is a favoured spot for recreational fishing and gets very busy in winter. Other visitors are attracted by the opportunity to live for a while on a true desert island as there are a few off the coast on which the enterprising locals have built accommodation.

Onslow and Old Onslow → *Colour map 5, grid A2. Population: 800. 140 from Nanutarra roadhouse, 310 km from Karratha.*

The town's few attractions include a folksey museum (part of the VIC), the 'sunset' beach, 2 km north, which is also the site of a salt loading jetty, surprisingly attractive at night, and the abandoned remains of **Old Onslow**, a 50-km 4WD excursion off the main road. Old Onslow was a pearling port dating from 1863, but the town site was moved in 1925 and many buildings relocated. Only the crumbling courthouse and gaol buildings survive at the original site. Services include a post office, supermarket (closed Sunday afternoon) and fuel. The **VIC** ⓘ *Second St, T9184 6644, Mon-Sat 0900-1200 and 1300-1600, museum $2.*

Mackerel and Montebello islands

These island groups are more or less due north of Onslow at a distance of 20 km and 110 km respectively. Both are surrounded by rich and pristine coral reefs, providing spectacular opportunities for fishing, snorkelling and diving. Whales, dolphins and turtles are often see in these remote waters. The Montebellos were used by the British government for nuclear weapon tests in 1952 and 1956. Some low-level radiation exists but the islands are considered perfectly safe. There are currently three options for staying on or near the islands – including one where you get a whole island to yourself! For fishing and sightseeing day charters out to the Montebello islands, see page 274.

Fortescue roadhouse → *Colour map 5, grid A2.*

Alongside the wide Fortescue River the **Fortescue Roadhouse and Tavern** ⓘ *T9184 5126*, is the only stop on a long and lonely stretch of highway. It has cheap dongas and campsites, and serves fuel and snacks from 0630-2030. The bar is open until midnight. Fuel is considerably cheaper than at Nanutarra (160 km away), and usually on a par with Karratha (110 km).

Karratha and Dampier → *Colour map 5, grid A2. Populations: Karratha 10,000, Dampier 1,400. Karratha 635 km from Carnarvon, 245 km from Port Hedland.*

The industrial towns of Karratha and Dampier, 20 km apart, were created in the late 1960s to service the mining of Pilbara iron ore, salt and natural gas and oil. Dampier was established first by the mining company Hamersley Iron and although it remains a major industrial port its residential space was quickly outgrown and Karratha was chosen as a better place for a regional capital. Karratha is now a thriving mining and administrative centre between the tidal flats of Nickol Bay and the low dark red Karratha Hills. There is little to interest visitors in Karratha itself, except the large air-conditioned shopping mall, **Karratha City**, which has the interesting Pilbara Fine Art Gallery. Karratha is a useful base, however, for trips to the Millstream-Chichester and Karijini national parks, and the islands of the Dampier Archipelago just offshore. There are also ancient aboriginal rock carvings to see in the Karratha Hills and on the Burrup Peninsula, where you can also take in the mind-boggling scale of Dampier's port facilites and natural gas plant.

Sights

The Aboriginal Jaburara people, who were custodians of the land from the Burrup Peninsula to an area west of Wickham at the time of European settlement, produced thousands of **rock engravings** in the area, thought to be about 6,000 years old and now the only remaining trace of the people and their culture. The **Jaburara** ('Yabura') **Heritage Trail** has been developed in the hills behind the VIC and this is a very accessible place to see some of the engravings. The walk is 3.5 km one way and very hot and exposed so try to do it before 0800 or after 1600. From the car park by the water tanks, you can find engravings within 500 m but the best are

A brochure on the Jaburara Heritage Trail available from the VIC ($2).

halfway along at the **Rotary Lookout**. If you can't arrange a pick-up at the far end of the trail, you won't miss much by just reaching this lookout and then retracing your steps to the VIC. The engravings are very faint and not signposted so you will have to look carefully for figures such as fish and kangaroos on large rock faces.

The other main sights in these towns are not exactly traditional. The giant industrial installations of Dampier, the **Hamersley Iron Port Facility** and **Dampier Salt Field**, can be visited on tours, and the **North-West Shelf Gas Project** has a lookout and interesting visitor centre ① *1000-1600 Apr-Oct, 1000-1300 Nov-Mar*, with lots of information and cool models. The Project is the biggest of its kind in the country and it is worth the drive out to see it if you're in the vicinity. It's halfway up the **Burrup Peninsula** (signposted 'North-West Shelf Gas Project'), a range of red shattered hills extending out into the Indian Ocean, and marks the end of the sealed road. There are some great beaches further up but

Karratha

Sleeping	Karratha
Caravan Parks 5	Caravan Park 4
Karratha Apartments 3	Karratha
Karratha Backpackers 1	International 2

The Pilbara Pilbara coast

this is 4WD territory only. Over 10,000 rock engravings still exist on the Burrup Peninsula, but few are easily found. The best collection is in the evocative **Deep Gorge**, reached via a short, rough unsealed track off the road to **Hearson's Cove**, a fairly average beach and not good at low tide. The right turn to the gorge is just before the sealed road ends.

There are 42 low rocky islands in the **Dampier Archipelago**, about 20 km west of Karratha, and a wonderfully rich marine life. Turtles nest on the beaches and whales, dolphins and dugongs inhabit island waters. Fringing coral reefs provide great diving and much of it has hardly been explored. CALM have estimated that there are 600 species of fish in the archipelago and naturally this is a popular local fishing ground. There are current plans to create a marine conservation reserve for the area from the Dampier Archipelago to Cape Preston but the state government is yet to make a decision on the proposal. A shipping channel has been included in the proposal but it is thought that locals may oppose any limits on fishing in the archipelago. For fishing and diving charters out to the islands see Activities and tours.

The cheapest fuel after Karratha is at Port Hedland.

The **VIC** ① *Karratha Rd, T9144 4600, info@tourist.karratha.com, Mon-Fri 0830-1700, Sat-Sun 0900-1600 (Apr-Nov), Mon-Fri 0900-1700, Sat 0900-1200 (Dec-Mar)*, is very well organized and helpful, and is found just by the main junction into town. If coming from the west take the second left-hand turn off the main highway signposted Karratha.

Roebourne and around

European settlement of the Pilbara was first established in this area and the sleepy remnants of the 19th century can still be found in Cossack and Roebourne. Cossack is not even a town anymore; just a charming group of old buildings maintained by caretakers that make an unusual and peaceful overnight or lunch stop. Many of Roebourne's grand buildings are still used for their original purpose, such as the police station, Holy Trinity Church and the post office, but aside from these the town lacks any attraction. The largest town is Wickham, in the centre of the peninsula, a modern town built to house iron-ore workers for the nearby loading facility. At the end of the peninsula is the laid-back seaside village of Point Samson where life revolves around fish, fishing and fish and chips.

Roebourne → *Colour map 5, grid A3. Population: 1,000. 40 km from Karratha, 205 km from Port Hedland.*

The original regional capital when the first pastoral leases were granted in the 1860s, Roebourne has declined to a small scruffy junction town straddling the main highway. Some impressive colonial buildings survive, notably the gaol which is now a **museum** and the area's **VIC** ① *T9182 1060, roebourne_tourist@kisser.net.au, Mon-Fri 0900-1700, Sat-Sun 0900-1600 (May-Oct); Mon-Fri 0900-1500, Sat 0900-1200 (Nov-Apr), museum entry by gold coin donation*. The gaol is notable for an unusual hexagonal design, the work of innovative government architect George Temple Poole, who also designed the bond store in Cossack and other interesting buildings in York, Albany and Perth. The gaol holds a small collection of historical photographs and prison memorabilia and sells local arts and crafts.

Cossack → *Colour map 5, grid A3. 12 km from Roebourne.*

Once a thriving port servicing Roebourne and the surrounding pastoral stations, Cossack declined dramatically in the early 1900s and now only a handful of colonial government buildings remain. These are all magnificently solid buildings of the 1890s, made from the local bluestone, that have survived years of cyclones to give

Cossack an air of faded dignity. The settlement is part-way along a rocky promontory
that protrudes east through sand-flats and mangrove swamps, and it's well worth
driving or walking the 2 km out to the lookout at the far end. Since the 1980s the
remaining buildings have been gradually restored and have now been put to use. The
old courthouse is now a **museum** ① *0900-1700, gold coin donation*, with an
interesting collection of local memorabilia and photographs. Other buildings are now
an aboriginal **art workshop** and a **gallery**. The impressive bond store opens as a **café**,
also the location for the Cossack Art Award, an annual exhibition of more than 200
works held in August. The police quarters have been converted into the peaceful
Cossack Backpackers. This is a great place to relax as there's little to do but wander
the museum, watch the tides change from the jetty, or go swimming and fishing.

Wickham → *Colour map 5, grid A3. Population: 1,600. 12 km from Roebourne, 5 km from Cossack.*

A service town for the local **Robe** iron-ore loading facility, Wickham has nothing to
offer visitors except a good supermarket, an ATM and the Red Rock café. A private
company road leads out to Cape Lambert where Robe has built one of the largest
piers in Australia, visible from Point Samson. Robe run tours ① *T9182 1060, free,
departs the Robe visitor centre at 1030 Mon-Wed and Fri (2 hrs) from May-Oct*, around
the peninsula (including Cossack) and out to their modern port facilities.

Point Samson → *Colour map 5, grid A3. Population: 200. 20 km from Roebourne.*

This small community on the eastern edge of the peninsula is a commercial fishing
port and mellow seaside home for those working in other parts of the region. It
attracts many recreational fishermen and is well known for great fish and chips at
Moby's Kitchen. The sandy beaches of Honeymoon Cove, Back Beach and Main
Beach are good for swimming but Point Samson has a tidal range of about 5 m and
you can only swim at high tide. At low tide you can snorkel at Honeymoon Cove on
coral reef 20 m from shore or explore the rock pools at the other beaches. There are no
hire facilities so bring your own snorkel gear and make sure you wear shoes on the
rocks as stone fish and other nasties are found on the Pilbara coast. To head out into
deeper water, charters are available

Roebourne to Port Hedland

The only stop on this route is the **C-E-F Whim Creek Hotel** ① *T9176 4914*, a great old
two-storey pub of corrugated iron, with loads of atmosphere. It dates back to the
1870s when **Whim Creek** was a copper mining town but nothing else but ruins survive
from that time. The pub can boast a warm welcome, excellent food, a shady beer
garden and even has orphaned kangaroos wandering about. Meals of burgers, steak
and fish served Tuesday-Saturday 0730-1430, 1800-2000, Sunday 0730-1500; they
include the 'Barra Burger', a towering mouthful of barramundi and bun. Hotel rooms
have air-conditioning, TV and fridge and there are also cheap backpacker rooms
(without air-conditioning so only bearable May-September). Beyond the hotel the
scenery becomes very dull.

Port Hedland → *Colour map 5, grid A3. Population: 12,900. 265 km from Auski Village (Karijini), 610 km from Broome.*

Named for its discoverer in 1863, Port Hedland was soon pressed into service as a
port servicing the local pastoral and small-scale mining industries, while also
developing its own pearling fleet. It remained a relatively small town until 1965 when
it was earmarked as a major terminal for the export of the considerable tonnage of
ores that was starting to flood out of the Pilbara. Today several 300-m long ore carriers
visit the port every day, and watching them creep in and out of the harbour is a

favourite pastime for locals and visitors alike (a notice board outside the VIC advises their movements and size). Port Hedland is dominated by huge stockpiles of ore, heavy industry and loading facilities. Some of these can actually prove quite fascinating sights, however, and Port Hedland also makes a very good base for taking a tour into the **Karijini National Park**, 250 km to the south. There is certainly enough to fill a day or two while waiting for or recovering from a bush trip. Its sister town, South Hedland, 20 km inland, was established as a dormitory town for the burgeoning industry and is now several times bigger than Port Hedland itself.

Sights

Dalgety House ① *Anderson St, Mon-Fri 1000-1400, $3, children and concessions $2*, is the restored former manager's residence of Dalgety & Co, the company that for generations handled much of the importation of the area's supplies and the export of commodities such as wool. It is now a museum cleverly portraying the town's history prior to the advent of large-scale mining. Behind the VIC is an **Observation Tower** ① *open as VIC, $2.50*, with a good view over the town and port. Best ascended after the town tour. Enclosed shoes must be worn. The **Courthouse Arts Centre and Gallery** ① *Edgar St, Mon-Fri 0900-1700*, exhibits usually good quality local art and craft. **The Rock Shed** ① *T9173 3375, Mon-Fri 0900-1700, Sat 0900-1300*, takes many of the ancient, richly coloured rocks of the Pilbara and cuts and shapes them into display pieces, clock mounts and wine racks. They're not cheap, but a visit includes a short, informal but informative tour of the shop and processing area. Some of the rocks on display (and for sale, though not for export) are fossilized 3.5 billion year-old stromatolites. **Cemetery Beach**, opposite the Mercure, is the scene of turtle nesting and hatching from November-March, a must-see if you're in the vicinity. Activity coincides with high tide, contact the VIC for guidance on seeing the turtles. Adjacent to the Shell station on Wilson Street, **Don Rhodes Open-air Museum**, is a simple collection of vehicles, including giant diesel train engines, used in various local mining operations over the last few decades. Worth stopping by on the way past. Almost opposite the museum, abutting the railway line, is the unlikely site of some beautiful **Aboriginal rock engravings**. The site is fenced off but a key is available from the Centre of Aboriginal Affairs in South Hedland. Contact the VIC for advice on how to go about borrowing it. Both the **Royal Flying Doctor Service** ① *Mon-Fri 0900-1400*, and **School of the Air** are based at the airport and visitors are welcome. Contact the VIC to find out the best visiting times for the school.

The VIC ① *Wedge St, T9173 1711, www.porthedlandtouristbureau.com, Mon-Fri 0830-1700, Sat 0830-1600 Jun-Oct, 0830-1300 Nov-May, Sun 1200-1600 Jun-Oct*.

> ✦ *Free heritage trail walk/drive map available at VIC.*

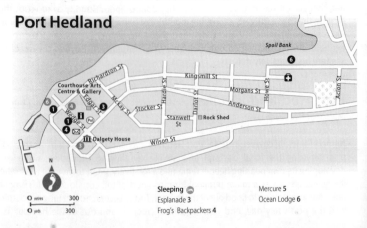

Port Hedland

Sleeping 🛏
Esplanade **3**
Frog's Backpackers **4**

Mercure **5**
Ocean Lodge **6**

66 99 There are sections where the vegetation struggles to get above knee-high, and the endless flat vista can be quite mesmerizing...

Port Hedland to Broome

This is one of the most tedious stretches of road in WA, particularly the last 300 km or so. There are sections where the vegetation struggles to get above knee-high, and the endless flat vista can be quite mesmerizing. Take plenty of water, even if you don't plan on any stops, and allow a full day.

Fuel around $0.10 more expensive than Port Hedland and Broome along this stretch.

The first roadhouse, **D Pardoo** ① *T9176 4916, 150 km from Port Hedand*, has air-conditioned singles and doubles in the usual dongas, is open for fuel 0600-2200, has a licensed bar, a small range of supplies and serves meals to 2000. Showers for non-residents are $2.50, and drinking water is also available (20 litres maximum). The roadhouse is close to the junction with two unsealed roads. To the north is the 14-km track to the wide inlet of **Cape Keraudren**, an exposed camping area very popular in winter with fishing families. Facilities are limited to drop toilets, camping is $5 per night. The unsealed road heading south winds its way to **Marble Bar** via Shay Gap, half the distance of the 300-km sealed route for those travelling down from Broome. If you do choose this way ask the roadhouse for directions and phone the Marble Bar police or your accommodation to let them know you're heading that way.

The next place of interest on the road is **Eighty Mile Beach**, 10 unsealed km off the highway and 105 km from Pardoo. The beach stretches as far as the eye can see in either direction and slopes gently down to the water, a favoured fishing spot though not recommended for a swim. One of the beach's chief claims to fame is the number and variety of shells that get washed up, and many collectors will head down at low tide for the pick of the day's offerings. Adjacent to the beach is the Eighty Mile Beach Caravan Park.

The **C-E Sandfire roadhouse** ① *T9176 5944*, 140 km from Pardoo, is the last before the junction with Broome Road, 290 km up the track, so make sure you have enough fuel. Accommodation in en suite, air-conditioned motel units and much simpler dongas. Fuel and meals 0600-2200. The small bar is definitely worth a look in.

The Pilbara Pilbara coast

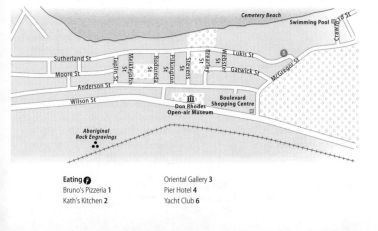

Eating ⓔ
Bruno's Pizzeria **1**
Kath's Kitchen **2**

Oriental Gallery **3**
Pier Hotel **4**
Yacht Club **6**

● Sleeping

Onslow and Old Onslow *p266*

There are 2 motels and a couple of caravan parks in Onslow.

B Mackerel Motel, Second Av, T9184 6586. Top of the range with some pleasant foreshore units, continental breakfast included.

C Sun Chalets, Second Av, T9184 6058. Has a few well presented motel units with ocean views, several shabbier self-contained chalets and a swimming pool.

D-E Ocean View, at the north end of the main street, T9184 6053, is the principal caravan park, has a/c cabins and on-site vans.

Mackerel and Montebello islands *p266*

To stay on either of two the islands below contact Mackerel Islands, T9184 6444, www.mackerelislands.com.au.

Direction Island, another part of the group, has a single A-frame cabin, sleeping up to 8, as its only man-made structure! This can be hired (sans food) for $1,400-2,000 depending on season.

Thevenard Island, part of the Mackerels, has a 30-room 'village' with bar, restaurant etc and a few well-appointed self-contained cabins, sleeping up to 10 people each. Cabin prices start at $2,000 for a couple for a week, dropping by about 20 per cent per person if you can get a large group together. The village is a cheaper option.

A MonteBello Island Safaris, T9314 2034, www.montebello.com.au. Takes parties of up to 16 out to their houseboat, moored permanently in a sheltered cove of **Hermite Island**, 1 of the 100 or so islands that make up the Montebello group. Price (high) includes all food and some activities.

Karratha and Dampier *p267, map p267*

There are a handful of high-standard motels in both Karratha and Dampier (generally cheaper in the latter) catering for the large business market. Karratha has 3 caravan parks, none close to the town centre, and Dampier has a sites-only park.

L Karratha International, corner of Hillview and Millpoint rds, Karratha,

T9185 3111, www.kih.com. au. Sets the benchmark for the region with excellent rooms and facilities.

B Karratha Apartments, Galbraith Rd, 2 km from Karratha, T9143 9222, www.karratha apartments.com.au. Has 10 fully self-contained, spacious chalets grouped around a pleasant pool and BBQ area.

C Peninsula Palms, The Esplanade, Dampier, T9183 1888. The best balance between price and quality can be found here. It also has male-only budget 'singles', a/c but not en suite.

D-E Karratha Backpackers, 110 Wellard Way, Karratha, T9144 4904, www.kisser.net. au/backpackers. A cheerful hostel, which is a brick ex-motel with 30-odd beds in 10 rooms, including 1 double. Courtyard BBQ, games room. Rooms a/c, but coin-operated ($1 per hr).

Karratha Caravan Park, near the industrial estate off Karratha Rd, Karratha, T9185 1012. Has the cheapest on-site vans and cabins.

Pilbara Big 4 Holiday Park, Rosemary Rd, Karratha, T9185 1855, is the next closest and a smarter alternative. Lots of spacious cabins (**C**) and en-suite vans (**D**), pool and shop with takeaways.

Roebourne *p268*

A relatively cheap **caravan park**, T9182 1063, lies on the far side of the river from the town. It has sites, on-site vans and a pool.

Cossack *p268*

E Cossack Backpackers, T9182 1190. The police quarters here have been converted into this peaceful peaceful, which has 1 large dorm and 3 doubles, and a shady veranda and garden (free pick-ups from Roebourne). Thick walls, high ceilings and fans ensure the lack of a/c is rarely a hardship.

Point Samson *p269*

L-A Point Samson Lodge, T9187 1052, www.pointsamson.com. Has 12 pricey but very comfortable self-contained garden chalets, each sleeping up to 4. It also has an expensive alfresco café, **Tata's**, open to

● *For an explanation of sleeping and eating price codes used in this guide, see inside the*
● *front cover. Other relevant information is found in Essentials, see pages 40-46.*

non-residents daily for dinner, 1830-2100. Asian-influenced seafood, curries and soups are the specialities.

C **Amani Cottage**, McLeod St, T9187 1085. One of a couple of self-contained cottages available in the town, and very good value.

Samson Beach General Store and Caravan Park, T9187 1414. Has a good spot next to the pub, overlooking the beach, with mostly sites and a couple of on-site vans. The place seems to be almost constantly full so book ahead, particularly in winter.

Port Hedland *p269, map 270*
Contact the VIC for additional options in South Hedland.

A **Mercure**, Lukis St, T9173 1511, www.accor hotels.com/mercure_inn_port_hedland. Has 1 of the best spots on the northern foreshore. It's well-maintained, has a pool and a patio dining area overlooking the sea. Mid-range meals are generally the best in town, available 0600-0900, 1200-1400 and 1800-2100. Of the 60 rooms it's the slightly smaller older ones that have ocean-view balconies.

C-E **Esplanade Hotel**, the Esplanade, T9173 1798. A large traditional pub with a range of simple upstairs a/c rooms plus a kitchenette, and several motel rooms. The large courtyard bar has karaoke Fri-Sat, regular live bands and a rare 2-up session on late Sun afternoons. Cheap counter meals 0600-0730, 1130-1330 and 1800-2000 when the mid-range dining room is also open.

D **Ocean Lodge**, behind Bruno's, Richardson St, T9173 2635. Has the best value motel-style a/c en-suite rooms in town. Nothing fancy, but clean, comfortable and well-equipped.

D-E **Frog's Backpackers**, Richardson St, T9173 3282, www.frogsbackpackers.com.au. Small and friendly.

D-E **Oasis Backpackers and Budget Motel**, 2 Turner River Dr, T9172 5666, www.dingo trek.com.au. Further afield in South Hedland, but well worth considering as it runs regular shuttles to Port Hedland. The owners run the excellent **Dingo's Treks** tours to the Karijini. The closest **caravan park** to the centre, 6 km away, is at Cooke Point, T9173 1271.

Port Hedland to Broome *p271*
B-C **Eighty Mile Beach Caravan Park**, T9176 5941. Adjacent to Eighty Mile Beach, has a few a/c cabins and a cottage, several dongas

and hundreds of shady camping sites. Facilities are surprisingly good, including a small store, takeaway and a renowned bakery with superb bread and pastries. Book well ahead for the Jun-Sep peak season.

● Eating

Onslow and Old Onslow *p266*
The below are situated in Onslow.
♥ **Nikki's**, First Av, T9184 6121. The town's only restaurant and has a wide deck overlooking the ocean. The mid-range menu is understandably brief, but a high standard is thereby maintained, and the seafood is very good. Licensed, Tue-Sun 1830-2000.

♥ **Coastal Café**, back on the main street, a standard takeaway with a few tables. Breakfasts from 0730 Mon-Sat, 0830 Sun, snacks and takeaways to 2000.

♥ **Fish Shack**, a few kilometres east, by Beadon Creek wharf. A fish and chip take-away and casual BYO café, Fri-Sun 1730-2030.

Karratha and Dampier *p267, map p267*
A couple of the motels in Karratha have bistros. There are licensed Chinese restaurants in both Dampier and Karratha. Karratha has the better cafés.

♥♥♥ **Etcetera**, Karratha, T9185 3111, at the **Karratha International**. The area's undisputed best bistro, a contemporary open space overlooking the hotel's central pool courtyard. An extensive menu of rich and sophisticated modern food compliments the excellent service. Meals 0600-0930, 1200-1400 and 1800-2100.

RR-R **Gecko's**, also situated in Karratha International, is the best of Karratha's watering holes. Unpretentious, it also serves good quality counter meals from 1130-2100 Mon-Sat and 1200-2000 Sun.

♥♥ **Barnacle Bob's**, The Esplanade, Dampier, T9183 1053. An alfresco fish restaurant that overlooks the Dampier Yacht Club and harbour. Licensed, Sat-Sun 1200-1400 and Tue-Sun 1700-210.

♥ **Dampier Chinese Restaurant**, opposite the shopping centre, Dampier, T9183 1555. 1130-1330 Mon-Fri and 1700-2100 daily.

Café
Boomerang, in Karratha City. Has internet access, open daytime only.

The impressive bond store opens as a café between 1000-1400, daily from May-Oct, otherwise at weekends. Snacks, drinks and wonderful scones.

Wickham *p269*
Red Rock is a friendly little café serving cheap pizzas, pasta, salads, curries and seafood. Open 1700-2200 Wed-Sun.

Point Samson *p269*
Moby's Kitchen, T9187 1435. The town is best known for this place. It's a legendary spot for the freshest, tastiest fish and chips imaginable, served at outdoor wooden benches overlooking the sea. BYO but you can buy drinks upstairs. Open Mon-Fri 1100-1400, 1700-2030, Sat-Sun 1100-2030. Recommended.
Point Samson Lodge, T9187 1052. Has an expensive alfresco café, **Tata's**, open to non-residents daily for dinner, 1830-2100. Asian-influenced seafood, curries and soups are the specialities.
Samson Beach Tavern, T9187 1503. Worth going out of your way for the pub upstairs. Relaxed, friendly veranda bar that appeals to both locals and visitors alike. Meals Mon-Fri 1200-1430, 1800-2100 , Sat-Sun 1200-2100.

Port Hedland *p269, map 270*
Eating out in Port Hedland, even at the **Mercure**, falls quite a way short of what most folks would call fine dining, but it is generally good quality.
♦♦ **Bruno's Pizzeria**, Richardson St, T9173 2047. A friendly Italian restaurant serving good standard pizzas, pastas and grills. Licensed, it has a main indoor dining room and a few outside 'smoking' tables. Open 1730-0200, also takeaways.
♦ **Kath's Kitchen**, in Wedge St. A simple, unpretentious café and takeaway, open daily from 0600-1900.
♦ **Oriental Galley**, Edgar St, T9173 1272. A traditional Chinese, open for cheap lunch specials 1130-1330 Mon, Wed, Fri, and 1700-2130 daily.
♦ **Pier Hotel**, the Esplanade. Has a similar courtyard bar to the Esplanade but the nightly entertainment is considerably more 'exotic'. The dancing doesn't start before 2030, however, and the cheap counter

snacks and grills are definitely not to be sniffed at. Daily 1200-1400, 1800-2030. Note there is also a dance act on Fri lunchtime.
♦ **Yacht Club**, Fri is the popular fish and chip night.

▲ Activities and tours

Karratha and Dampier *p267, map p267*
Boat hire
Pilbara Island Charters, Karratha, book at VIC. Inflatable dinghy $90 ½ day, $120 day.

Diving
Karratha Dive Centre, Warrambie Rd, Karratha, T9185 2299. Hires out full gear and organizes dive trips to the Dampier Archipelago and the Montebello Islands. Also snorkelling tours, minimum 6 people. Winter is the best time for visibility.

Fishing
Norkat, Karratha, T9144 4922. Fishing and general charters in the Dampier Archipelago and Montebello Islands on a 12-m catamaran from $165 day per person (minimum 12).
Oceanus Fishing Charters operates a large boat – up to 10 passengers – and charge $195 per day. See VIC for details.

Industry tours
Note that enclosed footwear should be worn on all tours.
Hamersley Iron Port Facility Tour takes visitors on a bus around the iron-ore stockpiles, ship loading, train facilities and a good lookout point ($11, 1½ hrs). Bookings at the Karratha VIC but the tour starts from Dampier. Weekdays at 0900 (Apr-Oct).
Nor-West Explorer Tours runs tours of Dampier Salt, following the process from sea water to shipping ($20, ½ day). Only a few days a week, bookings and times from VIC.

National parks
Snappy Gum Safaris, T9185 1278, www. snappygum.karratha.com. Runs a range of trips into Karijini and Millstream-Chichester during the cool season of May-Oct. Karijini lookouts and gorges 2 days $290; 3-day adventure tour $390; North West Explorer into both national parks (staying in Tom Price motel), 3 days $490. Day tours into

Millstream run all year round, $75 including lunch and park fees. See VIC for departure dates and more tours.

Rock art tours
Burrup Rock Art Tours specializes in 4-hr tours to view the carvings ($80). Book at leave from VIC.

Swimming
There's an excellent outdoor municipal pool with gardens and BBQs on Sharp Av, T9186 8527, Karratha. 0900 or earlier to 1700 or later. $2.80, children and concessions $1.70. **Karratha International** allow daytime customers at the pool-side bar to take a dip.

Point Samson *p269*
Phantom, T9187 1052, www.pointsamson. com. Is an unusual charter boat as it departs daily, 0800, and does not require minimum numbers (8 hrs, $240).

Port Hedland *p269, map 270*
Boat tours
Big Blue, Wedge St, T9173 3202, www. bigbluedive.com.au. Heads out most days during the winter months on a tour of the harbour (1 hr) where you'll get to see the massive ore carriers up close and may even see dugongs. Its sunset tours (2 hrs) go most of the year round. Other tours available as per demand.

Bus tours
The VIC organizes 3 different coach trips. **BHP** tours depart daily at 0930, taking in the impressive port loading facilities and stockpiles.
Boodarie Iron tours head out at 1300 Tue and Thu and include the launch-pad like Boodarie works plus a trip to the Royal Flying Doctor Service and Bureau of Meteorology in South Hedland.
Town tours (same price and duration) leave at 1300 every Mon, Wed and Fri, and stops include Dalgety House and Don Rhodes Open-air Museum.

Diving, fishing and whale watching
Big Blue boat is available for good value trips as per demand, check on current programme. It runs dives out to a few excellent coral reefs and a couple of local

wrecks, and also offer PADI courses. It heads out most days during the Jul-Oct season to see the humpback whales migrating past the coast (3 hrs).

National parks
Dingo's Treks, T9173 1000, www.dingotrek. com.au. Run by the entertaining Chris, heads into the national park every week for 3 days of adventure ($450). Bush camp with a bonfire just outside the park and the trip involves lots of walking and swimming, including sections of the 'Miracle Mile'. Everything is included in the price.

Swimming
None of the beaches is particularly inviting, and can be dangerous thanks to stone fish, octopus and even salties.
Gratwick Memorial Swimming Pool T9173 3562. Much more preferable, open-air, open every afternoon, Sep-Apr. Entry $3, concessions $2.

Waterskiing
North West Water Sports, T04-0100 1116. Take groups of 4-10 out for lessons.

⊖ Transport

Karratha and Dampier *p267, map p267*
Air
Karratha Airport, roughly between the two towns, is one of Australia's busiest domestic airports, handling about 500 people a day, mostly workers. Bar, café and all the major hire car companies have manned desks. A taxi to Karratha will be about $15. **Qantas** and **Skywest** have daily flights to **Perth**.

Bicycle
Bike hire **Bike Force**, Sharp Av, Karratha, T9185 4455.

Bus
The daily **McCafferty's/Greyhound** Perth to Darwin service leaves the Shell Service Station for **Port Hedland** and **Broome** (11 hrs) at 0815. The Perth-bound service departs 2050.

Car
Cheapest fuel in the region is generally at the Shell road house on the highway oppo-

site the airport. Car servicing at **North West Mechanical**, T9185 1930. Tyres and parts from **Opposite Lock/Tyre Power**, T9144 4222.

Taxi
Call T9185 4444.

Port Hedland *p269, map 270*
Air
Qantas flies daily to **Perth** and, at weekends, to **Karratha**.

Bus
Local Hedland Bus Lines, T9172, runs a number of services around Port and South Hedland. Its 501 bus between the two, stopping at the Boulevard Shopping Centre and South Hedland Caravan Park, runs 4-5 times a day, Mon-Fri.
Long distance The daily McCafferty's/Greyhound **Perth** to **Darwin** service leaves the VIC for **Broome** (7 hrs) and the Northern Territory at 1150. The Perth-bound service departs 1610.

Car/4WD
Car servicing at **Pilbara Auto and Marine**, Hardy St, T9173 1815. Pilbara 4X4 Recovery,

T0418 951804, is the local recovery expert outfit. It also hires out 'Pilbara Packs' consisting of all the essential extra vehicle kit you wish you had but couldn't afford.

Taxi
Call T9172 1010.

◐ Directory

Karratha and Dampier *p267, map p267*
Banks All the major banks, with ATMs, on Hedland Pl, Karratha town centre.
Chemist Karratha Pharmacy, Karratha City, T9185 1316. Open 0900-1730 Mon-Fri, to 2100 Thu, 0830-1700 Sat. **Hospital** Nickol Bay, Dampier Rd, Karratha, T9144 0330.
Internet At VIC or Boomerang café in the shopping centre. **Police** Welcome Rd, T9144 2233. **Post** Opposite Karratha City, off Welcome Rd.

Port Hedland *p269, map 270*
Banks Main banks and ATMs in Wedge St.
Hospital T9158 1666. **Internet** Access at the VIC. **Chemist** Soul Pattinson, Wedge St, T9173 1132. Mon-Fri 0800-1700, Sat 0800-1300. **Police** T9173 1444.
Post Wedge St.

Pilbara interior

Despite a couple of mining towns, Aboriginal communities and a handful of stations, inland Pilbara is one of the least populated but still accessible regions in the country. This glorious emptiness helps make exploring the low gold and blood-red ranges a real delight and adventure: it is quite possible to head along the unsealed roads from Karratha, through Millstream, Karijini and Marble Bar and back to the highway without seeing another vehicle. Care is required, however. The iron-rich stone fractures to create small sharp shards, and it is these that make up the surface of many of the region's unsealed roads. Punctures are the norm, not the exception, and you should expect at least one during an extended drive around the area. ▸▸ *For Sleeping, Eating and other listings, see pages 281-282.*

Millstream-Chichester National Park → *Colour map 5, grid A3.*
Python Pool 125 km from Karratha, 90 km from Roebourne.

① *For more information contact CALM, Karratha, T9143 1488, park fees $9 car, camping $10 for 2, water available but must be treated, phone at homestead.*
As you approach this national park from the north you pass through classic Pilbara landscape and begin to see the unusual grandeur and beauty of this region. Flat-topped ranges and hills the colour of dried blood are dotted with yellow

Ins and outs

All access roads to the national park are unsealed and although rocky are generally fine for 2WD, except after heavy rain. Ask for current conditions at the Karratha VIC. If travelling from Karratha there are two main routes. The shire road is 30 km east of Roebourne and leads to Python Pool but there is also a Hamersley Iron company road that runs direct from Karratha through the western end of the park, joining the shire road midway between Python Pool and Millstream. It continues south to Tom Price (185 km). A permit must be obtained to use this road, from the Karratha VIC or Shell garage at Tom Price. Company road conditions on T9143 6464. ▶▶ *See Karratha, page 274, for details of tours.*

No petrol is available between Karratha/ Roebourne and Tom Price/Auski so plan carefully and also take plenty of water.

Sights

The park itself has two distinct visitor areas. The northern end provides stunning views over the landscape described above, from **Mount Herbert**, just beyond **Python Pool**, a deep pool below a sheer rock wall. The view from Mount Herbert is best at sunset and Python Pool is wonderful at sunrise so it's a good place to spend a night, although the Snake Creek campground is stony and shadeless.

Once your vehicle has climbed past Mount Herbert, you'll reach a plateau and travel 60 km over fairly featureless country to the freshwater oasis of Millstream, 145 km from Karratha, 220 km from Auski Roadhouse, at the southern end of the park. Here there are permananent spring-fed pools in the Fortescue River, lined with palm trees, rushes and tall gums – idyllic swimming and camping spots. This area was under a pastoral lease from 1865 until the 1960s and the park visitor centre is situated in the old farm homestead. The centre is not staffed but has interesting displays on the history and environment of the park and a box to put your park fees in. Kangaroos often rest in the shade of the homestead grounds, where there is also a pretty picnic spot. **Deep Reach Pool** and **Crossing Pool** both have shady campsites with toilets, BBQs and ladders into the river if you feel like a swim (you will). Crossing Pool, on the northern bank, tends to be the quietest camping spot although both are busy in the winter high season. There are a few walks detailed in the free park brochure.

Tom Price → *Colour map 5, grid B3. Population: 3,900. 335 km from Nanutarra, 155 km from Auski roadhouse.*

Owned by Hamersley Iron, a subsidiary of one of the world's largest mining companies Rio Tinto, Tom Price is an attractive company town surrounded by the Hamersley Ranges. Brilliant green grass and palm trees have been cultivated which makes a change from the film of red dust that coats most mining towns. Although increasingly employees prefer to work on a fly-in fly-out basis from Perth, the company tries to make life as comfortable as possible for the young families of Tom Price. This is good news for travellers as the huge supermarket contains the kind of goodies you may have forgotten existed. There is also a drive-in cinema showing films at weekends.

Day tours operate out of Tom Price to **Karijini National Park** and there are regular tours to the Hamersley Iron open-cut mine. There are fantastic views of the area from **Mount Nameless**, actually called Jarndrunmunhna for countless years, accessible both by foot and 4WD from the road to the caravan park. The walking track from the caravan park to the summit (1,128 m) takes about two to three hours return (and if you park here you'll avoid the very rough unsealed 2-km access road to the trail car park).

Tom Price is the highest town in WA at 747 m above sea level so the ascent of Mount Nameless is not too arduous.

The VIC ① *Central Rd, T9188 1112, tptb@norcom.net.au, Mon-Fri 0830-1730, Sat-Sun 0900-1200 (May-Sep), Mon-Fri 0830-1430, Sat 0900-1200 (Oct-Apr).*

Karijini National Park → *Colour map 5, grid B3. Central gorges 80 km from Tom Price, 110 km from Auski roadhouse.*

Northern and central Australia contain so many impressive red-walled gorges that some visitors get gorge fatigue but Karijini's gorges are the dessert course you'll find you still have room for. The park contains extraordinary deep and narrow gorges full of waterfalls, idyllic swimming pools and challenging walks, yet it is hardly known, even within Australia. The park sits within the heart of one of the world's most ancient landscapes, the Hamersley Plateau, where creeks have carved 100-m deep chasms into layers of 2,500 million year old sedimentary rock. Unusually, you enter the park from the plateau and descend into the gorges which means there are excellent lookouts above each gorge. The most spectacular feature of the park can be seen from Oxers Lookout, where four gorges meet below the golden spinifex and crooked white snappy gum trees of the plateau.

Ins and outs

Getting there If travelling northeast along the coast, turn off at the Nanutarra Roadhouse to reach Tom Price, close to Karijini's western border. Another alternative is to continue north to Karratha and take the unsealed Hamersley Iron company road that runs direct from Karratha to Tom Price (185 km), passing through Millstream-Chichester National Park. A permit must be obtained to use this road, from the Karratha VIC or Shell garage at Tom Price. Company road conditions on T9143 6464. Note that no petrol is available on this route. If travelling southwest, take the Great Northern Highway south shortly after Port Hedland to Auski Roadhouse and turn right after 35 km onto Karijini Drive. If you're comfortable with unsealed roads a pretty alternative is through Marble Bar. McCafferty's/Greyhound's bus service from Perth to Port Hedland stops at Auski roadhouse at 0655 on Saturday, in time to be picked up for a Dingo's three-day tour (returning to Port Hedland). A tour is a good way to see Karijini, especially if you want some adventure, but choose your tour carefully, checking that the age and activity level will suit you. ▸▸ *See Tours, page 281, for further details.*

❖ All access is via unsealed roads and punctures are notoriously common.

Getting around Although this is the state's second largest park, all of the facilities and walks are found fairly close to each other in the northern section of the park, above Karijini Drive. Head first for the innovative visitor centre, built with curved walls of rusted iron that both mirror and disappear into its landscape. An interpretive display explains the history and geology of the park and the viewpoint of its Banyjima, Yinhawangka, and Kurrama traditional owners. Maps, drinks and souvenirs are available and there are toilets, showers and phones. The park is generally open all year round, although most pleasant April-September. Visitor centre open daily 0900-1600 (limited hrs in summer). Park fees $9 car (per visit), camping $10 site (per night). T9189 8121. Roads are unsealed and rocky (2WD but remote driving rules apply and punctures are common). The Nanutarra-Wittenoom Road north of Hamersley Gorge may be impassable from December-April.

The gorges

Walking and swimming are the main activities but Karijini is also known for some very exciting adventure trails. Because some gorges are as narrow as 1-2 m wide, or filled with water, you cannot walk between the gorge walls but have to clamber along the steep sides on narrow ledges of dark red ironstone, swimming and climbing through difficult sections. The hair-raising **'Miracle Mile'** contains the most challenging terrain and some sections are considered extremely dangerous. The routes beyond Kermits Pool in **Hancock Gorge** and Handrail Pool in **Weano Gorge** should only be attempted with a guide, but if you crave adrenaline this could be the most fun you have outdoors in Australia. There are easy walks but you will not be able to see the best of this awesome park unless you are reasonably fit and agile.

There are two main areas to visit in the park. **Dales Gorge** is 10 km east of the visitor centre, where you can walk up the gorge to a wide cascade, Fortescue Falls, and beyond the falls to Fern Pool, a lovely large swimming hole (1 km). Return to the top of the gorge by the same path or walk down the centre of the gorge and turn left at the end to join the trail to **Circular Pool**, a lush rock bowl dripping with ferns. At the point where you turn a steep path joins the carpark to the pool (800 m) so you don't need to retrace your steps. There is also an easy rim trail overlooking Dales Gorge and Circular Pool (2 km).

The other main area is 29 km west of the visitor centre, at the junction of **Weano, Joffre, Hancock** and **Red gorges**. There are several lookouts here, including Oxer Lookout, and trails into Joffre (3 km), Knox (2 km), Weano (1 km to Handrail Pool) and Hancock Gorges (1½ km to Kermits Pool). These are all enjoyable and involve some scrambling but the latter two offer a taste of Karijini adventure that most people can manage without a guide.

One of the prettiest gorges to visit is **Kalamina Gorge**. The turn-off is 19 km west of the visitor centre, and it is also one of the easiest to explore. A short, steep track leads to the base of the gorge and a permanent pool. If you turn right and walk for a short distance you'll reach a small picturesque waterfall, if you turn left there is a lovely and flat walk downstream to Rock Arch Pool (3 km return).

Hamersley Gorge is another delightful spot, although on the far western border 100 km from the visitor centre. This is a large, open gorge with dramatically folded rock walls in shades of purple, green and pink. Fortescue River flows through the gorge, creating beautiful pools and waterfalls. If you head upstream you'll pass a deep 'spa' pool, scoured out by boulders, on the way to the fern-lined Grotto (1 km, difficult). Finally, to get a birds-eye perspective on the whole landscape you can climb **Mount Bruce**, WA's second highest mountain at 1,235 m. This is the island peak visible from the western end of Karijini Drive and the track is a long but rewarding slog up the western face (9 km, six hours return).

Wittenoom → *Colour map 5, grid A3. 130 km from Tom Price, 42 km from Auski roadhouse.*

Just on the northern border of Karijini, Wittenoom is a former mining town that has almost ceased to exist. It is a strange and controversial place that is only kept going by its dozen or so determined residents who live among deserted streets and empty lots where the rest of the town's houses and businesses once stood. Wittenoom was created in the late 1930s for the mining of blue asbestos (crocidolite) in nearby Wittenoom Gorge and provided services for several thousand people until the mine closed in 1966 due to high production costs and lack of ore. Although most residents quickly left town, those who remained transformed Wittenoom into a service town for visitors to the Hamersley Ranges. Unfortunately during the 1970s it was revealed that former asbestos miners were developing a fatal carcinogenic lung disease called mesothelioma up to twenty or thirty years after coming into contact with asbestos. Town residents were also vulnerable as the streets and playing fields of Wittenoom had been laid with asbestos tailings. In 1979 the government decided to 'close' Wittenoom, compensating residents and demolishing buildings. However, some

The Pilbara Pilbara interior

residents refuse to leave and claim that there is now little or no risk to visitors of inhaling asbestos fibres – at least no more than standing in Trafalgar Square inhaling traffic fumes (brake pads are still made of asbestos). Veins of asbestos in ironstone are found throughout Karijini but are only a health risk when the fibres are disturbed and become airborne.

The main attraction of the town is the beautiful **Wittenoom Gorge**, with permanent rock pools and an extended track along the creek bed that joins up with Red Gorge in Karijini. A 10-km sealed road threads up the gorge from the town. The government has not yet carried out threats to cut off power and water but it has built Karijini Drive to bypass the town and the nearby Yampire Gorge road into the park is closed. Only two businesses survive in Wittenoom. The **Wittenoom Gem Shop** ① T9189 7096, www.holiday-wa.net/gemshop, has an interesting rock collection and also acts as a **VIC**.

The government does not recommend visits to the town or gorge but advises visitors in Wittenoom to take the following precautions; keep to main roads, keep car windows closed, keep away from asbestos tailings and do not camp outside designated areas. VICs will not generally provide any information on Wittenoom.

Marble Bar → Colour map 5, grid A4. Population: 350. 200 km from Port Hedland, 250 km from Auski roadhouse.

If you've travelled this far you'll know that Australians often take a perverse pleasure in their continent of extremes and proudly boast of its isolation, dangerous creatures or whatever else is big, bad and ugly. The people of the Pilbara can really win at this game, with their huge ships, trucks and trains, and those of Marble Bar are no exception. They gladly proclaim that they live in the hottest town in Australia, not exactly a strong selling point. In the summer of 1923-1924 there were 160 days over 38.7°C, but any typical summer could boast at least a few months of days sweltering in the high 30s. Despite this Marble Bar is actually quite an attractive, if tiny, outback town with a wide main street of corrugated-iron buildings. The town is surrounded by spectacular Pilbara scenery of low spinifex-covered ranges and dark red ironstone ridges.

Ins and outs
The main route to the town drops south of the Great Northern Highway 40 km east of Port Hedland and is presently sealed for the first 100 km but should be sealed all the way to Marble Bar (150 km) by the time you read this. If coming west from the Kimberley there is an unsealed alternative 50 km past Pardoo. Take this left-hand turn, then right over the railway line after a couple of kilometres. This scenic road joins with the Marble Bar Road after 75 km, 50 km from the town, saving about 70 km off the sealed route. Watch for slippery concrete beds on a couple of creek crossings. The unsealed Hillside Road links Marble Bar to the Great Northern Highway (155 km). This is a remote route, sometimes closed during the wet, but one of the most scenic in the Pilbara. Also unsealed, the Marble Bar Road to the south connects the town with Newman (300 km).

Sights
Marble Bar was founded in 1893 after discoveries of alluvial gold nearby and had a population of 5,000 at its peak. The fine stone government buildings (1896) at the end of the main street are an indication of the optimism of the time.

Just outside Marble Bar is the beautiful rock bar of jasper across the Coongan River that gives the town its name and **Chinamans Pool** nearby where you can swim. Samples of jasper cannot be taken from the Marble Bar but there is a quarry (signposted **Jasper Deposit**), 4 km from town on the Hillside Road where you can chip away. On the same road, 8 km from town, is the **Comet Gold Mine** ① *T9176 1015, 0900-1600, $2, tours 1000, 1400, $10 (wear closed shoes)*. This mine operated from 1936 until 1955, and now is run as an interesting historic site, mineral display and gem shop. There are some other attractive natural sights around Marble Bar only accessible to 4WD, such as **Coppins Gap** and **Glen Herring Gorge**. Ask for directions at the shire office. Marble Bar has no VIC but information can be obtained from the shire office in the main street.

● Sleeping

Tom Price *p277*
A Tom Price Hotel, Central Rd, T9189 1101. Has more expensive motel-style rooms.
B Karijini Lodge Hotel, Stadium Rd, T9189 1110. Has pretty standard rooms.
C-E Tom Price caravan park, 2 km from town, T9189 1515. Has self-contained A-frame units, 4-bed dorms in dongas, and a campers' kitchen, friendly.

Karijini National Park *p278*
Dales, 10 km east of the visitor centre, is the only place to camp. It has gas BBQs, picnic tables, bush toilets, stony ground and limited shade and has caravan sites (unpowered) that allows use of generators. Campfires are not permitted within the park.

Outside the park, the closest options are Tom Price and, out on the Great Northern Highway, **B-D Auski Roadhouse**, T9176 6988, 265 km from Port Hedland, 200 km from Newman. On the northeastern border of the park, the roadhouse is a coach stop and a useful meeting point for tours. It has 20 comfortable motel rooms, budget twins without en suite, and powered and unpowered sites. Snacks all days and meals served 1800-2030. There is also budget accommodation at **Wittenoom**, north of the park (see below), but this is about 130 km from the park entry point via the eastern or western routes and unusual conditions apply.

Wittenoom *p279*
C Wittenoom Guest House, Gregory St, T9189 7060. Has twin and dorm rooms with shared facilities, and camping sites.

Marble Bar *p280*
There are only 3 places to stay in Marble Bar, all along or just off the main street.
C Marble Bar Travellers Stop, T9176 1166.

A roadhouse with motel rooms.
C-D Ironclad, T9176 1066, is one of the town's landmarks and much smarter inside than the corrugated-iron exterior suggests. A pub, it also has motel and budget rooms. The caravan park, T9176 1067, has sites only.

● Eating

Tom Price *p277*
The town also has an assortment of take-aways plus Thai and Chinese restaurants.
♥♥ **Tom Price Hotel**, Central Rd, T9189 1101. Serves both counter and restaurant meals from 1200-1400 and 1800-2000.
♥ **Karijini Lodge Hotel**, Stadium Rd, T9189 1110. The town's better dining facilities.

Marble Bar *p280*
♥ **Ironclad**, T9176 1066. Pub, does counter meals 1200-1330, 1800-2000.
♥ **Marble Bar Travellers Stop**, T9176 1166. Has a reasonable restaurant.

▲ Activities and tours

Tom Price *p277*
Lestok Tours, T9189 2032, lestok@nor com.net.au. Operates coach tours of the Hamersley Iron Mine most days and up to 3 times a day (1½ hrs, $15, children $7.50). They also run a regular day trip into Karijini, departing at 0800 ($100, children $50).

Karijini National Park *p278*
Dingo's Treks runs excellent 3-day adventure tours out of Port Hedland (see page 275, can pick up from Auski) into Dales, Weano, Hancock and Hamersley Gorges. Dingo's may also be able to offer a 'tag- along' option if you have your own transport (recommended if you would like to tackle the more adventurous parts of Weano and Hancock).

282 **Snappy Gum Safaris** operates out of Karratha and cover both the mature and adventure markets.

⊖ Transport

Tom Price *p277*
Car servicing at **Shell**, Mine Rd, T9188 1853. For a taxi call T9188 1202.

❶ Directory

Tom Price *p277*
Banks Challenge ATM, Central Rd. **Chemist** Amcal, same lane as **Coles** entrance, T9189 1202. Mon-Fri 0830-1730, Sat 0830-1230. **Hospital** Hospital Dr, T9189 1199. **Internet** Access at the VIC, $3 for 15 mins. **Police** Court Rd, T9189 1344. **Post** Same lane as Coles entrance.

Broome and around

Introduction

The shark's tooth of the Dampier Peninsula marks the start of WA's Kimberley region and the northerly tip of the west coast before it breaks into a maze of inlets and archipelagos. Fringed by intermittent mangrove estuaries and low, deep red sandstone cliffs, the interior is a plain of low scrub and sparse woodland, usually dry but occasionally soaked by passing cyclones. A sealed highway connects Broome at its southwest corner with Derby in its southeast, and a rough unsealed track heads up through the middle connecting isolated Aboriginal communities. Broome is home to a unique blend of European, Asian and Aboriginal people, with an architecture, culture and history like nowhere else in Australia. Slipping into 'Broometime' can be a seductive experience.

Don't miss...

1 **Pearl Luggers** Learn all about Broome's pearling history, page 287.
2 **Broome Historical Museum** Visit the small but fascinating town museum, page 288.
3 **Cable Beach** Watch the sun setting from Old Mac's, page 288.
4 **Town Beach Café** Kick back and tuck into a pancake, a smoothie or even a fish supper, page 291.
5 **Sun City** Watch a movies in one of the oldest cinemas in the world, page 292.
6 **Astronomical tour** Spend an evening gazing at the stars and planets, page 292.
7 **Dampier Peninsula** Explore the peninsula on a 4WD tour, pages 292 and 295.
8 **Broome Bird Observatory** Time it right and you will be rewarded with the memorable sight of thousands of birds migrating, page 295.

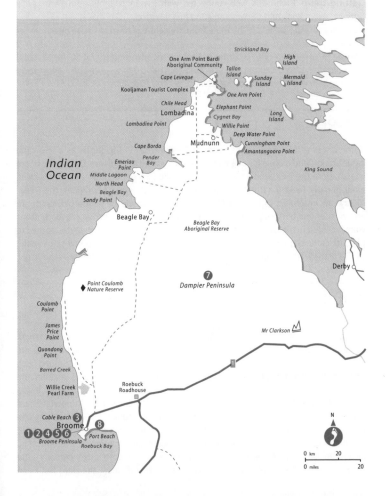

Broome & around

Broome → *Colour map 6, grid B2. Population: 12,000.*

Turquoise water, red cliffs, white sand and green mangroves; Broome is a town full of vivid colour and tropical lushness, with an interesting history and composition quite unlike any other Australian town to boot. Founded because of its proximity to vast beds of the southern ocean's magnificent large oyster, the Pinctada maxima, Broome's past and present is wrapped up in the pearl. In recent years, the refined and expensive resorts at Cable Beach have brought the town much attention and sophistication. Broome's international renown causes a lot of envious mumbling from other towns in the region and many people will tell you that the town has changed beyond recognition in the last decade or so, becoming too crowded and commercial. Although it is probably true that Broome has lost some of its unique character, it remains a fascinating oasis and a very enjoyable place to spend a few days. ▸▸ *For Sleeping, Eating and other listings, see pages 290-295.*

Ins and outs → *610 km from Port Hedland, 1,060 km from Kununurra.*

Getting there Broome is well connected with frequent flights from Perth, Alice Springs, Ayers Rock and Darwin and good bus links too.

Getting around Buses ply the route from the centre of town to Cable Beach. ▸▸ *See Transport, page 294, for further details.*

Tourist information VIC ① *corner of Broome Highway and Bagot St, T9192 2222, www.broomevisitor centre.com.au, Mon-Fri 0800-1700, Sat-Sun 0900-1600 (Apr-Sep); Mon-Fri 0900-1700, Sat-Sun 0900-1300 (Oct-Mar).*

History

Broome was established on the shore of Roebuck Bay in the 1890s as a telegraph cable station and a base for pearl shell merchants and their divers. During the boom years before the First World War Broome supplied 80 per cent of the world's pearl shell, mostly used for buttons. The first pearl divers were Aboriginal, then later Malaysian, Indonesian, Chinese or Japanese. Consequently the people of Broome are an unusual mix of Aboriginal, Asian and European heritage. When plastic buttons were invented in the 1950s Broome was in trouble but the pearling industry learned to produce cultured pearls with the help of the Japanese and has prospered since on the profits of the world's largest and most lustrous pearls, and more recently by tourism.

Sights

Chinatown

Chinatown is the oldest part of town and is still the main focus of Broome. **Carnarvon Street** and **Dampier Terrace** are lined with architecture that is characteristic of the town and its history. Australian corrugated iron and verandas are blended with Chinese flourishes such as red trims and lattice. Except for the architecture Chinatown bears little resemblance to the days of the late 19th century when it was full of billiard saloons, opium dens, noodle houses and pearl sheds. Carnarvon Street is the main street, lined with tourist shops and cafés, and most of the buildings on this street are original. About halfway down there are monuments to those involved in the pearling industry. The **Cultured Pearling Monument** remembers Kuribayashi, Iwaki and Dureau, men who helped to pioneer the cultured pearl industry after demand for pearl shell fell away. Opposite these three figures, the **Hard Hat Pearl**

Diver is a reminder of those who did all the hard, dangerous work underwater, and a plaque has also been erected by the Aboriginal community in memory of all the Aboriginal pearl divers forced into the job.

Walk through Johnny Chi Lane, lined with historical markers, to Dampier Terrace. At the northern end is the **Streeter Jetty**. This unprepossessing narrow wooden jetty among the mangroves was once the major jetty for pearl luggers. The shell was unloaded here onto rail carts and the luggers would moor in the creek, lying on their bellies in the mud when the tide receded. Modern boats now use the jetty at the Deep Water Port but two luggers survive and can be seen at **Pearl Luggers** ① *T9192 2059, www.broomecam.com/gold/pearlluggers, tours Mon-Fri 1100, 1400, Sat-Sun 1100, $18.50, children $9, concessions $16.50; bookings essential for Thu tour (1800-2030, $48)*, at the other end of Dampier Terrace. This is the best place to learn about the pearling industry of the old days. A former pearl diver tells riveting tales that leave nothing to the imagination. On Thursdays there is a special evening tour that includes the chance to taste pearl meat.

Broome town

A succession of roads follow the mangrove coast down towards the town beach. On the way they pass Matso's bar and, next door, the **Monsoon Gallery** ① *corner of Hamersley St and Carnarvon St, 1000-1600, free*. The gallery is housed in a fine old pearling master's residence and is worth a visit to see an example of early Broome architecture as well as the fine collection of art and jewellery.

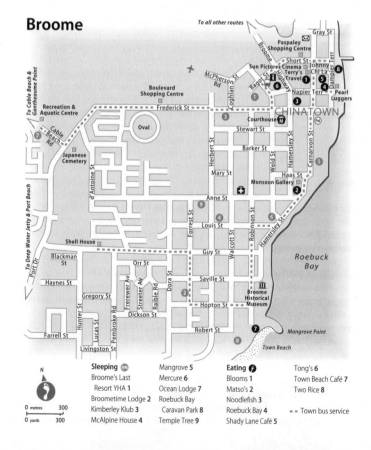

Broome

Sleeping
Broome's Last Resort YHA 1
Broometime Lodge 2
Kimberley Klub 3
McAlpine House 4
Mangrove 5
Mercure 6
Ocean Lodge 7
Roebuck Bay Caravan Park 8
Temple Tree 9

Eating
Blooms 1
Matso's 2
Noodlefish 3
Roebuck Bay 4
Shady Lane Café 5
Tong's 6
Town Beach Café 7
Two Rice 8

■ ■ Town bus service

0 metres 300
0 yards 300

About 1 km south is the **Broome Historical Museum** ⓘ *Hamersley St, T9192 2075, 1000-1300, $5, children $1, concessions $3*, which houses a small but well arranged and quite fascinating collection of artefacts, memorabilia and photographs charting the whole history of the European and Asian colonists. All sorts of themes are explored, but most of the displays focus on early colonials, the pearling industry, the Second World War and cyclones.

Not far away is **Town Beach**, a small shallow bay with warm golden sand and Broome's amazing opaque turquoise water, fringed by a low rocky headland on one side and mangroves on the other. A grassy foreshore has a few picnic tables but most people choose to patronize the wonderful café. Swimming is fine here but note the tide times as at low tide the sea retreats into the far distance. Town Beach is the best place to see the phenomenon called **Staircase to the Moon**, when the moonlight shines on pools of water left behind by the tide to create the illusion. Like so much in Broome this is tide-dependent and only happens about once a month for half the year. It also depends on lack of cloud of course. Pick up a monthly visitor guide from the VIC for 'staircase' dates and tide times.

Heading west from the water, along Guy Street, takes you to the **Shell House** ⓘ *95 Guy St, T9192 1423, Mon-Fri 0900-1700, Sat-Sun 0900-1300*. Here the owners display their compact collection of 6,000 shells from hundreds of mostly local species. The main business of the place is as a shop selling shells and mother-of-pearl jewellery (great for souvenirs and presents), so entry is free.

Via a short maze of roads to the north are the Chinese and Japanese cemeteries. The **Japanese Cemetery** is particularly striking, with its simple rough-hewn headstones. Over 900 Japanese pearl divers are buried here and very few of them made old bones.

Broome peninsula

Broome's deep water port lies right at the southern end of the peninsula, on Roebuck Bay. Apart from port facilities there are a couple of reasons to come down here. **The Wharf** restaurant does good fish and chips overlooking the bay and the jetty is a popular local fishing spot. The beach to the right of the jetty is a good place for a swim at high tide but at low tide it is great fun to fossick among the rocks. Wear shoes and peer around and under rocks to see octopus, starfish and crustaceans. An unsealed road leads west around the foot of the peninsula to the ocean-facing Gantheaume Point and Cable Beach. It is also possible to reach the area directly from town by following sealed Gantheaume Point Road southwest to the point. **Gantheaume Point** is a jumble of red rock stacks that make a striking contrast to the turquoise sea beyond. It is one of many areas around Broome where dinosaurs left their footprints in the tidal flats. The **dinosaur footprints** are just at the base of the cliff but can only be seen at very low tide. Check the tide times as this only happens once or twice a month. There is also a rather uninspiring concrete-lined rock pool at the point, **Anastasia's Pool**, built by a former lighthouse keeper for his arthritic wife to bathe in. All that remains of the lighthouse keeper's house is the brick chimney by the car park. The modern house on the point is a private house. Around the corner, **Reddell Beach** runs along the southern edge of the peninsula. It's known for interesting rock formations and sheer pindan cliffs above the beach. *Pindan* is an Aboriginal name for the intensely red dirt landscape of the area.

> ⁑ *Gantheaume Point is a lovely place to watch the sun set, although the light for photography is best in the morning.*

Cable Beach

Synonymous with holiday luxury in the northwest, Cable, 6 km from the town centre, on the opposite side of the peninsula, is a long, wide white sand beach that faces west and the setting sun. It was once the point at which the state's telegraph cable

Beware of the croc

There are two species of crocodile inhabiting Australia's northern waterways. The **Estuarine Crocodile**, commonly known as the Saltwater croc, or 'saltie', is far and away the most dangerous. Growing up to 6 m long a big one will think nothing of grabbing a cow or horse given the opportunity and will happily take a human for elevenses. Because of this they were shot on sight for decades by European pastoralists, though their numbers seem to have held up well until someone clicked that both hides and meat could be valuable. Professional hunting started with a vengeance in the 1950s and the population soon crashed. Protected since 1971 it was feared that they would become extinct anyway, but they have recovered well and are now even culled in the Northern Territory. You need to start watching out for them north of Port Hedland and keep watching as far as Maryborough in Queensland. That they are only found in the sea or at the mouths of rivers is a myth, unfortunately propagated by their common name. In fact they will stake territories anywhere suitable upriver, and have been found 600 km inland. They are not fans of cross-country travel, however, and tend to stick to the water. A general rule of thumb for swimming in creeks and pools in the north is to get above a decent sized waterfall – though this is still no guarantee. If in any doubt whatsoever simply steer well-clear of rivers, riverbanks and waterholes. Absence of a warning sign does not mean absence of a crocodile.

The **Freshwater Crocodile** is considerably smaller than the saltie and is not territorial. As such it tends to keep away from people and usually only attacks if trod upon or threatened. They are not found as far west as the salties and are found in and east of the Fitzroy River.

It is easy to tell the difference between the two types of crocodile if you look at their snouts. The feshwater crocodile has a very narrow snout, tapering to a point at the end. The saltie has a much wider, chunkier snout.

headed into the sea on its way to Indonesia and the rest of the world, but the name is now the only reminder of that era. A long grassy foreshore sits atop the ridge at the back of the beach, and there are toilets, picnic tables and a café. It is a relatively safe place to swim and there is usually a lifeguard patrol in winter. If you prefer being on the water rather than in it, then a couple of options present themselves. A small beach shack hires out surf and boogie boards (from $3-10 per hour) and is open daily 0830-1630. It also hires out umbrellas and deckchairs. A little further down the beach you can hire surfcats and slightly larger catamarans for the more experienced (both $30 per hour, T0412 087080). If the staff aren't too busy they'll be happy to throw in an informal lesson for your first half hour or so until you get the hang of it. The classic way to watch the sunset at Cable Beach is, unlikely as it may sound, on the back of a camel. There are a couple of operators who offer the experience, see Activities and tours page 292.

The beach was developed by British Lord McAlpine in the late 1980s. He built the **Cable Beach Club** resort and over the last 15 years Cable Beach has become a satellite village of holiday accommodation and facilities. In the centre of this is **Broome Crocodile Park** ① *Cable Beach Rd, T9192 1489, www.malcolmdouglas.com.au, Apr-Oct, Mon-Fri 1000-1700, Sat-Sun 1400-1700; tours daily 1500 and, during Jun-Oct, 1100 Mon-Fri; spiced with croc feeding at 1500 Wed-Sun, $15 including tour,* *children $8, concessions $12,* the public arm of a large commercial crocodile farming operation. Dozens of pens hold hundreds of crocs and alligators from five species, but mostly the big estuarine (or saltwater) crocodiles of northern Australia. A 5-m long 'saltie' hungrily grabbing a chicken is a sight well worth making time for. The tours are fascinating and you usually get to see and feel a baby croc. Allow 1½ hours. On Sanctuary Road there is a **Willie Creek** pearl and jewellery shop, open daily.

● Sleeping

Broome *p286, map p287*
Broome has easily the widest range of accommodation north of Perth. The following is a small selection from what is available. Contact the VIC for other options, and if you're around for a while consider a spell out on the Dampier Peninsula. Book well ahead for the peak Apr-Sep season.
LL-L Cable Beach Club Resort, Cable Beach Rd, Cable Beach, T9192 0400, www.cable beachlub.com. Broome's premier holiday accommodation, an exquisitely designed resort hotel with excellent facilities and restaurants. Traditional Broome architecture is complemented by polished wooden floors, Asian furniture and antiques, and endless lush landscaped gardens. One of the country's few large hotels that manages to feel like a small boutique hideaway.
LL-L McAlpine House, 84 Herbert St, T9192 3886, www.mcalpinehouse.com. The most exclusive B&B in town, this townhouse dates back to 1910 when it was built by a local pearling master, and is one of the very best examples of Broome's distinctive architecture. The 6 exquisite rooms are well-equipped though the 3 least expensive share 2 bathrooms. Tropical breakfast in the open-air dining room next to the courtyard pool. Evenings meals, from $35 per head, by arrangement. It also has a guest kitchen. Recommended.
L-A Mangrove, Carnarvon St, T19192 1303. A large resort-style hotel occupying the best shoreside location in town. The architecture is unremarkable but the food is very good and the luxury suites are quite striking.
A Cable Beachside Resort, Murray Rd, Cable Beach, T9193 5545, www.cablebeachside. com.au. Fully self-contained, well-equipped units grouped around a central pool area.
A-B Mercure, Weld St, T9292 1002, www.accorhotels.com. Equally bland, cannot boast the same outlook but does have a notable surprise feature: an Irish bar serving a good

pint of the black stuff and hearty Irish style meals. Food served 1200-1400, 1800-2030, live music most nights in peak season, Thu-Sat in the wet.
B Cable Beach Caravan Park, Millington Rd, Cable Beach, T9192 2066. Even caravan park sites need to be booked well ahead in peak season.
C Broometime Lodge, 52 Forrest St, T9193 5067, broometimelodge@australiamail.com. Simple but comfortable motel rooms, many en suite, and a range of facilities including a simple kitchen area, dining room, television room and pool. The cheapest en-suite, a/c rooms in town.
C Ocean Lodge, 1 Cable Beach Rd, T9193 7700, www.oceanlodge.com.au. Reasonably priced motel with good facilities. All rooms are en suite, a/c and have kitchenettes.
C Temple Tree, 31 Anne St, T9193 5728, www.templetreebnb.com.au. A modest but welcoming B&B with 2 en-suite rooms and a stately spreading frangipani shading the back garden. Breakfasts and optional cheap dinners are superb. Very good value. Recommended.
C-D Kimberley Klub, Frederick St, T9192 3233, www.kimberleyklub.com. A superb large hostel, and very much a party destination. Modern, well-maintained and clean, it centres around a large open-plan games, dining and pool area. Facilities include a bar and cheap café, internet access, bike hire, volleyball and well-equipped kitchen. Beds in spacious 10 and 5-bed dorms, plus a few doubles. Beds are pricey, but include breakfast. No a/c, but still recommended.
D Cable Beach Backpackers, Sanctuary Rd, Cable Beach, T9193 5511, www.cablebeach backpackers.com. Another resort-style hostel along similar lines to the Klub. Facilities are very good, lots of freebies and cheap deals are thrown in, including a regular town centre shuttle. Some rooms are a/c.

D Roebuck Bay Caravan Park, T9192 1366, roebuckbaycp@broome.wn.com.au. Has foreshore camping sites and a good number of basic a/c on-site vans.

D-E Broome's Last Resort YHA, Bagot St, T9193 5000, www.broomeslast resort.com.au. Tired and slightly grungy hostel favoured by seasonal workers as the cheapest and most convenient to town. Communal facilities are pretty good, however, and include a pool. The management work hard to ensure guests enjoy their stay. A constant flow of evening activities frequently include fancy-dress parties. Rooms are non-a/c.

Broome Bird Observatory, see Excursions, is also a good budget place to stay.

❷ Eating

Broome *p286, map p287*
Evening bookings advisable at most restaurants between May-Sep.

❦ **Blooms**, 31 Carnarvon St, T9193 6366. Casual and stylish licensed café with a good range of meals available all day. Breakfast, baguettes, laksas, salads, pizza and pasta. Generous serves and friendly service. Licensed, open daily 0700-2130. Mon-Sat 1800-2100.

❦ **Matso's**, Hamersley St, T9193 5811. This pub/restaurant has the best setting in town – a classic breezy Broome house with wraparound verandahs overlooking Roebuck Bay. Imaginative Modern Australian cooking, great service and their own range of coolers and beers to taste, including a refreshing alcoholic ginger beer. A beer on the veranda in the late afternoon is highly recommended. Open daily 0700-2100.

❦ **Noodlefish**, Frederick St, T9192 5529. Simple outdoor setting but the fresh modern Asian food is excellent. Menu changes frequently to reflect the best of local fish, seafood and local produce. BYO and cash only.

❦ **Tong's**, 10 Napier Terr, T9192 2080. The best of the town's many Chinese restaurants though you wouldn't think so from the outside. Licensed, open daily 1730-2130.

❦ **2 Rice**, Dampier Terr, is run by the same team that operate the **Town Beach Café**, and the Asian-style food is excellent. Also very good value. Open 0930-1430 Mon-Fri, 1800-2100 Mon-Sat.

❦ **Roebuck Bay**, Dampier Terr, T9192 1221. Large, lively pub with hearty meals daily 1200-1400, 1800-2000, particularly popular on Sun when they serve up a substantial tasty roast. They also have motel rooms and scruffy backpacker accommodation.

❦ **Shady Lane Café**, Johnny Chi Lane, between Carnarvon St and Dampier Terr. Funky place popular with locals serving breakfast and fresh wraps, rolls and salads, as well as juices and smoothies from its adjacent juice bar. Outdoor tables are quiet and cool under a profusion of palms. Daily 0700-1500.

❦ **Town Beach Café**, Robinson St, T9193 5585. Another local favourite, this laid-back, unpretentious café is equally at home serving you a pancake and smoothie for breakfast or a superb fish supper. All the tables are out front, covered by sailcloth and overlooking the beach. Open from 0730-2100 Tue-Sat, 0730-1300 Sun, and 1730-2100 Mon. Recommended.

❦ **Wharf**, Port Drive, adjacent to the deep water jetty, T9192 5800. A no-frills licensed restaurant serving fresh and generous serves of fish, seafood, Asian dishes and salads at a price achieved with paper plates and plastic cutlery. The smart outdoor tables overlook the deep water jetty and Roebuck Bay. Daily 1100-2200.

Cable Beach *p288*
❦ **Cable Beach SandBar & Grill**, Cable Beach, T9193 5090. Has a prime position on the grassy foreshore overlooking the beach, with tables both on a shaded patio and in the open dining room. Both main restaurant and the adjacent takeaway kiosk are open for meals 0700-2100 daily, licensed.

❦ **Old Mac's Sunset Bar**, part of the **Club Resort**, Cable Beach, is the perfect spot to watch the sun sink romantically into the ocean. The problem is everyone knows this is the top spot so arrive early in peak season. The light meals don't embarrass the resort's high standards and are consequently very good value. Food 1600-2100.

● *For an explanation of sleeping and eating price codes used in this guide, see inside the*
● *front cover. Other relevant information is found in Essentials, see pages 40-46.*

¶¶ **Old Zoo Café**, Sanctuary Rd, Cable Beach, T9193 6200. The most intimate of Cable's eateries with an open dining room and small deck overlooking its modest surrounding gardens and ponds. Excellent juices, smoothies, breakfasts and light lunches by day, the expensive evening menu offers inventive takes on traditional Australian themes. Licensed, all the wines are available by the glass. Meals 0700-2200 (closed Mon, Oct-Mar).

¶ **Divers Tavern**, Cable Beach Rd, Cable Beach, T9193 6066. Large and open-plan, this is the best of the town's true Aussie pubs with local cover bands every Fri and Sun, and good hearty meals, including excellent steaks, between 1200-1400 and 1800-2030.

¶ **Munchies**, Cable Beach, the cheapest option at the beach. Takeaways, cheap meals to eat in, some supplies and internet at $2.50 for 15 mins. BYO, open 0700-2000.

☻ Entertainment

Broome p286, map p287
Sun Pictures, Carnarvon St, T9192 3738. One of the oldest original picture houses in the world. Built in 1916 the screen is outdoors and most of the deckchair seats are out under the stars.

☻ Festivals and events

Broome p286, map p287
The Festival of the Pearl, known as **Shinju Matsuri**, is celebrated for a week in **Sep** and this is when you'll see Broome's multicultural community out in force. Events include parades, dragon boat racing and the Shinju Ball. A detailed programme of events can be obtained from the VIC in the weeks preceding the festival.

○ Shopping

Broome p286, map p287
Books
Kimberley Bookshop, 6 Napier Terr, T9192 1944. Excellent range of new books, especially on Aboriginal culture and Broome history.
Woody's Book Exchange, Johnny Chi Lane. A good spot for second hand or exchange.

Pearls and jewellery
There are half a dozen exclusive pearl boutiques on Dampier Terr. Prices start at $500 and head for the moon.
Georgia Morgan is the place to go for more contemporary designs.
Linneys sells fine traditional pearls and the business is owned by a local family.
Paspaley Pearl, Carnarvon St. Very welcoming, professional and play an informative video on request.
Shell House, Courthouse Markets. Cheaper, casual jewellery made of pearl shell can be found here, Sat 0800-1300, and Johnny Chi Lane market, Sun 0800-1230.

Outdoor
Kimberley Camping and Outback Supplies, 65 Frederick St, T9193 5354, kcaos@tpg.com.au. Has an excellent range of gear. Much essential kit is available for hire, and they make up good value hire packs for camping and 4WD expeditions.

Shopping centres
Boulevard, Frederick St. Essentially a huge **Action** supermarket with a few other retailers attached, including a CD store, newsagent and several clothes shops.
Paspaley, Chinatown. Has a 24-hr **Coles** supermarket and a **Target**.

▲ Activities and tours

Broome p286, map p287
Aboriginal culture tours
Mamabulanjin Aboriginal Tours, 640 Dora St, T9192 2660, mabtours@wn.com.au. Broome through Aboriginal eyes – tours can include bush tucker, weapon throwing and learning about hunting techniques.

Aerial tours
Broome Aviation, T9192 1369, www. broomeaviation.com. Flies around the Broome peninsula and Willie Creek (25 mins, $150).
Windrider Safaris, T0407 010772. Take budding pilots up in their micro-light trikes for a mini-lesson and aerial sightsee. Options include going up to see the sunrise or sunset. A 30-min intro and flight is $145, with an optional extra 30 mins for another $65.

Astronomical tours

Astro Tours, T9193 5362, mail@astrotours.net. Heads about 10 km out of Broome once or twice an evening up to 4 nights a week between Apr-Nov. Its guided tour of the night sky is both animated and fascinating, one of the country's very best, and 8 telescopes means plenty of viewing time. $50, children $25.

Boat/sailing trips

Dampier Creek Boat Tours, T9192 1669. Heads up the town creek through the mangroves, dipping in fishing lines along the way (3 hrs, $70).

Oceanic Cruises, T9193 6679, www.oceaniccruises.com.au. Takes out their impressive 35-m schooner every day, Sun-Fri, from May-Sep. Lunch cruises leave at 1000 (4 hrs, $69) and include a simple but good quality BBQ lunch, while the sunset cruise heads out at 1600 (2 hrs, $35). Staying aboard all day ($95) is one of WA's best value day sailing experiences.

Spirit of Broome, T9193 5025. Breakfast or sunset tours by hovercraft.

Willie Pearl Lugger Cruises, T0418 919781. Takes their original lugger out most days between Jun-Sep for sunset and afternoon 'boom net' cruises (both $60).

Camel/horse safari

Cable Stables, T04-0108 8473, offers beach and bush horse-rides, $50 for 2 hrs.
Ships of the Desert, T9192 6383, 1 hr, $30, also full day expeditions for $75.

Dampier Peninsula trips

4WD **Over the Top**, T9192 5211, www.4wdtourswa.com. On s 4WD, this outfit heads out on both day and overnight trips that include stops at Beagle Bay, Lombadina and Cape Leveque. Day tours every Tue and Fri, Apr-Dec, overnight trips every Mon-Tue, Apr-Nov. The guides are good fun and all food and equipment included.

Diving

Workline, Short St, T9192 2233, workline@optusnet.com.au. Organizes local trips off Gantheaume Point, around $150 for a 2-dive trip, but only once a fortnight when the tide is very low. It also hires out gear and runs PADI courses. It can also advise on who to consider booking with to dive on the Rowley Shoals, 3 coral atolls 170 km northwest of Broome that are considered one of the very best, and most pristine diving sites in the world. The season for the shoals is very short, generally Sep-Nov. Trips out are a minimum 5 nights and cost around $500-800 per day.

Kimberley trips

See also 'routes east' below. Flights and tours over and into the Kimberley are usually better value from Derby.

4WD and bus **Broome Day Tours**, T1800 801068. Head out for a day to Tunnel Creek and Windjana, leaving around 0645 every Fri, Apr-Nov. They also offer a day trip out to Geike Gorge every Mon, Wed and Fri during the same season but note that this involves over 800 km of sitting in the coach and not much sightseeing!

Kimberley Adventure Tours, T/F9168 3368. Specialize in one-way trips along the Gibb River Road to Kununurra and Darwin (9 days, Apr-Oct, around $1,500).

Over the Top, offer a more adventurous overnight trip every Sun and Wed from Apr-Nov that takes in all these sights. Their excellent 5 day west Kimberley adventure safari leaves every Mon, May-Oct.

Air A flight over the Kimberley and its off-shore islands is visual adventure of the highest order, especially if you cannot afford the time or money to take a boat cruise around the coast. Check whether the operator has high-winged aircraft and whether window seats are standard.

Broome Aviation, T9192 1369, www.broomeaviation.com. Also have a number of Kimberley options including, in the off-season, a good-value day trip to the Buccaneer Archipelago and Cape Leveque. This includes lunch and 2½ hrs flying time (0900, 6½ hrs).

King Leopold Air, T9193 7155, www.kingleopoldair.com.au. Offer a variety of flights over the western Kimberley and over the Bungle Bungles via Windjana Gorge, plus a connection to Cockatoo Island. Costs are around $150 per hr. They also fly from Derby.

Coastal cruises A handful of companies offer 1-2 week cruises around the Kimberley coast, usually from Broome to Wyndham or the reverse, during the Apr-Sep season. The

Kimberley coast is a riot of deep red rock headlands and islands, wide tree-lined estuaries, crystal blue waters and beautiful beaches. Cruises usually put a premium on exploring this as much as possible, seeking out the wildlife, including the big 'saltie' crocodiles, looking at ancient Aboriginal rock art, and eating freshly caught fish and molluscs. Some have their own on-board helicopters so that passengers get to see some of the Kimberley interior as well. Needless to say, none of this is cheap, though there are a couple of shorter duration cruises from Derby from around $1,000 for 3-night trips.

The Great Escape, T9193 5983, www.kimberleyescape.com. Travel with 16 passengers and are one of the less expensive options at $7,250 per person. Both of these operators also offer diving expeditions to the Rowley Shoals from Oct-Nov.

North Star Cruises, T9192 1829, www.northstarcruises.com.au. Shuttle their *True North* luxury cruiser back and forth between Broome and Wyndham every 2 weeks, with prices ranging from $7,500 to $16,000, depending on the standard of cabin.

Local sightseeing tours

Broome Day Tours, T1800 801068. Buses trundle around both the town and lower peninsula, taking in Gantheaume Point, the Deep Water Jetty, Town Beach and Chinatown. Departs around 0800 every day from May-Oct, Mon, Wed, Fri and Sun from Nov-Apr (4 hrs).

Broome Sightseeing Tours, T9192 5041. Interesting look at Broome's history and main sights, maximum of 4 (3 hrs). Mon-Fri 0815. Also can hire CD/cassette for self-guided tour.

Swimming pool

Broome Recreation and Aquatic Centre, Cable Beach Rd, T9193 7677. Leisure pool and 25-m saltwater pool.

Wildlife tours

Kimberley Birdwatching, T/F9192 1246, kimbird@tpg.com.au. Offers regular and custom tours from 3 hrs to 3 weeks. George Swann's enthusiastic and deeply knowledgeable trips are a must for visiting

bird-watchers and well worth considering for anyone wanting to see more of the area and its wildlife. Programmes vary. Also see Broome Bird Observatory.

⊖ Transport

Broome *p286, map p287*
Air

Qantas have a daily service to **Perth**. Air North fly daily to **Kununurra** and **Darwin**. Skywest, T1300 660088, fly to **Perth** Mon-Sat.

Bicycle/scooter

Hire from **Broome Cycle & Scoot**, 2 Hamersley St, T9192 1871. Bikes $15 day, also scooters and buggies. **Roadrunner**, Farrell St, T9182 1971, has a range including scooters and 1000cc tourers.

Bus

Local Town Bus Service, www.broome cam.com/gold/broomebus, operates its single winding route between **Broometime Lodge**, the town centre and Cable Beach, and back, daily every hour between 0720 and 1830. Some services extend to the Shell House. The last bus back from Cable Beach leaves at 1815.

Long distance Many 4WD tours heading east are one-way trips that will get you to **Kununurra** or **Darwin** but if money or time is tight there is a McCafferty's/Greyhound service to **Derby**, **Kununurra** (14 hrs) and the **Northern Territory**. Backpacker buses Easyrider, T9226 0307, www.easyridertours. com.au, has several ticket options west, including **Exmouth** and **Perth**. Travelabout, T9244 1200, www.travelabout.au.com, runs several trips, some 4WD, to **Darwin** and **Perth**. See also Activities and tours above.

Car

All the major car hire companies and several inexpensive local operators including **Broome Broome**, T04-1794 9727, bbcrent @wn.com.au, who has a good range from 3-door hatchbacks to Landcruisers. If you're going to do a bit of distance check out **Just Broome**, T9192 6636, who have more free km and cheaper per km excess than most. **Willie Creek**, T9192 3311, has excellent packages for small 4WDs.

Car servicing from **Minishull**, Guy St, opposite Shell House, T9192 1168. Cheap fuel at **Woody's**, Dampier Terr.

Taxi
Call T9192 1133.

ⓘ Directory

Broome p286, map p287
Banks The major bank branches are in Chinatown, on Canarvon St.

Chemist Chinatown Pharmacy, Paspaley Shopping Centre, Canarvon St, T9192 1399. **Hospital** Broome District, Robinson St, T9192 9222. **Internet** Broome Telecentre, 40 Dampier Terr. Internet Outpost, 16 Carnarvon St. **Laundry** Broome Laundromat, Paspaley Shopping Centre. Daily 0600-2200. **Police** Hamersley St, T9192 1212. **Post** Canarvon St. **Useful contacts** CALM, West Kimberley HQ, 111 Herbert St, T9192 1036.

Around Broome

Willie Creek Pearl Farm

ⓘ *T9193 6000, www.williecreekpearls.com.au, half-day tours $59 including 37-km transfer from Broome, or $25 self-drive to Willie Creek (4WD recommended).*

> ⁑ *See above for details of tours available from Broome. The peninsula is becoming popular with 4WD travellers so book accommodation ahead.*

Strangely for these parts, Willie Creek is actually bigger than it sounds. This wide tidal inlet at the bottom of the Dampier Peninsula is the only Broome pearl farm that receives visitors. In fact it is a demonstration farm. The real business of pearl growing is carried out in a remote coastal spot further north because of security. Unfortunately, thousand dollar pearl oysters can't be left sitting in a public waterway, even if it is crocodile infested. Nevertheless, Willie Creek is a fascinating place to visit as the daily tours explain every aspect of the cultured-pearl industry, including a demonstration of the seeding technique in a fresh oyster. A quick boat trip allows visitors to see how the oysters are suspended in the creek and the tour ends with a look at the finished product in the showroom.

Broome Bird Observatory

ⓘ *T9193 5600, home.it.net.au/~austecol/observatories/broome, bookings essential for tours and accommodation.*

On the edge of Roebuck Bay, 25 km from Broome, on the highway opposite the Cape Leveque turn-off, this observatory is one of the best places in Australia to see migratory shorebirds. It was established as a research and education facility in 1998 and has counted over 300 bird species in the area since. The sight of thousands of migrating birds departing in April and returning in September-October is magnificent. Regular half-day tours are held that may include seeing the migrations, exploring the mangroves or bush, depending on the time of year ($73 from Broome, self-drive $48). It's also a peaceful place to stay. Accommodation includes self-contained chalets (**C**), double, single and bunk rooms (**D-E**) and bush campsites (both powered and unpowered). Return transfers from Broome for overnight guests cost around $30 per person. Twitchers should contact the observatory for details of current workshops and field trips.

Dampier Peninsula → *Colour map 6, grids B2/B3.*

The Dampier Peninsula forms a large triangle north of Broome, reaching east almost as far as Derby. It is a huge area and most of it is Aboriginal land, home to several Aboriginal communities, of about six different language groups. Access is limited but some communities offer tours and accommodation, an excellent way to spend time

66 99 The land is entirely covered in long grass and spindly trees but the coastline continues Broome's spectacular blend of red cliffs, white beaches and chalky blue sea...

with Aboriginal people and see the peninsula. The land is entirely covered in long grass and spindly trees but the coastline continues Broome's spectacular blend of red cliffs, white beaches and chalky blue sea. Just one dirt road traverses the peninsula from Broome to its tip at Cape Leveque (220 km) and it's a shocker. Corrugations, sand, rocks and pools of water make this a road for high-clearance 4WD vehicles only (usually closed in wet season).

The first turn-off, shortly after leaving the sealed road, leads to the **Willie Creek Pearl Farm**, see page 295. The next is the very scenic **Manari Road** (4WD) which follows the coast for about 50 km. This leads to a series of beaches, creeks and cliffs where you can explore, fish and camp though there are no facilities.

Following the Cape Leveque Road for about an hour, the next stop is **Beagle Bay** community ① *call into the office when entering the community, T9192 4913, $5.* Aboriginal people of the Dampier Peninsula were pursued in the 1860s and 1870s by 'blackbirders' who captured them to work as pearl divers but by the 1890s Europeans were after their souls. French trappists and German Pallottine monks arrived to found mission settlements and their legacy survives in the unusual church at Beagle Bay. Sacred Heart Church was built in 1917 and is notable for its altar, walls and floor lined with pearl shell. Fuel is sometimes available here but there is no accommodation.

After leaving Beagle Bay, it is 28 km to the **Middle Lagoon** turn-off ① *T9192 4002, day visitors $8 car*, then another 33 km to reach this beautiful and peaceful sandy cove where you can swim and snorkel. Accommodation is available in beach shelters (**D**), self-contained cabins (**A-B**) or campsites. There is no fuel or supplies but ice and drinks are available.

Continuing north for about 50 km, you'll reach the Aboriginal community of **Lombadina** ① *T9192 4936, www.ibizwa.com/lombadina, day visitors $5 car, payable at office or craft shop*. This is also a former mission settlement and many of the 60 people who live here are still Catholic. Visitors can look at the lovely timber church with bark roof and buy local work from the craft shop. The settlement clusters around neat lawns, mango trees and ghost gums, and is very picturesque and friendly. The Bard people offer the best range of accommodation and tours, including fishing and whale-watching charters (from $275 per person per day), tours such as mud crabbing and bush walking (from $33-66 per half day) and 4WD day tours ($99). Accommodation in four-bed backpacker dorms (**D**) and self-contained units (**B**). There are no transfers from Broome but drop-offs/pick-ups can be arranged with Over the Top tours.

Cape Leveque lies at the end of the road, capped by red cliffs, rocky coves and white beaches. **Kooljaman** ① *T9192 4970, www.kooljaman.com.au*, is a popular resort at the cape, owned by the Djarindjin and One Arm Point communities but usually run by non-Aboriginal managers. Accommodation is in beach shelters (**D**), units (**C**), open paperbark cabins (**B**) and safari tents (**A**). Although it's very busy here

● *Aborigine is a Latin word meaning 'from the beginning'; the Romans used it to describe the*
● *first inhabitants of Latium and it can be used for any people living in a country from its earliest period.*

Northern star

Broome lies at the very western edge of the Kimberley, an area larger than Germany with a population of 30,000. It's a wild and rugged region of gorges and waterfalls, cattle stations and diamond mines, spectacular coastline and ancient Aboriginal art. The Kimberley is part of Australia's tropical north with a summer monsoon that throws a green cloak over the grassy plains and scrub covered ranges, and turns the rivers into powerful torrents. During the dry season the rivers shrink to a series of pools, waterfalls slow to a trickle and heat and humidity drop to a comfortable level. There are only three major roads in the Kimberley and just one of them is sealed, the Great Northern Highway from Broome to Kununurra. Kununurra, on the eastern edge of the state, is surrounded by typically beautiful Kimberley range country and fertile land fed by the Ord River. The Gibb River Road connects the same towns and provides access to some of the region's most beautiful gorges in cattle station country but this is a challenging dirt route. Within the Kimberley are places so remote that you can only see them by boat, plane or 4WD, such as the extraordinary western coast, Mitchell Plateau, Buccaneer Archipelago and beehive domes of the Bungle Bungle Range.

in high season it still feels wild and isolated, helped by the Robinson Crusoe style huts. Facilities include a kiosk, restaurant, scenic flights and boat tours but most people just come to swim, walk, fish and relax. Units, cabins and tents sleep four for price quoted, no discount for double. There is another community, **One Arm Point**, on the eastern side of the peninsula but they do not encourage visitors. Just south of this community is **Mudnunn** community ① *T9192 4121*, who allow unpowered camping and sometimes run mud-crabbing tours in the mangroves ($55), which is a pretty memorable experience.

Routes east → *Derby 220 km from Broome.*

From Broome the Great Northern Highway heads east across the foot of the Dampier Peninsula and then forks, giving the traveller two very different alternative routes to the Northern Territory. The northerly fork heads up to Derby and the Gibb River Road, while directly east the Great Northern Highway curls around the bulk of the Kimberley, skirting the deserts to the south.

Derby

Derby ① *T9191 1426, www.derbytourism.com*, sits on a narrow spur of land surrounded by tidal mud flats, close to where the mighty Fitzroy River flows into King Sound. Although the town has few attractions for visitors, its position at the start of the Gibb River Road and close to the spectacular Kimberley coast means that tours and cruises from Derby are very good value.

Great Northern Highway

This long run between Derby and Kununurra is split into two very different scenic sections. The first 550 km to Halls Creek are frankly pretty tedious and have little to distract the traveller other than impressive **Geike Gorge** near Fitzroy Crossing, 260 km along the way. After a couple of hours or so spent at the Gorge, **Halls Creek** is a popular stopover and offers a small but broad range of options. The resort-style Kimberley Hotel ① *Roberta St, T9168 6101, kimberleyhotel@bigpond.com*, has both standard and large motel-style rooms, plus a couple of en-suite, air-conditioned, four-bunk backpacker rooms. **Halls Creek Motel** ① *main highway, T9168 0001, hallscreekmotel@westnet.com.au*, has similar rooms to the **Kimberley** standard at a very similar price. Its budget rooms are well-equipped and available as twins or good value singles. The **caravan park** ① *T9168 6169*, has reasonably priced on-site vans and cabins.

❢ *Talk to the Derby VIC before tackling this route.*

The 365 km between Halls Creek and Kununurra has far more striking scenery than that of the Gibb River Road; indeed it is one of the most scenic bits of road in the whole country, and it also gives you a chance to see the magnificent **Purnululu National Park** (the **Bungle Bungles**). Helicopter flights over the Bungles ① *T9168 7337, 45 mins, $200*, are available at **Warmun** (Turkey Creek Roadhouse), 165 km from Halls Creek.

Kununurra ① *T9168 1177, www.eastkimberley.com, 510 km from Katherine*, is WA's northeastern outpost. Surrounded by range country and the bountiful waters of the Ord River, Kununurra has the most picturesque setting of any town in the Kimberley, and makes an excellent base for the adventurer's playground of the East Kimberley. From the town 4WD, flight, canoe and boat tours head out to sights as diverse as the Ord River, Lake Argyle, the Argyle Diamond Mine, The Bungles, El Questro Wilderness Park and Wyndham.

The Gibb River Road

This legendary unsealed Kimberley road is both an experience and a challenge. It was created in the 1960s as a way for the cattle stations of this region to get their stock to Derby and Wyndham ports. Although now used more frequently by travellers, the alarming sight of a huge cattle road train barrelling along in clouds of dust is still common. The Gibb River Road traverses about 660 km between Derby and Kununurra (about 250 km shorter than the highway route but it takes much longer because of the condition of the road) and passes through remote range country and grass plains, threaded with creeks, gorges and waterfalls. Part of the Gibb River Road experience is also staying at the cattle stations along the way, meeting their owners and perhaps taking a tour or scenic flight to explore privately owned landscapes seen by few. There are also good campsites close to several beautiful gorges, where you can go for a walk or swim. Remember this is a rugged road though, and travelling it is less than comfortable. Dusty and bone-jarring conditions means a 4WD is recommended and you should allow at least four days to cross. If you don't have your own vehicle there are plenty of operators offering adventure tours for about $150 a day (see Broome, page 292, for a couple of options).

Road conditions vary along the route, during the season and from year to year so it is essential to check current conditions before setting out (Main Roads WA ① *T1800-013314*). Generally the road is only passable in the dry (May-November) and the eastern section is much rougher and more corrugated than the western section. Although you can sometimes travel the road in a 2WD, the road is very rough and stony, there are many creek crossings, and many of the stations and gorges off the road are found at the end of even rougher tracks. Finally, the Pentecost River crossing at the eastern end is long and hazardous, and unless the river is dry or extremely low 2WD vehicles will not have the clearance to cross it. Vehicles need to be in excellent condition and you'll need to carry extra fuel, water and spare wheels. For more information see the *Gibb River and Kalumburu Roads Travellers Guide* ($3), produced every year by the Derby Tourist Bureau, which lists current facilities. Available from Derby and Broome VICs, it can also be ordered by phone. If the worst happens, for road rescue from Derby call T9193 1205, or from Kununurra T9169 1556. The website www.exploroz.com has some good tips and travellers' comments.

History

The arrival of man

Meganesia, the then-joined landmass of Australia and New Guinea, was undoubtedly the first landmass to be reached by humans using boats. From their evolution in Africa *Homo erectus*, and then *Homo sapiens* walked into Asia but the latter's expansion from these strongholds to the 'new worlds' was barred by either water or ice for hundreds of thousands of years. It is true that parts of New Guinea and north west Australia are tantalizingly close to the islands of south east Asia, but even during the severest of ice ages there have always been deep channels between them: it has never been possible to walk from Asia to Meganesia.

The Aboriginal ancestors' certain passage by boat is one of three relatively new pieces of key information that have jarred the traditional picture of Aboriginal history. The second is when this happened. There are no dates, not even any folk memories of the first coming of humanity to Meganesia, and that's probably because the time of first migration has been pushed back by slowly accumulating evidence to over 45,000 and possibly as much as 60,000 years ago. Finally it is also now certain that Australian Aboriginals and the original New Guineans are one and the same people, separated by just a few thousand years of cultural divergence, and New Guineans were amongst the earliest and most intensive farmers on the planet.

There is little doubt that the peoples who finally crossed from Asia to Meganesia around 55,000 years ago carried with them one of the most, if not the most, technologically advanced cultures of the time. That they already had a grasp of the potential of agriculture seems likely, as some of those that settled in the northern highlands, later to become isolated as island New Guinea, had developed intensive farming systems by as much as 10,000 years ago. Population expansion amongst the early settlers in the new fertile New Guinean lands would have been exponential, and it cannot have been long before groups were heading south in search of new land. It is quite possible that people had reached the very southern tip of WA within a thousand years of their ancestors reaching the northern coasts.

The early Aborigines carried with them a notable firepower. Stone, bone and wooden weapons honed to perfection during the many generations of island-hopping from Asia. These hunter-gatherers had encountered, for the first time in human history, lands where they were the undisputed top predator. One of their new weapons would have been psychological, a new feeling of unbridled power, a sense of their own dominance. The Australian animals they met would have been woefully ill-prepared for such an encounter.

The few, relatively small mammalian predators could not hope to compete with such a powerful new force, either in direct confrontation or for prey as the human population increased. As for the giant reptiles, the awesome *Megalania* (imagine a Komodo Dragon weighing in at about a tonne) and the giant snake *Wonambi* (6 m long with a head the size of a serving tray) were ambush predators, strictly territorial. They would have been a serious hazard to the lone hunter, but in the face of collective competition were as doomed as their mammalian counterparts. The only large Australian predator to survive to the present day is the saltwater crocodile, the feared 'saltie', probably protected by its primarily aquatic habitat. As for the herbivores, the now-vanished giants of the vast Australian plains, there can surely be little doubt that the coming of humanity was the decisive factor in the extinction of so many.

An ecological crisis?

Evidence is also mounting that the coming of humanity had an extraordinarily profound effect on Australian flora. First indirectly and then, in the face of calamity, purposefully. Core samples from around Australia, but particularly in the east, seem to indicate that the now dominant **eucalypts** were surprisingly rare prior to around 60,000 years ago. These cores also sometimes show high concentrations of carbon – ash – at the point at which the gums began their ascendancy. Could this be another climate-driven coincidence? Again, some researchers think not.

A powerful, and frightening scenario may well have followed the local demise of the large grazers. With very little to eat it the forest undergrowth and plains brush would have proliferated, in wet times an impenetrable green morass, in the dry a huge store of kindling. Forest fires are natural, lightening-ignited phenomena on every continent, and especially common in hot, dry Australia. Massive build-ups of combustible fuel would have resulted in equally massive, and quite catastrophic forest and bushfires, deadly to the native flora and fauna, and humans alike.

In the face of this crisis the early peoples of Australia would have realized they had to keep the brush low artificially. They would have been forced to fight fire with fire, continuously lighting small scale blazes to prevent large scale conflagrations. Whatever the cause, the adoption of fire for more than just cooking, heating and protection was to have many and widespread consequences.

Most important for the pioneering Australians was the realization that fire could have multiple uses. Not only did it prevent large-scale, life-threatening bushfires, but it was also discovered that controlled blazes had a multiplicity of uses. They could be used for offence or defense against antagonistic neighbours, or to signal distant groups or relations. They could also be used to drive and herd game to favoured trapping areas, and burn-offs encouraged new growth with many of the succulent shoots favoured by many of the Aboriginals' prey. It would also not have been lost on them how much more easily they could navigate, travel and hunt.

A more-or-less constant regime of small-scale bushfires had other less useful consequences. Crucially for the future development of Australian flora, it naturally favoured fire-resistant and fire-promoting species. Foremost amongst these are the eucalypts, the ubiquitous gum trees that once were minor players in the ecology of the continent, but are now almost all-pervading. Dry and wet rainforests have been driven back to relatively tiny refuges around Australia's eastern periphery, while the great gum woodlands have marched on triumphantly.

The Catch-22 of the Aboriginal fire-regime may have helped to lock Australia yet further into another ecological cul-de-sac. The total number of animals a landmass can support, its faunal biomass, depends on a number of factors. Two of these Australia already had a paucity of: water and nutrients. The fire regime would have accelerated erosion, further depleting soil nutrient levels, and would also have significantly lowered the amount of water and nutrients locked up within the plants themselves. Most obviously of all, the potential number of animals is crucially constrained by the sheer biomass of plant material available for feed. With much of this being continually burned off, the amount of prey available to both humans and their competitors would have had a much reduced upper limit.

Partnership with the land

The early pioneers into each part of the continent would have had a relatively easy time of it, but once the honeymoon was over the challenges that faced the first Australians were immense. The extinction of the large herbivores and the bushfire crisis were huge blows to an already very specialized, and hence vulnerable ecology. Without human intervention, massive bushfires could have decreased the viability of many other animal species. As it was, the introduction of the fire regime seems to have stabilized the situation and prevented further degradation of the environment. It was a fix, but a fix that stood the test of time.

As well as coping with a damaged environment and a much reduced quantity of game, most Aboriginal peoples faced challenges rarely faced by humanity. Paramount amongst these was the scarcity and unpredictably of water supply, and the consequent boom-and-bust fluctuations of many of the species of animals hunted for food. Almost against logic this actually seems to have resulted in a better standard of diet than that experienced by many peoples in more stable environments.

That they did so has two chief causes. The relative scarcity of food resulted in the early Australians becoming experts in everything that could possibly have nutritional value, from plant roots to roos, and moths to mussels. In most parts of the continent people could draw on a variety of in-season fruits and animals, more than sufficient to sustain them. In the process they also discovered an extensive natural medicine chest that helped keep them healthy. That this natural larder was not over-stretched is paradoxically because of the boom-and-bust ecology. In many environments the really bad times are rare. Humans, though slow breeders, can build populations that make the most of relatively long periods of prosperity. The ENSO (El Niño Southern Oscillation) driven Australian climate dictated the reverse pattern, with Aboriginal populations kept at the low levels possible in the periods of drought. In times of plenty there was more than enough to go around.

This pegging of population and resultant 'abundance' of food is perhaps one of the reasons why farming was rarely employed by Aboriginal peoples, even though the seeds of agriculture were probably in their cultural baggage. ENSO also makes farming extremely difficult, with attempts at planting crops frequently foiled by drought conditions, but one of the key factors that mitigated against Aboriginal agriculture was the lack of suitable species. It is now becoming accepted that under the experimental conditions of our early ancestors only a handful of plants and animals would have had exactly the right characteristics for domestication. In Australia all the large herbivores that may have been suitable quickly disappeared and to this day only one indigenous crop has been cultivated to any extent by Europeans: the macadamia nut. The unrelated factors of no domesticated animals and continental isolation were to later combine to make the Aboriginals horrifically susceptible to European diseases.

As is now widely appreciated, it is agriculture that has eventually provided any human culture with the excess labour required to build the urban trappings of civilization. Leading a nomadic or semi nomadic, hunter-gatherer lifestyle with little incentive or opportunity for farming, the Australian peoples rarely created permanent settlements. Over most of the continent not even clothes, let alone buildings were required for warmth. Buildings were also unnecessary for either safety, keeping animals or the storage of foodstuffs. Only in the colder south were some of these trappings adopted. Here some peoples sewed together blankets and clothes from skins and embarked on intensive aquaculture, building sophisticated canals and traps to catch fish and eels.

With strong parallels with the peoples in North America, the Aboriginal peoples came to place a great value on their relationship with the land. Disturbances to their environment, or deviation from the fire regime (sometimes called 'fire-stick farming'), were recognized as threats to survival, and this relationship came to be regarded as a sacred stewardship. Nomadic peoples rarely develop the concept of land ownership, but the peoples of Australia did maintain strict 'territories', each carefully tended and managed by its resident people. Embarking on a journey through another people's land involved careful negotiation, but even so this was not a rare event.

In environments as difficult as most that Australia has to offer, isolation can be lethal. Regional contact was maintained through constant trading, mostly for ochre or precious materials used in the making of jewellery. These were mined in a large number of sites across Australia. There were also great regional meetings, social *corroborees* that usually coincided with an abundant, seasonal food source. Over tens of thousands of years this helped maintain a remarkable consistency of culture across such a vast area.

Given such a prodigious tenure it is hardly surprising that a folk memory of their ancestors' coming to Australia has been lost. Aboriginal history is passed from generation to generation in the form of oral stories, part of the all-pervasive culture of 'dreaming' that also encompasses law, religion, customs and knowledge. These stories talk of a period when powerful ancestors, both human and animal, strode the land, creating natural features, plants, animals and peoples alike. Parts of the dreaming were also immortalized, and illustrated to younger generations through songs and dances, rock art and carvings. It is probable that Australia now has the oldest such art on the planet.

Aboriginal culture is the longest uninterrupted culture the modern world has witnessed. Over tens of thousands of years the first peoples of Australia developed unique strategies to ensure their survival in the face of some of the world's most difficult environments. They built a rich cultural heritage, a phenomenal knowledge of their land and its natural resources, prodigious internal trade routes, a carefully managed environment, and a stable population in harmony with that environment rather than stressing it.

Early European exploration

On the far side of the world, European trading interest in Asia matured in the 15th and 16th centuries, and at last brought Europeans into contact with the only habitable continent they had not yet seen. By the end of the 16th century the published information on the new land was still negligible. Just a few charts that clearly rely more on guesswork than actual knowledge, and a small passage written in 1598 by one Cornelius Wytfliet that begins, "The Australis Terra is the most southern of lands, and is separated from New Guinea by a narrow strait." The situation was, however, about to change. In 1601 the Dutch ship *Duyfken* encountered Cape York Peninsula, and in a nearly aborted voyage of discovery in 1606 the Spaniard Luis de Torres negotiated his way through the strait that now bears his name. That the certain knowledge of Torres Strait remained, for whatever reason, unavailable to the other sea-faring nations for over 150 years, had a profound effect on how the exploration of Australian shores proceeded.

This is to jump the gun, however, for we need to look at the first really important date of 1584. In that year the overbearing king of Spain, Phillip II, decided to punish the Dutch for their religious heresies by barring their ships to Lisbon, a port that had latterly come into his control. Hitherto the Dutch had done a roaring trade as the hauliers of Europe, picking up the goods the Portuguese brought back from the far east and transporting them all over western seaboard. Phillip, having failed to subjugate them with the sword, was now trying to cut their economic base from under them. The Dutch were nothing if not wilful, however, and instead they set about fetching the goods from the far east themselves. In 1597 the first fleet returned in triumph and in 1611 Hendrik Brouwer discovered that sailing due east from the Cape of Good Hope for 3,000 miles, and then turning north, cut about two months off the Holland-Java journey time. Five years later Dirk Hartog, in the trading ship *Eendracht*, overshot the mark and found his namesake island off Shark Bay. This is the first time that we know for certain Europeans stepped onto Western Australian soil. He left an inscribed pewter dinner plate nailed to a post, thus setting something of a trend for plate souveniring among early explorers. A visible landmark really opened the route up, and soon the Dutch were establishing a fair picture of the west coast of what came to be called New Holland, wrecking many of their ships on it in the process, including the infamous *Batavia*.

The next sea captain to purposefully arrive at WA's shores was William de Vlamingh of the Dutch East India Company, in 1697, who removed Hartog's plate and nailed up his own. William Dampier had been the first Englishman on the continent in 1688, landing near Broome, and he visited the northwest again in 1699, naming Shark Bay for its abundance of sharks while exploring in the *Roebuck*. (Despite the name, the sharks in the bay have plenty to eat and a shark attack on humans has never been known in these waters).

In 1772 Francois de St Allouarn landed at Cape Inscription and, ignoring Vlamingh's plate, claimed the land for France (though Cook had landed at Botany Bay two years earlier). More Frenchmen arrived in 1801 and again in 1803 on Baudin's voyages of scientific discovery. The *Geographe* and *Naturaliste* spent 70 days exploring Shark Bay and named most of its geographical features. Captain Hamelin of the *Naturaliste* found time to re-erect Vlamingh's plate, which had slipped into the sand, and added one of his own.

All of these explorers were unimpressed with what seemed to be barren land and had trouble finding freshwater. Their negative reports meant that European settlers stayed away. Of course to the local Aboriginal people the west coast was a cornucopia of seafood and they harvested shellfish, turtles, and dugongs as well as the land mammals.

Two of the pewter dinner plates finally found resting places well away from the harsh sun of Shark Bay. Hartog's plate of 1616 lives in the Rikjsmuseum of Amsterdam and Vlamingh's plate of 1697 now belongs to the Maritime Museum in Fremantle. The French government returned it to Australia in 1947. The youngest plate, Hamelin's of 1801, has never been found.

The process of colonization

European designs on Australia only became serious after Captain James Cook was sent by the English government to observe a transit of Venus in Tahiti in 1770. By now the English were very much caught up in the European exploratory spirit and he was instructed, while in the area, to check out New Zealand and, if possible, chart the hitherto unexplored eastern coast of New Holland. In all this he was completely successful, spending six months charting New Zealand and then sailing west as planned. This east coast was sufficiently far from the western coasts that it was entirely possible the two were actually unconnected, and he named the 'new' territory New South Wales. He must have seen the Australian environment at its best and gave glowing descriptions of it in his reports to his government. His positive, though fateful and misinformed opinions were summarized in *The Voyages of Captain Cook*:

"The industry of man has had nothing to do with any part of it, and yet we find all such things as nature hath bestowed upon it in a flourishing state. In this extensive country it can never be doubted but what most sorts of grain, fruit, roots, etc, of every kind, would flourish were they brought hither, planted and cultivated by the hands of industry; and here is provender for more cattle, at all seasons of the year, than can ever be brought into the country."

Two of the most different cultures imaginable were now on an inevitable collision course. No sooner had the British Empire nonchalantly claimed a large new territory than it was ignominiously turfed out of an old one. In 1782 the American colonies successfully gained independence by prosecuting a war against the empire, carving a new future for themselves and creating all sorts of problems for the aghast British government. Not least amongst these issues was what to do with tens of thousands of convicts, who continued to be sentenced to 'transportation', now that the traditional dumping ground was off limits. The other colonies swiftly declined to accept them, and the practice of dropping them off in West Africa was given up on the grounds that this simply meant a nastier death for the transportees than they could have otherwise enjoyed at the end of a noose back home.

Sir Joseph Banks, Cook's wealthy and influential botanist on the *Endeavour*, had suggested New South Wales as early as 1779, but it wasn't until 1786 that Prime Minister William Pitt agreed to the suggestion, then formally put forward by Lord Sydney, the minister responsible for felons. The following year Arthur Phillip's 'first fleet' set out for Botany Bay, less a grand colonial voyage than a handy solution to a pressing problem.

Some forty years later the British, partly scouting for a penal settlement for re-offenders and partly to counter perceived French ambitions, finally made a small encampment in the western half of the continent, at King William Sound (now Albany) in 1826. In 1828 they dispatched a warship to the Swan River to formally claim western New Holland as a colonial territory, and Captain James Stirling, after much persistent lobbying and government vacillation, was finally sent to found the Swan River Colony in 1829.

As is not unusual in the history of the British invasions of Australia, Stirling discounted the local Aboriginal peoples, offering no treaty and ignoring them entirely in his planning. It took decades for Europeans to even begin to understand the Aboriginals' complex relationship with their land. It is ill understood even today. Most did not care and some, particularly the poor or emancipated, were happy that there were people on a rung lower than theirs. It was assumed that as the Aboriginals did not farm they had no concept or right of ownership; that since they were nomadic they could simply move out of the way; that as their technology was relatively simple so was their culture and indeed so were they as people. From the very beginning there were settlers who considered them sub-human, and right up to the 1960s many Aboriginals believed themselves, not unreasonably, regarded as 'fauna'.

Today it is vigorously debated how much the early authorities were guided by the policy of *terra nullius*, the idea that Australia was an empty land, free for the taking. *Terra nullius* was a legal fiction based on the premise that land ownership was only proved by land cultivation. The colonial authorities did not think that Australia was empty, but that Aboriginal people had no legal claim upon it. At the time it seems likely that whatever angst was occurring in the minds of liberal societies and authorities in England or urban Australia, the reality on the crucial frontier was promoted by the pioneering settler, over which the authorities had little control. For many that reality was one of conflict. *Terra nullius* was immaterial, there was a future to secure and it was 'either us or them'.

Disease did a lot of the damage, with thousands of Aboriginals undoubtedly dying of smallpox and flu, syphilis and typhoid. The Europeans' long association with domestic animals had fermented a rich brew of the beasties and, like the native Americans before them, the native Australians had little defense. Sometimes, however, there were survivors, and some of these could not be persuaded to join a Christian mission or work as a farm hand or join the native police. Then some of the of the most intense confrontations took place. Some Aboriginals fought back, spearing settlers and attempting to drive them back from whence they had come. The response, both official and not, was often savage. There are known instances of whole groups being rounded up and shot wholesale as retribution for something as trivial as the death of a bullock. On the other hand some groups simply tried to maintain their existence, living off the land as their ancestors had done. Here less brutal tactics were sometimes employed by the Europeans, such as the poisoning of their waterholes.

By the late 1860s it was all over bar the shouting. Aboriginal peoples reached some of their lowest populations ever, driven almost entirely from the southwest and with only fragmented peoples clinging to existence on the fringes of European society over much of the rest of the state. Only deep in the northwest deserts and in the Kimberley did their traditional way of life persist relatively untarnished into the 20th century, in parts as late as the 1950s. When in the late 19th century Charles Darwin's theories gained widespread notice, it was widely expected that Aboriginals would become extinct. Their perceived inferiority meant they could not survive in the face of a more 'advanced' people. It was simply a case of the 'survival of the fittest'.

Captain Stirling also committed the usual Australian mistake of grossly exaggerating the excellence of the potential port facilities and the suitability of the local land for agriculture. Partly as a result of these misplaced notions, the early settlements of Fremantle and Perth got off to a very slow start, despite considerable private backing from English speculators. The finding of the relatively fertile Avon Valley in 1830 and the decisive crushing of Aboriginal opposition at the 'battle' of Pinjarra (see page 131) in 1834 did open doors for some settlers, leading to the establishment of a reasonable wool industry, but a generation later in 1850 the entire colony could still only boast a population of 5,500 Europeans and the addition of just a couple of other industries including the cutting and export of local sandalwood to China.

Aboriginal people have lived in the southwest, a rich source of vegetation and wildlife, for many thousands of years and a lot of local landscape features are still known by the names given by *Nyoongar* people. The region was the first of any distance from Perth's Swan River Colony to be prospected by pastoralists and woodsmen, the earliest in the 1830s. In the decades until the turn of the century settlements gradually developed and wool, timber and horses which were all exported from Koombana Bay.

The convict era

Following strong urging from some of the few thriving Perth businessmen, who appreciated the possibilities cheap labour would present, the colony accepted its first consignment of convicts in 1850 and 10,000 more over the next 18 years. The convicts were considered a most unsavoury addition by many of the settlers, but undoubtedly did help to open up parts of the immense colony at a time when many were to tempted to abandon it in favour of the new eastern goldfields around Ballarat and Bendigo in Victoria. The southwest saw renewed energies with the coming of the convicts, but it was the coastal region between Perth and Shark Bay that was first largely exploited using convict labour. The land known as Greenough Flats proved reasonably fertile, and soon much of this whole stretch of land was being claimed by pastoralists at the expense of the local Aboriginal people. Small ports developed at places like Denison, Geraldton and Gregory, though most swiftly fell into disservice thanks to their relatively poor situations. Mineral prospectors accompanied the pastoralists, and some significant discoveries were made, such as those around Northampton, though gold – the holy grail – eluded them. Later in the 1850s bay islands in the Gascoyne region were mined for guano and the potential of local pearl shell realized. Many pearling settlements sprang up in the north, such as Cossack and Broome, during the 1870s to 1890s. The industry brought many Chinese, Filipinos, Japanese and Malay people and Aboriginal people also worked as pearl divers, although there are reports that some were kidnapped and forced to dive. The pearls were over exploited, however, and the industry crashed during the depression of the 1930s.

The state government encouraged pastoralists to take up land further and further north in the Pilbara and Kimberley regions during the late 1850s and 60s. Most of the land in the more fertile and temperate regions of the south had been claimed and the government knew that the success of the colony depended on further expansion. Surveyor Francis Gregory was sent to explore the Pilbara region in 1861 and established a base camp at Nickol Bay, near the modern town of Karratha. He believed conditions in the Pilbara were suitable for pastoralists and made enthusiastic reports to the government who quickly offered generous leasing terms. The first pastoralist, Walter Padbury, arrived in 1863 and settled on the De Grey River just north of Port Hedland. The Withnell family arrived the following year at the Tien Tsin harbour (later known as Cossack) and settled by a freshwater pool in the Harding River. A settlement grew around their home and became the first town of the northwest in 1866, when it was named Roebourne after the state Surveyor-General, John Septimus Roe. All over the state pastoralists and settlers found conditions tough, however, and supplemented their income by fishing and harvesting native timber. The pastoral industry struggled, particularly in the north, until an artesian basin was discovered in 1900, ensuring a reliable supply of water for stock.

Of course all of this new land for sheep and wheat was far from empty. Aboriginal people are thought to have continuously inhabited Western Australia for the last 20,000 years at least, and as the British settlers moved in to new areas their traditional way of life came under unrelenting pressure. Even in the more remote areas waterholes were ruined by stock, sacred sites destroyed and native animals depleted. Violent conflict persisted and many more Aboriginal people were killed in battle or massacred by terrified European settlers, determined to protect themselves and what they perceived to be their legal property. European diseases also continued to devastate many groups and others moved away from their inland country to the new coastal settlements; the combination of a massively disrupted society and the lure of European goods contributing to the decision (or necessity) to move off their land.

The white population of WA slowly climbed, and as did it so the colony began to prosper, thanks largely to thriving wool and timber industries, and by 1892 there were around 50,000 non-indigenous West Australians thinly spread over the enormous colony. Despite the low population, agricultural progress was matched by important social advances. In 1861 about one in four European Australians were illiterate, a figure reduced to one in 40 by 1892. The unions forced a shorter working day, then a shorter working week, opening up Saturday afternoons for sport and leisure. The outdoor climate, large accessible spaces, and large urban populations contrived to ensure that sport itself became almost a religion, those competing successfully at international level were the new gods. By 1900 Australians were avid followers of home-grown boxers, skullers, horses, cricketers, athletes and footballers. With the rise in sport came a rise in gambling, a habit Australia has never lost. At the same time there was a growing appreciation of indigenous flora and fauna. Bushwalking societies formed and there were moves to declare reserves around outstandingly beautiful natural landmarks. These forerunners of the National Parks began to be established in the 1870s and 1880s.

Societies very much at odds with the natural environment were also formed. A nostalgia for 'home' led groups of misguided amateur naturalists to import countless species of plants and animals in the hope that the alien landscape of Australia could be transformed into one huge English garden. Other animals were brought over as pets or for stock, and these too often escaped into the wild. Foxes were introduced, for example, so that people could participate in an authentic hunt. Today dozens of these species have gone feral, each one disturbing the native ecology to a greater or lesser degree.

That much of this progress was at the expense of the traumatized indigenous peoples and the environment they had so carefully managed went largely unnoticed and unremarked. Their cultures were almost fatally fractured and reservoirs of knowledge were disappearing fast. They were rarely actively hunted down any more, though cold-blooded massacres allegedly occurred well into the 1900s, but a decline in aggression did not mean an increase in acceptance. That they would themselves soon disappear entirely still seemed entirely likely to the white population, so there was little need to include them in the colony's future.

Gold and Federation

In 1890 Western Australia finally became self-governing, and as if in celebration (and strangely echoing events in Victoria 40 years before) gold was found near to the modern site of Coolgardie. Other states were experiencing economic chaos, but thanks to the Coolgardie and Kalgoorlie-Boulder gold finds Western Australia finally made the big leap forward in the 1890s that it had witnessed the other colonies make in the 1850s and 1860s. Within months tens of thousands of people had made their way over from the eastern states, from even as far as Britain, China and the United States. One of those from the US was a young Herbert Hoover. They camped in canvas cities, all desperately seeking the big find that would make them their fortune. The gold was there in prodigious quantities, and many did indeed become rich. Many more, however, died of disease or accident and a stroll around the cemetery at Coolgardie is a sobering experience – only a handful of the hundreds interred between 1890 and 1920 were over 35.

As well as experiencing gold fever in the 1890s, WA politicians kept a wary eye on the debate over whether Australia should federate or not. Up to about 1890 the six Australian colonies and New Zealand had jealously guarded their independence from each other. Proud of their differences they each operated their own institutions, governments, services and military forces, united only by currency, the environment and a shared heritage. Their military forces were scant, however, and the colonies still relied heavily on the navy of the British Empire for defence. During the late 1800s other nations such as France, Germany, Japan and Russia were becoming powerful, challenging the Empire for hegemony over maritime and continental trade routes. In Australia there were very real fears that some of these powers might have designs on Australian territory, and in the late 1880s Britain pointed out that the colonies' military forces were hugely inadequate and would be far more effective if united under a single command structure.

In 1889 the Prime Minister of New South Wales made a bold step. He suggested that the proposed federation of armed forces be given far greater scope, that it should be widened to a political federation of the colonies. The Commonwealth officially came into existence on 1 January 1901 and it effectively ushered in nationhood. Colonies became states, and the relationship with the 'mother country' became more complex. On the one hand ties had never been stronger. Many who held high office were British born, Britain was still Australia's biggest market for most of its exports, and British rather than Australian history was still considered more important in schools. On the other hand a British visitor to the new nation had to be careful not to offend local sensibilities. He or she would perhaps be called a 'pommy' (suspected to be a cockney derivative of 'immigrant' from 'pomegranate') instead of the warmer 'new chum' that had been in vogue since the eastern goldrushes of the 1850s. They would also have noticed signs encouraging people to 'buy Australian' and shun imported goods from the Empire and elsewhere. That they could be encouraged so was a sign of Australia's growing self-sufficiency and a surge of confidence.

Federation also ushered in a raft of legislation that smoothed out policy across the nation. Paramount amongst these was that which gave women the vote in 1902. Another was the formal introduction of a 'White Australia' policy which, although in line with many nations of the day, seems shocking now and also jars given that the island continent was so manifestly 'Non-White Australia' just 125 years before.

Immigration restarted in earnest in the mid-1900s, an integral part of the process being a dictation test in the European language of the immigration official's choice! In the northern regions of Australia where the colonial frontier was still advancing, Aboriginal people were increasingly devastated by violence, disease, starvation and exploitation. The colonial governments had begun to worry that they were witnessing the destruction of Aboriginal people and introduced a raft of legislation to 'protect' them by confining them to certain areas away from Europeans. Additional legislation meant that Aboriginal people could be forced to move to a reserve, were denied citizenship and the vote, and were prohibited sexual relations with 'Europeans'.

Between 1890 and 1910 a lot of the remaining land in WA that could be useful to the colonists was utilized, in the south for wheat and wool, in the north for cattle. Pearl shell began to be harvested in massive quantities off the northern coast and a string of small ports was established both for the lugger fleets and to ship cattle. By 1912 WA's population had increased sharply to over 300,000 'whites' plus an uncounted and declining number of Aboriginal people no longer seen as significant.

War and peace

The still very British people of WA rallied to the standard of the Empire during the First World War like almost no other former colony. The state provided nearly four times as many soldiers and auxiliary workers as its agreed share, and those that went suffered higher casualty rates than any other soldiers in the British Empire. It has been said that because of their extreme courage and resilience they were commonly used as front-line 'shock troops'. Significant monuments in Kings Park, Perth, honour their sacrifice and there is also an avenue of gum trees there, each marked by a plaque commemorating one of the dead.

The Australian Imperial Force (AIF) were all either regular army or volunteers, but had still mustered 300,000 by the end of the First World War. They figured in many theatres of the war, the most celebrated of which has come to be known as Gallipoli. On 25 April 1915 the Anzacs (Australia and New Zealand Army Corps) constituted a large part of a force sent to win control of the banks of the Dardanelles, the narrow channel that connects the Aegean and Marmara seas. The expedition's success would open the allies' supply line through the Mediterranean to the Black Sea and so to Russia.

Though finally forced to retreat, the chief legacy of the campaign was profound for Australians. The Anzacs were seen to display a degree of bravery, mateship and humour not expected in such an untried force. In a seminal moment for the nation, its unbloodied and untested soldiers had faced the fire for the first time and not been found wanting. It is sometimes thought that these expressions of national character were forged on the beaches of Gallipoli, but it is truer to say that it is during the campaign that foreign journalists first saw and publicized these traits that had been slowly maturing for decades. Unseen by the rest of the world, and even by many urban Australians, Australian toughness, independence and cooperation had been won on the pastoral and mining frontiers over the previous century. Of the 300,000 Australians who went to war over 50,000 were killed, a greater number than was lost by America. Many of these were the bravest, most resourceful, most inspiring men of their time. Their loss was profoundly felt, eliciting a huge outpouring of national pride and grief, given substance by literally thousands of memorials erected all over the country.

After the war, returned servicemen and post-war immigrants from Britain and parts of western Europe had to be quickly and efficiently housed and found work. One obvious solution was to grant settlements of bush for clearing and cultivation. In WA's southwest region the timber was largely gone by the end of the First World War and in one scheme the government decided to try to use the region for dairy farming. The Minister for Lands proposed the Group Settlement Scheme in 1921 and 3,391 hungry migrants from post-war Britain arrived, keen to have their own piece of earth. Few realized how tough it would be and there are reports of tears when they saw the rough huts and dirt floors they had to live in. They cleared some land, built fences and houses and tried to make a go of it, but by 1924 a third of the 'groupies' had walked off their land with nothing. The depression finished off many of those who stayed on into the 1930s.

There was a significant expansion of the burgeoning 'wheat-belt' throughout the 1920s, though, with new machinery and technology enabling the clearing and farming of huge tracts of land with comparatively few workers. Cattle and sheep farming in the north also boomed with high prices commanded on the world's markets. The good times were not set to last, however, as the global depression of the 1930s certainly did not spare WA. Up to a third of the state's workforce was laid off during the decade, and considerable government assistance was required to stave off actual starvation. The only industry that benefited was Kalgoorlie's gold-mining, which was able to hire labour very cheaply and increase production when every other industry saw output collapse.

The 1930s were also marked by increased misery for many Aboriginal people. Influenced by popular notions of eugenics and racial purity in Europe, Australian state governments thought that 'full bloods' would eventually die out and 'half castes' could be bred out. It was thought that if a woman of both Aboriginal and European descent took a European partner, and her children did the same, then the 'Aboriginal blood' would eventually become so diluted as to be invisible. It was also thought that if children of mixed descent with fairly pale skin could be taken from their Aboriginal mothers at an early age and raised within the white community it would give the child every material advantage and help 'half-castes' to be absorbed into the community. Thus in the Western Australian Aboriginal Act (1936) provisions relating to permission to marry and sexual relations between Aboriginal people and Europeans were strengthened. The state's powers of guardianship were increasingly used to remove children of mixed descent from their mothers and rear them in missions, orphanages or foster homes. This process and some of its consequences are movingly and powerfully portrayed in the film *Rabbit Proof Fence*. In 1937 a conference of the state government Protectors decided '*the destiny of the natives of aboriginal origin, but not of the full blood, lies in their ultimate absorption by the people of the Commonwealth, and it therefore recommends that all efforts be directed to that end.*' However, anthropologists working with Aboriginal people in the 1930s did begin to try to educate the rest of society about their culture, and various humanitarian groups and Aboriginal protest groups also began to agitate for a change in attitudes.

The advent of world war in 1939 again proved a huge draw to young men of WA, though this time Australia itself was to become geographically involved. Japanese bomber aircraft repeatedly attacked some of the northern towns during 1942-1943, including Broome, and there was widespread belief that an invasion was imminent. This sharp recognition of vulnerability had a deep impression on the Australian psyche and is an aspect of national psychology to this day. The Second World War also marked a reversal in the state's financial fortunes. Wool and wheat prices climbed steadily, and continued to do so after 1945. Returning soldiers who moved onto the land in the late 1940s and 1950s had a much better time of it than their predecessors 30 years before.

Post-war prosperity

Prime Minister Ben Chifley's Australia of the late 1940s was a careful nation. Although beaten by the bomb, it was felt that Japan still had considerable potential for aggression and Australia played a leading role in garrisoning the defeated country and prosecuting its war leaders. There was a deep feeling that peace could not last. Russia and China were deemed the major new threats and it was universally felt that a large population would be the best disincentive to invasion, and defence against any such attempt.

The old 'White Australia' policy was energized once more. Chifley's chief minister for immigration, Arthur Calwell, instigated and pursued the most vigorous such programme Australia has ever seen. The nation must 'populate or perish'. It was originally thought that the Brits, still seen as the best 'stock', could make up 90 per cent of the numbers but this proved over-ambitious – they eventually made up around a quarter of the immigrants of the period, and some of those were unwittingly expatriated orphans. Calwell had to relax his criteria and was soon fishing in the vast refugee camp that central and southern Europe had become. The net would be thrown no wider: those of African or Asian origin were definitely not welcome.

Non-British immigrants had to put up with a fair amount of social antagonism. 'Refos' (refugees), 'DPs' (displaced persons) and 'dagos' were taunts frequently slung at the newcomers. The few non-European immigrants and descendants of the earlier Chinese gold-miners fared much worse, suffering at times outright racial vilification. The non-British were, however, to form the foundation of a vibrant and successful urban multi-cultural society.

In 1949 the giant of 20th-century Australian politics, Robert Menzies, strode back into the limelight, leading his new national Liberal party to election victory. A staunch monarchist, he welcomed Queen Elizabeth II to Australia in 1954, the first reigning monarch to make the trip. In 1962 she came to Perth to open the Commonwealth Games which the city was proudly hosting. The games were a huge success, televised all over the world, and proved a showcase for WA.

Post-war migration helped swell the population of WA to over 700,000 by 1960. The wheat-belt became vast, producing huge quantities of grain for export and an even more valuable amount of wool. Gold production stuttered occasionally but reached its peak in 1961, and the Kimberley and Pilbara cattle runs matured and prospered. Pastoralism struggled with water shortages, disease, cyclones and isolation but remained the major industry in the north until the 1960s. Then minerals other than gold, but almost as valuable, began turning up in the north. Amongst them nickel, iron-ore, bauxite and oil were found in massive quantities, and today they have been joined by the discovery of almost indecent numbers of premium grade diamonds in the eastern Kimberley. The government lifted an embargo on the export of iron ore in 1960 and scientists confirmed that the Pilbara contained massive quantities of high grade ore. Mining companies quickly established new mines, ports, railways and towns to exploit these resources. Dampier, Karratha, Wickham and the inland mining towns of Newman, Tom Price and Paraburdoo were all developed during the 1960-1970s. The Pilbara is now responsible for 40 per cent of Australia's mineral exports, and the Kimberley for 30 per cent of the world's diamonds.

The impact on the culture and environment that existed prior to 1829 cannot be understated. Entire peoples had vanished over much of this sub-continent. Huge tracts of land were cleared of native vegetation to make way for wheat and wool, and much of this has resulted in a rising water table, bringing with it enough salt to ruin huge areas of land for anything, let alone agriculture. Species loss amongst both plant and animal life, particularly in the southwest, will never be accurately known but was certainly substantial. Immediate prosperity also had a radical impact on WA's colonial cultural heritage when much of historic central Perth was bulldozed in the 1960-1970s to make way for modern office blocks.

The life of the remaining Aboriginal people also changed greatly during this period. Since the 1860s many Aboriginal people had lived and worked on pastoral stations, maintaining links with their traditional lands. However pastoralists' exploitation of Aboriginal workers led to resentment and in 1946 Aboriginal pastoral station workers went on strike for equal wages and conditions. They finally got them in 1968 but this meant that station owners simply couldn't or wouldn't employ as many workers. The result was an urban Aboriginal population who had little contact with their own country and the further breakdown of their culture and identity.

Culture shock

Their was, however, a flip-side to post-war optimism. Although the Japanese had failed to establish a modern Asian Empire the 'western' world became convinced that either China or the Soviets might succeed, and many Australians believed that their beloved homeland would be firmly in the sights of any nation with such ambitions.

This fear of communism had two profound effects, which between them later engendered a counter consequence of equal, if not greater importance. Anti-communist hysteria goes a long way to explaining the firm grip that conservative governments were to have on Australian politics for a quarter of a century, with Labor Party members and supporters frequently suspected of being communist sympathizers and even spies. In 1950 Robert Menzies held a national referendum on whether the Communist Party should be banned outright and its members jailed. To the nation's credit the result was a comfortable 'no'. The other major effect of the national mood was an enthusiastic willingness to back up any Asian military efforts against the 'red tide' with practical support. The same year as the referendum saw Australian troops join those from the USA and their other allies in fighting the 'commies' in Korea. A little later, in the year of the Melbourne Olympics, the Soviet Union invaded Hungary and anti-communist fears in Australia were bolstered further by a stream of frightened refugees.

The conservative cauldron simmered on through the height of the Cold War in late 1950s and early 1960s, thus ensuring that Australia, unlike Britain, was ready to send troops in support of another Asian crusade, this time in Vietnam. The Australian commitment was never huge in military terms, committing some 8,000 people, but Prime Minister Harold Holt's famous statement, "all the way with LBJ", neatly illustrates the depth of conservative political support. It was also an indication that Australia was shifting from British influence to follow an American lead. Although only a few troops made the journey, some of them were conscripts. This sat uneasily with much of the general public, and when conscripts started getting killed unease turned to anger.

The nation became embroiled, for the first time in decades, in serious discussions about the direction and fitness of the national government and its policies. Demonstrations against the war were organized and some marches became violent. Governments frequently clamped down hard, prompting further discussion and protests on the subject of civil liberties. Some people demonstrated simply to express their view that they had a right to demonstrate. A heady brew of general anti-establishment feeling began to ferment, particularly amongst the youth of the day, inspired by their cousins in Europe and the US who were discovering a new independence from their 'elders and betters'.

Aboriginal people were also part of the protest movement and increasingly demanded change. In the early 1960s new legislation appeared in all states that largely removed the paternalistic and restrictive laws relating to Aboriginal people. The federal government enfranchised Aborigines of the Northern Territory (the only region under their control) and WA followed the federal lead. Previously citizenship had only been available to those who applied for it and was subject to certain conditions: in Western Australia that meant not keeping company with any Aboriginal people except the applicant's immediate family for two years before applying and after being granted citizenship.

The granting of rights such as equal wages had to be fought for in some cases, even when the legislation existed, and this could be the catalyst for further activism. When the Gurindji people failed to obtain equal wages from the powerful Lord Vestey of Wave Hill Station in the Northern Territory they walked off the land, led by stockman Vincent Lingiari, and decided to make a land rights claim for some of Vestey-owned land. As one of his people later said, "*We were treated just like dogs. We were lucky to get paid the fifty quid a month we were due, and we lived in tin humpies you had to crawl in and out on your knees. There was no running water. The food was bad – just flour, tea, sugar and bits of beef like the head or feet of a bullock. The Vesteys were hard men. They didn't care about blackfellas.*" Just ten years earlier Lingiari and his Gurindji people would probably have been ignominiously, forcefully and quietly evicted, but this was 1966 and sections of society were prepared to listen and help. The ruling conservative Liberal-Country Party rejected the Aboriginals' claim, wary of their own land-owning voters and perhaps of the effects a positive outcome might have on future mineral exploitation. The political wind was, however, changing. The Australian people had soon had enough of the conservatives and were ready for a new broom. In 1972 they finally elected the Labor Party back into power, and with it the charismatic and energetic Gough Whitlam.

Modern Australia

In many ways the brief tenure of Gough Whitlam as national Prime Minister was the coming of age for Australia. He came to power unencumbered by decades of the politics of fear, and with a zeal to be his own man and make Australia her own nation. Within days the troops were recalled from Vietnam and conscription ended, women were legally granted an equal wage structure, 'White Australia' formally abandoned, and a Ministry of Aboriginal Affairs created. Whitlam's policy was "to restore to the Aboriginal people of Australia their lost power of self-determination in economic, social and political affairs". Whitlam spurned the prime ministerial Bentley, ended the old imperial honours system and dumped *God Save the Queen* as the national anthem. He was a political dynamo, and exacted an unprecedented work-rate from his colleagues. His policies were not everyone's cup of tea, but no one could argue that his every effort was not aimed at the betterment of Australia and Australians. In 1975 the Gurindji people were given 2,000 sq km from the Vestey leases and Whitlam flew to Wave Hill to personally hand over the deeds, symbolically pouring a handful of sand into the palm of Vincent Lingiari as he did so. Even Whitlam's sacking a few months later, a controversial affair involving the Governor-General and so the British Crown, had the effect of galvanizing public opinion on the subject of republicanism. Whitlam had permanently altered the mood of the nation, and of Australian politics.

In some ways these events were peripheral to matters in WA. The state's residents – known as 'sandgropers' – refer to the rest of Australia as 'the eastern states', sometimes with no little contempt. However, WA soon had a vibrant but highly conservative premier of its own. Liberal Sir Charles Court was Prime Minister from 1974 until 1982, and helped channel WA's undoubted wealth and vitality as no-one had done before. By the end of his tenure over a million people could call themselves Western Australians. The spirit of raw Western Australian entrepreneurship was colourfully personified by Alan Bond, an English immigrant of the late 1950s who was a multi-millionaire by the 1970s. In 1983 Perth famously hosted the world's most famous sailing race, the America's Cup, and Alan decided that the USA's 132 year-old cast-iron hold on the cup needed to be dislodged. As a result of his enthusiasm and determination, his yacht *Australia II* did just that, triumphing in the event to the delight of the whole country.

The 1980s also saw interstate and international tourists start to pay more attention to WA, until then the poorest tourist relation of the popular east coast. Mirroring the early European invasion of the state 150 years before, tourists first made for Perth, its hinterland and the southwest Cape-to-Cape region, widely known to travellers as simply 'Margaret River'. Gradually more and more travellers have ventured further and further from the capital: around the south coast, and north to Kalbarri, Shark Bay, Coral Bay and Broome. In the last decade or so more of the west coast has been 'discovered', as have the whale sharks visiting the Ningaloo Reef and the incredible gorges of Karijini in the Pilbara.

The 1990s was a tumultuous decade for issues involving Aboriginal people. In 1992 the High Court made what was probably the most important decision of the century in the Mabo land rights case. The court ruled that native title (or prior indigenous ownership of land) was not extinguished by the Crown's claim of possession in the Murray Islands of Torres Strait. In other words the legal fiction of *Terra nullias* was overturned after 222 years and the decision was later enshrined in the Native Title Act (1993). This was a major victory for Aboriginal people, although land owners had to be able to prove a continuous relationship to the land and claims could only be made on Crown land. A land fund was suggested to buy land for the majority of Aboriginal people who were unable to claim land under the Act. Despite the limited nature of native title conservatives were horrified and lobbied hard against it.

As Australia moved toward a new century, two campaigns aimed at moving the country in a new direction built a considerable head of steam; that for a republic and another for reconciliation. One sought to sunder further the ties with Britain, the other to build better ties between white and black Australians. Reconciliation was seen as important for the future health of the nation. A gesture that would heal the divisions between black and white and allow Australians to move into the future together. The Council for Aboriginal Reconciliation worked on a Declaration of Reconciliation that was presented to the government in 2000. In the same year there were large reconciliation marches all over the country by sections of the community who wanted to say 'sorry' for past injustices, despite the government's refusal to do so. The issue of the republic was to be decided by a 1999 national referendum. The question asked, however, was controversially worded in a way that prevented many republicans assenting to it, and the result was 'no', despite polls showing a majority in favour of a republic.

A new century

The Olympics went to Sydney in 2000, and must be ranked as one of the greatest games ever. The Aboriginal athlete Kathy Freeman won gold in the women's 400-m track sprint, sending the nation into a frenzy of joy. Following the reconciliation movement the victory seemed, to many, serendipitous. However, the huge optimism created by the successful staging of the Olympics seemed to fizzle out with the failure of the republic and the failure to achieve any meaningful reconciliation between indigenous and non-indigenous Australians. Aboriginal people are still coming to terms with the effects of dispossession and the government policies that have affected their lives from 1788 until the present day. By almost every measure of social welfare they are less well off than non-indigenous Australians, for example the life expectancy of an indigenous person is 20 years less than other Australians, and rectifying this inequality is the great challenge of the future for all Australians.

In the Federal election of November 2001 the Liberal-National government under John Howard was returned to power despite the unpopularity of the Goods and Services Tax introduced in 2000, and he was returned again in 2004, shortly thereafter becoming Australia's second-longest serving Prime Minister. The first campaign was run amid the uncertainty caused by the terrorist attacks of September 11 and issues of border protection highlighted by the government's handling of the *Tampa* crisis. Border protection and the detention of asylum seekers had become the hot issues and, as in much of the world, Australian political affairs have continued to be largely dominated by the international threat of terrorism and war rather than local issues. In October 2002 terrorism hit very close to home for Australians, and particularly Western Australians, when two nightclubs were bombed in Bali, killing around 200 people. The proportion of Western Australian holidaymakers killed was high sending shockwaves through the state's small population. Despite the on-going world climate of fear, the 2004 Federal election was fought rather more on domestic issues with the economy seemingly uppermost in the minds of most voters. As in the rest of the country, WA's prosperity continues to surge, and the voting population is loathe to rock the boat. The WA government has also been stable – though for Labor not Liberal, and its response to the state's environmental insults has finally turned a corner. Logging of old-growth forests has been stopped by the government, as has the potential development of a huge and hugely controversial tourist complex near Coral Bay. The 'salt-pan' crisis has been recognized as such and both government and private initiatives are under way to combat it.

Politics

Australian politics is of great importance to many Australians, a conversation topic on a par with the weather or sport. This is partly because of the sheer volume of government the country bears, partly because of the colourful characters and events Australian politics seems to throw up, and partly because everyone, by law, has to vote.

Australia's head of the state is one and the same as the reigning monarch of England, a throwback to when that monarch was the head of the British Empire, which the historical Australian colonies were very much part of. The Queen's principle representative in Australia, now usually Australian born, is the Governor-General, appointed by the Australian Prime Minister. His or her role is largely ceremonial though in theory they are invested with considerable powers. In 1975 the serving Governor-General, Sir John Kerr, demonstrated some of these by dismissing the government of Gough Whitlam during an unprecedented political crisis.

In practical terms the business of governing the whole country is undertaken by the Federal ('Commonwealth') Parliament based in Canberra. Its 'lower' House of Representatives is constituted by members directly elected from electorates with approximately equally sized populations. The electorates range in size from a small city suburb to that of Kalgoorlie which encompasses most of WA and is, in fact, the biggest electorate for any MP in the world. The 'upper' house, the Senate, is elected by a form of proportional representation that guarantees each state 12 members, and each territory two. The lower house formulates government policy and the upper house either vetoes or passes it. Both houses are voted for every three years.

There are two major parties which sit either side of the political fence. The Australian Labor Party ('ALP') and the Liberal Party are the two chief protagonists, the ALP being the rough equivalent of the British Labour Party or American Democrats, the Liberals the equivalent of the Conservatives or Republicans. Over the last 70 years the ALP have generally polled slightly higher than the Liberals, but have usually been kept out of office by the latter's alliance with the smaller National Party. The leader of the majority in the lower house forms the country's government and is its Prime Minister. In 2004 John Howard's Liberal/National coalition won their fourth consecutive election and are currently in office. The upper house is even more evenly balanced, and here the voting system usually allows the smaller significant parties, prevusouly Democrats and now more so the Greens to win more seats and so to effectively hold the balance of power. The last election, however, has finally delivered John Howard the majority in this chamber that he has sought for the best part of a decade.

Most of the nation's tax dollar ends up in the Commonwealth coffers. About a third of the Federal budget goes in benefit payments, about a fifth on the machinery of government and state institutions, and about a quarter is distributed as payments to individual states. A constant grievance between Federal and state governments is the relative proportion of each state's Federal income compared to the amount of tax its residents have paid, with bitter (and not untruthful) claims that some states subsidize the others.

In a second tier of government most states also have their own upper and lower houses, and also Governors. These too are elected on a three-year cycle, and much the same political parties vie for election. In Western Australia the current government is Labor and Geoff Gallup the Prime Minister.

Culture

Aboriginal art and culture

From the beginning

Aborigine is a Latin word meaning 'from the beginning'; the Romans used it to describe the first inhabitants of Latium and it can be used for any people living in a country from its earliest period. It may seem strange that the first Australians are known by a generic name but its meaning is certainly appropriate for Australian Aboriginal people. Although anthropologists believe that Aboriginal people arrived in Australia 50-60,000 years ago from Southeast Asia, Aboriginal people believe that they have always been here, that they were created here by their spirit ancestors. Before Europeans arrived in Australia Aboriginal people had no collective sense of identity. Their identity was tied to their own part of the country and to their extended family groups. Hence no name existed to describe all of the inhabitants of Australia, in the same way that until relatively recently the inhabitants of Europe would have had no conception of being 'European'.

A continent of many nations

When the First Fleet arrived with its cargo of convicts in 1788 there were 300,000 to 750,000 Aboriginal people living in Australia, who belonged to about 500 peoples or groups. It is difficult to make generalizations about Aboriginal people because each group had its own territory, its own language or dialect and its own culture. There were broad cultural similarities between these groups just as different nationalities in Europe had more in common with each other than they had with Chinese or African people for example. Naturally neighbouring groups were more similar to each other; perhaps speaking dialects of the same language and sharing some 'Dreamtime' myths linked to territory borders such as rivers and mountains. However, if a man from Cape York had found himself transported to the Western Desert he would have been unable to communicate with the desert people. He would have found them eating unfamiliar food and using different methods to obtain it. Their art would have been incomprehensible to him and their ceremony meaningless. If he had been able to speak their language he would have found that they had a different explanation of how they came into existence and his own creation ancestors would have been unknown to them. Each group was almost like a small state or nation.

Dreaming

Every traveller in Australia will encounter the concept of the 'Dreaming' or the 'Dreamtime'. These words attempt to explain a complex concept that lies at the heart of Aboriginal culture and should not be understood in the English context of something that is not real. Most Aboriginal groups believe that in the beginning the world was featureless. Ancestral beings emerged from the earth and as they moved about the landscape they began to shape it. Some of them created humans by giving birth to them or moulding them from incomplete life forms. Ancestral beings were sometimes human in form but also often animals, rocks, trees or stars, and could transform from one shape to another. Nor were they limited by their form; kangaroos could talk, fish could swim out of water. Wherever these beings went, whatever they did left its mark on the landscape. A mountain might be the fallen body of an ancestor speared to death, a waterhole may be the place a spirit emerged from the earth, a rock bar may show where an ancestor crossed a river, yellow ochre may be the fat of an ancestral kangaroo. In this way the entire continent is mapped with the tracks of the ancestor beings.

Although the time of creation and shaping of the landscape is associated with the temporal notion of 'beginning', it is important to understand that Dreaming is not part of the past. It lies within the present and will determine the future. The ancestral beings have a permanent presence in spiritual or physical form. The ancestors are also still involved in creation. Sexual intercourse is seen as being part of conception but new life can only be created if a conception spirit enters a woman's body. The place where this happens, near a waterhole, spring or sacred site, will determine the child's identification with a particular totem or ancestor. In this way Aboriginal people are directly connected to the ancestral world.

Aboriginal people belonged to a territory because they were descended from the ancestors who formed and shaped that territory. The ancestral beings were sources of life and powerful performers of great deeds but were also capable of being capricious, amoral and dangerous. Yet in their actions they laid down the rules for life. They created ceremony, song and designs to commemorate their deeds or journeys, established marriage and kinship rules and explained how to look after the land. In the simple forms related to outsiders, Dreaming stories often sound like moral fables. Knowledge of the land's creation stories was passed on from generation to generation, increasing in complexity or sacredness as an individual aged. With knowledge came the responsibility to look after sacred creation or resting places. Ceremonies were conducted to ensure the continuation of life forces and fertility. Aboriginal people had no idea of owning the land in the sense that it was a possession that could be traded or given away, but saw themselves as custodians of land in which humans, animals and spirits were inseparable, in fact were one and the same. Consequently Aboriginal people of one group had no interest in possessing the land of another group. Strange country was meaningless to them. To leave your country was to leave your world.

The bonds of kin

In their daily life Aboriginal people usually hunted, gathered and socialized within a small band, perhaps 50 people belonging to one or two families. These bands or clans only came together to form the whole group of several hundred people for ceremonial reasons and at places or times when food was plentiful. Group behaviour and social relations were governed by an intricate kinship system, and guided by the superior knowledge and experience of the elders. This is one of the reasons that the word 'tribe' is not used to describe groups of Aboriginal people, as a tribe by definition is led by a chief and Aboriginal society did not operate in this way. The rules of kinship are far too complicated to explain here, and also varied in different regions, but in essence the kinship system linked the whole group as family. You would call your birth mother 'mother' but you would also call your mother's sisters 'mother' and they would take on the obligations of that role. The same applied for sisters, fathers, uncles and so on. There were specific codes of behaviour for each kin relationship so you would know the appropriate way to behave towards each member of your group. For example, in many Aboriginal societies mothers-in-law and sons-in-law were not allowed to communicate with each other. A neat solution to an age-old problem in human relations!

Kinship also determined whom an individual could marry. In one type of kinship system each person in a group belongs to one of several sections or moieties. The moiety category is inherited from the father and so contains all of an individual's patrilineal relations. That individual can only marry someone from another moiety. Kinship links also exist between people of the same totem or ancestor. People born from the goanna ancestor would be related to all other 'goannas'. Each kinship relationship carried specific responsibilities and rights such as initiating a 'son' or giving food to a 'sister', creating a strong collective society where everyone is tied to each other. By this method food and possessions are distributed equally and because of these kinship obligations it is almost impossible for an individual to accumulate material wealth. This major difference between Aboriginal culture and the dominant ethic in Australian society of Western materialism still creates problems for those trying to live in both worlds. For example a young Aboriginal footballer will often move from his close-knit rural community to Melbourne to play in the AFL, and find it very difficult to balance the material demands of his family against the demands of his team who teach him to pursue personal wealth and glory.

Environment
The laws of the Dreaming provided a broad framework for spiritual and material life but of course Aboriginal culture was not static. Although their society valued continuity above change, parts of their culture were the result of adapting to their environment. Aboriginal people have lived in Australia for so long that they have seen major environmental changes such as climate change, dramatic changes in sea level caused by the last ice age and even volcanic eruptions in southern Australia. The picture that many people have in their minds of an Australian Aboriginal is of a desert-dwelling nomad with few possessions and only a roof of stars over his head at night. Of course some people lived like this but others sewed warm skin cloaks, built bark or stone huts or lived in the same place for several seasons. The ways in which Aboriginal people differed from each other very much depended on the environment that they lived in. Naturally, tools were developed to match the territory; boomerangs were not known to people who lived in areas of dense woodland, nor elaborate fish traps known to inland people. Conversely, Aboriginal people also changed their environment with methods such as 'fire-stick farming' (see page 302).

Hunting and gathering
Aboriginal people were generally semi-nomadic rather than true nomads but they did not wander about aimlessly. They moved purposefully to specific places within their territory to find food that they knew to be ripening or abundant at certain times of the year. Their long tenure and stable society meant that they knew the qualities of every plant, the behaviour of every animal and the nature of every season intimately. Men hunted large game such as kangaroos with their toolkit of spears, clubs or boomerangs, and women gathered fruit, vegetables, seeds, honey, shellfish and small game such as lizards using their own kit of bags, bowls and digging sticks. Each gender had its own responsibilities and knowledge, including the ceremonies to ensure continuing fertility by commemorating the Dreaming. The need to 'look after country' in this way also determined their movements. Although men were generally more powerful than women, having more authority over family members and ritual,

women had their own power base because of their knowledge and the reliability of the food they provided. Although hunting and gathering was labour intensive anthropologists estimate that Aboriginal people only had to spend three to five hours a day working for food, leaving plenty of time for social life and ceremony.

Ceremony and art

Ceremony and art were at the very heart of life for these were the ways in which Aboriginal people maintained their connection with the ancestors. During ceremonies the actions and movements of the ancestors would be recalled in songs and dances that the ancestors themselves had performed and handed down to each clan or group. Not only did the ancestral beings leave a physical record of their travels in the form of the landscape but also in paintings, sacred objects and sculptures that might be shown or used as part of a ceremony. Ceremonies maintained the power and life force of the ancestors thus replenishing the natural environment. Some ceremonies, such as those performed at initiation brought the individual closer to his or her ancestors. Ceremonies performed at death made sure that a person's spirit would re-join the spiritual world. Some were public ceremonies or art forms, others were secret and restricted to those who were responsible for looking after a certain piece of country and the ancestors and stories associated with it.

Function of art

When a person painted and decorated his or her body, they did so with designs and ornaments that the ancestral beings had created. The individual was almost transformed into the ancestor, bringing these beings to life in the present, as do carvings and paintings of spirit beings such as the Rainbow Serpent or an ancestral bandicoot. Art was also a product of the kinship system for one of its obligations was the giving and receiving of goods. The value of the gift was not important in fulfilling this obligation, only the act of giving. As a result Aboriginal people were continually engaged in making material objects such as body ornaments, baskets, tools and weapons, all of which can be considered secular forms of art or craft. Of course these items also needed to be made again as they wore out. One of the features of Aboriginal art was its ephemeral nature; it existed to perform a function rather than be hoarded or kept as a perfect example of the form. Elaborate body paintings that took hours to complete could be smudged by sweat in minutes. They were also sometimes deliberately wiped off to hide or lessen the power of the ancestral image. The same applied to bark paintings that would be discarded or destroyed. Ground sculptures were often temporary, made in sand, or left to decay like the carved and painted pukunami burial poles of the Tiwi people. The most permanent forms were rock engravings and paintings but even these were eroded or painted over in time. Some Aboriginal art was like a blackboard, used to teach and then wiped clean.

A symbolic landscape

The most immediately obvious feature of Aboriginal art is its symbolic nature. Geometric designs such as circles, lines, dots, squares or abstract designs are used in all art forms and often combine to form what seems to be little more than an attractive pattern. Even when figures are used they are also symbolic representations, an emu may be prey or an ancestral being. The symbols do not have a fixed meaning; a circle may represent a waterhole, a camping place or an event. In Aboriginal art symbols are put together to form a map of the landscape. But this is not a literal map where if you could read the 'key' you would see the topography of a piece of countryside, but a mythological map. Features of the landscape are depicted but only in their relation to the creation myth that is the subject of the painting. A wavy line terminating in a circle might represent the journey of the Rainbow Serpent to a waterhole. That landscape may also contain a hill behind the waterhole but if it is not relevant to the serpent's journey it will not be represented, although it may feature in other paintings related to different ancestral beings. Unlike a conventional map, scale is not consistent. The size of a feature is more likely to reflect its importance rather than its actual size or there may be several scales within a painting. Nor is orientation fixed; Aboriginal artists often paint sitting on the ground or at a table and work on the nearest side so there may be no top or bottom to these works.

Artistic licence

As art was a means of expressing identity it follows that only those who belonged to an area of landscape and its Dreaming stories, could paint those stories. No one else would know them. An artist must have the right to paint the image he has in mind and these rights are carefully guarded. This idea is refined further within the clan or group. A father and son of the same clan may know the same story but the father will be able to paint more powerful ancestral beings with more knowledge and detail, because it can take a lifetime to learn all of the knowledge connected to an ancestral being. Rights to paintings can also be established through kinship links, living in an area or taking part in ceremony. To many people Aboriginal art is recognized by its style – dots, X-ray or cross hatching – but what is painted is just as important as how it is painted. Aboriginal people working in traditional forms simply do not paint landscapes, figures or people that they are not spiritually connected to. The idea of painting a landscape simply because it is pretty is utterly foreign to Aboriginal art. Even an artist like Albert Namatjira who painted European landscape watercolours in the 1940s never painted anything but his own Arrernte land in central Australia, although he travelled widely outside it.

Interpretation

How does the viewer understand the meaning of a work of Aboriginal art? Because of the use of symbols and the fact that Dreaming stories are only known to the ancestral descendants, only the painter, and perhaps his close relatives, will be able to fully understand the meaning of a painting. In some areas the whole group may be able to interpret the painting. When you look at Aboriginal art in a gallery it will labelled with the name of the artist, and often his clan or group name, dates and location but the meaning of the painting is not usually revealed. As knowledge of the creation myths illustrated relates to ownership it is not appropriate for the artists to pass on important cultural knowledge to strangers, although sometimes a very simple or limited explanation will be given to buyers. Some artists do interpret their paintings in more detail to anthropologists, land rights lawyers or art experts in order to educate non-indigenous people about Aboriginal culture. Looking at examples of Aboriginal art alongside an interpretation is the best way to comprehend the many layers of meaning possible; these can be found in art books such as the excellent **Aboriginal Art** by **Howard Morphy**.

Culture in the 21st century

After the British arrived in Australia, many Aboriginal people died from unfamiliar diseases. Those who did not were often moved off their land to missions or reserves, or killed while resisting the strangers attempting to farm or live on their land. The British acted as they did for a variety of reasons; sometimes for their own material gain, sometimes just following orders and sometimes from the genuine desire to help or protect Aboriginal people. Unfortunately the British had no understanding of Aboriginal culture and did not comprehend that separating Aboriginal people from their land was about the most destructive action possible. In unfamiliar country there was no land to look after, no reason to perform ceremony, hand down knowledge or maintain kinship ties. In missions and reserves people had to live with groups who were perhaps recent enemies, who spoke another language, who did not share their

religious beliefs. In the missions they were often forbidden to speak their own
language and to practice any aspects of ceremonial life that had survived the
sundering from their source. It says much for the strength of Aboriginal culture that
many aspects of it still exist. Since the paternalism of the Australian government was
abandoned in the 1970s and a policy of self-determination implemented, many
Aboriginal people from northern and central Australia have moved from government
reserves back to their land to live in small remote communities. The production of art
for sale in these communities helps them achieve financial independence but also
revives their cultural life as the art is used to instruct young people in their Dreaming.
Art has always been an integral part of the life of Aboriginal people and all over
Australia people continue to express their Aboriginality in a variety of art forms.
Aboriginal culture survives but continues to change and adapt as it has for countless
thousands of years.

Art forms

When travelling across Australia it is possible to glimpse the regional variation of
Aboriginal art. Most of Western Australia's Bradshaw and Wandjina **paintings**, in the
Kimberley, can only be found with a guide, however it is possible to find ancient **rock
engravings** at easily accessible sites in the Pilbara. The state museum and gallery
have superb collections of both traditional and contemporary Aboriginal art and
these are excellent places to learn about Aboriginal culture and art. There are also
many commercial galleries. The art centres owned and run by Aboriginal communities
help build self-sufficiency for Aboriginal people, offer the indigenous perspective and
you may be able to see artists at work. Works produced for sale in Australia include
bark paintings from Arnhem Land, the dot paintings, batik fabric and wood carvings
of the desert regions of Central Australia, baskets and didjeridus from northern
Australia, and wood carvings and screen-printed fabric from the Tiwi Islands. In
Western Australia the unique works of artists of the Warmun community in the
Kimberley, with their bold forms and textured ochre surface, are highly sought after
and there are many talented contemporary Aboriginal artists such as Sally Morgan.

Rock paintings and rock engravings found all over the country constitute
Australia's most ancient and enduring art form. Early rock engravings in Koonalda
Cave on the Nullabor have been dated to 20,000 years ago but engravings are eroded
over time and it is possible that rock engravings were being made 40,000 or even
60,000 years ago. Common forms are circles, lines, and animal tracks or animal
figures. Many are so ancient that Aboriginal people of the area can not explain their
meaning. Rock painting can also be dated back to many thousands of years ago and
was practised until the last few decades. The finest and most extensive rock painting
galleries are found in the great rocky escarpment and range country of the north,
including the thousands of engravings in the Pilbara.

Painting styles have also changed over the millennia and these help to date
paintings too because paintings are generally layered on top of each other. The
earliest art forms are stencils, where a mouthful of ochre is spat over the hand, foot or
tool to leave a reverse print on the wall. Figures in red ochre (or blood) are also some
of the oldest works as red ochre lasts longer than any other colour, seeping into the
rock to bond with it permanently.

Dot paintings are the most widely recognized of Aboriginal art forms, highly
sought after by international collectors, but also one of the newest forms. Dot
paintings are made in the western and central desert regions and relate to an older
form used by desert people. In the desert there are few rock surfaces and no trees
suitable for stripping off large pieces of bark so the desert people used the ground to
commemorate the travels and actions of their ancestral beings. Drawings, or perhaps
more correctly sculptures, were created by placing crushed plant matter and feather
down on a hard-packed surface. The material would be coloured with ochre or blood.

Common designs were spirals or circles and lines. These works were always ceremonial and created by old and knowledgeable men. In the 1970s many desert people were living at Papunya, a community northwest of Alice Springs. An art teacher, Geoff Bardon, encouraged local men to paint a mural on the school wall. A Honey Ant Dreaming painting was created that led to great interest and enthusiasm from men in the community. They began painting their stories on boards, using ochres or poster paints, in the symbolic manner of ground sculptures and ceremonial body painting. Over the next few decades these paintings, increasingly on canvas using acrylic paints, were offered for sale and became incredibly successful, both in Australia and outside it. There is great diversity of colour and style in contemporary desert paintings but the qualities of symbolism and ownership discussed earlier also apply. They are popularly known as dot paintings because the background is completely filled in by areas of dots. These can represent many elements of a landscape; for example clouds, areas of vegetation, the underground chambers of a honey ant's nest, or all three at once. In galleries look out for the incomparable work of **Clifford Possum Tjapaltjarri** and **Kathleen Petyarre**.

Aboriginal people all over Australia produced string and fibre from the plants in their region to make functional and ceremonial objects. These **baskets** and other **works of string** have only recently been considered works of art as non-indigenous fibre and textile work has gained in status and as the importance of these objects is increasingly understood. Fibre work is a woman's art, although men sometimes made strong ropes for fishing. Palm leaves, reeds, vines, bark, and hair were all used to make string and fibre that was then made into a variety of baskets and bags. These were primarily used to carry food collected during a day's foraging but also held personal possessions. String was also used to made body ornaments such as belts and fringes, armbands and necklaces. Baskets and bags are still made by the women of northern Australia and today's techniques show how new technology is adapted to continue traditional ways. Before the British arrived Aboriginal people had no steel or clay containers and therefore were not able to boil water. Fibre work was coloured by rubbing ochre into the fibre when making it or by painting the finished object with ochre. Now the fibre is dyed in boiling water but the dyes are made by the weavers from natural sources, such as roots and grasses, with great skill and subtlety.

Weapons and utensils made of **wood** were often carved with designs that symbolized an ancestor, thus identifying the land of the owner. The beauty of these carvings carries them beyond the purely functional, as does their origin in the Dreaming. Carvings of ancestral figures were also made to be used in ceremonies such as funeral rites. In many communities weapons are no longer made because Aboriginal people now hunt with guns. Shields and clubs are not needed, but nothing has replaced the spear, and people still make clapping sticks or carrying dishes. As well as making the pukunami poles, the Tiwi carve wonderful wooden sculptures of totemic animals and ancestral beings for sale, as do people along the coast and islands of Arnhem Land. People in central Australia also make wooden animal carvings and these are often decorated with pokerwork, a burn from a hot wire. The didjeridu is still made and used in ceremony in Arnhem Land, where it is called the *yidaki*. The didjeridu is made from a tree trunk that has been hollowed out by termites so each one is unique and the bumps and knots inside influence the sound it makes.

Contemporary Aboriginal art

The art that is produced in northern and central Australia is contemporary art. Although it has its foundation in an ancient culture, it is also shaped by its present. Contemporary art is also produced by Aboriginal people who live in the urban societies of the south and east. These people may have lost their land, language, religion and families but they still have an Aboriginal identity. The people sometimes

called urban Aboriginal artists may have trained in art school and their art possesses
the 'Western' quality of reflecting the experience of the individual. They are united in
their experience of surviving dispossession, by their personal history and experience
of being Aboriginal in a dominant non-indigenous society. Some of the common
themes in their work are events of the colonial past, such as massacres, or
contemporary issues that affect Aboriginal people such as the fight for land rights or
the disproportionately high number of Aboriginal prisoners. Some urban artists have
tried to reconnect with their past or, like the late **Lin Onus**, establish links with artists
working in more traditional forms and to incorporate clan designs or symbolic
elements into their work. To see powerful contemporary Aboriginal art look for the
work of **Robert Campbell Jnr, Sally Morgan, Lin Onus, Gordon Bennett, Trevor Nikolls,
Fiona Foley** and **Donna Leslie**.

Other Australian art

Australia was colonized during the century of Romanticism in Western Europe when
interest in the natural world was at its height. Much of the earliest colonial art came
from scientific expeditions and their specimen drawings. Most of these early images
look slightly odd as if even the best draughtsman found himself unable to capture the
impossibly strange forms of unique Australian species such as the kangaroo. Indeed
art from the whole of the first colonial century portrays Australia in a soft northern
hemisphere light and in the rich colours of European landscapes. In these finely
detailed landscapes the countryside was presented as romantically gothic or neatly
tamed, even bucolic with the addition of cattle or a farmer at work, as seen in the work
of **John Glover, Louis Buvelot** and **Eugene von Guérard**. In some there would also be
quaint representations of a bark hut or black figure belonging to the peaceful
'children of nature'. Given the violence of what was happening to Aboriginal people at
the time and the British impression that the new colony was a nasty, brutish place full
of convicts, these paintings can be seen as an attempt to portray Australia as
peaceful, beautiful and civilized. Things began to change in the 1880s and 1890s, by
which time a majority of colonists had been born in Australia.

The Heidelberg School and Australian Impressionism

Increasing pride in being Australian and European Impressionism inspired
Australian artists to really look at their environment and cast away conventional
techniques, prompting a dramatic change in how the country was portrayed. Truth
in light, colour and tone was pursued by artists such as **Arthur Streeton, Charles
Conder, Tom Roberts** and **Frederick McCubbin**, who began painting *en plein air*. In
their paintings bright light illuminated the country's real colours; the gold of dried
grass, the smoky green of eucalypts and the deep blue of the Australian sky. These
artists were known as the Heidelberg School because they painted many of their
bush scenes around Heidelberg and Box Hill, just outside Melbourne. Some of
Australia's most iconic and popular images were painted at this time. They
portrayed the nobility of a hard but independent life in the bush. *Down on his luck*
(1889) by Frederick McCubbin is a classic image of a bushman and his swag, staring
into his campfire among gum trees. In Tom Roberts' *A break away!* (1891) a heroic
lone horsemen tries to control the rush of sheep to a waterhole in drought-
stricken country. The same painter's *Shearing the Rams* (1888-1890) again
celebrates the noble masculinity of the bush with a shearing-shed scene portraying
the industry and camaraderie of the pastoral life. These paintings all represent a
golden age that belie the end of the boom times in Victoria, where the economy
crashed in the early 1890s, and the reality that most Australians were urban workers
rather than bushmen.

Modernism and the Angry Penguins

After Federation in 1901 Australian landscapes became increasingly pretty and idyllic, typified by the languorous beauties enjoying the outdoors in the work of **E. Phillips Fox** or **Rupert Bunny**. However, the Great War shocked the sensibilities of those who witnessed it and Australian artists followed the lead of Britain and Europe in embracing Modernism. **Margaret Preston** was influenced by the modernist focus on 'primitive' art to incorporate elements from Aboriginal art into her works, *Aboriginal flowers* (1928) and *Aboriginal Landscape* (1941). **Grace Cossington Smith** looked to Van Gogh for her short brushstrokes of intense colour in interior works such as *The Lacquer Room* (1936). **Hans Heysen** worked in the tradition of Streeton and McCubbin, glorifying the South Australian landscape with images of mighty old gum trees and the ancient folds of the Flinders Ranges, but other painters of the 1940s and 1950s were looking at the landscape differently. The outback is presented as a harsh and desolate place in the work of **Russell Drysdale** and **Sidney Nolan**. During the 1940s Nolan produced a famous series of paintings on bushranger Ned Kelly in a whimsical, naïve style in which he expressed a desire to paint the 'stories which take place within the landscape' - an interesting link to Aboriginal art. Nolan belonged to a group of artists called the 'Angry Penguins', along with **Albert Tucker**, **Joy Hester** and **Arthur Boyd**. These artists worked under the patronage of John and Sunday Reed at Heide outside Melbourne, the same area that had inspired the Heidelberg School. Their work reflects the ugliness and uncertainty of the war period. Tucker painted the nightmarish evil that the Second World War had brought to society in paintings like *The Victory Girls* (1943). Boyd worked on moral themes amongst light-sodden landscapes. Other artists were portraying the alienation of urban lives, in stark paintings like **John Brack's** *Collins Street 5 p.m.* (1955).

Contemporary art

During the 1960s and 1970s Australian artists were influenced by the abstract movement. Artists such as **John Olsen** and **Fred Williams** still produced landscapes but in an intensely personal, emotional and unstructured way. **Brett Whiteley** painted sensuous, colour-drenched Sydney landscapes and disturbing works such as the *Christie Series* (1964) in a surreal or distorted manner reminiscent of Salvador Dali or Francis Bacon. Painting became a less dominant form in this period and the following decades with many artists working in sculpture, installations, video and photography. The 1980s and 1990s were also marked by an intense interest in Aboriginal art, leading to its inclusion within the mainstream venues and discourse of contemporary Australian art.

Literature

Australia has a rich literary culture and an admirable body of national literature. Until recently this reflected only the European experience of the country, but increasingly includes Aboriginal voices and those of migrants. Awareness and exploration of the Asia-Pacific cultures of the region is also a new theme. It is not surprising that the main concern for Europeans has been the alien nature of the country they had so recently arrived in; to examine how it was different from their own country and to find both meaning and their own place within it. As in so many cultural fields it has taken a long time for an Australian identity to develop and in literature it has been primarily within the last 50 years. As questions of national identity are resolved Australian writers move towards regional and local identity. One of the features of contemporary Australian literature is the strong sense of place it conveys. The writers and poets discussed below are significant figures of Australian literature who have built up a substantial collection of work but of course there are many more fine writers. See page 340 for more state-based suggestions.

A B 'Banjo' Paterson and Henry Lawson

Paterson and Lawson were both journalists of the 1890s and have done more to define the character of the Australian bushman than any other writers. Both were nationalists, although there were important differences in their work. Paterson wrote the country's most famous bush ballads such as *Waltzing Matilda*, *Clancy of the Overflow* and *The Man from Snowy River*. The latter still outsells all other volumes of Australian poetry. Paterson's was a romantic vision; brave and cheerful men on noble horses worked companionably across this wide land or stood firm against figures of authority. Lawson criticized Paterson in the literary journal, *The Bulletin*, for his idealism saying "the real native outback bushman is narrow minded, densely ignorant, invulnerably thick-headed" and that heat, flies, drought and despair were missing from Paterson's poetry. Lawson was a part of the republican movement of the late 1880s and a prolific writer of poetry and prose based on the people of the bush. His well-crafted short stories present the bush in the clear light of realism and their qualities of understated style, journalistic detail, sympathy for broken characters and ironic humour mean that Lawson's stories are considered among the finest in Australian literature. His best stories are found in the collections *Joe Wilson and His Mates* and *While the Billy Boils*.

Patrick White

Patrick White detested what he saw as the emptiness and materialism at the heart of Australian life yet it inspired his visionary literature with its characters searching for meaning. He wanted to convey a transcendence above human realities, a mystery and poetry that could make an ordinary life bearable. His major novels are *The Tree of Man*, *Voss*, *Riders in the Chariot*, *The Solid Mandala*, *The Vivisector*, *Eye of the Storm* and *Fringe of Leaves*. Never very popular in Australia because of his critical eye and 'difficult' metaphysical style, White won the Nobel Prize for Literature in 1973 for *The Tree of Man* and began to receive more attention at home. His original vision, the dynamism and poetic language of his work are some of the elements that make him a giant of Australian literature.

Thomas Keneally

An energetic and prolific writer with a great store of curiosity, Keneally has ranged all over the world in subject matter yet at the core of his fiction is the individual trying to act with integrity in extreme situations. One of his most important 'Australian' novels is *The Chant of Jimmy Blacksmith*, a fictional representation of the late-19th century figure, part-Aboriginal Jimmy Governor, who married a white girl and was goaded into murder. Other subjects include Armistice negotiations (*Gossip from the Forest*), Yugoslav partisans in the Second World War (*Season in Purgatory*) and the American Civil War (*Confederates*) but Keneally's best known novel is *Schindler's Ark*. He won the Booker Prize for this novel, although some complained that the book was hardly fictional, and it was made into the highly successful Spielberg film, *Schindler's List*. Keneally manages to capture historical moments vividly and is that rare kind of writer who is popular yet serious.

Les Murray

Contemporary poet Les Murray can be linked back to the 1890s poets Paterson and Lawson in his central theme of the bush as the source of Australian identity. Respect for pioneers, the laconic and egalitarian bush character, the shaping influence of the land and dislike for the urban life all run through his work. The city verses country theme is informed by Murray's own experience of moving between the two; he grew up on a farming property in NSW, leaving it for university and work, but later managing to buy back part of the family farm in the Bunyah district. The larger-than-life poet is often called the 'Bard of Bunyah'. Murray writes in an accessible and popular style,

Background Culture

but is a contemplative and religious thinker of great originality. Murray's reverence for land has led to an interest in Aboriginal culture, expressed in *The Bulahdelah-Taree Holiday Song Cycle*, a series of poems echoing the style and rhythm of an Arnhem Land song cycle. Other major works include the collections *The People's Otherworld* and *Translations from the Natural World*.

Peter Carey

Carey grew up in Victoria, lived for a while in Sydney, but now lives in New York. Being an expatriate writer has only focused his view of Australia, a fairly dark vision that wonders what can grow out of dispossession, violence and a penal colony. Carey is a dazzling writer who never repeats himself; each novel is entirely different in genesis, period and character. His earlier novels had magic-realist elements, such as *Bliss* in which advertising man Harry Joy is re-born several times into new realities. Other qualities include surrealism, comedy, the macabre, and a concern for truth and lies. Carey won the Booker Prize in 1988 for *Oscar and Lucinda*, a Victorian novel with echoes of George Eliot and Edmund Gosse, set in 19th-century NSW and centering on the love between two unconventional gamblers. *True History of the Kelly Gang* won Carey the Booker Prize again in 2001 for a feat of language and imagination that is simply breathtaking. Carey puts flesh on the bones of history by getting inside the mind of bushranger Ned Kelly. His other novels are *Illywhacker*, *The Tax Inspector*, *The Unusual Life of Tristan Smith*, *Jack Maggs* and the latest, *My Life as a Fake*.

David Malouf

An elegant and lyrical writer, Malouf is preoccupied by the question of Australian identity. He believes writers need to create mythologies that are the means of a spiritual link between landscape and lives. Places need to be mapped by imagination to acquire meaning or belonging. His own themes are often played out against the background of his own childhood in Brisbane, a richly imagined slow and lush city of the past. In his novels characters are forced by circumstance to find a new way of seeing. *The Great World* follows the lives of Vic and Digger through Second World War prisoner of war camps to examine layers of history and identity. *An Imaginary Life* deals with the Roman poet Ovid in exile from Rome and his relationship with a wolfchild, a poetic novel that explores Australian issues of exile, place and belonging. These themes are continued in *Remembering Babylon*, set in the 1840s when a white boy who has lived with Aborigines for 16 years encounters the first settlers to reach northern Queensland. Malouf also writes poetry and short stories; forms that suit his economic yet powerfully descriptive language.

Tim Winton

Tim Winton is a West Australian author who writes very successfully for both adults and children. His work is marked by a sense of place, particularly the WA coast, and a tight focus on character within an environment. Winton has said of his work "if I can get a grip on the geography, I can get a grip on the people". He certainly does so – his characters are intensely imagined and powerfully 'real', often reinforced by Winton's open endings as if the rest of their lives really are still to be lived. Loneliness and self-doubt are common to his characters as they search for identity and a sense of purpose. *Cloudstreet* is a funny and affectionate tale of two very different families sharing a house in post-war Perth and the dark undercurrents of their ordinary lives. In *The Riders* Fred Scully makes a frantic search across an alien and unfamiliar Europe for his wife. *Dirt Music* is a moving story of loss and loneliness set in the crayfishing towns of the west coast. Luther and Georgie belong to nowhere and nobody and are drawn together, although Luther is determined to be left alone.

Kate Grenville

Grenville's novels are sharply observed, funny and sometimes gothic explorations of what makes people tick and how they create their own destiny. This writer sees Australian history as a rich source of material; full of stories still to be told, landscape to be described and ways of being 'Australian' to explore. For *Lilian's Story* Grenville was inspired by Sydney eccentric Bea Miles to write the story of an uninhibited woman who makes her own myth at a time when women are supposed to be passive. *Dark Places* is about Lilian's monstrous father and how he distorts truth and reality to justify his actions. *Joan Makes History* re-writes Australian history in the image of women. Joan imagines she is present at all the big moments of Australia's past. *The Idea of Perfection* is about two middle-aged and unattractive people drawn together because they value history and its imperfections. This novel won the Orange Prize for Fiction in 2001.

Language

When Europeans arrived in Australia there were about 250 Aboriginal languages and many more dialects. These were as different from each other as English and Bengali. Most Aboriginal people spoke three or four languages: including those of neighbouring groups, kin or birth place. Because Aboriginal languages were oral they were easily lost. About 100 languages have disappeared since 1788, another 100 or so are used only by older people and will die out within 10-20 years. Only about 20 languages are commonly spoken today. Many Aboriginal people still speak several languages, of which English may be their second or third language. Aboriginal English is widely spoken; this is a form of English with the structure of Aboriginal languages or English words that do not correspond to the English meaning.

English is the official language of Australia, and it has developed a rich vocabulary all its own in its two centuries of linguistic experimentation. The words and terms listed in the Glossary are mostly unique to Australia. American visitors will also find a lot of unfamiliar British terms and slang words in use. Unfortunately many colourful Australian phrases are gradually disappearing under the dominant influence of American television and film.

Music

Popular music

Australian popular music has been heavily influenced by the British and American scenes but has also produced exciting home-grown sounds that are distinctively Australian. The industry suffered from the 'cultural cringe' for some time – the idea that anything Australian is only any good if Britain and America think so. In the last three decades Australians have embraced their own music and there have been many bands that are extremely successful in Australia but unknown outside the country. Australian musicians are limited by their tiny market; if they want to make serious money they must pursue success overseas.

Australian music first came to the notice of the rest of the world in the 1970s, when glam rock outfits **Sherbert** and the **Skyhooks** toured America. **Little River Band** did well in the US with their catchy commercial pop while punk outfit **The Saints** were simultaneously making it big in the UK. However the real success story of the decade was **AC/DC**, one of the greatest heavy-rock bands in the world. Their album *Highway to Hell* was a huge success in 1979 though they lost their lead singer Bon Scott in 1980 to a tragic rock star death.

The 1980s was the decade of the hardworking pub rock band, the sexy funk rock of **INXS**, the stirring political anthems of **Midnight Oil,** and the working class onslaught of **Cold Chisel**. Of these bands INXS had the most success overseas while Midnight Oil and Cold Chisel were huge at home, singing about Australian places, issues and experiences. **Men at Work** had a hit with the quirky *Down Under* and **Crowded House,** led by the master singer-songwriter and New Zealander **Neil Finn,** seduced the world with tracks like *Don't Dream It's Over*. Singer-songwriters **Richard Clapton** and **Paul Kelly** also came to prominence at this time and both continue to influence the music scene. Paul Kelly's album *Gossip* is a classic – full of finely observed stories about life in Sydney and Melbourne.

Record companies became less willing to take a chance on unproved Australian bands in the 1990s and the decade is marked by developments on the local scene. Strangely, there was a rash of success for ex-soap stars **Kylie Minogue** and **Natalie Imbruglia,** but more so in the UK than at home. Kylie even got serious when she teamed up with ex-**Birthday Party** frontman, **Nick Cave,** on a track for his typically downbeat *Murder Ballads* album. Cave's dark, philosophical stylings have always gone down better in the UK and Europe than down under. **The Whitlams,** meanwhile, appealed to sophisticated punters with witty and melodic funk. At the noisier end of the spectrum, **Regurgitator** appeared with an influential and original sound, **Spiderbait** and **Powderfinger** and **Savage Garden** also all made it big. The band that really caught the public imagination though was **Silverchair,** a trio of schoolboys who won a competition to record their grunge classic *Tomorrow*. Aboriginal musicians also had commercial success; look out for bands **Yothu Yindi, Saltwater** and **Coloured Stone,** and the soulful ballads of **Archie Roach** or energetic pop of Torres Strait Islander **Christine Anu.**

In the first couple of years of this decade Kylie Minogue just got bigger, Savage Garden split up but singer Darren Hayes started up a solo career. **Superjesus, Bodyjar, Even,** and **Killing Heidi** are all doing well locally and a handful of Australian singer/songwriters look set to make a significant international impact, particularly **Missy Higgins** and **Pete Murray.**

Cinema

First steps

Although Australia produced the world's first feature film in 1906, *The Story of the Kelly Gang*, its budding film industry was soon overwhelmed by a flood of British and American films. It wasn't until the 1970s, when Australia was exploring its cultural identity, that the industry revived. Government funding commonly paid for as much as half of the production costs and Australian themes were encouraged. During this period some classics were made, such as *Picnic at Hanging Rock*. Directed by **Peter Weir,** this is a story of a schoolgirls' picnic that goes horribly wrong when some of the girls disappear into the haunting and mysterious landscape, one of many Australian films to suggest that perhaps the outback has the spiritual power that Aboriginal people believe it does. Weir went on to become a very successful Hollywood director (*Witness, Dead Poets Society, Truman Show*). *My Brilliant Career* was the beginning of brilliant careers for director **Gillian Armstrong** and actor **Judy Davis**. Davis played an independent young woman of the late 19th century who wanted to escape from the farm and live an intellectual life. The decade was also marked by 'ocker' films made for the home audience portraying the crass, uncouth and exaggerated Australian, like *The Adventures of Barry McKenzie*.

Glamour and heroes

Things changed in the 1980s when the government brought in tax incentives to encourage private investment in the film industry. Direct government funding dropped away to low levels. Naturally under these conditions the emphasis switched to profit rather than artistic merit and many big budget commercial films were made such as *Crocodile Dundee*. In 1981 Peter Weir's *Gallipoli* was a much-loved film about the sacrifices and stupidity of events at Gallipoli, starring a young **Mel Gibson**. In a completely different role Gibson also starred in another successful film that year, *Mad Max II*, shot around Broken Hill in outback NSW. Australian high-country life was romanticised in *The Man from Snowy River*, featuring a lot of handsome, rugged horsemen and spectacular scenery. In 1987 the thriller *Dead Calm* brought **Nicole Kidman** much attention and *Evil Angels* did the same for Uluru in a film about Lindy Chamberlain who claimed that a dingo took her baby from the campsite at the base of the rock in 1980. Even Meryl Streep failed to master an Australian accent to play Chamberlain. Despite these big flashy films, Australian film makers also managed some smaller interesting films looking at relationships, such as *Monkey Grip*, *High Tide*, *My First Wife*, and the extraordinary *Sweetie* in 1989. The first feature film directed by New Zealand born **Jane Campion**, it focuses on the sisters Sweetie and Kay in their dysfunctional suburban family life. Sweetie is perhaps the first of the freaks and misfits that would feature in films of the 1990s.

Money and misfits

The industry changed again in the 1990s when the generous tax concessions of the 1980s were retracted and the country suffered through economic depression in the early years of the decade. Australian film makers had to look overseas for finance and increasingly encourage American producers to use Australian facilities and locations. The new *Fox Studios* in Sydney attracted *The Matrix*, *Star Wars Episode II* and *Mission Impossible II*. The joint finance and production arrangements made it difficult to define an 'Australian' film. Cross-fertilization of talent and general optimism in the industry led Australian film makers to produce some bold and risk-taking films in the 1990s. Issues of identity and gender came to the fore in films that weren't afraid to celebrate the daggy, the misfits or oddballs like *Strictly Ballroom*, *The Adventures of Priscilla, Queen of the Desert*, and *Muriel's Wedding*. In less subtle films, like *The Castle* or *Holy Smoke*, Australians were portrayed as well-meaning but hopelessly naïve fools and bumpkins. Other films pursued more serious issues but got less attention outside the country, like *Romper Stomper*, a harrowing look at a gang of racist skinheads in Melbourne starring **Russell Crowe**, or *Dead Heart*, a confronting look at the clash of cultures in central Australia starring **Bryan Brown.**

Beyond 2000

Despite the successes and attention of the 1990s, the Australian film industry still struggles against the behemoth of Hollywood. International financing is still a feature of the industry and it is difficult for distinctively Australian films to get made as they are still perceived as not very marketable outside the country. There is no shortage of suberb talent but many of the best Australian actors and directors need work overseas to get the most opportunities. Indeed at present Australian actors are better known than Australian films; Nicole Kidman, Cate Blanchett, Russell Crowe, Guy Pearce, Toni Collette, Geoffrey Rush, Judy Davis, Hugh Jackman and more are all in huge demand in Britain and America. The most recent standout film was *Moulin Rouge*, made by visionary director **Baz Luhrmann** and starring Nicole Kidman and Ewan McGregor. This love story set in the Paris of Toulouse-Lautrec is a riot of colour and music. Luhrmann has singlehandedly reinvented the musical film in *Strictly Ballroom*, *Romeo and Juliet* and *Moulin Rouge*. His next film, focusing on the career of *Alexander the Great*, is greatly anticipated. Other films worth looking out for are *Lantana*, an immensely sophisticated tangle of love and betrayal; *Rabbit Proof Fence*, a film bringing alive the trauma of the 'stolen generation' in recreating the true stories of three Aboriginal girls escaping from their mission and walking thousands of miles to find their mother; *Japanese Story*, the moving and visually spectacular tale of an Australian woman's roller-coaster relationship with a Japanese businessman in the Pilbara; and *Yolgnu Boy*, an interesting look at contemporary Aboriginal society, following three teenage boys in Arnhem Land as they try to exchange petrol sniffing for something better.

Religion

In many areas the ancient Aboriginal belief system has persisted to the present day. The British immigrants, their captives and hangers-on of the 18th and 19th centuries brought with them two forms of Christianity; Protestantism and Catholicism. These are still Australia's two main religions as we enter the 21st century, though in the 1990s Catholics, for the first time, outnumbered the Protestants, who now more usually call themselves Anglicans. Most of these are nominal Christians only, and do not practice or attend church. The constitution of 1901 steered Australian government in a secular, rather than religious direction, though most successive governments throughout the 20th century took Christian beliefs as a major source of inspiration and had significant Christian sympathies.

With the opening up of immigration policy in the 1970s came a broadening of the religious spectrum in Australia. There are now substantial numbers of people following Jewish, Islamic, Hindu and Buddhist and other beliefs.

Land and environment

Geography

There are bits of Western Australia that are staggeringly old. There have been rocks found in the south that date back over four billion years. In fact most of that corner of the continent is made up of something called the Yilgarn Block, a vast chunk of bedrock over two billion years old, and much of Western Australia is nearly as ancient. The coastal areas are younger, and a couple of the deserts are composed of more recent sedimentary rocks, but much of the state is a billion years old or more. The biggest mass of young rock is the great limestone block that we loosely call the Nullarbor. Much of the western coastal areas are also relatively young, formed while India was pulling away from Western Australia, a process that was complete by about 160 million years ago. As well as being old, the region has also been incredibly stable, with no appreciable seismic activity for hundreds of millions of years.

This ancient provenance goes a long way to explaining why Western Australia, compared with other landmasses, and even the east coast, is so flat. Hundreds of millions of years of weathering have steadily taken their toll, relentlessly grinding down mountain ranges and flattening out the plains. This isn't quite the whole story, however. Australia was once part of the super-continent Gondwana, a huge landmass that broke up between 270 and 40 million years ago to become South America, Antarctica, Africa, India, and the Middle East, as well as the Australasian islands. All this pulling and pushing helped create great vertical movement as well as horizontal. Several eastern and southern parts of the continent sank, creating huge depressions that were periodically inundated. One of these, the Eucla Basin, filled with a sediment that has become the Nullarbor limestone.

Fauna and flora

The isolation, age, and position of Australia have had a tremendous impact on the flora and fauna that have evolved. Until Australia started heading north 40 million years ago, much of it lay within the Antarctic circle and had done so for hundreds of millions of years before that. The Antarctic was not glaciated at this warmer time, but was still very cold with average temperatures of no more than 10°C, and a long dark polar winter. Thus, although animals and plants could in theory migrate from South America to Australia and vice-versa until about 70 million years ago, any such migration would have been extremely slow compared to movements on other landmasses. Hence for many types of plants and animals the effective isolation has been far longer than is immediately apparent.

There have been three particularly decisive factors in the subsequent history of life on the landmass. The first is the relative degradation and leaching of the soils compared with all the other continents. Nutrient rich soils are formed through three primary agents: mountain-building, volcanic activity and glaciation. Western Australia particularly has seen very little of these for hundreds of millions of years. At the same time the constant weathering and extraction of nutrients by plants and animals has steadily leached nutrients from the soils. In short, there is little goodness to go around.

The second major effect on the evolution of Australian life is the long-term climatic stability of the continent. The world has gradually cooled over the last 40 million years. On most continents this has resulted in successive waves of appropriately evolved creatures and plants. Australia, however, has been drifting north toward the equator, more-or-less counterbalancing the cooling. Just one of the results of these first two factors is the diversity of flora in the south of Western Australia. The paucity of nutrients encourages intense specialization, for example some plants settle for more saline soils, others for sandier soils. The long-term climate stability has allowed evolution to experiment to an astounding degree, creating thousands of different species. It may be counter-intuitive to anyone who visits the area, but there is as much diversity of life in south-western Australia as almost anywhere in the world.

The third major factor is the type of climate the continent experiences. First and foremost it is dry. Even with the monsoonal rains of the far north this is still the world's driest landmass after Antarctica, and has been for millions of years. During the recent ice-ages it became dryer still, most of the interior becoming one vast dune-covered desert. To make matters worse the short-term climate dances only weakly to a seasonal tune, and is crucially affected by one of the world's most powerful weather phenomena, ENSO (El Niño Southern Oscillation). This delivers rain and drought to the continent in unpredictable cycles of two to eight years, though the effects are weaker in the west than the east.

Both plants and animals have had to develop unique strategies to cope with this terrible combination of low nutrient levels and sparse, unpredictable rainfall. Paleontologists have found evidence for both placental and marsupial mammals on the early island continent, and indeed a few placental rats and mice have survived down to the present day, but it is tempting to suspect that Australia's unique harsh conditions actually favoured the marsupial way of life. Kangaroos and wallabies have a fascinating approach to procreation. As soon as she has given birth a mother will conceive, but the embryo is not necessarily immediately developed. If drought conditions are in play it will be held in a sort of suspended animation until rains come, and only then will it be born and make its way to the pouch.

When it comes to vertebrate creatures Australian conditions actually seem to have favoured reptiles rather than mammals. This is hardly surprising as reptiles live on around 20 per cent of the food required by mammals of a similar size, and can go without food and water for considerable periods when they have to.

If we could have taken a 4WD trip around Western Australia 60,000 years we would have witnessed a fascinating biota. It is thought that dry rainforests were much more in evidence, covering large areas of the sub-continent, but with undergrowth, and hence the fire risk, kept low by huge herds of herbivores. Some of these were species of kangaroos, but the larger ones were of the now extinct *Zygomaturus* and *Diprotodon* families which weighed up to 2 tonnes and were very distant relatives of the wombats. Larger wombats there were too, pig-sized creatures that dug the largest burrows the world has ever witnessed, as well as titanic tortoises and behemoth birds. Very few attained anywhere near the size of their ecological counterparts on other continents, though the sight of them would still have been impressive.

Mammalian carnivores have long found the Australian conditions difficult, with prey species following boom-and-bust population cycles, but some evolved, mostly from vegetarian ancestors. Most impressive was the 'marsupial lion', *Thylacoleo*, while one of the most extraordinary in terms of evolutionary convergence was the *Thylacine*, commonly known as the Tasmanian Tiger, which survived on that island until at least the 1930s. However, these would probably have fled at the sight of the average human tourist, and certainly at the approach of the real top dog in the Australian hierarchy. That was *Megalania prisca*, an awesome relative of the Komodo dragon that could reach 7 m in length and a tonne in weight. It was probably an ambush predator like its cousin, capable of taking practically anything it wanted, and would have made getting out of our 4WD for a stroll a far more hazardous experience than it is today.

Wildlife

Wildlife is inevitably very much a part of the Western Australian holiday experience. There is no doubt that Australia's rich bio-diversity is among the most remarkable and specialist on the planet. Despite the destructive effects that humans have had on the Australian ecosystem for 40,000 years, in particular the last 200 years since the arrival of the Europeans, much of that unique ecology remains.

Provided you remain observant, cautious and have respect, your Australian wildlife experience can be an extremely positive and pleasant one. A visit to a couple of the many wildlife parks and zoos around the state will familiarize you with what exactly is out there, especially Perth Zoo and Aqwa in Perth and Broome Crocodile Park, but the best way of encountering WA's wildlife is to get out into the bush. Try to camp in as many National Parks as you can and snorkel wherever the chance arises. This will inevitably result in many unexpected and truly memorable wild encounters. The Department of Conservation and Land Management (CALM) is an invaluable source of information and has offices in most major towns and cities (listed in the travelling text). Despite the almost unbearable temptation, do not feed any wild animals, since this merely makes them more dependent on humans and indirectly places them under greater threat.

Marsupials
Marsupials (derived from the Latin word 'marsupium', meaning 'pouch') can essentially be described as mammals that have substituted the uterus for the teat. Their reproductive system is complex, the females have not one, but three vaginas and there is a short gestation and a long lactation. In essence it is a specialist

system, almost opportunistic, that has developed to meet harsh environmental demands. At any one time when it comes to kangaroos (as the saying goes), 'there is a bun in the oven, one in the pouch and one young at foot'.

The most famous of the marsupials are of course the **kangaroos** and **wallabies**. There are over 50 species of kangaroos, wallabies and tree kangaroos in Australia. The most well known and commonly seen in WA are the western grey and the red. The red kangaroo, which is the largest, is the one most synonymous with the outback. Joseph Banks, the naturalist on board Captain Cook's ship the *Endeavor*, first described the kangaroo to modern science in 1770. We can only

> ✷ See www.calm.wa. gov.au/plants_animals, or www.austmus.gov.au, for more information, and page 51 for advice on tracking down WA's wildlife.

imagine him standing there in front of his peers perhaps having to resort to an impersonation? Your encounters with these, the most famous of Australian creatures, will be frequent and highly entertaining, especially with the greys in the wildlife parks, golf courses and national park campsites. In wildlife parks they are notoriously tame and obsessed with the contents of your pockets, while in the national parks you can sit and have breakfast with them nibbling the grass nearby. Sadly, in the outback your encounters with kangaroos will also commonly be of the dead variety. There are literally thousands of road kills each year involving kangaroos, since they are very inept at avoiding moving vehicles. When traveling in the outback you should avoid dawn and dusk and about an hour either side, since this is the worst time for accidents. Wallabies are generally smaller than their kangaroo cousins, and tend to specialize in exploiting rocky country and thick scrub. Five of 15 species of rock wallabies are found in the northwest and the Karijini and Millstream-Chichester national parks are good places to see them.

Another, very familiar family of marsupials are the possums. There are numerous species with the most commonly encountered being the doe-eyed **brushtail possum** and the smaller **western ring-tailed possum**. Both are common in urban areas and regularly show up after dusk in campsites. Ironically the brushtail possum is protected in Australia, but after being introduced for the fur trade in New Zealand in the 19th century have reached plague proportions there with an estimated 70 million causing havoc to native species.

Other marsupials include Rottnest's delightful **quokka** (like a miniature wallaby), also found in small numbers around Dwellingup and in the Stirling Ranges; the beautifully striped carnivorous **numbat** (endangered, and also unique to WA) which might be seen, with patience in the Dryandra Woodlands; the rat-like **bandicoot**; and the hugely eared and very rare desert-living **bilby**. Remarkably (although maybe not for Australia), there is also a **marsupial mole** that lives in the desert. **Quolls** are meat-eating marsupials, the largest on the mainland, about the size of a cat with a brownish coat with attractive white spots that may, if you are very lucky, be encountered in the wild.

Monotremes

There are only three living species of monotremes in the world: the duck-billed platypus and the short-beaked echidna, both of which are endemic to Australia, and the long-beaked echidna that is found only on the islands of New Guinea. They are unique in many ways; the word monotreme means 'one hole'. But, suffice to say, the most remarkable feature is that they are mammals that lay eggs. They have also been around for over 100 million years. The only one now native to WA is the **short-beaked echidna**. Although it is in no way related to the hedgehog, it looks decidedly like one. Although relatively common they can be quite shy and your best chance of seeing one is probably in the Avon Valley National Park or the Dryandra Woodlands. If approached they adopt the same defence tactics as hedgehogs by curling up, erecting their spines and remarking in gruff 'Echidnaese': 'bugger off'.

They are immensely powerful creatures not dissimilar to small spiny tanks, are mainly nocturnal and hunt for insects by emanating electrical signals from the long snout, before catching them with a long sticky tongue.

Eutherians

Although you may be an avid *Star Trek* fan and think you know your Klingons from your Vulcans, you may still not be aware that you yourself are not only a *Homo sapiens*, but also a Eutherian: a placental mammal. Perhaps the most well known placental mammal in Australia is the **dingo**. Although not strictly endemic to Australia, having being introduced (most probably) by Aboriginals over 3,000-4,000 years ago and derived from an Asian wild dog, they are now seen to be as Australian as Fosters. Found everywhere on the mainland continent, though commonest in the north, they are highly adaptable, opportunist carnivores, which makes them very unpopular with farmers. Interesting features of this sub-species are that they do not, like other dogs, hunt or live in packs and cannot bark or jump, although substantial interbreeding with domestic dogs is blending these traits back in.

The most common native placental mammals, however, are bats and mice. There are 85 species of **bat** in Australia, eight of which can be seen in Perth, the most common being the white-striped mastiff whose metallic tik-tik-tiks can be heard at half-second intervals.

Birds

With one of the most impressive bird lists in the world, Australia is a bird watcher's paradise and even if you are indifferent, you cannot fail to be impressed by their diversity, their colour and their calls. They also enter the 'safe' department, which is something many paranoid folks find profound comfort in. Perhaps the most famous of Australian birds is the **Kookaburra**. Although not native to WA it has made its way across here following the advent of colonial migration. Both cheeky and enchanting, they look like huge kingfishers and are indeed the largest of that family. Other than their prevalence, their fearlessness and their extrovert behaviour, it is their laughing call that will remain forever in your psyche. At dawn, when a family group really gets going, it can sound so much fun that you almost feel inclined to rise immediately and share the joke.

Next up is the equally melodic Australian **magpie**. Looking like some smart waiter or wedding groom in their black and white attire they are another common sight, but again it is their fluid carol-like call that remains truly memorable. In the breeding season they are also known to attack people that have the misfortune to stray into their territory by swooping with determination at your head. Just how many bad hair days the dear magpie has caused one can only imagine. If you think one is attacking you, wave your arms about your head as this seems to put them off but the best advice is to move out of their territory which may be as small as one or two trees.

From the cryptic to the colourful, Australia is famous for its psittacines (the **parrot** family), including parakeets, lorikeets, cockatiels, rosellas and budgerigars. There can perhaps be no better demonstration that these species should not be confined to cages, like goldfish are to bowls, than in the vast outback of Australia, their true and natural domain. Out there, against oceanic skies, huge colourful flocks roam in search of food. Largest are the **cockatoos**, which come in sulphur-crested brilliant white, or deepest black, the latter species differentiated by flickers of red, yellow or white in their tails. The smallest are the desert-loving **budgerigars**, shimmering green and yellow in the heat haze. In the far north the **rainbow lorikeet**, looking like some award-winning invention by some manic professor of colour, is a common sight (and sound) while the **northern rosellas** appear like blue and yellow fireworks. **Western rosellas**, seen commonly in the southwest, are the smallest of that family and have very different male and female colours: the former largely vibrant red, the latter mostly green. Other parrots common around the southwest include the yellow-collared green **28s**, and the pink and grey **galahs**.

Also in the southwest look out for the metallic blue, iridescent hues of the tiny **fairy wrens** that when first seen simply take your breath away. One of the commonest is the splendid fairy wren, a bird that could hardly be more aptly named.

The largest flighted Australian birds, seen around the far northern lakes and wetlands are the **brolgas** and the black-necked storks, or jabirus. The brolga is a distinctly leggy, grey crane with a dewlap (flap of skin under the chin) and a lovely splash of red confined to its head. The **jabiru** is equally leggy but has a lovely iridescent purple-green neck set off with a daffodil yellow eye and a very impressive rapier-like beak.

Hugely impressive in the beak department (in fact, perhaps possessing the most remarkable of all) is the **pelican**, that large, doleful, webby white character so synonymous with a day at the beach. They are simply wonderful to watch, behaving as if they would love you forever for a mere fish scrap. As well as hanging around wharfs and boat ramps for free handouts they are also regularly seen sleeping on the top of lampposts, seemingly oblivious to the chaotic urbanity beneath. Lakes and harbours in the south are also the favourite haunt of the **black swan**, the faunal emblem of Western Australia. The Australian black swan is the only uniform black swan in the world with the other seven species being predominantly white.

Almost a match when it comes to wingspan is the white-breasted **sea eagle**, which is a glorious sight almost anywhere along the coast, or around inland lakes and waterways. Like any eagle they are consummate predators and in this case are highly adept at catching fish with their incredibly powerful talons. Fairly common in the northern part of the state are the equally huge **wedge-tailed eagles** (or 'wedgies'), Australia's largest raptors with a wingspan of up to 2½ m. Smug and smirking, they know that for them there is absolutely no need to flee from anyone, or anything. Wedgies are most commonly sighted feeding on road kills, especially kangaroos, which is an ironic twist of our impact on nature, the outback and the Australian environment. Another common raptor in the north is the **whistling kite**, an even more opportunistic feeder on carrion.

The largest Australian bird of all is of course the flightless **emu**, distant cousin to the African ostrich. With long powerful legs they are prevalent all over the state, usually quite shy unless water is scarce, often running off like a group of hairy basketball players on a first time shoplifting spree. Don't try to get too close as they can get very aggressive.

We leave the avian roll-call with a major surprise: the **fairy penguin**, the smallest penguin in the world. Like some interminably cute, chubby little pigeon in a wetsuit, they are found all along the southern coastline of Australia and are easily seen at Penguin Island, off Rockingham. Their scientific name '*Eudyptula*' is Greek for 'good little diver'.

Reptiles

The range of reptile, amphibian and insect species is, not surprisingly, as diverse as any other in Australia and perhaps the group of animals most feared by travellers. For it is here you have the teeth, the fangs and the stingy bits that can potentially cause consummate grief to humans. Many myths and misconceptions exist, but it is true to say that within this group there are some creatures that could bring down a horse, eat it and spit out the empty skin! But let's face it; since they are not out to get us and are merely protecting their ilk and their domain, one cannot fail to be impressed.

First up is the largest and a 'living dinosaur', the crocodile. There are two species in Australia: the **estuarine crocodile** (or 'saltie' as they are known), which is found throughout the Indo-Australian region, and the smaller **freshwater crocodile**, which is endemic. Your best chance of seeing one in the wild is around Broome. Only the saltwater crocodile is partial to meat. The largest was measured at a fearsome 10 m and the largest human 'feeding frenzy' occurred when one thousand Japanese soldiers vanished in a swamp between Burma and Romree Island to escape the British during the Second World War. By morning only 20 were left! Greatly hyped by films and television since the creation of Tarzan, it is a sobering thought that a large saltie would eat a lion or tiger for breakfast, could probably handle a grizzly for lunch and even the feared great white shark would think twice about taking one on. Maybe it is their size generally, or their admirable dentition, but either way, there is no doubt they demand our respect. In northern WA warning signs next to rivers and estuaries are a common sight, extolling various recommendations for your due safety, including... 'If out in a boat, DO NOT dangle arms or legs in the water'. Take note that these signs are in deadly earnest.

The enchanting **goanna**, or monitor, is a common sight, especially in campsites. There are actually many species of goanna in Australia (also know as perenties, monitors and bungarras). The biggest, in lizard terms second only to Indonesia's Komodo Dragons, can reach up to 2 m in length, are carnivores and if threatened run towards anything upright to escape. Of course, this is usually a tree, but not always, so be warned!

There are many other species of lizard that you may encounter on your travels, including the **blue-tongued lizard** (six species, usually referred to as a 'stumpy' or 'bob-tail' in WA), which is about 50 cm in length. If you get too close a blue-tongue will no doubt show you how it got its name. Sitting on a balcony of a late afternoon, you are likely to notice tiny flesh-coloured lizards plastered to the roof or busy catching insects. These are **geckos**, and there are many species in Australia. They manage to cling to smooth surfaces using an incredible adaptation, in the form of tiny hairs on their feet called setae. On a single toe there can be over one million.

When it comes to Australian snakes there is no alternative really but to be honest. Australia has 140 species of land snake and about 32 species of sea snake. The bad news? Of these about 100 are venomous with about a dozen able to cause a human fatality. Of the eleven most venomous snakes in the world, Australia has seven of them. These include the rather innocuous looking **taipan**. There are two species, the coastal variety, once considered the most dangerous land snake in the world, and the related western taipan, found later to be worse still. The taipan is particularly dangerous because they are intelligent, have 'a 'nervous' disposition, a 'snap-release' bite and a venom potent enough to reduce a horse to a quivering heap. It does gets worse: during an attack they can actually launch themselves off the ground towards their target and until 1955 – wait for it – they enjoyed the unenviable reputation of a 100 per cent kill-rate in human victims. The good news is that, remarkably, you can survive a taipan attack. This is because they can actually recognize that you are human and in doing so be merciful as to bite you, but not release the venom. In fact fatalities are very rare with, at worst, only one or two deaths per year. Hospitals all stock antivenin so there is hope even if you are. If you do get bitten, to lessen the spread of the venom, tie a tourniquet around the affected limb and stay as still and as calm as possible. Then send a companion for help. If you are alone obviously you must seek help as best you can. Do not suck out the venom from a stricken companion: this will only potentially result in two obituaries.

Other snakes found in WA that you might be better off not seeing include the brown and lightly striped **southern death adder**, the yellow and black **tiger snake**, the small **dugite**, and the uniformly coloured **king brown** (also known as the **mulga**).

Spiders

There are around 2,000 species of spiders in Australia, the best known being the diminutive **red back**, a close relative of America's black widow. Common throughout Australia, it is shiny black with a distinctive red mark on its back – a clear warning to keep well clear. They are extremely poisonous but actually quite timid and as long as you desist from sticking your fingers at it or under rocks you would be unlucky to be bitten. The **huntsman** is a very common species seen almost anywhere in Australia, especially indoors. Although not the largest spider on the continent, they can grow to a size that would comfortably cover the palm of your hand. Blessed with the propensity to shock, they are an impressive sight and do bite, but only when provoked and are not venomous.

Marine mammals and turtles

Although whaling was once practiced in Australia to the very point of extinction, it is now thankfully whale watching that is big business. Along the western seaboard of Australia, **humpback whales** are commonly sighted on passage between the tropics and Antarctica between the months of July and October. The **southern right whale** is another species regularly seen in Australian waters, and can be seen off the Cape-to-Cape region between July and December. Several species of dolphin are present including the **bottlenose dolphin,** which is a common sight off almost any beach. There are a number of places along the west coast where you can not only see wild dolphins, but also encounter them personally, notably Monkey Mia in Shark Bay, and Rockingham, Mandurah and Bunbury. Another less well-known sea mammal clinging precariously to a few locales around the coast is the **dugong** or sea cow which browses exclusively on underwater sea-grass meadows. Shark Bay is the best place to see them, though they can also be seen off Port Hedland. Australia is also a very important breeding ground for **turtles**. It is not unusual to see them on snorkelling trips off the northern coast, but the most memorable way to see these creatures is to quietly visit during the nesting season (October-May). The females haul themselves up at night to lay their eggs, and hatchlings emerge to make a mad dash for the waves. There are nesting beaches near to both Exmouth and Port Hedland. Talk to local tourist or CALM offices before organizing an expedition.

Sharks

There are dozens of sharks inhabiting the seas all around Australia, including the large **tiger sharks**, and the common **grey nurse** and **reef** sharks. Virtually all are completely harmless, but there are a handful of species that definitely aren't, including the best known of them all, the **great white shark** of *Jaws* fame. This is found in waters all around southern Australia, and is known to occasionally attack humans. Our physical make-up is, however, not to their taste and even those rare attacks only lead to a death about 10 per cent of the time – less than one a year in Australian waters. It is the largest of the carnivorous sharks, growing up to 6 m in length, and surely the most scary to see (this is possible, believe it or not, in South Australia - see www.divedirectory.com.au). If anything could be more jaw-dropping than seeing a great white up close, however, then it has to be eyeballing the incomparable **whale shark**, a huge, gentle filter-feeder. This, the largest fish in the world's oceans, can reach 18 m in length - around the size of a single-decker bus. This prodigious size, coupled with its effortless grace and beautiful colouration make it an intensely exciting creature up close, and this is more than possible (in fact practically guaranteed) if you can get yourself up to Exmouth or Coral Bay between May and July. This is when the sharks come in to feed on the spawn being produced by the corals of the Ningaloo Reef.

Introduced fauna and the future

There is no doubt that your experience of Australian wildlife will be both exciting and memorable. But that experience and its celebration must be replete with the realities of the true state of the Australian environment, which of course also holds true to any other country on earth. It is something we must all bear in mind. A host of introduced animals have combined to have the greatest and most negative impact on the Australian environment since its separation from Gondwanaland 80 million years ago. Species that are currently causing havoc and have done so for some time include the **rabbit**, the **fox** and the **cat**.

There is no doubt that sterling conservation efforts are being made to halt the destruction and that ecotourism plays an important role in conservation generally, but since conservation is a drain on money not a money maker, it inevitably suffers. In WA you can actually help turn the tide by joining one of CALM's *Landcare* expeditions (see Essentials, page 20).

Vegetation

A visit to the southwest of Western Australia will reveal one of the richest plant communities in the world with an immense variety of plants growing within a wide range of habitats. The southwest botanical province is approximately bordered by a line drawn between Shark Bay and Cape Arid and it is within this region that well in excess of 8,000 native plant species are found, many of them growing nowhere else on earth.

The area enjoys a Mediterranean type climate with winter rainfall and warm dry summers. North of Perth the rainfall gradually decreases and summer temperatures are quite high while the southwest corner to the south of Perth has quite a high rainfall and this is reflected in the vegetation.

The term wildflower is often misunderstood and only applied to members of the **everlasting** or **paper daisy** family. These are small annuals with papery petals which have an extremely long life when picked and dried, they come in reds, pinks, white and yellow and flower in spring. But wildflower is more widely accepted as the floral display of any native plant, shrub or tree and the range in colour, shape and size of these is enormous and fascinating. A word of warning: it is an offence in WA to pick wildflowers from any roadside, reserve, national park or other public land, so photograph and enjoy but leave them for others to see.

When planning a trip to view the wildflowers remember the species north of Perth flower first, with peak flowering being August and September; while to the south of Perth September and October is the best time to visit. Having made this comment it is also true to say that whenever or wherever you go in Western Australia there will be some wildflowers in bloom and often spectacular displays occur at the most unexpected times.

Some striking flowers to the north include the **Banksias**, more than 70 species of which exist and most of them are endemic. They vary from small prostrate plants to tall trees and the large bottle brush shaped flowers may be red, orange or yellow. The flower spikes on some banksia species grow to 12 cm in diameter and 30 cm long. **Feather flowers** with their brilliant rich colours and soft feathery petals are greatly admired and are among the most beautiful of flowers and are usually small to medium shrubs. The northern inland areas are where the best displays of paper aisies or everlastings are to be found, after a good season they flower profusely and it is common to see hundreds of hectares of them forming solid blocks of colour along the roadsides, a truly captivating spectacle. This is also the habitat of the rare and unusual **wreath lechenaultia**; this little prostrate plant spreads out evenly from its centre to a diameter of 40 cm or so and the red and yellow flowers form only at the ends of the branchlets. Seeing these beautiful little wreaths growing on the bare red soil at the roadside is a sight you will always remember. The **kangaroo paw** is another strange-looking plant, long stems emerge from a clump of long green leaves and the flowers at the top of the stems may be green, yellow or red. A red and green flowering kangaroo paw is the Western Australian floral emblem and is the most attractive of the species. The **West Australian christmas tree** is a sturdy single trunk tree and grows to about 8 m, it is unusual in being a partial parasite, some of its nutrient is obtained by its roots tapping into those of nearby plants and drawing off what it needs. In December masses of large brilliant orange yellow flowers appear and the trees are then a magnificent sight.

South of Perth the **karri** forests are amongst the most beautiful on earth, the tall straight trees with their patchy pale orange to white bark grow to almost 90 m with very few side branches till the crown is reached. They are a significant timber species which yield longer lengths of hardwood than any other hardwood species. The **jarrah** forests are also found in this area, another very important timber tree producing an even more durable timber than the karri. They do not grow as tall and straight as the karri and the bark is dark grey and fibrous and held in longitudinal strips. As a change from looking up at the colossal trees try finding some of the tiny **orchids** on the forest floor, many of them only a few centimetres tall. Over 300 species in all shapes and colours imaginable occur in the southwest. In one of the more bizarre forms the flower imitates the shape of a species of female wasp, the real wasp is fooled and attempts to mate with them so ensuring that pollen is distributed from flower to flower. While at ground level check out the tiny **sun dews** which trap insects within their dewy tentacles and then digest them for additional nutrient; and around Albany way the **pitcher plant** which traps insects within special pitcher-shaped leaves and metes out a similar fate to its prey. Adding a wealth of blue to the understorey, **blue lechenaultia** is a small shrub which displays clusters of sky-blue flowers in spring time. An unusual plant is the **grass tree** or **balga** (sometimes still referred to as Blackboys), which have a dense fibrous stem of about 30 cm in diameter and up to 3 m long, often branched. From a dense crown of thin green metre-long leaves the white flowers are carried on a stout spike above the foliage. A skirt effect is achieved by the old dry leaves hanging down from the crown. Mention must be made of the **wattles** or **acacia** plants with their masses of beautiful yellow flowers in spring. More than 800 species of them occur in Western Australia varying from small prostrate shrubs to fairly tall trees. Some wattle species were once an important resource for the Aboriginal people, seeds were ground to make a type of flour, the sticky sap was gathered and chewed, bark strips were used for nets and bags and various implements were made from the very hard, dense wood.

Books

Australian history

Diamond, Jared *Guns, Germs and Steel.* A fascinating explanation of why it is that the British invaded Australia in 1788, rather than an Aboriginal fleet that sailed up the Thames, wide-ranging, a global look at the trends of human development and history.
Flannery, Tim, editor *The Explorers.* An amazing insight into the minds of the early

European pioneers is given in these eyewitness accounts.
Macintyre, Stuart *A Concise History of Australia.* A general history.

Books detailing the impact of the British invasion on the indigenous peoples include:
Broome, Richard *Aboriginal Australians.* A good general history of what has happened to Aboriginal people since 1788 and how they have responded to their situation.

McGrath, Ann, editor *Contested Ground.* The Aboriginal voice itself is starting to be heard in books such as this.

Reynolds, Henry *The Other Side of the Frontier* or *An Indelible Stain.* Very fine work, utilizes a lot of compelling primary sources.

Culture

Berndt, Ronald and Catherine *The World of the First Australians.* The classic work on Aboriginal culture.

Flood, Josephine *Riches of Ancient Australia.* A superb look at archaeological and art sites by region. *Archaeology of the Dreamtime.* An account of how people first came to Australia and how they lived. *Rock Art of the Dreamtime.* For those interested in rock art.

Knightley, Phillip *Australia: A Biography of a Nation.* Short but snappy, this is in essence a modern history, but also goes a long way to getting inside the minds of today's Australians.

McCulloch, Alan and Susan *The Encyclopedia of Australian Art.* The major reference book at a hefty 800 pages.

Morphy, Howard *Aboriginal Art.* An excellent overview of its subject.

Sayers, Andrew *Australian Art.* A new history of all Australian art forms from 1788 to the present.

Penguin Good Australian Wine Guide. Those intending to drink a lot of Australian wine may find this annual useful.

Travelogues and memoirs

de Bernières, Louis *Red Dog.* English novelist who couldn't resist the tales he heard of an independent kelpie in the Pilbara who hitched rides with mine workers, and so turned them into a novella.

Bryson, Bill, *Down Under.* Written by an American, this is probably the best-selling account of a journey around Australia, and certainly one of the funniest.

Connolly, Billy *World Tour of Australia.* It goes without saying that this is also very funny.

Davidson, Robyn *Tracks.* A moving and honest account of the author's solo camel trip across central and western Australia.

Jacobson, Howard *In the Land of Oz.* Written in the 1980s by this Englishman, but is an amusing, perceptive and thoughtful account, and still pertinent.

Morgan, Sally *My Place.* Her autobiographical classic account of growing up in Perth in the 1950s and 1960s and exploring her Aboriginal heritage.

Winton, Tim *Land's Edge.* A powerfully evocative account of his love of the Western Australian coast.

Western Australia in fiction

One of the best ways of getting a flavour of Western Australian history and culture is to dive into a great novel. If you only read one Western Australian novelist it should be the incomparable Tim Winton. See also Literature, page 324.

Drewe, Robert *The Drowner.* A meditative piece centred on the son of a water diviner working to bring water to the WA goldfields at the turn of the century. *Shark Net.* A gripping memoir about a series of murders in Perth in the 60s.

Jolley, Elizabeth Another well known WA novelist who writes about the lonely and invisible in a darkly comic and unsettling way.

Scott, Kim *Benang.* An award-winning fictional account of a man of Nyoongar and European heritage trying to cope with being bred as his family's 'first white man born'.

Winton, Tim *Cloudstreet.* Describes growing up in a ramshackle family house in suburban Perth. *Dirt Music.* His newest novel tells of love between 2 drifters amid a passionate evocation of the West Australian coastline. Winton is by no means the only great WA writer, however.

Ecology, the outdoors and wildlife

The best place to find and order Australian wildlife books from afar is the Australian Geographic website, www.australian geographic.com.

Absalom, Jack *Safe Outback Travel.* A trusted manual of driving and camping advice if getting right off the beaten track.

Flannery, Tim *Future Eaters.* A fantastic ecological history of the continent, focusing on its fauna, flora and people, and how they have shaped, and been shaped by the environment.

Hiddin, Les *Bush Tucker Field Guide.* For those worried about getting lost in the bush who may want to brush up on bush tucker.

Low, Tim *Feral Future.* An interesting and alarming study of the current biological invasion of Australia.

Zborowski, Paul *Australia's most dangerous spiders, snakes and marine creatures: Identification and First Aid.* Those who are a little nervous of getting close to Australia's wildlife may be soothed (or terrified) by this useful field guide.

Good generalist wildlife books include: **341**
Menkhorst, Peter *Field Guide to Mammals of Australia.* Another fine field guide et al.
Simpson, Ken *Birds of Australia.* A new and comprehensive guide that is on a par with *Slater.*
Slater, Peter *Slater Field Guide-Australian Birds.* Tried and trusted by et al (now out of print but worth searching for).

Immigration Visas
Employment - pay scales
Cost of living - Bills / food / car
House prices - triplex + Duplex land
kit houses
dragging one here across

Footnotes

Common words and phrases

B&S Ball	Bachelors and Spinsters Ball – young person's excuse to get as drunk as possible and get off with anything that moves
Back of Bourke	Middle of nowhere
Bananabender	Someone from Queensland
Barbie	Barbeque (BBQ)
Arvo	Afternoon
Bail up	Hold up, forcibly halt
Beauty	('Bewdy') Fantastic, wonderful (also "You beauty")
Billy	Kettle, usually non-electric
Blowies	Blow flies
Bludger	Layabout, non-worker
Bottleshop	Off-licence
Bull bar/Roo bar	Extra front vehicle bumper
Bush	Generally any non-urban, non-agricultural area
Bushranger	Bush-based outlaw, eg Ned Kelly
Centralian	Someone from central Australia, eg Alice Springs
Chips	Potato crisps
Chook	Chicken
Chunder	Vomit – 'hurl', 'spew' and 'ralph' are also used
Cobber	Friend, friendly term for non-acquaintance ("G'day cobber")
Cocky	Cockatoo, cockroach or farmer
Cray	Crayfish, lobster
Croweater	South Australian
Cyclone	Hurricane
Dag, daggy	Bit of dirty wool around sheep's backside, also uncool or silly
Digger	Goldrush miner, also soldier of the world wars
Dob in	Report on someone to the authorities
Donger	Converted shipping container used for sleeping in
Doona	Duvet
Drongo	Idiot
Dunny	Toilet
Esky	Portable cool box
Fair dinkum	Fair enough, a good show, the truth
Feral	Non-indigenous animal or person who has become 'wild'
Flush	Having plenty of money
Footy	Aussie Rules or Rugby League football
G'day	Hello (corruption of the greeting 'good day')
Give it a burl	Give it a try
Good on us/you	General term of satisfaction, endearment or thanks
Goodo	OK, Fine
Grommet	Very young surfer
Hard yakka	Hard physical work
Hot chips	Thick potato chips, french fries
Ice-block	Ice lolly (flavoured ice or ice cream on a stick)
Jackeroo/Jilleroo	Worker (usually young) on a station
Jumbuck	Sheep

Knocker/knock	Person who puts things down, to criticize
Larrikin	Mischievous person
Lay-by	Keep aside (by a shop) until paid for
Lollies	Sweets, candy
Mate	Friend, friendly term for non-acquaintance ("G'day mate")
Mob	Large number of animals or people
Moleskins	Jeans, of brushed cotton
Morning tea	Mid morning break for cake and tea
Mullet	Popular country hairstyle short on top, long at back
No worries	Do not worry, no problem
Op-shop	Second-hand clothing shop, proceeds go to charities
Outback	Australia's interior
Park	Parking place
Pokers/pokies	Slot or gambling machines
Property	Often used to denote a large outback farm
Rego	Car registration document
Ripper	Excellent!
Sandgroper	Western Australian
Score	Secure something for free, though this has recently been hijacked by advertisers to simply mean getting a bargain ("score this for $20")
She'll be right	Everything will turn out ok, honest
Skerrick	A tiny amount
Slab	Case of beer, usually 24 bottles
Smoko	Cigarette break, tea break
Snag	Sausage
Station	Often used to denote a large outback farm
Stubbie	Small bottle of beer
Stubbie holder	Keeps small bottles (or cans) of beer cold
Swag	Canvas sleeping bag and mattress, for outdoor use
Sydneysider	Someone from Sydney
TAB	State bookmakers, similar to the UK's Tote
Tassie	Tasmania, or a Tasmanian
Territorian	Someone from the Northern Territory
Thongs	Flip-flops (footwear)
Tinnie	Can of beer
Tucker	Food – bushtucker is gathered or hunted food
Ute	('Yoot') Utility vehicle with a flat-bed rear
Wet (the)	Northern monsoon season
Willy-willy	Small, harmless swirl of air
Yabby	Edible freshwater crustacean, like a small lobster

Index

Map index

Acknowledgements

Andrew and Katrina would like to thank the staff of the many tourist offices and commissions around WA who gave us their time generously to ensure that we made the best of ours. There are too many to mention, but we are particularly grateful to Karen Priest and Sascha Turner from South West WA.

Our thanks too to those we met along the way who helped us out and showed us genuine warmth and hospitality. Again too numerous to list fully, but special mention must be made of: June Anderson, Robbie Atkinson, Chris Ferris, Tony Park, Rob and Julie Saunders, Sandy and Simon Watkin, Corry Westlake, Diving Ventures and everyone at Murchison House Station.

Mention must be made of our contributors. Darroch Donald provided most of the background information on wildlife, and was our original inspiration for researching Australia for the Footprint guides in the first place. Don Bellairs drew on his extensive knowledge of WA flora to provide the section on wildflowers.

Also thanks to the team at Footprint for their commitment, patience and passion. Finally a big thanks to our friends and family: Dennis and Alexandra, whose enthusiastic support helped to make this project possible; Bryan, Mary and Terry, for a constant ear and encouragement; Morag Kerr and Jim and Jo Tippetts for their support, kindness and comfy beds in Perth; and Cliff for his tremendous friendship and bringing Andrew to Oz in the first place.

Dr Charlie Easmon wrote the health section. His aid and development work has included: Raleigh International (Medical Officer in Botswana), MERLIN (in Rwanda his team set up a refugee camp for 12,000 people), Save the Children (as a consultant in Rwanda), ECHO (The European Community Humanitarian Office review of Red Cross work in Armenia, Georgia and Azerbaijan), board member of International Care and Relief and previously International Health Exchange. In addition to his time as a hospital physician, he has worked as a medical adviser to the Foreign and Commonwealth Office and as a locum consultant at the hospital for tropical diseases travel clinic, as well as being a specialist registrar in Public Health. He now also runs Travel Screening services (www.travelscreening.co.uk) based at 1 Harley Street.

Credits

Footprint credits

Editor: Stephanie Lambe
Production assistant: Emma Bryers
Map editor: Sarah Sorensen
Picture editor: Claire Benison

Publisher: Patrick Dawson
Editorial: Alan Murphy, Sophie Blacksell, Sarah Thorowgood, Claire Boobbyer, Felicity Laughton, Laura Dixon, Nicola Jones
Cartography: Robert Lunn, Claire Benison, Kevin Feeney, Angus Dawson, Esher Monzón García, Thom Wickes
Series development: Rachel Fielding
Design: Mytton Williams and Rosemary Dawson (brand)
Advertising: Debbie Wylde
Finance and administration: Sharon Hughes, Elizabeth Taylor, Lindsay Dytham

Photography credits

Front cover: Boab tree
Photobank
Back cover: Perth Skyline
Alamy
Inside colour section: Alamy, Powerstock

Print

Manufactured in Italy by LegoPrint
Pulp from sustainable forests

Footprint feedback

We try as hard as we can to make each Footprint guide as up to date as possible but, of course, things always change. If you want to let us know about your experiences – good, bad or ugly – then don't delay, go to **www.footprintbooks.com** and send in your comments.

Publishing information

Footprint West Coast Australia
2nd edition
© Footprint Handbooks Ltd
May 2005

ISBN 1 904777 45 7
CIP DATA: A catalogue record for this book is available from the British Library

® Footprint Handbooks and the Footprint mark are a registered trademark of Footprint Handbooks Ltd

Published by Footprint

6 Riverside Court
Lower Bristol Road
Bath BA2 3DZ, UK
T +44 (0)1225 469141
F +44 (0)1225 469461
discover@footprintbooks.com
www.footprintbooks.com

Distributed in the USA by

Publishers Group West

Every effort has been made to ensure that the facts in this guidebook are accurate. However, travellers should still obtain advice from consulates, airlines etc about travel and visa requirements before travelling. The authors and publishers cannot accept responsibility for any loss, injury or inconvenience however caused.

Map symbols

Administration

- □ Capital city
- ○ Other city/town
- International border
- Regional border
- Disputed border

Roads and travel

- ── National highway, motorway
- ── Main road
- ── Minor road
- ---- Track
- ...... Footpath
- ⊷ Railway with station
- ✈ Airport
- 🚌 Bus station
- Ⓜ Metro station
- ---- Cable car
- ┼┼┼┼ Funicular
- ⛴ Ferry

Water features

- ≈ River, canal
- ⬭ Lake, ocean
- ⩔ Seasonal marshland
- ▨ Beach, sand bank
- ⦚ Waterfall

Topographical features

- ⬭ Contours (approx)
- ⩍ Mountain
- ⩕ Volcano
- ⇌ Mountain pass
- Escarpment
- Gorge
- Glacier
- Salt flat
- Rocks

Cities and towns

- ══ Main through route
- ══ Main street
- ══ Minor street

Pedestrianized street

- ⊐⊏ Tunnel
- → One way street
- ▥ Steps
- ⇌ Bridge
- ▟▟▟ Fortified wall
- ▨ Park, garden, stadium
- ● Sleeping
- ⊙ Eating
- ◑ Bars & clubs
- ⊙ Entertainment
- ▨ Building
- ▪ Sight
- ✝ ✝ Cathedral, church
- ☗ Chinese temple
- ⊞ Hindu temple
- 𝘈 Meru
- ☖ Mosque
- △ Stupa
- ✡ Synagogue
- ▪ Tourist office
- ⛪ Museum
- ✉ Post office
- Ⓟ Police
- Ⓢ Bank
- @ Internet
- ♪ Telephone
- ☍ Market
- ✚ Hospital
- Ⓟ Parking
- ⛽ Petrol
- ⛳ Golf
- Detail map
- ◁ Related map

Other symbols

- ⸫ Archaeological site
- ♦ National park, wildlife reserve
- ✿ Viewing point
- ▲ Campsite
- ⌂ Refuge, lodge
- ▥ Castle
- ⚓ Diving
- ♠♣♠ Deciduous/coniferous/palm trees
- ⌂ Hide
- ♠ Vineyard
- ⚱ Distillery
- ⋈ Shipwreck
- ✕ Historic battlefield

West Coast Australia

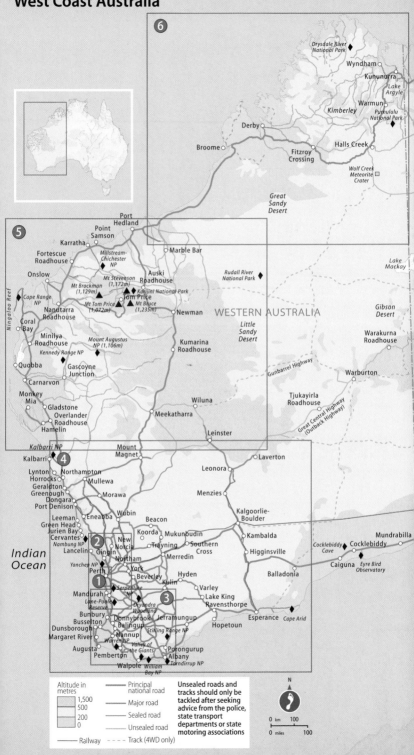

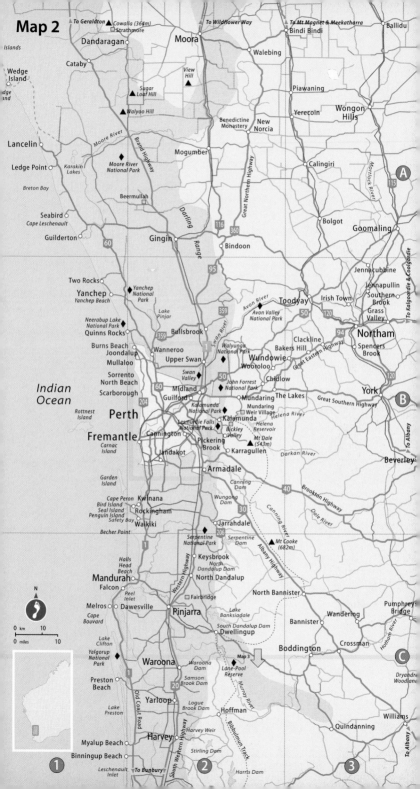

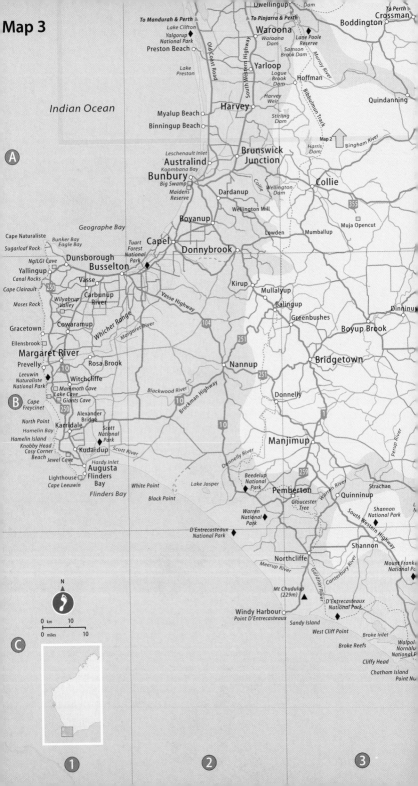